ACTIVISM ACROSS BORDERS SINCE 1870

New Approaches to International History

SERIES EDITOR: THOMAS ZEILER, *Professor of American Diplomatic History, University of Colorado Boulder, USA*

Series Editorial Board:

ANTHONY ADAMTHWAITE
University of California at Berkeley (USA)

KATHLEEN BURK
University College London (UK)

LOUIS CLERC
University of Turku (Finland)

PETRA GOEDDE
Temple University (USA)

FRANCINE MCKENZIE
University of Western Ontario (Canada)

LIEN-HANG NGUYEN
University of Kentucky (USA)

JASON PARKER
Texas A&M University (USA)

GLENDA SLUGA
University of Sydney (Australia)

Published:

DECOLONIZATION AND THE COLD WAR
edited by Leslie James and Elisabeth Leake (2015)

COLD WAR SUMMITS
Chris Tudda (2015)

THE UNITED NATIONS IN INTERNATIONAL HISTORY
Amy Sayward (2017)

LATIN AMERICAN NATIONALISM
James F. Siekmeier (2017)

THE HISTORY OF UNITED STATES CULTURAL DIPLOMACY
Michael L. Krenn (2017)

INTERNATIONAL COOPERATION IN THE EARLY 20TH CENTURY
Daniel Gorman (2017)

WOMEN AND GENDER IN INTERNATIONAL HISTORY
Karen Garner (2018)

INTERNATIONAL DEVELOPMENT
Corinna Unger (2018)

THE ENVIRONMENT AND INTERNATIONAL HISTORY
Scott Kaufman (2018)

SCANDINAVIA AND THE GREAT POWERS IN THE FIRST WORLD WAR
Michael Jonas (2019)

CANADA AND THE WORLD SINCE 1867
Asa McKercher (2019)

THE FIRST AGE OF INDUSTRIAL GLOBALIZATION
Maartje Abbenhuis and Gordon Morrell (2019)

EUROPE'S COLD WAR RELATIONS
edited by Urlich Krotz, Kiran Klaus Patel and Federico Romero (2019)

UNITED STATES RELATIONS WITH CHINA AND IRAN
edited by Osamah F. Khalil (2019)

PUBLIC OPINION AND TWENTIETH-CENTURY DIPLOMACY
Daniel Hucker (2020)

GLOBALIZING THE US PRESIDENCY
edited by Cyrus Schayegh (2020)

THE INTERNATIONAL LGBT RIGHTS MOVEMENT
Laura Belmonte (2021)

GLOBAL WAR, GLOBAL CATASTROPHE
Maartje Abbenhuis and Ismee Tames (2021)

AMERICA'S ROAD TO EMPIRE
Piero Gleijeses (2021)

MILITARIZATION AND THE AMERICAN CENTURY
David Fitzgerald (2022)

REBUILDING THE POSTWAR ORDER
Francine McKenzie (2023)

LEFTIST INTERNATIONALISMS
edited by Michele Di Donato and Mathieu Fulla (2023)

SOLDIERS IN PEACEMAKING
edited by Beatrice de Graf, Frédéric Dessberg and Thomas Vaisset (2023)

Forthcoming:

THE FEAR OF CHINESE POWER
Jeffrey Crean

CLIMATE CHANGE AND INTERNATIONAL HISTORY
Ruth A. Morgan

NON-ALIGNED MOVEMENT SUMMITS
Jovan Čavoški

FROM WORLD WAR TO POSTWAR
Andrew N. Buchanan

CHINA AND THE UNITED STATES SINCE 1949
Elizabeth Ingleson

ACTIVISM ACROSS BORDERS SINCE 1870

CAUSES, CAMPAIGNS AND CONFLICTS IN AND BEYOND EUROPE

Daniel Laqua

BLOOMSBURY ACADEMIC
LONDON • NEW YORK • OXFORD • NEW DELHI • SYDNEY

BLOOMSBURY ACADEMIC
Bloomsbury Publishing Plc
50 Bedford Square, London, WC1B 3DP, UK
1385 Broadway, New York, NY 10018, USA
29 Earlsfort Terrace, Dublin 2, Ireland

BLOOMSBURY, BLOOMSBURY ACADEMIC and the Diana logo
are trademarks of Bloomsbury Publishing Plc

First published in Great Britain 2023

Copyright © Daniel Laqua, 2023

Daniel Laqua has asserted his right under the Copyright, Designs and
Patents Act, 1988, to be identified as Author of this work.

For legal purposes the Acknowledgements on pp. xii–xiii constitute an
extension of this copyright page.

Cover image © CND demonstration in Hyde Park, 16 July 1983.
Photo by Geoff Garrett/Daily Mirror/Mirrorpix/Getty Images.

All rights reserved. No part of this publication may be reproduced or transmitted
in any form or by any means, electronic or mechanical, including photocopying,
recording, or any information storage or retrieval system, without prior
permission in writing from the publishers.

Bloomsbury Publishing Plc does not have any control over, or responsibility for, any third-party
websites referred to or in this book. All internet addresses given in this book were correct at the
time of going to press. The author and publisher regret any inconvenience caused if addresses
have changed or sites have ceased to exist, but can accept no responsibility for any such changes.

A catalogue record for this book is available from the British Library.

A catalog record for this book is available from the Library of Congress.

ISBN: HB: 978-1-3502-6280-5
PB: 978-1-3502-6279-9
ePDF: 978-1-3502-6282-9
eBook: 978-1-3502-6281-2

Series: New Approaches to International History

Typeset by Integra Software Services Pvt. Ltd.
Printed and bound in Great Britain

To find out more about our authors and books visit www.bloomsbury.com
and sign up for our newsletters.

CONTENTS

List of figures   x
Acknowledgements   xii
List of abbreviations   xiv

Introduction: Making sense of transnational activism   1
    'Activism': social movements, voluntary action and amorphousness   2
    'Across borders': transnational activism, internationalism and cosmopolitanism   6
    'Since 1870': historical contexts of transnational activism   10
    Analysing transnational activism: connectedness, ambivalence,
        transience and marginality   13

1 Empire and activism   25
    The transnational dynamics of anti-slavery before 1870   26
    Imperialism and Cardinal Lavigerie's 'anti-slavery crusade' in the 1880s   30
    Targeting atrocities in the age of imperialism, 1890s–1900s   33
    Empire and activism during and after the First World War   37
    Anticolonialists on the move   40
    Political and intellectual contexts of anti-imperialism, 1920s to 1950s   42
    Liberation struggles, 1950s to 1980s   45
    Combating neo-colonial relations in a postcolonial world   49

2 Humanitarianism in war and peace   65
    Helping the victims of conflict   66
    Humanitarianism and the politics of solidarity   69
    Helping refugees in the age of total war   73
    Aid in the face of famine and natural disasters   77
    Activist humanitarianism since the 1970s   81

3 Building a peaceful world   93
    Organizational pacifism and its features   95
    Integral pacifism in an age of total war   99
    The nation as a subject in transnational peace activism   101
    Socialist and communist perspectives on war and militarism   105
    The rise of feminist pacifism   107
    Overcoming Cold War binaries   110

	Mobilizing against 'American' wars	114
	Confronting 'new wars'	117
	Building peace in post-conflict societies	121
4	**Class, revolution and social justice**	**139**
	Mobility, exile and the left	140
	Organization-building before the First World War	146
	A culture of internationalism	150
	The boundaries of internationalism	152
	International communism	155
	Fascism and anti-fascism	158
	Socialist alternatives in a Cold War world	162
	Protest cultures in and beyond the 1960s	166
	Global social justice	169
5	**The politics of gender and sexuality**	**189**
	Transnational bonds and organizational efforts	191
	Diversity and congruence within the international women's movement	196
	Engaging with international organizations – from the League of Nations to the UN	201
	New attitudes and the shift from rights to liberation	203
	Towards gay liberation	206
	Division and unity since the 1990s	209
6	**Encountering racism and discrimination**	**223**
	The making of Jewish internationalisms	224
	Combating anti-Semitism in the age of extremes	228
	Questioning 'race' and articulating Black identity	233
	The transatlantic dimensions of African American struggles	236
	Challenging apartheid	239
	A multicultural Europe	245
7	**The rights of others**	**259**
	Activism and connected conceptions of human rights	261
	International organizations and human rights	264
	Amnesty International and the 'prisoners of conscience'	266
	Between human rights and left-wing solidarity	269
	Human rights and Eastern Europe	272
	A broadening or a narrowing?	275

8	**Going green**	**287**
	A concern for nature	288
	New associations, new forms of campaigning	291
	Challenging nuclear power	295
	Green politics	298
	International organizations, NGOs and sustainable development	301
	Tackling climate change	303

Conclusion   **315**

Select bibliography   324
Index   358

LIST OF FIGURES

1.1	Cardinal Lavigerie at Saint-Sulpice church in Paris, 21 September 1890	32
1.2	Members of the International African Friends of Abyssinia at a rally held in Trafalgar Square, London, on 25 August 1935	40
1.3	Activists from the Swiss 'Nicaragua – El Salvador Committee' holding up a banner 'against US colonialism in Central America' at a demonstration in Zürich, 1 May 1986	48
1.4	Opening of *Deerde Wereldwinkel* ('Third World Shop') in Amsterdam, 18 September 1971	49
2.1	Delegates at an international congress of Workers' International Relief committees, held in Berlin, July 1922	71
2.2	Vietnamese 'boat people' on *L'Île de Lumière*, a 'floating hospital' run by *Médecins Sans Frontières*, 9 July 1979	82
3.1	Bertha von Suttner in 1911	94
3.2	Anti-nuclear demonstration in Thessaloniki, 1983	111
3.3	International Vietnam Congress, held at the Technical University of Berlin on 11–12 February 1968	116
4.1	Emma Goldman, depicted with members of the *Federacion Anarquista Ibérica* (Iberian Anarchist Federation) and the anarchosyndicalist *Confederación Nacional de Trabajo* (National Confederation of Labour), Spain, 1938	161
4.2	*Solidarność* banner held up during a mass celebrated by John Paul II in Szczecin, 11 June 1987	166
4.3	Participants of the First European Social Forum (Florence, 11 August 2002)	171
5.1	Poster advertising the Budapest congress of the International Woman Suffrage Alliance in 1913	194
5.2	Members of the Women's Peace Party (USA), including Jane Addams, travel to the Women's Peace Congress at The Hague, 28 April 1915	199
5.3	Gay Pride Parade in Warsaw, 15 June 2013	210
6.1	Zionist Congress held in Basel, Switzerland, from 29 to 31 August 1897	226
6.2	Participants of the Pan-African Congress held at Chorlton-on-Medlock Town Hall, Manchester, 1 October 1945	235
6.3	Poster against the purchase of South African Outspan oranges (Paris, *c.* 1976)	242
7.1	Amnesty International poster protesting against Argentina's use of torture on the occasion of the FIFA World Cup of 1978	268
7.2	Dutch demonstration against Pinochet's coup in Chile (Amsterdam, 15 September 1975)	270

7.3	Lyudmila Alexeyeva at a human rights protest in Moscow, 31 October 2009	277
8.1	The Greenpeace boat 'Rainbow Warrior' at Auckland harbour, 10 July 1985	293
8.2	Russian security forces arrest a participant of the 'Walk Across Europe for a Nuclear-Free World', Moscow, 12 October 1995	298
8.3	Greta Thunberg and other participants of the 'School Strike for Climate' outside the Swedish parliament, Stockholm, 28 August 2018	304
9.1	Walter Crane, 'Solidarität der Arbeit' (Solidarity of Labour), lithograph to mark May Day 1890	316
9.2	Latvian participants in the 'Baltic Way' human chain, 23 August 1989	317
9.3	Participants in a human chain that linked the Women's Peace Camp outside the airbase at Greenham Common with the Nuclear Weapons Establishment at Aldermaston (both in Berkshire, UK), 1 April 1983	319

ACKNOWLEDGEMENTS

This book covers a wide range of movements, ideas and historical events, and it would have been impossible to write it in isolation. Countless interactions and experiences have contributed to this work, and I am grateful to the many people who have shaped it, in many cases without knowing that they did. Thanks go to all the archivists and librarians who have supported my research, and to the many people who have discussed history and/or activism with me. I am particularly indebted to several colleagues who have commented on sections of this book: Charlotte Alston, Jennifer Aston, Constance Bantman, Georgina Brewis, Ann-Marie Einhaus, Maria Framke, André Keil, Nikolaos Papadogiannis, Anne-Isabelle Richard, Katharina Rietzler, Avram Taylor, Anna-Katharina Wöbse and Julian Wright. I am humbled by the time they have taken to read my work and by their willingness to offer such perceptive remarks on it. Obviously, all remaining errors are my own. In addition, my book has benefited from other kinds of input – from conversations about particular questions to various forms of collaborative work. I therefore extend my thanks to Grace Brockington, Jodi Burkett, Martin Conway, Stefan Couperus, Thomas Davies, Sarah Hellawell, Axel Körner, Isabella Löhr, Jessica Reinisch, Pierre-Yves Saunier, Christophe Verbruggen, among many others who could be mentioned here.

I have been fortunate to present this project in several settings. Kiran Klaus Patel hosted a fruitful discussion on my project as part of his research colloquium at the Ludwig Maximilian University of Munich. Furthermore, a 'work in progress' reading group in my department (organized by Dominic Williams) enabled me to discuss the introduction. Finally, half a day after submitting the first draft of my manuscript to the publisher, I discussed the project with the members of the 'Voluntary Action History' seminar of London's Institute of Historical Research – a great way to prepare for the final stretch.

I am grateful to Northumbria University for supporting my research ever since I joined the institution as a Lecturer in 2009. A particular 'thank you' goes to the students who have taken my undergraduate module on transnational activism or who have written dissertations and doctoral theses under my supervision. I am grateful for their enthusiasm and for the inspiration that their own work has provided to me. This book is very much the result of the fruitful exchanges with them.

At two crucial points in time, external fellowships boosted my work: a Senior Visiting Research Fellowship at the Leibniz Institute of European History in Mainz coincided with the genesis of this project, while a Simone Veil Fellowship at Project House Europe in Munich helped me enter the principal writing phase. Johannes Paulmann and Kiran Klaus Patel provided wonderful hospitality at these institutions, and I appreciated everyone who created an intellectually stimulating and socially enriching environment during those sojourns.

As a publisher, Bloomsbury Academic has been delightful to work with, and I am grateful to everyone involved. I especially thank Maddie Holder, who has been supportive and helpful throughout the entire process. Moreover, I value the suggestions from the series editor (Thomas Zeiler) and the detailed reports from the anonymous reviewers: their comments were thoughtful, helpful and have undoubtedly strengthened this book.

Friends and family have been an important part of this project, be it by sharing their interest in the subject or by offering welcome distractions. Three people, however, have a special part in this story. The first two are my parents, who have been loving and unstinting in their support. When I boarded a plane to the UK back in 1998, they probably did not expect that, twenty-five years later, I would still live abroad! In a different way, the question of travel also concerns the person who has a special place in these acknowledgements, Sare Aricanli. In 2022, the year that I finished most of the manuscript, Sare and I crossed various borders together – repeatedly and happily. This book is dedicated to her.

LIST OF ABBREVIATIONS

AI	Amnesty International
AIU	Alliance Israélite Universelle [Universal Israelite Alliance]
Attac	Association pour la Taxation des Transactions financières et pour l'Action Citoyenne [Association for the Taxation of Financial Transactions and Citizens' Action]
BFASS	British and Foreign Anti-Slavery Society
BPP	Black Panther Party
Comintern	Communist International
CISC	Confédération internationale des syndicats chrétiennes [International Confederation of Christian Trade Unions]
CND	Campaign for Nuclear Disarmament
CRA	Congo Reform Association
END	European Nuclear Disarmament
FoE	Friends of the Earth
GDR	German Democratic Republic
HCA	Helsinki Citizens' Assembly
ICRC	International Committee of the Red Cross
ICW	International Council of Women
IGA	International Gay Association
ILGA	International Lesbian and Gay Association / International Lesbian, Gay, Bisexual, Trans and Intersex Association
IPPNW	International Physicians for the Prevention of Nuclear War
IR	International Relations
IWSA	International Woman Suffrage Alliance
IUCN	International Union for Conservation of Nature
KOR	Komitet Obrony Robotników [Workers' Defence Committee]
LAI	League against Imperialism
LDH	Ligue des droits de l'homme [Human Rights League]
LGBT	lesbian, gay, bisexual and transgender
LSI	Labour and Socialist International
MSF	Médecins Sans Frontières [Doctors without Borders]
NAFTA	North American Free Trade Agreement
NATO	North Atlantic Treaty Organization
NGO	non-governmental organization
PAC	Pan Africanist Congress of Azania

SNoRE	Support Network on Renewable Energy
UN	United Nations
UNESCO	United Nations Scientific, Cultural and Educational Organization
UNRRA	United Nations Rehabilitation and Relief Administration
WASU	West African Students' Union
WCTU	Women's Christian Temperance Union
WIDF	Women's International Democratic Federation
WILPF	Women's International League for Peace and Freedom
WIR	Workers' International Relief
WRI	War Resisters' International
WTO	World Trade Organization
WUNC	worthiness, unity, numbers, commitment
WWF	World Wildlife Fund/World Wide Fund for Nature

INTRODUCTION
MAKING SENSE OF TRANSNATIONAL ACTIVISM

In recent years, transnational activism has repeatedly captured the media's attention – from the Occupy protests of 2011 and the launch of the 'Friday for Future' school strikes in 2018 to the summer of 2020, when activists targeted statues in Belgium, Britain and France in the wake of the American 'Black Lives Matter' protests.[1] Notwithstanding their considerable differences, these movements resemble one another in one respect: they reflect activists' conviction that particular problems are not confined to one country and that they therefore require alliances that transcend individual nations.

Neither global interdependence nor transnational activism is a recent phenomenon. If, for example, one shifted the gaze to the late 1880s and early 1890s, one could observe protagonists of the women's, peace and labour movements gather at international congresses – sometimes in close physical and temporal proximity to each other.[2] In that period, activists also consolidated their ties by forming international associations.[3] Moreover, the creation of such formal settings for interactions was but one aspect. From humanitarians undertaking relief work across imperial boundaries to anarchists maintaining clandestine networks to evade the authorities, activists in the late nineteenth century crossed borders in different ways and for different reasons.[4] Such efforts were often underpinned by a sense of connectedness and a conviction that the world was becoming smaller – a perception that was partly informed by an accelerating process of global integration.[5]

Different as these past contexts are from our present-day circumstances, they point at a wider issue: as long as there have been borders, activists have sought to cross them. But how exactly did individuals, groups and organizations foster bonds as part of their quest for political and social change? And to what extent did national or ideological boundaries affect their activism? This book addresses such questions by analysing political movements whose internationalism was a conspicuous feature – from feminism and socialism to anti-war campaigns and green politics. It also discusses groups and individuals who did not articulate visions of global change, but whose movements and collaborations nonetheless transcended national boundaries.

While the focus is on Europe, the subjects in question can only be understood within a global context. Many forms of activism were shaped by imperial or postcolonial settings and by the dynamics of globalization. Thus, even actors who confined their actions to Europe and who perceived particular causes through a Eurocentric lens were connected to other parts of the world. Moreover, for many individuals who feature in this study, moving between continents and cultures formed part and parcel of their political practice. As a whole, the book therefore considers how activists navigated, negotiated, contested and reshaped particular boundaries or understandings of nationhood, region, empire and civilization.

There are, of course, many accounts that trace specific forms of activism across different countries, regions and time spans. Examples include major surveys on the European left, the women's movement and pacifism.[6] Moreover, various historians have explored ideas about global governance and international cooperation within their broader historical contexts.[7] Yet, as Stefan Berger and Sean Scalmer have acknowledged, 'The role of transnational activists in deeper historical perspective has perhaps inspired less systematic and concentrated scholarly interest' than work on social movements, organizations and institutions.[8] While some studies bring together research on different varieties of activism, these largely take the shape of edited volumes.[9] As a monograph, the present book sets multiple causes and campaigns in relation to one another, analysing them within an overarching framework. In doing so, it traces how different principles, objectives and forms of collective action intersected or collided.

At first sight, the book title *Activism across Borders since 1870* may seem self-explanatory. Yet it is worth disaggregating its components – not only because it clarifies the terms of the overall enquiry, but also because it allows us to acknowledge some important complexities. This introduction will therefore define 'activism', consider how we might approach different movements and processes 'across borders', and then explain why and how this book explores them 'since 1870'. Following on from this, I identify four major analytical lenses that are crucial for understanding transnational activism: connectedness, transience, ambivalence and marginality.

'Activism': social movements, voluntary action and amorphousness

According to the historian Martin Conway, the period between the end of the Second World War and the upheavals of 1968 amounted to a 'democratic age' in Western European history. In exploring the meanings and practices of democracy, he has noted how activism transformed the nature of politics during the 1960s: 'democracy was, in effect, changing sides within European politics' because instead of being 'the defining characteristic of the established order, it was becoming the legitimation of the new politics of protest'.[10] Such an interpretation associates activism with both democracy and dissent. It is possible to develop this point further and argue that today, activism is a phenomenon through which many of us perceive politics in general and movements for democratic change in particular. At a time when traditional parties and institutions struggle to mobilize and enthuse, activism may appear as an ever-prominent framework for understanding and experiencing politics. Google's N-gram viewer – which analyses the occurrence of specific terms in items on Google Books – suggests a growth in the usage of 'activists' and 'activism', with a rapidly rising curve since the 1960s.[11] While such visualizations are hardly precise tools – and while the picture looks more complex in other languages – they suggest that at least in English, these expressions are enjoying ongoing, if not growing, currency.

Likewise, the figure of 'the activist' appears to be an ever-prominent feature of contemporary politics. In some instances, the image of particular individuals can help us render abstract political processes and ideas tangible. The Swedish environmentalist Greta Thunberg and the Pakistani educational rights campaigner Malala Yousafzai are but two activists who have attracted widespread media coverage for their dedication to a specific cause.[12] At the same time, the phenomenon in question has a much deeper history, and one could cite a variety of individuals who seemed to embody the causes that they promoted, from Mohandas Gandhi and Indian independence to Nelson Mandela and the struggle against apartheid.[13] In some instances, specific acts by one person reverberated very widely, as illustrated by Rosa Parks's refusal to vacate her seat on a Montgomery bus.[14] According to the political scientist Thomas Olesen, activists can become 'global political icons' as they 'have acquired meaning for audiences in several national contexts'.[15]

In light of its contemporary and historical resonances, it is important to specify what we mean when we speak of activism. As defined in this book, 'activism' describes a variety of efforts to effect political, social or cultural change through practical or symbolic action. As such, it is based on visible expressions of support – be it the gathering of signatures for a petition, the distribution of leaflets, the participation in a march or the act of addressing a meeting.[16] The phenomenon of 'hashtag activism' is a more recent development, which has given 'counterpublic groups and their allies on Twitter' new ways of making 'political contentions about identity politics that advocate for social change, identity redefinition, and political inclusion'.[17] While activism does not necessarily require mobility, it is closely entwined with communication.

Many forms of activism are associated with particular social movements. According to one definition, social movements are 'based on a sense of collective identity' and 'seek to bring about social change (or resist social change) primarily by means of collective protest'.[18] The campaigns waged by the labour movement seem to epitomize such activism and its connection to social movements. The promotion of other causes – from environmentalist concerns to LGBT rights – has grown in prominence more recently. The term 'new social movements' as an umbrella term for such concerns is linked to the notion that since the 1970s, post-material values and matters of identity have become more central than they had been in earlier social movements. Various aspects of this distinction have attracted scholarly critique, for instance the question 'whether contemporary movements are specifically a product of postindustrial society'.[19] Donatella della Porta and Mario Diani have argued that, notwithstanding some conceptual limitations, research on new social movements has been useful in putting 'actors at the center of the stage' and in recognizing 'the innovative characteristics of movements which no longer defined themselves principally in relation to the system of production'.[20]

Some forms of activism can be seen as manifestations of 'contentious politics' – a concept that figures prominently in the literature on social movements. To scholars in the field, the term describes different ways of seeking to advance 'shared interests or programs'; since such contention is a form of politics, it usually involves governments as either 'targets, the objects of claims or third parties'.[21] Many activists who feature in this book engaged in forms of claim making, as they pursued particular causes – from war resistance to women's rights – by placing pressure on governments and other target authorities. Such cases of collective action depended on the specific political environment, and contentious politics often manifests itself 'when patterns of political opportunities and constraints change'.[22]

Because of the inherent connection to activism, approaches from social movement theory can help us gauge particular dimensions of activism. According to Charles Tilly's influential typology, a social movement combines three features: it engages in 'campaigns', draws on particular 'repertoires' and makes use of so-called 'WUNC displays'.[23] Campaigns typically seek to attain their objective through a concerted attempt at generating publicity for a cause. They are indeed an important focus of this book. Moreover, my study acknowledges the wider-ranging nature of activist repertoires, with a tool kit that comprised petitions, public appeals, marches, congresses, the formation of associations and much more. Finally, Tilly's concept of 'WUNC' displays – standing for 'worthiness, unity, numbers and commitment' – is useful in highlighting how activists cast themselves and their cause. Many of them undoubtedly emphasized the serious nature of their objectives and of the protagonists involved in their movement (*worthiness*) and stressed their embrace of a common agenda (*unity*). In their effort to mount pressure on political authorities, they highlighted the broad support for their cause (*numbers*) and affirmed their motivation to pursue it, even in the face of external obstacles (*commitment*).[24] As activism is driven by a desire to make a difference, the effective projection of WUNC increases the likelihood of a response.

While social movements tend to generate various forms of activism, not all activists are part of a social movement. Dieter Rucht, for instance, has contrasted 'comprehensive social movements' with 'political campaigns' that 'are more limited in their thematic scope and duration'.[25] The present book covers campaigns that were driven by social movements but also ones that seemed to derive from very specific, more limited conditions and concerns. Moreover, the discussion extends to acts that are less easily interpreted as 'contentious politics' but that instead focus on specific and sometimes quite personal efforts to support others.

For this reason, it is worthwhile to approach activism not only through the theoretical framework of social movements, but to add another perspective: voluntary action. As Colin Rochester has argued, the latter term tends to be approached in two ways: on the one hand through a 'voluntary sector paradigm' that 'involves the assumption that voluntary agencies operate in the general area of social welfare'; on the other hand through the lens of 'volunteering', which focuses on 'philanthropic activity to help someone less fortunate than oneself' and is often seen 'essentially as unpaid work'.[26] He has argued, however, that we need to consider voluntary action much more broadly.[27] In doing so, we can see that volunteering could be a form of activism. In Rochester's own 'three perspectives' model, volunteering can be 'unpaid work or service', 'activism' or 'serious leisure', with various overlaps between these three strands.[28] Alison Penn has noted two different impulses – one being 'collective self-help', as exemplified by 'mutual aid organizations'; the other being 'the value of altruism, or helping others'.[29] The concept of voluntary action allows us to acknowledge forms of activism that are less spectacular than protests and nonetheless resonated widely, with various philanthropic endeavours being a case in point.[30]

This is not to ignore potential issues raised by the concept of 'voluntary action'. The term suggests that those who engaged in it did so without being forced to. For the vast majority of activists, these observations hold true, yet some grey areas need to be acknowledged. For instance, under dictatorships, participation in voluntary organizations could be a form of fulfilling state expectations. This, for instance, was the case with the quasi-official 'peace' committees in the Soviet Union and other state-socialist countries, as such organizations essentially affirmed the state-sponsored discourse along Cold War lines.[31] Even in democratic systems, voluntary action may have non-voluntary dimensions, as states deploy it as part of a 'mixed economy of welfare' in which some provision is delegated to the 'third sector'.[32] At times, this semi-official role raises questions about the 'voluntary' dimensions of such action, as states may incentivize or even compel individuals to undertake such work.[33]

Another grey area concerns the question of employment. As volunteering and philanthropy are often treated as manifestations of voluntary action, the term might suggest that individuals did not engage in it for pecuniary gain. Yet some activists made a living by working for organizations that were dedicated to their cause. While in many cases, this may appear as an expression of their full-time commitment, in others it may not be quite so clear. The professionalization of non-governmental organizations (NGOs) has also resulted in 'NGO professionals' who may be employed because of their aptitude in running a secretariat, mounting a publicity effort and liaising with various agencies, rather than their personal activism. The emergence of such a field of employment is illustrated by the existence of dedicated career guidance for this sector.[34]

As a whole, this book adopts a broad understanding of activism. It encompasses various degrees of participation in social movements and covers different forms of voluntary action. It also acknowledges that activism is an amorphous phenomenon. This becomes particularly evident when considering three areas: its political orientation, its relationship with religion and the question of legality.

As for the first of these three points – namely political amorphousness – it is worth emphasizing that activists can occupy different locations on the political spectrum. After all, activism is not just the pursuit of progressive causes: it is a set of tools and approaches to politics. While many cases tackled in this book were associated with the left, conservatives and the far right also mounted public campaigns, used activist repertoires and displayed 'WUNC'.[35] As a result, the word 'activist' had multiple meanings and connotations, depending on both language and historical context. For instance, during the German occupation of Belgium in the First World War, Flemish nationalists who collaborated with the occupiers were labelled 'activists'.[36] In National Socialist Germany, the term 'activist' was used positively by some National Socialists, with the Nazi propaganda organ *Völkischer Beobachter* envisioning the creation of 'a unified bloc', forged by 'the activists of the National Socialist idea who campaign for this task with all their strength'.[37] Moreover, when looking at specific campaigns, it becomes clear that the promotion of a particular cause can involve

5

politically heterogeneous alliances. A recent example is provided by the 'anti-lockdown' protests of 2020–1 in which far-right elements were joined by segments of the libertarian left.[38]

Secondly, the relationship between activism and religion is by no means clear-cut. Some forms of activism were driven by secular political goals and visions – indeed, anticlericalism or secularism constituted activist causes in their own right.[39] Yet at the same time, religious beliefs were central for many activists, from humanitarians to war resisters.[40] The rise of Catholic lay action in the twentieth century illustrates how religion informed a broad spectrum of activities, involving different constituencies and stretching from the local to the international.[41] Various forms of Muslim activism provide further examples, ranging from support efforts within migrant communities to humanitarian relief.[42]

Thirdly, there is the question of the relationship between activism and legality. During the time period covered in this study, many activists operated within systems that severely curtailed legal expressions of dissent. The threat of persecution put some individuals in conflict with the law and potentially drove them underground. In such instances, illegality formed part of what sociologists describe as a limitation of activists' 'political opportunity structure'.[43] However, even in pluralistic systems that safeguarded basic freedoms, some activists engaged in selective rule-breaking, for instance to prevent particular measures or to generate publicity. While such action often involved non-violent forms of protest, not all activists rejected violence. From anarchists who embraced the 'propaganda of the deed' to groups that saw their cause as a 'liberation struggle', various activists accepted political violence as a potential tool.[44] Thus, the boundary between activism and terrorism was sometimes blurry. As Charles Tilly has argued, violence 'emerges from the ebb and flow of collective claim making and struggles for power'; as such, it 'interweaves incessantly with non-violent politics'.[45] In this respect, the particular course that a movement or activist might adopt may partly be shaped by the nature of the political regime in question.[46] The book acknowledges such complexities and notes the use of violence in some instances, even if it largely focuses on peaceful – but not necessarily legal – forms of protest and change-making.

'Across borders': transnational activism, internationalism and cosmopolitanism

This book does not endeavour to cover all forms of activism. Instead, it deals with efforts that ranged 'across borders'. As such, it focuses on *transnational* activism. Over the last two decades, transnational history has become an increasingly prominent field of study that covers various processes, issues and events that reached beyond individual nations.[47] Such lines of enquiry have attracted interest for the insights they can generate. For instance, Fiona Paisley and Pamela Scully have argued that 'working with spaces and scales beyond national and imperial borders and boundaries can reveal more about the fractured and uneven nature of authoritative historical events'.[48] Seen from this angle, transnational approaches can help us reassess familiar narratives as they do not take the national framework as their starting point.

Studying activism from a transnational perspective means to explore how ideas and practices were disseminated beyond national contexts and how activists forged alliances with individuals in other countries.[49] It also means to consider how activists themselves crossed borders – in some instances out of necessity, for instance the need to escape persecution, and in other cases as a conscious effort to spread their cause. Transnational activism thus encompassed different ways of thinking, living or acting transnationally. The historians Sonja Levsen and Kiran Klaus Patel have highlighted three kinds of spaces that shaped such activism: 'imagined spaces of belonging and solidarity; spaces of knowledge circulation; and finally, spaces of social experience and concrete political engagement'.[50] This distinction acknowledges that even when activists affirmed notions of a global community, their practical endeavours or personal experiences could operate in more confined settings. My book is sensitive to the tensions that manifested themselves when activists navigated these different spaces.

One may ask what distinguishes the terms 'transnational' and 'international' from one another, seeing that both terms have been applied to political causes and campaigns. In some cases, scholars have spoken of both the 'international women's movement' and 'transnational feminism' within the same book.[51] One way of making sense of such differences in usage is to consider 'international' in terms of the *scale* (people coming together from several different nations) whereas the term 'transnational' refers to specific *characteristics* (activists cooperating with each other beyond national borders, borrowing ideas from abroad or travelling to meetings with activists). In many instances, it is entirely appropriate to use both expressions, as activism could at once be international and transnational. Thus, the choice of such terms partly depends on whether one wants to highlight the international breadth of a movement or the transnational patterns of the interactions that characterized it.

The deliberate use of the term 'transnational' has an additional benefit: it draws attention to the fact that some action within the international realm was not confined to states and governments interacting with one another – it was more than a matter of diplomats and state leaders speaking to one another. Indeed, within the field of International Relations (IR), the term 'transnational relations' was first used to highlight the role of non-state actors, which in turn has inspired research in international history that looks at a variety of players and parties.[52]

Among IR scholars, transnational relations have been of particular interest to protagonists of the 'constructivist' school, who argue that inter-state relations are not only driven by self-interest but also by norms which, in some cases, are constructed by actors other than states.[53] One way of tracing such processes in the international realm is through a focus on 'transnational advocacy networks'. In a pioneering study on this subject, the political scientist Margaret Keck and the IR scholar Kathryn Sikkink have examined how activists mobilized on issues such as human rights in Latin America, the environment and violence against women.[54] One of their analogies is useful in highlighting a particular incentive to work transnationally: Keck and Sikkink refer to a 'boomerang effect' whereby activists work through partners and institutions abroad, in the hope that this will ultimately yield changes at home.

In practice, international movements and transnational campaigns were manifestations of internationalism – a term that covers a variety of movements and processes that promoted cooperation, both internationally and transnationally.[55] As I have argued elsewhere, internationalism was a movement, a process and an outlook.[56] It generated transnational interactions at several levels and provided spurs for different forms of activism. Both historical agents and historians used the term 'internationalism' – a word whose emergence in the nineteenth century reflected an awareness of international links and a commitment to forging them. From the beginning, its usage proved elastic. Some forms of internationalism were driven by ideology – mostly associated with the 'red' varieties of the socialists or communists.[57] In other contexts, internationalism involved efforts to foster closer cooperation through institutions such as the League of Nations or the United Nations (UN).[58] To yet others, internationalism was a practice, for instance the participation in congresses and exhibitions, which meant that scientists and artists could also engage in it.[59] In some instances, the very act of organizing such ventures was supposed to foster peaceful relations, leading Akira Iriye to speak of 'cultural internationalism'.[60] Given the plethora of meanings associated with the term, a volume edited by Glenda Sluga and Patricia Clavin refers to 'internationalisms' and thus underscores 'the plurality of internationalisms that fed political faith and disillusionment'.[61]

Regardless of whether or not one places 'internationalism' in the plural, it is crucial to acknowledge its variegated nature. Just because something or someone was focused on international cooperation did not mean that such actions were necessarily benign. At one level, this is evident when one considers the role of internationalism within imperial projects.[62] Moreover, historians such as Madeleine Herren have highlighted the existence of fascist internationalisms.[63] Seen from this angle, the literature on internationalism chimes with my earlier observation regarding the way in which 'activism' was a politically amorphous phenomenon. It means that transnational activism in this book cannot be reduced to the European left and to causes that were portrayed or perceived as 'progressive'. Even nationalists who decried intercultural encounters and denied global interdependence forged transnational links to advance their agenda.

While nationalists could engage in internationalism, the reverse observation also holds true: many protagonists of internationalism viewed the world through a national lens. Glenda Sluga has persuasively argued that national categories were central to many internationalists.[64] This aspect is also important when considering activism that in some ways ranged across borders: often, such 'border crossings' were only partial ones. As Levsen and Patel have pointed out, even those who engaged in transnational activism 'often had an interest in keeping their spaces delineated by hard and soft edges'.[65] It is therefore important to acknowledge the intrinsic barriers that characterized many internationalist ventures.

In considering such limitations, it is possible to distinguish internationalism from a phenomenon that is subject to an extensive research literature in its own right, namely cosmopolitanism.[66] In the nineteenth and twentieth centuries, cosmopolitanism could sometimes have positive associations, especially in the realm of culture and aesthetics.[67] Yet it was also deployed as a term of abuse, sometimes with anti-Semitic connotations.[68] Some activists were eager to counter suspicions of being cosmopolitans while to others, it formed part of their self-fashioning.[69] Stefan Berger and Sean Scalmer have argued that the term may be 'ideologically too narrow to describe all forms of transnationalism connected to social movements': it appears 'so much connected in European intellectual traditions with humanism and the Enlightenment that it seems to suggest an open, tolerant, and intercultural approach to transnationalism'.[70] In this respect, the term may be less useful in capturing the less benevolent forms of transnational practice. Nonetheless, cosmopolitanism can help us approach activism across borders in two major ways.

Firstly, it allows us to capture the attitudes, visions and experiences of activists for whom nationhood was a less overt reference point. To some individuals, a sense of belonging derived from sources other than the nation, for instance unity in the struggle against external domination, including oppression that was conducted in the name of nations.[71] Sidney Tarrow has coined the term 'rooted cosmopolitans' for activists who, during the 1990s and 2000s, combined their action in the global realm with an attachment to local contexts. To him, these are individuals who 'move physically and cognitively outside their origins but who continue to be linked to place, to the social networks that inhabit that space, and to the resources, experiences, and opportunities that place provides them with'.[72] In his definition, transnational activists are 'a subgroup of rooted cosmopolitans'.[73] The present era of globalization has in some ways provided new opportunities for this form of cosmopolitanism.[74]

Secondly, cosmopolitanism is a useful category because in political science and sociology, it has been deployed in a normative way – namely in terms of promoting universal principles.[75] This understanding of cosmopolitanism allows us to acknowledge visions and ideas that clearly transcended the nation and thus differed from internationalism. This overarching perspective can be useful when considering manifestations of global civil society – a term that has enjoyed some currency within political science circles but that has also been historicized.[76] Indeed, one of the prominent theorists of global civil society, Mary Kaldor, was involved in ventures that sought to link peace campaigners in East and West during the 1980s. Such transnational activism, according to Kaldor, provides an example of global civil society in action.[77]

While terms such as 'transnational', 'internationalism' and 'cosmopolitanism' are useful in offering greater precision as to the type of border crossings that are being studied, they are no ends in themselves. We need to be conscious of the pitfalls that are inherent in using such terminology: there is a risk of superimposing a particular kind of language – and the ideas that it implies – upon earlier periods. Some individuals could be viewed as 'internationalists', others as 'cosmopolitans', and in some cases, the label may be a matter of one's vantage point or, indeed, the specific audience that activists sought to address.

'Since 1870': historical contexts of transnational activism

One of the premises of Sidney Tarrow's 2005 book on *The New Transnational Activism* is that the phenomenon under consideration is not novel since 'transnational activism has a history'.[78] While Tarrow's study starts with a vignette from the 1920s and 1930s and occasionally ranges back in time, the bulk of his material covers phenomena between 1999 and 2005. This is linked to his argument that the 'new' form of transnational activism derived from 'its connection to the current wave of globalization and its relation to the changing structure of international politics'.[79] Obviously, what appeared 'new' back in 2005 can itself be historicized by now. Moreover, there is still scope to substantiate Tarrow's premise by exploring transnational activism in its historical dimensions. My study provides a historical perspective for a field in which overarching interpretations largely come from other disciplines, in particular sociology, political science and international relations.

The title refers to the period 'since 1870'. To some extent, any starting point can only be notional: I do not mean to suggest that earlier campaigns were any less significant or that we can disregard them. Indeed, the first chapter ranges back further in time when it discusses anti-slavery activism which, as a transnational phenomenon, can be traced back to the late eighteenth century.[80] Moreover, if one thinks of different forms of mobilization in the European revolutions of 1848, a starting point in the mid-nineteenth century would also be justifiable.[81] That said, the choice to focus on developments since 1870 is by no means arbitrary: it allows me to shed light on three important processes, namely globalization, nationalization and Europeanization. Neither of these phenomena unfolded in a consistent or compatible manner; indeed, in some cases, the interplay between them could generate substantial tensions.

As for the first of these processes, it is clear that the late nineteenth and early twentieth centuries were an age of global integration. In this period, imperial expansion coincided with greater connectivity in terms of trade, transport and communication. Admittedly, it is possible to note such patterns and forces for the period *before* 1870. But, as Emily Rosenberg has argued, in the period between 1870 and 1945, 'the global flows of migrants, commodities, and ideas surges through circuity that, generally, became denser', even if this happened 'at different levels and with various effects'.[82] Jürgen Osterhammel's large-scale examination of nineteenth-century history refers to the '1880s threshold', which heralded 'a time of especially radical change' on a global level.[83]

In the late nineteenth century, activists increasingly evoked such interconnections as an argument for their own approach to politics. Traditionally, the era of the two World Wars is often seen as a time of 'de-globalization', whereas a more recent wave of globalization is associated with the period since the 1970s, with a particular focus on forces that gathered momentum from the 1990s onwards. Seen from this perspective, both the start and end point of this study fall into eras of globalization. Recent research, however, forces us to abandon a 'rise, fall and rise again' narrative of globalization. Despite protectionist measures and nationalism, the interwar years were also a globalizing era, driven for instance by new international institutions and other global actors.[84] Even when focusing on the economic realm, it has been argued that the 'internationalisation efforts' of many businesses as well as economic developments outside of Europe mean that 'the thesis of an economic deglobalisation during the interwar period is barely tangible in its absolute form'.[85] Meanwhile, from an intellectual history perspective, Or Rosenboim has shown that 'globalist' thinking gathered momentum during and after the Second World War.[86] When it comes to the post-1945 years, the Cold War evidently generated fresh global impacts and developments.[87] In this respect, it is more useful to treat globalization as an important dynamic *throughout* the period under consideration, albeit in different ways.

Secondly, nationalization became an important factor in Europe in the period under consideration. Of course, national movements grew throughout the 'long nineteenth century', reclaiming and constructing national pasts, promoting the use of national languages and launching new political projects.[88] But 1870 is a useful starting point because, by then, this process had started to transform the political map of Europe. In the wake of the Franco-Prussian War, a unified German state was formally established in January 1871. Meanwhile in Italy, the capture of Rome by Giuseppe Garibaldi's troops in September 1870 completed the political unification of Italy. A few years earlier, the Austro-Hungarian Compromise of 1867 had changed the political set-up of the Habsburg empire by turning it into a Dual Monarchy, partly in response to a growing desire for autonomy in Hungary. Within both halves of the Habsburg Monarchy, new movements increasingly challenged the dominance of German Austrians and Hungarians. Furthermore, by 1878, the declining powers of the Ottoman Empire resulted in the emergence of new states in South-Eastern Europe. These geopolitical shifts are important when one considers the relationship between state actions and nationalism: in some ways, states themselves could become driving forces for nationalization.[89]

This is not to say that nationalism was all-important in the decades after 1870, and recent work has noted that a focus on national tensions risks obscuring the extent of 'national indifference'.[90] Nonetheless, national ideas became increasingly powerful in mobilizing larger groups of people, with Eric Hobsbawm stressing that national issues acquired greater prominence 'in the forty years preceding 1914'.[91] In the aftermath of the First World War, the frequent reference to national principles and the rise of ultra-nationalist movements highlighted the appeal of national persuasions. Whether they liked it or not, activists increasingly operated in a world of nations and nationalisms.

Looking at these broader contexts, it is clear that any movement or campaign that ventured beyond national borders had to deal with the interplay between globalization and nationalization. In some cases, activists directly referenced these processes. For instance, protagonists of the peace movement evoked global integration in describing war as futile and in arguing for the creation of international institutions. Writing in 1905, the Austrian pacifist Alfred Hermann Fried suggested that peace activism was rooted 'in the complete transformation of modern humanity, in the great technological and intellectual achievements of the final decades of the previous century, and in the upheavals caused by it'. In this context, 'the internationality of the economic and intellectual life of the present' appeared like a major factor.[92] One century later, activists attacked aspects of globalization that they deemed 'neoliberal' and juxtaposed this process with their own, alternative vision of global change.[93] Likewise, the growing appeal of national principles forced activists to position themselves when acting within the international realm – either by denouncing the dangers of nationalism or by asserting their own national credentials.

To nationalization and globalization, one can add a third aspect: Europeanization. This concept is primarily associated with the history of European integration since the end of the Second World War, yet recent work has drawn attention to forms of Europeanization from below.[94] If 'Europe' was more than an abstract idea but a set of particular practices, activists could be involved in constructing it. This was not just a question of people who promoted visions of European unity, for instance the Pan-Europeanists of the interwar years or campaigners who championed the vision of a socialist Europe.[95] In times when political borders seemed very pronounced, it was activists who helped to give meaning to Europe and the mental maps associated with it. This, for instance, was the case during the Cold War years, when dissidents in Central and Eastern Europe envisaged their own future within a new Europe.[96]

Patricia Clavin has argued that writing history from a transnational perspective allows us to reconsider 'time, manner, place'.[97] The history of transnational activism is a good example of how such a reframing might occur, as it raises questions about the nature of politics ('manner') and draws attention to the ways in which 'Europe' was being conceived and constructed ('place'). With regard to the latter, this book acknowledges that 'Europe' could have very different meanings: to some, it ultimately amounted to a narrow, Western European 'core' while others conceived it in much broader terms. In some cases, it encompassed parts of the European empires or overseas constituencies with whom activists felt a commonality of interest. For this reason, this book is based on a fluid understanding of 'Europe': it acknowledges that its boundaries cannot be clearly defined and that they were partly being reshaped in the rhetoric and praxis of different activists.[98]

Obviously, there are major differences between the late nineteenth and the early twenty-first centuries, and one must remain alert to the significance of specific historical settings. Nonetheless, the approach taken here also allows us to reconsider 'time' in European history, as it cuts across some of the existing periodizations in European history: the *fin de siècle* (lasting from the late nineteenth century to the First World War), the interwar period, the Cold War and the global present. This broader chronological approach allows us to trace the resonance of particular ideas and tropes. For example, many activists stressed their relationship to existing intellectual traditions, as illustrated by activists who evoked Marxist ideology or revolutionary pasts.[99] In studying such phenomena over a longer period of time, we can see how they were recast and reconfigured.

Moreover, a broader historical perspective allows us to trace how much empire affected the scope and nature of transnational activism – which is also the reason why the first chapter focuses on the interplay between activism and empire. Some historians have spoken of 'imperial humanitarianism' in the period of up to 1945 and 'imperial internationalism' during the interwar years.[100] Certainly, many activists took empire for granted or even viewed it as a vehicle for progress. Others, however, engaged in transnational campaigning precisely because they opposed imperial domination. Even after most former colonies had gained their independence, empire remained an important trope in activist mobilizations, from challenging particular forms of domination as 'neo-colonialism' to protesting against American 'imperialism'.[101]

International organizations formed another important thread that covered a large time span. Already in the late nineteenth century, many campaigners demanded the creation of international organizations that would lay the foundations for a more peaceful order. At the same time, they founded voluntary international associations of their own. International organizations of different kinds grew in number from the 1870s onwards.[102] The foundation of the League of Nations in 1920 was at one level also the outcome of the efforts of activists to promote a new world organization while in another sense, this new body provided a potential target and forum for activists. After the Second World War, the United Nations (UN) in some ways built upon the experiences of the League and provided a potential audience for campaigners who, for instance, mobilized on the occasion of UN summits. In these respects, a broader historical perspective allows us to understand how the contemporary world of international NGOs and UN agencies developed out of particular historical experiences and contexts.[103]

As a whole, the book's broader chronological approach makes it possible to trace shifting alliances, to identify ideological and rhetorical continuities and to highlight the importance of geopolitical contexts in shaping campaigners' agendas and actions. At the same time, we must not to fall into the teleological trap of casting the history of activism in terms of the purposeful 'rise' of a particular set of causes, concerns or actions. For this reason, the book eschews narratives of progress: it does not present earlier forms of activism as preludes to the contemporary world. Instead, the emphasis is on ruptures and transformations caused by wars and ideological dispute.

Analysing transnational activism: connectedness, ambivalence, transience and marginality

The preceding sections have explained this book's intention to develop an overarching perspective on the history of transnational activism since 1870. As the discussion has shown, the phenomenon under consideration was often contradictory and highly malleable. To recognize its complexity, I propose the combination of four analytical lenses: connectedness, ambivalence, transience and marginality.

The first of these dimensions, *connectedness*, is important in several respects. At a basic level, the history of transnational activism is a history of activists connecting with one another. Indeed, the spaces in which activists gathered, from congress halls to the street, had their own sociabilities that could reinforce certain ties, even if they also revealed divisions.[104] Yet to this, one must add another dimension that is equally crucial – namely the connectedness of causes. We cannot put activism into neat boxes: many activists construed different causes as intertwined, for instance by championing feminist pacifism or by insisting on the entwined nature of the struggles for social justice and human rights. This is not to say that all causes were connected. It does, however, suggest that such linkages provided a basis for further mobilization. The alertness to such cross-connections is one reason why the present book seeks to cover a broad array of phenomena within a few hundred pages.

Secondly, the book highlights the *ambivalence* that characterized many forms of transnational activism. Public portrayals tend to treat activists in the international realm as idealists and 'do-gooders'. By contrast, the book problematizes transnational action by highlighting its manifold blind spots and by noting how it could also be a vehicle for prejudices and exclusionary agendas. A recognition of ambivalence means that my analysis incorporates points raised earlier on in this introduction: the politically amorphous nature of activism and the way in which internationalism encompassed practices and attitudes that were far from benign. Because of this emphasis on ambivalence, I have chosen not to include a separate chapter on exclusionary or oppressive forms of transnational activism because such forms feature throughout the book, also when discussing campaigns that, at first sight, may have appeared 'progressive' or benevolent.

Thirdly, an acknowledgement of *transience* is important because the alliances formed by activists often ended up being temporary in nature and sometimes ended in discord. The availability of associational records as well as the tendency of international organizations to highlight past achievements may create temptations to write the history of activism in institutional terms and thus may risk privileging organization that proved durable. Rather than adding to the well-established literature on the history of NGOs, the book focuses on coalitions and campaigns that were often temporary in nature, as well as discussing the idiosyncratic trajectories of individual activists.

Finally, *marginality* plays an important role when considering the nature and development of transnational activism. The creation of transnational bonds was a potential strategy for actors who were being marginalized at the national level. By acting transnationally, they forged partnerships and thus amplified their voices. In this respect, transnational activism had particular potentials and roles precisely because it was not confined to the national arena and its existing hierarchies. At the same time, some groups were more successful than others when seeking backing abroad.[105] Moreover, we must bear in mind the insight that activism could reflect or even reinforce discriminatory practices.

In acknowledging the role of connectedness, transience, ambivalence and marginality, this book draws on a rich array of sources. The material in this book builds on many years of researching and reflecting on the subjects in question. As such, I have used material from a range of international archival collections as well as many published sources, from congress proceedings to memoirs. That said, I am conscious of my own biases and linguistic limitations. There cannot be a comprehensive study of transnational activism, and the present book constitutes just one possible history of transnational activism: it is well possible to imagine a study on the same subject with very different examples and emphases. While each chapter surveys wider developments, I have selected examples of specific campaigns or even individuals in order to illustrate broader points. This consideration of individual figures is helpful because, as Donatella della Porta has noted, 'the focus on transnational activists in historical perspective addresses a gap in social movements that have focused (much) more on the macro- and the meso-levels than on the micro-level'.[106]

The overarching structure of this book is thematic, with eight chapters that cover different forms of activism. Within the individual chapters, however, I have sought to combine thematic and chronological approaches. Thus, the chapters allow the reader to see how particular strands of actions developed and how particular currents gained in prominence over time. Moreover, when looking at the book as a whole, the chapter sequence retains a certain chronological thrust, as the first chapter ('Empire and Activism') goes back furthest in time and has substantial sections on the nineteenth century, while the final chapter ('Going Green') ends in the twenty-first century.

It is possible to approach the structure of this book in two different ways. Perhaps most obviously, it can be read in terms of particular causes – for instance anti-slavery and anticolonialism (Chapter 1), humanitarian aid (Chapters 1 and 2), pacifism (Chapter 3), socialism and social justice (Chapter 4), feminism and sexual equality (Chapter 5), anti-racism (Chapter 6), human rights (Chapter 7) and, finally, environmentalism (Chapter 8). Such a list inevitably raises question about notable absences: what about prison reform, Esperanto, temperance, vegetarianism, animal rights – to cite but some examples? While such movements may be touched upon, they do not feature in depth, and further examples of such gaps could easily be added. This study is not encyclopaedic: instead, the aim is to trace some prominent causes and themes on which people campaigned.

We can also read the structure in a second way, namely in terms of broader contexts that solicited responses and thus generated activism. In this respect, a consideration of these dimensions starts with empire (Chapter 1) and military conflict (Chapters 2 and 3), then traces experiences of inequality on the grounds of class, gender, sexuality, ethnicity and nationality (Chapters 4, 5 and 6), highlights the role of state power (Chapter 7) and, finally, draws attention to the environment (Chapter 8). Of course, there are no neat dividing lines; instead, it is a question of some contexts being foregrounded at specific points in the book. Taken together, however, the chapters offer an alternative history of modern and contemporary Europe, with the subject of transnational activism providing the overarching conceptual unity.

Notes

1. On these movements, see The Social Movement Studies Editorial Collective, ed., *Occupy! A Global Movement* (Abingdon: Routledge, 2015); Sebastian Haunss and Moritz Summer, eds, *Fridays for Future – Die Jugend gegen den Klimawandel: Konturen der weltweiten Protestbewegung* (Bielefeld: transcript Verlag, 2020); the special journal issue edited by Audrey Célestine, Nicolas Martin-Breteau and Charlotte Recoquillon, 'Black Lives Matter: un mouvement transnational?', *Esclavages et post-esclavages*, no. 6 (2022): 1–18; and Kevin Gaines, 'Global Black Lives Matter', *American Quarterly* 74, no. 3 (2022): 626–34.

2. See, for example, the congresses staged by the socialist, peace and women's movements in Paris in 1889, as discussed in Karen Offen, *Debating the Women Question in the French Third Republic* (Cambridge: Cambridge University Press, 2018), 133–52.
3. Akira Iriye, *Global Community: The Role of International Organizations in the Making of the Contemporary World* (Berkeley, CA: University of California Press, 2004); Thomas Davies, *NGOs: A New History of Transnational Civil Society* (London: Hurst, 2014).
4. For historiographical overviews that acknowledge transnational dimensions of humanitarianism, see Abigail Green, 'Humanitarianism in Nineteenth-Century Contexts: Religious, Gendered, National', *The Historical Journal* 52, no. 4 (2014): 1157–75; Aoife O'Leary McNeice, 'Towards a History of Global Humanitarianism', *The Historical Journal* 63, no. 5 (2020): 1378–89. For a discussion of anarchist mobilities, see e.g. Isabelle Felici, 'Anarchists as Emigrants', in *Reassessing the Transnational Turn: Scales of Analysis in Anarchist and Syndicalist Studies*, ed. Constance Bantman and Bert Altena (New York: Routledge, 2015), 83–99.
5. Jürgen Osterhammel and Niels Petersson, *Globalization: A Short History* (Princeton, NJ: Princeton University Press, 2009), 81–9.
6. To cite but one example for each of these three fields: Geoff Eley, *Forging Democracy: The History of the Left in Europe, 1850–2000* (Oxford: Oxford University Press, 2002); Karen Offen, *European Feminisms, 1750–1950: A Political History* (Stanford, CA: Stanford University Press, 2000); David Cortright, *Peace: A History of Movements and Ideas* (Cambridge: Cambridge University Press, 2008).
7. Mark Mazower, *Governing the World: The History of an Idea* (London: Penguin, 2012); Glenda Sluga, *Internationalism in the Age of Nationalism* (Philadelphia, PA: University of Pennsylvania Press, 2013); Daniel Gorman, *International Cooperation in the Early Twentieth Century* (London: Bloomsbury, 2018).
8. Stefan Berger and Sean Scalmer, 'The Transnational Activist: An Introduction', in *The Transnational Activist: Transformations and Comparisons from the Anglo-World since the Nineteenth Century*, ed. Stefan Berger and Sean Scalmer (Cham: Palgrave, 2018), 5.
9. Martin Geyer and Johannes Paulmann, eds, *The Mechanics of Internationalism: Culture, Politics, and Society from the 1840s to the First World War* (Oxford: Oxford University Press, 2001); Glenda Sluga and Patricia Clavin, eds, *Internationalisms: A Twentieth-Century History* (Cambridge: Cambridge University Press, 2017); David Brydan and Jessica Reinisch, eds, *Internationalists in European History: Rethinking the Twentieth Century* (London: Bloomsbury, 2021); and Stefan Berger and Holger Nehring, eds, *The History of Social Movements in a Global Perspective* (London: Palgrave, 2017).
10. Martin Conway, *Western Europe's Democratic Age: 1945–1968* (Princeton, NJ: Princeton University Press, 2020), 277.
11. The n-gram viewer is available at https://books.google.com/ngrams (last accessed 9 January 2023).
12. Ingrid Hoofd, 'Malala and the Politics of Feminist New Media Activism', in *Doing Gender in Media, Art and Culture: A Comprehensive Guide to Gender Studies*, ed. Rosemarie Buikema, Liedeke Plate and Kathrin Thiele (Abingdon: Routledge, 2018), 222–32; Patrick D. Murphy, 'Speaking for Youth, Speaking for the Planet: Greta Thunberg and the Representational Politics of Eco-Celebrity', *Popular Communication* 19, no. 3 (2021): 193–206.
13. Sean Scalmer, *Gandhi in the West: The Mahatma and the Rise of Radical Protest* (New York: Cambridge University Press, 2011); Rita Barnad, ed., *The Cambridge Companion to Nelson Mandela* (Cambridge: Cambridge University Press, 2014).

14. Holloway Sparks, 'Dissident Citizenship: Democratic Theory, Political Courage, and Activist Women', *Hypatia* 12, no. 4 (1997): 74–110.
15. Thomas Olesen, *Global Injustice Symbols and Social Movements* (New York: Palgrave, 2015), 41.
16. See e.g. Clare Saunders, 'Activism', in *The Wiley-Blackwell Encyclopedia of Social and Political Movements*, ed. David A. Snow et al. (Hoboken, NJ: Wiley-Blackwell, 2014), available online via https://doi.org/10.1002/9780470674871.wbespm002 (last accessed 9 January 2023).
17. Sarah J. Jackson, Moya Bailey and Brooke Foucault Welles, *#Hashtag Activism: Networks of Race and Gender Justice* (Cambridge, MA: The MIT Press, 2020), xviii.
18. Dieter Rucht, 'Studying Social Movements: Some Conceptual Challenges', in Berger and Nehring, *The History of Social Movements in Global Perspective*, 43.
19. Nelson A. Pichardo, 'New Social Movements: A Critical Review', *Annual Review of Sociology* 23 (1997): 411–30, 425.
20. Donatella Della Porta and Mario Diani, *Social Movements: An Introduction* (Malden, MA: Blackwell, 2006), 10.
21. Charles Tilly and Sidney Tarrow, *Contentious Politics* (2nd edn; Oxford: Oxford University Press, 2015), 236.
22. Sidney Tarrow, *Power in Movement: Social Movements and Contentious Politics* (3rd edn; Cambridge: Cambridge University Press, 2013), 28–9.
23. Charles Tilly, Ernesto Castañeda and Lesley J. Wood, *Social Movements, 1768–2018* (New York: Routledge, 2020), 6.
24. Tilly et al., *Social Movements*, 7.
25. Rucht, 'Studying Social Movements', 43.
26. Colin Rochester, *Rediscovering Voluntary Action: The Beat of a Different Drum* (Basingstoke: Palgrave, 2013), 6–7.
27. Rochester, *Rediscovering Voluntary Action*, 179.
28. Ibid., 181.
29. Alison Penn, 'Social History and Organizational Development: Revisiting Beverdige's Voluntary Action', in *Understanding the Roots of Voluntary Action: Historical Perspectives on Current Social Policy*, ed. Colin Rochester (Eastbourne: Sussex Academic Press, 2011), 19.
30. For studies using a 'voluntary action' perspective to consider different forms of activism, see Georgina Brewis, *A Social History of Student Volunteering: Britain and Beyond, 1880–1980* (Basingstoke: Palgrave, 2014); Peter Grant, *Philanthropy and Voluntary Action in the First World War: Mobilizing Charity* (New York: Routledge, 2014); Eve Colpus, *Female Philanthropy in the Interwar World: Between Self and Other* (London: Bloomsbury, 2018).
31. See e.g. the Soviet Peace Committee, a quasi-official organization: Irina Gordeeva, 'Solidarity in Search of Human Agency: "Détente from Below", and Independent Peace Activists in the Soviet Union', *Labour History Review* 86, no. 3 (2021): esp. 345–9.
32. Rochester, *Rediscovering Voluntary Action*, 69–84. See also Georgina Brewis et al., eds, *Transformational Moments in Social Welfare: What Role for Voluntary Action?* (Bristol: Policy Press, 2021).
33. With examples from Estonia, see Piret Tõnurist and Laidi Surva, 'Is Volunteering Always Voluntary? Between Compulsion and Coercion in Co-Production', *Voluntas* 28, no. 1 (2018): 223–47.
34. Tracy Brown Hamilton, *Nongovernmental Organization (NGO) Professionals: A Practical Career Guide* (Lanham: MD: Rowman & Littlefield, 2021).

35. See e.g. Kevin Passmore, 'Fascism as a Social Movement in a Transnational Context' and Fabian Virchow, 'Post-Fascist Right-Wing Social Movements', both in Berger and Nehring, *The History of Social Movements*, 579–618 and 619–47 respectively. See also Charles Tilly's comments on the 'right-wing appropriation of social movement forms' in Tilly et al., *Social Movements*, 93–4.
36. On 'activists' in the context of Belgium during the First World War, see Sophie de Schaepdrijver, *De Groote Oorlog: het Koninkrijk België tijdens de Eerste Wereldoorlog* (Amsterdam: Atlas, 1997).
37. 'Der "Völkische Beobachter" gehört in jedes deutsche Haus!', *Völkischer Beobachter*, 4 November 1938, 2. Other pieces in the National Socialist paper also used the term 'activist'.
38. 'Anti-Lockdown Protests: Opposites Attract', *The Economist*, 3 July 2021, 24.
39. Carolin Kosuch, ed., *Freethinkers in Europe: National and Transnational Secularities, 1789–1920s* (Berlin: De Gruyter, 2020).
40. On religion and humanitarianism, see e.g. Peter Stamatov, *The Origins of Global Humanitarianism: Religion, Empires, and Advocacy* (Cambridge: Cambridge University Press, 2013); Silvia Salvatici, *A History of Humanitarianism, 1755–1989: In the Name of Others*, trans. Philip Sanders (Manchester: Manchester University Press, 2019), e.g. 16 and 42–6. On religion and war resistance, see e.g. Anna Hamling, 'Three Apostles of Non-Violence: An Introduction to the Religious Thinking of Tolstoy, Gandhi, and Abdul Ghaffar Khan', in *The Routledge History of World Peace since 1750*, ed. Christian Philip Peterson, William Knoblauch and Michael Loadenthal (Abingdon: Routledge, 2019), 85–97; Cortright, *Peace*, 183–209; Patricia Applebaum, *Kingdom to Commune: Protestant Pacifist Culture between World War I and the Vietnam War* (Chapel Hill, NC: University of North Carolina Press, 2009).
41. Lex Heerma van Voss, Patrick Pasture and Jan De Maeyer, eds, *Between Cross and Class: Comparative Histories of Christian Labour in Europe 1840–2000* (Bern: Peter Lang, 2005); Gerd-Rainer Horn, *Western European Liberation Theology: The First Wave (1924–1959)* (Oxford: Oxford University Press, 2008).
42. Ahmet Yüklezen and Gökçe Yurdakul, 'Islamic Activism and Immigrant Integration: Turkish Organizations in Germany', *Immigrants & Minorities* 29, no. 1 (2011): 64–85; Bruno De Cordier, 'Faith-Based Aid, Globalisation and the Humanitarian Frontline: An Analysis of Western-based Muslim Aid Organisations', *Disasters* 33, no. 4 (2009): 608–28.
43. For a discussion of 'political opportunity structures', see Marco Giugni, 'Political Opportunity: Still a Useful Concept?', in *Contention and Trust in Cities and States*, ed. Michael Hanagan and Chris Tilly (Dordrecht: Springer, 2011), 271–83.
44. For a broader consideration, see Donatella Della Porta, *Clandestine Political Violence* (Cambridge: Cambridge University Press, 2013). For historical perspectives, see for instance the examples gathered in Wolfgang Mommsen and Gerhard Hirschfeld, eds, *Social Protest, Violence and Terror in Nineteenth- and Twentieth-Century Europe* (London: Macmillan, 1982).
45. Charles Tilly, *The Politics of Collective Violence* (Cambridge: Cambridge University Press, 2003), 238.
46. On the role of regimes, see Tilly, *The Politics of Collective Violence*, 50–3 and 231–2.
47. For an overview, see Pierre-Yves Saunier, *Transnational History* (Basingstoke: Palgrave, 2013). The sheer breadth of aspects that are part of transnational history is illustrated by the contributions to Akira Iriye and Pierre-Yves Saunier, eds, *The Palgrave Dictionary of Transnational History: From the Mid-19th Century to the Present Day* (Basingstoke: Palgrave, 2010).

48. Fiona Paisley and Pamela Scully, *Writing Transnational History* (London: Bloomsbury, 2019), 4.
49. From a social science perspective, such processes can be seen as 'transnationalization': Dieter Rucht, 'The Transnationalization of Social Movements: Trends, Causes, Problems', in *Transnational Movements in a Globalizing World*, ed. Donatella Della Porta, Hanspeter Kriesi and Dieter Rucht (Basingstoke: Palgrave, 1999), 206–22.
50. Sonja Levsen and Kiran Klaus Patel, 'Imagined Transnationalism? Mapping Transnational Spaces of Political Activism in Europe's Long 1970s', *European Review of History* 29, no. 3 (2022): 372. See also Kiran Klaus Patel and Sonja Levsen, 'The Spatial Contours of Transnational Activism: Conceptual Implications and the Road Forward', *European Review of History* 29, no. 3 (2022): 548–61.
51. See e.g. the use of these terms, and the author's clarification on the approach, in Marie Sandell, *The Rise of Women's Transnational Activism: Identity and Sisterhood between the World Wars* (London: I.B. Tauris, 2015), 4–5.
52. For a pioneering example, see Joseph Nye and Robert Keohane, 'Transnational Relations and World Politics: An Introduction', *International Organization* 25, no. 3 (1971): 329–49. See also Thomas Risse-Kappen, ed., *Bringing Transnational Relations Back In: Non-State Actors, Domestic Structures and International Institutions* (Cambridge: Cambridge University Press, 1995). For the adoption of this perspective among historians, see Patricia Clavin, 'Defining Transnationalism', *Contemporary European History* 14, no. 4 (2005): 421–39; Patricia Clavin, 'Conceptualising Internationalism between the World Wars', in *Internationalism Reconfigured: Transnational Ideas and Movements between the World Wars*, ed. Daniel Laqua (London: I.B. Tauris, 2011), 1–14; Sandrine Kott, 'Les Organisations internationales, terrains d'étude de la globalisation: Jalons pour une approche socio-historique', *Critique internationale* 52 (2011): 9–16; Karen Gram-Skjoldager, Haakon Ikonomou and Torsten Kahlert, eds, *Organizing the 20th-Century World: International Organizations and the Emergence of International Public Administrations, 1920s–1960s* (London: Bloomsbury, 2020); Madeleine Herren, *Internationale Organisationen seit 1865: Eine Globalgeschichte der internationalen Ordnung* (Darmstadt: Wissenschaftliche Buchgesellschaft, 2009).
53. Martha Finnemore and Kathryn Sikkink, 'Taking Stock: The Constructivist Research Program in International Relations and Comparative Politics', *Annual Review of Political Science* (2001): 391–416. The concept of 'epistemic communities' occupies a distinct space in this literature. See e.g. Peter M. Haas, *Epistemic Communities, Constructivism, and International Environmental Politics* (Abingdon: Routledge, 2016).
54. Margaret E. Keck and Kathryn Sikkink, *Activists beyond Borders: Advocacy Networks in International Politics* (Ithaca, NY: Cornell University Press, 1998), 12–13.
55. See e.g. Johannes Paulmann and Martin Geyer, 'Introduction: The Mechanics of Internationalism', in Paulmann and Geyer, *The Mechanics of Internationalism*, 1–26; David Brydan and Jessica Reinisch, 'Introduction: Internationalists in European History', in Brydan and Reinisch, *Internationalists in European History*, 1–13; Clavin, 'Conceptualising Internationalism'.
56. Daniel Laqua, *The Age of Internationalism and Belgium, 1880–1930: Peace, Progress and Prestige* (Manchester: Manchester University Press, 2013), 5. I have further expanded on internationalism in Daniel Laqua, 'Internationalism', in Leibniz Institute of European History (IEG), *European History Online (EGO)*, 4 May 2021, http://www.ieg-ego.eu/laquad-2021-en (last accessed 9 January 2023).
57. The literature on left-wing internationalisms is vast. For overviews, see Patrizia Dogliani, 'The Fate of Socialist Internationalism' and Talbot Imlay, 'Socialist Internationalism after

1914', both in Sluga and Clavin, *Internationalisms*, 61–84 and 213–42 respectively. For a longer discussion of, respectively, socialist and communist internationalism, see Talbot Imlay, *The Practice of Internationalism: European Socialists and International Politics, 1914–60* (Oxford: Oxford University Press, 2018); and Silvio Pons, *The Global Revolution: A History of International Communism 1917–1991*, trans. Allan Cameron (Oxford: Oxford University Press, 2014).

58. For a detailed analysis of these strands of internationalism, see Sluga, *Internationalism in the Age of Nationalism*; Mazower, *Governing the World*. On intersections between liberal and socialist internationalism, see Daniel Laqua, 'Democratic Politics and the League of Nations: The Labour and Socialist International as a Protagonist of Interwar Internationalism', *Contemporary European History* 24, no. 2 (2015): 175–92.

59. Grace Brockington, ed., *Internationalism and the Arts in Britain and Europe at the Fin de Siècle* (Oxford: Peter Lang, 2009); Charlotte Ashby et al., eds, *Imagined Cosmopolis: Internationalism and Cultural Exchange, 1870s–1920* (Oxford: Peter Lang, 2019); Anne Rasmussen, 'L'Internationale scientifique, 1890–1914' (PhD thesis, EHESS, Paris, 1995).

60. Akira Iriye, *Cultural Internationalism and World Order* (Baltimore, MD: Johns Hopkins University Press, 2000).

61. Glenda Sluga and Patricia Clavin, 'Rethinking the History of Internationalisms', in Sluga and Clavin, *Internationalisms*, 13.

62. Miguel Bandeira Jerónimo and José Pedro Monteiro, 'Pasts to Be Unveiled: The Interconnections between the International and the Imperial', in *Internationalism, Imperialism and the Formation of the Contemporary World: The Pasts of the Present*, ed. Miguel Bandeira Jerónimo and José Pedro Monteiro (Cham: Palgrave, 2018); Miguel Bandeira Jerónimo and Damiano Matasci, 'Imperialism, Internationalism and Globalisation in Twentieth Century Africa', *Journal of Imperial and Commonwealth History* 48, no. 5 (2020): 793–804.

63. Madeleine Herren, 'Fascist Internationalism', in Sluga and Clavin, *Internationalisms*, 191–212; Arnd Bauerkämper and Grzegorz Rossolinski-Liebe, eds, *Fascism without Borders: Transnational Connections and Cooperation between Movements and Regimes in Europe from 1918 to 1945* (New York: Berghahn, 2017); Sandrine Kott and Kiran Klaus Patel, 'Fascist Internationalism: Nazi Social Policy as an Imperial Project – an Introduction', in *Nazism across Borders: The Social Policies of the Third Reich and Their Global Appeal*, ed. Sandrine Kott and Kiran Klaus Patel (Oxford: Oxford University Press, 2018), 1–25.

64. Sluga, *Internationalism in the Age of Nationalism*.

65. Patel and Levsen, 'The Spatial Contours of Transnational Activism', 550.

66. For an overview of the literature on cosmopolitanism, see Maria Rovisco and Magdalena Nowicka, eds, *The Ashgate Research Companion to Cosmopolitanism* (Farnham: Ashgate, 2011); Gerard Delanty, ed., *Routledge International Handbook of Cosmopolitanism Studies* (2nd edn; Abingdon: Routledge, 2019); Steven Vertovec and Robin Cohen, eds, *Conceiving Cosmopolitanism: Theory, Contexts, and Practice* (Oxford: Oxford University Press, 2002). For examples of the relevance for historians, see Glenda Sluga and Julia Horne, 'Cosmopolitanism: Its Pasts and Practices', *Journal of World History* 21, no. 3 (2010): 369–74; Bernhard Gißibl and Isabella Löhr, eds, *Bessere Welten: Kosmopolitismus in den Geschichtswissenschaften* (Frankfurt/Main: Campus, 2017).

67. Vincenzi Cicchelli, Sylvie Octobre and Viviane Riegel, eds, *Aesthetic Cosmopolitanism and Global Culture* (Leiden: Brill, 2020).

68. Robert Phone and Philip Spencer, *Cosmopolitanism and Antisemitism* (London: Bloomsbury, 2015).
69. I have elaborated on these dimensions in Daniel Laqua, 'Cosmopolitanism and the Individual', in Ashby et al., *Imagined Cosmopolis*, 15–34.
70. Berger and Scalmer, 'The Transnational Activist', 6.
71. Nico Slate, *Colored Cosmopolitanism: The Shared Struggle for Freedom in the United States and India* (Cambridge, MA: Harvard University Press, 2012).
72. Sidney Tarrow, *The New Transnational Activism* (Cambridge: Cambridge University Press, 2005), 42.
73. Tarrow, *The New Transnational Activism*, 43.
74. Craig Calhoun, 'Cosmopolitanism and the Modern Social Imaginary', *Daedalus* 137, no. 3 (2008): 105–14.
75. David Held, *Cosmopolitanism: Ideals and Realities* (Cambridge: Polity, 2010); Ulrich Beck, *The Cosmopolitan Vision*, trans. Ciaran Cronin (Cambridge: Polity, 2006).
76. Andrew Arsan, Su Lin Lewis and Anne-Isabella Richard, 'The Roots of Global Civil Society and the Interwar Moment', *Journal of Global History* 7, no. 2 (2011): 157–65.
77. Mary Kaldor, *Global Civil Society: An Answer to War* (Cambridge: Polity, 2003).
78. Tarrow, *The New Transnational Activism*, 3.
79. Ibid., 5.
80. See e.g. John R. Oldfield, *Transatlantic Abolitionism in the Age of Revolution: An International History of Anti-Slavery, c. 1787–1820* (Cambridge: Cambridge University Press, 2013).
81. Axel Körner, ed., *1848: A European Revolution? International Ideas and National Memories of 1848* (rev. edn; Basingstoke: Macmillan, 2003). See also Patrick J. Kelly, 'The European Revolutions of 1848 and the Transnational Turn in Civil War History', *The Journal of the Civil War Era* 4, no. 3 (2014): 431–43.
82. Emily Rosenberg, 'Introduction', in *A World Connecting: 1870–1945*, ed. Emily Rosenberg (Cambridge, MA: Belknap Press, 2012), 7.
83. Jürgen Osterhammel, *The Transformation of the World: A Global History of the Nineteenth Century*, trans. Patrick Camiller (Princeton, NJ: Princeton University Press, 2014).
84. See e.g. Sönke Kunkel and Christoph Meyer, eds, *Aufbruch ins postkoloniale Zeitalter: Globalisierung und die außereuropäische Welt in den 1920s und 1930er Jahren* (Frankfurt/Main: Campus, 2012).
85. Christof Dejung, 'Deglobalisierung? Oder Entcuropäisierung des Globalen? Überlegungen zur Entwicklung der Weltwirtschaft in der Zwischenkriegszeit', in Kunkel and Meyer, *Aufbruch ins postkoloniale Zeitalter*, 59.
86. Or Rosenboim, *The Emergence of Globalism: Visions of World Order in Britain and The United States, 1939–1950* (Princeton, NJ: Princeton University Press, 2018).
87. A seminal study in this field is Odd Arne Westad, *The Global Cold War: Third World Interventions and the Making of Our Times* (Cambridge: Cambridge University Press, 2005).
88. John Breuilly, ed., *The Oxford Handbook of the History of Nationalism* (Oxford: Oxford University Press, 2013). For an anthology featuring seminal texts on nationalism, see John Hutchinson and Anthony D. Smith, eds, *Nationalism* (Oxford: Oxford University Press, 1994).

89. John Breuilly, *Nationalism and the State* (2nd edn; Manchester: Manchester University Press, 1993).

90. Pieter Judson, *Guardians of the Nation: Activists on the Language Frontiers of Imperial Austria* (Cambridge, MA: Harvard University Press, 2006); Tara Zahra, *Kidnapped Souls: National Indifference and the Battle for Children in the Bohemian Lands, 1900–1948* (Ithaca, NY: Cornell University Press, 2011); Maarten van Ginderachter and Jon Fox, eds, *National Indifference and the History of Nationalism in Modern Europe* (Abingdon: Routledge, 2019).

91. Eric Hobsbawm, *Nations and Nationalism since 1870: Programme, Myth, Reality* (2nd edn; Cambridge: Cambridge University Press, 1994), 101.

92. Alfred Hermann Fried, *Handbuch der Friedensbewegung* (Vienna: Verlag der Oesterreichischen Friedensgesellschaft, 1905), 33–4.

93. Such examples feature prominently in Tarrow, *The New Transnational Activism*. See also Donatella Della Porta, Massimiliano Andretta, Lorenzo Mosca and Herbert Reiter, *Globalization from Below: Transnational Activists and Protest Networks* (Minneapolis, MN: University of Minnesota Press, 2006).

94. Donatella Della Porta and Manuela Caiani, *Social Movements and Europeanization* (Oxford: Oxford University Press, 2009); Martin Conway and Kiran Klaus Patel, eds, *Europeanization in the Twentieth Century: Historical Approaches* (Basingstoke: Palgrave, 2010).

95. Anne-Isabelle Richard, 'The Limits of Solidarity: Europeanism, Anti-Colonialism and Socialism at the Congress of the Peoples of Europe, Asia and Africa in Puteaux, 1948', *European Review of History* 21, no. 4 (2014): 519–37.

96. See e.g. Jessica Wardhaugh, Ruth Leiserowitz and Christian Bailey, 'Intellectual Dissidents and the Construction of European Spaces, 1918–1988', in Conway and Patel, *Europeanization in the Twentieth Century*, esp. 32–7. See also Kim Christiaens, James Mark and José M. Faraldo, 'Entangled Transitions: Eastern and Southern European Convergence or Alternative Europes? 1960s–2000s', *Contemporary European History* 26, no. 4 (2014): 577–99; Victoria Harms, 'Living Mitteleuropa in the 1980s: A Network of Hungarian and West German Intellectuals', *European Review of History* 19, no. 5 (2012): 669–92; and James Mark, Bogdan Iacob, Tobias Rupprecht and Ljubica Spaskovska, *1989: A Global History of Eastern Europe* (Cambridge: Cambridge University Press, 2019), 125–45.

97. Patricia Clavin, 'Time, Manner, Place: Writing Modern European History in Global, Transnational and International Contexts', *European History Quarterly* 40, no. 4 (2010): 624–40.

98. On this subject, see also the argument that 'Europeanization has no fixed geographical boundaries' and that it 'can only be conceptualized "in action" within history': Ulrike v. Hirschausen and Kiran Klaus Patel, 'Europeanization in History: An Introduction' and Martin Conway, 'Conclusion', both in Conway and Patel, *Europeanization in the Twentieth Century*, 4 and 273 respectively. See also Anne-Isabelle Richard, 'A Global Perspective on European Cooperation and Integration since 1918', in *The Cambridge History of the European Union*, vol. 2, ed. Mathieu Segers and Steven Van Hecke (Cambridge: Cambridge University Press, forthcoming 2023).

99. See e.g. David Priestland, *The Red Flag: Communism and the Making of the Modern World* (London: Allen Lane, 2009) and Robert Service, *Comrades! A History of World Communism* (Cambridge, MA: Harvard University Press, 2007). See also the resonance of particular events, for example the transnational celebration of the Paris Commune: Laura Forster, 'The Paris Commune in the British Socialist Imagination, 1871–1914', *History of European Ideas* 46, no. 5 (2020): 614–32.

100. Daniel Gorman, *The Emergence of International Society in the 1920s* (Cambridge: Cambridge University Press, 2012), 19–172; Michael Barnett, *Empire of Humanity: A History of Humanitarianism* (Ithaca, NY: Cornell University Press, 2011), 49–94. See also Caroline Shaw, *Britannia's Embrace: Modern Humanitarianism and the Imperial Origins of Refugee Relief* (Oxford: Oxford University Press, 2015); Valeska Huber and Jan C. Jansen, 'Dealing with Difference: Cosmopolitanism in the Nineteenth-Century World of Empires', *Humanity* 12, no. 1 (2021), https://muse.jhu.edu/article/788437. Miguel Bandeira Jerónimo, 'Developing Civilisation? Imperial Internationalism at the League of Nations (1920s–1930s)', *Histoire @ Politique*, no. 41 (2020), available online via http://journals.openedition.org/histoirepolitique/385 (last accessed 9 January 2023).

101. See e.g. Felix Germain, 'For the Nation and for Work: Black Africans in Paris of the 1960s', in *Migration and Activism in Europe since 1945*, ed. Wendy Pajman (New York: Palgrave, 2008), 15–32; Robert Gildea, James Mark and Anette Warring, eds, *Europe's 1968: Voices of Revolt* (Oxford: Oxford University Press, 2013).

102. The classic study in this field is John Boli and George M. Thomas, eds, *Constructing World Culture: International Non-Governmental Organizations since 1875* (Stanford, CA: Stanford University Press, 1999). For a discussion of the data sets used to trace this growth, see Martin Grandjean and Marco H.D. van Leeuwen, 'Mapping Internationalism: Congresses and Organizations in the Nineteenth and Twentieth Centuries', in *International Organizations and Global Civil Society: Histories of the Union of International Organizations*, ed. Daniel Laqua, Wouter Van Acker and Christophe Verbruggen (London: Bloomsbury, 2019), 233–8.

103. Simon Jackson and Alanna O'Malley, eds, *The Institution of International Order: From the League of Nations to the United Nations* (Abingdon: Routledge, 2018). For the literature on NGOs, see Iriye, *Global Community*; Davies, *NGOs*.

104. See, for example, recent work on international conferencing, as featured in Stephen Legg, Mike Heffernan, Jake Hodder and Benjamin Thorpe, eds, *Placing Internationalism: International Conferences and the Making of the Modern World* (London: Bloomsbury, 2022). Another example is the role of international organizations as 'settings for transnational sociability', as acknowledged in Sluga, *Internationalism in the Age of Nationalism*, 141.

105. Regarding the competition for international attention, see Clifford Bob, *The Marketing of Rebellion: Insurgents, Media, and International Activism* (Cambridge: Cambridge University Press, 2006).

106. Donatella della Porta, 'Afterword: Transnational Activisms in Social Movement Studies', in Berger and Nehring, *The Transnational Activist*, 341.

CHAPTER 1
EMPIRE AND ACTIVISM

In August 1900, the representatives of anti-slavery societies from France, Austria, Belgium, Britain, Italy and Spain gathered in Paris.[1] Their congress – which also featured speakers from Haiti and Brazil – was one of several international events that coincided with the world's fair held in the French capital that year. In itself, the event seemed to perpetuate a tradition of sporadic international meetings for anti-slavery activists: earlier congresses had taken place in 1840, 1843 and 1890. Indeed, in his opening speech, the French Senator Henri-Alexandre Wallon pointed to the past: he mentioned William Wilberforce and other British activists of the late eighteenth and early nineteenth centuries, the development of French abolitionism in the 1830s and 1840s as well as the efforts that had led to the proclamation of abolition in Brazil.[2] Wallon himself embodied the history of the anti-slavery movement: he had been the president of the commission that instigated the French emancipation measures of 1848.

In evoking a sense of continuity, Wallon's comments were somewhat misleading. By the time of the Paris congress, the transatlantic slave trade, which had galvanized activists in earlier generations, was a matter of the past, having largely ended in the second half of the nineteenth century. By contrast, many of the delegates in Paris came from groups whose creation in the 1880s had denoted a shift of attention towards the trans-Saharan and East African slave trade. Their activism was by no means unproblematic, as it adopted a language that could justify imperial policies at a time of European expansion in sub-Saharan Africa.[3]

Precisely because of its ambivalent context, the 1900 congress constitutes a suitable starting point for examining the relationship between activism and empire. As Silvia Salvatici has argued, abolitionism is 'an important component in the archaeology of humanitarianism' because of its long history.[4] Moreover, the specific case of anti-slavery at the turn of the century draws attention to a form of 'humanitarian imperialism' that – either consciously or implicitly – perpetuated imperial domination.[5] From another angle, it shows how colonialism and empire created issues that nourished transnational action. Both the earlier campaign against the transatlantic slave trade and the subsequent focus on Africa were entwined with the history of European colonial expansion. Empires generated globalizing dynamics, which in turn created issues and awareness that activists responded to.

This chapter considers different ways in which empire and colonialism shaped the development and nature of transnational activism. Because of activists' reference to historical precedents – and the prominence of anti-slavery as a transnational movement – the discussion begins with efforts that predate the book's notional starting point of 1870. After first considering efforts that, in many ways, operated *within* imperial paradigms, the middle section of this chapter shifts to currents that challenged them, drawing attention to the rise of anti-colonial currents. However, even after decolonization, empire did not disappear from activist agendas, as the final section – which focuses on the postcolonial era – shows. In later periods, activists framed some of their efforts as a challenge to neo-colonial forms of external domination. On the whole, then, the chapter addresses the imperial dynamics of transnational activism, while remaining conscious of its manifold contradictions and inconsistencies.

The transnational dynamics of anti-slavery before 1870

Anti-slavery has often been memorialized in national terms. For example, in 2007, the bicentenary of Britain's Abolition of the Slave Trade triggered commemorations that, as the historian Andreas Eckert has put it, amounted to 'self-celebrations', characterized by images of a 'British love of freedom'.[6] These activities perpetuated a national tradition of publicly remembering abolition and emancipation.[7] Such representations were often selective: they tended to gloss over the fact that after proclaiming the end of British involvement in the slave trade in 1807, it took parliament until 1833 to end the legal institution of slavery across the empire. Celebratory narratives are further complicated by the large-scale compensation offered to British slaveowners as well as the use of Indian indentured labour from 1834 onwards.[8]

In some respects, the temptation of approaching anti-slavery by focusing on individual nations and empires is understandable. After all, the course of abolition and emancipation in the Atlantic world varied widely across time and territory, from the first short-lived slave emancipation in the French colonial empire (1794–9) to the end of slavery in Spanish-ruled Cuba (1884) and the Empire of Brazil (1888). Yet if anti-slavery is cast as a story of national activism, it risks obscuring its transnational and transimperial dimensions. The present section therefore discusses some of the ways in which the anti-slavery movement operated transnationally and then considers potential explanations why this was the case.

Although anti-slavery associations usually acted as local or national entities, their members did maintain contacts with likeminded groups and individuals abroad. For example, from the 1780s, communication between British and American abolitionists arguably created a 'transnational advocacy network'.[9] Some links were transient, as close cooperation was followed by periods when groups remained more distant from one another. Nonetheless, these exchanges helped with the dissemination of ideas and strategies. For example, in 1826, the British activist Elizabeth Heyrick made an influential contribution to transnational anti-slavery when she promoted the boycotting of slave-produced sugar as means to effecting abolition.[10] The historian Julie Holcomb has highlighted the impact of Heyrick's ideas in the United States, arguing that her efforts gave rise to 'an international movement against the products of slave labour'.[11] In some ways, such activism was an early manifestation of a wider concern for ethical consumption and production.[12]

Seymour Drescher has suggested that 'Continental' anti-slavery in Europe differed from the British and American movements in that it did not exercise mass appeal and was led by groups that adopted a cautious approach.[13] Yet the position of these groups also meant that, in some cases, ties to their counterparts across the Channel proved important. As the historian Nelly Schmidt has argued, 'British abolitionists were present at each major stage in the history of the French abolitionist movement'.[14] In the 1820s and 1830s, the principal groups driving French abolitionism – namely the *Société de la Morale Chrétienne* (Society of Christian Morals, founded in 1821) and the *Société française pour l'abolition de l'esclavage* (French Society for the Abolition of Slavery, 1834) – corresponded and met with British activists.[15] As with the Anglo-American case, these Anglo-French contacts involved the transfer of strategies: the success of petitioning within British anti-slavery inspired French abolitionists to launch petitions themselves, albeit to more limited effect.[16] In their gradualist approach, the leaders of the *Société française* differed from the most celebrated figure in French anti-slavery, Victor Schœlcher, who joined the government of the Second Republic in 1848 and led the French abolition measures that year. Prior to this, his views had been influenced by the American abolitionist William Lloyd Garrison; moreover, well into old age, Schœlcher remained in dialogue with British activists.[17]

The contacts between British, French and American campaigners reflected efforts by the British anti-slavery movement to extend its influence. In 1839, activists founded the British and Foreign Anti-Slavery Society (BFASS) with the 'ambition to attack foreign slavery'.[18] Shortly after its foundation, BFASS treasurer George William Alexander travelled to the Netherlands and Sweden, both to gather information on the anti-slavery movements in these countries and to address local audiences. Alexander reported back from his visits at the World's Anti-Slavery Convention of 1840.[19] Staged in London, the event exemplified the transnational ambitions of the BFASS. Along with a successor event in 1843 – also held in London – the gathering underscored the growing role of international congresses as vehicles for transnational cooperation among social reformers.[20] Indeed, the 1843 event was followed by an international peace congress, organized by the British abolitionist and pacifist Joseph Sturge.[21]

The mid-century congresses reveal both the extent and limitations of the anti-slavery movement. While most delegates came from the host country – as tended to be the case at such events – the 1840 anti-slavery convention also attracted a sizeable American presence as well as delegates from British colonies in the Caribbean and representatives from the *Société française pour l'abolition de l'esclavage*.[22] Nonetheless, the congress had clear limitations. Although it did feature emancipated slaves among the delegates, the congress only provided a limited space for Black voices: the published minutes merely record a brief intervention from Henry Beckford, an emancipated slave from Jamaica.[23] Moreover, the attitudes of many male activists were a major source of division. Famously, the congress ruptured over the presence of women abolitionists from the United States. The majority of delegates refused their request to be seated on the conference floor – an experience that stimulated the growth of organized feminism in the United States.[24] More generally, John Oldfield has estimated that the event deepened cleavages within the movement.[25]

The case of the Irish campaigner Daniel O'Connell illustrates the challenges for activists who sought to promote different causes at once. In 1840, his frequent and well-received speeches had made O'Connell 'the international star' of the London convention.[26] After the event, O'Connell further increased his profile in the United States: his biographer has spoken of his 'unparalleled role in the transatlantic anti-slavery movement'.[27] Yet this development was by no means unproblematic. Among some American audiences, O'Connell's pronouncements on slavery caused controversy. This, in turn, threatened to undermine his endeavours in another field – namely the quest for American support in his campaign to repeal the Act of Union between Britain and Ireland.

O'Connell's concern with the subject of American slavery reflected ongoing efforts to maintain transnational contacts in the wake of the 1840 convention. Not all of these attempts were equally successful. For instance, plans for an international anti-slavery congress in France came to nothing: at short notice, the French authorities prohibited the meeting, deeming it inopportune 'under the present circumstances'.[28] Anglo-French tensions ran high at the time, partly because of British efforts to expand international provisions for the 'right of search'. Such arrangements would have allowed the Royal Navy to search foreign vessels that were suspected of carrying slaves, touching on delicate matters of French sovereignty.[29] This political context created a difficult environment for French campaigners. As the secretary of the *Société française pour l'abolition de l'esclavage* put it, they struggled with perceptions 'regarding the supposedly Anglomaniac spirit of French abolitionists'.[30]

The case indicated that transnationalism could be a disadvantage. As Laurent Dubois put it, 'Accusations of Anglophilia were ... constant thorns in the side – sometimes deadly ones – of French abolitionists from the 1790s on.'[31] With regard to Dutch abolitionism, the picture is equally ambivalent. Dutch anti-slavery remained a peripheral force, notwithstanding financial support and repeated visits from British campaigners during the 1840s and 1850s.[32] In fact, the historian Maartje Janse has noted counterproductive aspects of such contacts: 'The deliberate attempts of the British to engender direct transfer, and their somewhat arrogant assumptions about the superiority of British methods, raised suspicions and irritation, and often triggered explicitly negative responses, reaffirming "otherness" of continental politics and culture.'[33]

By comparison, the transatlantic exchanges between British and American campaigners were more extensive. After the enactment of emancipation in the British Empire, the ongoing existence of American slavery attracted significant interest in Britain, supported by tours from visiting American speakers. The role of the African American activist Frederick Douglass was a case in point. Having escaped from slavery, Douglass travelled to Britain and Ireland in the 1840s, and British supporters helped to fund the formal acquisition of his liberty.[34] Douglass's status within the abolitionist movement meant that his return visits generated significant expectations. For example, in 1860, a local anti-slavery group – the Halifax Ladies' Anti-Slavery Society – hoped that Douglass would 'stimulate the energy and increase the efficiency of existing Societies, and … lead to the formation of many new ones'.[35] That year, Douglass did indeed travel to the West Yorkshire town, coinciding with an 'anti-slavery bazaar' that raised funds for American abolitionists.[36] Looking back, the organizers concluded that his 'timely visit to England and repeated lectures on slavery in this town … contributed materially to the success of the bazaar', attracting 'the attention of the people of Halifax to the subject and thus inducing them to come forward liberally and to buy generously'.[37] Of £255 raised at the event, £150 went to Douglass's anti-slavery newspaper. The donation indicated the reciprocal value of such visits. While foreign guests generated local interest, they in turn received support from their hosts – and not just materially. The friendships forged on such occasions offered visiting campaigners relief from the divisions they encountered at home.[38] Moreover, even after American emancipation, these transatlantic connections continued, with African American visitors educating British audiences about the ongoing legacies of slavery and experiences of racism.[39]

How, then, can we account for such ties? Three particular factors need acknowledging – namely global contexts, activist affinities and the national meanings that could be ascribed to a transnational cause. First, as far as the contexts are concerned, debates on slavery occurred in a globalizing world. This included easier means of communication between activists, but it extended to other realms. For example, if one supports Eric Williams's argument that economic motives drove the shift from slavery to free labour in the Caribbean, one can also acknowledge that international (and inter-imperial) economic competition created a global context for debates on abolition.[40] Moreover, specific experiences with both slavery and abolition in one colonial empire affected the perspective of activists and political leaders elsewhere. There has been much scholarly debate on the question of how far slave rebellions contributed to the end of slavery – yet such challenges to the institution of slavery were certainly observed by other colonial powers.[41]

Secondly, activists emphasized shared values and portrayed their cause as overriding the boundaries of empire, nation and race. This discourse was exemplified by Josiah Wedgwood's medallion that represented a kneeling Black slave with an inscription asking 'Am I not a man and a brother?'. The image had figured prominently in the British abolitionist movement from the 1780s but was also adopted by activists elsewhere.[42] While rhetoric about shared humanity needs to be probed critically, the concept of 'brotherliness' evoked a Christian discourse that resonated across different countries. Indeed, in several cases, religious ties sustained transnational contacts. The connections between British and American Quaker abolitionists were one example.[43] Moreover, the proportion of Protestants within French anti-slavery substantially outweighed their share of the French population; their involvement made for religious affinities with British campaigners.[44] In the Netherlands, members of the Protestant *Réveil* movement actively participated in debates on abolition during the 1840s.[45] Religious motivations could put activists at odds with secular activists, but they also meant that some protagonists spoke a common, religiously infused language.

Thirdly, the prominence of British activists in maintaining transnational ties was linked to the emergence of anti-slavery as a particular *national* discourse – which partly explains the commemorative practices that have been noted earlier on in this chapter. With regard to British abolitionists in the late eighteenth and early nineteenth centuries, Christopher Brown has argued at a time of imperial 'decline' – especially following the loss of the American colonies – an embrace of humanitarianism could help with the acquisition of 'moral capital'.[46]

This aspect draws attention to the potential coexistence of national and transnational motivations. Rather than remembering their country's slave-trading past, British activists forged a vision of British moral leadership in the world. This was more than mere rhetoric: between 1817 and 1880, a series of bilateral treaties – as well as abortive attempts at an international agreement – saw British governments seek to combat the slave trade at sea. The historian Fabian Klose has argued that these ventures constituted an early form of humanitarian intervention.[47] Such government action had unexpected impacts. For example, when Britain's policing of transatlantic slave trade precipitated a diplomatic conflict with Brazil, the so-called 'Christie Affair' of 1863, it nourished an 'insurgent abolitionism' in Brazil, with a 'steady stream of activism and hope that fed on fragmented news about Atlantic geopolitics and looked at every conjuncture for abolitionist opportunity'.[48] Yet British leadership in this field was not unproblematic as it coincided with, and sometimes supported, imperial expansion.[49] As Richard Huzzey has argued, 'anti-slavery ideas shaped the use and abuse of British power by successive governments'.[50] The subsequent section elaborates on such issues by considering humanitarian ventures in the era of 'high imperialism'.

Imperialism and Cardinal Lavigerie's 'anti-slavery crusade' in the 1880s

The relationship between national designs, visions of international leadership and the politics of imperialism became strikingly evident during a new wave of anti-slavery activism in the late nineteenth century, associated with the efforts of Cardinal Lavigerie. The French clergyman was well known as the founder of the White Fathers (*Pères blancs*), a Catholic missionary society whose initial focus was on North Africa. Having served as Archbishop of Algiers from 1867 onwards, Lavigerie ascended to the re-established See of Carthage in 1884 and, in this capacity, became the Catholic Church's Primate of Africa. In 1888, he launched an international campaign against the trans-Saharan and East African slave trade. In doing so, he responded to growing European awareness of events in Africa: explorers and missionaries provided harrowing accounts of slave raids in Central Africa and described how captives were trafficked to Abyssinia, the Sudan and the Indian Ocean coast, both for domestic markets and for shipment to the Arabian Peninsula, often via the island of Zanzibar.[51]

In instigating an international movement, Lavigerie received financial backing from the Vatican. In 1888, he visited several European capitals, appealing to the 'Christian piety and patriotism' of his audience.[52] His efforts sparked the formation of new, largely Catholic anti-slavery societies in Italy, France, Belgium, Germany and Spain. The initiative created new activist spaces, notably in Italy, where the Catholic protagonists of the newly founded *Società Antischiavista* engaged in public action 'at a time when religious influence on society was curtailed'.[53] Yet Lavigerie also visited Britain, where the membership, outlook and history of anti-slavery groups differed significantly from the new Catholic ventures. His appeal to British audiences evoked the 'noble crusade' waged by earlier generations of British abolitionists and pointed to the notion that 'noblesse oblige': 'England, which has made every effort to destroy slavery in the colonies, cannot remain indifferent to slavery in Africa, which is a thousand times more horrible.'[54] The BFASS responded favourably, not least because a financial donation from Lavigerie helped the association overcome 'its dire financial situation'.[55]

According to the historian Amalia Ribi Forclacz, these efforts produced 'a new type of faith-based humanitarian imperialism that cut across religious lines and combined the traditional Nonconformist and Protestant networks with new Catholic groups'.[56] Indeed, some activists interpreted this movement as a broad coalition. The BFASS described Lavigerie's financial support as 'tangible proof that in the great cause of human freedom, no political or religious differences are allowed to interfere'.[57] Accordingly, the British association corresponded with the leaders of the French, Italian and Belgian groups.[58] There were limits to this cooperation, however: while the mostly evangelical Swiss Anti-Slavery Society initially collaborated with Lavigerie's movement, a subsequent rupture indicated that denominational differences continued to matter.[59]

William Mulligan has seen the appeal of Lavigerie's campaign in terms of its relationship to 'popular preoccupations, such as missionary activities, geographic exploration, colonial expansion, and colonial interests'.[60] Two particular aspects make it necessary to problematize this form of activism. Firstly, the campaign conflated ideas about religion, 'race' and civilization. In doing so, it reflected and reinforced particular European images of Africa. Lavigerie and the groups that he inspired cast their humanitarian activism in terms of a 'civilizing mission', resonating with prominent imperialist tropes.[61] Moreover, many activists adopted a staunchly anti-Muslim discourse that set up the figure of the 'Arab slave-trader' as the antagonist. Seen from this angle, Lavigerie's references to an anti-slavery 'crusade' waged by Christendom were far from coincidental. Indeed, in naming their periodical *Gott will es!* ('God wills it'), the leaders of the German anti-slavery society borrowed its leitmotif from the Crusades. They cast their cause as one in which 'the honour of the Christian world is at stake' and claimed that Arabs were conscious that a 'movement against them is underway in Christian countries'.[62] Praising Lavigerie in 1889, the British Jesuit Richard Clarke argued that previous anti-slavery expeditions in Africa had 'failed because of the deadly enmity of the Crescent to the Cross, and of the double-dealing, rapacity and Corruption of Egyptian officials in the Soudan and on the Upper Nile'.[63] In portraying Europeans as liberators, activists played down own Europe's slave-trading past and glossed over colonial labour practices. They thus constructed highly selective accounts about the complex relationship between empire, religion and slavery.

Secondly, the new abolitionist wave tied in with imperial politics. Based on initiatives from the British government and Leopold II of Belgium – whose imperialism is discussed further in the next section – European powers addressed the African slave trade through the Brussels Anti-Slavery Conference of 1889–90, which resulted in the adoption of the Brussels General Act.[64] The signatories to this international agreement – which also included the Ottoman Empire, Persia and Zanzibar – agreed to allow mutual checks of the papers of ships sailing under foreign flags. Countries where slavery had not yet been outlawed agreed to end the import, transit and export of slaves. In addition, the General Act contained provisions on asylum for fugitive slaves and restricted the importation of

Figure 1.1 Cardinal Lavigerie at Saint-Sulpice church in Paris, 21 September 1890.
Source: Engraving by Henri Thiriat (as featured in *La Ilustracion Espanola y Americana*), via Getty Images.

arms and spirits to parts of Africa. Activists largely depicted these measures as a validation of their efforts. In September 1890, an international anti-slavery congress in Paris became a largely celebratory affair.[65] Prior to the formal congress opening, Lavigerie returned to Saint-Sulpice church, where he had previously preached in support of his cause. Enthusiastically, Lavigerie proclaimed that the politicians and diplomats at the Brussels Conference had 'discussed, adopted and consecrated, on principle, all the measures for which, in the name of nature, in the name of pity, we had so loudly petitioned'.[66] Seven months later, a leading figure of the French *Société Antiesclavagiste* argued at another international meeting that the Brussels Conference had allowed Lavigerie 'to consider the first part of his endeavour, which was surely the most audacious and most difficult one, to be accomplished'.[67]

Notwithstanding the humanitarian rhetoric, these practices were highly ambivalent. The historian Suzanne Miers has described the Brussels Act as 'ostensibly a humanitarian treaty' whose authors 'had far from humanitarian motives': their agreement 'enabled the colonial powers to justify the entire conquest of Africa in humanitarian terms'.[68] Indeed, while referencing the Brussels Act in the context of colonial warfare in Africa, European powers were reluctant to adopt emancipation measures in African territories under their control, fearing that such actions might destabilize their rule. As Paul Lovejoy has noted, 'European rhetoric pushed in the direction of abolition and emancipation; European experience encouraged complicity and often openly supported slavery on the pretext that "domestic slavery" was different from slavery elsewhere.'[69]

All in all, then, the activism associated with the anti-slavery campaigns of the 1880s and 1890s fed into the agendas of European governments, rather than challenging their practice. This is not to say that activists and governments always marched in lockstep. For Christian activists, missionary efforts trumped the politics of imperial rule and could therefore put them at odds with governments.[70] Moreover, humanitarians did steer governments towards action in some areas, as was the case with the rising prominence of the African liquor traffic, which featured at the Brussels Conference following an extensive petitioning campaign.[71] Nonetheless, the convergence of activist and government agendas is notable.

Targeting atrocities in the age of imperialism, 1890s–1900s

In the run-up to the Parisian anti-slavery congress of 1900, the periodical of the Belgian *Société Antiesclavagiste* recalled 'the civilizing task undertaken by our compatriots on African soil, and the countless difficulties which our missionaries and soldiers had to vanquish at each step of their glorious march'.[72] Yet, at the meeting itself, one speaker challenged such claims. The British activist Henry Fox Bourne, secretary of the Aborigines' Protection Society, argued that, notwithstanding European measures against the Arab and African slave trades, 'other, even greater crimes' had 'taken the place of what has, to a certain degree, been suppressed', noting the different 'ills that are being excused by alleging philanthropic motives'.[73] In elaborating on this issue, Fox Bourne particularly highlighted the conditions in the Congo Free State.[74]

The conflicting views of the Belgian *Société Antiesclavagiste* and Fox Bourne draw attention to the relationship between humanitarianism and Belgian imperialism. In 1876, Leopold II, King of the Belgians, had convened the Brussels Geographical Conference, which brought together academics, clergymen, military officers but also protagonists of the anti-slavery movement. The gathering laid the groundwork for Belgian expansion in Central Africa. The result was a private company, the International Congo Association, which, after a series of treaties during and after the Berlin Africa Conference (1884–5), became recognized as the Congo Free State – a kingdom ruled by King Leopold. The hosting of the Anti-Slavery Conference in Brussels in 1889–90 built on the monarch's attempts to cast his expansionism as a humanitarian undertaking. Even at the time of the Brussels Conference, some campaigners noted differences between rhetoric and practice, including the use of slaves by the Free State's agents.[75] By and large, however, Leopold managed to portray his Congo venture as a humanitarian undertaking during these early years.

At a time when Leopold's actions still received widespread praise, the monarch and his backers established a system that was based on the large-scale, brutal exploitation of the Congo's population.[76] The violence of European rule in the Congo was particularly connected to the rubber boom, the extensive use of forced labour and indiscriminate killings. In this respect, the Congo scandal demonstrated the contrast between lofty rhetoric and murderous practice – and it ultimately inspired a fresh wave of activism. Missionaries played an important role in revealing these atrocities: the Baptists John and Alice Harris, who were based at the Congo Balolo Mission, collected photographic evidence that they shared with British audiences, through both publications and a series of lantern lectures.[77] Meanwhile, the journalist E. D. Morel denounced Leopold's regime in a range of speeches, articles, pamphlets and books. His discourse exemplified how this cause was invested with the language of abolitionism, as he cast forced labour in the Congo as a 'new slavery' and described the Congo Free State as a 'slave state'.[78] In 1904, Morel established the Congo Reform Association (CRA) which provided the movement with 'the resilience, resources, and institutional impact of a voluntary association'.[79]

Among historians of Congo reform, there has been some disagreement as to the respective influence of Morel, the CRA and missionaries.[80] Undisputedly, however, transnational contacts played an important role in the campaign. Recent research has emphasized the role of African testimony which via missionaries and official enquiries helped to shape the campaign.[81] Moreover, similar to abolitionist campaigning, there was a significant transatlantic dimension to Congo reform, as highlighted by the formation of an America CRA in 1904. That year, Morel travelled to the United States, where he presented a petition to US president Theodore Roosevelt and addressed the Universal Peace Congress in Boston, which also included competing representations from backers of King Leopold's regime.[82]

While the Congo reform movement had pronounced Anglo-American features, the activists' transnational contacts extended to Europe. For instance, Morel maintained links with some of the most outspoken Belgian critics of the Free State.[83] Such connections were important as some of them were able to generate pressure within the Belgian parliament. Moreover, in 1908, activists in Switzerland and France formed associations for the 'protection of the indigenous people of the Congo basin'.[84] British Congo reformers corresponded with these activists, and René Claparède, founder of the Swiss league, stressed the example that Morel had set for his own activism.[85] In the same year, Morel addressed public meetings in France and Switzerland.[86]

These efforts resulted in the formation of an international organization, the *Ligue internationale pour la défense des indigènes au basin conventionnel du Congo*, counting key figures such as Morel and the Belgian socialist leader Emile Vandervelde among its committee, with the Norwegian author (and recipient of the Nobel Prize for Literature) Bjørnstjerne Bjørnson as the honorary president. The historian Dean Pavlakis has noted that such ties did not give rise to a fully fledged international organization 'because of the need to operate through national governments'.[87] Activists therefore settled for an international committee, stating that each national association would 'maintain its absolute independence of action'.[88] Moreover, the agendas of Congo reformers did not converge in all respects. The religious background of British missionaries and of some American Congo reformers sat uneasily with the secular agenda of activists such as Morel.[89] Furthermore, parts of the American CRA were rooted in American anti-imperialism; they thus represented an outlook that contrasted with British humanitarians, many of whom continued to think in imperial terms.[90]

In the very year that the international league was being formed, Belgium annexed the Congo Free State, following on from a parliamentary enquiry that vindicated the claims of the Congo reformers. While forced labour and other forms of repression did not cease, the Free State's transformation into a Belgian colony did end the most violent practices and thus meant that Congo reform soon evaporated, with the CRA winding down its work in 1913. Congo reform groups from France and Switzerland joined with the BFASS and the Aborigines' Protection Society in creating the *Bureau international pour la défense des indigènes* (International Bureau for the Defence of Indigenous People) in Geneva, which continued to promote the rights of colonial subjects during the interwar years.[91]

Notwithstanding its role in highlighting imperial brutality, one must acknowledge the limitations of the Congo reform campaign. In addressing a French audience, Morel maintained that occasional demands for public works in the French and British colonial empires did not qualify as 'forced labour' and stated emphatically that 'all in all, France and Britain currently undertake good work in West Africa'.[92] In this respect, Morel clashed with some French Congo reformers, who explicitly denounced the situation in the French Congo as a 'pernicious system'.[93] In criticizing their own governments, French activists such as Félicien Challaye and Pierre Mille were somewhat exceptional: most Congo reformers cast events in the Congo Free State as a deviation from acceptable imperial practice, rather than an indication of the murderous dimensions of empire itself.[94] Indeed, supporters of King Leopold were able to point to ties between Congo reformers and British business, arguing that Morel and his allies were serving the interests of 'Liverpool merchants' who were keen to extend their influence in West Africa.[95] While these claims aimed to undermine the accurate criticisms of Congo atrocities, it is true that some business figures from Liverpool helped to fund the campaign, pointing to the potential convergence of financial and humanitarian designs.[96]

In a somewhat different way, business connections also mattered for another supporter of Congo reform, namely the businessman and philanthropist William Cadbury. Between 1901 and 1909, his chocolate company came under attack because of the Portuguese use of forced labour on its cacao islands. The historian Kevin Grant has suggested that his support for Congo reform served to 'divert attention from his own company's slavery scandal'.[97] Cadbury's case was a complex one: he funded an investigation in Portuguese labour conditions, engaged with humanitarian critics of his business practices and in 1909 announced his company's boycott of cocoa that had been produced through forced labour.[98] However, the apparent tardiness of Cadbury's actions did raise suspicions and revealed some inconsistency in his approach to humanitarian matters.

These observations draw attention to the wider question of activists' attitudes. E. D. Morel presented himself as a defender of Africans – but after the First World War, his pronouncements on the French occupation of the Rhineland betrayed his racist prejudices as he attacked the presence of soldiers from the French colonial empire.[99] Indeed, Morel has been described as 'a key figure in the internationalisation of the "Black Shame".[100] The latter involved a wider alliance – with protagonists ranging from journalists to women's groups – that denounced the deployment of African troops on German soil. Such examples illustrate how both 'race' and place shaped the perspective of many activists even when they were willing to criticize some imperial practices. A recent study of the American and British Congo reform movements has shown how such preconceptions were already present during the campaign itself.[101]

The case of the British author Arthur Conan Doyle illustrates how activists' ambivalent views extended to the subject of empire. Doyle was a vociferous critic of conditions in the Congo Free State and even continued his campaign after the Belgian annexation of 1908, personally funding French and English translations of his pamphlet on *The Crime of the Congo*.[102] Yet he was also a long-time supporter of British imperialism.[103] In line with these views, he defended British actions during a particularly infamous episode in British imperial history, namely the Second South African War, or 'Boer War' (1899–1902).[104]

Doyle's writings on the Boer War contrasted with mounting criticisms of British actions in this conflict, notably the 'scorched earth' policy and the conditions in British-run concentration camps. This debate was an international one, with pro-Boer committees emerging in several countries. As the Boers were descendants of Dutch settlers, the presence of pro-Boer activism in the Netherlands is, perhaps, less surprising – although Dutch interest in the Boers was a relatively recent phenomenon, having been ignited by the Transvaal War of 1880–1.[105] Other activists attacked the imperial war effort from within Britain, where the campaign stirred radical circles that had previously been concerned with external forces, notably the Ottoman Empire.[106] Facing hostility at home, some activists built significant transnational links. The journalist Emily Hobhouse visited South Africa to report on the conditions in concentration camps, undertook humanitarian work through the Distress Fund for South African Women and Children and published testimony from Boer women.[107] The historian Rebecca Gill has viewed this activism in terms of Hobhouse's 'cosmopolitan concern for the welfare of humanity'.[108] Hobhouse's activism was part of a wider history of personal activism, from charity for miners in the United States during the 1890s to reconstruction efforts after the Boer War.[109]

All in all, humanitarianism was a highly ambivalent phenomenon in the age of empire. Moreover, it is also striking what activists did *not* campaign about. For instance, while the German genocide in South West Africa (1904–8) attracted criticisms among German social democrats, it did not trigger an international campaign. Arguably, these silences highlighted a wider problem: Western actions within the framework of colonial warfare were often perceived as a legitimate use of violence.[110] Such examples therefore indicate the manifold blind spots of humanitarian activism in the age of empire.

Empire and activism during and after the First World War

The First World War had several implications for the relationship between empire and activism. Firstly, as a global conflict, it involved the mobilization of imperial networks and resources.[111] Activism also figured in these contexts. For example, the German government supported some Indian nationalists with a view to destabilizing the British imperial war effort. Yet it soon became clear that these activists – who also maintained a committee in Berlin – were 'not as easily malleable' as German officials had thought.[112] Indeed, while some Indian anticolonialists built strategic wartime alliances in Germany, their transnational networks ranged much further and predated the war.[113]

Secondly, the war had major consequences for humanitarian action, as further discussed in Chapter 2. Much research on post-war humanitarian relief has focused on Europe and the former parts of the Ottoman Empire.[114] Yet European colonial empires also mattered in these contexts, notably in terms of efforts to deploy imperial networks for humanitarian fundraising and to stage such action in terms of imperial unity.[115] With regard to the humanitarian association Save the Children, the historian Emily Baughan has noted that its growing focus on relief in Africa during the 1920s 'represented an attempt to graft old imperial ideas and traditions onto the "new imperial order" of the interwar years'.[116]

A third aspect was the transformation of the international order, characterized by the collapse of the Austro-Hungarian, German, Ottoman and Russian empires and the border re-drawings carried out through the Paris Peace Conference of 1919. The historian Erez Manela has spoken of a 'Wilsonian moment' – a time when a variety of activists took up the language of national self-determination associated with the US president and thus challenged imperial hierarchies, but with obvious disappointments.[117] Moreover, as discussed further below, the international reverberations of the Russian Revolution added another dimension to the changing nature of global politics after the war.

These different factors made the interwar period a highly ambivalent era for European empires: it is possible to interpret the years after the Great War both in terms of an 'imperial zenith' and as a 'post-war crisis of empire'.[118] The latter development was related to the fact that the former German colonies and parts of the Ottoman Empire became League of Nations Mandates, with Britain and France as the largest mandatory powers and smaller roles for Australia, Belgium, Japan, New Zealand and the Union of South Africa. The Mandates system was based on notions of trusteeship: the mandatory powers supposedly acted on behalf of the international community and were accountable to the League's Mandates Commission. As the historian Susan Pedersen has shown, these arrangements created openings for activists. One such aspect was petitioning, as 'diasporic groups, humanitarian organizations and even a few early anti-colonialists' submitted petitions on behalf of the populations of mandatory territories, as did some of the inhabitants.[119] The likelihood of official responses depended on the petitioner, with a greater likelihood of success for established actors in the international realm, notably the *Bureau international pour la défense des indigènes* and the British and Foreign Anti-Slavery and Aborigines' Protection Society (which had resulted from a merger between the two principal British abolitionist associations and is hereafter referred to as the Anti-Slavery Society).[120]

The Mandates system highlighted the persistence of ideas surrounding a 'civilizing mission', which had characterized many forms of humanitarian activism in the age of empire. Most obviously, this was the case with Mandates being divided into A, B and C categories according to their perceived readiness for self-government. Indeed, the Covenant of the League of Nations explicitly evoked 'the prohibition of abuses such as the slave trade, the arms traffic and the liquor traffic' as a reason for direct rule by European powers, citing the 'stage of development' of particular peoples, 'especially in Central Africa', in this context.[121] Activists of the Anti-Slavery Society largely accepted these categorizations.[122] Such language means that the efforts of the 1920s and 1930s can be inscribed into wider histories of 'imperial internationalism' and 'internationalist imperialism'.[123]

Interwar practices had significant continuities with earlier humanitarian ventures. Even beyond references to the slave trade in the League Covenant, anti-slavery remained subject to transnational activism. One reason was the reluctance of European powers to challenge domestic slavery in their own colonies. The creation of the League of Nations allowed for new transnational interactions between pressure groups and officials in Geneva. One organization that pursued the cause both at home and by targeting the League was the Anti-Slavery Society, which had some success in putting slavery on the League agenda: over the subsequent years, the League of Nations maintained a series of expert committees charged with tackling slavery. Action within the international realm produced new legal instruments, notably the Slavery Convention (1926) and the

Forced Labour Convention (1930), the latter under the auspices of the International Labour Organization.[124] The problem was that the implementation of anti-slavery measures depended on colonial officials. Moreover, even amongst themselves, activists were divided: the Anti-Slavery Society rejected designs by the *Bureau international pour la défense des indigènes* to take the lead in international lobbying and in 1929, it stopped subsidizing the bureau.[125]

There was another way in which anti-slavery re-emerged on the international agenda: in 1923, Abyssinia applied for admission to the League of Nations. With the exception of Liberia, Abyssinia had been the sole African country to evade colonial rule: in 1895–6, Italy's attempt to colonize it had suffered a heavy defeat in the Battle of Adwa. In debates on Abyssinia's potential admission to the League, the persistence of domestic slavery was repeatedly cited as an objection – both by humanitarians and by the Italian government.[126] In the end, Abyssinia did join the League, following promises by Emperor Haile Selassie to end slavery. However, given the imperialist designs of Mussolini's government, Italian criticism of Abyssinia continued. In Italy itself, the *Società Antischiavista d'Italia* increasingly aligned itself with the fascist regime.[127]

Italy invaded Abyssinia in October 1935 and completed its conquest in May 1936. Italy's violation of Abyssinia's sovereignty, its use of mustard gas as well as the bombing of hospitals and other civilian targets caused international outrage. Even before the Italian attack, a range of committees protested against Italian aggression, involving anticolonial nationalists, communists and humanitarians. These included groups such as the *Comité international pour la défense du peuple éthiopien* (International Committee for the Defence of the Ethiopian People), which in the summer of 1935 began to mobilize against the prospect of an Italian attack, bringing together trade unionists as well as leaders from political, cultural and pacifist organizations, in order to 'defend the Abyssinian people against Italian fascist aggression' and 'to support the League of Nations against warmongers'.[128] Its meetings highlighted the extent to which Abyssinia provided a rallying cause: Paulette Nardal – a journalist and activist from Martinique – played a leading role in various Paris-based efforts; Algerian activists helped to host the campaign; and the first public meeting of the *Comité international* attracted nearly 1,000 participants, including representatives from various women's organizations.[129]

At the same time, the events in Abyssinia demonstrated the limitations of efforts to effect change through the League of Nations. Hopes that economic sanctions under the League's auspices would force the Italian government to end its aggression were soon disappointed.[130] Moreover, the conflict exposed the limitations of the anti-slavery movement, with British campaigners such as Kathleen Simon, a key figure in the Anti-Slavery Society, not speaking out against the Italian invasion.[131] These developments created disillusionment among anti-colonial nationalists, with Abyssinia becoming a touchstone for activists.[132] This context nourished the rise of activist currents that sought a more radical transformation of the existing global order, which was exemplified by groups such as the International African Friends of Abyssinia (International African Friends of Ethiopia).

Figure 1.2 Members of the International African Friends of Abyssinia at a rally held in Trafalgar Square, London, on 25 August 1935. *Source:* Daily Herald Archive/SSPL, via Getty Images.

Anticolonialists on the move

The International African Friends of Abyssinia were spearheaded by the intellectual and activist C. L. R. James. Born in Trinidad, James had moved to Britain in the 1930s and emerged as a central figure in anti-imperialist circles. James's writings show how anti-imperialist critiques could evoke abolitionist struggles of the past, but with a focus on slave resistance rather than metropolitan reformers. In 1936, his play on Toussaint Louverture – leader of the Haitian Revolution, which had begun as a slave rebellion in 1791 – premiered in London, featuring the African American actor Paul Robeson among the cast.[133] Three years later, James published his seminal study on the Haitian Revolution, *The Black Jacobins*. The final section of his book drew a link to contemporary struggles, with James proclaiming the readiness of Black Africans to rise up against their oppressors.[134] He later commented that 'the book was written not with the Caribbean but with Africa in mind'.[135] As the historian Christian Høgsbjerg has argued, James's historical work cannot be separated from his activism: 'his study of the Haitian Revolution clearly fired his imagination about how the coming war against Italian imperialism might be won'.[136] Around the same time, another Trinidadian intellectual and occasional collaborator of James's, Eric Williams, was conducting doctoral research in Oxford, working on his influential reassessment of the reasons for abolition in the Caribbean.[137]

James's case shows that anticolonialism had several transnational dimensions at once: it connected activists on the move; it was driven by ideologies and ideas that posited themselves in global terms; and it involved a sensitivity to events and conditions in different empires. The first of these aspects – 'activists on the move' – points to an apparent paradox: empires facilitated the movement of some colonial subjects to the imperial metropole, where they could build expertise and alliances that would serve the anticolonial struggle, and hence challenge the very structures that had facilitated their mobility. James's activism in London was not a solitary case but reflected the presence of various anti-imperialist circles in the British capital.[138] Likewise, interwar Paris has been interpreted as an 'anti-imperial metropolis', with diasporic groups playing an important role in this context. As the historian Michael Goebel has put it, 'migration, condensed in imperial hubs such as Paris, formed the social bedrock on which this idea [of an anti-imperialist solidarity spanning several continents] was formulated'.[139] Paris-based activists from French Indochina included Nguyen Ai Quoc, who as Ho Chi Minh would later lead the Vietnamese independence struggle.[140] Algerian workers who had temporarily moved to the metropole were able to spread anticolonial nationalism upon their return.[141]

The presence of colonial subjects challenged the stereotypical representations that had long characterized European imperialism. For example, diasporic groups led protests against the British Empire Exhibition at Wembley Park in 1924.[142] Their criticisms focused on the 'African village' that displayed colonial subjects for the amusement of Western spectators, building on a tradition of such representations.[143] Likewise, in 1931, diasporic activists and artists contributed to an exhibition on the 'Truth about the Colonies', which French communists staged in opposition to the Colonial Exhibition that was held in Paris that year.[144]

The West African Students' Union (WASU) exemplified the growing political voice of diasporic groups. Having been founded in London in 1925, it provided welfare services but also maintained ties to political movements, including the Universal Negro Improvement Association led by the radical Jamaican activist Marcus Garvey.[145] WASU's activism draws attention to the role of colonial students as protagonists within the wider cohort of migrant activists. While student mobility had been facilitated by the attempts of colonial administrators to nurture future elites, some students built a very different leadership while overseas – namely by assuming prominent roles in anticolonial ventures. This was the case with some WASU members, but also with Indonesian students in the Netherlands, whose organization, *Perhimpoenan Indonesia*, became a breeding ground for anticolonial leaders.[146]

At the same time, many activists who engaged in such mobility continued to work within imperial parameters, aiming at reform rather than a wholesale eradication of imperial rule. A case in point is the activism of Paul Panda Farnana, who founded the *Union Congolaise* in Belgium in 1919. Having been the first Congolese to receive a university education in Belgium, Farnana promoted the rights of Africans in Belgium as well as educational opportunities in the Belgian Congo, without advocating fully fledged independence. In the same period that Farnana was active in the imperial metropole, a Christian messianic movement in Congo – led by Simon Kimbangu – generated fears among officials that the Black nationalism of Marcus Garvey was spreading in Africa.[147] Farnana himself sought to avoid radical associations, which did not prevent pro-colonial Belgian papers from speculating about potential links with Kimbangu and Garvey.[148] Notwithstanding his desire to fend off such accusations, Farnana did speak out against the – later commuted – death sentence for Kimbangu.[149]

While the examples of activists have focused on those who migrated *within* imperial settings, many anti-imperialists had trajectories that took them even further. For example, the Indian nationalist M. N. Roy spent time in the United States, Mexico, Germany, the Soviet Union and China. Such experiences mattered, as he drew connections between, for example, patterns of oppression in India and Mexico, notwithstanding their different political contexts.[150] Moreover, during his time in Weimar Germany, Roy's encounter with a non-Bolshevik variant of communism proved influential for his perspective on revolutionary strategy in the late 1920s.[151] Another prominent anti-imperialist, the Trinidadian activist George Padmore, moved to Britain in the 1930s, after sojourns in the United States, the Soviet Union and Germany, where he was imprisoned and then deported by the Nazi authorities. In Britain, Padmore cooperated with C L. R. James, for instance in the International African Service Bureau, which had emerged from the International African Friends of Abyssinia.[152]

Political and intellectual contexts of anti-imperialism, 1920s to 1950s

The Soviet sojourns of individuals such as Roy and Padmore demonstrated communism's appeal as an anti-imperialist ideology. In line with Lenin's critique of imperialism, Russian communists positioned their country as a champion of anti-imperialism. Anticolonial activists could receive support and training, both through the Comintern and through ventures such as the Communist University of the Toilers of the East, which opened in Moscow in 1921.[153]

In 1927, communists played an influential role in the formation of the League Against Imperialism (LAI). This alliance attracted substantial interest among anticolonial activists – but also by the authorities, which placed such efforts under surveillance.[154] The Comintern and its front organizations shaped the LAI's development in several respects. For instance, the German publisher and communist politician Willi Münzenberg provided funding and ran the League's offices in Berlin which, partly in connection with such efforts, became a major site for anti-imperialist ventures.[155] In France, the most prominent figure in the LAI was the Senegalese communist Lamine Senghor.[156] Senghor's speech at the LAI's founding congress in Brussels explicitly linked anti-imperialism to the earlier struggle against slavery: as David Murphy has highlighted, Senghor cast 'twentieth-century colonialism as a modern form of slavery' and thus challenged 'the civilizing rhetoric of the European powers'.[157]

At least in its early years, the LAI was far more than a communist venture: it provided a platform for a range of non-communists, for whom such involvement proved significant in several ways. The historian Michele Louro has argued that for Jawaharlal Nehru, the 'months serving the LAI in Europe produced a more nuanced conceptualization of the relationship between India and the world: one which built upon the formative ideas in Brussels about international comradeship, the link between nationalism and the struggle of the proletariat, and Nehru's notion of an anti-imperialist geography of the world'.[158] Meanwhile for Mohammad Hatta and his organization, the *Perhimpoenan Indonesia*, participation in the LAI's founding event 'was beneficial to the small student organization, and elevated it to an important anti-colonial player'.[159]

Moreover, even anticolonial activists with communist affiliations or sympathies were not simply following Moscow's orders. For example, having travelled to China on behalf of the Comintern in 1926-7, M. N. Roy criticized the tactics and influence of Soviet advisers.[160] By 1928, his divergent views resulted in a rupture that culminated in his expulsion from the Comintern. While this development separated him from Indian communists, it made for closer contact with other anticolonial activists, including Nehru.[161] Other groups maintained ties with communists without being absorbed into the communist world. For instance, Messali Hadj, founder of the *Étoile Nord-Africaine* – which promoted Algerian independence from its base in France – addressed the Brussels congress in 1927. According to historian Martin Thomas, Hadj's party 'came of age' at this event.[162] At the time, the Comintern supported the campaign for Algerian independence.[163] However, by 1935, communists prioritized anti-fascism over anticolonialism, provoking the *Étoile*'s 'anger' at the communists' 'toadying to bourgeois non-Communist groups in France' and 'revulsion at the hypocrisy of the Algerian Communist Party'.[164]

The Comintern's shifting politics also affected other activists. George Padmore had been a key figure in a Comintern-led organization, the International Trade Union Committee of Negro Workers, but in 1933-4 broke with the Comintern over its shifting stance on empire.[165] Looking back on his interactions with Padmore during the 1930s, C. L. R. James stressed continuities in his political beliefs: 'Padmore was a great admirer of Marxism, and although he had left … the Moscow people, he made me understand that Marxism still remained the centre of his political ideas.'[166]

The friendship and political collaboration between Padmore and James were striking because the latter's persuasions were Trotskyist. Both were united in drawing on another current that helped to sustain transnational activism – namely Pan-Africanism, which sought to promote unity among people of African descent, both in Africa and in the diaspora.[167] The historian Hakim Adi has stressed the diversity of convictions and aims that were subsumed under the Pan-African moniker, noting that 'there has never been one universally accepted definition of what constitutes Pan-Africanism'.[168] The multidimensional nature of Pan-Africanism means that Chapter 6 will return to it from a different angle, discussing its role in anti-racist struggles, whereas the following discussion focuses on its relationship to empire.

Pan-Africanism posed an implicit challenge to the power relations and cultural notions associated with European imperialism. While initially associated with the Trinidad-born, Britain-based activist Henry Sylvester-Williams, it gained momentum in the interwar period.[169] In the aftermath of the First World War, the African American scholar and activist W. E. B. Du Bois organized a series of congresses, starting in Paris to coincide with the Peace Conference of 1919.[170] As promoted by Du Bois, Panafricanism could accommodate both anticolonialists and those who did not question empire as such.

Such diversity bred disagreement and ruptures, as exemplified by the 1921 Pan-African Congress, which comprised consecutive sessions in London, Brussels and Paris. While the multi-site nature affirmed the movement's transnational scope, it revealed differences between the ambitions of local organizers and audiences. An initial resolution in London denounced the exploitation of Africa by European powers and argued for African self-government. Yet the subsequent Brussels session – co-organized by Panda Farnana – was divided on these issues, as some delegates were wary of anticolonial pronouncements. This scepticism extended to the chair, Blaise Diagne, a Senegalese politician who represented four West African municipalities in the French Chamber of Deputies, having previously served within the colonial administration. Diagne pushed through a resolution that omitted the more radical statements of the earlier London meeting. The African American campaigner Jessie Fauset departed from Belgium 'in thoughtful and puzzled mood'.[171] In Brussels, she had observed 'the unspoken determination of the Belgians to let nothing interfere with their dominion in the Congo', noting that 'the careful Belgian eye watched and peered' and that 'the Belgian ear listened' during the proceedings.[172] Her disappointment with the turn of events was evident:

> How great was this smothering power which made it impossible for men even in a scientific Congress to be frank and to express their inmost desires? Not one word, for instance, had been said during the whole Congress by Belgian white or black, or French presiding officer which would lead one to suspect that Leopold and his tribe had ever been other than the Congo's tutelary angel. Apparently not even an improvement could be hinted at.[173]

It took until the final congress session in Paris for the earlier, more critical resolution to be re-adopted.[174] But while there was hence more overt criticism of colonialism than some would have liked, the early Pan-African congresses did not seem to mark a radical departure from past practice. A recent study has noted the 'paternalistic overtones' of many congress resolutions and suggested that these documents 'reflected a nineteenth-century tradition which viewed African liberation as a liberal humanitarian or philanthropic concern, rather than a political imperative'.[175] Even some humanitarians who themselves continued to think in imperial terms noted the reluctance of some Pan-Africanists when it came to particular matters in the early 1920s: John Harris of the Anti-Slavery Society complained that Du Bois was 'unwilling to listen to anything against French colonial policy' and claimed that his 'extraordinary defence of French Colonial practice' had 'made a very bad impression'.[176]

In this respect, the Pan-African ventures of the 1920s differed from more radical strands of Pan-Africanism that gained prominence in the 1930s, as associated with the likes of James, Padmore, Amy Ashwood Garvey and the organization that they co-founded in 1937, the International African Service Bureau.[177] The rise of an explicitly anticolonial interpretation of Pan-African ideas manifested itself at the 1945 Pan-African Congress, held in Manchester and commonly seen as a major episode on the road to African decolonization.[178] The event was driven by figures from the African diaspora in Britain, and it featured several individuals who subsequently led their countries to independence, for instance Kwame Nkrumah (Gold Coast/Ghana) and Jomo Kenyatta (Kenya).[179]

Both communism and Pan-Africanism integrated anticolonial activism into broader narratives of global change. This aspect points to a wider issue – namely the way in which we can interpret anticolonial activism as a form of internationalism. Recent research has shown how Indian activists conceived their own activism within an internationalist framework.[180] In the 1930s, Nehru and other members of the Indian National Congress embraced visions of solidarity that, for example, included aid to Republican Spain during the Spanish Civil War and support for China in the Sino-Japanese War.[181] Notions of solidarity cut both ways. For example, when Indian trade unionists were subjected to the Meerut Trial (1929–33), it sparked strategy discussions as well as solidarity campaigns among trade unionists in Europe.[182] Such observations should not obscure the politically diffuse nature of transnational anticolonial ties. For instance, some Indian nationalists embraced ideas which, during the 1930s and 1940s, resulted in contacts and cooperation with German National Socialists.[183] This strand clashed with the anti-fascism of Nehru and other Congress leaders, yet it highlighted the political variegation of Indian anticolonialism and the malleability of transnational action more broadly. Transnational ties could be formed for different reasons, be it ideological proximity, notions of a shared struggle or the search for temporary allies to achieve one's objectives.

Liberation struggles, 1950s to 1980s

While India attracted great attention among activists in and beyond Europe, the same can be said about the Algerian independence struggle. The presence of the *pieds-noirs* – the descendants of French settlers in Algeria – and Algeria's status as a *département* of the French state meant that the entanglements between metropole and colony were particularly pronounced in the Algerian case. The protracted Algerian War (1954–62) caused significant tremors in France, resulting in the collapse of the Fourth Republic and raising wider questions about French identity.[184] The use of torture became a major issue on which activists in metropolitan France mobilized, especially after death of French communist Maurice Audin in Algeria.[185] Algeria's acquisition of independent statehood met with enthusiasm: the persistence and ultimate outcome seemed to offer broader promises of a Third World revolution. As Jeffrey James Byrne has put it, 'For those disillusioned with both the Western and Eastern examples, Algeria seemed to fulfil the Third World's sense of a third way, a better way.'[186] The Algerian government actively promoted this sense of a wider mission, which involved activities such as the staging of a Pan-African Cultural Festival in 1969.[187]

The transnational resonance of specific liberation struggles was entwined with the attention for the methods of resistance that were associated with them. Gandhian non-violent resistance constituted one potential method of protest that exercised significant influence, from Western European pacifists to African American civil rights activists.[188] By contrast, the Algerian case provided the example of anti-imperialism as an armed struggle. The emphasis on violent resistance as a path to liberation from European domination underpinned Frantz Fanon's book *Les Damnés de la terre* (known in English as *The Wretched of the Earth*).[189] Fanon's own trajectory mapped onto some of the wider histories of transnational activism examined in this chapter – not least in terms of him being an activist on the move. Born in the French Caribbean colony of Martinique and having fought for the Free French during the Second World War, Fanon received his tertiary education in France, where he also trained as a psychiatrist before moving to Algeria in 1953.[190] As further noted in Chapter 5, following its publication in 1961, Fanon's book became an international phenomenon and provided an inspiration for activists who viewed themselves as part of a liberation struggle, even after decolonization.[191]

The appeal of Fanonist ideas in the 1960s overlapped with activists' enthusiasm for the 'Third World'. The French academic Alfred Sauvy had coined the term in 1952 – with 'Third World' evoking, on the one hand, distinctness from the 'First' and 'Second' worlds of the Cold War and, on the other hand, pointing to the 'Third Estate' that had represented the majority of the population in revolutionary France.[192] Three years later, the African-Asian Conference in Bandung, Indonesia, seemed to herald the rise of the Third World as a force in global politics.[193] Many participants at this event were former anticolonial activists who had become political leaders, from Nehru to Zhou Enlai who, after his early political activism as a Chinese student in France, had become one of Mao's key allies. In his opening speech, the Indonesian president Sukarno referred back to the LAI's congress in 1927, commenting that several participants of Bandung had previously met in Brussels.[194] Moreover, recent research has revealed a deeper history of African–Asian solidarity in the Bandung era.[195] For example, less than a fortnight before the Bandung conference, a meeting in New Delhi brought together activists who sought the 'Relaxation of International Tensions', indicating new attempts to build internationalist alliances.[196]

Third World politics generated significant enthusiasm among European activists who sought an alternative path between Western-style capitalism and Soviet-style communism.[197] Such activism extended into milieus that were less frequently associated with radical critiques of empire. Whereas in the 1880s, Catholic anti-slavery had provided a discourse that resonated with European expansionism, by the 1960s, liberation theology meant that some Catholic activists actively sought to overcome structures of exploitation.[198]

European interest in the Third World manifested itself in different ways. One form involved solidarity with political struggles against the remnants of colonial rule, for instance during the independence wars in the Portuguese colonies of Angola (1961–74) and Mozambique (1964–74).[199] Yet activists could also cast other conflicts in anti-imperialist terms. As discussed further in Chapter 3, protests against the American war in Vietnam cast US foreign policy as imperialist in nature. They were but one example of such representations. Developments in Cuba predated those in Vietnam and illustrated how criticisms of the United States could tie in with broader notions of anti-imperialist solidarity. In December 1959, revolutionaries disposed the US-backed dictatorship of Fulgencio Batista. US-backed attempts to overthrow the new administration – starting with the failed Bay of Pigs invasion of 1961 – generated expressions of solidarity, with a legacy that included the formation of Cuba solidarity groups in various countries. Activists' veneration for the Argentinian radical Che Guevara also dated back to his role in the Cuban Revolution. Significantly, his appeal extended to oppositional circles in Central and Eastern Europe, as his revolutionary example seemed to contrast with the rigid nature of state socialism.[200] More generally, Cuba solidarity movements coincided with attempts by the Cuban government to present itself as a vanguard of liberation movements, which also involved funding for allied movements in Africa and Latin America.[201]

Interest in the Cuban case reflected and nourished the growing prominence of Latin America within activist circles in Europe. This development was driven by the view that US policies in the region amounted to imperialism. In the 1970s and 1980s, one strand of activism focused on solidarity with movements that were targets of US foreign policy. For example, after the Sandinista revolution in Nicaragua had ended the US-backed Somaza dictatorship in 1979, the US-funded Contras sought to overthrow the new left-wing government. There were several transnational dimensions to subsequent solidarity activism. At one level, such campaigns built on ties that members of the Nicaraguan left had built whilst still in pre-revolutionary exile.[202] Moreover after 1979, Western activists travelled to Nicaragua to express their solidarity and provide practical aid. In 1982, the pronouncements of a Swiss 'solidarity brigade' typified the links between anti-imperialist rhetoric and transnational practice. Its members saw the Sandinistas' achievements as being 'threatened by the intervention of North American imperialism'. They suggested that their action would help 'development projects in support of the Nicaraguan population' but also ensure 'mass mobilization against the USA's intervention in Central America'.[203]

These criticisms of US foreign policy occurred in a Cold War context, with the Soviet Union re-affirming its support for liberation struggles and seeking to foster ties with newly independent nations in Africa.[204] Yet such aspects were not purely driven from the top. For example, within communist-inspired organizations such as the Women's

Figure 1.3 Activists from the Swiss 'Nicaragua – El Salvador Committee' holding up a banner 'against US colonialism in Central America' at a demonstration in Zürich, 1 May 1986. *Source*: photo by Gertrud Vogler, via Sozialarchiv Zürich.

International Democratic Federation (WIDF) – which included activists in both East and West – mobilization along anti-imperialist lines played a major role, for example in attacking the Portuguese colonial wars in Africa.[205]

Along such ties, attacks on Western foreign policy as imperialist were a staple of official rhetoric. Not all expressions of solidarity depended on state sanctioning. The historian Kim Christiaens has drawn attention to the way in which dissidents within the state socialist regimes of the Eastern bloc likened their own quests for liberation to events in the Third World.[206] However, the official rhetoric complicated matters. Responses to the Vietnam War exemplified this aspect. On the one hand, many Eastern European dissidents sympathized with Vietnamese resistance to the United States.[207] On the other hand, official denunciations of Western imperialism appeared to lack credibility. Jan Kavan, a Czechoslovak student leader during the Prague Spring of 1968, later articulated this point: 'the US war against Vietnam was condemned by the communist regimes, and the majority of the people had unquestionable personal experience of how communist leaders lied, deceived and regularly distorted even the most obvious truths. So why should they be right about this war?'[208] Indeed, the subsequent events in Czechoslovakia, including the invasion by Warsaw Pact states, sharpened some activists' awareness of Soviet imperialism.

These observations highlight a wider issue: the language of anti-imperialism was highly malleable. It could be used against the United States and the Soviet Union, and it overlapped with other discourses. Especially after the Six-Day War of 1967, some solidarity activists viewed the Palestinian case as an anti-imperial struggle, in some cases supporting the armed resistance of the Palestinian Liberation Organization and

Empire and Activism

other militant groups.²⁰⁹ In Europe itself, some forms of left-wing solidarity with Irish nationalism in Northern Ireland could also be cast in such terms. This discourse is illustrated by the claims of a British Maoist faction that cast Northern Ireland in terms of an 'imperialist struggle', arguing that Ireland's partition had been carried out 'to leave the south as a desolate backwater – an agricultural hinterland with little industry of its own, and a prey to neo-colonialist plunder'.²¹⁰ While coming from a small, marginal group, it illustrated a wider phenomenon: as the historian Stephen Howe has argued, during the Troubles, 'the discourse of anticolonialism became truly widespread in, and in relation to, Ireland' and Frantz Fanon became 'an increasingly ubiquitous father-figure for analyses of an Irish "colonial situation"'.²¹¹ Thus, the language of anti-imperialism could be applied to a range of different settings and scenarios.

Combating neo-colonial relations in a postcolonial world

Anti-imperialism did not depend on formal colonial rule or even military action: it could also involve a critique of economic forms of domination. A variety of activists denounced European and North American practices as 'neo-colonialist' or 'neo-imperialist'.²¹² In some ways, empire continued to be a frame for activists even in the 1990s and 2000s. Critics of globalization likened the emerging new power structures to empire, as epitomized by a bestselling book by the American philosopher Michael Hardt

Figure 1.4 Opening of *Deerde Wereldwinkel* ('Third World Shop') in Amsterdam, 18 September 1971. *Source:* photo by W. Punt, File 924-9458, Fotocollectie Anefo, Nationaal Archief, The Netherlands, via Wikimedia Commons.

49

and Antonio Negri, the latter a veteran of the Italian left.[213] Twenty years afterwards, both appreciated the efforts of the global justice movement while calling for further struggle.[214]

Rather than framing their rejection of exploitative relations in terms of resistance, some activists focused on practical attempts to challenge economic exploitation, with alternative forms of consumption as a major vehicle. This tendency was exemplified by the Dutch *Wereldwinkels* ('World Shops', initially also known as *Deerde Wereldwinkels*, or 'Third World shops'), which featured goods from developing countries and became associated with a wider phenomenon: the promotion and sale of 'fair trade' products from the 1960s onwards, in which Dutch activists played a prominent role.[215] Fair trade was transnational in more than one way. At one level, it targeted 'global inequality' and thus implied the vision of a different international order.[216] Furthermore, it depended on links between local producers, intermediaries and Western groups that organized the distribution and sale of fair-trade goods. Transnational exchanges boosted these developments, with the Dutch initiatives inspiring similar action in other Western European countries as well as the development of international organizational structures.[217] Religious groups actively contributed to the development of distribution networks, with Christian youth associations helping to inspire action in this field.[218] At the same time, such forms of activism were not entirely detached from political campaigns: in many cases, Third World shops were also hubs of groups that engaged in political solidarity. For example, the Swiss 'solidarity brigades' in Nicaragua during the 1980s featured not only members of trade unions and political groups, but also activists from local Third World shops.[219]

A focus on ethical consumption enabled local consumers to engage in a form of everyday activism, and at times it extended beyond fair trade. For example, in the 1980s, the Swiss company Nestlé came under scrutiny for the marketing of baby milk power in developing countries. A widespread campaign to boycott Nestlé put ethical consumption centre stage but has also been interpreted in the context of postcolonial legacies.[220] This was but one example of how empire continued to shape activism in a postcolonial age. More generally, however, ethical consumption and a concern for impacts on living conditions in the Global South point to notions of humanitarian relief, which the next chapter explores in further depth.

Notes

1. Société Antiesclavagiste de France, *Congrès international antiesclavagiste tenu à Paris les 6, 7, 8 août 1900: Compte rendu des séances* (Paris: Société antiesclavagiste de France, 1900). See also Nelly Schmidt, *L'abolition de l'esclavage: Cinq siècles de combats, xvie – xxe siècles* (Paris: Fayard, 2005), 288–9.
2. Henri-Alexandre Wallon, 'Allocution de M. le Président', in *Congrès internationale antiesclavagiste*, 5.
3. Daniel Laqua, 'The Tensions of Internationalism: Transnational Anti-Slavery in the 1880s and 1890s', *The International History Review* 33, no. 4 (2011): 705–26.

4. Salvatici, *A History of Humanitarianism*, 21.
5. Amalia Ribi Forclaz, *Humanitarian Imperialism: The Politics of Anti-Slavery Activism, 1880–1940* (Oxford: Oxford University Press, 2015).
6. Andreas Eckert, 'Europa, Sklavenhandel und koloniale Zwangsarbeit: Einleitende Bemerkungen', *Journal of Modern European History* 7, no. 1 (2009): 34–5. On the ambiguous nature of these celebrations, see also *History Workshop Journal*'s special issue 'Remembering 1807: Histories of the Slave Trade, Slavery and Abolition', *History Workshop Journal*, no. 64 (2007); and James Walvin, 'The Slave Trade, Abolition and Public Memory', *Transactions of the Royal Historical Society*, 19 (2009): 139–49.
7. John Oldfield, *Chords of Freedom: Commemoration, Ritual and British Transatlantic Slavery* (Manchester: Manchester University Press, 2007). For a discussion of French commemorations of abolition, see Françoise Vergès, 'The Slave Trade, Slavery, and Abolitionism: The Unfinished Debate in France', in *A Global History of Anti-Slavery in the Nineteenth Century*, ed. William Mulligan and Maurice Brigg (Basingstoke: Palgrave, 2013), 198–213.
8. On the compensation measures for British slave owners, see Nicholas Draper, *The Price of Emancipation: Slave-Ownership, Compensation and British Society at the End of Slavery* (Cambridge: Cambridge University Press, 2010) and the subsequent 'Legacies of British Slave Ownership' project at University College London. On the use of indenture, see Kay Saunders, ed., *Indentured Labour in the British Empire, 1834–1920* (London: Croom Helm, 1983); Marika Sherwood, *After Abolition: Britain and the Slave Trade since 1807* (London: I.B. Tauris, 2007); Ashutosh Kumar, *Coolies of Empire: Indentured Indians in the Sugar Colonies, 1830–1920* (Cambridge: Cambridge University Press, 2017).
9. Huw David, 'Transnational Advocacy in the Eighteenth Century: Transatlantic Activism and the Anti-Slavery Movement', *Global Networks* 7, no. 3 (2007): 367–82. See also Oldfield's comments that in this period, interactions between French, British and American campaigners 'reinforced a sense that abolitionism transcended narrow national boundaries': Oldfield, *Transatlantic Abolitionism*, 19.
10. Elizabeth Heyrick, *Immediate, Not Gradual, Abolition; or, an Enquiry into the Shortest, Safest and Most Effective Means of Getting Rid of West Indian Slavery* (Leicester: T. Combe, 1824).
11. Julie Holcomb, *Moral Commerce: Quakers and the Transatlantic Boycott of the Slave Labor Economy* (Ithaca, NY: Cornell University Press, 2016), 148.
12. Bronwen Everill, *Not Made by Slaves: Ethical Capitalism in the Age of Abolition* (Cambridge, MA: Harvard University Press, 2020).
13. Seymour Drescher, 'Two Variants of Anti-Slavery: Religious Organization and Social Mobilization in Britain and France, 1780–1870', in *Anti-Slavery, Religion, and Reform: Essays in Memory of Roger Anstey*, ed. Christine Bolt and Seymour Drescher (Folkestone: Wm. Dawson & Sons, 1980), 44.
14. Schmidt, *L'abolition de l'esclavage*, 142. See also Lauren Dubois, 'The Road to 1848: Interpreting French Anti-Slavery', *Slavery & Abolition* 22, no. 3 (2001): 150–7 and various examples in Lawrence Jennings, *French Anti-Slavery: The Movement for the Abolition of Slavery in France, 1802–1848* (Cambridge: Cambridge University Press, 2000), e. g. 21.
15. For contacts between 1835 and 1847, see the documents collected in Nelly Schmidt, *Abolitionnistes de l'esclavage et réformateurs des colonies, 1820–1851* (Paris: Katharla, 2000), 465–525.
16. For the text of fourteen French petitions covering the period from 1820 to 1848, see Schmidt, *Abolitionnistes de l'esclavage*, 845–89.

17. Nelly Schmidt, *Victor Schœlcher et l'abolition de l'esclavage* (Paris: Fayard, 1994), 64, 67 and 224. For letters between Schœlcher and British abolitionists such as Thomas Clarkson, see Nelly Schmidt, ed., *La Correspondance de Victor Schœlcher* (Paris: Maisonneuve et Larose, 1995), 338–54.
18. Richard Huzzey, *Freedom Burning: Anti-Slavery and Empire in Victorian Britain* (Ithaca, NY: Cornell University Press, 2012), 12.
19. Speech by William Alexander, 16 June 1848, as reprinted in *Proceedings of the General Anti-Slavery Convention, Convened by the Committee of the British and Foreign Ant-Slavery Society, and Held in London, from Friday, June 12th to Tuesday, June 23rd, 1840* (London: British and Foreign Anti-Slavery Society, 1841), 181–8. On Anglo-Dutch links in this period, see Maartje Janse, '"Holland as a Little England"? British Anti-Slavery Missionaries and Continental Abolitionist Movements in the Mid-Nineteenth-Century', *Past & Present*, 229, no. 1 (2015): 123–60.
20. Jakob Kihlberg, 'European Reform Movements and the Making of the International Congress, 1840–1860', *The International History Review* 43, no. 3 (2021): 488–507.
21. Martin Ceadel, *The Origins of War Prevention: The British Peace Movement and International Relations 1730–1854* (Oxford: Oxford University Press, 1996), 337–45.
22. The event also featured a Swiss delegate and an observer from Russia. For a full list, see Wilson Anti-Slavery Convention, British and Foreign Anti-Slavery Society, 'Convention, June 12th, 1840', available online via https://www.jstor.org/stable/60228328 (last accessed 9 January 2023).
23. *Proceedings of the General Anti-Slavery Convention*, 22. The other non-white delegates depicted in Benjamin Robert Haydon's famous painting of the Anti-Slavery Convention were Edward Barrett (like Beckford an emancipated slave from Jamaica); Louis Celeste Lecesne (originally a 'free man of colour' from Jamaica who settled in Britain after the Jamaican authorities targeted him for his activism), Samuel Jackman Prescod (Barbados) and Jean-Baptiste Symphor Linstant de Pradine (Haiti). See 'The Anti-Slavery Convention, 1840', *National Portrait Gallery Website*, https://www.npg.org.uk/collections/search/portraitExtended/mw00028/The-Anti-Slavery-Society-Convention-1840 (last accessed 9 January 2023).
24. On this event, see e.g. Maurice Bric, 'Debating Slavery and Empire: The United States, Britain and the World's Anti-Slavery Convention of 1840', in Mulligan and Bric, *A Global History of Anti-Slavery*, 59–77; Huzzey, *Freedom Burning*, 14–15.
25. Oldfield, *The Ties That Bind*, 158.
26. Christine Kinealy, *Daniel O'Connell and the Anti-Slavery Movement: 'The Saddest People the Sun Sees'* (London: Pickering & Chatto, 2011), 86.
27. Ibid., 95. See also Douglas Riach, 'Daniel O'Connell and American Anti-Slavery', *Irish Historical Studies* 20, no. 77 (1976): 3–25.
28. Tanneguy Duchâtel, Minister of the Interior, to Duc de Broglie, 1 Mach 1842, as featured in Schmidt, *Abolitionnistes de l'esclavage*, 502.
29. Lawrence Jennings, 'France, Great Britain, and the Repression of the Slave Trade, 1841–1845', *French Historical Studies* 10, no. 1 (1977): 101–25.
30. François Isambert to John Scoble, 27 August 1842, as featured in Schmidt, *Abolitionnistes de l'esclavage*, 492.
31. Dubois, 'The Road to 1848', 152. See also John Oldfield's comments on the suspicions encountered by French abolitionists in the 1790s: Oldfield, *Transatlantic Abolitionism*, 103.

32. P. C. Emmer, 'Anti-Slavery and the Dutch: Abolition without Reform', in *Anti-Slavery, Religion, and Reform*, ed. Bolt and Drescher, 86–7.
33. Janse, 'Holland as Little England', 151.
34. Hannah-Rose Murray and John McKivigan, eds, *Frederick Douglass in Britain and Ireland, 1845–1895* (Edinburgh: Edinburgh University Press, 2021). On speaker tours more broadly, see Hannah-Rose Murray, *Advocates of Freedom: African American Transatlantic Abolitionism in the British Isles* (Cambridge: Cambridge University Press, 2020).
35. 'Halifax Anti-Slavery Bazaar' (January 1860), in the Wilson Anti-Slavery Collection, available via https://www.jstor.org/stable/10.2307/60239568 (last accessed 9 January 2023).
36. As features in the activist repertoire, anti-slavery 'bazaars' had been pioneered in the United States. See John Oldfield, *The Ties That Bind: Transatlantic Abolitionism in the Age of Reform, c. 1820–1865* (Liverpool: Liverpool University Press, 2020), 101–7.
37. 'Third Annual Report of the Halifax Ladies' Anti-Slavery Society', in Wilson Anti-Slavery Collection, https://www.jstor.org/stable/60239630 (last accessed 9 January 2023).
38. Simon Morgan, 'The Political as Personal: Transatlantic Abolitionism *c.* 1833–67', in Mulligan and Bric, *A Global History of Anti-Slavery in the Nineteenth Century*, 78–96.
39. Murray, *Advocates of Freedom*, 292–317.
40. Eric Williams, *Capitalism and Slavery: With a New Foreword by William A. Daity Jr; Introduction by Colin A Palmer* (Chapel Hill, NC: University of North Carolina Press, 2021 [orig. 1944]).
41. For example, as John Oldfield has noted, 'the slave rebellion in Saint Domingue reframed debates about slavery and the slave trade': Oldfield, *Transatlantic Abolitionism*, 96.
42. On British activists' use of medallions with this image, see Oldfield, *The Ties That Bind*, 93–5. The image's use by Spanish abolitionists in the 1860s has been noted in Arthur Corwin, *Spain and the Abolition of Slavery in Cuba, 1817–1886* (Austin, TX: University of Texas Press, 1967), 158.
43. David, 'Transnational Advocacy', 370.
44. On the role of Protestants within the *Société de Morale Chrétienne*, see e.g. Serge Daget, 'A Model of the French Abolitionist Movement and Its Variations', in Bolt and Drescher, *Anti-Slavery, Religion, and Reform*, 71–2; Drescher, 'Two Variants of Anti-Slavery', 53.
45. Emmer, 'Anti-Slavery and the Dutch', 85–6.
46. Christopher Leslie Brown, *Moral Capital: Foundations of British Abolitionism* (Chapel Hill, NC: University of North Carolina Press, 2006).
47. Fabian Klose, *In the Cause of Humanity: A History of Humanitarian Intervention in the Long Nineteenth Century*, trans. Joe Kroll (Cambridge: Cambridge University Press, 2022).
48. Isadora Moura Mota, 'On the Verge of War: Black Insurgency, the "Christie Affair", and British Antislavery in Brazil', *Slavery & Abolition* 43, no. 1 (2022): 122.
49. For perspectives on this relationship, see Raphaël Cheriau, *Imperial Powers and Humanitarian Interventions: The Zanzibar Sultanate, Britain, and France in the Indian Ocean, 1862–1905* (Abingdon: Routledge, 2021); Suzanne Miers, *Britain and the Ending of the Slave Trade* (London: Longman, 1975). On the use of antislavery for both 'British imperial aggression' and 'anti-imperialist critics of expansion or exploitation', see Huzzey, *Freedom Burning*, 77.
50. Huzzey, *Freedom Burning*, 6.

51. See e.g. Henri Morton Stanley, *Through the Dark Continent, or the Source of the Nile around the Great Lakes of Equatorial Africa and Down the Livingstone River to the Atlantic Ocean* (orig. 1878, repr. London: Constable, 1988) and his subsequent *In Darkest Africa, or the Great Rescue and Relief of Emin, Governor of Equatoria* (New York: Scribner, 1890). For numbers and assessments of the East African slave trade, see e.g. Paul Lovejoy, *Transformations in Slavery: A History of Slavery in Africa* (3rd edn; Cambridge: Cambridge University Press, 2012), 140–64; William Gervase Clarence-Smith, ed., *Economics of the Indian Ocean Slave Trade in the Nineteenth Century* (London: Routledge, 1989); Ralph A. Austen, 'The 19th Century Islamic Slave Trade from East Africa (Swahili and Red Sea Coasts): A Tentative Census', *Slavery & Abolition* 9, no. 3 (1988): 21–44.

52. Cardinal Lavigerie, *L'Esclavage Africain: Conférence sur l'esclavage dans le Haut Congo* (Brussels: Société antiesclavagiste, 1888), 2.

53. Ribi, *Humanitarian Imperialism*, 25.

54. Charles Lavigerie, *Slavery in Africa: A Speech. Made at the Meeting Held in London July 31, 1888* (Boston: Cashman, Keating and Company, 1888).

55. Ribi Forclacz, *Humanitarian Imperialism*, 20.

56. Ibid., 7.

57. Bodleian Libraries, Oxford, MS. Brit. Empire: Minute Book 6 of the British and Foreign Anti-Slavery Society (E2/11), entry for 7 December 1888.

58. Ribi notes contacts between Britain, France and Italy: Ribi, *Humanitarian Imperialism*, 28. There were also contacts between the BFASS and the *Société Antiesclavagiste de Belgique*: Bodleian Libraries, MSS Brit. Emp. S. 18: Letter exchanges between Charles Allen and Hypolite d'Ursel (C. 68) and Louis Delmer (C. 56).

59. Thomas David and Janick Schaufelbuehl, 'Swiss Conservatives and the Struggle for the Abolition of Slavery at the End of the Nineteenth Century', *Itinerario* 34, no. 2 (2010): 87–103.

60. William Mulligan, 'The Anti-Slave Trade Campaign in Europe, 1888–1890', in Mulligan and Bric, *A Global History of Anti-Slavery*, 151. See also Susan Zimmermann, *GrenzÜberschreitungen: Internationale Netzwerke, Organisationen, Bewegungen und die Politik der globalen Ungleichheit vom 17. bis zum 21. Jahrhundert* (Vienna: Mandelbaum, 2010), 26–71.

61. Laqua, 'The Tensions of Internationalism', esp. 313–19. On the role of 'civilizing missions', see Boris Barth and Jürgen Osterhammel, eds, *Zivilisierungsmissionen: Imperiale Weltverbesserung seit dem 18. Jahrhundert* (Konstanz: UVK-Verlag, 2005).

62. 'Wo stehen wir in der Antisklaverei-Bewegung?', *Gott will es!*, 1 (December 1889): 443.

63. Richard F. Clarke, *Cardinal Lavigerie and the African Slave Trade* (London: Longmans, Green & Co., 1889), v–vi.

64. On the conference and congress, see Laqua, *The Age of Internationalism and Belgium*, 47–52.

65. *Documents relatifs au Congrès libre anties-clavagiste, tenu à Paris, en septembre 1890* (Paris: Direction générale de l'oeuvre anti-esclavagiste, 1890).

66. 'The Anti-Slavery Congress: Cardinal Lavigerie at St. Sulpice', *The Tablet*, 27 September 1890, 502.

67. Antonin Lefèvre-Pontalis, 'Les Frères du Sahara: À la réunion des Sociétés antiesclavagistes, 29 avril 1891', in Lefèvre-Pontalis, *Conférences antiesclavagistes* (Saint Cloud: Imprimerie Berlin Frères, 1891), 18.

68. Suzanne Miers, 'Humanitarianism at Berlin: Myth or Reality?', in *Bismarck, Europe, and Africa: The Berlin Conference 1884–1885 and the Onset of Partition*, ed. Stig Förster, Wolfgang Mommsen and Ronald Robinson (Oxford: Oxford University Press, 1988), 344. See also Miers, *Britain and the Ending of the Slave Trade*; Matthew Unangst, 'Manufacturing Crisis: Anti-Slavery "Humanitarianism" and Imperialism in East Africa, 1888–1890', *Journal of Imperial and Commonwealth History* 48, no. 5 (2020): 805–25; Mairi McDonald, 'Lord Vivian's Tears: The Moral Hazards of Humanitarian Intervention', in *The Emergence of Humanitarian Intervention: Ideas and Practice from the Nineteenth Century to the Present*, ed. Fabian Klose (Cambridge: Cambridge University Press, 2016), 121–41.

69. Lovejoy, *Transformations in Slavery*, 246.

70. Andrew Porter, *Religious versus Empire? British Protestant Missionaries and Overseas Expansion, 1700–1914* (Manchester: Manchester University Press, 2004); James P. Daughton, *An Empire Divided: Religion, Republicanism and the Making of French Colonialism, 1880–1914* (Oxford: Oxford University Press, 2006); Vincent Viaene, Bram Cleys and Jan De Maeyer, eds, *Religion, Colonization and Decolonization in Congo, 1885–1960* (Leuven: Leuven University Press, 2020).

71. Archives of the Ministry of Foreign Affairs, Brussels: 'Conférence Anti-Esclavagiste de Bruxelles', dossier 373 ('Pétitions'), vols. 18 and 19, microfilms 304 and 305.

72. 'Le congrès antiesclavagiste de 1900', *Le Mouvement antiesclavagiste* 12, no. 7 (25 December 1900): 294.

73. Henry Fox Bourne, 'L'esclavage et ses formes dissimulées en Afrique', in *Congrès international antiesclavagiste*, 51.

74. Ibid., esp. 57–64.

75. Bodleian Libraries, MSS Brit. Emp. 20: Minute Book 6 of the British and Foreign Anti-Slavery Society (E2/11), entries for 6 June 1890 and 4 July 1890.

76. For a pioneering Belgian study on this subject, see Daniël Vangroenweghe, *Rood rubber: Leopold II en zijn Kongo* (Brussels: Elsevier, 1985). In the 2000s, the subject attracted wider attention among Anglophone audiences after the publication of Adam Hochschild, *King Leopold's Ghost: A Story of Greed, Terror, and Heroism in Colonial Africa* (London: Papermac, 2000). For a more recent study that brings together key findings on Belgium's role in Central Africa, see Guy Vanthemsche, *Belgium and the Congo, 1885–1980*, trans. Alice Cameron and Stephen Windross (Cambridge: Cambridge University Press, 2012).

77. Kevin Grant, *A Civilised Savagery: Britain and the New Slaveries in Africa, 1884–1926* (New York: Routledge, 2005), 39–78; Kevin Grant, 'The Limits of Exposure: Atrocity Photographs in the Congo Reform Campaign', in *Humanitarian Photography: A History*, ed. Heide Fehrenbach and Davide Rodogno (Cambridge: Cambridge University Press, 2015), 64–88.

78. E. D. Morel, *The Congo Slave State: A Protest against the New African Slavery; and an Appeal to the Public of Great Britain, of the United States, and of the Continent of Europe* (Liverpool: J. Richardson and Sons, 1903).

79. Dean Pavlakis, *British Humanitarianism and the Congo Reform Movement, 1896–1913* (Farnham: Ashgate, 2013), 67.

80. In contrast to Pavlakis's emphasis on Morel and the CRA, see Grant, *A Civilised Savagery*, 39–78. For an earlier account that emphasizes Morel's role, see Wm. Roger Louis, 'E. D. Morel and the Triumph of the Congo Reform Association', in Wm. Roger Louis, *The Ends of British Imperialism: The Scramble for Empire, Suez and Decolonisation* (London: I.B. Tauris, 2007), 153–82.

81. Robert Burroughs, *African Testimony in the Movement for Congo Reform: The Burden of Proof* (London: Routledge, 2019).
82. Jules Marchal, *E. D. Morel contre Léopold II: L'histoire du Congo 1900–1910*, vol. 1 (Paris: L'Harmattan, 1996), 277–84.
83. Laqua, *The Age of Internationalism and Belgium*, 60–1.
84. Ribi, *Humanitarian Imperialism*, 39–40. On the Swiss league, see 'La Ligue Suisse pour la défense des Indigènes dans le bassin conventionnel du Congo', *Journal de Genève*, 7 July 1908.
85. LSE Archives and Special Collections, London, Morel Papers, F8/131, letter from René Claparède, 7 June 1908. For Morel's correspondence with Félicien Challaye of the French league, see F8/27.
86. 'E.D. Morel en France' and 'E. D. Morel en Suisse', *Bulletin trimstestriel (Ligue internationale pour la protéction des indigènes au bassin conventionnel du Congo)* 2, no. 4 (1909): 35–9 and 40.
87. Pavlakis, *British Humanitarianism*, 164.
88. 'Comité international pour la défense des indigènes du Congo', *Bulletin Trimestriel* 4, no. 2 (1909): 1.
89. On divisions in the American context, see Dean Clay, 'Transatlantic Dimensions of the Congo Reform Movement, 1904 – 1908', *English Studies in Africa* 59, no. 1 (2016): 18–28. On the British case, see Grant, *A Civilised Savagery*, 62–3.
90. Michael Cullinane, 'Transatlantic Dimensions of the American Anti-Imperialist Movement, 1899–1909', *Journal of Transatlantic Studies* 8, no. 4 (2010): 301–14.
91. Emmanuelle Sibeud, 'Entre geste impériale et cause internationale: défendre les indigènes à Genève dans les années 1920', *Monde(s)*, no. 6 (2014): 23–43.
92. E. D. Morel, 'Les indigènes du Congo Belge et du Congo Français: un appel à la France', *Bulletin Trimestriel* 1, no. 1 (1908): 8–9.
93. See, for example, the piece by the president of the French league, Pierre Mille, 'La question du Congo Français', *Bulletin Trimestriel* 2, no. 5 (1909): 2, originally featured in the French periodical *Action Nationale*. For the criticisms of Mille's ally, the French activist Félicien Challaye, see Emmnuelle Sibeud, 'Intellectuals for Empire: The Imperial Training of Félicien Challaye, 1899–1914', in *The French Colonial Empire, vol. 1: Mental Maps of Empire and Colonial Encounters*, ed. Martin Thomas (Lincoln: University of Nebraska Press, 2011), 26–48.
94. Dirk Moses, *The Problems of Genocide: Permanent Security and the Language of Transgression* (Cambridge: Cambridge University Press, 2021), 85–93.
95. Dean Clay, 'The Congo Free State Propaganda War, 1890–1909', *The International History Review* 43, no. 1 (2021): 457–74; Marchal, *E. D. Morel contre Léopold II*, e. g. 216.
96. Dean Clay, '"A Clash of Titans": Big Business and the Congo Reform Movement', *History* 107, no. 374 (2022): 97–120. Dean Pavlakis has shown, however, that the share of merchants backing the CRA was lower than has sometimes been assumed: Pavlakis, *British Humanitarianism*, 125–6.
97. Grant, *A Civilised Savagery*, 66.
98. Catherine Higgs, *Chocolate Islands: Cocoa, Slavery and Colonial Africa* (Athens, OH: Ohio University Press, 2012); Lowell Satre, *Chocolate on Trial: Slavery, Politics and the Ethics of Business* (Athens, OH: Ohio University Press, 2005). For the broader context, see Miguel Bandeira Jerónimo, *The 'Civilising Mission' of Portuguese Colonialism, 1870–1930*, trans. Stewart Lloyd-Jones (Basingstoke: Palgrave, 2015).

99. E. D. Morel, *The Horror on the Rhine* (London: Union of Democratic Control, 1920). See also Robert Reinders, 'Racialism on the Left: E. D. Morel and the "Black Horror on the Rhine"', *International Review of Social History* 13, no. 1 (1968): 1–28.

100. Iris Wigger, *The 'Black Horror on the Rhine': Intersections of Race, Nation, Gender and Class in 1920s Germany* (London: Palgrave, 2017), 7.

101. Felix Lössing, *A 'Crisis of Whiteness' in the 'Heart of Darkness': Racism and the Congo Reform Movement* (Bielefeld: transcript, 2020).

102. Arthur Conan Doyle, *The Crime of the Congo* (London: Hutchinson & Co., 1909). See also Marchal, *E. D. Morel contre Leopold I*, 407; Moses, *The Problems of Genocide*, 89–91.

103. Kenneth Wilson, 'Fiction and Empire: The Case of Sir Arthur Conan Doyle', *Victorian Review* 19, no. 1 (1993): 22–42.

104. Arthur Conan Doyle, *The Great Boer War* (London: Smith, Elder & Co., 1900); Arthur Conan Doyle, *The South African War: Its Cause and Conduct* (London: Georg Newnes, 1902).

105. Vincent Kuitenbrouwer, *War of Words: Dutch Pro-Boer Propaganda and the South African War (1899–1902)* (Amsterdam: Amsterdam University Press, 2012), 35.

106. Rebecca Gill, *Calculating Compassion: Humanity and Relief in War, Britain 1870–1914* (Manchester: Manchester University Press, 2013), 128.

107. Emily Hobhouse, *The Brunt of the War, and Where It Fell* (London: Methuen, 1902). On the importance of testimony, as well as selective representations and 'degrees of concern' that manifested themselves on such occasions, see Gill, *Calculating Compassion*, 158–60.

108. Rebecca Gill, 'Networks of Concern, Boundaries of Compassion: British Relief in the South African War', *Journal of Imperial and Commonwealth History* 40, no. 5 (2012): 838.

109. Rebecca Gill and Cornelis Muller, 'The Limits of Agency: Emily Hobhouse's International Activism and the Politics of Suffering', *Safundi* 19, no. 1 (2018): 16–35.

110. Moses, *The Problems of Genocide*, 94–135. See also Eric Weitz's discussion on the way in which the German colonial authorities cast their actions, and how this related to notions of rights in this period: Eric Weitz, *A World Divided: The Global Struggle for Human Rights in the Age of Nation-States* (Princeton, NJ: Princeton University Press, 2019), 206–41.

111. Robert Gerwarth and Erez Manela, eds, *Empires at War 1911–1923* (Oxford: Oxford University Press, 2014). See also Robert Frank, '1914–1918: une guerre mondiale ou une "guerre-monde"?', *Monde(s)*, no. 16 (2016): 9–21.

112. Kris Manjapra, 'The Illusions of Encounter: Muslim "Minds" and Hindu Revolutionaries in First World War Germany and After', *Journal of Global History* 1, no. 3 (2006): 371.

113. Harald Fischer-Tiné, 'Indian Nationalism and the "World Forces": Transnational and Diasporic Dimensions of the Indian Freedom Movement on the Eve of the First World War', *Journal of Global History* 2, no. 3 (2007): 325–44; Jennifer Jenkins, Heike Liebau and Larissa Schmid, 'Transnationalism and Insurrection: Independence Committees, Anti-Colonial Networks, and Germany's Global War', *Journal of Global History* 15, no. 1 (2020): 61–79.

114. Bruno Cabanes, *The Great War and the Origins of Humanitarianism, 1918–1924* (Cambridge: Cambridge University Press, 2014); Keith Watenpaugh, *Bread from Stones: The Middle East and the Making of Modern Humanitarianism* (Oakland, CA: University of California Press, 2015).

115. Emily Baughan, 'The Imperial War Relief Fund and the All British Appeal: Commonwealth, Conflict and Conservatism within the British Humanitarian Movement, 1920–25', *The Journal of Imperial and Commonwealth History* 40, no. 5 (2012): 845–61.

116. Emily Baughan, *Saving the Children: Humanitarianism, Internationalism, and Empire* (Oakland, CA: University of California Press, 2022), 79.
117. Erez Manela, *The Wilsonian Moment: Self Determination and the International Origins of Anticolonial Nationalism* (New York: Oxford University Press, 2007).
118. Martin Thomas, *Fight or Flight: Britain, France, and Their Roads from Empire* (Oxford: Oxford University Press, 2014), 11–43.
119. Susan Pedersen, *The Guardians: The League of Nations and the Crisis of Empire* (Oxford: Oxford University Press, 2015), 90.
120. Ibid., 93.
121. Covenant of the League of Nations, Article 22, available online at the Avalon Project: Documents in Law, History and Diplomacy, https://avalon.law.yale.edu/20th_century/leagcov.asp (last accessed 9 January 2023).
122. Grant, *A Civilised Savagery*, 153–4.
123. Bandeira Jerónimo, 'Developing Civilisation?'.
124. For a detailed analysis of these initiatives, see Suzanne Miers, *Slavery in the Twentieth Century: The Evolution of a Global Problem* (Walnut Creek, CA: AltaMira, 2003). See also Ribi Forclaz, *Humanitarian Imperialism*, 46–76; and Amalia Ribi, '"The Breath of a New Life"? British Anti-Slavery Activism and the League of Nations', in Laqua, *Internationalism Reconfigured*, 93–113.
125. On these tensions, see Ribi Forclacz, *Humanitarian Imperialism*, 50–5. For the termination of subscriptions, see Bodleian Libraries, Oxford, MSS Brit. Emp. 20, Minute Book 11 of the Anti-Slavery Society (E2/16), 7 October 1929.
126. United Nations Library and Archives, Geneva, League of Nations Archives, R4157, dossier 6B (Slavery): Advisory Committee of Experts on Slavery, *A Précis of the Information Supplied to the League of Nations Upon Slavery in Ethiopia* (prepared by Sir George Maxwell), 8 February 1935.
127. Ribi Forclaz, *The Politics of Anti-Slavery Activism*, 108–38.
128. International Institute of Social History, Amsterdam (hereafter: IISG), Rassemblement Universel pour la Paix archives (ARCH01165), folder 'Dossier sur le Comité international pour la défense du peuple éthiopien (et de la paix), Paris 1935–1936': Letter from the Comité international pour la défense du peuple éthiopien, 20 August 1935.
129. Marc Matera and Susan Kingsley Kent, *The Global 1930s: The International Decade* (Abingdon: Routledge, 2017), 84; Bibia Pavard, Florence Rochefort and Michelle Zancarini-Fournel, *Ne nous libérez pas, on s'en charge: Une histoire des féminismes à nos jours* (Paris: La Découverte, 2020), 204. On Nardal, see also Hakim Adi, *Pan-Africanism: A History* (London: Bloomsbury, 2018), 102–3.
130. Cherri Wemlinger, 'Collective Security and the Italo-Ethiopian Dispute before the League of Nations', *Peace & Change* 40, no. 2 (2015): 139–66.
131. For a detailed discussion, see Susan Pennybacker, *From Scottsboro to Munich: Race and Political Culture in 1930s Britain* (Princeton, NJ: Princeton University Press, 2009), 103–45.
132. Maria Framke, 'Anti-Koloniale Solidarität? Der Abessinienkrieg, Indien und der Völkerbund', in Kunkel and Meyer, *Aufbruch ins postkoloniale Zeitalter*, 190–208; Priyamvada Gopal, *Insurgent Empire: Anticolonial Resistance and British Dissent* (London: Verso, 2019), 319–54; Theo Williams, *Making the Revolution Global: Black Radicalism and the British Socialist Movement before Decolonisation* (London: Verso, 2022), 75–122.

133. C. L. R. James, *Toussaint Louverture: The Story of the Only Successful Slave Revolt in History*, ed. Christian Høgsbjerg (Durham, NC: Duke University Press, 2013).

134. C. L. R. James, *The Black Jacobins: Toussaint L'Ouverture and the San Domingo Revolution* (London: Penguin, 1980 [orig. 1938]), 303. See also Christian Høgsbjerg, *C. L. R. James in Imperial Britain* (Durham, NC: Duke University Press, 2014), 158–98.

135. This quote is taken from the foreword, dated January 1980: James, *The Black Jacobins*, xvi.

136. Høgsbjerg, *C. L. R. James in Imperial Britain*, 97.

137. The PhD thesis on which Williams's *Capitalism and Slavery* was based is in itself now available: Eric Williams, *The Economic Aspect of the Abolition of the West Indian Slave Trade and Slavery*, ed. Dale Tomich (Lanham, MD: Rowman & Littlefield, 2014). For an analysis of the intellectual and political contexts, see Pepijn Brandon, 'From Williams's Thesis to Williams Thesis: An Anti-Colonial Trajectory', *International Review of Social History* 62, no. 2 (2017): 305–27.

138. Marc Matera, *Black London: The Imperial Metropolis and Decolonization in the Twentieth Century* (Oakland, CA: University of California Press, 2015).

139. Michael Goebel, *Anti-Imperial Metropolis: Interwar Paris and the Seeds of Third World Nationalism* (Cambridge: Cambridge University Press, 2015), 279.

140. Sophie Quinn-Judge, *Ho Chi Minh: The Missing Years* (London: Hurst, 2003).

141. Rabah Aissaoui, 'Exile and the Politics of Return and Liberation: Algerian Colonial Workers and Anti-Colonialism in France during the Interwar Period', *French History* 25, no. 2 (2011): 214–23.

142. Sarah Britton, '"Come and See the Empire by the All Red Route!": Anti-Imperialism and Exhibitions in Interwar Britain', *History Workshop Journal* 69, no. 1 (2010): 68–89, at 71–5.

143. See e.g. Gilles Boetsch, Nanette Jacomijn Snoep and Pascal Blanchard, *Human Zoos: The Invention of the Savage* (Arles: Actes Sud, 2012); Annie Combes, *Reinventing Africa: Museums, Material Culture and Popular Imagination in Late Victorian and Edwardian England* (New Haven, CT: Yale University Press, 1994).

144. Jodi Blake, 'The Truth about the Colonies, 1931: Art Indigène in Service of the Revolution', *Oxford Art Journal* 25, no. 1 (2002): 35–58.

145. Hakim Adi, *West Africans in Britain 1900–1960: Nationalism, Pan-Africanism and Communism* (London: Lawrence and Wishart, 1998), 45–7.

146. Adi, *West Africans in Britain*, 96–101; Klaas Stutje, *Campaigning in Europe for a Free Indonesia: Indonesian Nationalists and the Worldwide Anticolonial Movement, 1917–1931* (Copenhagen: NIAS Press, 2019).

147. Muzong W. Kodi, 'The 1921 Pan-African Congress at Brussels: A Background to Belgian Pressures', *Transafrican Journal of History* 13 (1984): 48–73.

148. See e.g. the article in *L'Avenir Colonial Belge*, 17 July 1921, as featured in Robert Hill, ed., *The Marcus Garvey and Universal Negro Improvement Association Papers, vol. 11: Africa for the Africans 1921–1922* (Berkeley, CA: University of California Press, 1997), 97–100.

149. Jeremy Rich, 'Paul Panda Farnana', in *Dictionary of African Biography*, ed. Emmanuel Akyeampong and Henry Louis Gates (Oxford: Oxford University Press, 2011), https://www.oxfordreference.com/view/10.1093/acref/9780195382075.001.0001/acref-9780195382075-e-0649 (last accessed 9 January 2023).

150. Michael Goebel, 'Geopolitics, Transnational Solidarity or Diaspora Nationalism? The Global Career of M.N. Roy, 1915–1930', *European Review of History* 21, no. 4 (2014): 485–99.

151. Kris Manjapra, *M. N. Roy: Marxism and Colonial Cosmopolitanism* (Abingdon: Routledge, 2010), e.g. 64 and 79.
152. Leslie James, *George Padmore and Decolonization from Below: Pan-Africanism, the Cold War, and the End of Empire* (Basingstoke: Palgrave, 2015), e.g. 42–5; and Williams, *Making the Revolution Global*.
153. Irina Filatova, 'Indoctrination or Scholarship? Education of Africans at the Communist University of the Toilers of the East in the Soviet Union, 1923–1937', *Paedagogica Historica* 35, no. 1 (1999): 41–66; Masha Kirasirova, 'The "East" as a Category of Bolshevik Ideology and Comintern Administration: The Arab Section of the Communist University of the Toilers of the East', *Kritika* 18, no. 1 (2017): 7–34; See also Vijay Prashad, *Red Star Over the Third World* (London: Pluto, 2019); Holger Weiss, ed., *International Communism and Transnational Solidarity: Radical Networks, Mass Movements and Global Politics, 1919–1939* (Leiden: Brill, 2016); Brigitte Studer, *Reisende der Weltrevolution: Eine Globalgeschichte der Kommunistischen Internationale* (Frankfurt/Main: Suhrkamp, 2020), 237–97.
154. Daniel Brückenhaus, *Policing Transnational Protest: Liberal Imperialism and the Surveillance of Anticolonialists in Europe, 1905–1945* (Oxford: Oxford University Press, 2017), 139–68.
155. Frederick Petersson, 'Hub of the Anti-Imperialist Movement: The League against Imperialism and Berlin, 1927–1933', *Interventions* 16, no. 1 (2014): 49–71.
156. David Murphy, 'Defending the "Negro Race": Lamine Senghor and Black Internationalism in Interwar France', *French Cultural Studies* 24, no. 2 (2013): 161–73; Lamine Senghor, *La Violation d'un pays, et autres écrits anticolonialistes*, ed. David Murphy (Paris: L'Harmattan, 2012 [orig. 1927]).
157. David Murphy, 'No More Slaves! Lamine Senghor, Black Internationalism and the League against Imperialism', in *The League against Imperialism: Lives and Afterlives*, ed. Michele Louro, Carolien Stolte, Heather Streets-Salter, and Sana Tannoury-Karam (Leiden: Leiden University Press, 2021), 218.
158. Michele Louro, *Comrades against Imperialism: Nehru, India, and Interwar Internationalism* (Cambridge: Cambridge University Press, 2018).
159. Klaas Stutje, 'Heralds of a Failed Revolt: Mohammad Hatta in Brussels, 1927', in Louro et al., *The League against Imperialism*, 319.
160. M. N. Roy, *Revolution und Konterrevolution in China*, trans. Paul Frölich (Berlin: Soziologische Verlagsanstalt, 1930). This German version predated the publication of Roy's work in English.
161. Manjapra, *M. N. Roy*, 88.
162. Martin Thomas, *The French Empire between the Wars: Imperialism, Politics and Society* (Manchester: Manchester University Press, 2005), 258.
163. Céline Marangé, 'Le Komintern, le Parti communiste français et la cause de l'indépendance algérienne (1926–1930)', *Vingtième Siècle* 131, no. 3 (2016): 53–70.
164. Thomas, *The French Empire between the Wars*, 278.
165. Pennybacker, *From Scottsboro to Munich*, 77–87. On Padmore's Comintern-related trade unionism prior to this, see Holger Weiss, *Framing a Radical African Atlantic: African American Agency, African Intellectuals and the International Trade Union Committee of Negro Workers* (Leiden: Brill, 2013).
166. C. L. R. James in conversation with Stuart Hall, Channel 4, 1984, available online at https://www.youtube.com/watch?v=_Gf0KUxgZfI&t (last accessed 9 January 2023).

167. Hakim Adi, *Pan-Africanism and Communism: The Communist International, Africa and the Diaspora, 1919–1939* (Trenton: Africa World Press, 2013).
168. Adi, *Pan-Africanism*, 2.
169. Marika Sherwood, *Origins of Pan-Africanism: Henry Silvester Williams, Africa, and the African Diaspora* (New York: Routledge, 2011).
170. For an overview of these congresses, see Adi, *Pan-Africanism*, 46–71.
171. Jessie Fauset, 'Impressions of the Second Pan-African Congress', *The Crisis* 23, no. 1 (1921): 15.
172. Fauset, 'Impressions of the Second Pan-African Congress', 13 and 14.
173. Ibid., 15.
174. W. E. B. Du Bois, 'The Pan-African Movement', in *W. E. B. Du Bois Speaks: Speeches and Addresses 1920–1963*, ed. Philip Foner (New York: Pathfinder, 1970), 199–203.
175. Jake Hodder, 'The Elusive History of the Pan-African Congress, 1919–27', *History Workshop Journal* 91, no. 1 (2021): 124.
176. Bodleian Libraries, Oxford, MSS Brit. Emp. S22, dossier G.432: quotes taken from letters by John Harris to E. N. Bennett, 22 August 1928 and to H. M. Nevison, 17 October 1921.
177. Adi, *Pan-Africanism*, 111–13. On the activities of the International African Service Bureau, see in particular Williams, *Making the Revolution Global*.
178. Hakim Adi and Marika Sherwood, *The 1945 Manchester Pan-African Congress Revisited* (London: New Beacon Books, 1995).
179. Jonathan Derrick, *Africa's 'Agitators': Militant Anti-Colonialism in Africa and the West, 1918–1939* (New York: Columbia University Press, 2008).
180. Louro, *Comrades against Empire*; Carolien Stolte, 'South Asia and South Asians in the Worldwide Web of Anti-Colonial Solidarity', in *Routledge Handbook of the History of Colonialism in South Asia*, ed. Harald Fischer-Tiné and Maria Framke (Abingdon: Routledge, 2021), 463–73.
181. Maria Framke, 'Political Humanitarianism in the 1930s: Indian Aid for Republican Spain', *European Review of History* 23, nos. 1–2 (2016): 63–81; Maria Framke, '"We Must Send a Gift Worthy of India and the Congress!": War and Political Humanitarianism in Late Colonial South Asia', *Modern Asian Studies* 51, no. 6 (2017): 1969–98.
182. Carolien Stolte, 'Trade Unions on Trial: The Meerut Conspiracy Case and Trade Union Internationalism, 1929–32', *Comparative Studies of South Asia, Africa and the Middle East* 33, no. 3 (2013): 345–59.
183. Benjamin Zachariah, 'Indian Political Activities in Germany, 1914–1945', in *Transcultural Encounters between Germany and India: Kindred Spirits in the Nineteenth and Twentieth Centuries*, ed. Joanne Miyang Cho, Eric Kurlander and Douglas McGetchin (Abingdon: Routledge, 2014), 141–55; Benjamin Zachariah, 'A Voluntary Gleichschaltung? Indian Perspectives towards a Non-Eurocentric Understanding of Fascism', *Journal of Transcultural Studies* 5, no. 2 (2014): 63–100; Maria Framke, *Delhi – Rom – Berlin: Die indische Wahrnehmung von Faschismus und Nationalsozialismus 1922–1939* (Darmstadt: WBG, 2013); Baijayanti Roy, 'At the Crossroads of Anti-Colonialism, Axis Propaganda and International Communism: The Periodical Azad Hind in Nazi Germany', *Media History* (advance access online 2022), https://doi.org/10.1080/13688804.2022.2158793 (last accessed 9 January 2023).
184. Todd Shepard, *The Invention of Decolonization: The Algerian War and the Remaking of France* (Ithaca, NY: Cornell University Press, 2006).

185. François-René Julliard, 'Le Comité Maurice Audin: s'organiser contre la torture', *Le Mouvement Social*, no. 267 (2019): 63–79.
186. Jeffrey James Byrne, *Mecca of Revolution: Algeria, Decolonization and Third World Order* (New York: Oxford University Press, 2016), 3.
187. Tolan Szkilnik Paraska, 'Flickering Fault Lines: The 1969 Pan-African Festival of Algiers and the Struggle for a Unified Africa', *Monde(s)*, no. 9 (2016): 167–84.
188. Sean Scalmer has traced these inspirations with regard to Britain and the United States which, he argues, 'were the most fully engrossed in Gandhi's activities and in the subsequent career of Gandhism': Scalmer, *Gandhi in the West*, 6.
189. Frantz Fanon, *Les Damnés de la terre* (Paris: François Maspero, 1961).
190. David Macey, *Frantz Fanon: A Biography* (London: Verso, 2012).
191. Kathryn Batchelor and Sue-Ann Harding, eds, *Translating Frantz Fanon across Continents and Languages* (New York: Routledge, 2017).
192. Marcin Wojciech Solarz, '"Third World": The 60th Anniversary of a Concept That Changed the World', *Third World Quarterly* 33, no. 9 (2012): 1561–73.
193. Prashad, *The Darker Nations*, 31–50.
194. Asian-African Conference, *Selected Documents of the Bandung Conference: Texts of Selected Speeches and Final Communique of the Asian-African Conference, Bandung, Indonesia, April 18–24, 1955* (New York: Institute of Pacific Relations, 1955), 2.
195. Su Lin Lewis and Carolien Stolte, 'Other Bandungs: Afro-Asian Internationalisms in the Early Cold War', *Journal of World History* 30, no. 1 (2019): 1–19.
196. Carolien Stolte, '"The People's Bandung": Local Anti-imperialists on an Afro-Asian Stage', *Journal of World History* 30, no. 1 (2019): 12–56.
197. Robert Gildea, James Mark and Niek Pas, 'European Radicals and the "Third World"', *Cultural and Social History* 8, no. 4 (2011): 449–71. See also Quinn Slobodian, *Foreign Front: Third World Politics in Sixties West Germany* (Durham, NC: Duke University Press, 2012); Eleanor Davey, *Idealism beyond Borders: The French Revolutionary Left and the Rise of Humanitarianism, 1954–1988* (Cambridge: Cambridge University Press, 2015).
198. Gerd-Rainer Horn, *The Spirit of Vatican II: Western European Progressive Catholicism in the Long Sixties* (Oxford: Oxford University Press, 2015), 100–10; Chris Dols and Benjamin Ziemann, 'Progressive Participation and Transnational Activism in the Catholic Church after Vatican II: The Dutch and West German Examples', *Journal of Contemporary History* 50, no. 3 (2015): 465–85.
199. This also extended to active support by Eastern European governments for these struggles: see Lena Dallywater, Chris Saunders and Helder Adegar Fonseca, eds, *Southern African Liberation Movements and the Global Cold War 'East': Transnational Activism 1960–1990* (Berlin: De Gruyter, 2019).
200. See e.g. James Mark, Nigel Townson and Polymeris Voglis, 'Inspirations', in Gildea et al., *Europe's 1968*, 94 and 101–2.
201. Piero Gleijeses, 'Cuba's First Venture in Africa: Algeria, 1961–1965', *Journal of Latin American Studies* 28, no. 1 (1996): 159–95; Margaret Randall, *Exporting Revolution: Cuba's Global Solidarity* (Durham, NC: Duke University Press, 2017); Jeremy Friedman, 'Reddest Place North of Havana: The Tricontinental and the Struggle to Lead the "Third World"', in *The Tricontinental Revolution: Third World Radicalism and the Cold War*, ed. Joseph Parrott and Mark Atwood Lawrence (Cambridge: Cambridge University Press, 2020), 193–215.

202. Kim Christiaens, 'Between Diplomacy and Solidarity: Western European Support Networks for Sandinista Nicaragua', *European Review of History* 21, no. 4 (2014): 617–34.

203. Sozialarchiv, Zürich, AR 201.259.1: Schweizerische Internationalistische Arbeitsbrigade in Nicaragua, 'Pressemitteilung' 7 September 1982. On the Swiss solidarity movement for Nicaragua, see Thomas Kadelbach, *Les brigadistes suisses au Nicaragua (1982–1990)* (Fribourg: Academic Press Fribourg, 2006).

204. James Mark et al., *Socialism Goes Global: The Soviet Union and Eastern Europe in the Age of Decolonisation* (Oxford: Oxford University Press, 2022); James Mark and Péter Apor, 'Socialism Goes Global: Decolonization and the Making of a New Culture of Internationalism in Socialist Hungary, 1956-1989', *Journal of Modern History* 87, no. 4 (2015): 852–91.

205. See e.g. the coverage of this issue in the WIDF newsletter, as featured in AMSAB – Institute of Social History, Ghent, Émilienne Brunfaut papers (343): *Bulletins* 9 and 10 (1973) of the Women's International Democratic Federation. Organizations such as WIDF provided activists from Angola and Mozambique with 'crucial opportunities for tapping into transnational networks of women's solidarity': Andreas Stucki, *Violence and Gender in Africa's Iberian Colonies: Feminizing the Portuguese and Spanish Empire, 1950s–1970s* (Cham: Palgrave, 2019), 263. See also Yulia Gradskova, *The Women's International Democratic Federation, the Global South, and the Cold War: Defending the Rights of Women of the 'Whole World'?* (Abingdon: Routledge, 2021), 77–97.

206. Kim Christiaens, 'Europe at the Crossroads of Three Worlds: Alternative Histories and Connections of European Solidarity with the Third World, 1950s–1980s', *European Review of History* 24, no. 6 (2017): 932–54.

207. James Mark, Péter Apor, Radina Vučetić and Piotr Osęka, '"We Are with You, Vietnam": Transnational Solidarities in Socialist Hungary, Poland and Yugoslavia', *Journal of Contemporary History* 50, no. 3 (2015): 439–64.

208. Jan Kavan, 'Czechoslovakia 1968: Revolt or Reform? 1968 – A Year of Hope and Non-Understanding', *Critique* 36, no. 2 (2008): 289–301.

209. Colin Shindler, *Israel and the European Left: Between Solidarity and Delegitimization* (London: Continuum, 2012).

210. 'Revolutionary Anti-Imperialist Struggle in Ireland: Build Solidarity', *New Age*, no. 15 (August/September 1979), transcribed/edited by Sam Richards and Paul Saba and available online via https://www.marxists.org/history/erol/uk.hightide/cwm-ireland-2.htm (last accessed 9 January 2023).

211. Stephen Howe, *Ireland and Empire: Colonial Legacies in Irish History and Culture* (Oxford: Oxford University Press, 2000), 169 and 134. See also Marc Mulholland, 'Northern Ireland and the Far Left, c. 1965–1975', *Contemporary British History* 32, no. 4 (2018): 542–63.

212. See, for example, Kwame Nkrumah, *Neo-Colonialism: The Last Stage of Imperialism* (London: Nelson, 1965).

213. Michael Hardt and Antonio Negri, *Empire* (Cambridge, MA: Harvard University Press, 2000).

214. Michael Hardt and Antonio Negri, 'Empire, Twenty Years On', *New Left Review*, no. 120 (November/December 2019): 67–92. See also A. K. Thompson, *Black Bloc, White Riot: Anti-Globalization and the Genealogy of Dissent* (Oakland, CA: AK Press, 2010).

215. Peter van Dam, *Wereldverbeteraars: een geschiedenis van fair trade* (Amsterdam: Amsterdam University Press, 2018); Peter van Dam, 'Moralizing Postcolonial Consumer Society: Fair Trade in the Netherlands, 1964–1997', *International Review of Social History*

61, no. 2 (2016): 223–50; Peter van Dam, 'Attracted and Repelled: Transnational Relations between Civil Society and the State in the History of the Fair Trade Movement since the 1960s', in *Shaping the International Relations of the Netherlands, 1815–2000: A Small Country on the Global Stage*, ed. Ruud van Dijk et al. (Abingdon: Routledge, 2018), 83–200. See also Matthew Anderson, *A History of Fair Trade in Contemporary Britain: From Civil Society Campaigns to Corporate Compliance* (Basingstoke: Palgrave, 2015).

216. Peter van Dam, 'Challenging Global Inequality in Streets and Supermarkets: Fair Trade Activism since the 1960s', in *Histories of Global Inequality: New Perspectives*, ed. Christian Olaf Christiansen and Steven L. B. Jensen (Cham: Palgrave, 2019), 255–75.

217. Ruben Quaas, *Fair Trade: Eine global-lokale Geschichte am Beispiel des Kaffees* (Cologne: Böhlau, 2015), 84–6.

218. Quaas, *Fair Trade*, 82.

219. See the material in Sozialarchiv, Zürich, AR 201.259.1, for example coverage in a leftist newspaper: 'Dämme bauen, Brunnen graben', *Volksrecht*, 11 August 1982.

220. Tehila Sasson, 'Milking the Third World? Humanitarianism, Capitalism, and the Moral Economy of the Nestlé Boycott', *The American Historical Review* 121, no. 4 (2016): 1196–224. For the broader context of Nestlé's activities in Africa, see Lola Wilhelm, 'One of the Most Urgent Problems to Solve: Malnutrition, Trans-Imperial Nutrition Science and Nestlé's Medical Pursuits in Late Colonial Africa', *Journal of Imperial and Commonwealth History* 48, no. 5 (2020): 914–33.

CHAPTER 2
HUMANITARIANISM IN WAR AND PEACE

As a delegate for the International Committee of the Red Cross (ICRC), the Swiss medic Marcel Junod was present at several sites of human suffering: he visited Abyssinia in the aftermath of the Italian attack of 1935–6, inspected concentration camps in Nazi Germany, helped to coordinate aid efforts during the Spanish Civil War and saw the impact of nuclear warfare in Japan. Unsurprisingly, these encounters were on his mind as he wrote his memoirs in 1947: 'In the shadows around me I seem to divine all those suffering bodies, all those anxious faces lined with pain, which haunted me during the twelve years of my long journey on their behalf.'[1] In listing the scenes that he had observed – from 'the Abyssinians seared by the burns of mustard gas helplessly' to 'the horror rising from the white desert which was once the thriving town of Hiroshima' – Junod argued that 'these pictures are not merely out of the past'.[2] As he suggested, the victims of these events sent a message to future humanitarians, urging them to help those in distress.

Junod's example indicates how the history of humanitarianism maps onto major developments in modern and contemporary history, with humanitarian activists and organizations responding to the crises of their day and serving as historical witnesses. At the same time, humanitarian actors have crafted narratives about their own past. Junod's memoirs are one example; the involvement of humanitarian organizations in publishing accounts of their own history is another.[3] Yet an awareness of the different pasts of humanitarianism is not confined to activists and their organizations: in recent years, political scientists and historians have shown great interest in humanitarianism as a historical phenomenon.[4] Recent work has highlighted the insights that academic work can yield for practitioners.[5] Examinations of, for instance, the media strategies of humanitarians or the gendered dimensions of humanitarianism evidently relate to the concerns faced by present-day humanitarian actors.[6]

Humanitarianism is multifarious in nature, as it can range from seemingly pragmatic responses in the face of an acute crisis to more overtly political appeals for supporting the victims of particular regimes.[7] Yet, while humanitarianism may be diffuse in some respects, its transnational features are clearly evident, as captured in Michael Barnett's definition of humanitarianism as comprising 'assistance beyond borders, a belief that such transnational action was related in some way to the transcendent, and the growing organization and governance of activities designed to protect and improve humanity'.[8]

With its emphasis on European theatres of humanitarian action, this chapter does not suggest that any discussion of humanitarianism can be easily confined to Europe. Indeed, it has been argued that a 'new conceptualization of humanity', which underpinned the rise of humanitarianism from the eighteenth century onwards, 'was closely linked to the colonial experience and led to the broadening of the scope of care for others'.[9] After all, European empires were major spaces for humanitarian action.[10] As a result, imperial contexts gave rise to humanitarian tropes and repertoires that applied elsewhere, including in Europe itself.[11] In other words, this chapter needs to be read in conjunction with the preceding one, parts of which have covered humanitarian campaigns in terms of their relationship to empire. Rather than providing a chronological narrative, I will start by contrasting two seemingly competing visions of humanitarianism: the Red Cross and the discourse of 'neutrality' on the one side, and framings of humanitarianism that were based on political affinities on the other. The chapter subsequently considers two fields of humanitarian action in which narratives of impartiality coexisted with expressions of solidarity, namely support for refugees on the one hand, and famine and disaster relief on the other. The chapter concludes with a consideration of 'activist humanitarianism' since the 1960s.

Helping the victims of conflict

In 1862, Henry Dunant's *Memoir of Solferino* recounted his observations of the Second Italian War of Independence (1859), detailing the suffering on the battlefield and the inadequate arrangements for the care of wounded soldiers. His celebrated account concluded with an appeal to establish new structures for the provision of aid in such emergencies. As he envisaged it, national committees would be 'animated by an international spirit of charity' and 'although independent of one another' would 'know how to understand and correspond with each other, to convene in congress and, in event of war, to act for the good of all'.[12] In 1863, Dunant's vision resulted in the foundation of the ICRC, followed by the formation of national committees over the subsequent decades. Given the undeniable prominence of the Red Cross as a humanitarian actor, it is worth outlining the features that shaped its activism.[13]

First of all, the Red Cross sought to project an image of neutrality in its commitment to addressing human needs and thus acting 'above politics'. In his book, Dunant presented the women of Castiglione, a small Italian town near Solferino, as caring for wounded soldiers irrespective of the background of the people under their care.[14] The fact that many histories of the Red Cross point to this episode testifies to the powerful notion of impartial aid.[15] One can justifiably be sceptical about such origin stories and the discourse employed by humanitarians.[16] The principles of the Red Cross evolved over time and had to adapt to changing global circumstances.[17] Nonetheless, notions of a shared humanity certainly mattered for many activists. For example, in tracing the origins of the Japanese Red Cross movement, Sho Konishi has spoken of 'the humanitarian ethic of medical care and philanthropy for ordinary people without association with the nation-state, war, or religion'.[18]

Secondly, the case of the Red Cross draws attention to the complex relationship between identity and humanitarianism. The organization originated in Geneva, the city of Calvin, and many of its founding members professed their attachment to Christian notions of charity. In his *Memoir of Solferino*, Dunant claimed that the women of Castiglione had used the phrase *tutti fratelli* ('all brothers') – thus citing words associated with the medieval friar and theologian Francis of Assisi. While the Red Cross subsequently established itself as a secular actor, its use of the cross caused tensions and necessitated the creation of a separate symbol for the Muslim world, with the Red Crescent becoming the emblem first in the Ottoman Empire (1869) and subsequently in other regions with Muslim populations – although it took until 1929 before Western Red Cross societies and governments accepted this symbol as equal to the Red Cross.[19] Moreover, even beyond imagery or religious backgrounds, culture and identity shaped humanitarian responses. These differences were illustrated by conflicting responses to the partition of Palestine and the establishment of Israel in 1948. In this context, the divergent views of actors within the wider movement – from the International Committee to the Egyptian Red Crescent – indicated how 'the attempt of transnational cooperation with countries that had just overcome colonial dependence amounted to an innovative, but difficult experiment'.[20] At the conference of Red Cross societies in 1948, relations with Israel became a major bone of contention.[21]

A third element in the development of the Red Cross was its symbiotic relationship with the development of international law. In 1864, Dunant and his Genevan associates convinced the Swiss government to initiate a diplomatic conference, giving rise to the Geneva Convention for the Amelioration of the Condition of the Wounded and Sick in Armed Forces in the Field. This international agreement became the basis of Red Cross operations, yet the Red Cross also saw itself as a guardian of the Convention. International law on matters of war and peace expanded in subsequent years, although the introduction of special provisions for civilians only occurred in 1949. The time lag in extending the Geneva Conventions highlighted the challenges of relying on international law – and the question of how to deal with violations of the agreements affected the Red Cross movement early on.[22] In his memoirs, Marcel Junod acknowledged the limitations of a dependence on governments' willingness to implement international law: looking at the start of the Second World War, he asked himself 'what weapons, what means were at the disposal of the strictly humanitarian cause we had been called upon to serve against this sudden explosion of violence which was rapidly spreading over the world?'.[23] He answered this question himself: 'Nothing but the two Conventions which we had already seen in action in Abyssinia and Spain; the one concerned the protection of the wounded and the other the protection of prisoners of war.' Moreover, the era of decolonization, this focus on international law posed particular challenges when it came to Red Cross intervention during wars of decolonization, given the policy of European powers to portray them as 'internal' rather than international conflicts.[24]

Fourthly, transnational cooperation was central to Red Cross operations. The Red Cross was far from the first organization to promote care for sick and wounded soldiers. However, such medical care had traditionally been linked to military structures and mostly delivered to compatriots. With its international remit, the Red Cross played a pioneering role, even though much of its work was channelled through national Red Cross societies. The formation of such national groupings was in itself the outcome of transnational contacts. For example, the American nurse Clara Barton founded the American Red Cross Society after observing Red Cross operations during the Franco-Prussian War of 1870–1.[25] In 1919, the different Red Cross societies strengthened their ties by forming the International Federation of Red Cross and Red Crescent Societies.

Notwithstanding its transnational scope, national ideas and state structures clearly shaped the Red Cross movement. The ICRC had a peculiar status – being on the one hand defined as 'international' but on the other hand composed exclusively of Swiss citizens and sometimes acting in line with Swiss foreign policy considerations.[26] Moreover, by the outbreak of the First World War, underlying tensions within the Red Cross movement became evident. The historian Heather Jones has highlighted the constrast between, on the one hand, the ICRC's transnational orientation and, on the other hand, individual Red Cross societies that construed their role in national terms.[27] With a focus on the American Red Cross, Julia Irwin has shown how humanitarian action reinforced a sense of American mission and tied in with state policies: even when relief efforts came from private actors, 'diplomatic and military officials came to recognize the strategic importance of aid … [and] they facilitated these voluntary efforts in myriad ways'.[28] The interaction between state agencies and Red Cross societies meant that the latter could be appropriated by regimes of very different political shades. For instance, in 1933, the German Red Cross was quickly absorbed into the structures of the National Socialist state, while continuing to maintain ties to the ICRC and the Red Cross societies in other countries.[29]

These considerations indicate both the extent and limitations of humanitarian action. Beyond the institutional perspective, it is possible to trace the ambiguities of Red Cross aid through the individuals who were involved in it. In this vein, the historian Francesca Piana has analysed the activities of the Swiss medic and anthropologist George Montandon, who headed the ICRC mission to Siberia during the Russian Civil War and visited Austrian, Hungarian and Ottoman soldiers in Russian prisoner of war camps.[30] Montandon had experience of working abroad: an interest in ethnography had previously taken him to Abyssinia and resulted in speaker engagements in Switzerland, France, Italy and Britain.[31] Having arrived in Russia, Montandon operated with considerable independence: he 'transformed the fact-finding mission into a relief mission and organised the distribution of clothing, medication, food and money'.[32] After his brief had been extended to cover the repatriation of prisoners of war, Montandon made arrangements without prior authorization from ICRC leaders. He was aware of tensions under these circumstances, describing the period as being 'rich' in internal disputes – and, in a seeming departure from the Red Cross discourse of impartiality, referred to his excitement 'in observing the new Bolshevik world'.[33] Montandon's case highlights both the limits of Red Cross oversight even half a century into its existence and the personal motivations of some actors. Montandon used his Russian mission as an opportunity to pursue his ethnographical interests, gathering various objects for his private collection.[34]

In later years, Montandon became associated with the championing of scientific racism. Moreover, following the German invasion of France, he collaborated with the

National Socialists, for instance in an anti-Semitic exhibition and publication on 'how to recognize the Jew'.[35] By then, he had long ended his involvement in the Red Cross movement. Yet, while his own collaboration was an extreme case, it draws attention to the circumstances of the 1940s. Red Cross actions in this period have attracted much criticism, especially regarding the question whether the organization served as a bystander to the Holocaust. Critics have pointed to the ICRC's silences, while others have suggested that limited means and the wider political circumstances prevented the organization from mounting an effective response.[36] One aspect, however, was evident well before the Second World War: claims of impartiality sounded hollow in the face of intense ideological struggles and genocide.

Humanitarianism and the politics of solidarity

Michael Barnett has distinguished between two strands of humanitarianism, namely 'emergency humanitarianism', which focuses on practical help and the saving of lives; and 'alchemical humanitarianism', which, as he puts it, 'involves saving lives at risk and addressing the root causes of suffering'.[37] The latter supposedly involves a wider vision, be it the articulation of a particular political project or the championing of a new international order. Yet 'emergency humanitarianism' sometimes took on explicitly political contours, too. Even when humanitarians stressed their neutrality, there were political implications to their stance – either by speaking out or by remaining silent. For this reason, any claims by humanitarians who cast themselves as 'apolitical' need to be questioned.

Moreover, already in the nineteenth century, an important strand of humanitarian activism was characterized by professions of solidarity – which involved taking sides. Like its Red Cross counterpart, this form of humanitarianism can be traced back to the nineteenth century, to efforts that have often been viewed as forerunners to contemporary ideas of humanitarian intervention.[38] During the late nineteenth and early twentieth centuries, the fate of minorities in the crisis-ridden Ottoman Empire became a matter of particular concern to activists in different parts of Europe. Many of them adopted a discourse of scandal, barbarism and atrocity that also characterized some of the campaigns that have been discussed in Chapter 1. Protests against the Ottoman Empire's treatment of its Christian minorities indicated that real or imagined proximity to the objects of humanitarian concern was an important mobilizing factor. Conversely, Ottoman Turks were presented as 'other'. As the historian Davide Rodogno has noted, such campaigns were informed by the conviction 'that massacres and atrocities were the direct consequence of the "barbarous" Ottoman government', yet over time, 'imperial racism toward Muslims played a recurring role in moving European humanitarians and some policy-makers to action'.[39] In this respect, activism involved multiple projections. For instance, the historian Rebecca Gill has shown how some British humanitarians 'bestowed an anachronistic nationhood' on populations that were in fact 'ethnically and religiously mixed'.[40] Seen from this angle, the 'emphasis on

Christian subject nations was to overlook the presence of Jews and Muslims in these lands – and of their suffering once they were forced to flee'.[41]

This is not to say that such representations were stagnant. For example, the historian Jo Laycock has traced the changing representations of Armenians: whereas late-nineteenth-century images were initially shaped by Armenian revolutionary activism against Ottoman rule, they subsequently shifted to an emphasis on Armenian victimhood.[42] This change was linked to the mass killings and displacement of Armenians by the Ottoman authorities in 1915 – events that the Polish lawyer Raphael Lemkin had in mind when he later coined the word 'genocide'.[43] By 1920, Armenians were the subject of a range of aid efforts, comprising medical support, food provision and accommodation for refugees. These undertakings signified the growth of a humanitarian field that included actors such as the Red Cross but also the nascent League of Nations.[44] While these endeavours were direct responses to human suffering, some activists viewed the Armenians as an oppressed national group deserving of solidarity.[45] The Armenian diaspora played a role in providing aid, especially through the Armenian Benevolent Union which, having been founded in Cairo, moved its seat to Paris after the First World War and undertook humanitarian work in Soviet Armenia during the 1920s.[46]

Soviet Armenia had come into existence after Ottoman and Russian forces had ended the short-lived Republic of Armenia (1918–20). In the same period, Soviet Russia became itself both an object and subject of humanitarian efforts, exemplified by the creation of Workers' International Relief (WIR) in 1921. With its secretariat in Berlin and the communist media magnate Willi Münzenberg as its principal organizer, WIR epitomized a form of humanitarianism with overtly political features.[47] Its first appeals focused on aid in the face of the Russian famine, but tied such action to support for the 'international class struggle'.[48] These efforts were driven by political sympathies, which were reinforced by the involvement of allied associations such as the US-based Friends of Soviet Russia. They constituted an explicit challenge to other relief efforts. For example, in 1921, the Comintern's *International Press Correspondence* complained that the American Relief Administration – which the US Congress had established two years earlier – 'stands in the limelight and monopolizes all publicity' regarding American aid in Russia.[49] Such accusations glossed over the fact that, in terms of the sheer scale, the American Relief Administration far eclipsed all other humanitarian agents, providing 'four-fifths of all foreign aid'.[50] Nonetheless, the protagonists of communist aid stressed that 'the American workers have organized and are putting into operation their own class relief organization, which is aiding the starving Russian workers and peasants without exacting humiliating and tyrannic conditions'.[51] In this respect, WIR and its related ventures cast humanitarian aid as part of a wider, emancipatory project based on class solidarity.

Early on, one key activity of national WIR committees revolved around the construction and funding of children's homes, initially with an emphasis on Russia at a time of civil war and famine. In focusing on children, WIR took up a staple of

Humanitarianism in War and Peace

humanitarian campaigns. After all, as the historian Katharina Stornig has pointed out, 'distant children in need' figured prominently in humanitarian endeavours well before the First World War.[52] In the post-war period, images of children proliferated in relief campaigns, from aid efforts in Hungary to the creation of the humanitarian organization Save the Children in Britain.[53]

Yet while other humanitarian ventures used children to affirm an 'apolitical' conception of aid, WIR adopted a perspective that cast such aid in political terms. For instance, the WIR children's homes in Russia were named after 'famous pioneers and leaders of the workers' struggles'.[54] According to WIR, suffering children were victims of both the post-war situation and capitalism. In 1924, the German WIR section launched a 'children's aid' initiative that exemplified this discourse.[55] To the activists, children – who had 'been born during the misery of the war years and curbed in their development by the hunger period of the post-war years' – were 'the first victims of the attack of capital'.[56] In practical terms, German WIR branches echoed the earlier Russia-based activities by opening their own children's homes. At the same time, they initiated leisure activities that were also cast as contributions to international understanding, as illustrated by vacation trips that took 160 German children to France.[57]

If WIR stood for an overtly political form of humanitarianism in the 1920s, such currents became particularly widespread in the 1930s. Activism during both the Spanish Civil War and the Sino-Japanese War shows that humanitarian responses to military conflict could involve the taking of sides. Militant solidarity – as expressed through the International Brigades – tends to dominate popular perceptions of transnational

Figure 2.1 Delegates at an international congress of Workers' International Relief committees, held in Berlin, July 1922. *Source*: Object F Fb-0004-29, Sozialarchiv Zürich.

activism in Spain. Yet alongside the action of volunteers who fought on the Republican side (and a smaller cohort of volunteers who supported Franco's troops), a range of humanitarian efforts were under way. In some cases, these were cast as impartial ventures, with the representation of child victims as a prominent feature.[58] Yet other forms of humanitarianism sat somewhere between militant solidarity and humanitarianism. For instance, the historian Maria Framke has noted how Indian nationalists provided aid to both Republican Spain and China as an expression of solidarity.[59] Another example is the case of the Australian communist Esme Odgers, who worked with refugee children from Republican Spain under the Foster Parents Plan.[60] Odgers joined a diverse group of women who provided aid in different ways. Winifred Bates – an East London woman who became involved in the United Socialist Party of Catalonia during her time in Spain – argued that 'girls who went to work in Spain as nurses, secretaries and interpreters' had different motivations and levels of knowledge:

> About half of them when they came out were quite unaware of the historical importance of the war and its international complications. They were just nurses, courageous women, willing to work under the most dangerous conditions. The other half knew what it was about, [and] had read a good deal on it.[61]

Politically grounded humanitarianism continued after the Second World War. Especially from the 1960s onwards, solidarity with liberation struggles employed humanitarian discourse alongside the anti-imperialist tropes that have been discussed in Chapter 1. An example was the campaign in 1966 by French activists to collect a billion old French francs – used as *centimes* after the currency revaluation of 1960 – in support of the North Vietnamese Red Cross. Their appeal noted the humanitarian needs of a population 'cruelly hit by American bombings'.[62] At the same time, the organizers acknowledged the dual purpose of their campaign, as humanitarian fundraising also sought 'to stimulate a national current of protest against the war in Vietnam within French public opinion'.[63] The newspaper *Le Monde* commented on this duality, but in the reverse way: to the paper, the fundraising dimensions underscored the aim to 'go beyond the framework of purely moral protest'.[64] While the initiative fell short of its target, a financial report from April 1967 recorded the considerable sum of 121.2 million *anciens francs*, with 80 million already passed on to the Red Cross in Vietnam.[65] Importantly, the initiative presented itself as a novel type of campaign, which was captured by *Le Monde*'s suggestion that the organizers were not 'familiar faces of protest'.[66] In fact, however, the undertaking included prominent political campaigners, for example the historian Madeleine Rebérioux, who had previously contributed to protests against the French war in Algeria.[67] In the end, the *milliard pour le Vietnam* initiative was absorbed by the 'Books for Vietnam' campaign, which was run by a network of activists with longstanding political commitments.

The *milliard* and 'Books for Vietnam' campaigns benefited from ties to the North Vietnamese government, which maintained a form of 'people's diplomacy' to gain allies in the West.[68] Such links were not confined to the Vietnamese case. For example, having overthrown the Somoza dictatorship in Nicaragua in 1979, the left-wing Sandinistas worked with activist groups in Europe; with a focus on Belgian solidarity groups, the historian Kim Christiaens has described this as a case of 'states going transnational'.[69] This development benefited from the contacts that some Sandinistas had built in their European exile during the years before the Nicaraguan Revolution.[70] While Chapter 1 has mentioned representations of Nicaragua as an anti-imperialist struggle, many groups and individuals who engaged in such actions cast their acts of solidarity as humanitarian, for instance by travelling to Nicaragua to support the construction of schools and hospitals. This dual aspect was aligned with Sandinista perspectives: as Christian Helm has noted, 'the Sandinistas established a leftist humanitarian master frame for the interpretation of their revolutionary politics'.[71]

Such efforts could be multi-layered. For example, in 1982, the Nicaragua trip of forty Swiss activists – previously mentioned in Chapter 1 – sought to support reconstruction efforts in areas devastated by recent floods. Yet participation also had a more personal dimension, with participants seeking to 'gain deeper insights into Nicaragua's reality three years after the victory of the revolution'.[72] Moreover, the political framing of humanitarian visits to Nicaragua became evident in the reference to such groups as 'brigades'. As a German activist recalled, when her group 'brokered the doctors and nurses of our health brigades for health centres in remote areas of the country', it evoked 'the spirit of the International Brigades in the Spanish Civil War'.[73] In such instances, humanitarian action was connected to the wider memory cultures of the European left.

Helping refugees in the age of total war

Military conflict did not only inspire humanitarian action because of the death and devastation that it caused: it also created refugees. In the twentieth century, total war – with its direct impact on civilian populations – and political repression triggered the mass displacement of people. The First World War eroded the boundaries between home front and battle front, with implications for humanitarian relief. Its protracted nature and its geographical spread resulted in the displacement of an estimated 10 million people.[74] The Russian Empire was a key site of wartime and post-war population movement. Not all such forced migration was transnational, with internal displacement being a key aspect. However, many practical aid efforts, even for internally displaced groups, had transnational features: as Peter Gatrell has pointed out, 'Most of imperial Russia's national minorities could count on material and other assistance from communities in self-imposed or voluntary exile overseas.'[75] Jewish suffering in the Russian Empire was particularly drastic during the war; moreover, the plight of Jewish refugees in Eastern Europe extended into the post-war years, with pogroms in Ukraine and elsewhere triggering further displacement in the early 1920s. The historian Jaclyn Granick has traced the wartime relief efforts for Russian Jews while noting that these undertakings built on 'preexisting and sophisticated, yet deeply threatened philanthropic networks'.[76] Since the 1890s, Jewish people from the Russian Empire had been subjects of humanitarian concern because of the refugee waves generated by anti-Semitic pogroms. As discussed further in Chapter 7, Jewish philanthropic organizations in Western Europe and North America provided aid in such circumstances, but Tobias Brinkmann has noted their ambivalent stances, 'ranging from genuine compassion to open disapproval', and often seeking 'to prevent the migration or to redirect it to distant destinations'.[77]

During the war, another major group of refugees resulted from the German attack on Belgium in August 1914. Initially, around 1.4 million Belgians fled to the neutral Netherlands, France and Great Britain. Of these, 600,000 spent an extended period in exile.[78] Whereas in France, Belgian refugees benefited from state help, and whereas in the Netherlands, they were housed in camps, the support infrastructure in Britain relied on private agency. Indeed, in the aftermath of the German attack, an outpouring of humanitarian sentiment manifested itself in the formation of around 2,000 support committees.[79] The case reveals, however, the ambiguities of humanitarian activism. First, the representation of 'gallant little Belgium' within the British war effort meant that support for refugees also reaffirmed civilian backing for the war effort.[80] Second, as in other situations, initial hospitality among broad sections of the population gave way to hostility, as reflected in anti-Belgian riots in London in May 1916.[81] Such antagonism coincided with representations of refugees as 'job stealers', indicating that the conditions for activism could change quite drastically.[82] The circumstances also proved challenging in other regards. Visiting Belgian refugees in the Dutch city of Amersfoort, the British Quaker and humanitarian Ruth Fry noted the presence of around 3,800 Belgian women and children for whom little support existed, but also observed the 'difficulty of co-operation between the Dutch and Belgians'. To Fry, it seemed 'obvious that there is little friendliness and that both look to us to bridge the differences'.[83]

While the First World War raised the issue of refugees on a new scale, refugeedom – and the need for humanitarian relief – did not cease with the Armistice of November 1918. Indeed, Claudena Skran has described the interwar period as a time when 'refugees first emerged as an international issue', partly because 'the development of immigration restrictions world-wide erected a new obstacle to the resolution of refugee problems'.[84] Such action came within limits: as Peter Gatrell has argued, 'little attempt was made to understand the root causes of their displacement'.[85]

Three factors were significant in making refugee aid a key issue in this period, with implications for transnational activism: the effects of the October Revolution in Russia; the break-up of the Ottoman Empire; and the rise of dictatorships across Europe. Refugee movements in the first two cases overlapped to some extent: for instance, in 1920 an estimated 148,000 Russian refugees arrived in Istanbul.[86] In the wake of the Armenian genocide, refugees from the Armenian territories under Turkish rule fled to Russia, with many others – 'approximately 200,000' – being 'scattered throughout Europe and the Middle East, principally located in Syria, France, Greece and Bulgaria'.[87] The multidirectional nature of this refugee wave to some extent contrasted with the movement of another large group, namely of Greek people to Greece: Greek refugees who fled the massacres in Turkey were followed by around 1.3 million Greeks who arrived under the population exchange between Greece and Turkey (1923).[88] The range of crises also gave rise to a new humanitarian initiative that built on the war experiences, namely Near East Relief.[89] In this period, aid for refugees was a mixed economy, involving ventures with quasi-official status alongside activists' efforts. According to the historian Daniel Maul, the sheer number of refugees in interwar Europe – an estimated 9.5 million – meant that 'governments were only rarely able or willing to look after them, meaning that 'the main burden rested … on the shoulders of NGOs'.[90]

To some extent, such efforts were boosted through the establishment of formal international structures within the framework of the League of Nations. The Norwegian humanitarian Fridtjof Nansen embodied this development. Having initially made his name as a polar explorer and been active in Norwegian circles that promoted the formation of a League of Nations, Nansen was appointed by the newly created League to deal with the repatriation of prisoners of war; he subsequently served as the League's High Commissioner for Refugees. As a League employee, Nansen may be seen a diplomat or international civil servant. Yet the nature of his efforts, and the multi-layered interactions he was involved in, demonstrates that the boundary between official work and activism could be blurry. This aspect was further underlined by the way in which private associations, rather than governments, had been 'a major driving force for the creation of a High Commissioner for Refugees' and 'subsequently carried the main financial burden for its work'.[91]

With migration affecting the concerns of states that were eager to safeguard their borders, the League's role in refugee relief was curtailed in several ways. For example, the Nansen International Office for Refugees – founded in 1930, shortly after Nansen's death – had no formal role in supporting two major refugee groups in 1930s Europe: those fleeing Germany after the National Socialists' ascent to power and those seeking to escape the Spanish Civil War. In 1933, governments agreed to appoint a separate High Commissioner for Refugees Coming From Germany, but under a limited remit. The official, James McDonald, soon pointed to the significant obstacles; in his widely publicized resignation letter of 1935, McDonald noted that '[t]he efforts of the private organisations and of any League organisation for refugees can only mitigate a problem of growing gravity and complexity', arguing that the issue had to 'be tackled at its source'.[92] The document generated a 'striking' response, yet it did not effect a change in international policy.[93]

Activists' rescue efforts operated within an environment that was inhospitable in several respects.[94] Jewish organizations in France and Britain therefore raised funds for refugees, seeking to prevent the impression that the arrivals would become 'burdens' on the host society.[95] In some cases, activists emphasized the utility of particular kinds of refugees, as exemplified by aid efforts for persecuted academics.[96] Government policies, however, posed significant obstacles to many humanitarians. In 1939, two veteran British campaigners, Dorothy Buxton and Norman Angell, discussed this issue, at a time when refugees had also been arriving from war-torn Spain. They pointed to the image of child refugees, 'even tiny children arriving at our ports, labelled like parcels, bundles of forlorn and helpless childhood, homeless, parentless, seeking refuge and sanctuary from the storm of cruelty and oppression which has swept their parents to penury, imprisonment, torture, death'.[97] Buxton and Angell highlighted the problems caused by official policies – namely an approach that was 'broadly one of exclusion tempered by the admission of relatively tiny numbers as an act of grace'.[98]

While national policies constituted an obstacle for refugee aid, international initiatives tackled the issue from a different angle. In 1943, the formation of the United Nations Relief and Rehabilitation Administration (UNRRA) was a major development – part of its novelty has been ascribed to the attempt to combine relief efforts, including refugee aid, with post-war development planning.[99] Until its closure in 1948, the organization ran refugee camps and supported the repatriation of former prisoners of war. As part of the nascent United Nations, UNRRA worked with existing humanitarian actors in helping refugees, but with the result that such associations 'were transformed in the process into nongovernmental organizations integrated into the United Nations'.[100] At the same time, the making of this sector highlighted the fluid boundaries between activism and humanitarian work: although UNRRA aimed for a professional image and sought to recruit qualified welfare workers, many individuals with backgrounds in voluntary action ended up joining the organization.[101]

While UNRRA dealt with the challenges of the post-war situation, Cold War conflict shaped refugee work in subsequent decades. Hungarian refugees were one example: after Soviet troops had crushed the Hungarian Uprising of 1956, 200,000 people fled the country, amounting to the largest refugee group since the immediate aftermath of the Second World War, with neighbouring Austria receiving by far the largest share – around 164,000.[102] As in previous cases, initial hospitality gave way to tensions, with complaints about 'ingratitude' as one factor.[103] At the same time, the case highlighted the Cold War dynamics that shaped responses to refugees. The Polish exile activist Stefan Korboński commented that 'the Western world' had not been 'sparring in expressions of sympathy for Hungary and various kinds of help', but attributed the hospitality for refugees across many Western countries to a guilty conscience, linked to their 'political inactivity' vis-à-vis the Soviet Union.[104] According to Korboński, expressions of solidarity had not been confined to Western countries, as members of the Polish opposition had 'spontaneously organized the collection of funds, medical aid and clothing for the rebels and had even offered care and hospitality for the orphans of those killed'.[105]

The Hungarian case illustrated how refugee aid could take on Cold War meanings. From a different angle, this point was exemplified when countries in the communist bloc welcomed Chilean victims of Augusto Pinochet's CIA-backed coup, which had overthrown Salvador Allende's leftist government in 1973. For instance, for the authorities of the German Democratic Republic (GDR), the hosting of around 2,000 Chileans fed anti-fascist narratives.[106] Yet alongside state-based endeavours, there was also grassroots support for the refugees, in both the GDR and other countries in the socialist world.[107] Meanwhile, as noted in Chapter 7, Western European support for Chilean exiles was often organized by groups with leftist sympathies. Their activism was informed by earlier hopes pinned on Allende's socialism – which differed from the Soviet variety and thus resonated with New Left thinking.[108] Such examples highlight the ongoing significance of a humanitarianism based on political sympathies.

Aid in the face of famine and natural disasters

Alongside support for the wounded and for refugees, famine relief has been a prominent strand of humanitarian action. Efforts to end hunger and starvation do not necessarily have to be transnational: they also fall into the domain of local and national administrations. At the same time, however, transnational cooperation is crucial – for instance, when state authority has broken down and when suffering is so widespread that national resources prove insufficient. In such instances, fundraising, food provision and technical help from abroad play an important role. While much of this work has been carried out by international institutions and development aid agencies, activists play an important role during such crises. In a recent study, Norbert Götz, Georgina Brewis and Steffen Werther have argued that we can analyse famine relief in terms of three major periods: 'ad hoc humanitarianism' in the nineteenth century, 'organized humanitarianism' during the first six decades of the twentieth century and a form of 'expressive humanitarianism' since around 1970.[109] This periodization helpfully highlights shifts that also affected the ways in which funds for famine and disaster relief were raised, spent and accounted for; at the same time, it draws attention to the changing ways in which activists sought to provide relief.

While 'organized humanitarianism' was already an established phenomenon before 1914, it gained momentum during the First World War. The large-scale American relief effort to support the population in German-occupied Belgium was the most prominent manifestation of this development, raising $900,000 through charity and loans and securing over 5 million tons of food provision.[110] Suffering across Europe continued in the aftermath of the conflict and inspired further humanitarian undertakings. As previously noted, Russia became one arena for such efforts. The Hoover-led American Relief Administration – which built on the experience of wartime relief in Belgium – was the largest actor, at its peak feeding 6.3 million adults in civil-war-striven Russia in 1922.[111] As in other humanitarian ventures, appeals suggested that the emergency transcended political affiliations. As a statement by British charities put it, 'Among these hungry and desperate peasants there are millions of children and of the elders not one in a hundred belong to any political party whatsoever.'[112]

The explicit reference to children picked up an element that, as previously noted, had figured prominently in humanitarian appeals of the past. In the face of famine, such aid proved particularly important, in more than one way. One aspect was the shape of these efforts. For instance, in post-war Poland, a number of actors – from the American Relief Administration to the Polish Red Cross – fed an estimated 1.3 million children by 1921 and combined such action with public health programmes.[113] The subsequent development of the relief activities in Poland showed that '[r]elief had become politicized even amongst people who explicitly claimed that they wanted to stay away from politics'.[114] This aspect points to a second aspect, namely political dimensions. As the historian Emily Baughan has noted, Dorothy Buxton – who co-founded Save the Children in 1919 – 'believed that publicizing the plight of children suffering in the aftermath of the Great War would draw the British public into a broader protest against the inequalities of the post-war order'.[115] Buxton was a critic of the post-war settlement: in 1920, her co-authored book on *The World after the War* argued that 'the Allied Governments, which had entered the war as the champions of democracy and of nationality, betrayed their high-sounding promises, and disappointed the generous hopes which those promises had excited'.[116] In this instance, Save the Children's policy of extending aid to former enemy nations was a political act. Meanwhile, visions of a different post-war order informed the work of European Student Relief, an initiative that initially involved Christian students who raised funds for their Austrian peers, before extending the remit to other countries. As its co-founder Ruth Rouse argued, such efforts were vital for building a more peaceful future, seeing that 'the hearts of students' were 'the danger zone of Europe': 'the burning of devotion of her students is each nation's hope but the patriotism of her future leaders passes easily into a Chauvinist solidarity'.[117]

As with the First World War, the Second World War and its aftermath generated manifold relief efforts, but also changes. For example, operating under difficult wartime circumstances, Save the Children shifted to a policy of expertise, rather than activism.[118] A separate venture, the Oxford Committee for Famine Relief (Oxfam), was founded in 1942, initially with a focus on Greece. In some respects, this initiative appeared to be a continuation of earlier impulses: its co-founder Gilbert Murray had been a prominent supporter for the League of Nations.[119]

Over the subsequent decades, famine and disaster relief were affected by the desire of different governments to project 'soft power'. During the Cold War, this aspect manifested itself in both American and Soviet contexts, yet it extended to other countries, as recent research on the two German states has illustrated.[120] This is not to say that all such efforts can simply be ascribed to ideological competition. In some cases, the notion of emergency relief as politically neutral allowed some actors to transcend Cold War boundaries. For instance, during natural disasters that struck Romania in the 1970s – two floods and one earthquake – Romanian Germans who had emigrated to West Germany were able to organize aid across the Iron Curtain along with other humanitarian actors.[121]

One major aspect of post-1945 relief efforts was the connection to the emergence of the United Nations system. UNRRA's work played a significant role in integrating famine relief with wider post-war planning.[122] Moreover, the subsequent development of the UN provided activists with a potential partner. In this context, recognition as a 'non-governmental organization' through the UN's Economic and Social Council offered a form of external validation. Kevin O'Sullivan has associated the heyday of humanitarian NGOs with the period from the late 1960s to the mid-1980s, interpreting this era as 'the point when a Westernized, NGO-led model of compassion became the dominant global expression of solidarity with the Third World'.[123] Moreover, UN initiatives could transcend institutional relationships and inform individual activism. For example, Anna Bocking-Welch has shown how the UN's 'freedom from hunger' campaign inspired or reinforced a variety of civil society efforts, including ones that engaged young people in international action.[124]

The UN's focus on global famine was relevant for wider shifts in famine relief: in contrast to the first half of the twentieth century, when international activism had often focused on European famines, the focus shifted to Africa, Asia and Latin America. This was, for instance, the case with the famine caused by the Biafran War of 1967–70, which was characterized by widely disseminated images of starving children. According to Norbert Götz, Georgina Brewis and Steffen Werther, the conflict was vital for the development of an 'expressive humanitarianism' in which mediatization played a prominent part.[125] The suffering in Biafra – the province that had declared its secession from Nigeria – was broadcast into European homes. As with other humanitarian campaigns, representations of the victims were selective. As Konrad Kuhn has argued, initial appeals from church aid agencies sought to cast the conflict as a 'religious war between Christians and Muslims', featuring 'discriminatory and racist calls for donations'.[126] Such activism stood in uneasy relationship with the realities and legacies of empire.

One of the most widely covered humanitarian efforts of the twentieth century emerged in response to the Ethiopian famine of the 1980s. Following civil war and draughts, the African country's population faced great suffering and a large death toll. In Götz, Brewis and Werther's typology, it sparked the full manifestation of 'expressive humanitarianism', while Kevin O'Sullivan has seen it as a case of 'populist humanitarianism'.[127] Such conceptualizations are connected to the role of Western celebrities in generating publicity for this cause. In December 1984, the Irish singer Bob Geldof and Scottish musician Midge Ure assembled a cast of British and Irish pop stars to record their song 'Do They Know It's Christmas?' to raise funds for Ethiopia. Similar charity singles followed in Brazil, Canada, Denmark, Finland, France, Ireland, Italy, Norway, the United States and Yugoslavia, as did the globally broadcast Live Aid concerts in London and Philadelphia (1985). This form of activism by pop stars was not altogether new: the Concert for Bangladesh (1971) – staged by George Harrison in New York – has often been seen as a forerunner.[128] In 1979, another ex-Beatle, Paul McCartney, cooperated with the UN in staging a concert series for the Cambodian population.[129] In later years, major disasters such as the Armenian Earthquake (1988), the Indian Ocean Tsunami (2004) and the Haiti earthquake (2010) all resulted in charity records or concerts.[130]

The celebrity activism associated with Band Aid has given rise to ongoing debates. Firstly, within a British context, the historian Lucy Robinson has argued that the growing number of charity singles in the 1980s highlighted a broader political and economic turn – which focused on individual responsibility in an age when neoliberal politics eroded state-led efforts.[131] Secondly, the resources generated by new celebrity-led vehicles such as Band Aid Trust could clash with existing efforts on the ground.[132] Thirdly, such initiatives have been criticized for not tackling the root causes of poverty and starvation and, in some cases, replicating stereotypical images of Africa. These criticisms were renewed on the occasion of the global 'Live 8' concerts of 2005 and a new Band Aid single in support of victims of the Ebola pandemic in West Africa in 2014.[133]

That said, the 'Live 8' concerts of 2005 occurred in a different context: rather than focusing on famine relief, the events related to a wider campaign, namely the Global Call to Action against Poverty, a major alliance of non-governmental organizations founded in 2003. The latter's focus on the UN's Millennium Development Goals highlighted its relationship with the UN system – even when it criticized international agencies for inadequacies in their provision. For instance, in 2011, the campaign's report on *The Word We Want* emphasized the need for 'substantive civil society and public participation in planning, implementation, budgeting and monitoring at all levels' when it came to working towards both the Millennium Goals and the safeguarding of human rights.[134] Such references highlighted a broader development: some humanitarian organizations in the 1960s and 1970s experienced a conceptual broadening that sought to incorporate visions of human rights – thus connecting with the themes that Chapter 7 will explore further.[135]

The Global Call absorbed one particular campaign that had appeared on activists' agendas in the late 1990s, namely the demand to cancel the foreign debt of developing countries. The main vehicle for this demand was Jubilee 2000, a coalition launched by several Christian and development NGOs in the 1990s. It was based on the idea to take the new millennium as an opportunity to wipe out Third World debt, building on the biblical notion of debt forgiveness in the Jubilee, the 'year of release'.[136] The campaign argued for unconditional debt relief, which differed from earlier measures in which relief had been tied to specific conditions, for instance market liberalization and budget controls. The campaign attained a significant scale: by 1999, it included representatives of thirty-nine national alliances, who met in Rome to discuss their strategies.[137] The transnational dimensions of Jubilee 2000 manifested itself in large-scale demonstrations at international summits, starting with the G8 meetings in Birmingham (1998) and Cologne (1999), while, at an organizational level, the campaign utilized the growing availability of internet technology.[138]

To many of its protagonists, Jubilee 2000 formed part of a wider history of humanitarian activism. A key Jubilee 2000 slogan urged to 'break the chains of debt', thus likening the campaign to the earlier humanitarian struggle against slavery. An editorial in *The BMJ* – the journal of the British Medical Association, which backed the campaign – was more explicit: it began with the observation that 'For the world's poorest countries debt burden is "the new slavery"' and concluded with the appeal to 'set the slaves free'.[139] To Ann Pettifor, an economist and leading figure in the campaign, it was possible to view these efforts in a wider context:

> Examples of great campaigns that harnessed movements against injustice, and achieved transformative change, include the movements to abolish slavery, to win the vote for women, to expand civil and political rights to African Americans, and in this case, to 'Drop the Debt'. All of these campaigns had a specific legislative goal that altered the balance of power: between slaves and their owners; between women and men; and between black people and white people.[140]

Looking back on the campaign, Pettifor concluded that 'Jubilee 2000 succeeded in one of its goals', namely 'getting about $100 billion of debt written off for 35 poor countries'. At the same time, she conceded that the movement had 'failed to alter the balance of power between international creditors and sovereign debtors'.[141] These critical remarks reflected tensions that had existed within the campaign from the start: some protagonists focused on the immediate aim of debt cancellation, while others saw the debt issue as a way of raising broader questions about global inequality. As early as 1999, a report noted 'somewhat different interpretations' between the Jubilee 2000 campaigns in over fifty countries. In this context, activists from the Global South 'cautioned that Jubilee campaigns in creditor countries, while understandably adapting their strategies to suit political realities at home, must be careful to respect and not inadvertently undercut … South Jubilee negotiating strategies and views'.[142] Recent research has suggested that in many ways, Jubilee 2000 did not manage to address underlying structural inequalities and the policies linked to them.[143] At one level, then, the Jubilee 2000 campaigns fitted into a broader history of humanitarian campaigns – and in this respect it differed from the further-reaching global justice movement that gathered momentum in the early 2000s and that features in Chapter 4 of this book.[144]

Activist humanitarianism since the 1970s

As noted earlier on, political humanitarianism was by no means a new phenomenon. But from the 1960s, a new form of politically engaged humanitarianism combined the strands that have been noted – conflict intervention, famine relief, refugee aid – in ways that, on the one hand, rejected Red Cross tropes of neutrality and, on the other, sat apart from expressions of humanitarianism that were rooted in political ideologies. Many accounts ascribe particular significance to the Biafran War, whose widespread media coverage triggered debate on the meaning and limitations of humanitarian action.[145] As Kevin O'Sullivan put it, activism in the face of this conflict was shaped by the 'entanglement of humanitarian compassion, interventionist impulses and continuities from the late-colonial and immediate postcolonial eras, allied to the political exigencies of local and international actors'.[146] Within activist circles, one consequence of Biafra was the creation of *Médecins Sans Frontières* (MSF, Doctors without Borders) in 1971. Founded in France following dissatisfaction with the Red Cross stance during the Biafra crisis, it adopted an ethos of activist humanitarianism. MSF endeavours were premised on the notion that any help would not just involve practical relief, but extended to bearing witness to the suffering and speaking out about it. This stance had a significant appeal among the European left invested in solidarity with the 'Third World'.[147] As the historian Eleanor Davey has shown, MSF contrasted with 'Third Worldism' as it was built on the 'rejection of political ideology'.[148] This position did not equal silence on political matters. During the 1980s, MSF's willingness to criticize human rights violations in Ethiopia contrasted with the reticence of other NGOs on this issue, leading to the organization's expulsion from the country in 1985.[149]

The methods of activist humanitarianism are illustrated by an initiative of the late 1970s, when large numbers of Vietnamese people fled their countries on boat. In France, left-wing intellectuals such as André Glucksmann and Jean-Paul Sartre supported the initiative 'A Boat for Vietnam'. While their involvement might suggest continuities with earlier forms of political humanitarianism, the action was explicitly framed in a way that

Figure 2.2 Vietnamese 'boat people' on *L'Île de Lumière*, a 'floating hospital' run by *Médecins Sans Frontières*, 9 July 1979. *Source:* Jacques Pavlovsky/Sygma, via Getty Images.

sought to overcome ideological polarization.[150] MSF was a key actor in this regard, raising funds for a 'floating hospital' and rescuing Vietnamese 'boat people' at sea.[151] In its turn, the French initiative inspired the creation of Cap Anamur, a West German initiative that also organized direct help to the 'boat people'. While such examples involved cooperation, the approach of MSF and Cap Anamur created tensions with established humanitarian actors: the Red Cross, which was also active in the Pacific, sought to avoid perceptions of being involved in politically sensitive rescue-at-sea efforts.[152]

Moreover, as Bertrand Taithe has shown, the boat initiative caused ruptures within the movement, with the majority of the organization arguing against the 'mediatisation of the conflict'.[153] In 1981, disputes within MSF triggered the formation of a new association, *Médecins du Monde* (Medics of the World), whose rhetoric evoked 'tropes of indignation, revolt against disease, poverty, war and incompetence', but also stressed a 'considerably lighter structure' that allowed it to 'intervene more rapidly'.[154] Such comments reflect a wider issue in humanitarian relief: namely the tension between professionalization on the one hand, and more ad-hoc campaigns on the other. While the former approach could put relief efforts on a more durable footing, it also meant that some aid organizations began to resemble international institutions – with the potential loss of flexibility that this might entail.

In 1987, *Médecins du Monde* adopted the 'duty to intervene' as its motto, based on pronouncements of its co-founder Bernard Kouchner. In the subsequent decade, this principle spoke to wider concerns, especially in the face of the genocides in Rwanda and

Bosnia. For instance, during the Bosnian War, both MSF and *Médecins du Monde* argued for direct intervention, publishing testimony to underscore their case.[155] Yet, despite shared positions, there were ongoing tensions. Looking back on this period, an MSF account pointedly noted that its report on ethnic cleansing in Bosnia went together with 'a series of video clips that were unfortunately released at the same time as a Médecins du Monde poster campaign comparing [Yugoslav president] Milošević to Hitler'.[156] These remarks suggest broader divisions as to the ways of attracting attention for issues of great urgency.

The Bosnian War gave rise to a major migration wave within Europe: around 2.5 million out of Bosnia's population of 4.4 million suffered displacement, with 700,000 fleeing to Western European countries.[157] The emergency meant that European refugee relief returned as a major issue on the political agenda, yet it coincided with growing hostility to immigration in many countries.[158] Such patterns continued in subsequent decades. Importantly, humanitarian activists not only faced issues vis-à-vis national border policies but also international institutions when it came to supporting refugees. As EU member states started to cooperate in policing the Union's external frontiers – exemplified by the creation of the Frontex agency in 2004 – activists articulated their criticisms of 'Fortress Europe' policies.[159] These tensions became particularly acute in 2015 when the Syrian Civil War and other crises caused international refugee numbers to rise significantly. While in many countries, support groups provided relief in local settings, some forms of activism involved the formation of transnational efforts, for instance the role of churches in creating a 'sanctuary network'.[160] Moreover, one form of activist humanitarianism focused on rescue-at-sea efforts in the Mediterranean, as carried out by groups such as Sea Watch (founded in 2015).[161] To many activists who undertook such endeavours, these efforts were intrinsically connected to wider issues of conflict and global injustice – themes that the next two chapters will explore further.

Notes

1. Marcel Junod, *Warrior without Weapons*, trans. Edward Fitzgerald (London: Jonathan Cape, 1951 [orig. 1947]), 311.
2. Junod, *Warrior without Weapons*, 311–12.
3. For an early example of institutional history-writing, see the account by American Red Cross activist Clara Barton, *The Red Cross: A History of This Remarkable International Movement in the Interest of Humanity* (Washington, DC: American National Red Cross, 1898) as well as the longstanding history of *the International Review of the Red Cross*, whose publication history dates back to 1896. For another example of historical accounts published by the organization that is its subject, see Maggie Black, *A Cause for Our Times: Oxfam – The First 50 Years* (Oxford: Oxfam and Oxford University Press, 1992).
4. Matthew Hilton, Emily Baughan, Eleanor Davey, Bronwen Everill, Kevin O'Sullivan and Tehila Sasson, 'History and Humanitarianism: A Conversation', *Past & Present* 241, no. 1 (2018): e1–e38; Kevin O'Sullivan, Matthew Hilton and Juliano Fiori, 'Humanitarianisms in

5. Eleanor Davey and Kim Scriven's special issue 'Aid in the Archives: Academic Histories for a Practitioner Audience', *Disasters* 39, no. 2 (2015); Bertrand Taithe, 'Humanitarian History?', in *The Routledge Companion to Humanitarian Action*, ed. Roger Mac Ginty and Jenny Peterson (Abingdon: Routledge, 2015); Bertrand Taithe and John Borton, 'History, Memory and "Lessons Learnt" for Humanitarian Practitioners', *European Review of History* 23, nos. 1–2 (2015): 210–24; John Nicholas Borton, 'Improving the Use of History by the International Humanitarian Sector', *European Review of History* 23, nos. 1–2 (2016): 193–209.

6. Johannes Paulmann, ed., *Humanitarianism and Media: 1900 to the Present* (New York: Berghahn, 2018); Esther Möller, Johannes Paulmann and Katharina Stornig, eds, *Humanitarianism in the Twentieth Century: Practice, Politics and the Power of Representation* (Cham: Palgrave, 2020).

7. I have previously used the metaphor of a 'humanitarian cloud', referring to its porous boundaries that might sometimes obscure deeper motivations: Daniel Laqua, 'Inside the Humanitarian Cloud: Causes and Motivations to Help Friends and Strangers', *Journal of Modern European History* 12, no. 2 (2014): 175–85.

8. Barnett, *Empire of Humanity*, 10.

9. Johannes Paulmann, 'The Dilemmas of Humanitarian Aid: Historical Perspectives', in *Dilemmas of Humanitarian Aid in the Twentieth Century*, ed. Johannes Paulmann (Oxford: Oxford University Press, 2016), 11.

10. See, for example, Emily Baughan and Bronwen Everill's themed issue on 'Empire and Humanitarianism' of *The Journal of Imperial and Commonwealth History* 40, no. 5 (2012).

11. See e.g. Shaw, *Britannia's Embrace*; Tehila Sasson, 'From Empire to Humanity: The Russian Famine and the Imperial Origins of International Humanitarianism', *Journal of British Studies* 55, no. 3 (2016): 519–37.

12. Henri [Henry] Dunant, *The Origins of the Red Cross: 'Un Souvenir de Solferino'*, trans. Anna Heylin Wright (Philadelphia: John Winston, 1911 [orig. 1862]), 90.

13. James Crossland, Melanie Oppenheimer and Neville Wylie, eds, *The Red Cross Movement: Myths, Practices and Turning Points* (Manchester: Manchester University Press, 2020); David Forsythe, *The Humanitarians: The International Committee of the Red Cross* (Cambridge: Cambridge University Press, 2005); Shai Dromi, *Above the Fray: The Red Cross and the Making of the Humanitarian NGO Sector* (Chicago: University of Chicago Press, 2020).

14. Dunant, *The Origins of the Red Cross*, 40.

15. As Michael Barnett has noted, the relevant section of Dunant's book 'is fondly cited by many histories of the origins of humanitarianism': Barnett, *Empire of Humanity*, 77.

16. See e.g. John Hutchinson, 'Rethinking the Origins of the Red Cross', *Bulletin of the History of Medicine* 63, no. 4 (1989): 557–78.

17. This, for instance, was the case in the context of decolonization: Andrew Thompson, 'Humanitarian Principles Put to the Test: Challenges to Humanitarian Action during Decolonization', *International Review of the Red Cross* 97, nos. 897–8 (2015): 45–76.

18. Sho Konishi, 'The Emergence of an International Humanitarian Organization in Japan: The Tokugawa Origins of the Japanese Red Cross', *The American Historical Review* 119, no. 4 (2014): 1129–53, at 1133.

19. Esther Möller, 'Between Globalization and Contestation: Humanity as a Polemical Concept within the Red Cross and Red Crescent Movement', in *Humanity: A History of European Concepts in Practice, 16th Century to the Present*, ed. Fabian Klose and Mirjam Thulin (Göttingen: Vandenhoeck & Ruprecht, 2016), 209–28. See also Adrian Ruprecht, 'The Great Eastern Crisis (1875–1878) as a Global Humanitarian Moment', *Journal of Global Hisotry* 16, no. 2 (2021): 159–84.

20. Esther Möller, 'Humanitarismus ohne Grenzen? Die Rotkreuz- und Rothalbmondbewegung und der Israel-Palästina-Konflikt 1948–1949', *Geschichte in Wissenschaft und Unterricht* 66, nos. 1–2 (2015): 69.

21. Möller, 'Humanitarismus ohne Grenzen?', 76.

22. Matthias Schulz, 'Dilemmas of "Geneva" Humanitarian Internationalism: The International Committee of the Red Cross and the Red Crecent Movement, 1863–1918', in Paulmann, *Dilemmas of Humanitarian Aid*, 35–62.

23. Junod, *Warrior without Weapons*, 138.

24. On attempts to navigate this situation, see Boyd van Dijk, 'Internationalizing Colonial War: On the Unintended Consequences of the Intervention of the International Committee of the Red Cross in South-East Asia, 1945–1949', *Past & Present* 250, no. 1 (2021): 243–83; Fabian Klose, *Human Rights in the Shadow of Colonial Violence: The Wars of Independence in Algeria and Kenya*, trans. Dona Geyer (Philadelphia: University of Pennsylvania Press, 2013), 128–37.

25. Julia Irwin, *Making the World Safe: The American Red Cross and a Nation's Humanitarian Awakening* (Oxford: Oxford University Press, 2013), 20.

26. Caroline Moorehead, *Dunant's Dream: War, Switzerland and the History of the Red Cross* (London: HarperCollins, 1998).

27. Heather Jones, 'International or Transnational? Humanitarian Actors during the First World War', *European Review of History* 16, no. 5 (2009): 697–713. On the ICRC's focus, see the observation that it was 'a highly active neutral intermediary among belligerents, and more identified with visits to detainees rather than only with medical aid to the war wounded': Forsythe, *The Humanitarians*, 31.

28. Julia Irwin, 'Taming Total War: Great War-Era American Humanitarianism and Its Legacies', *Diplomatic History* 38, no. 4 (2014): 766.

29. Stephanie Merkenich and Birgitt Morgenbrod, *Das Deutsche Rote Kreuz unter der NS-Diktatur 1933–1945* (Paderborn: Schöningh, 2008).

30. Francesca Piana, 'The Dangers of "Going Native": George Montandon in Siberia and the Intenrational Committee of the Red Cross, 1919–1922', *Contemporary European History* 25, no. 2 (2016): 253–74.

31. Piana, 'The Dangers of "Going Native"', 258.

32. Ibid., 264.

33. George Montandon, *Deux ans chez Koltchak et chez les bolchéviques pour la Croix-Rouge de Genève, 1919–1921* (3rd edn; Paris: Librairie Félix Alcan, 1923), 93.

34. Piana, 'The Dangers of "Going Native"', 268–70.

35. George Montandon, *Comment reconaïtre le juif* (Paris: Nouvelles Éditions Françaises, 1940). See also Marc Knobel, 'L'ethnologue à la dérive: George Montandon et l'ethnoracisme', *Ethnologie Française* 18, no. 2 (1988): 107–13; and Alice Conklin, *In the Museum of Man: Race, Anthropology, and Empire in France, 1850–1950* (Ithaca, NY: Cornell University Press, 2013).

36. For discussions of this subject, see Gerald Steinacher, *Humanitarians at War: The Red Cross in the Shadow of the Holocaust* (Oxford: Oxford University Press, 2017); Jean-Claude Favez, *The Red Cross and the Holocaust*, trans. John Fletcher and Beryl Fletcher (Cambridge: Cambridge University Press, 1999).
37. Barnett, *Empire of Humanity*, 39.
38. Brendan Simms and D. J. B. Trim, eds, *Humanitarian Intervention: A History* (Cambridge: Cambridge University Press, 2011); Davide Rodogno, *Against Massacre: Humanitarian Interventions in the Ottoman Empire, 1815–1914* (Princeton, NJ: Princeton University Press, 2012); Klose, *In the Cause of Humanity*, 162–207.
39. Rodogno, *Against Massacre*, 12.
40. Gill, *Calculating Compassion*, 94.
41. Ibid., 95.
42. Jo Laycock, *Imagining Armenia: Orientalism, Ambiguity and Intervention* (Manchester: Manchester University Press, 2016).
43. Peter Balakian, 'Raphael Lemkin, Cultural Destruction, and the Armenian Genocide', *Holocaust and Genocide Studies* 27, no. 1 (2013): 57–89.
44. For the broader developments see Rodogno, *Night on Earth*; Watenpaugh, *Bread from Stones*.
45. Charlie Laderman, *Sharing the Burden: The Armenian Question, Humanitarian Intervention, and Anglo-American Visions of Global Order* (Oxford: Oxford University Press, 2019); Joy Damousi, '"An Appeal from Afar": The Challenges of Compassion and the Australian Humanitarian Campaigns for Armenian Relief, 1900–30', in *Aid to Armenia: Humanitarianism and Intervention from the 1890s to the Present*, ed. Jo Laycock and Francesca Piana (Manchester: Manchester University Press, 2020), 50–65.
46. Vahé Tachjian, 'Humanitarian Diaspora? The AGBU in Soviet Armenia, 1920–30s', in Laycock and Piana, *Aid to Armenia*, 115–30; Jo Laycock, 'Saving the Remnant or Building Socialism? Transnational Humanitarian Relief in Early Soviet Armenia', *Moving the Social* 57 (2017): 77–96.
47. Kasper Braskén, *The International Workers' Relief, Communism, and Transnational Solidarity: Willi Münzenberg in Weimar Germany* (Basingstoke: Palgrave, 2015).
48. Norbert Götz, Georgina Brewis and Steffen Werther, *Humanitarianism in the Modern World: The Moral Economy of Famine Relief* (Cambridge: Cambridge University Press, 2020), 110.
49. 'American Workers' Relief for Russia', *International Press Correspondence* 1, no. 17 (16 December 1921): 135.
50. Götz et al., *Humanitarianism in the Modern World*, 52.
51. 'American Workers' Relief for Russia', 135.
52. Katharina Stornig, 'Promoting Distant Children in Need: Christian Imagery in the Late Nineteenth and Early Twentieth Century', in Paulmann, *Humanitarianism and Media*, 41–66. Children also featured prominently in WIR appeals for Russia: see Götz et al., *Humanitarianism in the Modern World*, 112.
53. Friederike Kind-Kovács, *Budapest's Children: Humanitarian Relief in the Aftermath of the Great War* (Bloomington, IN: Indiana University Press, 2022); Baughan, *Saving the Children*.
54. Warwick Digital Collections, 292/771.21/6/38: Workers' International Relief / British Joint Labour Aid Committee, 'The Workers' International Relief – What Is It?' (leaflet, c. 1925).
55. 'Zur Kinderhilfsaktion', *Not und Brot*, no. 31 (1 September 1924): 6.
56. 'Warum gerade Kinderhilfe?', *Not und Brot*, no. 31 (1 September 1924): 6.

57. 'Deutsche Ferienkinder der I.A.H. fahren nach Paris', *Not und Brot*, no. 31 (1 September 1924): 1; 'Kinderkreuzzug gegen den Völkerhaß durch die I.A.H.', *Not und Brot*, no. 31 (1 September 1924): 3–4; 'Katastrophaler Zustand und Abbau der bürgerlichen Kinder- und Jugendfürsorge und die Aufgaben der I. A. H.', *Not und Brot*, no. 31 (1 September 1924): 4.

58. See e.g. the case of Swiss Aid to Spanish Children: Dolores Martín-Moruno, 'Elisabeth Eidenbenz's Humanitarian Experience during the Spanish Civil War and Republican Exile', *Journal of Spanish Cultural Studies* 21, no. 4 (2020): 485–502; Rose Holmes, '"Make the Situation Real to Us without Stressing the Horrors": Children, Photography and Humanitarianism in the Spanish Civil War', in Paulmann, *Humanitarianism and the Media*, 67–89.

59. Framke, 'Political Humanitarianism in the 1930s'; Framke, 'We Must Send a Gift Worthy of India'. See also Louro, *Comrades against Imperialism*, 214–55.

60. Joy Damousi, *The Humanitarians: Child War Refugees and Australian Humanitarianism in a Transnational World, 1919–1975* (Cambridge: Cambridge University Press, 2022), 85–107.

61. Winifred Bates, 'A Woman's Work in Wartime', in *Women's Voices from the Spanish Civil War*, ed. Jim Fryth and Sally Alexander (London: Lawrence & Wishart, 1991), 64.

62. 'Mouvement du millard pour le Vietnam: Appel', *Tribune Étudiante*, no. 4 (November/December 1966): 28.

63. LDH Archives, La Contemporaine, Paris, ARCH/0103/758: Pierre Guetta, president of the Mouvement du Milliard, to the Ligue des Droits de l'Homme, 4 November 1966.

64. '1 Millard pour le Vietnam', *Le Monde*, 22 October 1966, 2.

65. ARCH/0103/758: 'Mouvement du Milliard pour le Vietnam, 6 May 1967'. A subsequent report referred to the total sum of 130 million: 'La campagne du Milliard pour le Vietnam se terminera le 20 juillet', *Le Monde*, 13 May 1967, 3.

66. '1 Millard pour le Vietnam', *Le Monde*, 22 October 1966, 2.

67. Ellen Crabtree, 'The Historical Militancy of Madeleine Rebérioux, 1920–2005' (PhD thesis, University of Newcastle upon Tyne, 2016), 130–1.

68. Harish Mehta, *People's Diplomacy of Vietnam: Soft Power in the Resistance War, 1965–1972* (Newcastle upon Tyne: Cambridge Scholars Publishing, 2019).

69. Kim Christiaens, 'States Going Transnational: Transnational State Civilian Networks and Socialist Cuba and Sandinista Nicaragua Solidarity Movements in Belgium (1960s–1980s)', *Revue belge de philologie et d'histoire* 89, nos. 3–4 (2011): 1277–305.

70. Christiaens, 'Between Diplomacy and Solidarity', 618–21.

71. Christian Helm, 'Booming Solidarity: Sandinista Nicaragua and the West German Solidarity Movement in the 1980s', *European Review of History* 21, no. 4 (2014): 599.

72. Sozialarchiv, Zürich, AR 201.259.1: Nationale Koordination der Nicaragua/El Salvador-Komitees der Schweiz, 'Pressecommuniqué: Schweizer Arbeitsbrigada nach Nicaragua' (2 July 1982).

73. Marita Hecker, 'Im Geist der internationalen Brigaden: Erinnerungen an die Nicaragua-Solidaritätsarbeit im Gesundheitsbereich', in *Aufbruch nach Nicaragua: Deutsch-deutsche Solidarität im Systemwettstreit*, ed. Erika Harzer and Willi Volks (Berlin: Christoph Links Verlag, 2008), 74.

74. Tammy Proctor, *Civilians in a World at War, 1914–1918* (New York: New York University Press, 2010), 115. See also Peter Gatrell, *The Making of the Modern Refugee* (Oxford: Oxford University Press, 2015), 21–51.

75. Peter Gatrell, *A Whole Empire Walking: Refugees in Russia during World War I* (Bloomington, IN: Indiana University Press, 1999), 169.
76. Jaclyn Granick, *International Jewish Humanitarianism in the Age of the Great War* (Cambridge: Cambridge University Press, 2021), 26.
77. Tobias Brinkmann, 'The Road from Damascus: Transnational Jewish Philanthropic Organizations and the Jewish Mass Migration from Eastern Europe, 1840–1914', in Rodogno et al., *Shaping the Transnational Sphere*, 153.
78. Michaël Amara, *Des Belges à l'épreuve de l'Exil: Les réfugiés de la Première Guerre mondiale; France, Grande-Bretagne, Pays-Bas 1914–1918* (Brussels: Éditions de l'Université de Bruxelles, 2008).
79. For an introduction to the literature on these relief efforts, see Jacqueline Jenkinson, 'Soon Gone, Long Forgotten: Uncovering British Responses to Belgian Refugees during the First World War', *Immigrants & Minorities* 34, no. 2 (2016): 101–12. For a pioneering study on this subject, see Peter Cahalan, *Belgian Refugee in England during the First World War* (New York: Garland, 1982).
80. Pierre Purseigle, '"A Wave on to Our Shores": The Exile and Resettlement of Refugees from the Western Front, 1914–1918', *Contemporary European History* 16, no. 4 (2007): 427–44.
81. Amara, *Des Belges à l'épreuve de l'Exil*, 346; Tony Kushner, 'Local Heroes: Belgian Refugees in Britain during the First World War', *Immigrants & Minorities* 18, no. 1 (1999): 16–17.
82. On such concerns, and wider tensions as traced through local case studies, see Rebecca Gill, '"Brave little Belgium" Arrives in Huddersfield: Voluntary Action, Local Politics and the History of International Relief Work', *Immigrants & Minorities* 34, no. 2 (2016): 132–50; Daniel Laqua, 'Belgian Exiles, the British and the Great War: The Birtley Belgians of Elisabethville', *Immigrants & Minorities* 34, no. 2 (2016): 113–13.
83. Swarthmore Peace Collection, Swarthmore College, Ruth Fry Papers (DG046), Box 2: Ruth Fry, 'Journey to Holland and Belgium 1915' notes.
84. Claudena Skran, *Refugees in Inter-War Europe: The Emergence of a Regime* (Oxford: Oxford University Press, 1995), 3 and 21.
85. Gatrell, *The Making of the Modern Refugee*, 54.
86. Rodogno, *Night on Earth*, 43.
87. Skran, *Refugees in Inter-War Europe*, 45. Inger Marie Okkenhaug, 'Protestant Missionaries, Armenian Refugees and Local Relief: Gendered Humanitarianism in Aleppo, 1920–1939', in Möller et al., *Humanitarianism in the Twentieth Century*, 61–84.
88. Skran, *Refugees in Inter-War Europe*, 46.
89. Watenpaugh, *Bread from Stones*, 91–123; Rodogno, *Night on Earth*, 72–105.
90. Daniel Maul, 'Humanitärer Aufbruch – Internationale Hilfe in der Zwischenkriegszeit', *Geschichte in Wissenschaft und Unterricht* 66, nos. 1–2 (2015): 55. See also Daniel Maul, *The Politics of Service: US-amerikanische Quäker und internationale humanitäre Hilfe 1917–1945* (Berlin: De Gruyter, 2022).
91. Maul, 'Humanitärer Aufbruch', 59. As noted in Gatrell, *The Making of the Modern Refugee*, 55, the ICRC had suggested the creation of a High Commissioner.
92. 'Letter of Resignation of James G. McDonald, High Commissioner for Refugees (Jewish and Other) Coming from Germany, addressed to the Secretary General of the League of Nations' (London, 27 December 1935), ix, available online on the Library of Congress website, https://www.loc.gov/item/2021666891/ (last accessed 9 January 2023).

93. Greg Burgess, *The League of Nations and the Refugees from Nazi Germany: James G. McDonald and Hitler's Victims* (London: Bloomsbury, 2016), 162.
94. Frank Caestecker and Bob Moore, eds, *Refugees from Nazi Germany and the Liberal European States* (New York: Berghahn, 2010).
95. See e.g. on French Jewish organizations: Vicki Caron, *Uneasy Asylum: France and the Jewish Refugee Crisis, 1933–1942* (Stanford, CA: Stanford University Press, 1999). For a broader discussion, with a focus on Britain, see Tony Kushner and Katherine Knox, *Refugees in an Age of Genocide: Global, National and Local Perspectives during the Twentieth Century* (London: Frank Cass, 1999), 126–71.
96. Shula Marks, Paul Weindling and Laura Wintour, eds, *In Defence of Learning: The Plight, Persecution, and Placement of Academic Refugees, 1933–1980s* (Oxford: Oxford University Press, 2011); Isabella Löhr, 'Solidarity and the Academic Community: The Support Networks for Refugee Scholars in the 1930s', *Journal of Modern European History* 12, no. 2 (2004): 231–46.
97. Norman Angell and Dorothy Buxton, *You and the Refugee: The Morals and Economics of the Problem* (Harmondsworth: Penguin, 1939), 11.
98. Angell and Buxton, *You and the Refugee*, 12.
99. Jessica Reinisch, 'Old Wine in New Bottles? UNRRA and the Mid-Century World of Refugees', in *Refugees in Europe, 1919–1959: A Forty Years' Crisis?*, ed. Jessica Reinisch and Matthew Frank (London: Bloomsbury, 2017), 147–75.
100. Gerard Daniel Cohen, *In War's Wake: Europe's Displaced Persons in the Post-War Order* (Oxford: Oxford University Press, 2012), 10.
101. Silvia Salvatici, 'Professionals of Humanitarianism: UNRRA Relief Workers in Post-War Europe', in Paulmann, *Dilemmas of Humanitarian Aid*, 235–59.
102. Peter Gatrell, *Free World? The Campaign to Save the World's Refugees* (Cambridge: Cambridge University Press, 2011), 50–1. See also Catherine Hobel, 'Frankreich und die Ungarnkrise 1956', in *Die Ungarnkrise 1956 und Österreich*, ed. Erwin Schmidl (Vienna: Böhlau, 2003), 175–86.
103. Becky Taylor, *Refugees in Twentieth-Century Britain* (Cambridge: Cambridge University Press, 2021), 92–148.
104. Stefan Korboński, *Warsaw in Exile*, trans. David Welsh (London: Gorge Allen & Unwin, 1966), 152.
105. Korboński, *Warsaw in Exile*, 153.
106. Sebastian Koch, *Zufluchtsort DDR? Chilenische Flüchtlinge und die Ausländerpolitik der SED* (Paderborn: Schöningh, 2016).
107. Jadwiga Pieper Mooney, 'East Germany: Chilean Exile and the Politics of Solidarity in the Cold War', James Mark and Bálint Tolmár, 'Hungary: Connecting the "Responsible Roads to Socialism"? The Rise and Fall of a Culture of Chilean Solidarity, 1965–89' and Yulia Gradskova, 'The Soviet Union: "Chile Is in Our Hearts": Practices of Solidarity between Propaganda, Curiosity, and Subversion', all in *European Solidarity with Chile, 1970s–1980s*, ed. Kim Christiaens, Idesbald Goddeeris and Magaly Rodríguez García (Frankfurt/Main: Peter Lang, 2014), 275–346.
108. Nicolas Progon, 'France: Welcoming Chilean Exiles, a Mark of the Resonance of the *Unidad Popular* in French Society?', in Christiaens et al., *European Solidarity with Chile*, 187–207.
109. Götz et al., *Humanitarianism in the Modern World*, 24.

110. For these statistics, see Jeffrey B. Miller, *Yanks behind the Lines: How the Commission for Relief in Belgium Saved Millions from Starvation during World War I* (Lanham, MD: Rowman & Littlefield, 2020), xx.
111. Götz et al., *Humanitarianism in the Modern World*, 181. On the major developments in this era, see also Cabanes, *The Great War and the Origins of Humanitarianism*.
112. Swarthmore Peace Collection, Swarthmore College, Ruth Fry Papers (DG046), Box 2: Russian Famine Relief Fund, 'The Russian Famine: An Appeal to the Nation'.
113. Davide Rodogno, Francesca Piana and Shaloma Gauthier, 'Shaping Poland: Relief and Rehabilitation Programmes Undertaken by Foreign Organizaitons, 1918–1922', in Rodogno et al., *Shaping the Transnational Sphere*, 268.
114. Rodogno et al., 'Shaping Poland', 271.
115. Baughan, *Saving the Children*, 18.
116. Charles Roden and Dorothy Buxton, *The World after the War* (London: George Allen & Unwin, 1920), 134.
117. Ruth Rouse, *Rebuilding Europe: The Student Chapter in Post-War Reconstruction* (London: Student Christian Movement, 1925), 15. On European Student Relief, see Isabella Löhr, 'Coping with a Post-War World: Protestant Student Internationalism and Humanitarian Work in Central and Eastern Europe during the 1920s', *Social History* 48, no. 1 (2023): 43–64; and Brewis, *A Social History of Student Volunteering*, 54.
118. Joëlle Droux, 'Life during Wartime: The Save the Children International Union and the Dilemmas of Warfare Relief, 1919–1947', in Paulmann, *Dilemmas of Humanitarian Aid*, 185–206.
119. Black, *A Cause for Our Times*, 1–21.
120. Young-Sung Hong, *Cold War Germany, the Third World, and the Global Humanitarian Regime* (New York: Cambridge University Press, 2015).
121. Cristian Capotescu, 'Migrants into Humanitarians: Ethnic Solidarity and Private Aid-Giving during Romania's Historic Flood of 1970', *East European Politics and Societies* 35, no. 2 (2021): 293–312; Luminita Gatejel, 'Bargaining for Humanitarian Aid across the Iron Curtain: Western Relief Workers in Romania in the late 1970s', *Cold War History* 22, no. 1 (2022): 41–57. On the case of the Romanian Germans more broadly, see James Koranyi, *Migrating Memories: Romanian Germans in Modern Europe* (Cambridge: Cambridge University Press, 2021).
122. Jessica Reinisch, '"Auntie UNRRA" at the Crossroads', *Past & Present* 218, suppl. no. 8 (2013): 70–97.
123. Kevin O'Sullivan, *The NGO Moment: The Globalisation of Compassion from Biafra to Live Aid* (Cambridge: Cambridge University Press, 2021), 5. See also Kevin O'Sullivan, 'A "Global Nervous System": The Rise and Rise of European Humanitarian NGOs', in *International Organizations and Development, 1945–1990*, ed. Marc Frey, Sönke Kunkel and Corinna Unger (Basingstoke: Palgrave, 2014), 196–219.
124. Anna Bocking-Welch, 'Imperial Legacies and Internationalist Discourses: British Involvement in the United Nations Freedom from Hunger Campaign, 1960–70', *Journal of Imperial and Commonwealth History* 40, no. 5 (2012): 879–96; Anna Bocking-Welch, 'Youth against Hunger: Service, Activism and the Mobilisation of Young Humanitarians in 1960s Britain', *European Review of History* 23, nos. 1–2 (2016): 154–70.
125. Götz et al., *Humanitarianism in the Modern World*, 57–9.

126. Konrad J. Kuhn, '"The Credibility of Our Humanitarian Effort Is at Risk": Tensions between Solidarity and Humanitarian Aid in the Late 1960s', in Paulmann, *Dilemmas of Humanitarian Aid*, 317.
127. O'Sullivan, *The NGO Moment*, 56–74.
128. Benjamin Möckel, 'Humanitarianism on Stage: Live Aid and the Origins of Humanitarian Pop Music', in *The Politics of Authenticity: Countercultures and Radical Movements across the Iron Curtain, 1968–1989*, ed. Joachim Häberlen, Mark Keck-Szajbel and Kate Mahoney (New York: Berghahn, 2019), 233–55.
129. Selections from these concerts were subsequently collected on Various Artists, *Concerts for the People of Campuchea* (double-album, Atlantic, 1981), and also documented in a concert movie.
130. See e.g. the different 'Rock Aid Armenia' initiatives from 1988, including Various Artists, *The Earthquake Album* (Life-Aid Armenia Records, 1990), as well as Artists for Haiti, 'We Are the World 25 for Haiti' (We Are the World Foundation / Interscope Records, 2010).
131. Lucy Robinson, 'Putting the Charity Back into Charity Singles: Charity Singles in Britain 1984–1995', *Contemporary British History* 26, no. 3 (2012): 405–25.
132. Götz et al., *Humanitarianism in the Modern World*, 211.
133. For one of many examples, see Julie Grant, 'Live Aid/8: Perpetuating the Superiority Myth', *Critical Arts* 29, no. 3 (2015): 310–26.
134. *The World We Want: GCAP Annual Report 2011*, 6, available at https://gcap.global/wp-content/uploads/2018/07/The-World-We-Want.pdf (last accessed 9 January 2023).
135. Matthew Hilton, 'International Aid and Development NGOs in Britain and Human Rights since 1945', *Humanity* 3, no. 3 (2012): 449–72.
136. Ruth Reitan, *Global Activism* (Abingdon: Routledge, 2007), 66–107.
137. Kamran Abbasi, 'Free the Slaves: Debt Relief for the World's Poorest Is Feasible but May Not Happen', *The BMJ* 318, no. 7198 (1999): 1568–9.
138. Reitan, *Global Activism*, 80.
139. Abbasi, 'Free the Slaves', 1568–9.
140. Interview with Ann Pettifor, as featured in Joan Walsh, 'Jubilee 2012? A Leader of the Global Debt-Relief Movement Says OWS Can Point to Restructuring America's Consumer Debt Crisis', *Salon.Com*, 12 October 2012, https://www.salon.com/2011/10/12/jubilee_2012/ (last accessed 9 January 2023).
141. Ibid.
142. Carole Collins, '"Break the Chains of Debt!": International Jubilee 2000 Campaign Demands Deeper Debt Relief', *Review of African Political Economy* 26, no. 81 (1999): 420, originally published in *Africa Recovery*, September 1999.
143. Hélène Baillot, 'A Well-Adjusted Debt: How the International Anti-Debt Movement Failed to Delink Debt Relief and Structural Adjustment', *International Review of Social History* 66, no. S.29 (2021): 215–38.
144. Peter van Dam, 'No Justice without Charity; Humanitarianism after Empire', *The International History Review* 44, no. 3 (2022): 653–74.
145. Lasse Heerten, *The Biafran War and Postcolonial Humanitarianism: Spectacles of Suffering* (Cambridge: Cambridge University Press, 2017).
146. O'Sullivan, *The NGO Moment*, 19.

147. Davey, *Idealism beyond Borders*, esp. 50–111.
148. Eleanor Davey, 'Famine, Aid, and Ideology: The Political Activism of Médecins Sans Frontières in the 1980s', *French Historical Studies* 34, no. 3 (2011): 531.
149. Davey, 'Famine, Aid, and Ideology', 546–54.
150. Philip Ther, *The Outsiders: Refugees in Europe since 1492*, trans. Jeremiah Riemer (Princeton, NJ: Princeton University Press, 2019), 205–6.
151. Bertrand Taithe, 'Reinventing (French) Universalism: Religion, Humanitarianism and the "French Doctors"', *Modern & Contemporary France* 12, no. 2 (2004): 152.
152. Michael Vössing, 'Competition over Aid? The German Red Cross, the Committee Cap Anamur, and the Rescue of Boat People in South-East Asia, 1979–1982', in Paulmann, *Dilemmas of Humanitarian Aid*, 345–68.
153. Taithe, 'Reinventing (French) Universalism', 152.
154. Ibid.
155. Claire Boulanger, Bernard Jacquemart and Philippe Granjon, *L'Enfer yougoslave: les victimes de la guerre témoignent* (Paris: Belfond, 1994).
156. Laurence Binet, ed., *MSF and the War in the Former Yugoslavia, 1991–2003* (Paris: MSF, 2015), 13.
157. Kirsten Young, 'UNHCR and ICRC in the Former Yugoslavia: Bosnia-Herzegovina', *International Review of the Red Cross* 83, no. 843 (2001): 783.
158. Ther, *The Outsiders*, 231–3.
159. Pierre Monforte, *Europeanizing Contention: The Protest against 'Fortress Europe' in France and Germany* (New York: Berghahn, 2014).
160. Katharyne Mitchell and Key MacFarlane, 'The Sanctuary Network: Transnational Church Activism and Refugee Protection in Europe', in *Handbook on Critical Geographies of Migration*, ed. Katharyne Mitchell, Reece Jones and Jennifer Fluri (Cheltenham: Edward Elgar, 2019), 410–24. For another form of religious activism, see the activities of the Christian charity World Vision: Kathryn Reid, with Chris Huber and Sevil Omer, 'Syrian Refugee Crisis: Facts, FAQs, and How to Help', *World Vision*, updated version of 12 July 2022, online via https://www.worldvision.org/refugees-news-stories/syrian-refugee-crisis-facts (last accessed 9 January 2023).
161. Vicki Squire, *Europe's Migration Crisis: Border Deaths and Human Dignity* (Cambridge: Cambridge University Press, 2020); Maurice Stierl, 'A Sea of Struggle – Activist Border Interventions in the Mediterranean Sea', *Citizenship Studies* 20, no. 5 (2016): 561–78.

CHAPTER 3
BUILDING A PEACEFUL WORLD

The Austrian baroness Bertha von Suttner was one the most famous peace campaigners of her age. In 1900, the French feminist paper *Le Fronde* described her as 'a European celebrity' whose novel *Die Waffen nieder!* (Lay Down Your Arms) had been 'a political event': the book had 'toured the world and been translated into all modern languages' after its original publication in 1889.[1] For a while, pacifism was so closely associated with the author that critics ridiculed it as 'Suttnerei'.[2] In 1905, Suttner became the first female recipient of the Nobel Peace Prize – an award whose very creation she had inspired.[3] Less than six weeks after her death in June 1914, the First World War broke out. Addressing peace campaigners in 1915, the Hungarian pacifist Vilma Glücklich admitted a certain 'envy' that Suttner had not been forced 'to experience the collapse of her hopes'.[4]

In more than one way, Suttner offers a suitable starting point to discuss efforts to build a more peaceful world. Firstly, her famous novel illustrates how campaigners sought to mobilize anti-war sentiment by depicting the horrors of military conflict. The female protagonist of *Die Waffen nieder!* witnesses suffering and personal loss through the Italian War of 1859, the Second Schleswig War (1864), the Austro-Prussian War (1866) and the Franco-Prussian War (1870–1). In other writings, Suttner combined references to past conflicts with future scenarios. For instance, her pamphlet on 'the barbarization of the air' noted both Italy's use of airborne missiles during the invasion of Libya (1911) and H.G. Wells's futuristic visions of aerial warfare.[5]

Secondly, Suttner concurred with campaigners who portrayed peace activism as rooted in an appraisal of 'facts'. During her lifetime, both the Polish economist Jan Bloch and the Russian sociologist Yakov Novicov (Jacques Novicow) reached international audiences with their writings on the economic and social costs of war.[6] Suttner herself disseminated such ideas. In 1891, she launched a monthly that covered Novicow and Bloch's work alongside many other pieces that sought to validate the pacifists' cause.[7] As editor, Suttner collaborated with the Austrian journalist Alfred Hermann Fried, who in 1899 established another periodical, *Die Friedens-Warte* and translated Novicow's books into German.[8] According to Fried, pacifism was a 'scientific' solution to growing global interdependence.[9] He occasionally reproached Suttner with seeking to solicit emotional rather than intellectual responses, revealing the gendered perceptions of Suttner's endeavours, even among allies.[10] In fact, her approach encompassed appeals to both sentiment and reason. In her final novel, she put the argument about a 'scientific' peace centre-stage, with a plot that revolved around a group of thinkers seeking to uncover solutions to the problem of war.[11]

Thirdly, Suttner's efforts demonstrate the importance of transnational contacts for peace activists. A German-speaker born in Prague, Suttner spent her life in a multinational empire. In 1891, she founded the Austrian Peace Society in Vienna; four years later, she helped to establish its Hungarian counterpart in Budapest. Moreover, her endeavours extended beyond Central Europe and involved cooperation with peace activists from across Europe and North America.

Figure 3.1 Bertha von Suttner in 1911. *Source:* Hutton Archive, via Getty Images.

To many activists, it seemed obvious that the promotion of peace had to be a transnational pursuit. Well before Suttner's lifetime, the first peace societies – launched in North America and Britain in the early nineteenth century – worked with likeminded individuals from other countries.[12] Enlightenment ideas and broader visions of social reform were important factors in forging transnational links in this earlier period. For example, the French *Société de la Morale Chrétienne* championed humanitarian causes and established new contacts during a trip to London in 1823.[13] Yet, at the time, such interactions did not produce a firmly organized international movement. Likewise, a series of international peace congresses in the mid-nineteenth century failed to create permanent ties.[14]

It was in the late nineteenth century – and hence in Suttner's era – that peace activists developed international structures and began to hold near-annual congresses, at which Suttner herself became a celebrated figure. For Suttner, attendance at these events was invested with both personal and political meanings: travelling to a congress was at once a 'festal journey into unfamiliar countries' and 'another stage of progress in the triumphant march of an Idea'.[15] In her publications, she extensively covered these gatherings and other activities that demonstrated the reach of the peace movement. A focus on documentation was particularly crucial for Suttner's associate Alfred Fried: by producing surveys on the peace movement and 'international life', he sought to show that pacifism had momentum on its side.[16]

The first parts of this chapter mostly – but not exclusively – focus on the period up to the Second World War and discuss several strands of peace activism, including a concern for international law, the embrace of non-violence as well as socialist and feminist approaches to the problem of war. The later sections then shift to the period after 1945, with an emphasis on the spectre of nuclear warfare, protests against American foreign policy as well as the 'new wars' of the post-1990 era. As a whole, the chapter acknowledges the importance of international structures and transnational ties while stressing pacifists' complex relationships with class, ideology and nationhood.

Organizational pacifism and its features

In 1901, the prominent French peace activist Emile Arnaud noted that 'none of the words in the dictionary are adequate for our programme', arguing that as a label, 'we require an -ism, like royalism, Bonapartism, imperialism, republicanism, radicalism, opportunism, progressivism, socialism, collectivism, anarchism'.[17] As a solution, he proposed the term *pacifisme*. The publication of Arnaud's piece in the daily *L'Indépendance Belge* was far from coincidental. In 1895, a group of French activists, including Arnaud, had acquired a stake in the Belgian newspaper, seeking to turn it into a voice for the peace movement. It seemed appropriate to enlist Belgium's most prominent liberal paper: Belgian elites were broadly supportive of internationalism, as the neutral country depended on respect for international norms.[18] In 1903, the newspaper's editors noted that it regularly 'published articles or studies on subjects that form part of the pacifist programme'.[19]

After Arnaud's intervention, it took several years before the English equivalent to the French neologism *pacifisme* gained currency.[20] As an actor's category in the early twentieth century, 'pacifism' amounted to a catch-all label. For analytical purposes, we therefore need to distinguish between two principal strands. One approach – which is sometimes described as 'absolute' or 'integral' pacifism – involves a radical rejection of violence, and nowadays is commonly associated with the term 'pacifism'.[21] Yet in the early twentieth century, many who considered themselves pacifists did not reject all forms of military action. Instead, they sought to prevent war by promoting international law and the creation of international institutions. For reasons of clarity, Martin Ceadel has championed the use of 'pacificism' for this second strand.[22] Another, equally fitting way of labelling this variety is 'organizational pacifism'. The German academic and politician Walther Schücking first proposed the latter term in 1912; after the First World War, he continued to promote the concept in theory and practice, publishing on international law, campaigning for the League of Nations and serving on the International Court of Justice.[23]

Since the nineteenth century, the protagonists of organizational pacifism had intersected with the nascent community of experts in international law.[24] Before the First World War, the focus on international law particularly manifested itself in the promotion of arbitration as a way of resolving disputes between states, arguably constituting 'the primary objective of internationalist and peace societies' in this period.[25] Some organizations explicitly proclaimed these principles in their names, as exemplified by two British initiatives, the International Arbitration League (1869) and the International Arbitration and Peace Association (1880), as well as the French association *La Paix par le Droit* ('Peace Through Law', 1889).[26]

A drive towards greater transnational ties between activists occurred from the 1880s. In this period, the co-founder of the International Arbitration and Peace Association, Hodgson Pratt, travelled to continental Europe to gain new affiliates.[27] Whereas his impact in Germany remained localized and temporary, Pratt's efforts spawned a durable Belgian peace society.[28] Internationalization efforts received further stimuli from the late 1880s onwards. Suttner's work and Fried's creation of the German Peace Society in 1892 consolidated the organized peace movement in the Habsburg Monarchy and Imperial Germany. It meant that subsequent gatherings of peace activists involved partner associations from Central Europe. Having been launched in 1889, the 'Universal Peace Congresses' became near-annual gatherings for peace activists; from 1891, the International Peace Bureau (IPB) coordinated such efforts from Bern. Arbitration featured prominently on the agenda of these meetings.

The historian Sandi Cooper has described Universal Peace Congresses and IPB as one of two pre-war 'peace internationals' – with the second 'peace international' being the Inter-Parliamentary Conferences and their coordinating body, the Inter-Parliamentary Union.[29] Launched in 1889, these inter-parliamentary ventures gathered deputies with an interest in international cooperation and arbitration. To the *Reichspost* – a conservative Viennese newspaper – these efforts appeared as '*Suttnerei* that has been carried into the legislative bodies'.[30] In the face of such attacks, key figures within the Inter-Parliamentary

Union emphasized the 'rigid exclusion of utopian aims'.[31] Despite the mixed responses, the alliance between legal scholars, peace activists and parliamentarians yielded results: it provided the promotion of arbitration with a degree of respectability.

In 1899, peace activists responded enthusiastically when Tsar Nicholas II invited governments to a conference to discuss agreements on arbitration and the conduct of war. As the historian Maartje Abbenhuis has argued, 'Few diplomatic announcements have caused as much international fervour as the release of Tsar Nicholas II's announcement.'[32] Suttner initially experienced the news as being 'like a dream, like a fairy tale' and received 'numberless congratulatory letters and telegrams' after the news about the Tsar's rescript.[33]

This is not to say that pacifists were oblivious to the obstacles. For instance, Suttner complained about 'general incomprehension, apathetic stupor and – still worse – hidden and open hostility' to the project of a peace conference.[34] She also noted the hypocrisy of governments that publicly supported the initiative while continuing to arm themselves.[35] Despite such concerns, the opening of the Hague Conference in May 1899 appeared to Suttner as 'an epoch-making date in the history of the world', even in retrospect.[36] Activists from different countries flocked to the Netherlands, aiming to influence the discussions of diplomats and politicians while strengthening their bonds through numerous political and social events.[37] On the occasion of the Second Hague Conference in 1907, the campaigning journalist William T. Stead even maintained a conference newspaper.[38] While many peace activists had hoped for further-reaching results from these diplomatic events, they did welcome some of their outcomes, especially the creation of the Permanent Court of Arbitration in 1899.

The outbreak of war in 1914 ruptured parts of the peace movement along national lines, yet it also led campaigners to renew their efforts.[39] Alfred Fried, for example, argued that as 'the result of international anarchy', the war had validated pacifists' insistence on international organization.[40] Moreover, peace activists participated in a broader dialogue on the post-war order, including the making of a future League of Nations.[41] A large stimulus for such discussions came from the United States, involving academics, activists and associates of US president Woodrow Wilson.[42] Further transatlantic influences came from charitable foundations such as the Carnegie Endowment for International Peace. Before the war, Carnegie funds had supported pacifist ventures in Europe, including the IPB. During the war, the Carnegie Endowment shifted its focus towards the 'scientific' study of international relations and, after the war, supported the newly founded League of Nations.[43]

The Carnegie Endowment's activities are but one example of the League's importance in the interwar period. After launching its operations in 1920, the League became a target for activist efforts. For example, champions of transnational disarmament focused their efforts on achieving their aims through the League.[44] Moreover, various organizations explicitly promoted the work of the Geneva institutions to domestic audiences. Among the former Central Powers, such efforts faced significant challenges. In Germany, the League was tarnished by its association with the Treaty of Versailles. By and large, the efforts of the *Deutsche Liga für Völkerbund* (German League for a League of Nations) therefore remained confined to scholarly and republican circles. In Austria, the *Völkerbundliga* operated within an 'almost exclusively male world of politicians, lawyers, and university professors' whose vision of Europe involved coming to terms with the post-Habsburg realities.[45]

In such instances, League-related activism seemed to perpetuate the earlier focus on expertise and intellectual exchange among organizational pacifists. Likewise, as a forum for the transnational cooperation of pro-League ventures, the International Federation of the League of Nations Societies lobbied politicians and ran events such as summer schools that put students from different countries in touch with representatives of the League.[46] However, a focus on the limits of pro-League activism risks underestimating the degree of popular mobilization in some countries. During the interwar years, League societies in France and Britain launched a plethora of activities, both within the population at large and among specific constituencies, from school children to veterans.[47] The League of Nations Union was a mass membership organization in interwar Britain. In 1934–5, it mobilized nearly 12 million British people in the Peace Ballot, an initiative that demonstrated public support for the League and that can be interpreted in the context of efforts to democratize foreign policy.[48]

Notwithstanding such expressions of support, the crises of the 1930s made the League's limitations painfully obvious. The writings of Helena Swanwick illustrate such disappointments. Born in Germany and raised in Britain, Swanwick became a well-known feminist and pacifist campaigner.[49] As a critical supporter of the Geneva institutions, she represented Britain at the League of Nations Assembly as a substitute delegate during the 1920s. By 1937, however, she considered even a reform of the League to be insufficient, arguing against 'legalism and a barren chop-logic' and seeking a deeper transformation in attitudes.[50]

While arbitration and international institutions were important objects of organizational pacifism, other activists focused on the development of federative structures. During the interwar years, different groups portrayed European integration as key to a more peaceful future and as a way of countering European 'decline'.[51] The Pan-European movement was one major manifestation of these ambitions. Its founder brought a cosmopolitan sensibility to this venture: born in Tokyo to a Japanese mother, with an Austro-Hungarian diplomat as his father, Richard Coudenhove-Kalergi described himself as a 'citizen of the world'.[52] His project of global organization was based on regional federations, with 'Pan-Europe' as one of them. This scheme was not uncontroversial among pacifists: at the Universal Peace Congress in Berlin in 1924, Coudenhove-Kalergi sought to counter suspicions that his ideas might undermine the League of Nations.[53]

Visions of European integration were driven by widely different political persuasions. For former aristocratic elites, a united Europe could be an answer to the demise of the multinational empires.[54] In other contexts, references to European unity masked militarism and nationalism: Italian and German fascists led various associations on 'European culture' that ultimately aimed at domination rather than exchange.[55] A degree of political amorphousness was not only characteristic of Europeanism at large, but also of Coudenhove-Kalergi's activism. He was an opponent of National Socialism and fled Austria after the *Anschluss* of 1938, yet he did not oppose all forms of repressive politics. Before 1938, he maintained positive relations with the Austrofascist leaders of his country, at a time when Austria sought international alliances in the face of the Pan-German challenge.[56] In his memoirs, he stated that Engelbert Dollfuss and he 'became friends at our first meeting and understood each other perfectly', with the Austrian chancellor accepting the honorary presidency of the Pan-European Movement.[57]

Three years after the end of the Second World War, the large-scale Europeanist congress at The Hague highlighted the renewed momentum for groups that promoted closer European ties.[58] Meanwhile, Western European advocates of a 'United Socialist States of Europe' forged links with anti-imperialists, informed by the project of a potential 'World Federation with socialists and democratic nationalists from Eastern Europe, Asia and Africa'.[59] The relationship between ideas and activism on the one hand, and the pursuit of (initially Western) European integration is subject to a large literature and different interpretations.[60] Even if the creation of European institutions was driven by political leaders and technocratic elites, it is clear that various forms of grassroots activism promoted the European idea across several decades.[61]

A different federal movement – namely world federalism – remained ephemeral. In the 1930s and 1940s, some campaigners promoted visions of world government. One key figure in these ventures was the Hungarian activist Rosika Schwimmer, initially known for her role in the Hungarian women's movement, but also a member of the Hungarian Peace Society.[62] During the First World War, Schwimmer played a major part in transnational women's campaigning for peace. Having briefly held a position in the post-war Hungarian government, she migrated to the United States when Béla Kun established the short-lived Hungarian Soviet Republic (1919). By the 1930s, she outlined the project for a 'world government' along with her American ally Lola Maverick Lloyd. During the Second World War, Schwimmer and Lloyd reiterated their commitment. Noting that government-led moves towards a 'world union' would not only be 'hopeless but even undesirable', they instead called for 'unofficial action', including grassroots action towards a 'Provisional World Government' and an end to war.[63]

Although these appeals represented a minority view, world federalism inspired a wide and diverse set of activists after the war had ended. In 1947, several groups of world federalists merged into the United World Federalists, which by 1949 boasted over 46,000 members who were organized within 720 chapters across the United States.[64] The world-federalist moment soon faded but testified to the ambition to 'organize the world' – in this instance, by turning the United Nations into the nucleus of a genuine world government.

Integral pacifism in an age of total war

Schwimmer's focus on world government maintained a connection to the organizational strand of pacifism. However, it was her personal commitment to non-violence that made her a widely known figure. In the United States, her refusal to swear to defend her adopted home country meant that she was refused US citizenship; after losing her landmark case 'United States vs. Schwimmer' (1929), she remained a stateless citizen for the rest of her life. Moreover, her pacifism also marginalized her from the international women's movement, in which she had played a prominent role before the Great War.

Schwimmer's stance draws attention to the 'integral' or 'absolute' strand of pacifism. Whereas for Schwimmer, non-violence was driven by secular political convictions, for others, it was shaped by religious beliefs. Such examples range from Quakerism to Leo Tolstoy's version of Christian anarchism. Contrasting with the focus on state-led cooperation among many organizational pacifists, integral pacifists maintained their distance from state authority which, to some of them, appeared inherently violent. Tolstoyans formed their own communities and practised non-violence on an everyday basis.[65] Such positions generated conflict when states claimed the right to enlist individuals for military service. On these occasions, support for conscientious objectors became a focus for pacifist and humanitarian groups. For example, during the 1890s, British Quakers mobilized on behalf of the Doukhobors, a Russian religious community whose members faced Tsarist repression because of their commitment to non-violence.[66]

The First World War brought the issue of conscientious objection to the fore. Although aid for conscientious objectors mostly operated within national settings, the increased prominence of this issue, as well as the broader impact of the war, triggered efforts to forge closer links between integral pacifists. The creation of the War Resisters' International (WRI) in 1921 was one manifestation of this process.[67] Another body that adopted this stance was the *Ligue internationale des combattants pour la paix* (International League of Combatants for Peace, 1931). This Paris-based organization reflected the growing appeal of the radical current which, in France, was described as a 'new-style pacifism'.[68] While noting the support of prominent pacifists from other countries, the organization primarily disseminated integral-pacifist ideas to French audiences, not only through periodicals but also through various cultural activities.[69]

Bart de Ligt – a Dutch former pastor – was a key figure in the WRI and exemplified the rise of more radical currents within the interwar peace movement.[70] Between 1928 and 1930, his public correspondence with Mohandas Gandhi highlighted divisions even among proponents of non-violence. De Ligt's initial criticism focused on Gandhi's role in recruiting volunteers to the Indian Ambulance Corps during the First World War. 'Didn't you recall that Tolstoy himself condemned the Red Cross because it formed part of the war system?', he asked.[71] To de Ligt, even humanitarian bodies such as the Red Cross formed part of 'the gigantic machinery of war'.[72] In subsequent letters, the Dutch pacifist reiterated these unfavourable comparisons between Tolstoy and Gandhi.[73] In doing so, he contradicted the French author Romain Rolland, whose highly influential book on Gandhi had cast Tolstoy as a 'John the Baptist' to Gandhi's 'Messiah' figure.[74]

In response, Gandhi reiterated his commitment to non-violence. He argued that he had sought to combine the principle of self-defence – in this case an external threat to Britain and its colonies – with the principle of not bearing arms.[75] Yet this explanation failed to convince de Ligt, to whom non-cooperation with any war-waging government was the only solution.[76] Tolstoy's erstwhile ally Vladimir Chertkov also intervened in the debate. In a letter to Gandhi, he expressed a classic Tolstoyan notion: 'if living as I live, I am allowed to assist the State in waging war, then I ought at all costs cease to live as I live, even if I had in doing so to sacrifice my life'.[77] In this respect, de Ligt's critique pointed back to older pacifist traditions, albeit in the context of the radical politics of the 1920s.

The Second World War produced major challenges for integral pacifists. With large parts of Europe experiencing dictatorship or occupation, the decision to refuse military service could have drastic consequences.[78] Moreover, in countries that were at war with the Axis Powers, the refusal to engage in military action raised questions: at one end, it could extend to collaboration, while at the other, it could involve different forms of resistance to the occupier.[79] In the eyes of integral pacifists, the conflict had not undermined the case for pacifism but demonstrated the need to foster nonviolent principles. The concept of nonviolent resistance offered a way of demonstrating that pacifism did not imply passivity or submission in the face of aggression. This broader context helps to explain the increasing interest in Gandhian principles after 1945. Sean Scalmer has noted that 'As alarm about nuclear weapons spread widely, so Gandhi's political tools beckoned in the battle for peace' and Holger Nehring has seen the 'engagement with the global legacy of Gandhian non-violence' as an important factor for British campaigns against nuclear weapons.[80]

The nation as a subject in transnational peace activism

Pacifist critiques of state policies must not be mistaken for a detachment from national categories. Indeed, many activists stressed their national credentials. As the historian Sandi Cooper has put it, they were 'patriotic pacifists' who 'struggled to coordinate their patriotic impulses with an internationalist vision'.[81] Their stance illustrates how visions of international cooperation were constructed on the back of nationhood in this period.[82] According to some designs, nationhood even appeared as a route towards future peace. The Geneva-based *Ligue internationale de la Paix et de la Liberté* (International League of Peace and Freedom) represented this line of thought. As one of the earliest international peace associations, its creation has been described as 'a fundamental turning-point for European pacifism'.[83] The *Ligue*'s link to democratic nationalism was evident at its founding congress in 1867: Giuseppe Garibaldi, the hero of the Italian Risorgimento, served as the honorary president and attracted a large audience when he visited Geneva for this occasion.[84]

Garibaldi's involvement points to visions in which nationalism, republican politics and peace intersected. Such ideas were also associated with his compatriot Giuseppe Mazzini, whose efforts to create a transnational radical network dated back to the 1830s and whose promotion of national liberation resonated far beyond the Italian peninsula.[85] In light of Garibaldi and Mazzini's influence, it is hardly surprising that the most prominent Italian pacifist of the pre-1914 era, Ernesto Teodoro Moneta, was also a nationalist. In 1860, Moneta had participated in Garibaldi's Expedition of the Thousand and in 1866, he had served in the war against Austria. As co-founder of the *Unione Lombarda per la Pace e l'Arbitrato* (Lombard Union for Peace and Arbitration, 1880), Moneta became a prominent figure in pacifist circles and the first Italian to receive the Nobel Peace Prize (1907).[86] To Moneta, involvement in the peace movement was compatible not only with the pursuit of national unification but also with national expansion: in 1911, he defended Italy's invasion of Libya.[87] Among peace activists, this stand proved controversial, leaving the Italian movement 'permanently scarred'.[88]

The espousal of national causes generated a paradox: while some activists viewed national liberation and unification as prerequisites for a peaceful future, the attainment of these national goals generated international tensions and potential military conflicts. Before the reconstruction of the Polish nation-state in 1918, many Polish nationalists remained sceptical of the peace movement, as they assumed that pacifists might accept the status quo to prevent another war.[89] However, the agenda of the *Ligue internationale de la Paix et de la Liberté* offered a potential way of reconciling these aims. For this reason, the exiled Polish general Jozef Hauke-Bosak – who had been a military leader during the Polish January Uprising of 1863–4 – participated in the *Ligue* until his death in 1871.[90]

The *Ligue*'s emphasis on national visions was evident to external observers, including peace leaders from the United States who 'were perplexed by the Europeans' ... militancy over national causes'.[91] Yet tension between national liberation and peace activism was not confined to the *Ligue*. Related questions emerged at later points and in other contexts. For example, the aforementioned debate between Bart de Ligt and Mohandas Gandhi during the late 1920s involved disagreements on the role of nationhood. While Gandhi accepted de Ligt's insistence on non-violence, he saw 'the unhuman competition for the exploitation of the so-called weaker races of the earth' as the main cause of war.[92] Although de Ligt affirmed his support for the struggle against colonial domination, he argued that pacifists would have to overcome national categories. He therefore proposed a 'united international front, formed of all races and all peoples, which would fight, not for out-of-date nationalist conceptions, but for the realisation of a universal and supranational community'.[93] While at face value, his statement seemed to emphasize internationalist principles, it did not acknowledge the particular circumstances under which anticolonial movements were forced to operate.

Given the divisiveness of national questions, one possibility was to sideline them in international settings. When peace activists gathered in Rome for the Universal Peace Congress of 1892, their debates revealed major differences regarding the national question – ranging from Polish delegates, who sought to put the national question centre stage, to the British activist Felix Moscheles, who wanted pacifists to reduce 'national sentiment'. Faced with diverging views, the congress created a committee to examine the phenomenon of nationhood in more abstract terms.[94] Subsequent congresses largely avoided national questions. Likewise, Habsburg pacifists – including Bertha von Suttner – eschewed open discussion of the role of national ideas in a multinational empire.[95]

Developments in south-eastern Europe proved challenging for many peace activists. Perceptions of the Ottoman Empire as an 'other' made it easier for peace activists and humanitarians to proclaim their solidarity with national struggles in the Ottomans' European provinces. After the Berlin Congress of 1878 and Austria-Hungary's assumption of the administration of Bosnia-Hercegovina, members of the *Ligue* hoped that a regional reorganization would produce a federation composed of Slavic, Romanian and Greek states.[96] When Austria-Hungary instead decided to annex Bosnia-Hercegovina in 1908, pacifist protests remained muted. By the early 1910s, pacifists and humanitarians struggled to reconcile their sympathy for national struggles in the Balkans with the realization that these were likely to produce another war.[97] During the Balkan Wars of 1912–13, the most prominent international response among peace activists focused on an established area of pacifist concern: the Carnegie Endowment for International Peace sent a commission of enquiry to the region and prepared a much-noted report on violations of international law.[98]

Apart from small bands of integral pacifists, peace activists continued to accept the validity of national categories and attachments, which explains why the Great War caused such severe rifts within organized pacifism. As the forum for the leaders of national peace societies, the IPB was severely hampered as many members sided with their own governments.[99] Among pacifist minorities, however, the war effected a detachment from the nation since political repression or public hostility forced them into exile. Neutral Switzerland became a key site of anti-war encounters as well as the home for anti-war publications, from Romain Rolland's anti-war polemic *Au-dessus de la mêlée* appearing in Geneva to the exiled Alfred Fried issuing his *Friedens-Warte* from Zürich.[100]

After the Great War, an important strand of peace activism sought to overcome national antagonisms. Some of these efforts were animated by Christian notions of fraternity, as exemplified by the efforts of the International Fellowship of Reconciliation, an association that originated in the wartime contacts of Christian pacifists.[101] Young people became a particular target of activist concern, as illustrated by the organization of various youth exchanges. For instance, in 1926, the French Catholic politician and pacifist Marc Sangnier staged a youth camp and peace congress – cast as a 'Locarno of Youth' – and, in subsequent years, launched a pacifist youth movement and founded the first French youth hostel.[102]

The case of the *Deutsche Liga für Menschenrechte* (German League for Human Rights) illustrates the challenges for activists who questioned national narratives. The association originated in the *Bund Neues Vaterland* (New Fatherland Alliance), a wartime forum for socialist, progressive radicals and academics who criticized their government's policies. After 1921, the DLM's new name stressed its links to the *Ligue des Droits de l'Homme* (Human Rights League; LDH), a major force for French republicanism.[103] The two leagues staged events that featured views and voices from the other side, even during the Ruhr Crisis of 1923. One year later, however, the German journalist Carl von Ossietzky – himself a member of the German association – concluded that most of his compatriots remained unaware that pacifism had 'grown to be a great force in the democratic nations of the world'.[104] Ossietzky welcomed the fact that Berlin hosted the Universal Peace Congress of 1924, which attracted 'foreign guests whose importance, seriousness and good patriotic intentions nobody can doubt'. As he argued, this presence forced the German public to question its perceptions – albeit only temporarily: 'The worthy citizen clutches his brow: "My God, and they are pacifists too! But they are quite sensible people!" And for minutes the deepest beliefs are shaken.'[105]

The *Deutsche Liga für Menschenrechte* remained a minority undertaking. Some of its members embraced positions that proved controversial in Weimar Germany, including the notion of German war guilt as well as suggestions that the Versailles Treaty might be less harsh than most German politicians claimed. They also documented German violations of the provisions of Versailles. Such activities provoked accusations of treason. The association's secretary turned these charges on their head, speaking of a 'duty to treason', as these efforts would ultimately strengthen the international system.[106] LDH president Victor Basch made a similar point when he addressed a German league meeting in 1928: 'Instead of putting people accused of high treason into prison, one should weave them laurel wreaths.'[107] While noting the select nature of the audience – 'fanatics of international understanding' – the Belgian ambassador, who reported on the event, was struck by the positive reaction to Basch's discourse: 'in no other country of the world could a speaker get the acclaim of his audience for proclamations so radical, so devoid of any patriotic sentiment'.[108]

Accusations of treason could have serious repercussions. Ossietzky's role in revealing secret German armaments led to his imprisonment in 1931–2, and after the National Socialists' ascent to power, he was incarcerated again. After five years in Nazi concentration camps, he died of tuberculosis in 1938. Ossietzky's captivity made him an international cause célèbre, which was also reflected in the award of a Nobel Peace Prize in 1935.[109] Meanwhile, many other peace activists – both in Germany and elsewhere – had to emigrate if they wanted to escape persecution.

By 1945, the horrors of war and genocide had demonstrated the destructive potential of nationalism. However, nationhood more generally remained a lens through which peace activists perceived their cause. Of course, their perspective differed drastically from the aggressive nationalism that had generated war and genocide. But it did mean that many Cold War pacifists remained 'national internationalists'.[110] Illustrating this dimension, the Campaign for Nuclear Disarmament (CND), which had been founded in 1958, embraced a discourse of British exceptionalism. CND's promotion of unilateral disarmament fed into a narrative of British moral leadership on the international stage, evoking the country's earlier role in the abolition of the slave trade.[111] A similar sense of mission manifested itself elsewhere, for instance in Norway, where peace activists portrayed 'peaceability' as an intrinsically national characteristic.[112]

In Greece, critiques of both NATO membership and the situation in Cyprus provided the Greek left – including the peace movement – with opportunities to 'present themselves as the true patriotic alternative'.[113] The idea of pacifism as a form patriotism also informed West German peace campaigns, especially in a context where direct references to the nation had been complicated by the legacies of Nazism.[114] The German past remained an important frame for German anti-war movements in subsequent decades. For example, many student activists justified their desire to protest against the Vietnam War in terms of their parents' silences under Nazism.[115] With regard to the 1980s, Benjamin Ziemann has noted that protests about NATO policies 'were bound up with symbols of the Allied bombing campaign' and thus involved a 'focus on the specific trajectory of German victimisation'.[116] Thus, national ideas remained an important factor, even when they were referenced indirectly rather than overtly.

Socialist and communist perspectives on war and militarism

Pacifism – whether absolute or organizational – can be distinguished from another phenomenon, namely antimilitarism. For socialists, communists and anarchists, 'antimilitarism' went beyond the rejection of military values or institutions: it treated military conflicts as products of class-based oppression. While antimilitarism sustained protests against specific wars, it did not entail a wholesale rejection of violence. In the nineteenth century, socialists embraced the concept of citizens' militias; in the twentieth century, communists and other parts of the left supported conflicts as long as they were able to cast them as revolutionary or anti-imperialist struggles.[117]

Socialist antimilitarism and 'bourgeois' pacifism maintained a complex relationship throughout the nineteenth and twentieth centuries. According to socialists, pacifists failed to address the root cause of war, namely the inequalities that were intrinsic to the capitalist system. In return, many pacifists remained wary about groups that advocated a fundamental transformation of the social and economic order. Peace leaders such as Suttner and Fried welcomed socialist anti-war pronouncements but complained about socialist attacks on 'bourgeois' pacifism.[118] For example, in 1908, *Die Friedens-Warte* approvingly published an antimilitarist speech by the French socialist leader Jean Jaurès, but added an editorial note that criticized the views of Jaurès's German comrades.[119]

Such tensions should not obscure the manifold intersections between socialist antimilitarism and 'bourgeois' pacifism. For instance, at the time of its formation in 1867, the *Ligue internationale de la Paix et de la Liberté* constituted 'a sort of radical International' and included exiled radicals of different political persuasions.[120] The *Ligue*'s founding congress featured the Russian anarchist Mikhail Bakunin, even though the organization did not endorse the International Workingmen's Association (or First International), in which Bakunin was active between 1868 and 1872. Another figure from the First International's early years, the British radical Randal Cremer, shifted towards peace activism from the 1870s but maintained a focus on appealing to working-class interests. Through his Workmen's Peace Association, Cremer promoted the cause of peace among British artisans.[121]

Socialists and pacifists could make common cause, for instance in criticizing the role of the military and in protesting against particular wars. Socialist congresses of the Second International often went hand in hand with local marches and large-scale public displays, as exemplified by a major anti-war demonstration in Basel in 1912.[122] Disarmament was another shared concern. Before the First World War, three socialists from, respectively, Britain, France and Germany – namely Walton Newbold, André Morizet and Karl Liebknecht – gathered evidence on the international munitions industry, thus linking disarmament to a critique of capitalist interests.[123] Yet, while many socialists and trade unionists favoured general strikes as a tool for war prevention, this approach did not become a binding policy for socialist parties.

In August 1914, large parts of the socialist movement split along national lines, in ways that seemed to mirror divisions within the pacifist camp.[124] The wartime ruptures created obstacles for transnational peace initiatives, as illustrated by the abortive project of a socialist peace conference in Stockholm in 1917.[125] This is not to say that all socialists rallied behind the national war effort. A vocal and increasingly prominent minority embraced anti-war policies and coordinated its actions through conferences in the Swiss villages of Zimmerwald (1915) and Kienthal (1916).[126] Meanwhile, anarchists launched their own transnational challenges to war policies.[127]

The 'Zimmerwald Left' is often seen as a forerunner of the Communist International, whose history is discussed further in Chapter 4. In the interwar years, the Comintern not only coordinated the work of communist parties but also sustained campaigns on matters of war and peace. Communists openly attacked the new international order, including the League of Nations and, in doing so, clashed with those who broadly viewed the Geneva institutions as a tool for peace – from pacifists to socialists.[128]

The rift between socialists and communists shaped the responses to the Amsterdam-Pleyel Movement, an initiative named after anti-war congresses in the Dutch capital (1932) and the Salle Pleyel in Paris (1933). Along with Romain Rolland, this venture was spearheaded by another French intellectual, Henri Barbusse. Like Rolland, Barbusse had risen to prominence as an anti-war author during the Great War. After the war, he was a prominent figure in French veteran politics and co-founded the *Internationale des Anciens Combattants* (Veterans' International) which, in classic antimilitarist terms, portrayed military conflict as 'the tool of an international caste' that was 'stealing wealth and glory from the countless hands of the poor and the sacrificed'.[129] Barbusse's stature within international communism was evidenced by his authorship of an officially sanctioned biography of Stalin, whom he had first met in 1927.[130] Such links help to explain why many socialists criticized 'Amsterdam-Pleyel' as a communist 'front' venture. The secretary of the Labour and Socialist International – the body that represented non-communist parties on the left – had 'no doubt that the experienced tacticians of the communist "United Front" manoeuvres have their hands in the affair or, for a certain time, have held the whole affair in their hands and that they have only used Romain Rolland as an instrument'.[131]

By the mid-1930s, Popular Front policies – which are explored further in Chapter 4 – and the threat of fascism produced alliances that in some cases transcended ideological divides.[132] In 1936, the willingness to overcome ideological divides manifested itself in the *Rassemblement Universel pour la Paix* (also known as the 'International Peace Campaign'). The venture had been launched by Lord Robert Cecil – a British Conservative peer and prominent supporter of the League of Nations – and brought together political leaders and activists from a range of causes. In February 1936, the Belgian socialist Louis de Brouckère, a leading figure within international socialism, concluded that the movement 'has moved beyond the phase at which it could be dominated by communist influences' – somewhat optimistically, as communists continued to play a leading role in it.[133]

The communist stance on war and fascism was far from unequivocal. In light of the Soviet Union's non-aggression pact with Nazi Germany, the Comintern initially portrayed the Second World War as a conflict between imperialist powers, calling on communist parties to oppose the Allied war effort.[134] While not all communists followed the Moscow line, and while the position shifted in 1941, these examples raised the question of how far communist positions on war and peace were determined by Soviet foreign policy.

After the end of the Second World War, competing visions of peace became a major topic in Cold War propaganda. Communists and fellow travellers on both sides of the Iron Curtain portrayed the United States and its allies as the principal risk to world peace while casting the Soviet Union as peace-loving. Between 1948 and 1950, congresses in Wrocław, New York, Paris, Prague and Warsaw sought to unite communists, fellow travellers and prominent intellectuals under the banner of peace. These initiatives gave rise to the communist-dominated World Peace Council as well as the Stockholm Appeal of 1950, a petition against nuclear weapons at a time when the Soviet Union itself had already conducted its first atomic tests.[135] While the World Peace Council brought together peace groups from both East and West, it largely cast the United States and its allies as responsible for the Cold War. Many of the Council's Eastern European members were quasi-officials who represented state-sanctioned peace committees. This context created significant challenges for peace activists as they faced suspicions 'that peace activity must be pro-Soviet'.[136] The question of communist influence, including potential funding from the East, also arose during the revival of anti-nuclear protests in the 1980s. Benjamin Ziemann and Holger Nehring have argued that it would be wrong to suggest that Moscow or East Berlin steered the peace movement.[137] Indeed, as we shall see further on in this chapter, many activists in East and West stressed their desire to overcome Cold War boundaries, challenging the ideological assumptions on which these binaries had been founded.

The rise of feminist pacifism

Not long before her death in 1914, Bertha von Suttner proclaimed that she was 'fully in sympathy with women's rights', expressing her 'hope that the triumph of the Suffrage cause will greatly help the cause of peace'.[138] While her statement illustrates how peace activists could view women's rights as a related concern, the reverse was the case, too. In 1899, the International Council of Women (ICW) – the first international federation of national women's organizations – launched a Standing Committee on Peace and Arbitration. Indeed, until 1904, peace and arbitration remained 'the only declared propaganda [object] of the International Council'.[139] On the occasion of its 1904 congress, the ICW reaffirmed its commitment by staging a large peace gathering in the Berlin Philharmonic Hall. Such interactions do not mean that women's peace activism was necessarily cast in feminist terms. Although Suttner addressed women's suffrage, especially in the final years of her life, she stressed the primacy of pacifism and its equal relevance for both sexes.[140] A later example is Peggy Duff, one of the most prominent British peace campaigners during the Cold War era. Duff rarely discussed the gendered dimensions of peace politics, maintained her distance from feminism and 'had little patience for women's liberation'.[141]

Nonetheless, an increasingly prominent strand of twentieth-century activism treated the causes of peace and women's rights as intertwined and inseparable. The significance of such views became evident during the First World War, when the dominant factions within the women's movement prioritized national unity over peace activism. In contradiction to their stance, some groups and individuals reinforced their transnational cooperation.[142] The Women's Peace Congress at The Hague was arguably the most dramatic manifestation of feminist pacifism during wartime. Held from 28 April to 1 May 1915, the event attracted more than 1,100 women. Although the leaders of many women's organizations remained absent, the gathering succeeded in bringing together activists from the warring nations. The Dutch feminist Aletta Jacobs stressed that the mere fact of the gathering was a substantial achievement: 'despite all the difficulties, the delays in the mail, the lost, censored, and confiscated letters, we still managed to organize an international conference in just two months that was to be attended by a great many women from twelve different countries'.[143]

At one level, the congress had a symbolic function. The activists' determination to overcome wartime divisions was epitomized by the spectacular arrival of a small Belgian delegation, whose members had left their German-occupied country and crossed the Dutch border by foot.[144] Moreover, the Women's Peace Congress had a lasting outcome as it created the International Committee of Women for Permanent Peace. Its members embarked on a large-scale effort of citizens' diplomacy, visiting different European capitals to lobby for a negotiated peace.[145] Transatlantic influences were important for this undertaking, as Jane Addams – who had led an American delegation at the congress – participated in these efforts alongside Aletta Jacobs.[146] The International Committee also spawned national committees that sought to promote women's internationalism to domestic audiences.[147]

Having emerged from over four years of bloodshed, the world looked very different in 1919: multinational empires had collapsed, new states taken their place and a complex international architecture was being erected. In May 1919, activists from the Women's Committee for Permanent Peace gathered in Zürich for their second congress. The event featured demonstrative acts of reconciliation of women from former enemy countries. Delegates also considered plans for the League of Nations and, in this context, argued for the inclusion of a Women's Charter in the Covenant of the League of Nations.[148] The Zürich congress transformed the Women's Committee into the Women's International League for Peace and Freedom (WILPF), which became a leading anti-war voice during and beyond the interwar years.[149] Its subsequent activities included lobbying the League from the newly established WILPF headquarters in Geneva, but also fact-finding missions, for example to investigate violence against the Ukrainian minority in Eastern Poland.[150]

WILPF was a prominent participant in the international disarmament campaign of the interwar years. According to Thomas Davies, 'the gathering of signatures to massive disarmament petitions' became WILPF's 'principal contribution to the movement for arms reduction'.[151] The most significant activity in this field coincided with the opening of the World Disarmament Conference in 1932: WILPF helped to collect over 8 million signatures for disarmament, having rallied fourteen other women's organizations for this initiative. While the single largest number of signatures came from the British Empire (over 2.1 million, not counting the Dominions, which were registered separately) and the United States (more than 1.1 million), the initiative also attracted over a million German signatories.[152]

WILPF was a forum in which different forms of internationalism – from liberal to socialist varieties – intersected.[153] Moreover, in 1934, the leader of the French WILPF section, Gabrielle Duchêne, co-founded the World Committee of Women Against War and Fascism, which was aligned with the communist-dominated Amsterdam-Pleyel Movement. Duchêne's role was far from uncontroversial within WILPF, reflecting concerns about communist ties as well as contrasting views on the role of antifascism within the organization.[154] The Dutch feminist Rosa Manus – a key figure during the early years of WILPF – was one critic of these ventures. Manus subsequently became a key figure in the *Rassemblement Universel pour la Paix* of 1936 but remained wary of communist influences within such campaigns.[155]

While these examples illustrate ideological ruptures within the field of feminist pacifism, the presence of different forces underneath one associational umbrella also highlighted its diversity. After 1945, WILPF's perspective became even broader, triggered by a growing engagement with 'race', decolonization and global inequality. The international relations scholar Catia Celia Confortini has seen WILPF as 'a Western liberal middle-class white women's organization' that increasingly 'stretched the boundaries of the liberal context within which it was inscribed'.[156]

Beyond matters of ideology, one area of diversification concerned the relationship between gender and peace. Traditionally, many campaigners had cast women's role in peacebuilding in maternalist terms, a discourse that emphasized links between motherhood and pacifist attitudes. There were, however, limitations to such views. In analysing the 'Conference of Concerned Women to End the War' – an event held in Paris in 1968 – the historian Jessica Frazer has noted the 'tensions over what constituted inherent maternal responses'.[157] Women Strike for Peace – an American group that had initiated the Paris meeting – adopted a largely maternalist perspective. Its visions contrasted with Vietnamese delegates, who eschewed portrayals of victimhood and celebrated the role of female revolutionary fighters during the Vietnam War.

Moreover, the rise of women's liberation from the late 1960s challenged maternalist pacifism as it questioned gendered expectations around motherhood. Nonetheless, different perspectives of women's peace activism could co-exist. During the 1980s, the Greenham Common Peace Camp in Britain brought together women of different generations. Some participants deployed maternalist arguments, emphasizing the protection of families from nuclear war. Yet for many others, Greenham Common was a space in which key principles of women's liberation were being put into practice. Significantly, the British camp was subject to external stimuli. It originated in a peace march from Cardiff which, in its turn, had been inspired by the Nordic Women's Peace March that took Danish, Norwegian and Swedish women from Copenhagen to Paris in 1981.[158] Moreover, after establishing the camp, 'Greenham women' engaged in manifold transnational encounters. Ann Pettitt, who had organized the initial march to Greenham, travelled to Moscow with two other activists. This trip fed into the wider project of facilitating encounters between 'ordinary people as citizens, with fears and hopes in common'.[159] Such ventures highlighted the ambition to address the Cold War contexts head-on – an issue that the next section will address further.

Overcoming Cold War binaries

In August 1945, the detonation of nuclear bombs over Hiroshima and Nagasaki highlighted the destructive power of nuclear warfare. The rise of Cold War antagonism and the ensuing nuclear arms race raised the spectre of a fully blown conflict between the rival power blocs. Campaigns against this threat peaked at two points when tensions ran particularly high: on the one hand in the late 1950s and early 1960s, and on the other hand during the early 1980s. Although activists used established tropes and methods, they faced a new geopolitical situation, launched new alliances and developed new ways of protesting. According to the historian Benjamin Ziemann, the Cold War generated 'a new form of peace movement activism' that was partly nourished by 'a broad coalition of independent socialist groups and individuals, Protestant Christians and other non-Communist oppositional groups'.[160]

From the outset, the campaign against nuclear warfare had important transnational dimensions. The so-called 'Easter marches' illustrate this aspect. On the Easter weekend of 1958, British anti-nuclear campaigners walked from London to a nuclear research facility in Aldermaston, Berkshire. This protest became an annual affair for the newly founded CND and spawned similar initiatives elsewhere. For example, in 1960, a German Quaker couple – Konrad and Helga Tempel – helped to organize the first anti-nuclear Easter March in the Federal Republic, having attended the Aldermaston march the previous year. As contributors to the British *Peace News* magazine, the Tempels had existing ties to Britain.[161] In staging the West German march, they worked with the West German affiliates of WRI, who had transnational links of their own.[162] Similar to the West German case, participation in an Aldermaston march inspired Danish activists to initiate an Easter march in their own country in 1961.[163]

One prominent endeavour inspired by Aldermaston was the attempt by Greek activists to walk from Marathon to Athens in April 1963. Shortly before this, the Greek anti-war politician Grigoris Lambrakis had attended the CND's annual march. The group that planned the Greek demonstration acknowledged its British influences by naming itself after the British philosopher and campaigner Bertrand Russell.[164] In the end, the Greek authorities banned the march, but parliamentary privilege enabled Lambrakis to carry the activists' banner into Athens. One month after this protest, he was killed by the far right, inspiring widespread protests in Greece.[165] Importantly, rather than falling into the communist camp, Lambrakis and his allies had built 'a non-aligned and inclusive Greek peace movement'.[166]

Aldermaston also had another transnational impact. During the 1960s, the 'CND logo', which had been created for this occasion, turned into an internationally recognized symbol. Early on, members of the US-based Committee for Non-Violent Action displayed the sign during their widely publicized 'March for Peace' (December 1960 to October 1961), which took them from San Francisco across the United States and Europe, concluding in Moscow.[167] By the late 1960s, the CND symbol had gained near ubiquity in countercultural circles because of its association with hippies and the use in protests against the Vietnam War.

Transnational ties continued to be a factor when activists in Western Europe took aim at NATO's Dual-Track Strategy (1979), which involved the stationing of nuclear missiles in NATO's European member states. A revived peace movement showcased its strength through demonstrations throughout the early 1980s, culminating in an October weekend of protests in several Western European capitals, mobilizing an estimated 2 million people.[168] In this period, peace activists not only coordinated their actions and exchanged speakers: they also shared ideas about possible solutions. For example, Norwegian, Danish and Finnish activists championed the concept of a 'nuclear-free Northern Europe'.[169] Campaigners in the Baltic Republics of the Soviet Union subsequently argued for their region's inclusion in such a nuclear-free zone.[170]

Figure 3.2 Anti-nuclear demonstration in Thessaloniki, 1983, with banners calling for 'peace, detente, disarmament' and protesting against foreign military bases. *Source:* Universal History Archive / Universal Images Group, via Getty Images.

What motivated the transnational protests against nuclear war? As earlier sections of this chapter have shown, a commitment to non-violence, political affinities and feminist visions all continued to be factors in the post-war period. Moreover, a key impetus for many Cold War-era activists was the idea of forging ties not only across national but also ideological borders. To do so, they evoked principles that they cast as being 'above' politics, for instance professional credentials and expertise.[171] The Pugwash Conferences on Science and World Affairs were one manifestation of this phenomenon. Inspired by Albert Einstein and Bertrand Russell's anti-nuclear manifesto of 1955 and launched in 1957, the Pugwash meetings provided a forum for scientists who discussed ways of halting the arms race with politicians and diplomats.[172] Their discourse regarding the 'universal' nature of science should not obscure the fact that 'views of the role of science' remained 'deeply embedded within specific *national* interpretations of the purposes and mission of science'.[173] Moreover, political leaders were selective in their engagement with scientific advice. Nonetheless, these efforts did have an impact, especially during the 1980s. According to Matthew Evangelista, their influence on Soviet foreign policy showed that 'the Soviet system … could under certain conditions be quite susceptible to transnational influences'.[174]

Evangelista's research has also drawn attention to another transnational venture, namely the International Physicians for the Prevention of Nuclear War (IPPNW).[175] At the national level, anti-nuclear medical groups had already existed during the 1950s, casting their political struggle as expressions of their concern for human life.[176] IPPNW built on these earlier undertakings but was explicitly construed as an East–West initiative, jointly launched by the Russian cardiologist Yevgeniy Chazov and his (Lithuanian-born) American colleague Bernard Lown. The different backgrounds and domestic contexts created some tensions within the organization. As Lown later recalled, some members 'aimed primarily to amass objective information to help educate our patients about the medical consequences of the nuclear arms race and nuclear war', whereas others 'envisioned a far wider agenda, believing that health problems were ultimately societal in scope and required political engagement for their solution'.[177] The more limited approach was exemplified by the Swedish branch, which had a large membership and 'avoided politically charged issues'.[178]

When IPPNW received the Nobel Peace Prize in 1985, it attracted controversy because of Chazov's role in the Soviet Union, including the revelation that in 1973, he had signed a collective letter against the Soviet nuclear physicist and dissident Andrei Sakharov.[179] The case highlighted dividing lines on how peace was being understood. To Lown, negative media coverage was part of 'a continuing effort to discredit the IPPNW antinuclear message'; he argued that collaboration with Soviet physicians who had 'government connections' was inevitable if one sought 'to influence Soviet nuclear policy'.[180] Yet the dispute also revealed a more fundamental difference. For the American activist, the campaign against nuclear warfare took priority over other issues because '[a]fter a nuclear holocaust, neither human rights nor civil liberties would have mattered'.[181] By contrast, for Sakharov – recipient of the Nobel Peace Prize in 1975 – the promotion of civil liberties and the critique of Soviet armament policies were entwined.[182]

During the 1970s, Sakharov's persecution by the Soviet authorities generated expressions of solidarity abroad, including among activist scientists for whom the struggle against nuclear weapons became more closely linked to notions of human rights.[183]

The creation of European Nuclear Disarmament (END) in 1980 epitomized both the ambition to transcend Cold War binaries and a growing appreciation of its connection with human rights, reflecting an insistence on the 'indivisibility of peace'.[184] END ascribed responsibility for the Cold War to both power blocs. This position facilitated dialogue with new dissident peace groups that were emerging in Central and Eastern Europe and that challenged Soviet armaments policies, thus contradicting the state-sanctioned 'peace committees' of the Soviet Union and other state-socialist countries.[185] To British END activists such as the peace researcher Mary Kaldor and the historian E. P. Thompson, cooperation with grassroots peace movements in Central and Eastern Europe was a way of promoting 'détente from below'.[186] As Greenham Common activist Ann Pettitt later put it, 'END ... brought something new into the nuclear disarmament movement: a fresh perspective on the Cold War'.[187]

To the quasi-official peace committees in the Eastern bloc and to communist activists in the West, the protagonists of 'détente from below' were capitalist agents. Even within END, there were disagreements as to whether Western activists should prioritize links with the official 'peace leaders' from the Eastern bloc or whether they should focus on the independent activists who faced repression under state socialism. In 1984, some END members seceded, creating the European Network for East–West Dialogue to work exclusively with dissidents.[188] Three years later, another END congress clashed over invitations that had been issued to communist parties in the Eastern bloc.[189] In looking back, E. P. Thompson argued that in most parts of Europe, END's non-aligned position ultimately prevailed over communist-dominated peace groups: 'We had stopped being just a bunch of intellectuals talking about a possible "third way". We were a real confederation of political forces, and we *were* the third way'.[190]

Unlike communist-dominated peace organizations, END members acknowledged grassroots movements in the Eastern bloc. For instance, Thompson and Kaldor raised awareness of the persecution of the Trust Group in the Soviet Union – non-conformists who sought to promote the idea of citizen actions that would generate 'trust' among people from both sides.[191] In 1983, members of the Greenham Common Peace Camp met with Trust activists, as part of the aforementioned trip to Moscow. Ann Pettitt noticed that the non-aligned position of the British visitors had facilitated this visit: as they were not perceived as 'anti-Soviet', they were able to travel to the Soviet Union and meet representatives of the official Soviet peace initiatives, while pursuing their ties to grassroots, dissident peace ventures at the same time.[192] Once the subversive character of their efforts became obvious, Soviet officials cancelled plans for a larger visit of British women.[193]

Peace activists in the Eastern bloc reciprocated END's interest in their efforts. For instance, the Hungarian peace activists László Rajk Jr. and Miklós Haraszti translated E. P. Thompson's *Beyond the Cold War*.[194] Such contacts were also important as some dissidents had been sceptical about the END agenda. For example, the Czech playwright and dissident Václav Havel initially 'found it difficult to imagine how peace could be achieved without first achieving civil rights and freedoms'.[195]

Shortly after the end of the Cold War, Mary Kaldor argued that the East–West contacts had triggered 'an intense learning process': 'We in the Western peace movement began to internalize the struggle for democracy in Eastern Europe, not only for its own sake, but also as way of ending the arms race.'[196] END members developed ties to dissidents even beyond the forging of links with independent peace groups. This, for instance, was the case with the Dutch *Interkerkelijk Vredesberaad* (Inter-Church Peace Council).[197] Moreover, the END of 1988 featured the prominent Polish dissident Jacek Kuroń among its speakers.[198]

Importantly, END also highlighted human rights violations in the West – thus contrasting with Cold War-era groups that only criticized one camp. For example, END addressed the wave of repression followed by the Turkish military coup of 1980. In 1982, it protested against the arrest of Mahmut Dikerdem and other members of the Turkish *Barış Derneği* (Peace Association), which had been founded in 1977. In doing so, END argued that Turkey had become 'the one place in Europe where the US can pursue its policy of nuclear rearmament without the inconvenience of massive public revulsion'.[199] Such comments also pointed to another issue: namely the critiques of American foreign policy that informed different forms of activism and protest.

Mobilizing against 'American' wars

According to Benjamin Ziemann, 'anti-Americanism was most crucial for the collective identity of peace movements in Europe and Japan from the 1960s to the 1990s', notwithstanding 'variations in timing and identity'.[200] While earlier Cold War tensions had certainly shaped perceptions of the United States' role in the world, negative portrayals of American foreign policy proliferated during the Vietnam War. Both in the Soviet bloc and among segments of the Western left, the conflict corroborated existing perceptions of the United States as an imperialist power.[201] Although such rhetoric might appear as an extension of Cold War-era peace propaganda, anti-war activism in communist countries did not necessarily follow the official line. For example, in 1971, a Vietnam demonstration by Russian hippies in Moscow led to them being rounded up by KGB officials.[202] In communist (albeit non-aligned) Yugoslavia, students staged protests against the Vietnam War, clashed with the authorities and – much like in the West – used the conflict in South East Asia as a symptom for wider societal problems.[203] Such observations point to a more general issue: although anti-American tropes certainly featured in the protests, 'Vietnam' held a multitude of meanings for activists in East, West and the Global South.[204]

Although Western European countries did not formally participate in the Vietnam War, their membership of NATO raised questions about implicit support for their American ally. British activists were therefore adamant to prevent their government from providing active backing for US policy – and they mobilized transnational contacts to maintain pressure on their government.²⁰⁵ Beyond the established repertoire of marches and declarations, activists also launched new ventures. For example, in September 1968, the British Campaign for Peace in Vietnam steered a 'peace boat' from southern England to Boulogne, cooperating with French activists and Vietnamese officials.²⁰⁶ With regard to contacts between West German and American anti-war campaigners, the historian Martin Klimke has spoken of a 'transatlantic anti-war alliance' that emerged in contrast to the existing NATO partnership.²⁰⁷ In West Germany, the presence of American troops provided opportunities for transnational action, for instance 'GI organizing' that ranged from leafleting near American army bases to support for deserters.²⁰⁸

Transnational contacts were vital for many campaigners. For instance, the British campaigner Peggy Duff maintained manifold links to the United States, as illustrated by her extensive correspondence with the anti-war intellectual Noam Chomsky. She also travelled to Vietnam and launched a new organization, the International Confederation for Disarmament and Peace.²⁰⁹ The latter sought to ally the anti-war cause to the older anti-nuclear movement. In 1967, the year of its foundation, Duff also attended the Stockholm Conference on Vietnam, which gave rise to annual meetings in the Swedish capital. Commenting on the American participants of these sessions, a CIA report noted that it featured activists whose 'political colorations have ranged from clerical pacifists ... to radical New Leftisits [sic] ... to members of the Communist Party, USA'.²¹⁰

As the American report indicates, protests against the Vietnam War were driven by different motivations, not all of them pacifist. Indeed, some of these protests are better understood through the lens of antimilitarism. In many instances, depictions of the United States as a 'militarist' power went together with expressions of support for the National Liberation Front of South Vietnam and its military struggle. However, antimilitarists and pacifists could unite in denouncing the nature of American warfare, from 'search and destroy' missions to the use of Napalm and Agent Orange. Even before the conflict's full medialization, some activists documented American abuses. In 1966, Bertrand Russell launched an 'international tribunal' to highlight American actions in Vietnam, attracting the support of prominent intellectuals such as Simone de Beauvoir, Jean-Paul Sartre and James Baldwin. As a private venture, the Russell Tribunal had no jurisdiction. Yet its sessions in Stockholm and Copenhagen in 1967 exemplified a form of transnational information politics that entailed the gathering of testimony and the presentation of evidence.²¹¹

The Russell Tribunal partly deployed a longstanding area of pacifist concern, namely international law – which, since the Nuremberg Trials of 1945, had expanded to include the concept of 'crimes against humanity'. According to Dirk Moses, anti-war activists were able to deploy Nuremberg 'as a normative standard with which to condemn the US'.²¹² The Tribunal connected longstanding campaigners such as Russell to a new generation of radical activists. Tariq Ali – a Pakistan-born activist who had risen to prominence as a student leader in Britain – and the African American civil rights campaigner Stokely Carmichael both contributed to the Russell Tribunal.²¹³

In February 1968, Tariq Ali participated in another international venture, the Vietnam Congress in West Berlin, which brought together 5,000 activists under the banner of anti-imperialist solidarity and facilitated a direct encounter between American activists and a delegation from North Vietnam.[214] The Berlin congress occurred at a time that seemed like the high watermark of European protests against the Vietnam War. For example, one month later, Ali organized a demonstration outside the American embassy in London. With violent clashes between protestors and the police, the event tends to be commemorated as an event in British protest history. Looking back, however, Ali also stressed the presence of French and German student leaders and the demonstrators' vision of 'a new world without wars, oppression and class exploitation, based on comradeship and internationalism'.[215]

The Vietnam War was the most obvious example of an international mobilization centring on a specific military conflict. Yet, well beyond the Cold War, US foreign policy attracted criticism and protest. In January 1991, the United States launched 'Operation Desert Storm' in response to the Iraqi invasion of Kuwait in August 1990. While Iraq's violation of international law served as a key argument for military intervention, peace activists argued that UN sanctioning merely provided a fig leaf for economic designs.[216] Following the rapid conclusion of direct military action, some campaigners focused on the impact of ongoing UN sanctions against the country. For example, in January 2001, the European branch of the Catholic relief organization Caritas sent a delegation to Iraq to investigate the situation. Its subsequent report denounced 'the immeasurable suffering in Iraq' and called for the immediate suspension of sanctions.[217]

Figure 3.3 International Vietnam Congress, held at the Technical University of Berlin on 11–12 February 1968. *Source:* Ullstein Bild, via Getty Images.

The aftershocks of the 9/11 attacks stimulated a new wave of anti-war activism. When a US-led international coalition invaded Afghanistan in October 2001, activist responses to this first episode in a wider 'war on terror' were mixed. On the one hand, al Qaeda's use of Afghanistan as a base had made it possible to interpret the attack as a response to external aggression. Moreover, the oppressive nature of the Taliban regime, including the brutal repression of women, seemed to give moral legitimacy to the intervention. On the other hand, a prominent strand of activism challenged the very notion of a 'war on terror'.[218]

In 2002, US foreign policy shifted its attention to Iraq, arguing that Saddam Hussein's regime posed an international threat because of the alleged presence of 'weapons of mass destruction'. The run-up to the attack – with UN weapons inspectors and debates within the UN Security Council – allowed an anti-war movement to build up and coordinate its activities. In February 2003, activists mobilized on an international day action, with demonstrations in Barcelona, London and Madrid that each attracted over a million marchers, while 2.5 million people gathered in Rome.[219] According to David Cortright, 'The campaign against the invasion of Iraq was the largest, most intensive mobilization of antiwar sentiment in history.'[220]

At one level, this mobilization drew on established elements – not only concerns about American power, but also an emphasis on the role of international institutions in war prevention. At the same time, it revealed changing contexts and patterns of activism. For example, the growth of Muslim communities in Western Europe meant that religious affinities shaped some involvement when military action against countries with Muslim majorities was concerned.[221] A second aspect was the rise of the global justice movement in the early 2000s, as some of the alliances that had emerged in this context supported the campaign against the Iraq War.[222] A third dimension was the increased use of the internet in the coordination of anti-war campaigns, highlighting how transnational technologies played a major role for many activists.[223]

Confronting 'new wars'

The Iraq War occurred at a time when illusions about a more peaceful world order had long been shattered: notwithstanding some optimism at the end of the Cold War, events in South-Eastern Europe soon dashed any hopes in this regard. In the summer of 1991, the Serbian-dominated leadership of the Yugoslav state reacted violently to Slovenia and Croatia's declarations of independence. Whereas military hostilities in Slovenia largely concluded after ten days, the Croatian War of Independence only ended in 1995. Moreover, the developments in Bosnia-Hercegovina caused widespread shock: during the Bosnian War of 1992–5, Bosnian Muslims (or Bosniaks) were faced by both Serbian and Croat forces, in a conflict marked by genocidal violence. The wars in the former Yugoslavia revealed the limitations of international institutions as vehicles for building peace, as the United Nations and the European Union struggled to respond to the unfolding humanitarian catastrophe. Along with the Rwandan genocide (1994) and the failed UN intervention in Somalia (1992–5), Bosnia demonstrated the shortcomings of UN peacekeeping approaches.

According to Mary Kaldor, events in the former Yugoslavia typified the phenomenon of 'new wars'. In Kaldor's view, such conflicts tend to 'take place in the context of the disintegration of states', feature 'networks of state and non-state actors' as combatants and involve a targeting of civilians 'as a consequence of counter-insurgency tactics or ethnic cleansing'.[224] Kaldor has acknowledged that these wars are not 'new' in all respects but has argued that they reflect a 'new reality' of conflict in a globalized age. Moreover, she has suggested that the concept highlights 'the need for a cosmopolitan political response – one that put[s] individual rights and the rule of law as the centrepiece of any international intervention (political, military, civil or economic)'.[225]

The question of what specific *type* of intervention might be appropriate, however, is a subject of ongoing controversy. Faced with the events in Bosnia, some argued for direct military support to the Bosnian Muslims. In May 1993, the philosopher Bernard-Henri Lévy claimed that 'a bit of our soul, and the soul of our future Europe' was at stake in Bosnia.[226] The next year, he launched an abortive attempt to present a list of candidates for the elections to the European Parliament, under the banner *L'Europe commence à Sarajevo* ('Europe begins in Sarajevo'). The campaigning of Lévy and other French intellectuals partly aimed to affect domestic public opinion and to force the French government to shift its position which, to some extent, had been sympathetic to the Serbian position.[227] Many activists, however, remained critical of military intervention, deeming states unable to promote genuine humanitarian intervention.[228]

With regard to the former Yugoslavia, some activists therefore focused on direct aid for civil society. Such efforts were multi-layered. For example, socialists and left-wing trade unionists in 1993 launched Workers' Aid for Bosnia, which perpetuated a political form of humanitarianism that was underpinned by an internationalist anti-war position.[229] There were continuations with earlier forms of transnational activism. In 1990, Kaldor and others had launched the Helsinki Citizens' Assembly (HCA) to translate the impetus of 'détente from below' into a post-Cold War world. After the outbreak of war in 1991, HCA organized a meeting in Belgrade, featuring the former Polish dissidents Adam Michnik and Bronisław Geremek, the British academic Ernest Gellner as well as the Yugoslav social theorist Milovan Djilas.[230] In 1992–3, HCA's efforts included the promotion of 'safe havens' in some Bosnian cities; Mient Jan Faber – formerly a key figure in both END and the *Interkerkelijk Vredesberaad* – portrayed this campaign as an example of 'human security from below'.[231]

Such endeavours need to be seen in conjunction with a diverse anti-war movement in the former Yugoslavia itself.[232] In its willingness to challenge the politics of ethnic division, such activism had intrinsically transnational features, although the character of these campaigns varied widely. At the same time, contacts to activists from other parts of Europe were also a factor.[233] The potential role of these interactions was illustrated by Women in Black Serbia, whose first peace vigil took place in Belgrade in October 1991. One of the Serbian activists, Lepa Mladjenović, noted that the Serbian initiative had been sparked by conversations about the Italian Women in Black – initially launched 'to protest the Italian government's involvement in the Gulf War' – which in turn had been inspired by Israeli women who campaigned on the subject of occupied Palestine.[234] Mladjenović and others had heard about these activities through an HCA initiative: in September 1991, a 'Peace Caravan' took several hundred activists from different European countries on a bus through Slovenia, Croatia, Serbia and Bosnia. Looking back, Sonja Licht – a Serbian HCA activist and organizer of this undertaking – commented on the contacts that were formed on this occasion: 'There were some Women in Black from Italy on board, continuing the tradition of the Israeli Women in Black, and they provided the first funds necessary to start off the Belgrade Women in Black.'[235]

Such examples must not lead us to idealize transnational contacts. Licht's account of the tour acknowledged very mixed responses in the different cities that it visited, from a reserved welcome in Ljubljana to a large-scale human chain in Sarajevo.[236] Some anti-war campaigners in Croatia criticized 'peace tourism' or 'peace safaris' for generating 'a lot of work for local activists' while 'bringing poor results.'[237] Moreover, while peace campaigners in the Balkans deployed transnational links, so did those who were promoting specific ethnic agendas. Diasporic groups from different parts of the former Yugoslavia sought to mobilize foreign support and, in some instances, formed a transnational 'war lobby.'[238]

While transnationalism thus generated rival attempts at mobilization, the question of military intervention continued to produce significant debates among campaigners. In 1999, NATO launched an attack on the Federation of Yugoslavia – by that stage only composed of Serbia and Montenegro. This action took place under the banner of humanitarian intervention, with the argument that it was needed to prevent genocide in Kosovo, whose autonomous status within Serbia had been suspended in 1989 and where since 1998, movements towards independence had met with violent suppression by Serbian forces.

As David Cortright has pointed out, news about the Kosovo intervention coincided with the Hague Appeal for Peace, a gathering of 10,000 activists on the anniversary of the Hague Peace Conference – the event that had enthused many peace activists in 1899.[239] Contrasting responses to the international situation caused ruptures at the centenary event. Cortright has spoken of 'a defining moment for many activists', with the situation in Kosovo provoking 'an intensive discussion within peace and human rights communities on the principles and standards of humanitarian intervention.'[240] This assessment is shared by Kaldor, who noted that the Kosovo conflict 'deeply divided civil society': many activists in The Hague viewed the bombing as an example of American imperialism, while others supported the intervention – if not necessarily its actual form, then at least its underlying principle.[241]

Kosovo revealed both continuities and discontinuities in the debate on war and peace. To some, the lesson of Bosnia and other genocides was that human life would have to be defended by force. To others, however, NATO's leadership made it appear as a case of Western aggression. This framing did, for instance, become evident in attempts to stage 'international tribunals' that sought to emulate Bertrand Russell's initiative during the Vietnam War era. For example, in September 1999, a 'hearing' in Berlin attracted various veteran campaigners, including former US Attorney General Ramsey Clark, who had become a controversial critic of US foreign policy. Several participants portrayed the Kosovo intervention as a form of imperialism. For instance, a speaker from the Czech Peace Society claimed that since the start of the 1990s, 'the governments of leading NATO states … have pursued the aim to divide the Federal Republic of Yugoslavia into smaller parts, to separate different national and ethnic groups from one another, and to provoke tensions and violence between them'.[242] To the German activist Marie Mies, talk of humanitarian intervention ultimately aimed at 'a recolonization of the world'.[243] Protests against NATO actions combined traditional antimilitarist and anti-imperialist language, yet they also evoked international law as a supporting argument.[244]

The events in Ukraine in 2014 were another example of the 'new wars'. While Russia's annexation of Crimea in February/March may have appeared like a traditional territorial conflict, the subsequent Donbas War fitted Kaldor's definition, as it was not a formally declared inter-state conflict until the Russian attack of 2022. In spring 2014, pro-Russian separatist forces proclaimed so-called 'people's republics' in the Donetsk and Luhansk *oblasti*, located in the Eastern parts of Ukraine. Early on, pro-peace forces in Russia helped to challenge the official narratives that denied Russian involvement. For example, the Union of the Committees of Soldiers' Mothers of Russia noted the number of Russian military personnel that were believed to be in Ukraine.[245] Founded in 1989, the Soldiers' Mothers had previously mobilized on the issue of the Chechen War and maintained relations with Western NGOs.[246] In contrast to these kinds of transnational links, other Russian groups and individuals maintained connections in support of a pro-war agenda. Alexander Dugin, a Russian far-right politician, promoted the concept of 'Euroasianism' in ways that supported Russian expansionism in Ukraine and, at the same time, connected him to the European far right.[247]

Transnational ties were clearly important to many Ukrainians. Russian military action had started after the resignation of the pro-Russian Ukrainian president Viktor Yanukovych. His step had been triggered by the Euromaidan protests of 2014, which had mobilized hundreds of thousands of Ukrainians for a closer relationship with the European Union. During the Euromaidan protests, transnational contexts played a role through the involvement of Ukrainian diasporic groups.[248] Moreover, after the war had started, some international structures helped to support local peacemaking efforts.[249] For example, in October 2019, activists staged a symbolic encounter between four women from opposing sides on the bridge at Stanytsia Luhanska.[250] The event originated in the efforts of Nina Potarska, a Ukrainian WILPF organizer, and was based on a prior meeting between Ukrainian, Russian, Finnish and Swedish activists during the 'Baltic Glory' peace camp.[251] In February 2022, however, the Russian attack on Ukraine demonstrated that civil society peacebuilding cannot stop aggressive powers by itself. Civil society perspectives, however, remain a concern for some activists. Two days before the Russian invasion – when the imminence of the attack on Ukraine was clear – Kaldor argued for the need to strengthen Russian civil society and to promote human rights.[252] These arguments suggested continuities in terms of concerns and strategies, as they evoked approaches that END had championed in the 1980s.

Building peace in post-conflict societies

During the 1990s and 2000s, many policymakers regarded civil society as a major component of post-conflict peacebuilding and emphasized the role of NGOs in this context. This perspective provided activists with opportunities for official support, yet it involved specific expectations as the type of venture that would merit funding. Mary Kaldor has argued that donors prioritized organizations that would place 'more emphasis on the transfer of skills from West to East than on the transfer of understanding from East to West, on the provision of services at a local level rather than campaigns at an international level, on offices rather than groups, and on professionalism rather than political mobilization'.[253]

The former Yugoslavia illustrates the debates surrounding the role of NGOs in peacebuilding. In the mid-1990s, a plethora of organizations – both domestic and international – were active in the Balkans. The ephemeral nature of their presence has led Patrice McMahon to speak of an 'NGO boom and bust' phenomenon, as the efforts of international NGOs 'did not create strong domestic actors committed to liberal goals and building peace – as internationals had hoped and promised'.[254] To both McMahon and the anthropologist Steven Sampson, the actions of Western NGOs in the Balkans amounted to a form of 'benevolent colonialism'.[255] With regard to EU support for peacebuilding in Bosnia, Stefanie Kappler and Oliver Richmond have noted the risk of 'romanticizing civil society' in ways that potentially marginalize some domestic actors.[256]

The case of Kosovo illustrates the complex dynamics shaped by transnational efforts in post-conflict societies. When the Yugoslav authorities terminated Kosovan autonomy in 1990, various bodies began to build 'parallel structures', as exemplified by 'everyday activism' in the field of healthcare.[257] Gani Demolli, a doctor involved in the Mother Teresa Society – one of the civil society groups in question – argued that 'everything changed' after the NATO intervention of 1999: 'international relief agencies flooded into Kosovo, bringing with them uncounted numbers of aid workers and massive amounts of funding'.[258] The international presence led some organizations to adapt to Western expectations so as to access financial support.[259] This situation did not create sustainable structures. Writing in 2002, Demolli argued that the massive hiring of personnel and subsequent departure of international actors had left local groups 'without means and without premises'.[260] Such assessments should not lead us to disregard the positive contributions of NGOs in post-conflict settings, yet they highlight the ambivalent nature of their role. As Ryerson Christie has noted, the scholarly literature on this subject largely adopts a position of 'friendly critique'.[261] Research in the field acknowledges that 'NGOs may not be representative of civil society' and stresses that they do not 'necessarily act in ways that are likely to achieve the presumed benefits of providing for a vibrant civil society'.[262]

In the former Yugoslavia, some protagonists demonstrated transnational inspirations without adopting NGO structures. For example, between 2006 and 2010, the Bosnian youth movement *Dosta!* ('Enough!') attacked corruption, democratic lacunae and nationalist politics while reflecting dissatisfaction with formal civil-society organizations.

Members of this largely urban movement had been influenced by their 'interaction with international solidarity movements and cultural initiatives' and drew on 'digital communication and proficiency in foreign languages'.[263] Their efforts had links to the peace movement, as some activists worked for *Zašto Ne* (Why Not), an organization that had initially campaigned on conscientious objection from 1999 onwards before broadening its remit.[264]

Dosta! activists were outlining their vision of a democratic future. At the same time, addressing the past is equally central to peacebuilding, as the extensive literature on transitional justice highlights.[265] As one manifestation of the latter approach, a 'Women's Court' initiative in Sarajevo brought thirty-six women from different parts of the former Yugoslavia to the Bosnian capital in 2015.[266] Unlike the International Criminal Tribunal at The Hague, the Women's Court did not adopt a criminal-justice approach to war crimes. Instead, it was a place for personal testimony: the organizers 'aimed to create a space for women to publicly voice their experiences of violence and injustice, and to highlight women's organised resistance to war, nationalism, and militarism'.[267] Groups such as Women in Black Belgrade backed the initiative. Moreover, the idea for this undertaking drew on events by the Asian Women's Human Rights Council in the early 1990s.[268] Back in 1889, Bertha von Suttner's novel had featured a female protagonist and highlighted female suffering during wartime. The Women's Court, however, directly addressed gendered experiences of conflict. Such contrasts invite further reflection on the shifting contexts and emphases of peace activism – while also pointing the connections to gender equality, which will be explored further in Chapter 5.

Notes

1. Camilla Theimer, 'La Tribune: Romancières autrichiennes', *La Fronde*, 15 May 1900, 2. The original publication of Suttner's bestselling novel was Bertha von Suttner, *Die Waffen nieder! Eine Lebensgeschichte* (Dresden: Edgar Pierson, 1889). The initial English version was *Lay Down Your Arms: The Autobiography of Martha von Tilling*, trans. Timothy Holmes (London: Longmans & Co., 1892). The reference to 'all modern languages' is an overstatement; one account speaks of sixteen translations (and forty German editions): Barbara Burns, 'Bertha von Suttner's Die Waffen nieder!: The Roots and Reception of a Pacifist Manifesto', in *Fontane and Cultural Mediation: Translation and Reception in Nineteenth-Century German Literature*, ed. Richie Robertson and Michael White (Cambridge: Legenda, 2015), 158–69.
2. Alfred Hermann Fried, 'Persönliches von Bertha von Suttner', *Die Friedens-Warte* 16, no. 7 (1914): 247.
3. Kenne Fant, *Alfred Nobel: A Biography*, trans. Marianne Ruuth (New York: Arcade, 1991), 265–72; Brigitte Hamann, *Bertha von Suttner: Ein Leben für den Frieden* (Munich: Piper, 1986), 330–68.
4. Internationales Frauenkomitee für dauernden Frieden, *Bericht – Rapport – Report: Internationaler Frauenkongress. Haag vom 21. April – 1. Mai 1915* (Amsterdam: IWCPP, 1915), 83.

5. Bertha von Suttner, *Die Barbarisierung der Luft* (Berlin: Verlag der Friedenswarte, 1912), 5 and 7. H. G. Wells's work on this subject was *The War in the Air: And Particularly How Mr. Bert Smallways Fared While It Lasted* (London: George Bell & Sons, 1908).

6. For English translations, see Jan Bloch, *Is War Now Impossible? Being an Abridgment of 'The War of the Future in Its Technical, Economic and Political Relations'* (London: Grant Richards, 1899); Jacques Novicow, *War and Its Alleged Benefits*, trans. Thomas Seltzer (New York: Henry Holt & Co., 1911). See also Grant Dawson, 'Preventing a "Great Moral Evil": Jean de Bloch's The Future of War as Anti-Revolutionary Pacifism', *Journal of Contemporary History* 37, no. 1 (2002): 5–19; Kevin Alleno, 'Un projet de paix perpétuelle: Fédéralisme et pacifisme chez Jacques Novicow', *Relations Internationales*, no. 154 (2013): 7–20. For another example of such arguments around the consequences of war, see Norman Angell, *Europe's Optical Illusion* (London: Simpkin, Marshall, Hamilton, Kent & Co., 1909), subsequently republished as *The Great Illusion: A Study of the Relation of Military Power in Nations to Their Economic and Social Advantage* (London: G.P. Putnam's Sons, 1910).

7. 'Sociales Gewissen und socialer Wille', *Die Waffen nieder!* 6, no. 1 (1897): 26–9; 'Das grosse Werk des Staatsrath v. Bloch', *Die Waffen nieder!* 8, no. 3 (1899): 86–8.

8. Jacques Novicow, *Der ewige Krieg: Antwort auf eine Schrift 'Der ewige Friede' des Herrn Prof. Karl Frh. v. Stengel*, trans. Alfred Hermann Fried (Berlin: Vita, 1899). Further Novicow translations by Fried included Jacques Novicow, *Die Föderation Europas* (Berlin: Edelheim, 1901); *Die Gerechtigkeit und die Entfaltung des Lebens* (Berlin: Wedekind, 1907); and *Das Problem des Elends* (Leipzig: Thomas, 1910).

9. Daniel Laqua, 'Alfred H. Fried and the Challenges for "Scientific Pacifism" in the Belle Époque', in *Information beyond Borders: International Cultural and Intellectual Exchange in the Belle Époque*, ed. W. Boyd Rayward (Farnham: Ashgate, 2014), 181–99.

10. Shelley E. Rose, 'Bertha von Suttner's Die Waffen nieder! and the Gender of German Pacifism', in *Women Writing War: From German Colonialism through World War I*, ed. Katherina von Hammerstein, Barbara Kosta and Julie Shoults (Berlin: De Gruyter, 2018), 143–62.

11. Bertha von Suttner, *Der Menschheit Hochgedanken: Roman aus der nächsten Zukunft* (Berlin: Verlag der Friedens-Warte, 1911), translated as *When Thoughts Will Soar: A Romance of the Immediate Future*, trans. Nathan Haskell Dole (Boston, MA: Houghton Mifflin, 1914). For a detailed analysis, see Geert Somsen, 'The Princess at the Conference: Science, Pacifism, and Habsburg Society', *History of Science* 59, no. 4 (2021): 434–60.

12. Sandi Cooper, *Patriotic Pacifism: Waging War on War in Europe, 1815–1914* (New York: Oxford University Press, 1991), 16–17.

13. Vanessa Lincoln Lambert, 'The Dynamics of Transnational Activism: The International Peace Congresses, 1843–51', *The International History Review* 38, no. 1 (2016): e.g. 128. On the Société's London trip, see 'Avis à Mm. les membres de la Société', *Journal de la Société de Morale Chrétienne*, no. 7 (1823): 3.

14. On these congresses, see Lambert, 'The Dynamics of Transnational Activism', 126–47; David Nicholls, 'David Cobden and the International Peace Congress Movement, 1848–1853', *Journal of British Studies* 30, no. 4 (1991): 351–76; Thomas Hippler, *Paradoxes of Peace in Nineteenth-Century Europe* (Oxford: Oxford University Press, 2015), 174–82.

15. Bertha von Suttner, *Memoirs of Bertha von Suttner: The Records of an Eventful Life*, vol. 2, trans. Nathan Haskell Dole (Boston, MA: Ginn and Company, 1910), 47.

16. Fried, *Handbuch der Friedensbewegung*; Alfred Hermann Fried, *Das internationale Leben der Gegenwart* (Leipzig: Teubner, 1908). For Fried's project of a 'yearbook of international life' – the *Annuaire de la Vie internationale* – and his cooperation with Belgian activists, see Laqua, 'Alfred H. Fried'.

17. Emile Arnaud, 'Le Pacifisme', *L'Indépendance Belge*, 15 August 1901, 2.
18. Laqua, *The Age of Internationalism and Belgium*, 145–80.
19. United Nations Library, Geneva, IPM/IPB/163, doss. 4: undated letter from *L'Indépendance Belge* to the International Peace Bureau, 1903.
20. Martin Ceadel, *Semi-Detached Idealists: The British Peace Movement and International Relations, 1854–1945* (Oxford: Oxford University Press, 2000), 158.
21. See e.g. April Carter, *Peace Movements: International Protest and World Politics since 1945* (London: Longman, 1992), 15.
22. See Martin Ceadel, 'Pacifism and Pacificism', in *The Cambridge History of Twentieth-Century Political Thought*, ed. Terence Bell and Richard Bellamy (Cambridge: Cambridge University Press, 2003), 471–92 and Ceadel's extensive body of work more generally. For another perspective on 'pacificism', see Nigel Dower, *The Ethics of War and Peace* (Cambridge: Polity, 2009), 137–60.
23. Walther Schücking, *Der Staatenverband der Haager Konferenzen* (Berlin: Duncker & Humblot, 1912), 4; Walther Schücking, 'Der Weg des Pazifismus', *Die Friedens-Warte* 23, nos. 1–2 (1923): 15–18.
24. Wouter De Rycke, 'In Search of a Legal Conscience: Juridicial Reformism in the Mid-19th Century Peace Movement', *Studia Iuridica* 80, no. 3 (2019): 355–74.
25. Cortright, *Peace*, 49.
26. Rémi Fabre, 'Un exemple de pacifisme juridique: "La Paix par le Droit" (1884–1950)', *Vingtième Siècle*, no. 39 (1993): 38–54.
27. On Pratt in Germany, see Roger Chickering, *Imperial Germany and a World without War: The Peace Movement and German Society, 1892–1914* (Princeton, NJ: Princeton University Press, 1975), 42–3. On Pratt in the Habsburg Monarchy, see e.g. 'Hodgson Pratt in Vienna', *The Herald of Peace*, 1 February 1888, 26.
28. For the Belgian impact of these activities, see Nadine Lubelski-Bernard, 'Les mouvements et les ideologies pacifists en Belgique 1830–1914' (PhD thesis, Université libre de Bruxelles, 1971), 33–4.
29. Cooper, *Patriotic Pacifism*, 8.
30. 'Friedens-Konferenz', *Reichspost*, 25 August 1904, 4.
31. Christian Lange, *The Interparliamentary Union* (New York: American Association for International Conciliation, 1913), 5.
32. Maartje Abbenhuis, *The Hague Conferences and International Politics, 1898–1915* (London: Bloomsbury, 2018), 21.
33. Suttner, *Memoirs*, 191–2.
34. Bertha von Suttner, 'Zeitschau', *Die Waffen nieder* 8, no. 4 (1899): 121.
35. Bertha von Suttner, 'Zeitschau', *Die Waffen nieder* 8, no. 5 (1899): 163.
36. Suttner, *Memoirs*, 249.
37. Alfred Hermann Fried, 'Unsere Freunde im Haag', *Die Waffen nieder* 8, no. 6 (1899): 228–31.
38. *Courrier de la Conférence de la Paix* (1907).
39. For an overview, see Martin Ceadel, 'Pacifism', in *The Cambridge History of the First World War*, vol. II: *The State*, ed. Jay Winter (Cambridge: Cambridge University Press, 2014), 576–605.

40. See e.g. Alfred Hermann Fried, 'Das Ziel', *Die Friedens-Warte* 6, no. 10 (1914): 321–3. Fried expanded on these ideas in Alfred Hermann Fried, *Europäische Wiederherstellung* (Zürich: Füssli, 1915).
41. See e.g. the documentation of various debates about a future League of Nations in the Switzerland-based internationalist periodical, which started with Leopold Katscher, 'Aus der Völkerbundbewegung', *Die Versöhnung* 2, no. 52 (10 August 1918): 3–4, and continued until June 1919.
42. Thomas Knock, *To End All Wars: Woodrow Wilson and the Quest for a New World Order* (new edn; Princeton, NJ: Princeton University Press, 2019).
43. Katharina Rietzler, 'From Peace Advocacy to International Relations Research: The Transformation of Transatlantic Philanthropic Networks, 1900–1930', in Rodogno et al., *Shaping the Transnational Sphere*, 173–93; Katharina Rietzler, 'Experts for Peace: Structures and Motivations of Philanthropic Internationalism in the Interwar Years', in Laqua, *Internationalism Reconfigured*, 45–66; Ludovic Tournès, *Philanthropic Foundations at the League of Nations: An Americanized League?* (Abingdon: Routledge, 2022).
44. Cecilia Lynch, *Beyond Appeasement: Interpreting Interwar Peace Movements in World Politics* (Ithaca, NY: Cornell University Press, 1999), 97–109; Thomas Davies, *The Possibilities of Transnational Activism: The Campaign for Disarmament between the Two World Wars* (Leiden: Brill, 2007); Andrew Webster, 'The League of Nations, Disarmament, and Internationalism', in Sluga and Clavin, *Internationalisms*, 139–69; Andrew Webster, 'The Transnational Dream: Politicians, Diplomats and Soldiers in the League of Nations' Pursuit of International Disarmament, 1920–1938', *Contemporary European History* 14, no. 4 (2004): 493–518.
45. Glenda Sluga, 'Habsburg Histories of Internationalism', in *Remaking Central Europe: The League of Nations and the Former Habsburg Lands*, ed. Peter Becker and Natasha Wheatley (Oxford: Oxford University Press, 2020), 22.
46. Anne-Isabelle Richard, 'Between Publicity and Discretion: The International Federation of League of Nations Societies', in Gram-Skjoldager et al., *Organizing the 20th-Century World*, 145–62.
47. Helen McCarthy, *The British People and the League of Nations: Democracy, Citizenship and Internationalism, c. 1918–1945* (Manchester: Manchester University Press, 2011); Susannah Wright, 'Creating Liberal-Internationalist World Citizens: League of Nations Union Junior Branches in English Secondary Schools, 1919–1939', *Paedagogica Historica* 56, no. 3 (2020): 321–40; Jean-Michel Guieu, *Le rameau et le glaive: Les militants français pour la Société des Nations* (Paris: Presses de Sciences Po, 2008); Christian Birebent, *Militants de la paix et de la SDN: les mouvements de soutien à la Société des nation en France et au Royaume Uni 1918–1925* (Paris: L'Harmattan, 2008).
48. Helen McCarthy, 'Democratizing British Foreign Policy: Rethinking the Peace Ballot, 1934–1935', *Journal of British Studies* 49, no. 2 (2010): 358–78.
49. For a discussion of Swanwick's activism, see Josephine Eglin, 'Women Pacifists in Interwar France', in *Challenge to Mars: Pacifism from 1918 to 1945*, ed. Peter Brock and Thomas Socknat (Toronto: University of Toronto Press, 1999), 149–68.
50. H. M. Swanwick, *Collective Insecurity* (London: Jonathan Cape, 1937), 21.
51. Mark Hewitson, 'The United States: The European Question in the 1920s', in *Europe in Crisis: Intellectuals and the European Idea, 1917–1957*, ed. Mark Hewitson and Matthew d'Auria (New York: Berghahn, 2012), 15–34.

52. Richard Coudenhove-Kalergi, *Crusade for Pan-Europe: Autobiography of a Man and a Movement* (New York: George Putnam's Sons, 1943), 1. See also Katherine Sorrels, *Cosmopolitan Outsiders: Imperial Inclusion, National Exclusion, and the Pan-European Idea, 1900–1930* (New York: Palgrave, 2016); and Anita Prettenthaler-Ziegerhofer, 'Richard Coudenhove-Kalergi, Founder of the Pan-European Union, and the Birth of a "New Europe"', in Hewitson and d'Auria, *Europe in Crisis*, 89–116.

53. Speech at the 23rd Universal Peace Congress, Berlin, as reprinted in Richard Coudenhove-Kalergi, *Kampf um Paneuropa: Aus dem 1. Jahrgang* (Vienna: Paneuropa-Verlag, 1925), 59–79.

54. Dina Gusejnova, *European Elites and Ideas of Empire, 1917–1957* (Cambridge: Cambridge University Press, 2016).

55. Benjamin Martin, *The Nazi-Fascist New Order for European Culture* (Cambridge, MA: Harvard University Press, 2016); Anthony Pagden, *The Pursuit of Europe: A History* (Oxford: Oxford University Press, 2021), 192–227.

56. Katiana Orluc, 'Caught between Past and Future: The Idea of Pan-Europe in the Interwar Europe', in *Reflections on Europe: Defining a Political Order in Time and Space*, ed. Hans-Åke Persson and Bo Stråth (Brussels: P.I.E. Peter Lang, 2007), 117. On Coudenhove-Kalergi's relations with the Austrofascist regime during the 1930s, see Anita Prettenthaler-Ziegerhofer, *Botschafter Europas: Richard Nikolaus Coudenhove-Kalergi und die Paneuropa-Bewegung in den zwanziger und dreißiger Jahren* (Cologne: Böhlau, 2004), 233–43.

57. Coudenhove-Kalergi, *Crusade for Pan-Europe*, 162.

58. On the range of individuals and forces that converged during the Congress of Europe at The Hague, see Jean-Michel Guieu and Christophe Le Dréau, eds, *Le 'Congrès de l'Europe' à La Haye (1948–2008)* (Brussels: P.I.E. Peter Lang, 2008).

59. Richard, 'The Limits of Solidarity', 520.

60. For recent overviews and interpretations, see Brigitte Leucht, Katja Sendel and Laurent Warlouzet, eds, *Reinventing Europe: The History of the European Union, 1945 to the Present* (London: Bloomsbury, 2023); Kiran Klaus Patel, *Project Europe: A History* (Cambridge: Cambridge University Press, 2020).

61. See e.g. the efforts of the Young European Federalists, as discussed in François-Xavier Lafféach, 'An Avant-garde for Europe? The Young European Federalists and the Emergence of a European Consciousness, 1948–1972', in *The Road to a United Europe: Interpretations of the Process of European Integration*, ed. Morten Rasmussen and Ann-Christina Knudsen (Brussels: P.I.E. Peter Lang, 2009), 39–52.

62. Dagmar Wernitznig, 'Living Peace, Thinking Equality: Rosika Schwimmer's (1877–1948) War on War', in *Living War, Thinking Peace (1914–1924): Women's Experiences, Feminist Thought, and International Relations*, ed. Bruna Bianchi and Geraldine Ludbrook (Newcastle upon Tyne: Cambridge Scholars Publishing, 2016), 123–38.

63. Lola Maverick Lloyd and Rosika Schwimmer, *Chaos, War, or a New World Order: What We Must Do to Establish the All-Inclusive, Non-Military, Democratic Federation of Nations* (4th edn; Chicago, IL: Campaign for World Government, 1942), 5.

64. Cortright, *Peace*, 117. See also Mazower, *Governing the World*, 230–5.

65. Charlotte Alston, *Tolstoy and His Disciples: The History of a Radical International Movement* (London: I.B. Tauris, 2014).

66. Luke Kelly, 'Christianity and Humanitarianism in the Doukhobor Campaign, 1895–1902', *Cultural and Social History* 13, no. 3 (2016): 339–55; Charlotte Alston, '"A Great Host of Sympathisers": The Doukhobor Emigration and Its International Supporters', *Journal of Modern European History* 12, no. 2 (2014): 200–15.
67. Cortright, *Peace*, 169.
68. Norman Ingram, *The Politics of Dissent: Pacifism in France, 1919–1939* (Oxford: Oxford University Press, 1991), 119.
69. Nicolas Offenstadt, 'Le pacifisme extrême à la conquête des masses: la Ligue Internationale des Combattants de la Paix (1931–1939) et la propagande', *Matériaux pour l'histoire de notre temps*, no. 30 (1993): 35–9.
70. Herman Noordegraaf, 'The Anarchopacifism of Bart de Ligt', in Brock and Socknat, *Challenge to Mars*, 89–100.
71. Bart de Ligt to Gandhi, May 1928, originally published in *The World Tomorrow* (May 1928), 445–6 and reprinted in *The Breath of My Life: The Correspondence of Mahatma Gandhi (India) and Bart de Ligt (Holland) on War and Peace*, ed. Christian Bartolf (Berlin: Gandhi-Informations-Zentrum, 2000), 27. Subsequent references to the correspondence are based on the original, with the exception of note no. 73.
72. Bart de Ligt, 'War against War', *Young India* 11, no. 18 (1929): 141.
73. Bart de Ligt, 'Cat and Mouse', *Young India* 12, no. 4 (1930): 30; Bart de Ligt, 'My Correspondence with Gandhi (19.7.1930)', originally published in *Die neue Generation* (July 1930) and reprinted in Bartolf, ed., *The Breath of Life*, 63.
74. Bart de Ligt, 'Meine Korrespondenz mit Gandhi', originally published in *Die neue Generation* (July 1930) and reprinted in Bartolf, *The Breath of My Life*, 63. For Rolland's portrayal of Gandhi, see Romain Rolland, *Gandhi* (Paris: Stock, 1924). For an overview of Rolland's engagement with Gandhi and another celebrated Indian thinker, Rabindranath Tagore, see Jean Biès, 'Romain Rolland, Tagore et Gandhi', *Littératures* 18 (1971): 45–66.
75. Mahatma Gandhi, 'My Attitude toward War', *Young India* 10, no. 37 (1928): 308; Mahatma Gandhi, 'A Complex Problem', *Young India* 11, no. 19 (1929): 148.
76. de Ligt, 'War against War', 142. In this letter de Ligt acknowledged 'the right of any oppressed class or race to liberate myself by means of arms', yet in such contexts, 'non-violent resistance' appeared to be 'the surest arm'. For de Ligt's comments on conscientious objection in Europe, see 'War against War II', *Young India* 11, no. 20 (1925): 153–6.
77. Letter of Vladimir Chertkov (transcribed as 'Tcherkoff'), *Young India* 11, no. 6 (1929): 45.
78. Peter Brock, 'Conscientious Objectors in Nazi Germany', in Brock and Socknat, *Challenge to Mars*, 370–9.
79. See e.g. Norman Ingram, '"Nous allons vers les monastères": French Pacifism and the Crisis of the Second World War', in *Crisis and Renewal in France*, ed. Kenneth Mouré and Martin Alexander (New York: Berghahn, 2002), 132–51, as well as the different contributions in Part II ('The Second World War') of Brock and Young, eds, *Challenge to Mars*, 241–423.
80. Sean Scalmer, 'Globalising Gandhi: Translation, Reinvention, Application, Transformation', in *Rethinking Gandhi and Nonviolent Relationality: Global Perspectives*, ed. Debjani Ganguly and John Docker (Abingdon: Routledge, 2007), 149; Nehring, 'Peace Movements', 508. See also Scalmer, *Gandhi in the West*.
81. Cooper, *Patriotic Pacifism*, 68.
82. Sluga, *Internationalism in the Age of Nationalism*, e.g. 16–17.

83. Donatella Cherubini, 'Si Vis Pacem Libertatem et Justitiam: Les Etats-Unis d'Europe, 1867–1914', in *Les Etats-Unis d'Europe: Un Project Pacifiste*, ed. Marta Petricioli, Donatella Cherubini and Alessandra Anteghini (Bern: Peter Lang, 2004), 3.

84. A. P. Campanella, 'Garibaldi and the First Peace Congress in Geneva in 1867', *International Review of Social History* 5, no. 3 (1960): 456–86; Hippler, *Paradoxes of Peace*, esp. 182–4.

85. On Mazzini's impact in the Slavic parts of Europe, see Anna Procyk, *Giuseppe Mazzini's Young Europe and the Birth of Modern Nationalism in the Slavic World* (Toronto: University of Toronto Press, 2019). While Mazzini and Garibaldi shared republican convictions and a discourse of universal fraternity, there were significant differences in their respective political visions, as discussed in Giuliana Limiti, 'Garibaldi and Mazzini: Thought and Action', *Journal of Modern Italian Studies* 13, no. 4 (2008): 492–502.

86. Alberto Castelli, *The Peace Discourse in Europe, 1900–1945* (Abingdon: Routledge, 2019).

87. Alberto Castelli, 'Between Patriotism and Pacifism: Ernesto Teodoro Moneta and the Italian Conquest of Libya', *History of European Ideas* 36, no. 3 (2010): 324–9.

88. Cooper, *Patriotic Pacifsm*, 68.

89. Leszek Kuk, 'La Ligue internationale de la Paix et de la Liberté et la "question polonaise"', in Petricioli et al., *Les Etats-Unis d'Europe*, 328.

90. Kuk, 'La Ligue internationale', 331–6.

91. Carole Fink, 'The *Ligue internationale de la Paix et de la Liberté*', in Petricioli et al., *Les Etats-Unis d'Europe*, 111.

92. Mahatma Gandhi, 'A Complex Problem', *Young India* 11, no. 19 (1929): 148.

93. de Ligt, 'Cat and Mouse', 30.

94. Bureau internationale de la Paix, *Bulletin Officiel du IVme Congrès Universel de la Paix, tenu à Berne (Suisse) du 22 au 27 août 1892* (Bern: Haller, 1892), 122–31.

95. Daniel Laqua, 'Pacifism in Fin-de-Siècle Austria: The Politics and Limits of Peace Activism', *The Historical Journal* 57, no. 1 (2014): 199–224, esp. 217–23.

96. Jasna Adler, 'Comment faire régner la paix dans les Balkans: *Les Etats-Unis d'Europe* et les Balkans, 1867–1913', in Petricioli et al., *Les Etats-Unis d'Europe*, esp. 353–4 and 358–9.

97. James Perkins, 'British Liberalism and the Balkans, *c.* 1875–1925' (PhD thesis, Birkbeck, University of London, 2014), 166.

98. Frances Trix, 'Peace-mongering in 1913: The Carnegie International Commission of Inquiry and Its Report on the Balkan Wars', *First World War Studies* 5, no. 2 (2014): 147–62.

99. Cooper, *Patriotic Pacifism*, 185–203.

100. Romain Rolland, 'Au-dessus de la mêlée', *Journal de Genève*, 22 September 1914. On Rolland's and Fried's wartime exile, see David James Fisher, *Romain Rolland and the Politics of Intellectual Engagement* (Berkeley, CA: University of California Press, 1988), 38–48; Petra Schönemann-Behrens, *Alfred H. Fried: Friedensaktivist – Nobelpreisträger* (Zürich: Römerhof, 2011), 258–66 and 338–42. On wartime exiles in Switzerland more generally, see Anja Huber, *Fremdsein im Krieg: Die Schweiz als Ausgangs- und Zielland von Migranten, 1914–1918* (Zürich: Chromos, 2017).

101. Brock and Young have called its American branch 'the most vigorous and intellectually alive exponent of pacifism' in this period: Peter Brock and Nigel Young, *Pacifism in the Twentieth Century* (Syracuse, NY: Syracuse University Press, 1999), 101.

102. Gearóid Barry, *The Disarmament of Hatred: Marc Sangnier, French Catholicism and the Legacy of the First World War, 1914–45* (Basingstoke: Palgrave, 2012), 128–52 and 158–62.

103. Daniel Laqua, 'Reconciliation and the Post-War Order: The Place of the Deutsche Liga für Menschenrechte in Interwar Pacifism', in Laqua, *Internationalism Reconfigured*, 209–38. On the activities of the *Ligue des Droits de l'Homme* in this period, see Norman Ingram, *The War Guilt Problem and the Ligue des Droits de l'Homme* (Oxford: Oxford University Press, 2019).

104. Carl von Ossietzky, 'The Pacifists' (orig. 9 October 1924), as featured in Bruno Frei, ed., *The Stolen Republic: Selected Writings of Carl von Ossietzky*, trans. John Peet (Berlin: Seven Seas, 1971), 155–6.

105. Ossietzky, 'The Pacifists', 156.

106. Kurt Großmann, 'Die Pflicht zum Landesverrat', *Die Menschenrechte*, 31 August 1927.

107. Archives du Ministère des Affaires Étrangères, Brussels, R1507, 'Allemagne 1928' (P733): Robert Everts to Paul Hymans, 15 May 1928.

108. Ibid.

109. Jean-Michel Palmier, *Weimar in Exile: The Antifascist Emigration in Europe and America*, trans. David Fernbach (London: Verso, 2006), 40–3, 207 and 325–6. The international campaign for Ossietzky is documented in Charmian Brinson and Marian Malet, eds, *Rettet Ossietzky! Dokumente aus dem Nachlaß von Rudolf Olden* (Oldenburg: Bibliotheks- und Informationssystem der Universität Oldenburg, 1990).

110. Holger Nehring, 'National Internationalists: British and West German Protests against Nuclear Weapons, the Politics of Transnational Communications and the Social History of the Cold War, 1957–1964', *Contemporary European History* 14, no. 4 (2005): 559–82.

111. Jodi Burkett, 'Re-defining British Morality: "Britishness" and the Campaign for Nuclear Disarmament 1958–68', *Twentieth Century British History* 21, no. 2 (2010): 84–205.

112. Benjamin Ziemann, 'A Quantum of Solace? European Peace Movements during the Cold War and Their Elective Affinities', *Archiv für Sozialgeschichte* 49 (2009): 357.

113. Benjamin Ziemann, 'Situating Peace Movements in the Political Culture of the Cold War', in *Peace Movements in Western Europe, Japan and the USA during the Cold War*, ed. Benjamin Ziemann (Essen: Klartext, 2007), 38. See also Dimitrios Tsakiris, 'State Repression against Peace Movements in Greece, 1950–1967', in Ziemann, *Peace Movements*, 147–64; Eirini Karamouzi, '"Out with the Bases of Death": Civil Society and Peace Mobilization in Greece during the 1980s', *Journal of Contemporary History* 56, no. 3 (2021): 617–38.

114. Holger Nehring, *Politics of Security: British and West German Protest Movements and the Early Cold War, 1945–1970* (Oxford: Oxford University Press, 2013), 173.

115. Wilfried Mausbach, 'Auschwitz and Vietnam', in *America, the Vietnam War, and the World: Comparative and International Perspectives*, ed. Andreas Daum, Lloyd Gardner and Wilfred Mausbach (Cambridge: Cambridge University Press, 2003), 279–98.

116. Ziemann, 'A Quantum of Solace', 364.

117. For this focus on militias and arming citizens, see e.g. Paul Miller, *From Revolutionaries to Citizens: Antimilitarism in France, 1870–1914* (Durham, NC: Duke University Press, 2002), 45; Nicholas Stargardt, *The German Idea of Militarism: Radical and Socialist Critics, 1866–1914* (Cambridge: Cambridge University Press, 1994), 50–1. For the relationship with ideas about conscription, see Kevin Morgan, 'Militarism and Anti-Militarism: Socialists, Communists and Conscription in France and Britain 1900–1940', *Past & Present* 202, no. 1 (2009): 207–44. On antimilitarist engagement with anti-imperialist struggles, see. e.g. the essays that were initially published in the Dutch journal *De Wapens Neder* in

1935 and recently re-edited: Ole Birk Laursen, ed., *Lay Down Your Arms: Anti-Militarism, Anti-Imperialism and the Global Radical Left in the 1930s* (Atlanta, GA: On Our Own Account, 2019).

118. Laqua, 'Pacifism in Fin-de-Siècle Austria', 214–16.
119. Jean Jaurès, 'Sozialdemokratie und Pacifismus', *Die Friedenswarte* 10, no. 11 (1908): 203–7.
120. Cherubini, 'Si Vis Pacem', 4–5.
121. Paul Laity, *The British Peace Movement 1879–1914* (Oxford: Clarendon Press, 2001), 25 and 112.
122. Kevin J. Callahan, *Demonstration Culture: European Socialism and the Second International, 1889–1914* (Leicester: Troubador, 2010), 257–91.
123. Stargardt, *The German Idea of Militarism*, 123–4.
124. For an overview of the wartime developments, see Imlay, *The Practice of Socialist Internationalism*, 17–48.
125. David Kirby, 'International Socialism and the Question of Peace: The Stockholm Conference of 1917', *The Historical Journal* 25, no. 3 (1982): 709–16.
126. R. Craig Nation, *War on War: Lenin, the Zimmerwald Left, and the Origins of Communist Internationalism* (Durham, NC: Duke University Press, 1989).
127. Ruth Kinna and Matthew S. Adams, eds, *Anarchism, 1914–18: Internationalism, Anti-Militarism and War* (Manchester: Manchester University Press, 2017).
128. See e.g. Laqua, 'Democratic Politics and the League of Nations'.
129. Henri Barbusse, *Paroles d'un combattant: articles et discours (1917–1920)* (Paris: Flammarion, 1920), 213–18. On Barbusse's involvement in transnational veterans' activism, see Ángel Alcalde, 'War Veterans as Transnational Actors: Politics, Alliances and Networks in the Interwar Period', *European Review of History* 25, no. 3–4 (2018): 494–5 and 500–1.
130. Henri Barbusse, *Staline: Un monde nouveau vu à travers un homme* (Paris: Flammarion, 1935). On his Soviet contacts, see Michael David-Fox, *Showcasing the Great Experiment: Cultural Diplomacy and Western Visitors to Soviet Russia, 1921–1941* (Oxford: Oxford University Press, 2012), 229–34.
131. Institut Emile Vandervelde, Brussels, EV/III/75: Friedrich Adler to Emile Vandervelde, 4 July 1932.
132. Serge Wolikow, 'Les gauches, l'antifascisme et le pacifisme pendant les années 1930', in *Histoire des gauches en France*, vol. 2, ed. Jean-Jacques Becker (Paris: La Découverte, 2005), 357–74.
133. IISG, ARCH01165, folder 19: Louis de Brouckère to Friedrich Adler, 9 February 1936.
134. Jonathan Haslam, 'The British Communist Party, the Comintern, and the Outbreak of War, 1939: "A Nasty Taste in the Mouth"', *Diplomacy & Statecraft* 3, no. 1 (1992): 147–54; Monty Johnstone, 'The CPGB, the Comintern and the War: Filling in the Blank Spots', *Science & Society* 61, no. 1 (1997): 27–45.
135. Günter Wernicke, 'The Communist-Led World Peace Council and the Western Peace Movements: The Fetters of Bipolarity and Some Attempts to Break Them in the Fifties and Early Sixties', *Peace and Change* 23, no. 1 (1998): 265–311.
136. Carter, *Peace Movements*, 33.
137. Holger Nehring and Benjamin Ziemann, 'Do All Paths Lead to Moscow? The NATO Dual-Track Decision and the Peace Movement – A Critique', *Cold War History* 12, no. 1

(2012): 1–24. See also Ziemann's argument against viewing the protests simply as part of a 'Soviet offensive': Ziemann, 'A Quantum of Solace?', 353.
138. This letter to the International Woman Suffrage Alliance was published in 'Letter from Baroness Suttner', *Ius Suffragii* 8, no. 9 (1914): 99.
139. May Ogilvie Gordon, *The International Council of Women and the Meetings of the International Council of Women in Berlin, 1904* (Aberdeen: Free Press, 1904), 6.
140. Laurie Cohen, 'Across a Feminist-Pacifist Divide: Baroness Bertha von Suttner's Tour of the United States in 1912', *L'Homme* 20, no. 2 (2009): 85–104.
141. Sophie Roberts, 'British Women Activists and the Campaigns against the Vietnam War, 1965–75' (PhD thesis, Northumbria University, 2018), 111.
142. The most extensive study on this phenomenon is Annika Wilmers, *Pazifismus in der internationalen Frauenbewegung (1914–1920): Handlungsspielräume, politische Konzeptionen und gesellschaftliche Auseinandersetzungen* (Essen: Klartext, 2008).
143. Aletta Jacobs, *Memories: My Life as an International Leader in Health, Suffrage, and Peace*, ed. Annie Wright and trans. Harriet Feinberg (New York: Feminist Press, 1996 [orig. 1924]), 83.
144. Emily Balch, 'Journey and Impressions', in *Women at The Hague: The International Congress of Women and its Results*, ed. Jane Addams, Emily Balch and Alice Hamilton (New York: Macmillan, 1915), 7.
145. David Patterson, *The Search for Negotiated Peace: Women's Activism and Citizen Diplomacy in World War I* (New York: Routledge, 2008).
146. For American impressions from this venture, see Alice Hamilton, 'At the War Capitals', in Addams et al., *Women at The Hague*, 22–54.
147. Sarah Hellawell, 'Antimilitarism, Citizenship and Motherhood: The Formation and Early Years of the Women's International League (WIL), 1915–1919', *Women's History Review* 27, no. 4 (2018): 551–64.
148. Women's International League for Peace and Freedom, *Report of the International Congress of Women, Report, May 12 to May 17, 1919* (Geneva: WILPF, 1919), 246–8.
149. Jo Vellacott, 'A Place for Pacifism and Transnationalism in Feminist Theory: The Early Work of the Women's International League for Peace and Freedom', *Women's History Review* 2, no. 1 (1993): 23–56.
150. Stefan Dyroff, 'Minority Rights and Humanitarianism: The International Campaign for the Ukrainians in Poland, 1930–1931', *Journal of Modern European History* 12, no. 2 (2014): esp. 221–2.
151. Davies, *The Possibilities of Transnational Activism*, 40.
152. Peace and Disarmament Committee of the Women's International Organisations, *Official Record of the Declarations and Petitions Presented by the Disarmament Committee of the Women's International Organisations to the Disarmament Conference, Geneva, February 6th, 1932* (Geneva: Imp. de la Tribune de Genève, 1932), 16–19. For these efforts, see Karen Garner, 'Global Visions: The Women's Disarmament Committee and the International Politics of Disarmament in the 1930s', in *Rosa Manus: The International Life and Legacy of a Jewish Dutch Feminist*, ed. Myriam Everard and Francisca De Haan (Leiden: Brill, 2016), 125–59.
153. Laura Beers, 'Bridging the Ideological Divide: Liberal and Socialist Collaboration in the Women's International League for Peace and Freedom, 1919–1945', *Journal of Women's History* 33, no. 2 (2021): 111–35.

154. For different perspectives, see Jasmine Calver, *Anti-Fascism, Gender, and International Communism: The Comité Mondial des Femmes Contre le Guerre et le Fascisme, 1934–1941* (Abingdon: Routledge, 2023); Emmanuelle Carle, 'Women, Anti-Fascism and Peace in Interwar France: Gabrielle Duchêne's Itinerary', *French History* 18, no. 3 (2004): 291–314; Lorraine Coons, 'Gabrielle Duchêne: Feminist, Pacifist, Reluctant Bourgeoise', *Peace & Change* 24, no. 2 (1999): 121–47.

155. Ellen Carol DuBois, 'Trying to Stem the Tide: Rosa Manus's Peace Activism in the 1930s', in Everard and De Haan, *Rosa Manus*, 160–83.

156. Catia Celia Confortini, *Intelligent Compassion: The Women's International League for Peace and Freedom and Feminist Peace* (Oxford: Oxford University Press, 2012), 118.

157. Jessica Frazier, *Women's Antiwar Diplomacy during the Vietnam Era* (Chapel Hill, NC: The University of North Carolina Press, 2017), 43.

158. On the initial march that led to Greenham Common, see Jill Liddington, *The Road to Greenham Common: Feminism and Anti-Militarism in Britain since 1820* (Syracuse, NY: Syracuse University Press, 1989), 224–30.

159. Ann Pettitt, *Walking to Greenham: How the Peace-Camp Began and the Cold War Ended* (Aberystwyth: Honno, 2006), 188.

160. Ziemann, 'European Peace Movements', 355

161. Interview with Konrad and Helga Tempel (conducted by Christoph Gunkel): '"Zur Not gehe ich alleine": 60 Jahre Ostermärsche', *Der Spiegel*, 12 April 2020, available online via https://www.spiegel.de/geschichte/corona-und-60-jahre-ostermaersche-zur-not-gehe-ich-allein-a-831c9aad-44c4-4425-9c97-f72c559c612e (last accessed 9 January 2023).

162. Nehring, *Politics of Security*, 120–1.

163. Carter, *Peace Movements*, 63.

164. On the formation of the Bertrand Russell Committee for Nuclear Disarmament in Greece, see Evi Gkotzaridis, '"Who Will Help Me to Get Rid of This Man?": Grigoris Lambrakis and the Non-Aligned Peace Movement in Post-Civil War Greece: 1951–1964', *Journal of Modern Greek Studies* 30, no. 2 (2012): 309. On Russell's impact within the anti-nuclear movement, see Lawrence Wittner, *Resisting the Bomb: A History of the World Nuclear Disarmament Movement 1954–1970* (Stanford, CA: Stanford University Press, 1997) e.g. 5–7, 20–5, 34–7 and 111–4.

165. Kostis Kornetis, *Children of the Dictatorship: Student Resistance, Cultural Politics and the 'Long 1960s' in Greece* (New York: Berghahn, 2013), 19–21.

166. Gkotzaridis, 'Who Will Help Me to Get Rid of This Man?', 322.

167. Günter Wernicke and Lawrence S. Wittner, 'Lifting the Iron Curtain: The Peace March to Moscow of 1960–1961', *The International History Review* 21, no. 4 (1999): 900–17. On the use of the CND logo on this occasion, see also Ken Kolsbun, with Mike Sweeney, *Peace: The Biography of a Symbol*, 59–61.

168. Paul Brown and Stpehen Cook, 'Millions in Europe March against Cruise', *The Guardian*, 24 October 1983, 28.

169. Carter, *Peace Movements*, 115.

170. Rein Taagepera, 'Citizens' Peace Movement in the Soviet Baltic Republics', *Journal of Peace Research* 23, no. 2 (1986): 183–92.

171. Christoph Laucht, 'Transnational Professional Activism and the Prevention of Nuclear War in Britain', *Journal of Social History* 52, no. 2 (2018): 439–67.

172. On Pugwash, see Alison Kraft and Carola Sachse, eds, *Science, (Anti-)Communism and Diplomacy: The Pugwash Conferences on Science and World Affairs in the Early Cold War* (Leiden: Brill, 2020).

173. Alison Kraft, Holger Nehring and Carola Sachs, 'Introduction', *Journal of Cold War Studies* 20, no. 1 (2018): 24. For case studies, see the contributions to the journal issue on 'The Pugwash Conferences and the Global Cold War' to which the piece by Kraft, Nehring and Sachs forms the introduction.

174. Matthew Evangelista, *Unarmed Forces: The Transnational Movement to End the Cold War* (Ithaca, NY: Cornell University Press, 1999), 18.

175. Evangelista, *Unarmed Forces*, 158–71.

176. Elizabeth Waterston and Frank Boulton, 'A History of British Health Professionals Working for the Abolition of Nuclear Weapons', *Medicine, Conflict and Survival* 34, no. 4 (2018): 350–9.

177. Bernard Lown, *Prescription for Survival: A Doctor's Journey to End Nuclear Madness* (San Francisco: Berrett-Koehler Publishers, 2008), 293.

178. Lown, *Prescription for Survival*, 293.

179. On this controversy, see e.g. 'Protest on Anti-Sakharov Letter Clouds Nobel Ceremony in Oslo', *New York Times*, 10 December 1985, 1; Thom Shanker, 'No Peace for a Nobel Winner', *Chicago Tribune*, 9 December 1985, 1.

180. Lown, *Prescription for Survival*, 352–3.

181. Ibid., 352.

182. Jay Bergman, 'Andrei Sakharov on Nuclear War and Nuclear Peace', in *The Routledge History of World Peace since 1750*, ed. Christian Philip Peterson, William Knoblauch and Michael Loadenthal (Abingdon: Routledge, 2018), 249–58.

183. Charles Rhéaume, 'Western Scientists' Reactions to Andrei Sakharov's Human Rights Struggle in the Soviet Union, 1968–1989', *Human Rights Quarterly* 30, no. 1 (2008): 1–21; Paul Rubinson, 'Scientists as Peace Activists', in Peterson et al., *The Routledge History of World Peace*, 259–69.

184. Patrick Burke, 'A Transcontinental Movement of Citizens? Strategic Debates in the 1980s Western Peace Movement', in *Transnational Moments of Change: Europe 1945, 1968, 1989*, ed. Gerd-Rainer Horn and Padraic Kenney (Lanham, MD: Rowman & Littlefield, 2004), 196.

185. For an overview of such groups, see Vladimir Tismaneanu, ed., *In Search of Civil Society: Independent Peace Movements in the Soviet Bloc* (New York: Routledge, 1990).

186. See e.g. Lawrence Wittner, *Toward Nuclear Abolition: A History of the World Nuclear Disarmament Movement, 1971–Present* (Stanford, CA: Stanford University Press, 2003), 238–41.

187. Pettitt, *Walking to Greenham*, 165.

188. Burke, 'A Transcontinental Movement of Citizens?', 189–206.

189. Carter, *Peace Movements*, 127.

190. E. P. Thompson, 'Ends and Histories', in *Europe from Below: An East-West Dialogue*, ed. Mary Kaldor (London: Verso, 1991), 10.

191. 'Appeal to the Governments and People of the USSR and the USA' (4 June 1982), in Staff of the Commission on Security and Cooperation in Europe, ed., *Documents of the Soviet Groups to Establish Trust between the U.S. and the USSR* (Washington, DC: CSCE, 1984), 1–3. On these links, see Gordeeva, 'Solidarity in Search of Human Agency', esp. 358–60.

192. Pettitt, *Walking to Greenham*, 200.
193. Ibid., 275.
194. Carter, *Peace Movements*, 192. The original is E. P. Thompson, *Beyond the Cold War* (London: Merlin Press and END, 1982).
195. Padraic Kenney, *A Carnival of Revolution: Central Europe 1989* (Princeton, NJ: Princeton University Press, 2002), 93.
196. Mary Kaldor, 'Introduction', in Kaldor, *Europe from Below*, 1.
197. Ziemann, 'A Quantum of Solace?', 36; Carter, *Peace Movements*, 188. For an example of such activism by members of the *Interkerkelijk Vredesberaad*, see Wim Bartels, ed., *Tussen Oost- en West-Europa* (Amersfoort: De Horstink, 1983), which provided a forum for oppositional voices from Czechoslovakia, Hungary and Poland.
198. Cortright, *Peace*, 282.
199. Jean Furtado, ed., *Turkey: Peace on Trial* (London: Merlin Press and END, 1984), 6.
200. Ziemann, 'Situating Peace Movements', 36. In a different context, Ziemann has argued that anti-Americanism was the 'frame' – and hence 'the common factor giving a sense of identity to the peace movement through the 1970s and 1980s': Benjamin Ziemann, 'The Code of Protest: Images of Peace in the West German Peace Movements, 1945–1990', *Contemporary European History* 17, no. 2 (2008): 248.
201. Alexandros Makris, 'The Greek Peace Movement and the Vietnam War, 1964–1967', *Journal of Modern Greek Studies* 38, no. 1 (2020): 159–83; Massimo De Giuseppe and Girogio Vecchio, 'Die Friedensbewegungen in Italien', *Mitteilungsblatt des Instituts für soziale Bewegungen* 32 (2004): 131–57; Günter Wernicke, 'The World Peace Council and the Antiwar Movement in East Germany', in Daum et al., *America, the Vietnam War, and the World*, 299–320.
202. Juliane Fürst, *Flowers through Concrete: Explorations in Soviet Hippieland* (Oxford: Oxford University Press, 2021), 83–93.
203. Radina Vučetić, 'Violence against the Antiwar Demonstrations of 1965–1968 in Yugoslavia: Political Balancing between East and West', *European History Quarterly* 45, no. 2 (2015): 255–74; Boris Kanzleiter, '1968 in Yugoslavia: Student Revolt between East and West', in *Between Prague Spring and French May: Opposition and Revolt in Europe, 1960–1980*, ed. Martin Klimke, Jacco Pekelder and Joachim Scharloth (New York: Berghahn, 2011), 84–100.
204. See the breadth of contributions in Alexander Sedlmaier, ed., *Protest in the Vietnam Era* (Basingstoke: Palgrave, 2022).
205. Sylvia Ellis, 'Promoting Solidarity at Home and Abroad: The Goals and Tactics of the Anti-Vietnam War Movement in Britain', *European Review of History* 21, no. 4 (2014): 557–76.
206. Sophie Roberts, 'British Women Activists and the Campaigns against the Vietnam War, 1965–75' (PhD thesis, Northumbria University, 2018), 65 and 146–7.
207. Martin Klimke, *The Other Alliance: Student Protest in West Germany and the United States in the Global Sixties* (Princeton, NJ: Princeton University Press, 2010), 75.
208. Klimke, *The Other Alliance*, 84–6.
209. Roberts, 'British Women Activists and the Campaigns against the Vietnam War', 75–115.
210. Richard Ober, memorandum for Robert Mardian, 'The Stockholm Conference on Vietnam', 11 March 1971, doc. 0005519967, CIA FOIA Collection (electronic reading room), available via https://www.cia.gov/readingroom/docs/DOC_0005519967.pdf.

211. John Duffett, ed., *Against the Crime of Silence: Proceedings of the Russell International War Crimes Tribunal* (Flanders, NJ: O'Hare Books, 1968).
212. Moses, *The Problems of Genocide*, 420.
213. For Ali's testimony, see Tariq Ali, 'Report from Cambodia and North Vietnam', in Duffet, *Against the Crime of Silence*, 130–5.
214. Klimke, *The Other Alliance*, 91–5.
215. Tariq Ali, *Street Fighting Years: An Autobiography of the Sixties* (new edn; London: Verso, 2005), 254.
216. Alan Riding, 'Crowds in European Cities Protest a War in Gulf Area', *New York Times*, 13 January 1991, 14; Tyler Marshal, 'German Peace Activists Roll Back into Action', *Los Angeles Times*, 20 January 1991, 9.
217. Caritas Europa, 'A People Sacrificed: Sanctions against Iraq' (report, 28 February 2021), available on *ReliefWeb* (maintained by the United Nations Office for the Coordination of Human Affairs), https://reliefweb.int/report/iraq/people-sacrificed-sanctions-against-iraq-report-caritas-europa (last accessed 9 January 2023).
218. For American examples, see Mary Susannah Robbins, *Peace Not Terror: Leaders of the Antiwar Movement Speak Out against U.S. Foreign Policy Post 9/11* (Lanham, MD: Lexington Books, 2008).
219. Tarrow, *The New Transnational Activism*, 15.
220. Cortright, *Peace*, 172.
221. Timothy Peace, 'British Muslims and the Anti-War Movement', in *Muslims and Political Participation in Britain*, ed. Timothy Peace (Abingdon: Routledge, 2015), 124–37.
222. Tarrow, *The New Transnational Activism*, 171; Cortright, *Peace*, 277.
223. Victoria Carty and Jake Onyett, 'Protest, Cyberactivism and New Social Movements: The Reemergence of the Peace Movement Post 9/11', *Social Movement Studies* 5, no. 3 (2006): 229–49.
224. Mary Kaldor, *Human Security: Reflections on Globalization and Intervention* (Cambridge: Polity, 2007), 3.
225. Mary Kaldor, *New and Old Wars: Organized Violence in a Global Era* (3rd edn; Cambridge: Polity, 2012), 3.
226. Bernard-Henri Lévy, *Le lys et la cendre: journal d'un écrivain au temps de la guerre de Bosnie* (Paris: Grasset, 1996), 163.
227. Anne Madelain, *L'expérience française des Balkans (1989–1999)* (Tours: Presses universitaires François Rabelais, 2019). For comparisons of different public and political responses, see e.g. Richard Sobel and Eric Shiraev, eds, *International Public Opinion and the Bosnia Crisis* (Lanham, MD: Lexington, 2003); Thomas Cushman and Stjepan G. Meštrović, eds, *This Time We Knew: Western Responses to Genocide in Bosnia* (New York: New York University Press, 1996).
228. Kaldor has spoken of a 'humanitarian peace' approach in this context. Kaldor, *Human Security*, 59.
229. Nicolas Moss, *Solidarity Is More Than a Slogan: International Workers Aid during and after the 1992–1995 War in Bosnia and Herzegovina* (Brussels: Rosa Luxemburg Stiftung, 2021).
230. Kaldor, *Human Security*, 31.
231. Mient Jan Faber, 'Human Security from Below: Freedom from Fear and Lifeline operations', in *The Viability of Human Security*, ed. Monica den Boer and Jaap de Wilde (Amsterdam: Amsterdam University Press, 2008), 160.

232. Bojan Bilić, *We Were Gasping for Air: (Post-)Yugoslav Anti-War Activism and Its Legacy* (Baden Baden: Nomos, 2012).
233. Vesna Jankovic, 'International Peace Activists in the Former Yugoslavia: A Sociological Vignette on Transnational Agency', in *Resisting the Evil: [Post-]Yugoslav Anti-War Contention*, ed. Bojan Bilić and Vesna Jankovic (Baden Baden: Nomos, 2012), 225–42.
234. Lepa Mladjenović, 'Women in Black against War (Belgrade)', in *Feminists under Fire: Exchanges across War Zones*, ed. Wenona Giles et al. (Toronto: Between the Lines, 2003), 41. For a detailed study of Women in Black Serbia, see Bilić, *We Were Gasping for Air*, 83–108.
235. Sonja Licht and Slobodan Drakulić, 'When the Word for Peacemaker Was a Woman: War and Gender in the Former Yugoslavia', originally published in 1996 and republished in the 'Selected Papers Anniversary Issue' of the *Belgrade Women's Studies Journal* (2002), https://web.archive.org/web/20210926055506/https://www.zenskestudie.edu.rs/en/publishing/online-material/women-s-studies-journal/296-when-the-word-for-peacemaker-was-a-woman-war-and-gender-in-the-former-yugoslavia (last accessed 9 January 2023).
236. Lucht and Drakulić, 'When the Word for Peacemaker Was a Woman'.
237. Paul Stubbs, 'Networks, Organisations, Movements: Narratives and Shapes of Three Waves of Activism in Croatia', *Polemos* 15, no. 2 (2012): 17.
238. Paul Hockenos, *Homeland Calling: Exile Patriotism and the Balkan Wars* (Ithaca, NY: Cornell University Press, 2003); Brad K. Blitz, 'Serbia's War Lobby: Diaspora Groups and Western Elites', in Cushman and Meštrović, *This Time We Knew*, 187–243.
239. Cortright, *Peace*, 289.
240. Ibid., 290.
241. Kaldor, *Human Security*, 51–2.
242. Stanislaw [sic] Patejdl, 'Die Anklage', in *Die Wahrheit über den NATO-Krieg gegen Jugoslawien: Schrift des Internationalen Vorbereitungskomitees für ein Europäisches Tribunal über den NATO-Krieg gegen Jugoslawien*, ed. Wolfgang Richter, Elmar Schmähling and Eckart Spoo (Schkeuditz: Schkeuditzer Buchverlag, 2000), 250.
243. Marie Mies, 'Der Zusammenhang zwischen neoliberaler Wirtschaftspolitik und Krieg', in Richter et al., *Die Wahrheit*, 42.
244. Internationales Europäisches Tribunal über den NATO-Krieg gegen Jugoslawien: Urteil vom 3. Juni 2000', *epd-Entwicklungspolitik*, nos. 14–15 (2000): 47–9.
245. Agence-France Presse, 'Thousands of Russian Soldiers Sent to Ukraine, Say Rights Groups', *The Guardian* website, 1 September 2014, https://www.theguardian.com/world/2014/sep/01/russian-soldiers-ukraine-rights-groups (last accessed 9 January 2023).
246. On earlier transnational contacts of the committee, see Anders Uhlin, *Post-Soviet Civil Society: Democratization in Russia and the Baltic States* (Abingdon: Routledge, 2006), 128.
247. Anton Shekhovtsov, *Russia and the Western Far Right: Tango Noir* (Abingdon: Routledge, 2018); Marlene Laruelle, ed., *Eurasianism and the European Far Right: Reshaping the Europe – Russia Relationship* (Lanham, MD: Lexington, 2015).
248. Roch Dunin-Wąsowicz and Joanna Fomina, 'The Euromaidan Moment: The Making of the Ukrainian Diasporic Civil Society in Poland' as well as Serhiy Kovalchuk and Alla Korzh, 'The Transnational Activism of Young Ukrainian Immigrants', both in *Democracy, Diaspora, Territory: Europe and Cross-Border Politics*, ed. Olga Oleinikova and Jumana Bayeh (Abingdon: Routledge, 2019), 91–11 and 127–43 respectively.

249. Ganna Bazilo and Giselle Bosse, 'Invisible Peacemakers: Civil Society and Reconciliation in the East of Ukraine', in *Civil Society in Post-Euromaidan Ukraine*, ed. Natalia Shapovalova and Olga Burlyuk (Stuttgart: ibidem 2018), 153–82.

250. OSCE Special Monitoring Mission to Ukraine, *Gender Dimensions of SMM Monitoring: Women's Perceptions of Security and Their Contributions to Peace and Security, 1 November 2018 – 15 June 2021* (Kiev: OSCE, 2021), 14–15, available via https://www.osce.org/files/f/documents/6/d/498108_0.pdf (last accessed 9 January 2023).

251. 'Organising for Peace in Ukraine: An Interview with Nina Potarska', *openDemocracy*, 15 January 2020, https://www.opendemocracy.net/en/odr/organising-peace-ukraine-interview-nina-potarska/ (last accessed 9 January 2023).

252. Mary Kaldor, 'The Ukraine Crisis: How to Respond', *Social Europe*, 22 February 2022, https://socialeurope.eu/the-ukraine-crisis-how-to-respond (last accessed 9 January 2023).

253. Kaldor, *Human Security*, 32.

254. Patrice McMahon, *The NGO Game: Post-Conflict Peacebuilding in the Balkans and Beyond* (Ithaca, NY: Cornell University Press, 2017), 2.

255. McMahon, *The NGO Game*, 121; Steven Sampson, 'Weak States, Uncivil Societies and Thousands of NGOs: Benevolent Colonialism in the Balkans', in *The Balkans in Focus: Cultural Boundaries in Europe*, ed. Sanimir Resic and Barbara Törnquist-Plewa (Lund: Nordic Academic Press, 2002), 27–44.

256. Stefanie Kappler and Oliver Richmond, 'Peacebuilding and Culture in Bosnia and Herzegovina: Resistance or Emancipation?', *Security Dialogue* 42, no. 3 (2011): 265.

257. Julie Nietsch, 'The Mother Teresa Society: Volunteer Work for the Kosovo–Albanian "Parallel Structures" in the 1990s', *Comparative Southeast European Studies* 68, no. 2 (2020): 200–24.

258. Gani Demolli, 'The Mother Teresa Society and the War in Kosovo', *Humanitarian Exchange*, no. 21 (July 2002): 14.

259. McMahon, *The NGO Game*, 124–5.

260. Demolli, 'The Mother Teresa Society', 14.

261. Ryerson Christie, *Peacebuilding and NGOs: State–Civil Society Interactions* (Abingdon: Routledge, 2013), 51.

262. Christie, *Peacebuilding and NGOs*, 65.

263. Heiko Wimmen, 'Divided They Stand: Peace Building, State Reconstruction and Informal Political Movements in Bosnia-Herzegovina, 2005–2013', in *Social Movements in the Balkans: Rebellion and Protest from Maribor to Taksim*, ed. Florian Bieber and Dario Brentin (Abingdon: Routledge, 2019), 14–15.

264. Wimmen, 'Divided They Stand', 14.

265. Catherine Baker and Jelena Obradovic-Wochnik, 'Mapping the Nexus of Transitional Justice and Peacebuilding', *Journal of Intervention and Statebuilding* 10, no. 3 (2016): 281–301.

266. Maria O'Reilly, *Gendered Agency in War and Peace: Gender Justice and Women's Activism in Post-Conflict Bosnia-Herzegovina* (London: Palgrave, 2013), 152.

267. O'Reilly, *Gendered Agency*, 151.

268. Ibid., 152.

CHAPTER 4
CLASS, REVOLUTION AND SOCIAL JUSTICE

What is the relationship between nationhood, class and the principle of international solidarity? To many socialists, this question has proven challenging, both in theory and in practice. In their *Communist Manifesto*, Karl Marx and Friedrich Engels famously proclaimed that workers had 'no country' and argued that 'the proletariat must first of all ... constitute itself the nation'.[1] Yet both the meaning and implications of this statement left room for interpretation. In 1965, the Ukrainian Marxist economist and historian Roman Rosdolsky discussed the famous passage in an article for the American journal *Science & Society*.[2] In his short piece, Rosdolsky argued against two contrasting interpretations. On the one hand, he dismissed those who ascribed notions of a 'proletarian nationalism' to Marx, in a way that 'reduced the internationalism of the working-class movement to the desire for international cooperation among peoples'.[3] On the other hand, he insisted that the *Manifesto* had not suggested 'that the proletariat should be indifferent with respect to national movements'. According to Rosdolsky, the *Communist Manifesto* was not anti-national, yet it had shown that a classless society would only be 'possible on an international scale'.[4] He also noted the importance of acknowledging 'the inherent cosmopolitan tendency of the worker's [sic] movement'.

As illustrated by Rosdolsky's reflections, the relationship between class-based action and the nation was far from clear-cut. Many socialists agreed that the pursuit of equality transcended national boundaries, yet they did so without rejecting national categories altogether. Indeed, Rosdolsky's own background testified to the significance of national ideas. Born in 1897 in the Galician part of the Austro-Hungarian empire, he came from a family in which Ukrainian national sentiment was strong. Rosdolsky himself later claimed that 'he had undergone an evolution from Ukrainian nationalism to internationalism'.[5] However, as a retrospective appraisal argued, 'everything that Rosdolsky wrote bore testimony that the author was a Ukrainian, the son of a nation with a difficult and so often tragic history'. As a theorist, he repeatedly addressed the relationship between socialism and nationalism, for instance in a piece that discussed Engels's dismissal of 'nonhistoric nations'.[6] Moreover, in the 1920s, Rosdolsky was active in the Communist Party of Eastern Galicia (later: Communist Party of Western Ukraine). Covering the areas that had become part of the Polish Second Republic, the party argued for Western Ukraine's integration into the Ukrainian Soviet Socialist Republic and thus into the Soviet Union.

Rosdolsky's life story and theoretical work were connected to the development and divisions of the communist movement, yet they point at wider issues in the history of the left, namely the manifold entanglements between individual mobility, ideological disputes and a concern for internationalism. In discussing 'the left', this chapter covers a broad spectrum of political thought and action, encompassing socialism, anarchism, communism, trade unionism and countercultural forms of activism. An inclusive approach makes sense: despite intense ideological conflict, different factions on the left and their protagonists had significant commonalities, including their rejection of the inequalities generated by capitalism. Importantly, left-wing practice rarely confined itself to one specific movement or ideology. As Geoff Eley has argued 'socialism was always the core of the Left; and the Left was always larger than socialism', since socialists 'always needed allies'.[7] Moreover, many individuals shifted political allegiances over time, because of outward pressures or personal disillusionment. This was also the case with Rosdolsky, who ruptured with the Comintern in the 1930s and aligned himself with Polish Trotskyism.[8]

Most crucially – as far as the subject of this book is concerned – transnational cooperation was important across the entire spectrum of the left. For example, Constance Bantman and Davide Turcato have demonstrated that both French and Italian anarchism in the late nineteenth and early twentieth centuries can be understood as transnational phenomena.[9] With regard to the interwar years, Brigitte Studer has shown how protagonists of international communism inhabited a 'transnational world' in the 1920s and 1930s.[10] Yet it was not only protagonists of revolutionary action who espoused internationalism. With regard to the aftermath of both world wars, Talbot Imlay has stressed the strength of socialist internationalism, with parties seeking 'to contribute to the task of recasting international relations in a new mould'.[11]

This chapter highlights different transnational and national dimensions of the quest for social change. It begins with a consideration of exile as a terrain for political activism and subsequently covers different efforts to place transnational alliances on an organizational footing. Later sections move on to forms of activism that avoid large-scale organization-building and instead focused on temporary coalitions that staged social and political protest.

Mobility, exile and the left

As Frank Jacob and Mario Keßler have argued, 'the possibilities and the wish for internationalization' were but one factor for '[t]he transnationality of … political radicals and their lives' as 'the transnational momentum was created by forced migration and state power intervention'.[12] Such observations also apply to Roman Rosdolsky. Faced with pressure from the Polish authorities during the early 1920s, he emigrated to Prague and then Vienna, where he became the Austrian correspondent for the Marx-Engels Institute in Moscow. In this period, he completed a doctorate at the University of Vienna and 'was intimately connected with the Austrian left' – which also meant that in the early 1930s, the repressive policies of the Dollfuss dictatorship forced his departure, with Rosdolsky returning to his birth city of Lviv/Lwów in the Republic of Poland.[13] Following Germany's invasion of Poland in 1939, he joined the anti-fascist resistance, was captured and survived imprisonment in Nazi concentration camps.[14] After the Second World War,

Rosdolsky moved to the United States, where he wrote the article that this chapter has started with. After his death, Trotskyists of the 'Fourth International' noted that although he had 'ceased to be active politically' after his move to the United States, 'he never stopped considering himself a sympathizer of the international Trotskyist movement'.[15]

Rosdolsky's case shows how both the threat of persecution and political affinities produced border crossings. He was hardly a solitary case. Well before his lifetime, exile and migration were key features of the European left. Between the mid-nineteenth century and the end of the First World War, three waves of exile had major consequences for the development of radical politics: the search for refuge after the 1848 revolutions, the transnational circulations of anarchists in the late nineteenth century and the impact of Russian exile politics.

The events of 1848 comprised a range of political movements, aims and ideas – and reconciling them proved difficult in practice: national liberation or unification, constitutional reform, parliamentarianism, a defence of basic freedoms as well as social emancipation all featured prominently on activists' agendas.[16] As such, not all protagonists of change in 1848 considered themselves part of 'the left', yet the European nature of the 1848 revolutions meant that it generated transnational publicity for a variety of causes.[17] For instance, Giuseppe Garibaldi's leadership in the struggle for a united and republican Italy inspired a veritable 'cult', turning the Italian radical into a figure with global appeal.[18] Lajos Kossuth, leader of the Hungarian Revolution, was another example, being revered as a hero in both Britain and the United States.[19] Indeed, support for national liberation – with regard to not only Italy and Hungary, but also Poland – nurtured transnational bonds.

The European public that manifested itself in 1848 enabled exiles to engage with audiences in their host countries. Exile groups played an increasingly prominent role because the defeat of the revolutionary movements in or after 1849 triggered a wave of political migration. For example, the historian Heléna Tóth has traced the move of activists from Hungary and South-West Germany to Switzerland, Britain, the United States and the Ottoman Empire.[20] Transnational mobility, whether in the cases examined by Tóth or by other groups, built upon earlier migrations. For example, already in the 1820s and 1830s, Italian radicals had constituted a 'Risorgimento in exile', which included the republican Giuseppe Mazzini, the followers of his Young Italy movement as well as members of the clandestine *Carbonari* network.[21]

By 1848, several countries were well-established destinations for political exiles, with new arrivals joining existing diasporic communities. This, for instance, was the case in Switzerland, which had an established German exile community.[22] On a larger scale, diasporic ties also mattered in the United States, which had absorbed a substantial immigrant population from Europe. When an estimated 3,000 to 4,000 German 'Forty-Eighters' crossed the North Atlantic, German Americans could help with the challenge of building both a new home and a sense of belonging.[23] Some German radicals established new forms of engagement overseas, as exemplified by Friedrich Hecker and Carl Schurz, two prominent leaders of the 1848 revolutions in south-west Germany: Hecker became a Union Army commander in the American Civil War, while Schurz attained political prominence as a Senator, Secretary of the Interior and vocal opponent of American imperial expansion.[24]

Meanwhile, Britain's role as a destination for exiles built on the country's liberal asylum policy: as Bernard Porter has pointed out, 'between 1823 and 1906 no refugee who came to Britain was ever denied entry, or expelled'.[25] Rosemary Ashton has noted that '[b]y 1848 ... no other country was more open to either the spokesmen or the practitioners of revolution than Britain'.[26] One example was Gottfried Kinkel, who had cooperated with Carl Schurz in the Rhineland and Palatinate. Having escaped prison, Kinkel settled in London, where he became a member of the Communist League – the very organization for which Marx and Engels had written their *Communist Manifesto*. Indeed, both Kinkel and Marx soon were on opposing sides of the disputes that ruptured the group.[27] In 1860, the former's wife, Johanna Kinkel, wrote a novel on 'refugee life in London' that pointed to such divisions: her text suggested that, without employment or other meaning to their new lives, many exiled men spent all their time dedicating themselves to political disputes that had taken the place of 'personal gossip'.[28]

Such observations reinforce Rosemary Ashton's characterization of exile life in London as being characterized by 'internecine battles and general impotence'.[29] This, however, does not make the influx of political refugees inconsequential. Exile in this period involved a significant degree of coalition-building, bringing together protagonists of national independence and advocates of social revolution. In the mid-nineteenth century, the boundaries between different oppositional currents remained fluid: in the 1840s and 1850s, the term 'democrat' encompassed a variety of stances, including socialism. The Democratic Friends of All Nations were one of these alliances, bringing together British socialists and exiles from France, Germany and Poland. Having been founded in 1844, this group 'formed a bridge and a transition between earlier forms of republican and democratic cosmopolitanism and late socialist internationalism in a more general sense'.[30] Several other associations of workers and democrats followed in the subsequent two decades, for instance the Brussels-based *Association Fédérative Universelle* in 1863.[31] These ventures were forerunners of the International Workingmen's Association – the 'First International' – and they indicate that the developments of the late 1840s continued to inform the exiles' political interests in the era of the First International's formation in 1864. Indeed, as one account noted, 'In London of 1864, the dominant passion among political exiles was not the founding of the International, but the organization of a tumultuously successful visit by Garibaldi.'[32]

Another major aspect of the transnational left – again with exile as a prominent feature – was the growth of the anarchist movement in the second half of the nineteenth century. The work of anarchist thinkers such as Pierre-Joseph Proudhon was widely discussed, also within the First International.[33] By the 1880s, anarchism constituted an international movement. As Benedict Anderson put it, after 'the collapse of the First International, and Marx's death in 1883, anarchism, in its characteristically variegated forms, was the dominant element in the self-consciously international radical Left'.[34] The ties and trajectory of the Italian anarchist Errico Malatesta illustrate anarchism's global and transnational features. The political scientist Carl Levy has portrayed the

Italian radical as 'a prime exemplar of the nomadic political left, which emerged in that antebellum era of globalisation between the late nineteenth century and 1914'.[35] Summarizing Malatesta's stints as an 'exilic intellectual revolutionary, tramping artisan and global labour organiser', Levy has noted his role as 'an erstwhile Garibaldian "freedom fighter" in Bosnia (1876) and Egypt (1882)', his stints as 'an anarchist and trade union and trade union organiser' in Argentina, the United States and Cuba (1885–90) as well as sojourns 'in Switzerland, Spain, France, Malta, Romania, the Levant (Egypt, Lebanon, Syria and Turkey), Romania and Belgium'. Yet, beyond these different places, London provided 'his main base'.[36]

Malatesta's presence in Britain was but one indication of the country's appeal to political radicals of all sorts. According to the Russian-born American anarchist Emma Goldman, the country was 'the haven for refugees from all lands, who carried on their work without hindrance' and argued that, in comparison to the United States, 'the political freedom in Great Britain seemed like the millennium come'.[37] The historians Pietro Di Paola and Constance Bantman have traced how Italian and French anarchists developed their respective ties and propaganda efforts in London.[38] Likewise, German anarchists formed a community that built on the earlier presence of socialist exiles.[39] In 1881, this transnational community staged a congress of 'socialist revolutionaries' in the British metropolis. According to the Austrian activist Josef Peukert, the event featured anarchists of 'nearly all European countries'.[40] Shortly after the congress, a report from the Prussian political police – which monitored socialist and anarchist action internationally – saw London as the centre of 'the entire European revolutionary agitation'.[41]

Attempts to forge more durable structures beyond sporadic anarchist congresses proved difficult.[42] This was not necessarily a question of failure. In Peukert's eyes, it merely reflected the anarchists' insistence on personal freedom: 'Up to that point, all assemblies of this kind had considered themselves a supra-authority, a legislating body that would decide for the masses what they would consider good and right, what they are to do and not do.' By contrast, the London congress 'broke with this authoritarian tradition', as it only considered itself 'a consultative assembly of individuals, whose common striving was for the emancipation of the exploited and fettered masses'.[43]

Instead of building international organizations, the anarchist experience amounted to something that the historian Constance Bantman has dubbed 'informal internationalism'.[44] In this context, the clubhouses set up by exile groups became sites of transnational encounters. For example, when German and Austrian anarchists planned a new venue in London, the Club Autonomie, in 1886, it attracted interest among other groups: according to its co-founder Peukert, 'the French, Italian and Slavic groups waited impatiently for its completion so as to make it their home'.[45] This statement was more than wishful thinking, as the club did indeed emerge as a meeting ground for anarchists from different countries.[46]

With a plethora of such social spaces, London remained a centre for anarchist activity in the 1890s and 1900s. On her first trip to Britain in 1895, Emma Goldman therefore sought to meet 'the outstanding personalities in the anarchist movement'.[47] In London, she encountered Malatesta – although communication was hampered by his lack of English – and Louise Michel, the widely admired French revolutionary who, during her London years, launched a range of political efforts, including a campaign to defend the right to asylum.[48] Most significantly, Goldman fulfilled her 'long-cherished dream, to meet my great teacher', the Russian anarchist Peter Kropotkin.[49] Goldman's reverence for Kropotkin exemplified his reputation within radical circles. For example, German-speaking anarchists in London issued translations of Kropotkin's texts as part of an 'anarchist-communist library' series while also featuring pieces by the Russian thinker in their weekly *Die Autonomie*.[50] Peukert, one of the journal's founders, noted that he had first encountered Kropotkin's writings in the French periodical *Le Revolté*, further illustrating the transnational reach of Kropotkin's ideas.[51] These observations also point to a wider issue – namely the role of well-connected activists and thinkers such as Malatesta and Kropotkin for the functioning of anarchism as a transnational movement.

By the late nineteenth century, anarchism's association with political violence – in particular the use of assassinations – alarmed many national authorities. Between 1878 and 1914, a range of attacks led to the death or serious injury of political leaders and monarchs. Several incidents had transnational dimensions: for example, Italian anarchists killed the French president Sadi Carnot (1894), the Spanish Prime Minister Antonio Cánovas del Castillo (1897) and Elisabeth, Empress of Austria (1898). In 1905, Armenian revolutionaries carried out an unsuccessful attempt on the Ottoman Sultan Abdülhamid II, having accessed training and tools in Bulgaria and Switzerland. They were aided by an Istanbul-based Belgian anarchist, Edward Joris, whose subsequent arrest by the Ottoman authorities caused protests in Belgium as well as diplomatic complications.[52] In an era of growing fears of 'anarchist terror', governments stepped up their efforts for transnational surveillance and took tentative steps to coordinate their efforts diplomatically.[53]

Not all anarchists supported the 'propaganda of the deed', yet the need to evade arrest meant that its proponents had transnational life stories. One prominent advocate of political violence – whose association with this strategy emerged whilst in exile – was Johann (John) Most, who initially rose to prominence as a Reichstag deputy for the German Social Democrats. Most arrived in London in late 1879, having been forced abroad by Bismarck's Anti-Socialist Laws. In exile, he moved towards socialist-revolutionary and, ultimately, anarchist positions, which he disseminated through his periodical *Freiheit* ('Freedom'). In 1882, Most was sentenced and imprisoned for publishing an editorial that rejoiced in the assassination of Tsar Alexander II.[54] While the British authorities largely tolerated the political activism of foreign subjects, their firmer response to Most can partly be attributed to the contemporaneous concerns about Fenian terrorism in both Ireland and England.[55] Shortly after his release from prison, he moved to New York, where he continued his activism as an anarchist publisher and orator. There, he also influenced Emma Goldman, although she subsequently criticized his intolerance of dissent.[56] Most was but one member of the diasporic communities that shaped American anarchism, with German, Italian and Eastern European Jewish immigrants all coming to play significant parts.[57]

Most's celebration of Alexander II's death was but one example of Russian events that seized the attention of activists in other countries. In 1879, Russian socialist revolutionaries had founded *Narodnaya Volya* ('The People's Will'), which adopted the 'propaganda of the deed' and planned the Tsar's assassination. Moreover, shortly before the group's formation, the revolutionary Vera Zasulich had attracted prominence for both her attempt to assassinate the governor of St Petersburg and her sensational acquittal. Having escaped Russia before her trial, Zasulich moved towards Marxism and opposed the use of assassinations. Notwithstanding this shift, British activists viewed her with fascination, being intrigued by the image of Russian women revolutionaries such as Sophia Perovskaya, the *Narodnaya Volya* member who had been executed for her role in the killing of Alexander II.[58]

The repressive nature of Tsarist policies meant that political migration from Russia predated the terror wave of the late nineteenth century.[59] For example, Alexander Herzen – a pioneering figure in Russian socialism – had emigrated in 1847, moving first to Risorgimento-era Italy and then onwards to France, before settling in Britain.[60] Similarly, Bakunin escaped his Siberian exile in 1861, with subsequent stints in Japan, Italy, France and Britain. By the 1880s, however, the growing association of Russian oppositional activity with the use of violence caused obstacles for exiles. For example, shortly after the assassination of Alexander II, the Swiss authorities expelled Peter Kropotkin, who had moved to Switzerland after escaping from a Russian prison in 1876. Yet Kropotkin's case also indicates that such rejection was far from universal: his own stance on terror remained diffuse, which did not prevent him from exercising appeal well beyond anarchist circles.[61] Moreover, as the historian Michael Hughes has shown, the nature of Tsarist repression meant that during the 1880s, British public opinion shifted towards sympathy with the Russian opposition.[62] Russian exiles were actively involved in forging a more positive image of their comrades. For example, the Russian anarchist Stepniak portrayed Russian revolutionaries sympathetically in his *Sketches from the Russian Underground*. In doing so, he argued that Russian revolutionaries were far from isolated in their rejection of the government: 'If the Government were not in such flagrant contraction with society, such a struggle would be absolutely impossible, for society would not remain indifferent, but would act as one man against the disturbers of its quiet and crush them in one instant.'[63] Even British liberals whose politics were quite distant from socialism or anarchism expressed support for Russian activists whom they considered victims of tyranny.[64]

Of the different kinds of Russian political emigration, the one to have the most durable impact was associated with the Russian Social Democratic Workers' Party, which had been formed along Marxist lines in 1893. Much of the party's history before 1917 was one of exile. During the period between 1903 and 1917, Lenin spent more than six years in Switzerland – repeatedly in Geneva, and later in Bern and Zürich.[65] Moreover, with the exception of its foundation in Minsk (1898), all pre-1917 party congresses were held outside the Russian Empire, in London, Brussels and Stockholm. Accordingly, the famous rift between Mensheviks and Bolsheviks occurred abroad, at the 1903 congress in London – and when the Russian socialists returned to London in

1907, it became obvious that Bolsheviks had increased their influence and that 'Lenin's star was in the ascendant'.[66]

The Russian socialists' exile operations coincided with the wider interest generated by the political changes in Russia. Emma Goldman described the Russian revolution of 1905 'as 'electrifying' and stated that these events had 'carried us to ecstatic heights'.[67] Angelica Balabanoff, a Russian Marxist who had studied in Belgium and then became involved in Italian socialism, later recounted her impressions of this period. She noted that news of the 1905 revolution attracted widespread enthusiasm in Italy, arguing that 'the Italian masses ... shared a solidarity with their Russian comrades which was unequalled by the workers of any other nation'.[68] Balabanoff herself sought to fuel such sentiments, undertaking various efforts aimed at 'gaining sympathy and raising funds for Russian revolutionaries in Italy'. This activism equipped her well for a subsequent role: in 1919–20, before her disillusionment with Bolshevism, she served as the Secretary of the Comintern, the body whose role as a vehicle for transnational cooperation is discussed later on in this chapter.

Organization-building before the First World War

While exile meant insecurity and instability for the activists who had been forced into it, it also nurtured efforts to place transnational ties on an organizational footing. In 1864, political refugees were prominently involved in founding the First International, bringing together followers of Marx but also trade unionists, anarchists and republicans.[69] Soon thereafter, the International ruptured into two camps – one led by Marx, the other by Bakunin. In 1872, the International's congress at The Hague expelled the anarchist faction; thereafter, a depleted International continued its work until 1876. While such rifts seemed to signify a lack of coherence, they showed that protagonists could form alliances, albeit transient in nature. This characteristic also applied to the short-lived international venture launched by Bakunin and his followers in St Imier, Switzerland (1872). While dominated by anarchists, its initial appeal extended to 'moderate British trade unionists', who were attracted by the greater degree of autonomy that this association promised when compared to the First International.[70]

Although several meetings sought to relaunch the International in the 1880s, it took until 1889 before such endeavours created the Second International. The circumstances of its formation revealed further divisions. Staged in Paris on the centenary of the French Revolution, two international socialist congresses competed with one another – one led by the French 'Possibilists', who pursued a reformist agenda; the other, larger one dominated by Marxist currents. While sympathetic to the latter venture, a report by London-based German socialists downplayed these ideological differences: it argued that the divisions were mostly due to 'questions of shape and organization, and only partially because of the tactic that is to be observed'. While conceding that such matters were 'of great importance to class-conscious workers of any country', they were not supposed to hold any 'major significance at an international congress'.[71] Such statements recognized the value of re-establishing socialist cooperation along transnational lines.

From 1890 onwards, Possibilists and Marxists did indeed join forces within the Second International. By contrast, anarchists were largely excluded from the proceedings. The anarchist Rudolf Rocker later stated that the 1891 congress – held in Brussels – had given him 'occasion for losing some of my youthful illusions' and regarded the 1896 congress in London as indicative of socialist intolerance, as reflected in its 'brutal trampling down on all freedom of opinion'.[72] At Brussels, the Dutch socialist Ferdinand Domela Nieuwenhuis – who was often cast as an anarchist, without describing himself as such – had opposed this step. In a sympathetic portrait, the British Labour politician Keir Hardie argued that Domela Nieuwenhuis believed 'that all who are engaged in any department of the Socialist movement ought to be free to attend an International Socialist Congress'.[73]

With anarchists absent, subsequent divisions in the Second International mostly involved disputes between, on the one side, Marxist advocates of class struggle and, on the other, reformists who sought progress by working through existing institutions. By the late 1890s, the dividing line no longer just pitted French Possibilists against German Marxists: Eduard Bernstein – the most prominent protagonist of reformist 'revisionism' – came from Germany. Bernstein's own ideological development coincided with several personal border crossings. Following the enactment of Bismarck's Anti-Socialist Laws in 1878, Bernstein joined other socialist leaders in moving to Switzerland, where he also met fellow exile Karl Kautsky, later the predominant theorist of German socialism. Over the subsequent years, Bernstein, Kautsky and the London-based Friedrich Engels 'laid the intellectual and programmatic fundament for the Marxification of German social democracy'.[74] One major role of Bernstein in this period was his editorship of the German socialists' exile periodical *Der Sozialdemokrat*. In 1888, diplomatic pressure led the Swiss authorities to expel the paper. Unsurprisingly, to socialists, this step suggested that 'formerly free Switzerland' had become 'the lackey of Prussian-German reaction'.[75]

Along with other German comrades, Bernstein moved to England, which he had previously visited – first in 1884 upon Engels's invitation, and then in 1887 'in order to negotiate with the English socialists in respect of a' Socialist and Labour Congress to be held the following year'.[76] His subsequent choice to settle in the city's Kentish Town area was influenced by the fact that Engels resided there.[77] In this era, Bernstein still promoted the Marxist currents that dominated his party, yet by the late 1890s, he departed from this position. At one level, Bernstein's critique of Marxism was on theoretical grounds – yet it also applied to questions of political practice, as his conclusions led him to champion parliamentary routes to power. Many observers ascribed Bernstein's changing position to his experiences in Britain. As the historian Roger Fletcher put it, 'The only explanation that made any sense to the vast majority of Bernstein's contemporaries – German and otherwise, friend and foe alike – was that his long years of exile in London had either addled his brain or distorted his vision, leading him to view the world through a Fabian, a Labourite, or a Liberal lens.'[78] While Fletcher has shown that such representations were an oversimplification, he has noted the influence of British radicals' views on free trade as an influential factor.

The emphasis on British influences indicated that Marxism was by no means the only current within the Second International. Amongst the latter's British members, only the Social Democratic Federation adopted Marxian principles, whereas 'the other British affiliates were not really in the European mould', being focused on social reform.[79] Meanwhile, the Belgian Workers' Party (*Parti Ouvrier Belge*) promoted a form of 'revolutionary reformism' that combined an embrace of strike action with an emphasis on franchise expansion.[80] Belgians played a prominent part in international socialism, with Brussels hosting the secretariat of the Second International, the International Socialist Bureau, from 1900 onwards.

Because of its structure with an international secretariat and national branches, the historian Moira Donald has described the Second International as 'a prototype of an international organisation'.[81] Moreover, its wider framework nurtured new transnational ventures. The Second International's Stuttgart congress in 1907 was a crucial event in this respect. In the run-up to the conference, German activists intensified preparations to create 'an international federation of organizations for socialist workers' youth'.[82] Initial steps included a 'provisional bulletin' and the establishment of a correspondence network under the leadership of the Belgian activist Henri de Man, at that point a student in Leipzig.[83] The formal creation of the Socialist Youth International then occurred at a meeting that coincided with the Second International's congress. De Man and in his successor as secretary of the new organization, Robert Dannenberg, later played prominent roles in, respectively, Belgian and Austrian socialism, illustrating how such activism could form part of a wider trajectory.

The Second International's 1907 congress also proved consequential in another respect: it went hand in hand with a women's conference that launched an International Bureau of Socialist Women. The debates in Stuttgart highlighted some of the divisions regarding women's suffrage and the broader relationship between socialism and feminism. Looking back at 1907, the Russian activist Alexandra Kollontai argued that 'not only male Social-Democrats, but even the women revealed their fundamental instability, their vacillation, and by their compromising attitude to this issue … demonstrated that this fundamental principle has not yet become an integral part of Social-Democracy'.[84] Kollontai's comments reflected two contrasting stances, both of which she rejected: the Russian activist opposed socialists who cooperated with 'bourgeois' feminists because, in her view, they had lost track of class struggle and its primacy; yet she also criticized those who downplayed the importance of gaining rights for working women.

Kollontai's views on the indivisibility of women's and worker's rights prevailed in 1907. As the author of the successful congress resolution on this issue, the German socialist Clara Zektin proclaimed that activists had, on the one hand, defeated the 'opportunistic, bourgeois conviction' that would have endorsed women's suffrage without addressing the fundamental issue of class and, on the other hand, ensured that socialist parties would support women's suffrage without qualification.[85] To Kollontai, these steps amounted to a 'courageous rejection of and revulsion towards compromise decisions', although in practical terms, the extent of active support for women's suffrage continued to vary significantly across different socialist parties.[86]

While the youth and women's ventures maintained a direct relationship with the Second International, labour internationalism also involved the construction of separate structures. For example, anarchists, revolutionary socialists and syndicalists came together in the Industrial Workers of the World, which had been founded in Chicago in 1905.[87] From the outset, immigrant workers played an important role within the organization, which ultimately sought to build an international trade union, dedicated to workers' direct action.

A different form of labour internationalism focused on individual trades and practical cooperation. Internationalism in some sectors was slow to develop, yet recent work has highlighted several endeavours, from an international congress of miners in Jolimont, Belgium, in 1890 to other forms of targeted cooperation.[88] From the 1890s, International Trade Union Secretariats served as vehicles for cooperation within specific industry sectors.[89] Moreover, in 1901, the Congress of Scandinavian Trade Unions in Copenhagen attracted foreign delegates who endorsed plans for regular international meetings, with a Dublin-based secretariat supporting such events from 1903 onwards. As the French trade unionist Léon Jonhaux later acknowledged, the remit of these bodies remained 'limited, at first extending only to the compilation of common statistics, the exchange of information on legislation affecting labor, and eventually to solidarity in the event of important strikes'.[90] Yet the reduced scale arguably facilitated the growth of these ventures, as the stakes for participation remained low. By 1913, eighteen national centres with altogether 7 million workers had affiliated to the Dublin secretariat.[91] After the First World War, a revival of such efforts led to the creation of the International Federation of Trade Unions – also known as 'Amsterdam International', in reference to the city where its secretariat was based. The historian Geert Van Goethem has argued that in terms of its overarching aim – namely the pursuit of peace – the Amsterdam International failed, yet he has also noted its resilience: the organization 'survived a succession of severe internal crises' and served as 'a forum for the discussions that caused dissension within international social democracy' during the interwar years.[92]

The 'Amsterdam International' was not the only international federation for trade unionists in this era. The late nineteenth and early twentieth centuries had seen the growth of a Christian labour movement, supported by the publication of *Rerum Novarum* (1891), Pope Leo XIII's encyclical on 'the rights and duties of capital and labour'.[93] In 1920, this movement established a separate International Federation of Christian Trade Unions (Confédération Internationale des Syndicats Chrétiens, CISC). The historians Frank Georgi and Lex Heerma van Voss have described the aims of CISC – which opposed both socialism and liberalism while promoting 'the principle of workers participating in economic decision-making' – as 'necessarily vague' and yet 'enduring'.[94] Both the 'Amsterdam International' and CISC pointed to post-war developments, as the World Federation of Trade Unions (1945), the World Federation of Labour (1945) and the International Confederation of Free Trade Unions (1949) continued the tradition of international trade union cooperation. The existence of these different organizations reflected ideological divisions: while founded as a successor to the 'Amsterdam International', the first of these bodies soon came under communist influence, triggering the creation of the International Confederation of Free Trade Unions; meanwhile, the World Federation of Labour continued CISC's work in the field of Christian trade unionism.

Alongside socialist and trade union cooperation, there was another movement that promoted workers' interests and built transnational organizational ties: consumer cooperation. The cooperative movement had arisen as a way of addressing the cost of food and other goods for workers, and developed across several countries. Such efforts had tangible benefits, as consumer co-operation 'acted as a check on the worst excesses of … globalization, helping to shield poor customers from the fluctuations of the market'.[95] There were significant variations, both in terms of the links between co-operation and socialism and in the models that were being pursued.[96] Notwithstanding such differences, by 1895, different national co-operative groups came together in founding the International Co-operative Alliance, which also benefited from the strength of individual co-operative movements, as illustrated by the prominent role of co-operators from the Nordic countries.[97]

A culture of internationalism

Internationalism was not just an ideological disposition, a rhetorical device or an impetus to create international organizations: it was actively maintained through publications, educational ventures and cultural activities. Importantly, transnational dissemination could help socialist and anarchist periodicals evade censorship and repression. For instance, having been forced to depart from their Swiss exile and moved to Britain, Bernstein and his fellow editors of *Der Sozialdemokrat* ensured the ongoing production and distribution of their paper.[98] Likewise, after Johann Most had left London for New York, his *Freiheit* continued to be distributed internationally, making its way from the United States to Germany via Britain.[99] In several cases, journal production abroad helped to sustain individual national movements. For example, *Iskra* ('The Spark') – the paper of the Russian Social Democratic Labour Party – was published from Germany, Switzerland and Britain between 1900 and 1905.[100]

Local and national organizing provided a framework for periodicals with an international reach. For example, as Emma Goldman noted, the German anarchist Rudolf Rocker was '[t]he moving spirit' of anarchist undertakings among the Eastern European Jewish community in the East End, constituting 'the peculiar phenomenon of a Gentile editor of a Yiddish paper'.[101] Goldman herself helped to raise funds for Rocker's publishing ventures.[102] In the early twentieth century, one of Rocker's ventures – the journal *Germinal* – also reached Yiddish-speaking anarchists abroad, thus amounting to a paper that was local and international at once: Rocker himself stated that it 'attracted a good circle of readers, not only in England and the British Isles, but in most of the big cities of America, and in Paris, Berlin, Bucharest, Sofia, Cairo, Alexandria, Johannesburg, Cape Town, Buenos Aires'.[103] From a different political angle, the socialist women's conference of 1907 designated *Die Gleichheit* ('Equality') – the main socialist women's periodical in Germany – as its international organ. In practice, its content remained focused on Germany, but with reports from other countries as well as broader theoretical debates. In 1910, the Second International Conference of Socialist Women concluded that *Die Gleichheit* had 'proven its worth as a central office and publication vehicle for [our] international correspondence'.[104]

Educational efforts complemented such publishing activities. In many countries, trade unions and socialist parties maintained their own libraries, study circles and schools, at a time when working-class access to educational opportunities remained limited. Yet the educational activities of the European left also had transnational dimensions. This was particularly the case for anarchists, who viewed education as central to fostering the attitudes and qualities that would sustain a future society. In some cases, their activities originated within specific political contexts. For example, in 1890, Louise Michel – whose prior life in France had included stints as a teacher and headmistress – created an International Anarchist School in London, aimed at the children of political exiles.[105] Other anarchists combined pedagogical thought and practice. In Spain, the anarchist Francisco Ferrer y Guardia implemented a pedagogy based on libertarian principles at his 'Modern School' in Barcelona.[106] Ferrer's activism had transnational features in more than one way: because of his suspected involvement in an attempted coup, he spent sixteen years in French exile (1885–1901), where he forged international contacts that supported the creation of Ferrer's International League for the Rational Education of Children.[107] Moreover, in 1909, his arrest and subsequent execution in Spain – having been blamed for the popular unrest of Barcelona's 'Tragic Week' that year – triggered an international solidarity campaign.[108] To Emma Goldman, who addressed a large-scale protest meeting in New York, Ferrer was being punished for his efforts 'to free the child from superstition and bigotry, from the darkness of dogma and authority'.[109] Well beyond his lifetime, Ferrer's educational ideas were widely discussed, not only among anarchists but also among pedagogues and activists who shared his emphasis on secular education.[110]

Publishing activities and educational work were but two ways in which left-wing activists forged a sense of their past and a vision of their future. Music played a part in this, too, exemplified by the widespread use of the *Marseillaise*, which had originated in the French Revolutionary Wars.[111] Moreover, two events loomed particularly large in the commemorative culture of the left: one was the crushing of the Paris Commune (1871) – in whose aftermath the words to another iconic song, namely the *Internationale*, were written.[112] The other event was the sentencing of eight anarchists who were blamed for detonating a bomb during a workers' demonstration on Chicago's Haymarket (1886).

Both the Commune and the Haymarket Affair were international matters in more than one sense. The former had involved adherents of the First International among its protagonists,[113] while the latter had included one British-born and six German-born anarchists among the accused. Moreover, both at the time and in subsequent years, these events were widely dissected. Many prominent thinkers and activists – including Marx, Bakunin and Lenin – analysed the Commune's defeat, and the Chicago events attracted widespread international attention, causing expressions of solidarity even among groups that were unsympathetic to anarchism as such.[114] The execution of 147 Commune soldiers on Père Lachaise cemetery in Paris as well as the execution of four of the Haymarket accused (and suicide in prison of one) in 1887 meant that commemorative activities focused on the 'martyrs' of the past. Both the crushing of the Commune and the date of the Haymarket demonstrations became fixtures in the international calendar of the left. Accordingly, in 1908, a German police report on radical activities in London noted 'the usual celebrations of the Commune rising and the "judicial murder" of Chicago'.[115]

From the 1890s, commemorations of the Haymarket Affair coincided with the celebration of International Workers' Day on 1 May: at its founding congress, the Second International had resolved that all member parties would mobilize on May Day.[116] After the first May Day celebrations in 1890, *Der Sozialdemokrat* argued that 'in its simultaneity and similarity', the initiative had been unprecedented.[117] By contrast, German police officials claimed that 'the celebration was neither as general nor as unified as had been originally intended, and has entirely missed the impression that it was supposed to make on the government and the governing classes'.[118] They also noted that at the Second International's Zürich congress, Germans had attracted criticism 'from different sides because of their half-heartedness' when it came to the issue of May Day mobilization.[119] In this early period, the meaning of May Day was contested between those who saw it as a vehicle for international strike action and those who favoured a more limited celebration. For this reason, the utility of May Day also attracted debate within anarchist circles.[120]

May Day was not the only date that the Second International added to the socialist calendar. At the Second International Conference of Socialist Women, held in Copenhagen in 1910, delegates adopted Clara Zetkin's resolution to celebrate an International Women's Day. In Alexandra Kollontai's words, it was conceived as 'a day of international solidarity in the fight for common objectives and a day for reviewing the organized strength of working women under the banner of socialism'.[121] It was on International Women's Day in 1917 – 8 March in the Gregorian and 23 February in the Julian calendar – that a women's demonstration in Petrograd resulted in the overthrow of the Russian Tsar, marking the starting point of the February Revolution in Russia.

The boundaries of internationalism

The emphasis on the transnational interactions of socialists should not obscure their limitations. For example, while socialists critiqued individual colonial practices – and in some instances denounced colonialism as a drain on national resources – many groups and parties did not commit to rejecting empire as such.[122] In this respect, they differed from other parts of the left. For instance, Benedict Anderson has highlighted the manifold connections between Spanish, Cuban and Filipino anarchists and anti-imperialists in this period.[123] Moreover, as noted in Chapter 1, communists forged links with anti-imperialists during the 1920s and 1930s.

Another boundary of internationalism concerned the relationship with nationhood – in some respects echoing tensions that Chapter 3 has discussed with regard to pacifists. Seen from this angle, Roman Rosdolsky's reflections on the proletariat and nationhood pointed at issues that were crucial for the left, not just for thinkers and activists in the Marxist vein. For instance, while many anarchists explicitly denounced national categories and developed a cosmopolitan sensibility, the anarchist rejection of nationhood was not categorical.[124] In his influential book on *Statism and Anarchy*, Mikhail Bakunin described nationality as 'an historical, local fact' with 'an undeniable right to general recognition'. At the same time, he warned against an overemphasis on nationality, arguing that people would benefit 'the less they think about themselves and the more they are filled with universal human content'.[125]

According to Marcel van der Linden, the era of the Second International marked the shift from the labour movement's 'transnational' to its 'national' phase.[126] With a focus on international labour, Susan Milner concluded that 'on a practical level … national priorities and interests were paramount'.[127] These developments manifested themselves in organizational terms. Unlike its forerunner – in which socialists had gathered as individuals – the Second International was composed of national parties that would send delegates to its meetings.[128] At one level, these features meant that individual parties could try to shape the International's agenda. Efforts by German social democrats – whose party was the largest of its kind – to dominate deliberations were one example. Moreover, the national features of socialist internationalism meant that protagonists from national movements could potentially work within the organization. For example, the Armenian Revolutionary Federation (*Dashnaktsutyun*), which operated in the Armenian diaspora and, covertly, in the Ottoman Empire, joined the Second International in 1907.[129] Yet within the organization, attitudes to such causes varied. In 1897 and 1903, Bulgarian socialists tabled demands to push for Armenian and Macedonian autonomy but met with a lukewarm response within the International, as some socialist leaders were concerned about the impact on international politics.[130] As Maria Todorova has shown in her study on 'socialists at Europe's margins', Bulgarians were also involved in imagining alternative forms of national and international organization, as exemplified by their vision of a Balkan federation, which by 1910 attracted broader support among socialists from the Balkans and beyond.[131]

The relationship between national movements and socialism gave rise to various internal disputes, with the question of Polish unification as a case in point. Having been founded in exile, the Polish Socialist Party promoted the reestablishment of the Polish nation-state and participated in the Second International from the outset. While some socialists had sympathies for the Polish case, Rosa Luxemburg rejected such concerns, notwithstanding her own Polish background. In 1905, she warned that 'the old traditions of nationalism' would 'divert the Polish working class from the path of class struggle to the utopian folly of Polish restoration'. To her, 'Social Democracy, sailing under the banner of international socialism' was better suited to 'the Polish national cultural heritage'.[132] In a subsequent article, she pointed to an inherent contradiction – namely that protagonists of national rights were often less willing to afford those rights to others: 'The very nationality which had to endure the bitter policy of extermination by the partitioning powers – Prussia and Russia – now refuses the right of independent existence to other nationalities', namely to Ukrainians and Lithuanians.[133]

During the First World War, Luxemburg was among those who rejected the stance adopted by many fellow socialists. In 1915, she concluded that despite the plethora of antimilitarist proposals within the pre-war International, its member parties had failed 'to back up these demands with a will and with deeds in the spirit of the class struggle and internationalism'.[134] Indeed, whereas pre-war socialist congresses had considered general strikes as a way of ending military conflict, socialist anti-war mobilization in 1914 remained limited, as many socialists swung behind the national war effort. In some respects, their positioning can be explained by the electoral growth of socialist parties, which increasingly shifted from extra-parliamentary activism to action within the parliamentary realm and, during the wartime, even government service in some cases. This trajectory contrasted with the anarchist movement, whose rejection of state institutions precluded such a development. As a result, anarchist anti-war activism was less equivocal, meeting with censorship or even imprisonment.[135]

However, wartime positions within the socialist movement were by no means uncontested, as Chapter 3 has already acknowledged. Talbot Imlay has rightly pointed out that the outbreak of war in August 1914 did not constitute 'a deadly blow' for socialist internationalism.[136] In March 1915, protagonists of the socialist women's movement, including Zetkin and Balabanoff, gathered in Bern. While relatively small in scale – with around thirty participants – it amounted to a significant initiative as it was 'the first time during the war [that] socialist representatives of belligerent powers had come together'.[137] Over the subsequent months, the anti-war camp within the Second International developed new structures through conferences in Switzerland, held in Zimmerwald (September 1915) and Kienthal (April 1916).[138] These meetings were prominently associated with Lenin who, from his Swiss exile, denounced the 'social chauvinism' of socialists who backed the war effort.[139]

Although the war divided socialists along both national and ideological lines, a durable rupture was not a foregone conclusion. As secretary of the Second International, the Belgian socialist Camille Huysmans sought to maintain its work – contrasting with his own party leaders who, after the German attack on their country, found it difficult to cooperate with socialists from the Central Powers.[140] Huysmans expressed his confidence that the war had 'no more destroyed the International Socialist organisation than it has caused the Catholic Church to disappear'.[141] In 1917, he contributed to a socialist peace initiative by Dutch and Swedish socialists who sought to gather socialists from neutral and enemy nations in a joint peace conference. Neutral Sweden thus became a major site of transnational socialist activism, with several preparatory meetings taking place in Stockholm. Such efforts coincided with popular mobilization. For instance, the Swedish May Day activities that year took place under the banner 'For peace, against the War and the high cost of living'.[142] During the main May Day demonstration in the Swedish capital, the Dutch socialist Pieter Jelles Troelstra – a driving force behind the conference plans – marched alongside the Swedish party leader Hjalmar Branting.

Plans for a broader socialist conference in Stockholm proved abortive. Many party leaders from the warring countries refused to meet their counterparts from enemy nations – partly for fear of appearing unpatriotic and partly because they were aggrieved by the wartime stance of their former comrades. In addition, national governments created obstacles for activists seeking to travel abroad. Finally, the Bolsheviks' growing prominence in international socialist debates proved challenging – and in the end, it was only a conference by the Zimmerwald Left that took place in Stockholm.[143] After the war, efforts to rebuild the Second International resulted in a successor organization, the Labour and Socialist International (LSI), which translated the principles of internationalism into the new international order.[144] The LSI certainly demonstrated the ongoing commitment to cooperation within the socialist movement, yet – in contrast to the wider 'demonstration culture' of the pre-war International – its main emphasis was on inter-party cooperation.[145] Most significantly, the LSI did not fully overcome the wartime rifts because the Zimmerwald Left had, in the meantime, given way to a new body: the Communist International.

International communism

Looking back in 1924, Clara Zetkin argued that the Second International had suffered from becoming 'a loose affiliation of political and industrial organisations of the various countries' rather than form 'a united and solid world-organisation with one goal and with strong and binding discipline', which explained why it had been 'incapable of carrying out any forceful actions upon an international scale'. To Zetkin, it was the Comintern's formation in 1919 that signalled a change from 'the international of the word to the international of the deed'.[146] This assessment reflected Zetkin's own political journey. As noted previously, she had been a central figure in the socialist women's movement, both in Germany and internationally. In 1914, she opposed the majority stance within the Social Democratic Party and joined other anti-war socialists in founding the Independent Social Democratic Party (USPD). Within the USPD, Zetkin worked with a left-wing faction around Rosa Luxemburg and Karl Liebknecht that gave rise to the German Communist Party. From 1919 until her death in 1933 – in the Soviet Union, to which she had emigrated after the Nazis' rise to power – Zetkin was a key figure within German communism.

This kind of trajectory was not unusual, as communist parties in the early 1920s were founded by activists who had previously been involved in social movements and socialist parties. To join the Comintern, the new parties had to adhere to the so-called Twenty-One Conditions, which included a commitment to evicting 'reformists' and 'centrists' as well as adopting a stance against 'social patriotism'. The Comintern principles also included an attack on 'social-pacifism'.[147] Used derogatorily, this term referred to the

League of Nations. As such, the communist position contrasted with the LSI, which supported the League, albeit with some reservations.[148]

At least in theory, the Comintern was meant to overcome national divisions: as Andrew Thorpe and Tim Rees have stressed, communist parties 'were seen as national sections of a world party'.[149] While there is ongoing debate about the degree of autonomy enjoyed by individual communist parties, attempts at control from Moscow existed early on, with attempts to 'Bolshevize' communist parties in the mid-1920s.[150] Soviet dominance within the Comintern was by no means surprising, given the enthusiasm for the October Revolution and the politics of Soviet Russia. In 1919, communists in Bavaria and Hungary established short-lived council republics. Even beyond their ambition to follow the Soviet model, their undertakings involved transnational links. For example, the Party of Communists in Hungary (*Kommunisták Magyarországi Pártja*) had been founded by Hungarian prisoners of war, including Béla Kun, who briefly led the Hungarian Soviet Republic. Meanwhile, protagonists within the Bavarian Soviet Republic included the Russian Bolshevik Eugen Leviné.[151] Although the Hungarian and Bavarian experiments in revolutionary politics soon succumbed to external force and internal tensions, they demonstrated the appeal of the events in Russia. To Zetkin, the October Revolution was a 'fiery token' that 'united the workers of all countries' and gave workers 'the rock of faith in international proletarian solidarity for the revolutionary fight against capitalism'.[152]

For some observers, however, the mismatch between socialist rhetoric and practice became apparent early on. Having moved to the Soviet Union after her expulsion from the United States, Emma Goldman recorded her disappointment in the book *My Disillusionment in Russia*.[153] At the time, her criticisms met with little sympathy among her target audience. Having addressed communist and anarchist trade unionists, she acknowledged her failure to show 'our own comrades in Europe and America ... the reverse side of the shiny Soviet medal'. She credited this response to the hopes that were being projected onto Soviet Russia: 'To the oppressed of the world the Bolsheviki had become the synonym of the Revolution itself. The revolutionists outside of Russia could not easily credit how far that was from the truth.'[154]

Importantly, it was not only communists who defended the revolutionary principles that they associated with Soviet Russia. For example, in 1919–20, the British 'Hands off Russia' campaign attracted a range of activists who opposed Allied intervention in the Russian Civil War. George Orwell later referred to this movement as one of the few instances when the British working class had 'thought or acted internationally'.[155] Such solidarity was no one-way street: the historian Gleb Albert has shown that principles of internationalism exercised considerable appeal in early Soviet Russia.[156] This appeal was particularly apparent in the Communist Youth League (or Komsomol), whose members expressed enthusiasm for principles of international solidarity during the organization's early years.[157]

The Communist Party of the Soviet Union was by far the largest and most influential party of its kind. Its counterparts elsewhere in Europe exercised more limited appeal during the 1920s, with only the German and Czechoslovakian parties attracting a mass membership in this period as well.[158] Precisely for this reason, practical support and leadership from Moscow played an important role for international communism. One major aspect involved Russian support to form future party cadres, as reflected in the educational ventures of the International Lenin School, the International University for the Toilers of the East and the Communist University of the National Minorities of the West.[159]

Transnational communist ties not only involved inter-party cooperation but sustained a wider network of associations, including organizations for youth (Young Communist International), trade unionists (Red International of Labour Unions, or Profintern, 1920), working-class sports (Red Sports International, 1921), support for communists facing political persecution (Red Aid International, 1922) and peasants (Red Peasants International, 1923). In this context, the Profintern seemed to indicate efforts to build a united workers' front 'from below'.[160] The notion of a 'united front' also informed ventures that have been discussed in earlier chapters – namely Workers' International Relief (founded in 1921) and the League Against Imperialism (1927) – which had the behind-the-scenes role of the German communist publisher Willi Münzenberg in common.[161]

By the early 1930s, non-communists had largely been excluded from leadership positions within the League Against Imperialism. This development reflected a broader shift that had started shortly after the LAI's formation: in 1928, the Comintern adopted its 'Class Against Class' strategy, based on the notion that the final crisis of capitalism had arrived and that the existing social conflicts needed reinforcing to accelerate the coming revolution. Rather than broadening their cooperation with different segments of the left, communist leaders embarked on a confrontational course that reserved particular scorn for socialists, whom they denounced as 'social fascists'. At this point in time, the Soviet Union itself had largely abandoned its promotion of world revolution, having adopted a policy of building 'socialism in one country' in the second half of the 1920s, partly under Stalin's growing influence.[162] By the 1930s, the Comintern became ever-more closely aligned with Soviet foreign policy interests. However, it was not a monolithic entity: there was some variation among communist parties in the late 1920s and 1930s, as 'different people in different countries interpreted applied the New Line in different ways amid different circumstances'.[163] Moreover, within local settings, internationalist principles were interpreted and practised in ways that could clash with Comintern policy.[164]

During the 1930s, communism pointed into opposing directions. On the one hand, communists and fellow travellers continued to visit the Soviet Union, professing their respect or admiration for the Soviet experiment, while frequently ignoring or downplaying Stalinist repression.[165] On the other hand, Stalin's political rise forced his opponents into exile, if they had not already fallen victim to Stalinist terror. One of the earliest anti-Stalinist exiles – and certainly the most famous one – was Leon Trotsky, who, after his expulsion from the Soviet Union in 1929, found temporary homes in Turkey, France, Norway and ultimately Mexico, where Soviet agents murdered him in 1940. In exile, Trotsky was a vocal critic of the Soviet state, which he accused of abandoning the revolutionary principles on which it had been founded.[166] Trotsky's criticisms extended to the practice of internationalism. After an initial period in which he still professed his loyalty to the Comintern, Trotsky established his rival Fourth International in 1933.[167] While remaining small in scale, it attracted support among disillusioned activists, with C. L. R. James calling it in 1937 'the only hope' for socialists.[168]

Emigration from communist Russia predated Stalinism, as the Russian Revolution and its aftermath generated several waves of emigration. While many of the initial émigrés in 1917–18 were former aristocrats, military leaders, Tsarist officials as well as liberal or conservative politicians, these groups were later joined by Mensheviks, Socialist Revolutionaries and the protagonists of national movements whose ambitions for self-determination were rejected by the early Soviet state. Thus, the exiles were a politically heterogeneous group. Among Russian exiles in Prague, there were conflicts between the first cohort of refugees and Socialist Revolutionaries who supported a policy of non-intervention in the Russian Civil War and thus disagreed with both the Bolsheviks and the Whites.[169] Such divisions, and the efforts to overcome them, reflected a wider phenomenon – namely 'calls for unity followed by rapid fragmentation', which were by no means confined to the experiences of Russian exiles.[170]

Notwithstanding their differences, exiles maintained a 'Russia Abroad' in many places, from France to Turkey and even China.[171] Publishing activities supported their political activism, as reflected by periodicals such as *New Russia* in London, *Golos emigranta* ('The Emigrant's Voice') in Berlin and *Russkoe Delo* ('Russian Affairs') and *Slavyanskaya Zarya* ('Slav Dawn') in Prague. The first of these was edited by the Russian Liberation Committee in London, which sought to mobilize Western support against the Bolsheviks.[172] The committee was but one of many such groups – and over subsequent years, further organizations emerged, for instance the National Alliance of the New Solidarists in 1930. The latter's base in Belgrade reflected the right-wing character of this venture: at the time, many Russian exiles saw Yugoslavia as 'an epitome of reaction, with the exception of the monarchist press, which defined Yugoslavia as a "haven for true patriots"'.[173] Such examples underscore the role of both political alliance-building and polarization in exile – albeit in ways that differed from the cases of exile politics that this chapter has discussed earlier on.

Fascism and anti-fascism

In Stalin's Russia, activists of different political shades faced internal banishment, forced labour or execution after show trials – with emigration as a potential way of escaping this fate. Yet, notwithstanding the Stalinist terror, the Soviet Union was also a destination for exiles who fled the fascist and authoritarian regimes elsewhere. In the Soviet Union, these activists faced surveillance – and in some cases later became victims of purges themselves.[174] Russian cities – notably Moscow and Leningrad – were but one potential destination for opponents of fascism, with cities such as Prague and Paris becoming centres for both communist and non-communist exiles.[175]

The connection between transnational activism and anti-fascism predated the 1930s. The historian Kasper Braskén, for example, has drawn attention to a range of anti-fascist efforts during the 1920s, which mostly focused on Mussolini's Italy.[176] Communists were not the only ones involved in such organizing. For example, in 1926, the LSI launched its Matteotti Fund, named after the Italian socialist Giacomo Matteotti, whom Italian fascists had murdered in 1924. By 1930, the IFTU had joined this initiative. In 1932, socialists and trade unionists gathered funds in support of the Austrian left, which was under attack by Chancellor Engelbert Dollfuss. One year later, the Nazis' ascent to power triggered further activism among socialists, but also caused significant challenges: by December, the organizers reported that the extensive work for German political refugees and ongoing work in Austria had prevented it from providing any support for activists elsewhere, demanding an urgent increase in funds.[177]

Meanwhile, Nazi actions also sparked communist ventures in transnational solidarity. Three Bulgarian communists – including Georgi Dimitrov, then secretary-general of the communist-dominated World Committee against War and Fascism – were accused of forming part of a plot that, in the Nazis' views, had been responsible for the Reichstag fire. At the time of their widely publicized trial, the German communist Willi Münzenberg published his *Brown Book*, which sought to expose Nazi duplicity as well as the broader structures of repression that were being established in Germany. Having previously been the driving force behind a variety of Comintern 'front' organizations, Münzenberg had fled Germany in March 1933; accordingly, his *Brown Book* was first published in France, where he had found temporary refuge.[178]

Münzenberg himself has alternatively been cast as a self-interested political entrepreneur, a willing tool of Stalinism and an anti-fascist hero.[179] His own death in 1940 remains shrouded in mystery: having ruptured with Stalinism in the second half of the 1930s, it is unclear whether or not he had committed suicide or been murdered by Soviet agents. In the early to mid-1930s, however, Münzenberg still acted in harmony with the Comintern, for which Dimitrov served as secretary-general after his release from Nazi captivity. In 1934, the Comintern abandoned its hostility to cooperating with 'class enemies' and adopted its 'Popular Front' strategy, encouraging broader alliances against the fascist threat. The initial steps in this direction were tentative and, given the history of past front ventures, attracted suspicion among socialists. For example, in January 1936 the LSI secretary Friedrich Adler rejected communist overtures to join forces with the Matteotti Fund, pointing out that Red Aid International was 'an auxiliary organization of the Communist International' and arguing that, in light of the political repression in the Soviet Union itself, the 'moral power conviction of the propaganda of the Red Aid' was 'very considerably diminished at the moment'.[180]

Over the subsequent years, however, the movement towards a Popular Front gained momentum, culminating in the election of Popular Front governments in both France and Spain in 1936. Subsequent events in Spain sparked one of the most striking manifestations of transnational solidarity in this period – namely the actions of volunteers who sought to defend Republican Spain after the Nationalist coup of July 1936.

Around 50,000 volunteers fought in the International Brigades, for which the Comintern had served as the recruiting tool.[181] Many members of the Brigades saw the Spanish conflict as part of a wider anti-fascist struggle. At the same time, recent research on these volunteers has highlighted the interplay between international solidarity and the local sociability that led individuals to sign up for the Brigades.[182] Not all forms of pro-republican solidarity had to take the form of military volunteering: a range of other activists provided practical support. Ruth Waller, an American nurse, viewed her teaching at a Spanish nursing school in political terms: 'We soon found out that the fight against illiteracy was a strong factor in the fight against fascism; that women and men alike, in throwing off their political fetters, were stirred also to overcome the old ignorance of which those fetters were the symbol.'[183] Such statements underscore the potential links between left-wing solidarity and the humanitarian ventures discussed in Chapter 2.

Volunteering for Republican Spain went beyond communists, with independent socialists, Trotskyists and anarchists travelling to Spain, too. Emma Goldman was among them. Noting the role of anarchists and anarcho-syndicalists in Catalonia, she described it as 'the freest place politically in the world' and reported that to her allies, it seemed that 'anarchism and libertarian communism' were 'ingrained in the Catalonian workers and peasants'.[184] Having returned to Britain, she saw it as her 'main quest here' to make their activism known because, despite all that 'was being done in England for the Anti-Fascist struggle', such aid efforts hardly extended to the Spanish anarchists.[185] To Goldman, solidarity with Republican Spain did not mean adopting the communist line; she concurred with those who deemed it fruitless 'to sacrifice one's ideal in the struggle against fascism, if it only means to make room for Soviet Communism'.[186] The conflict with communists became evident during the May Days of 1937, when the Republican government, Spanish communists and Soviet advisors cooperated to suppress the revolutionary government that Spanish anarchists and Trotskyists had established in Barcelona. Anarchists from other countries denounced these actions. For example, the British anarchist periodical *Spain and the World* printed a supplement to highlight the 'struggle between those who represent the anti-fascist front in the outside world'.[187]

While these developments indicate that transnational solidarity and political unity were by no means synonymous, the Spanish Civil War showed that transnational solidarity was not a prerogative of the left: Franco's Nationalists recruited international volunteers in their turn, albeit on a smaller scale.[188] Motivations for Francoist volunteering varied. For some Catholics, the anticlericalism of the Spanish left made the Nationalist troops appear as defenders of the Christian faith. In many other instances, support came from fascist or semi-fascist groups in other countries, for instance the Irish Green Shirts and the Romanian Iron Guard. Far-right activists saw their involvement as part of an international struggle against Bolshevism – which was a broader motivating factor for fascists in this period.[189]

Seen from this angle, right-wing volunteering seemed to continue a 'fascist internationalism' that also manifested itself in other respects. Early on, Italian fascism

Figure 4.1 Emma Goldman (*centre*) with members of the *Federacion Anarquista Ibérica* (Iberian Anarchist Federation) and the anarchosyndicalist *Confederación Nacional de Trabajo* (National Confederation of Labour), Spain, 1938. *Source:* IISG BG A5/529, International Institute of Social History, Amsterdam.

provided inspiration and, in some cases, financial support to anti-democratic groups.[190] By the early 1930s, Italian fascism was increasingly being framed as a 'universal', rather than national, project – something that has led the historian Daniel Hediger to speak of 'the first global movement of fascism'.[191] The Italian writer Asvero Gravelli exemplified this development when he argued for the creation of a 'fascist international' in 1932.[192] To Gravelli, fascism was a revolutionary force, whereas its opponents were 'counter-revolutionary, reactionary, conservative'.[193] His text included a survey of potential ideological allies in different countries, juxtaposing them with 'all those forces that we fight and deny', including 'communism, socialism, democracy, plutocracy, cartelism, European irreligiosity'.[194] This 'fascist international' remained inchoate, yet in 1936–7, the formation of the Axis marked a new point of convergence. While being a diplomatic alliance between Germany, Japan and Italy – rather than an activist venture – its framing as an 'Anti-Comintern Pact' evoked the Comintern's embrace of anti-fascism in the Popular Front era.[195]

Although attempts to build broader international structures among fascists proved abortive, fascists and other right-wing groups made common cause in different ways – a subject that will be further explored in Chapter 6.[196] Benito Mussolini's own trajectory from socialism to fascism was mirrored by some activists who had previously been involved in socialist or communist internationalism. In France, these included the former socialist Gustave Hervé, who had been a vocal antimilitarist within the pre-war debates of the Second International but shifted towards a Mussolini-inspired 'national' socialism in the 1920s.[197] Another example was the former French communist leader Jacques Doriot, who had been a member of the Comintern executive. In 1934, his party expelled him for championing cooperation with non-communists, at a point that predated the adoption of the Popular Front strategy. Two years later, an increasingly anti-communist Doriot founded the *Parti Populaire Français* (French Popular Party), which translated Nazi ideas into a French setting; accordingly, during the German occupation of France, he collaborated with the German authorities.[198]

Such spectacular ideological journeys contradicted the anti-fascist stance adopted by socialists and communists. Indeed, to many parts of the left, fascism seemed to be a tool of class rule. Yet antifascism was not always consistent. The Ribbentrop-Molotov Pact of 1939 meant that, upon Soviet instructions, the Comintern abandoned its anti-fascist line, causing consternation among some communists.[199] This position changed again after the German attack on the Soviet Union in 1941, but the Comintern itself was dismantled in 1943, underscoring the demise of communist internationalism, at least in organizational terms.

Socialist alternatives in a Cold War world

The Cold War was a transnational phenomenon in several respects. The establishment of communist rule in Central and Eastern Europe served Soviet interests; at the same time, it was facilitated by the existence of local communist movements whose members had maintained ties to Russia.[200] In some cases, these external factors undermined the work of communist activists who had become state leaders: as Mark Kramer has argued, 'the Soviet Union's role in establishing Communist regimes and the continued subordination of those regimes to Soviet preferences and policies thwarted efforts by the east European governments to acquire genuine legitimacy among their populations'.[201]

In the era of mounting Cold War tensions, conflict between the two power blocs had evident consequences for activists. Funding from the Soviet Union and its allies bankrolled activist groups in the West and at the international level, with peace as a prominent theme, as noted in Chapter 3.[202] In their turn, the CIA and other Western actors offered financial backing and covert support to various anti-communist ventures.[203] Taken together, these developments were key features of the 'cultural Cold War'.[204] Yet such activism was not just steered from above. For instance, Eastern European exile activists gathered in the Assembly of Captive European Nations and lobbied Western governments. In 1958, its then president Stefan Korboński – formerly a politician in the Polish Peasants Party and a member of the anti-Nazi resistance – embarked on a tour that took him to twelve, mostly Asian, countries, where he met 'a few hundred leaders of political parties, military leaders, writers, presidents and professors of universities' within less than three months. His journey sought to prevent the fate of the communist-ruled countries from being treated as 'an internal issue of the Soviet imperium'.[205] However, in 1982, the Polish dissident Adam Michnik – who never emigrated – argued that this earlier 'community of émigrés did not have a good reputation' among those who had stayed in Poland: there were suspicions that such individuals had chosen 'easy earnings, security, and property and who, for American money, told lies about Poland on Radio Free Europe'.[206] To Michnik, this form of exile activism differed from later currents that bound together dissident groups at home and in exile.

Even beyond oppositional activity, Cold War-era activism had various transnational features. Stalin's death in 1953 was followed by a revival of Soviet internationalism, with a renewed emphasis on fostering exchanges, both within the socialist world and beyond it.[207] Such efforts were not exclusively state-directed, as they also involved individuals who saw themselves as activists. Yet Soviet talk of international solidarity clearly contrasted with an unwillingness to grant independent agency to countries in the Soviet orbit. The crushing of both the Hungarian Uprising in 1956 and the Prague Spring in 1968 disillusioned many left-wing activists in other countries.[208]

This disenchantment with Soviet-style communism explains why the rise of the 'New Left' was a transnational phenomenon. A recent study has argued that although the term 'New Left' only gained traction in the 1960s, it had deeper ideological roots, as various earlier movements had explored how one might 'sustain the dynamism of a grassroots social movement without succumbing to hierarchy, centralized leadership, and banal political routine'.[209] For many, the term 'New Left' did not signify an abandonment of Marxist ideas, but a critique of state socialism as practised in Central and Eastern Europe.

The search for socialist alternatives pointed into different directions, with Trotskyism as one manifestation.[210] The intellectual and activist Ernest Mandel was a central figure in this regard. Born in Germany to Jewish parents from Poland, but raised in Belgium, he first gained prominence in the Belgian Trotskyist left and participated in the anti-fascist resistance during the German occupation of Belgium. After the war, Mandel became a well-known Marxist theorist and a key voice in the Fourth International. In these regards, he acknowledged the influence of the older Roman Rosdolsky: when the latter died in 1967, Mandel 'lost more than a kindred spirit and a mentor', namely 'a modest and affectionate friend'.[211] At one level, Mandel's transnational links proved helpful in disseminating his ideas. His biographer noticed his German connections: he had been 'raised in a family that spoke German with the political refugees who enjoyed their hospitality [in Belgium] in the 1930s'; moreover in 1966, he married the German student activist Gisela Scholtz.[212] In the second half of the 1960s, Mandel's ideas influenced the West German student movement. In other respects, his case revealed the limitations of transnational movement for political radicals, as Australia, France and the United States barred him in 1970, with West Germany expelling him in 1972.[213]

Alongside Trotskyism, there was a second current that provided a communist alternative to Soviet-style socialism – namely Maoism. While Maoist groups were small in membership, the historian Julia Lovell has noted that 'the influence of Maoism in Western Europe and North America during the 1960s and beyond was greater than the number of its supporters suggest' as its appeal extended to 'students, oppressed ethnic minorities (African, Asian, Hispanic Americans), urban terrorists, cultural celebrities, philosophers'.[214] This was particularly the case in France.[215] Further fragmentation occurred during the 1970s. For example, one faction of Maoists in the West championed the Albanian regime of Enver Hoxha, which had been aligned with the People's Republic of China but, after Mao's death, steered an independent cause, dismissing the new Chinese leadership as 'revisionist'.[216]

These examples suggest a splintering of the Western European left into ever smaller factions. Yet, when it came to the countries under state-socialist rule, the search for left-wing alternatives was far from inconsequential: it enabled activists to criticize the political system from within, on its own terms. For example, in 1963, the Polish activists Jacek Kuroń and Karol Modzelewski wrote an 'Open Letter to the Party' that challenged state-socialist practice on Marxist grounds, attacking party bureaucracy and other obstacles on the road to genuine socialism. In the same year, the Belgian Trotskyist Georges Dobbeleer visited Poland, distributed 1,000 translated copies of Ernest Manel's resolution on 'Stalinism in Crisis', and provided Kuroń and Modzelewski with a stencil machine that enabled them to produce copies of their letter.[217] Significantly, the 'Open Letter' did not remain confined to Poland: it was translated into other languages, with its first English version appearing in the Trotskyist periodical *International Socialism*, which combined the publication with some information on incarcerated Polish socialists.[218] Kuroń and Modzelewski's critique was a forerunner of the *Komitet Obrony Robotników* (Workers' Defence Committee, KOR), a Polish organization whose members – including Adam Michnik – challenged the political system in the 1970s, with publishing activities in the West.[219] Such ventures reflected a wider development in Central and Eastern Europe, namely the growth of a dissident Marxism that critiqued the bureaucratization and repressive policies associated with state-socialist practice.[220]

Despite being far from anti-communist, dissident Marxists still faced persecution in countries under communist rule. At the same time, they found support in the West, with New Left activists as natural allies. Moreover, during the mid-1970s, the development of reform currents within some Western communist parties – a direction known as 'Eurocommunism' – raised the question whether there might also be new spaces to challenge communist orthodoxies in state-socialist countries.[221] In a letter to the Eurocommunist parties in France, Italy and Britain, the Soviet dissident Petro Grigorenko spoke of the 'little glimmer of hope that the [communist] movement could find a way out of the cul-de-sac in which the policy of totalitarianism had led it' but argued that their stance would only be consequential if they did not shy away from criticizing conditions in the Soviet Union for fear of meddling in 'internal affairs'.[222] Meanwhile, from a Trotskyist perspective, Ernest Mandel criticized Eurocommunist parties both for their reformism and for their emphasis on an independent national course, which to him seemed a case of 'betraying proletarian internationalism'.[223]

The different currents discussed thus far still claimed a Marxist heritage, albeit in contrasting ways. However, in the 1960s, such older traditions were joined by other strands of leftist thinking. In the 1940s, various left-wing Catholic groups emerged in Western Europe, yet they largely failed to forge a durable alliance with other organizations and actors in the Christian realm.[224] In the 1960s, however, Catholic lay activists, 'worker priests' and theologians all developed different forms of 'left Catholicism' that engaged with the political and social transformations of the era, including in some cases an engagement with Marxist ideas or Third Worldist currents.[225]

While left-wing Catholicism was important in the West, a different form of Christian politics mattered in the Eastern bloc. Given the state's hostility to the churches, Christian communities found themselves under scrutiny. Within their ranks, they could host oppositional activity, and they also developed transnational links: for instance, evangelical Christians in Hungary and the GDR maintained covert relations with one another.[226] The most prominent case of religion supporting oppositional forces, however, was Poland. In 1978, the elevation of Karol Wojtyła, Archbishop of Krakow, to the papacy (as John Paul II) met with enthusiasm, and papal visits to the country of his birth led to events where mass displays of devotion stood alongside expressions of political discontent. Ideologically, the Polish opposition was wide-ranging – 'from post-Marxists and social democrats to Christian democrats and nationalists' – and it maintained 'good contacts in the [Roman Catholic] Church'.[227] At a time when he was imprisoned for his oppositional activities, Michnik noted the support that the church had given to 'the persecuted and their families' as well as its role in creating 'new islands of autonomy'.[228]

The developments in Poland had important transnational dimensions because in the early 1980s, the Polish opposition attracted widespread attention abroad. In 1980, Polish labour activists defied the authorities by founding the independent and vastly popular trade union *Solidarność* ('Solidarity') – with the Polish state responding to the growing unrest by imposing martial law (1981–3). In the West, expressions of support for *Solidarność* were facilitated by the fact that different ideas could be projected onto it: leftist notions of self-government, conservative anti-communism but also human rights discourses that had gained prominence in the preceding years.[229] Such backing was particularly appealing to the Christian labour movement in Western Europe, both because of its opposition to communism and because of Catholic involvement in the Polish opposition. Among socialist trade unions, expressions of solidarity varied in their forcefulness.[230] Trotskyists, in their turn, paid close attention to the events of Poland as 'Eastern Europe and anti-Stalinism formed part of the Trotskyist identity'.[231]

The activities of exiled dissidents, the international echo to *Solidarność* and the growing debates about reform in the late 1980s indicate that the challenge to state socialism was not confined to national boundaries. When the state-socialist regimes collapsed in 1989, it was the consequence of several factors – the economic crisis within the countries, the influence of Gorbachev's policies as well as popular unrest. But the demise of the regimes did not cause issues just for the old left, but also for the New Left, since the hopes for a socialist alternative were soon disappointed.[232]

Figure 4.2 *Solidarność* banner held up during a mass celebrated by John Paul II (Szczecin, 11 June 1987). *Source*: Marcel Mochet / AFP, via Getty Images.

Protest cultures in and beyond the 1960s

The historian Padraic Kenney has described 1989 as a 'carnival of revolution', drawing attention to the imaginative way in which activists expressed their discontent.[233] Seen from that angle, such mobilizations also had a broader context, namely the protest cultures that had developed since the 1960s. This section will return to the 1960s and focus on a point in time that, like 1989, was a 'transnational moment of change': 1968.[234] That year, protests shock societies in East and West, and in North and South. Importantly, many contemporary observers were conscious of the global nature of the events. The French singer and activist Dominique Grange expressed this sense of connectedness: in her song 'À bas l'état policier' ('Down with the police state'), she juxtaposed a global effort to suppress dissent with the solidarity of protesters:

> It is easy to recognise you
> You, cops of the entire world
> The same raincoats
> The same mentality
> But we are from Paris
> From Prague and Mexico

And from Berlin to Tokyo
Millions are shouting at you:
Down with the police state!'[235]

Indeed, the events of 1968 were not a set of more or less simultaneous events but characterized by manifold transnational exchanges. Politics was only part of the equation. The 1960s were a period of drastic changes for music, fashion and sexual politics, which had the potential to become vehicles for political change.[236] Importantly, the appeal of rock music, alternative lifestyles and countercultural expressions did not remain confined to Western Europe and North America.[237] That said, processes of transnational reception and adaption were uneven, partly linked to the wider political constellations. With regard to young people under the right-wing military dictatorship in Greece, the historian Kostis Kornetis has noted that 'news of what was happening abroad travelled to Greece, sometimes exaggerated and sometimes understated' but has argued that the political conditions prevented an emergence of the 'sort of pop politics that appeared in Western Europe'.[238] Nikolaos Papadogiannis, however, has shown that for 'left-leaning students', cultural elements of the 'Global Sixties' did matter.[239]

The scale and variety of protests in and beyond Europe make a monocausal explanation impossible. Two aspects were, however, particularly notable. First, young people – and university students in particular – were major protagonists in the quest for social and political change. For them, the post-war baby boom, the expansion of higher education as well as unresolved questions about the recent past of war and dictatorship were important factors. For this reason, 1968 is sometimes seen in terms of a generational revolt – although this interpretation should not obscure cross-generational cooperation in this period.[240] The historian Richard Ivan Jobs has stressed that mobility created a shared sense of identity among youths from different countries: to him, 1968 was 'a turning point in the emergence of a cohort of young people who had come, through travel, to conceive of themselves not merely as members of a particular nation, but as a continent-wide, transnational social group'.[241]

Secondly, in political terms, the 1968 protests reflected disappointment with both the capitalist order in the West and state socialism in the East. This quest for alternatives meant that the theoretical developments of the New Left mattered. For instance, Ernest Mandel 'served not only as a theoretician and political analyst but also as an agitator directly involved in the debate – as in Berlin – and as a participant in combat during the Paris "night of the barricades"' of May 1968.[242] Another influence was Herbert Marcuse who, after emigrating from Nazi Germany, had settled in the United States, where he became an academic at the University of California at Berkeley. Marcuse's book on *The One-Dimensional Man* became widely popular in student circles, turning Marcuse himself into a key inspiration for younger activists. As the historian Jeremy Suri has put it, 'Marcuse's language, like rock-and-roll music, became an incredibly popular antidote to the political rhetoric that alienated many young citizens.'[243]

The quest to build a different system also manifested itself in conflicts between established communist parties and the protestors. The pronouncements of Daniel

Cohn-Bendit illustrate this aspect. Born to Jewish parents who had fled Nazi Germany and survived the Holocaust in France, Daniel Cohn-Bendit was a student activist at the university in Paris-Nanterre, and became a figure of international renown when these local protests snowballed into a nationwide affair with occupied universities, mass demonstrations and street battles. Cohn-Bendit's activism in May 1968 led to his expulsion from France, whereupon he continued his activism in West Germany.[244] Shortly after the May events, he placed the upheavals into a wider context by publishing a book on *Obsolete Communism* with his brother Gabriel. Similar to other accounts, he started by acknowledging the 'world-wide' nature of the revolt, which was 'spreading like wildfire, and authorities everywhere are frantically asking themselves what has hit them'.[245] Yet, having discussed the Parisian events, the book shifted towards a particular target: the French Communist Party – which had maintained its distance from the protests – and Soviet-style communism more generally. To Cohn-Bendit, communist hostility to genuine revolutionary action was not a new phenomenon. He sought to demonstrate that, 'far from leading the Russian Revolution forwards, the Bolsheviks were responsible for holding back the struggle of the masses between February and October 1917, and later for turning the revolution into a bureaucratic counter-revolution'.[246] Beyond drawing parallels between 1917 and 1968, Cohn-Bendit made a wider point that any form of leadership would undermine a genuinely democratic revolution.[247] Given the heterogeneity of European student movements, Cohn-Bendit's comments were but one perspective, but they reflected wider tensions. For instance, competing visions between student radicals and the 'old left' became evident when a group of West German student leaders attended the communist-backed World Festival of Youth in Sofia.[248]

In 1969, Fred Halliday – then a twenty-one-year-old student at the School of Oriental and African Studies in London, and later a prominent IR scholar – surveyed the international student protests of the preceding year and described students as 'the internationalist social group par excellence under present conditions'.[249] According to Halliday, the events in Europe, Latin America and East Asia demonstrated 'the potential richness of forms of protest'.[250] Indeed, around 1968, activists from different countries actively shared strategies and ideas. For instance, the historian Martin Klimke has highlighted the manifold contacts between West German and North American student activists.[251] Such an awareness meant that concepts such as 'teach-ins' were adopted in different countries. In several instances, activists also sought to translate particular activist concepts from other countries into their own local settings. For instance, having settled in Frankfurt/Main, Cohn-Bendit formed the group *Revolutionärer Kampf* ('Revolutionary Struggle') which sought to send students into factories. The aim was to undertake revolutionary agitation and forge an alliance between students and workers, based on the example of the Italian *Lotta Continua* (Continuous Struggle).[252]

Processes of transnational reception, adoption and adaptation also extended to the minority of activists who endorsed or used political violence. For instance, the prominence of the American counterculture meant that the actions of the Weather Underground – who planned arson attacks as political signals – were noted among radical circles in Europe.[253] Ideological inspirations could also be a factor in the shift towards violence, as illustrated by the role of '[t]he rhetorical militancy of Maoism and the Cultural Revolution' as an inspiration for some of the West German and Italian radicals who embraced political violence.[254] During the 1970s, notions of a shared ideological struggle generated ties between left-wing terrorist groups such as the Italian Red Brigades and the West German Red Army Faction, but they also extended to links with organizations that, in their eyes, were engaged in national liberation struggles, from Northern Ireland and the Basque Country to Palestine.[255]

Global social justice

The collapse of the state-socialist regimes in Central and Eastern Europe caused significant ruptures for those who had believed in the prospects for a socialist society. At the same time, it did not signal an end to other forms of transnational cooperation on the left – and in many ways, such efforts were sparked by wider shifts that were connected to these transformations. While economic and cultural globalization was well underway before the 1990s, the end of the Cold War provided further stimuli to this process.[256] After the collapse of communism, most countries in Central and Eastern Europe introduced market reforms, further contributing to a global reduction in trade barriers. Yet it soon became clear that, rather than leading to a spreading of wealth, globalization created new inequalities. This situation gave rise to a movement that was sometimes described as 'anti-globalization' – although many activists rejected this label, arguing that they were merely opposed to forms of globalization that served the interests of multinational corporations.[257] An alternative approach has therefore been to frame such activism as a movement for global justice. One of its features has been to treat issues such as North–South inequality, human rights and the environment as interconnected. As one account has put it, 'environmental, workers', women's immigrant, minority, indigenous, and peace networks are all becoming entwined with those struggling against neoliberal globalization'.[258]

Participation in this movement took different shapes, with international solidarity campaigns as one feature that connected it to earlier forms of left-wing activism. One major case was the interest generated by the uprising in Chiapas, Mexico, which coincided with the implementation of the North American Free Trade Agreement (NAFTA) in 1994. In their rebellion, the Zapatistas – indigenous activists from Chiapas, with a name that evoked the Mexican Revolution of 1910 – linked different issues: the situation of Mexico's indigenous population as well as wider struggles for democracy and social equality. To this end, the Zapatistas adopted an international media strategy that appealed to activists in different countries. According to political scientist Thomas Olesen, the Zapatistas avoided a 'distinction between first, second and third worlds that has inspired so many analyses in the preceding decade' and instead cast their action as part of a wider protest against neoliberalism.[259]

Indeed, in the 1990s and 2000s, activists staged various protests against the course of globalization, often in conjunction with international summits. Activist gatherings on such occasions predated this period, with NGOs also running side events to UN summits in earlier decades.[260] But by the 1990s, a more radical protest culture targeted the meetings of bodies that seemed embody the global economic order, from the G7/G8 – as the organization of leading industrial nations – to the World Bank and the International Monetary Fund. This growing movement gained widespread attention when the World Trade Organization (WTO) held its ministerial conference in Seattle in 1999. A large-scale coalition of NGOs, religious groups and trade unions staged workshops and demonstrations. As a report in the British *Guardian* put it, 'Opposition to the WTO is becoming the end-of-century battle cry, and Seattle '99 is seen as the Woodstock of growing dissent against the excesses of capitalism.'[261] While the overwhelming number of demonstrators acted peacefully, some groups sought direct confrontation with the police, in an event that came to be known as the 'Battle of Seattle'.

While the Seattle protests took place in North America, they provided a model for activists in Europe. In 2001, both Gothenburg and Genoa hosted summits that involved demonstrations. In anticipation, the hosts of the G8 summit in Genoa had created an exclusion zone that was meant to minimize the risk for another conflagration, yet the heavy-handed actions of the Italian police as well as violent actions by the anarchist 'black bloc' resulted in clashes and rioting that saw one demonstrator killed and many injured. Such actions overshadowed the considerable amount of peaceful mobilization by global justice activists: around 800 groups worked together on a Genoa Social Forum that sought to create an alternative to the high-level meeting of state leaders.[262]

The protests against neo-liberal globalization benefited from another global development, namely the spread of the internet. In 1999, activists who were planning the Seattle protests set up the Indymedia platform – a network of websites that allowed protesters to share news on their different activities. Such ventures were part of a diverse media strategy that not only aimed at internal communication but also at gaining external coverage – although in 2011, over a decade after Seattle, a study suggested that the correlation between media efforts and the extent of media coverage itself was unclear.[263] Since then, the rise of social media has evidently changed the dynamics entirely, with both traditional print media and websites becoming a less prominent feature than direct interactions between campaigners.

Alongside the summit protests of the late 1990s and early 2000s, another major campaign was led by the *Association pour la Taxation des Transactions financières et pour l'Action Citoyenne* (Attac, Association for the Taxation of Financial Transactions and for the Aid of Citizens), which was founded in France 1998 and soon developed into an international organization. By the summer of 2001, Attac was seen 'as the central player in the global justice movements … in Germany' while in Italy, the formation of a national Attac chapter received the backing of 'a broad section of associations traditionally close to the left'.[264] While it soon developed into a broader campaign, one major focus for Attac was the demand to tax the profits from currency speculation and to use the resulting revenue to reduce global inequalities.

From the beginning, Attac was involved in a major initiative of the global justice movement: the World Social Forum. Proclaiming that 'another world is possible', the

Forum sessions were large-scale gatherings for protagonists from global civil society. Its name deliberately established a contrast with the World Economic Forum – the annual gathering of global political and business leaders at Davos, Switzerland. In contrast to Davos, the World Social Forum was conceived as an assembly of the people. The first such event took place in January 2001, in the Brazilian city of Porto Alegre. Indeed, there was a strong Latin American presence from the start and since Porto Allegre, all host cities – with the exception of Montreal in 2016 – have been in the Global South. Yet European activists were involved not only as participants but also by creating a regional variant, the European Social Forum. Held in Florence in 2002, the first such event attracted 60,000 participants, with a flagship demonstration that involved a million people.[265]

While there was a significant amount of contention in the late 1990s and early 2000s, political mobilization relating to the economic order gained particular force in the wake of the global economic crisis that began in 2008, which in several countries triggered the implementation of austerity policies. Donatella della Porta has spoken of a 'wave of protest that started in 2011' and that 'was especially visible in those countries that had been particularly hard hit by the finical crisis of 2008'.[266] The urban activism of the *Indignados* in Spain and the 'Occupy Wall Street' movement were key features of this movement, turning from localized urban protests to international phenomena. Such growth reflected shared experiences – a sense of lacking meaningful political representation in the face of powerful economic forces – but also cross-connections between the movements.[267] Indeed, when 'Occupy Wall Street' arrived on the scene in October 2011, external observers were struck by the resemblance to the *Indignados*. As

Figure 4.3 Participants of the First European Social Forum (Florence, 11 August 2002).
Source: Alain Buu / Gamma-Rapho, via Getty Images.

the journalist Ishaan Tharoor put it, 'The similarities between the Occupy Wall Street crowd and the indignados are legion', both in their use of social media and in 'the chaotic, decentralized nature of their movements'.[268] The simultaneous events of the 'Arab Spring' – the democratic protests across the Arab World – also meant that protesters in the West could construe themselves as part of a wider moment of global resistance.

This was also the case with the protests that emerged in Greece following the imposition of rigid austerity policies by the EU. As one study has pointed out, mobilization in this context 'has linked to and been influenced by the rhythms of economic and political contention in the Arab, Indignado and Occupy protests'.[269] Importantly, in challenging the policies of the Troika – the European Commission, the European Central Bank and the International Monetary Fund – Greek activists also sought to elicit solidarity from other countries. One such example was the occasion of a 'European Union Strike Day Versus Austerity' in November 2012. In a way, these contemporary mobilizations contain elements of past forms of collective action. While being removed from the efforts to build formal 'Internationals', they do evoke the 'informal internationalism' of various activist groups in the nineteenth century, the adoption of international days of action by earlier left-wing groups as well as the development of new protest cultures in the 1960s.

Notes

1. Karl Marx and Friedrich Engels, *The Communist Manifesto* (Oxford: Oxford University Press, 2008 [orig. 1848]), 23.
2. Roman Rosdolsky, 'The Workers and the Fatherland: A Note on a Passage in the "Communist Manifesto"', *Science and Society* 29, no. 3 (1965): 330–7.
3. Rosdolsky, 'The Workers and the Fatherland', 336.
4. Ibid., 337.
5. Janusz Radziejowski and William Leogrande, 'Roman Rosdolsky: Man, Activist and Scholar', *Science & Society* 42, no. 2 (1978): 199.
6. Roman Rosdolsky, *Engels and the 'Non-Historic' Peoples: The National Question in the Revolution of 1848* (Glasgow: Critique Books, 1986). On Rosdolsky's engagement with these issues, see Anson Rabinbach, 'Roman Rosdolsky 1897–1967: An Introduction', *New German Critique* 1, no. 3 (1974): 57.
7. Eley, *Forging Democracy*, 8.
8. Radziejowski and Leogrande, 'Roman Roslosky', 206.
9. Constance Bantman, *Jean Grave and the Networks of French Anarchism, 1854–1939* (Cham: Palgrave, 2021); Constance Bantman, 'The Dangerous Liaisons of Belle Epoque Anarchists: Internationalism, Transnationalism, and Nationalism in the French Anarchist Movement (1880–1914)', in Bantman and Altena, *Reassessing the Transnational Turn*, 174–92; Davide Turcato, 'Italian Anarchism as a Transnational Movement, 1885–1915', *International Review of Social History* 52, no. 3 (2007): 407–44.
10. Brigitte Studer, *The Transnational World of the Cominternians* (Basingstoke: Palgrave, 2015). See also Studer, *Reisende der Weltrevolution*.

11. Imlay, *The Practice of Socialist Internationalism*, 9.
12. Frank Jacob and Mario Keßler, 'Transatlantic Radicalism: A Short Introduction', in *Transatlantic Radicalism: Socialist and Anarchist Exchanges in the 19th and 20th Centuries*, ed. Frank Jacob and Mario Keßler (Liverpool: Liverpool University Press, 2021), 7.
13. Radziejowski and William Leogrande, 'Roman Roslosky', 205.
14. Roman Rosdolsky, 'A Memoir of Auschwitz and Birkenau', *Monthly Review* 39, no. 8 (1988): 33–8.
15. 'Roman Rosdolsky – A Genuine Marxist Scholar', *Intercontinental Press* 6, no. 22 (1968): 513. The piece originally appeared in *Quatrième Internationale*, a periodical issued by the Fourth International.
16. R. J. W. Evans, 'Liberalism, Nationalism and the Coming of the Revolution', in *The Revolutions in Europe 1848–1849: From Reform to Reaction*, ed. R. J. W. Evans and Hartmut Pogge von Strandmann (Oxford: Oxford University Press, 2000), 9–26; Jonathan Sperber, *The European Revolutions, 1848–1851* (2nd edn; Cambridge: Cambridge University Press, 2005).
17. Axel Körner, ed., *1848: A European Revolution? International Ideas and National Memories of 1848* (rev. edn; Basingstoke: Palgrave, 2003).
18. Lucy Riall, *Garibaldi: Invention of a Hero* (New Haven, CT: Yale University Press, 2008).
19. Simon Morgan, 'Heroes in the Age of Celebrity: Lafayette, Kossuth, and John Bright in 19th-Century America', *Historical Social Research*, S.32 (2019): 165–85; Zsuzsanna Lada, 'The Invention of a Hero: Lajos Kossuth in England (1851)', *European History Quarterly* 43, no. 1 (2013): 5–26.
20. Heléna Tóth, *An Exiled Generation: German and Hungarian Refugees of Revolution, 1848–1871* (New York: Cambridge University Press, 2014), 172–85.
21. Maurizio Isabella, *Risorgimento in Exile: Italian Émigrés and the Liberal International in the Post-Napoleonic Era* (Oxford: Oxford University Press, 2009).
22. Tóth, *An Exiled Generation*, 172–85.
23. Sarah Panter, 'Zwischen Verlust und Aneignung von "Heimat": Transatlantische Reflexionen deutscher Revolutionsflüchtlinge nach 1848/49', *The Germanic Review: Literature, Culture, Theory* 96, no. 3 (2021): 276–92.
24. Heike Bungert, 'The German Forty-Eighters in American Society and Politics', in *Yearbook of Transnational History*, vol. 4, ed. Thomas Adam (Madison, NJ: Fairleigh Dickinson University Press, 2021), 69–112. On Hecker, see also Sabine Freitag, *Friedrich Hecker: Two Lives for Liberty*, trans. Steven Rowan (St Louis: St Louis Mercantile Library, 2006).
25. Bernard Porter, *The Refugee Question in Mid-Victorian Politics* (Cambridge: Cambridge University Press, 1979), 8.
26. Rosemary Ashton, 'The Search for Liberty: German Exiles in England in the 1850s', *Journal of European Studies* 13, no. 3 (1983): 188.
27. Christine Lattek, *Revolutionary Refugees: German Socialism in Britain, 1840–1860* (Abingdon: Routledge, 2006), 83–109. See also Rosemary Ashton, *Little Germany: German Refugees in Victorian Britain* (Oxford: Oxford University Press, 1989).
28. Johanna Kinkel, *Hans Ibeles in London: Ein Familienbild aus dem Flüchtlingsleben* (Stuttgart: J.G. Cotta'scher Verlag, 1860), 171. See also Ashton, 'The Search for Liberty', 192–3; Carol Diethe, 'Keeping Busy in the Waiting-Room: German Women Writers in London following the 1848 Revolution', in *Exiles from European Revolutions: Refugees in Mid-Victorian Politics*, ed. Sabine Freitag and Rudolf Muhs (New York: Berghahn, 2003), 253–74.

29. Ashton, 'The Search for Liberty', 194.
30. Christine Lattek, 'The Beginnings of Socialist Internationalism in the 1840s: The "Democratic Friends of All Nations" in London', in *Internationalism in the Labour Movement 1830–1940*, vol. 1, ed. Frits van Holthoon and Marcel van der Linden (Leiden: Brill, 1988), 282.
31. On different forerunners, see Fabrice Bensimon, 'The IWMA and Its Precursors in London, c. 1830–1860', in *'Arise Ye Wretched of the Earth': The First International in a Global Perspective*, ed. Fabrice Bensimon, Quentin Deluermoz and Jeanne Moisand (Leiden: Brill, 2018), 21–38.
32. James Billington, *Fire in the Minds of Men: Origins of the Revolutionary Faith* (New York: Basic Books, 1980), 333.
33. Edward Castleton, 'The Origins of "Collectivism": Pierre-Joseph Proudhon's Contested Legacy and the Debate about Property in the International Workingmen's Association and the League of Peace and Freedom', *Global Intellectual History* 2, no. 2 (2017): 169–95.
34. Benedict Anderson, *Under Three Flags: Anarchism and the Anti-Colonial Imagination* (London: Verso, 2005). On the development of anarchism in this period as well as its underpinnings, see Ruth Kinna, *The Government of No One: The Theory and Practice of Anarchism* (London: Pelican, 2019).
35. Carl Levy, 'The Rooted Cosmopolitan: Errico Malatesta, Syndicalism, Transnationalism and the International Labour Movement', in *New Perspectives on Anarchism, Labour and Syndicalism: The Individual, the National and the Transnational*, ed. David Berry and Constance Bantman (Newcastle upon Tyne: Cambridge Scholars Publishing, 2010), 62.
36. Levy, 'The Rooted Cosmopolitan', 75.
37. Emma Goldman, *Living My Life* (New York: Alfred Knopf, 1930), 165.
38. Pietro Di Paola, *The Knights Errant of Anarchy: London and the Italian Diaspora (1880–1917)* (Liverpool: Liverpool University Press, 2013); Constance Bantman, *The French Anarchists in London, 1880–1914: Exile and Transnationalism in the First Globalisation* (Liverpool: Liverpool University Press, 2013).
39. Daniel Laqua, 'Political Contestation and Internal Strife: Socialist and Anarchist German Newspapers in London, 1878-1910', in *The Foreign Political Press in London: Politics from a Distance*, ed. Constance Bantman and Ana Cláudia Suriani da Silva (London: Bloomsbury, 2017), 135–54.
40. Josef Peukert, *Erinnerungen eines Proletariers aus der revolutionären Arbeiterbewegung* (Frankfurt/Main: Verlag AV, 2002 [orig. 1913]), 57.
41. 'Übersicht über die allgemeine Lage der sozialdemokratischen und revolutionären Bewegung, Berlin 12. January 1882', in *Dokumente aus geheimen Archiven: Übersicht der Berliner politischen Polizei über die allgemeine Lage der sozialdemokratischen und anarchistischen Bewegung 1878-1913*, vol. 1: *1878–1889*, ed. Dieter Fricke and Rudolf Knaack (Weimar: Herman Böhlaus Nachfolger, 1983), 120.
42. Another attempt to form an 'international bureau' – featuring, inter alia, Malatesta, Rocker and the Russian anarchist Alexander Schapiro – occurred during an international congress held in Amsterdam in 1907: Goldman, *Living My Life*, 404.
43. Peukert, *Erinnerugen*, 58.
44. Bantman, *The French Anarchists in London*, 10.
45. Peukert, *Erinnerungen*, 176.

46. Bantman, *The French Anarchists in London*, 39; Di Paola, *The Knights Errant*, 71; Lattek, *Revolutionary Refugees*, 195. On anarchist clubs, see also Charlotte Jones, 'Pandæmonium as Parallax: Metropolitan Underworlds and Anarchist Clubs in Nineteenth-Century London and Its Literature', in *The Literature of Hell: Essays and Studies 2021*, ed. Margaret Kean (Cambridge: D. S. Brewer, 2021), 37–68.
47. Goldman, *Living My Life*, 166.
48. Constance Bantman, 'Louise Michel's London Years: A Political Reassessment (1890–1905)', *Women's History Review* 26, no. 6 (2017): 994–1012.
49. Goldman, *Living My Life*, 168.
50. For a list of publications in the 'anarchist-communist library', see *Die Autonomie* 6, no. 119 (31 January 1891): 1. A serialized translation of a French text by Kropotkin began with Peter Krapotkine [sic], 'Anarchistische Moral', *Die Autonomie* 6, no. 138 (1891): 1–2. It concluded in *Die Autonomie* 6, no. 149 (1891): 1.
51. Peukert, *Erinnerungen*, 159.
52. Houssine Alloul, Edhem Eldem and Henk de Smaele, eds, *To Kill a Sultan: A Transnational History of the Attempt on Abdülhamid II (1905)* (London: Palgrave, 2018).
53. Richard Bach Jensen, *The Battle against Anarchist Terrorism: An International History, 1878–1934* (Cambridge: Cambridge University Press, 2014), 131–84; Pietro Di Paola, 'The Spies Who Came in from the Heat: The International Surveillance of the Anarchists in London', *European History Quarterly* 37, no. 2 (2007): 189–215.
54. Johann Most, 'Endlich', *Freiheit*, 19 March 1881, 1.
55. Bernard Porter, 'The *Freiheit* Prosecutions, 1881–1882', *The Historical Journal* 23, no. 4 (1980): 833–56.
56. Goldman, *Living My Life*, 40 and 379–80.
57. Tom Goyens, *Beer and Revolution: The German Anarchist Movement in New York City, 1880–1914* (Urbana, IL: University of Illinois Press, 2007); Kenyon Zimmer, *Immigrants against the State: Yiddish and Italian Anarchism in America* (Urbana, IL: University of Illinois Press, 2015).
58. Lara Green, 'Russian Revolutionary Terrorism in Transnational Perspective: Representations and Networks, 1881–1926' (PhD thesis, Northumbria University, 2019), e. g. 49.
59. Woodford McClellan, *Revolutionary Exiles: The Russians in the First International and the Paris Commune* (London: Frank Cass, 1979); Charlotte Alston, 'News of the Struggle: The Russian Political Press in London 1853–1921', in Bantman and Suriani da Silva, *The Foreign Political Press*, 155–74.
60. For documents relating to his early period of exile, see Alexander Herzen, *Letters from France and Italy, 1847–70*, trans. and ed. Judith E. Zimmerman (Pittsburgh, PA: University of Pittsburgh Press, 1995).
61. Green, 'Russian Revolutionary Terrorism', 149–80. See also Haia Shpayer-Makov, 'The Reception of Peter Kropotkin in Britain, 1886–1917', *Albion* 19, no. 3 (1987): 373–90.
62. Michael Hughes, 'British Opinion and Russian Terrorism in the 1880s', *European History Quarterly* 41, no. 2 (2011): 255–77.
63. Stepniak, *Underground Russia: Revolutionary Profiles and Sketches from Life* (New York: Charles Scribner's Sons, 1883), 252.
64. Lara Green, 'Russian Revolutionary Terrorism, British Liberals, and the Problem of Empire (1884–1914)', *History of European Ideas* 46, no. 5 (2020): 633–48.

65. For an account of this period in Lenin's life, see Helen Rappaport, *Conspirator: Lenin in Exile* (New York: Basic Books, 2010).

66. Robert Henderson, *The Spark That Lit the Revolution: Lenin in London and the Politics That Changed the World* (London: Bloomsbury, 2020), 169.

67. Goldman, *Living My Life*, 372.

68. Angelica Balabanoff, *My Life as a Rebel* (New York: Harper and Brothers, 1938), 53.

69. Bensimon, 'The First International and Its Precursors in London'.

70. Murray Bookchin, *The Third Revolution: Popular Movements in the Revolutionary Era* (London: Cassell, 1998), 258.

71. 'Zur Eröffnung der beiden Pariser Arbeiterkongresse', *Londoner Freie Presse*, 13 July 1889, 1. Debates about a potential unification featured at the congresses themselves: see *Protokoll des Internationalen Arbeiter-Congresses zu Paris. Abgehalten vom 4. bis 20. Juli 1889* (Nuremberg: Wörlein, 1890), 13–23.

72. Rudolf Rocker, *The London Years*, trans. Joseph Leftwich (Nottingham: Five Leaves, 2005 [1956]), 29.

73. 'Domela Nieuwenhuis', *Labour Leader*, 8 August 1896, 276. The paper of Britain's Independent Labour Party discussed the presence of anarchist delegates at the London congress from a perspective that was broadly sympathetic to their participation: 'Welcome to Anarchist Delegates', *Labour Leader*, 1 August 1896, 271; 'Between Ourselves', *Labour Leader*, 8 August 1896, 274; J. Bruce Glasier, 'The Congress', *Labour Leader*, 8 August 1896, 277.

74. Christina Morina, *Die Erfindung des Marxismus: Wie eine Idee die Welt eroberte* (Munich: Siedler, 2017), 199.

75. 'Die schwarz-weiße Internationale', *Londoner Freie Presse*, 5 May 1889, 4.

76. Eduard Bernstein, *My Years of Exile: Reminiscences of a Socialist*, transl. Bernard Miall (New York: Harcourt, Brace and Howe, 1921), 168 and 170–1.

77. Bernstein, *My Years of Exile*, 174.

78. Roger A. Fletcher, 'Cobden as Educator: The Free-Trade Internationalism of Eduard Bernstein, 1899–1914', *The American Historical Review* 88, no. 3 (1983): 562.

79. Graham Johnson, 'Making Reform the Instrument of Revolution: British Social Democracy, 1881–1911', *Historical Journal* 43, no. 4 (2000): 978. See also Douglas J. Newton, *British Labour, European Socialism and the Struggle for Peace 1889–1914* (Oxford: Clarendon Press, 1985).

80. Janet Polasky, *The Democratic Socialism of Emile Vandervelde: Between Reform and Revolution* (Oxford: Berg, 1995).

81. Moira Donald, 'Workers of the World Unite? Exploring the Enigma of the Second International', in Geyer and Paulmann, *The Mechanics of Internationalism*, 188.

82. IISG, Sozialistische Jugend-Internationale archives (ARCH01370), A1: circular letter from Henri de Man to socialist youth organizations, 13 March 1907.

83. IISG, ARCH01370, A1: see e.g. 'Provisorische Ausgabe des internationalen Bulletins der sozialistisciehn Jugendorganisationen', 15 February 1907.

84. Alexandra Kollontai, 'International Socialist Conferences of Women Workers [1907–1916]', in Alexandra Kollontai, *Selected Articles and Speeches*, trans. Cynthia Carlile (New York: Progress Publishers, 1984), 39. On these conflicts, see Susan Zimmermann, 'A Struggle over Gender, Class and the Vote: Unequal International Interactions and the Formation of the "Female International" of Socialist Women (1905–1907)', in *Gender History in a*

Transnational Perspective: Networks, Biographies, Gender Orders, ed. Oliver Janz and Daniel Schönpflug (New York: Berghahn, 2014), 101–27.
85. Clara Zetkin, 'Der Internationale Sozialistenkongress zu Stuttgart', *Die Gleichheit*, 2 September 1907, 1.
86. Kollontai, 'International Socialist Conferences of Women Workers', 45. For overview of different socialist attitudes in this period, see Eley, *Forging Democracy*, 99–107; and Zimmermann, *GrenzÜberschreitungen*, 137–86.
87. Peter Cole, David Struthers and Kenyon Zimmer, eds, *Wobblies of the World: A Global History of the IWW* (London: Pluto, 2017).
88. Marion Fontaine, 'L'Internationale des syndicalistes: quel sens donner à l'internationalisme? Le cas des mineurs', *Cahiers Jaurès*, nos. 212–13 (2014): 91–103; Nicolas Delalande, *La Lutte et l'entraide: l'âge des solidarités ouvrières* (Paris: Seuil, 2019), 212–20.
89. Rolf Neuhaus, *International Trade Secretariats: Objectives, Organisation, Aims* (Bonn: Friedrich-Ebert-Stiftung, 1981).
90. Léon Jouhaux, 'Fifty Years of Trade-Union Activity in [sic] Behalf of Peace: Nobel Lecture, December 11, 1951', in *Nobel Lectures in Peace (1951–1970)*, ed. Frederick Haberman (Singapore: World Scientific Publishing, 1999), 17.
91. Susan Milner, *The Dilemmas of Internationalism: French Syndicalism and the International Labour Movement, 1900–1914* (New York: Berg, 1990), 87 and 91.
92. Geert Van Goethem, *The Amsterdam International: The World of the International Federation of Trade Unions, 1913–1945* (Aldershot: Ashgate, 2006), 3.
93. 'Rerum Novarum: Encyclical of Pope Leo XIII on Capital and Labor', https://www.vatican.va/content/leo-xiii/en/encyclicals/documents/hf_l-xiii_enc_15051891_rerum-novarum.html (last accessed 9 January 2023). For its impact on Christian trade unions, see e.g. Wlihelm Damberg, Claudia Hiepel and Alfredo Canavero, 'The Formation of Christian Working-Class Organizations in Belgium, Germany, Italy and the Netherlands (1840s–1920s)', in Heerma van Voss et al., *Between Cross and Class*, 66; and Patrick Pasture, *Histoire du syndicalisme chrétien international: La difficile recherche d'une troisième voie* (Paris: L'Harmattan, 1999).
94. Frank Georgi and Lex Heerma van Voss, 'Christian Trade Unionism and the Organization of Industry: From the Organized Profession to Democratic Planning and Self-Management' in Heerma van Voss et al., *Between Cross and Class*, 236.
95. Mary Hilson, Silke Neunsinger and Greg Patmore, 'A Global History of Consumer Co-operation since 1850: Introduction', in *A Global History of Consumer Co-operation since 1850: Movements and Businesses*, ed. Mary Hilson, Silke Neunsinger and Greg Patmore (Leiden: Brill, 2017), 8.
96. Mary Hilson, 'Origins and Models: Introduction to Section 1', in Hilson et al., *A Global History of Consumer Co-operation*, 49–58.
97. Mary Hilson, *The International Co-operative Alliance and the Consumer Co-operative Movement in Northern Europe, c. 1860–1939* (Manchester: Manchester University Press, 2018). See also John Birchall, *The International Co-operative Movement* (Manchester: Manchester University Press, 1997).
98. Horst Bartel, Wolfgang Schröder, Gustav Seeber and Heinz Wolter, *Der Sozialdemokrat 1879–1890: Ein Beitrag zur Rolle des Zentralorgans im Kampf der revolutionären Arbeiterbewegung gegen das Sozialistengesetz* (Berlin: Dietz-Verlag, 1975), 105.
99. Police report for the year of 1898, in *Dokumente aus geheimen Archiven: Übersichten der Berliner politischen Polizei über die allgemeine Lage der sozialdemokratischen und anarchistischen Bewegung 1878–1913*, vol. 2: *1890–1906*, ed. Dieter Fricke and Rudolf Knaack (Weimar: Hermann Böhlaus Nachfolger, 1989), 148.

100. Henderson, *The Spark That Lit the Revolution*, 83–116.
101. Goldman, *Living My Life*, 254.
102. Rocker, *The London Years*, 71.
103. Ibid., 73.
104. 'Die Zweite Internationale Konferenz Sozialistischer Frauen zu Copenhagen', *Die Gleichheit*, 12 September 1910, 387. On *Die Gleichheit*'s links to British women socialists, see Karen Hunt, *Equivocal Feminists: The Social Democratic Federation and the Woman Question 1884–1911* (Cambridge: Cambridge University Press, 1996), 69.
105. Bantman, 'Louise Michel's London Years', 1002–4.
106. For a recent selection of his writings, see Mark Bray and Robert H. Haworth, eds, *Anarchist Education and the Modern School: A Francisco Ferrer Reader* (Oakland, CA: PM Press, 2019).
107. Geoffrey Fidler, 'The Escuela Moderna Movement of Francisco Ferrer: "Por la Verdad y la Justicia"', *History of Education Quarterly* 25, nos. 1–2 (1985): 103–32.
108. Daniel Laqua, 'Freethinkers, Anarchists and Francisco Ferrer: The Making of a Transnational Solidarity Campaign', *European Review of History* 21, no. 4 (2014): 467–84.
109. Goldman, *Living My Life*, 458.
110. Paul Avrich, *The Modern School Movement: Anarchism and Education in the United States* (Princeton, NJ: Princeton University Press, 1980); Jean-François Marchat, 'Francisco Ferrer, un solidariste libertaire en Education nouvelle', in *L'Éducation nouvelle: histoire, presence et devenir*, ed. Annick Ohayon, Dominique Ottavi and Antoine Savoye (2nd edn; Bern: Peter Lang, 2007), 67–92.
111. Axel Körner, *Das Lied von einer anderen Welt: Kulturelle Praxis im französischen und deutschen Arbeitermilieu 1840–1890* (Frankfurt/Main: Campus, 1997).
112. With regard to the tune and the symbol of the red flag, Dogliani has argued that 'Having failed as an organizational structure, the "International" ... assumed the value of a symbolic identity for the working classes': Patrizia Dogliani, 'The Fate of Socialist Internationalism', in Sluga and Clavin, *Internationalisms*, 41.
113. Quentin Deluermoz, 'The IWMA and the Commune', in Bensimon et al., *'Arise Ye Wretched of the Earth'*, 107–26; Delalande, *La Lutte et l'entraide*, 154–65.
114. Karl Marx, *The Civil War in France: Address of the General Council of the International Working-Men's Association* (London: Edward Truelove, 1871); Mikhail Bakunin, 'The Paris Commune and the Idea of the State' (1871), in *Bakunin on Anarchy: Selected Texts by the Activist-Founder of World Anarchism*, ed. Sam Dolgoff (London: George Allen & Unwin, 1973), 259–74; Lenin, 'Lessons of the Commune' (March 1908), in *Collected Works*, vol. 13: *June 1907–April 1908*, trans. Bernard Isaacs and ed. Clemens Dutt (Moscow: Foreign Languages Publishing House, 1962), 475–8. On responses to the Haymarket Affair, see e.g. Hubert Perrier, Catherine Collomp, Michel Cordillot and Marianne Debouzy, 'The "Social Revolution" in America? European Reactions to the "Great Upheaval" and to the Haymarket Affair', *International Labor and Working-Class History* 29 (1986): 38–52.
115. 'Übersicht über die allgemeine Lage der sozialdemokratischen und anarchistischen Bewegung im Jahre 1908', in *Dokumente aus geheimen Archiven: Übersichten der Berliner Polizei über die allgemeine Lage der sozialdemokratischen und anarchistischen Bewegung 1878–1913*, vol. 3: *1906–1913*, ed. Dieter Fricke and Rudolf Knaack (Berliner: Berliner Wissenschaftsverlag, 2004), 164.

116. The decision to celebrate 1 May did not, however, explicitly reference the Haymarket Affair: *Protokoll des Internationalen Arbeiter-Congresses zu Paris*, 123.
117. 'Die Maifeier des Proletariats', *Der Sozialdemokrat*, 19 May 1890, 2.
118. 'Übersicht über den Verlauf der sozialdemokratischen Bewegung in Deutschland seit der Aufhebung des Reichsgesetzes gegen die gemeingefährlichen Bestrebungen der Sozialdemokratie, 2. September 1893', in Fricke and Knaack, *Dokumente aus geheimen Archiven*, vol. 2, 13.
119. Ibid., 13
120. 'Zur 1. Mai-Bewegung', *Die Autonomie*, 10 January 1891, 1–2; 'Der Maitag', *Die Autonomie*, 9 May 1891, 1–2; R. W. Burnie, 'The First of May', *The Commonweal* 7, no. 260 (1891): 25–6.
121. Alexandra Kollontai, 'A Militant Celebration' (1920), trans. Alix Holt, online via the https://www.marxists.org/archive/kollonta/1920/womens-day.htm (last accessed 9 January 2023).
122. For caveats on this subject, see Jens-Uwe Guettel, 'The Myth of the Pro-Colonialist SPD: German Social Democracy and Imperialism before World War I', *Central European History* 45, no. 3 (2012): 452–84.
123. Anderson, *Under Three Flags*.
124. Carl Levy, 'Anarchism and Cosmopolitanism', in *The Palgrave Handbook of Anarchism*, ed. Carl Levy and Matthew Adams (Cham: Palgrave, 2019), 125–48.
125. Michael Bakunin, *Statism and Anarchy*, trans. and ed. Marshall Shatz (Cambridge: Cambridge University Press, 1990), 46.
126. Marcel van der Linden, *Transnational Labour History: Explorations* (Aldershot: Ashgate, 2003), 12.
127. Milner, *The Dilemmas of Internationalism*, 230.
128. Donald, 'Workers of the World Unite?', 187.
129. Louise Nalbandian, *The Armenian Revolutionary Movement: The Development of Armenian Political Parties through the Nineteenth Century* (Berkeley, CA: University of California Press, 1963), 171.
130. Maria Todorova, *The Lost World of Socialists at Europe's Margins: Imagining Utopia, 1870s–1920s* (London: Bloomsbury, 2020), 55–6.
131. Todorova, *The Lost World*, 60–2.
132. Rosa Luxemburg, 'Foreword to the Anthology *The Polish Question and the Socialist Movement*' (1905), in *The National Question: Selected Writings* by Rosa Luxemburg, ed. Horace Davis (New York: Monthly Review Press, 1976), 98. See also Jie-Hyun Lim, 'Rosa Luxemburg on the Dialectics of Proletarian Internationalism and Social Patriotism', *Science & Society* 59, no. 4 (1995/1996): 498–530.
133. Rosa Luxemburg, 'The National Question and Autonomy: 2. The Nation-State and the Proletariat' (1909), in Davis, *The National Question*, 164.
134. Rosa Luxemburg, 'Rebuilding the International', *Die Internationale*, no. 1 (1915), as reproduced in https://www.marxists.org/archive/luxemburg/1915/xx/rebuild-int.htm (last accessed 9 January 2023).
135. Kinna and Adams, eds, *Anarchism, 1914–18*.
136. Imlay, *The Practice of Socialist Internationalism*, 18.

137. Nation, *War on War*, 70.
138. Eley, *Forging Democracy*, 127–31; and Nation, *War on War*.
139. See e.g. Lenin, 'Opportunism and the Collapse of the Second International' (January 1916), in *Lenin Collected Works*, vol. xix: *1916–1927*, trans. Moissaye Olgin and ed. Alexander Trachenberg (London: International Publishers, 1942), 15–27.
140. G. D. H. Cole even went so far as calling the Belgian socialists as 'the most intransigent element in the International taking a strong stand against meeting the German socialists as long as the war continued': G. D. H. Cole, *Communism and Social Democracy 1914–1931* (London: Macmillan, 1958), 39.
141. Camille Huysmans, *The Policy of the International: A Speech of and Interview with the Secretary of the International*, trans. Fred Gorle (London: Allen & Unwin, 1916), 6.
142. Jonas Harvard, 'Socialist Communication Strategies and the Spring of 1917', *Scandinavian Journal of History* 44, no. 2 (2019): 183.
143. Kirby, 'International Socialism and the Question of Peace'; Masao Nishikawa, *Socialists and International Actions for Peace* (Berlin: Frank & Timme, 2010), 51–64; Elisa Marcobelli, 'Stockholm Conference', in Ute Daniel et al., eds, *1914–1918 Online: International Encyclopedia of the First World War* (2020), https://encyclopedia.1914-1918-online.net/article/stockholm_conference (last accessed 9 January 2023).
144. Imlay, *The Practice of Internationalism*, esp. 51–150; Laqua, 'Democratic Politics and the League of Nations'.
145. The term 'demonstration culture' is taken from Callahan, *Demonstration Culture*.
146. Clara Zetkin, 'From the International of the Word to the International of the Deed', *The Communist International*, new series, no. 1 (1924), via https://www.marxists.org/archive/zetkin/1924/xx/international.htm (last accessed 9 January 2023).
147. 'Conditions of Admission into the Communist International', as featured in Osip Piatnitsky, *The Twenty-One Conditions of Admission into the Communist International* (New York: Workers Library Publishers, 1934), 29.
148. Laqua, 'Democratic Politics and the League of Nations', 181–3.
149. Tim Rees and Andrew Thorpe, 'Introduction', in *International Communism and the Communist International 1919–1943*, ed. Tim Rees and Andrew Thorpe (Manchester: Manchester University Press, 1998), 1.
150. Norman LaPorte, Kevin Morgan and Matthew Worley, eds, *Bolshevism, Stalinism and the Comintern: Perspectives on Stalinization, 1917–53* (Basingstoke: Palgrave, 2008).
151. Martin Geyer, 'Munich in Turmoil: Social Protest and the Revolutionary Movement 1918–19', and Zsuzsa Nagy, 'Budapest and the Revolutions of 1918 and 1919', both in *Challenges of Labour: Central and Western Europe 1917–1920*, ed. Chris Wrigley (London: Routledge, 1993), 51–71 and 72–86 respectively.
152. Zetkin, 'From the International of the Word to the International of the Deed'.
153. Emma Goldman, *My Disillusionment in Russia* (Garden City: Doubleday, Page & Co., 1923).
154. Goldman, *Living My Life*, 800.
155. George Orwell, *The Lion and the Unicorn: Socialism and the English Genius* (London: Penguin, 1982 [orig. 1941]), 48.
156. Gleb Albert, *Das Charisma der Weltrevolution: Revolutionärer Internationalismus in der frühen Sowjetgesellschaft 1917–1927* (Cologne: Böhlau, 2017).

157. Matthias Neumann, 'Youthful Internationalism in the Age of "Socialism in One Country": Komsomol'tsy, Pioneers and "World Revolution" in the Interwar Period', *Revolutionary Russia* 31, no. 2 (2018): 279–303.

158. On German communism, see Norman LaPorte and Ralf Hofrogge, eds, *Weimar Communism as Mass Movement 1918–1933* (London: Lawrence & Wishart, 2017); Eric Weitz, *Creating German Communism, 1890–1990: From Popular Protests to Socialist State* (Princeton, NJ: Princeton University Press, 1997).

159. For contrasting views on the Lenin School and its relationship with British communism, see Gidon Cohen and Kevin Morgan, 'Stalin's Sausage Machine: British Students at the International Lenin School, 1926–37', *Twentieth Century British History* 14, no. 4 (2002): 327–55; John McIlroy, Alan Campbell, Barry McLoughlin and John Halstead, 'Forging the Faithful: The British at the International Lenin School', *Labour History Review* 68, no. 1 (2003): 99–128; as well as the subsequent debate between the authors of these articles. On the other two institutions, see Kirasirova, 'The "East" as a Category of Bolshevik Ideology and Comintern Administration'; Filatova, 'Indoctrination or Scholarship?'; Julia Köstenberger, 'Die Geschichte der "Kommunistischen Universität der nationalen Minderheiten des Westens" (KUNMZ) in Moskau 1921–1936', *Jahrbuch für Historische Kommunismusforschung* 6/7, no. 14 (2000/2001): 248–303; Studer, *The Transnational World of the Cominternians*, 90–3.

160. Kevin McDermott and Jeremy Agnew, *The Comintern: A History of International Communism from Lenin to Stalin* (New York: St Martin's, 1997), 34.

161. Braskén, *The International Workers' Relief*.

162. McDermott and Agnew, *The Comintern*, 50–2 and 79.

163. Matthew Worley, 'Courting Disaster? The Communist International in the Third Period', in *In Search of Revolution: International Communist Parties in the 'Third Period'*, ed. Matthew Worley (London: I.B. Tauris, 2004), 15.

164. Joachim Häberlen, 'Between Global Aspirations and Local Realities: The Global Dimensions of Interwar Communism', *Journal of Global History* 7, no. 3 (2012): 415–37.

165. Sophie Cœuré and Rachel Mazuy, *Cousu de fil rouge: Voyages des intellectuels français en Union soviétique. 150 documents inédits des Archives russes* (Paris: CNRS Éditions, 2012); David-Fox, *Showcasing the Great Experiment*, 203–46.

166. The most famous articulation of this critique is Leon Trotsky, *The Revolution Betrayed: What Is the Soviet Union and Where Is It Going?*, trans. Max Eastman (London: Faber & Faber, 1937).

167. J. Arch Getty, 'Trotsky in Exile: The Founding of the Fourth International', *Soviet Studies* 38, no. 1 (1986): 24–35.

168. C. L. R. James, *World Revolution, 1917–1936: The Rise and Fall of the Communist International*, ed. Christian Høgsbjerg (Durham, NC: Duke University Press, 2017 [orig. 1937]), 387–400.

169. Catherine Andreyev and Ivan Savický, *Russia Abroad: Prague and the Russian Diaspora, 1918–1938* (New Haven, CT: Yale University Press, 2004), 30.

170. Andreyev and Savický, *Russia Abroad*, 32.

171. Marc Raeff, *Russia Abroad: A Cultural History of the Russian Emigration, 1919–1939* (Oxford: Oxford University Press, 1990).

172. Charlotte Alston, 'The Work of the Russian Liberation Committee in London, 1919–1924', *Slavonica* 14, no. 1 (2008): 6–17.

173. Andreyev and Savický, *Russia Abroad*, 180.
174. Brigitte Studer and Berthold Unfried, 'Private Matters Become Public: Western European Communist Exiles and Emigrants in Stalinist Russia in the 1930s', *International Review of Social History* 48, no. 2 (2003): 203–23.
175. Palmier, *Weimar in Exile*, 135–40 and 184–218.
176. Kasper Braskén, 'Making Anti-Fascism Transnational: The Origins of Communist and Socialist Articulations of Resistance in Europe, 1923–1924', *Contemporary European History* 25, no. 4 (2016): 573–96.
177. IISG, Labour and Socialist International Archives (ARCH01368), folder 3439: 'Bericht an die Exekutive der S.A.I. und den Vorstand des I. G. B. erstattet vom Komitee zur Verwaltung des Matteottifonds über das Jahr 1933'.
178. Willi Münzenberg, *Livre Brun sur l'incendie du Reichstag et le terreur hitlérienne* (Paris: Éditions Carrefour, 1933). On Münzenberg's activities in Paris, see also Studer, *Reisende der Weltrevolution*, 392–415.
179. Münzenberg remains a highly controversial figure. For vastly different interpretations, see John Green, *Willy Münzenberg: Fighter against Fascism and Stalinism* (Abingdon: Routledge, 2020); Sean McMeekin, *Red Millionaire: A Political Biography of Willy Münzenberg, Moscow's Secret Propaganda Tsar in the West* (New Haven, CT: Yale University Press, 2003); Stephen Koch, *Double Lives: Stalin, Willi Munzenberg and the Seduction of the Intellectuals* (New York: Enigma, 2004).
180. Warwick Digital Collections, 292/946/9/25: 'Draft translation: Adler's proposed answer submitted to IFTU EC mtg, 16.1.35'.
181. The literature on the Spanish Civil War is vast, and there are also many different studies of individual contingents within the International Brigades. For a broader survey, see Giles Tremlett, *The International Brigades: Fascism, Freedom and the Spanish Civil War* (London: Bloomsbury, 2021).
182. Fraser Raeburn, 'Politics, Networks and Community: Recruitment for the International Brigades Reassessed', *Journal of Contemporary History* 55, no. 4 (2020): 719–44.
183. Ruth Waller, 'A School for Nurses' (1938), in Fryth and Alexander, *Women's Voices from the Spanish Civil War*, 163.
184. Emma Goldman to *Spain and the World*, 21 January 1937, 4, as digitized by the Emma Goldman Papers Project, UC Berkeley Library, https://www.lib.berkeley.edu/goldman/pdfs/letter24.pdf (last accessed 9 January 2023).
185. Emma Goldman to *Spain and the World*, 21 January 1937, 1.
186. Emma Goldman, 'Ideas and Realities' (1937), in Fryth and Alexander, *Women's Voices from the Spanish Civil War*, 301.
187. 'Anarchists Maligned Once More', *Spain and the World* 1, no. 14, supplement (1937): 1.
188. Judith Keene, *Fighting for Franco: International Volunteers in Nationalist Spain during the Spanish Civil War, 1936–1939* (London: Hambledon Continuum, 2001); Christopher Othen, *Franco's International Brigade Adventurers, Fascists, and Christian Crusaders in the Spanish Civil War* (London: Hurst, 2013).
189. Rob May, 'Saving Our Empire from the Bolsheviks: The British Fascisti from a Transnational Perspective', *The Journal of Imperial and Commonwealth History* 49, no. 1 (2021): 70–92; Liam Liburd, 'Thinking Imperially: The British Fascisti and the Politics of Empire, 1923–35', *Twentieth Century British History* 32, no. 1 (2021): 46–67.

190. Ángel Alcade, *War Veterans and Fascism in Interwar Europe* (Cambridge: Cambridge University Press, 2017), 95–111. See also Bauerkämper and Rossoliński-Liebe, eds, *Fascism without Borders*; Federico Finchelstein, *Transatlantic Fascism: Ideology, Violence, and the Sacred in Argentina and Italy, 1919–1945* (Durham, NC: Duke University Press, 2010).
191. Daniel Hedinger, *Die Achse: Berlin – Rom – Tokio* (Munich: C.H. Beck, 2021), 77.
192. Asvero Gravelli, *Verso l'internazionale fascista* (Rome: Nuova Europa, 1932).
193. Gravelli, *Verso l'internazionale fascista*, 23.
194. Ibid., 210.
195. Hedinger, *Die Achse*, 187.
196. Aristotle Kallis, 'The Transnational Co-production of Interwar "Fascism": On the Dynamics of Ideational Mobility and Localization', *European History Quarterly* 51, no. 2 (2021): 189–213. For a regional case study, see Samuel Huston Goodfellow, 'Fascism as a Transnational Movement: The Case of Inter-War Alsace', *Contemporary European History* 22, no. 1 (2013): 87–106.
197. Michael Loughlin, 'Gustave Hervé's Transition from Socialism to National Socialism: Another Example of French Fascism?', *Journal of Contemporary History* 36, no. 1 (2003): 5–39.
198. Laurent Kestel, *La Conversion politique: Doriot, le PPF et la question du fascisme français* (Paris: Éditions Raisons d'agir, 2012).
199. Morgan, 'Militarism and Anti-Militarism'; Pons, *The Global Revolution*, 91–111.
200. Vladimir Tismaneanu, ed., *Stalinism Revisited: The Establishment of Communist Regimes in East-Central Europe* (Budapest: CEU Press, 2009). For initial local discretion, and the limits thereof, see Silvio Pons, 'Stalin and the European Communists after World War Two (1943–1948)', *Past & Present* 210, suppl. 6 (2011): 121–38.
201. Mark Kramer, 'Stalin, Soviet Policy, and the Establishment of a Communist Bloc in Eastern Europe, 1941–1948', in *Stalin and Europe: Imitation and Domination, 1928–1953*, ed. Timothy Snyder and Ray Brandon (Oxford: Oxford University Press, 2014), 277.
202. Wernicke, 'The Communist-Led World Peace Council'. For the divisions that emerged at various points, see also Günter Wernicke, 'The Unity of Peace and Socialism? The World Peace Council on a Cold War Tightrope between the Peace Struggle and Intrasystemic Communist Conflicts', *Peace & Change* 26, no. 3 (2001): 332–51.
203. Frances Stonor Saunders, *The Cultural Cold War: The CIA and the World of Arts and Letters* (new edn; New York: New Press, 2013); Karen Paget, *Patriotic Betrayal: The Inside Story of the CIA's Secret Campaign to Enroll American Students in the Crusade against Communism* (New Haven, CT: Yale University Press, 2015); Joël Kotek, *Students and the Cold War*, trans. Ralph Blumenau (Basingstoke: Palgrave, 1996).
204. Luc van Dongen, Stéphanie Roulin and Giles Scott Smith, eds, *Transnational Anti-Communism and the Cold War: Agents, Activities, and Networks* (Basingstoke: Palgrave, 2014).
205. Korboński, *Warsaw in Exile*, 184.
206. Adam Michnik, 'Why You Are Not Emigrating …: A Letter from Białołęka' (March 1982), in Adam Michnik, *Letters from Prison and Other Essays*, trans. Maya Latynski (Berkeley, CA: University of California Press, 1985), 17.
207. Elonory Gilburd, 'The Revival of Soviet Internationalism in the Mid to Late 1950s', in *The Thaw: Soviet Society and Culture during the 1950s and 1960s*, ed. Denis Kozlov and

Elonory Gilburd (Toronto: University of Toronto Press, 2013), 362–401; Tobias Rupprecht, *Soviet Internationalism after Stalin: Interaction and Exchange between the USSR and Latin America during the Cold War* (Cambridge: Cambridge University Press, 2015); Patryk Babiracki and Austin Jersild, eds, *Socialist Internationalism in the Cold War: Exploring the Second World* (Cham: Palgrave, 2016).

208. Maud Bracke, *Which Socialism, Whose Détente? West European Communism and the Czechoslovak Crisis of 1968* (Budapest: Central European University Press, 2007).

209. Terence Renaud, *New Lefts: The Making of a Radical Tradition* (Princeton, NJ: Princeton University Press, 2021), 5.

210. Robert Jackson Alexander, *International Trotskyism, 1929-1985: A Documented Analysis of the Movement* (Durham, NC: Duke University Press, 1991).

211. Jan Willem Stutje, *Ernest Mandel: A Rebel's Dream Deferred*, trans. Christopher Beck and Peter Drucker (London: Verso, 2009), 131.

212. Stutje, *Ernest Mandel*, 136.

213. Ibid., 137.

214. Julia Lovell, *Maoism: A Global History* (New York: Alfred A. Knopf, 2019), 269.

215. Richard Wolin, *The Wind from the East: French Intellectuals, the Cultural Revolution, and the Legacy of the 1960s* (2nd edn; Princeton, NJ: Princeton University Press, 2018).

216. Robert Alexander, 'Maoism', in *Dictionary of Twentieth-Century Communism*, ed. Robert Service and Silvio Pons (Princeton, NJ: Princeton University Press, 2022), 509; and David Spreen, 'Signal Strength Excellent in West Germany: Radio Tirana, European Maoist Internationalism and Its Disintegration in the Global Seventies', *European Review of History* 29, no. 3 (2022): 391–416. See, for instance, the shifting stance among the KPD/ML, a small Maoist party in West Germany: Gerd Koenen, *Das rote Jahrzehnt: Unsere kleine deutsche Kulturrevolution, 1967–1977* (Cologne: Kiepenheuer & Witsch, 2001), 300.

217. Stutje, *Ernest Mandel*, 107–8.

218. Jacek Kuron and Karol Modzelewski, 'A Socialist Manifesto for Poland', *International Socialism*, no. 28 (1967): 25–7.

219. Anna Delius, 'Translating Human Rights between Local Workers and Transnational Activism in Late 1970s Poland', *East Central Europe* 46, nos. 2–3 (2019): 188–211; Robert Brier, 'Broadening the Cultural History of the Cold War: The Emergence of the Workers' Defence Committee and the Rise of Human Rights', *Journal of Cold War Studies* 15, no. 4 (2013): 104–27.

220. Thomas Oleszczuk, 'Dissident Marxism in Eastern Europe', *World Politics* 34, no. 4 (1982): 527–47. See also Daniel Laqua and Charlotte Alston, 'Activism and Dissent under State Socialism: Coalitions and Campaigns in the 1970s and 1980s', *Labour History Review* 86, no. 3 (2021): 295–311.

221. Eley, *Forging Democracy*, 408–17.

222. Pjotr [Petro] Grigorenko, 'Brief an die französische, italienische und britische KP (Auszug), in *Menschenrechte: Ein Jahrbuch zu Osteuropa*, ed. Jirí Pelikán and Manfred Wilke (Reinbeck b. Hamburg: Rohwolt, 1977), 414 and 417.

223. Ernest Mandel, *From Stalinism to Eurocommunism: The Bitter Fruits of 'Socialism in One Country'*, trans. Jon Rothschild (London: New Left Books, 1978), 37.

224. Martin Conway, 'Left Catholicism in the 1940s: Elements of an Interpretation', in *Left Catholicism 1943-1955: Catholics and Society in Western Europe at the Point of Liberation*,

ed. Gerd-Rainer Horn and Emmanuel Gerard (Leuven: Leuven University Press, 2001), 269–81.

225. See e.g. the case of the 'turn towards Marx' of the Italian priest Ernesto Balducci or the role of debates on the 'Third World' at the International Christian Solidarity Congress in Amsterdam (1970): Gerd-Rainer Horn, *The Spirit of Vatican II: Western European Progressive Catholicism in the Long Sixties* (Oxford: Oxford University Press, 2015), 47–50 and 100–2.

226. Edit Király, 'An der Grenze des Erlaubten: Ungarische Kontakte der Aktion Sühnezeichen in den 1980er Jahren', *Journal of Modern European History* 8, no. 2 (2010): 221–42.

227. Andrzej Paczkowski, *Poland, 1980–1989: Solidarity, Martial Law, and the End of Communism in Europe*, trans. Christina Manetti (Rochester, NY: University of Rochester Press, 2015), 6 and 7. See also Bernd Schaefer, 'The Catholic Church and the Cold War's End in Europe: Vatican *Ostpolitik* and Pope John Paul II, 1985–1989', in *Europe and the End of the Cold War: A Reappraisal*, ed. Frederic Bozo et al. (Abingdon: Routledge, 2008), 64–77.

228. Adam Michnik, 'On Resistance: A Letter from Białołęka' (May 1982), in Michnik, *Letters from Prison*, 59.

229. Robert Brier, *Poland's Solidarity Movement and the Global Politics of Human Rights* (Cambridge: Cambridge University Press, 2021).

230. Stefan Berger, 'Solidarność, Western Solidarity and Détente: A Transnational Approach', *European Review* 16, no. 1 (2008): 75–84; Idesbald Goddeeris, 'The Transnational Scope of Western Labour's Solidarity with Solidarność', *Labour History Review* 75, no. 1 (2010): 60–75; Idesbald Goddeeris, ed., *Solidarity with Solidarity: Western European Trade Unions and the Polish Crisis, 1980–1982* (Lanham, MD: Lexington, 2010).

231. Stutje, *Ernest Mandel*, 226.

232. Padraic Kenney, 'Borders Breached: The Transnational in Eastern Europe since Solidarity', *Journal of Modern European History* 8, no. 2 (2010): 179–95.

233. Padraic Kenney, *A Carnival of Revolution: Central Europe 1989* (Princeton, NJ: Princeton University Press, 2002).

234. Horn and Kenney, eds, *Transnational Moments of Change*. On the breadth of causes and campaigns as well as contrasting currents in 1968, see Gerd-Rainer Horn, *The Spirit of '68: Rebellion in Western Europe and North America, 1956–1976* (Oxford: Oxford University Press, 2007).

235. Dominique Grange, 'À bas l'état policier', as featured on Dominique Grange / Les Barricadiers, *Chansons de Mai 68* (Expression Spontanée LP, 1968).

236. Detlef Siegfried, 'Music and Protest in 1960s Europe', in *1968 in Europe: A History of Protest and Activism, 1956–1977*, ed. Martin Klimke and Joachim Scharloth (Basingstoke: Palgrave, 2008), 57–70; Timothy Scott Brown, *Sixties Europe* (Cambridge: Cambridge University Press, 2020).

237. See the examples in Gildea et al., *Europe's 1968: Voices of Revolt*, and the case of the Soviet hippie movement, as discussed in Fürst, *Flowers through Concrete*.

238. Kornetis, *Children of the Dictatorship*, 53 and 59.

239. Nikolaos Papadogiannis, *Militant around the Clock? Left-Wing Youth Politics, Leisure, and Sexuality in Post-Dictatorship Greece, 1974–1981* (New York: Berghahn, 2015), 49.

240. Detlef Siegfried, 'Understanding 1968: Youth Rebellion, Generational Change and Postindustrial Society', in *Between Marx and Coca-Cola: Youth Cultures in Changing*

European Societies, 1960–1980, ed. Axel Schildt and Detlef Siegfried (New York: Berghahn, 2006), 59–81.

241. Richard Ivan Jobs, *Backpack Ambassadors: How Youth Travel Integrated Europe* (Chicago, IL: University of Chicago Press, 2017), 98.
242. Stutje, *Ernest Mandel*, 170.
243. Jeremy Suri, *Power and Protest: Global Revolution and the Rise of Détente* (Cambridge, MA: Harvard University Press, 2003), 127. For his most influential text, see Herbert Marcuse, *One-Dimensional Man: Studies in the Ideology of Advanced Industrial Society* (London: Routledge & Kegan Paul, 1964).
244. On Cohn-Bendit's transnational mobility, see Jobs, *Backpack Ambassadors*, 108–14.
245. Daniel Cohn-Bendit and Gabriel Cohn-Bendit, *Obsolete Communism: The Left-Wing Alternative*, trans. Arnold Pomerans (London: André Deutsch, 1968), 23.
246. Cohn-Bendit, *Obsolete Communism*, 201.
247. Ibid., 250.
248. Nick Rutter, 'Look Left, Drive Right: Internationalisms at the 1968 World Youth Festival', in *The Socialist Sixties: Crossing Borders in the Second World*, ed. Anne Gorsuch and Diane Koenker (Bloomington, IN: Indiana University Press, 2013), 193–212.
249. Fred Halliday, 'Students of the World Unite', in *Student Power: Problems, Diagnosis, Action*, ed. Alexander Cockburn and Robin Blackburn (London: Penguin, 1969), 324.
250. Halliday, 'Students of the World Unite', 325.
251. See e.g. the links between the Socialist German Student Alliance on the one hand and Students for a Democratic Society on the other: Klimke, *The Other Alliance*, 10–39.
252. Koenen, *Das rote Jahrzehnt*, 319–20.
253. Jeremy Varon, *Bringing the War Home: The Weather Underground, the Red Army Faction, and Revolutionary Violence in the Sixties and Seventies* (Berkeley, CA: University of California Press, 2004).
254. Lovell, *Maoism*, 297–8.
255. Kieran McConaghy, 'Transnational Connections: Militant Irish Republicans and the World', in *The Cambridge History of Terrorism*, ed. Richard English (Cambridge: Cambridge University Press, 2021), 477–500.
256. Philip Ther, *Europe since 1989: A History*, trans. Charlotte Hughes-Kreutzmüller (Princeton, NJ: Princeton University Press, 2018), 77–160.
257. For a discussion of this contested terminology at a time when these movements gathered prominence, see e.g. Catherine Eschle and Bice Maiguashca, 'Introduction', in *Critical Theories, International Relations and 'the Anti-Globalisation Movement': The Politics of Global Resistance*, ed. Catherine Eschle and Bice Maiguashca (Abingdon: Routledge, 2005), 27.
258. Reitan, *Global Activism*, 1–2.
259. Thomas Olesen, 'Globalising the Zapatistas: From Third World Solidarity to Global Solidarity?', *Third World Quarterly* 25, no. 1 (2004): 256.
260. For a comparison with these earlier forms, see Mario Pianta and Raffaele Marchetti, 'The Global Justice Movements: The Transnational Dimension', in *The Global Justice Movement: Cross-National and Transnational Perspectives*, ed. Donatella della Porta (Abingdon: Routledge, 2007), 29–51.

261. John Vidal, 'How the Young Battalions Hatched the Battle of Seattle', *The Guardian*, 30 November 1999, 1.
262. Herbert Reiter et al., 'The Global Justice Movement in Italy', in Della Porta, *The Global Justice Movement*, 55.
263. Dieter Rucht, 'Global Justice Movements and the Mass Media: Conceptual Reflections and Empirical Findings', in *Power and Transnational Activism*, ed. Thomas Olesen (Abingdon: Routledge, 2011), 190–213.
264. Dieter Rucht, Simon Teune and Mundo Yang, 'The Global Justice Movements in Germany', in Della Porta, *The Global Justice Movement*, 157; Reiter et al., 'The Global Justice Movement in Italy', 57.
265. Donatella della Porta, 'The Global Justice Movement: An Introduction', in della Porta, *The Global Justice Movement*, 3.
266. Donatella della Porta, 'Riding the Wave: Some Conclusions', in *Global Diffusion of Protest: Riding the Protest Wave in the Neoliberal Crisis*, ed. Donatella della Porta (Amsterdam: Amsterdam University Press, 2017), 215.
267. Jérôme E. Roos and Leonidas Oikonomakis, 'They Don't Represent Us! The Global Resonance of the Real Democracy Movement from the *Indignados* to Occupy', in *Spreading Protest: Social Movements in Times of Crisis*, ed. Donatella della Porta and Alice Mattoni (Colchester: ECPR Press, 2014), 117–36.
268. Ishaan Tharoor, 'From Europe with Love: U.S. "Indignados" Occupy Wall Street', *Time*, 5 October 2011, https://world.time.com/2011/10/05/from-europe-with-love-the-u-s-indignados-have-arrived/ (last accessed 9 January 2023).
269. Maria Kousis, 'The Transnational Dimension of the Greek Protest Campaign against Troika Memoranda and Austerity Policies, 2010–2012', in della Porta and Mattoni, *Spreading Protest*, 146.

CHAPTER 5
THE POLITICS OF GENDER AND SEXUALITY

In 1985, the Italian socialist Ivanka Corti suggested that 'the struggle and the new consciousness of women involved in many women's and feminist organizations' had helped to challenge 'the global polarisation into two spheres of activity, determined by the biological concept of "male" and "female"', although she argued that 'there still remains much to do, in order to secure women's inclusion (with equal rights) in the social world and their way out of the domestic sphere'.[1] Moreover, to Corti, the promotion of women's equality was also crucial in another respect – namely to address '[t]he decisive challenge of our time, the struggle for peace and for controlled disarmament' as such an aim could 'never be achieved … as long as a deep gulf exists between the perception and the reality of women (c. 53% of the total world population), between policies and practices in the fields affecting women'.

Corti's statement is instructive in several respects. Firstly, it illustrates how women activists could connect their cause to other concerns. In linking gender equality and peace, Corti used arguments that had also featured in other historical contexts, as noted in Chapter 3. Her insistence on this connection occurred at a time when renewed Cold War tensions had added particular urgency to such issues. Yet Corti's own political background also pointed to socialism: her remarks featured in a pamphlet by Socialist International Women, a federation for the women's sections of various socialist, social democratic and labour parties. In formal terms, the history of the organization dated back to 1958, when it had been founded as the International Council of Social Democratic Women. Politically, however, it had its roots in the International Conference of Socialist Women of 1907 which, as noted in Chapter 4, sought to organize socialist women activists.[2] Socialist International Women was not the only organization that was anchored in left-wing feminism. In 1945, communist women and peace activists had founded the Women's International Democratic Federation (WIDF). Whereas Corti insisted on women's equality as a requirement for attaining peace, the WIDF adopted a different perspective: according to the historian Francisca de Haan, it viewed peace as 'the necessary precondition for its other three aims: anti-fascism/democracy, women's rights and children's rights'.[3]

Beyond pointing to the linkages between different activist concerns, Corti's comment highlighted a second aspect, namely the role of the United Nations as a potential partner for women's organizations. Corti's remarks featured in a pamphlet that commented on the UN Decade for Women which, between 1976 and 1985, had sought to focus and coordinate international efforts on women's rights and development.[4] Women's organizations played an important role during the International Decade – indeed, the WIDF had been a driving force behind the launching of this venture.[5]

Thirdly, in speaking of a 'new consciousness', Corti alluded to the impact of changing attitudes in generating and facilitating political change. Many such efforts occurred outside of the institutional frameworks that connected women's organizations and the UN. One therefore needs to think of these institutional ventures alongside other activist currents, such as the role of women's liberation movements in the 1970s.

The term 'feminism' is sometimes used as shorthand for the women's movement. Like 'pacifism', it was based on a French neologism (in this instance, *féminisme*) that originated in the fin-de-siècle period.[6] Its meanings, however, varied across time and place. Some protagonists used it as a synonym for the cause of women's rights. However, in the course of the twentieth century, it became increasingly associated with activism on matters of sexuality – as exemplified by growing activism on reproductive rights.[7] The latter stance has sometimes been described as 'second wave' feminism. The 'wave' metaphor has had its critics, partly for the way in which it downplays continuities in activists' concerns.[8] Nonetheless, it has proven remarkably durable: in the 1990s, US feminists used the term 'third wave' to describe an individualistic perspective that stressed generational difference vis-à-vis earlier activists.[9] In the 2010s, 'fourth wave' feminism, with its focus on intersectionality and the use of social media, became an international phenomenon.[10] In adopting a broad approach, the present chapter looks beyond individuals who described themselves as 'feminists' as it considers different ways in which gender and sexuality generated activism that cut across national borders.[11]

Notwithstanding semantic differences between terms such as 'women's movement', 'women's rights' and 'feminism', it is clear that these were political phenomena aimed at empowerment. They gained their resonance from the fact that they challenged attempts to silence or disregard women's voices. Indeed, the writing of women's history but also of lesbian, gay, bisexual and transgender (LGBT) histories could in itself be both a scholarly and an activist endeavour, giving a voice to groups and individuals who had been 'hidden from history'.[12] The fact that the marginalization of women and repression of sexual minorities were not confined to one country helped to nurture a sense of solidarity across national boundaries. The chapter acknowledges this impetus while also noting how such activism could be subject to internal conflicts and divisions.

This chapter first considers the emergence of an international women's movement, tracing its consolidation in organizational terms as well as its divisions. The second half then adopts a thematic approach, shifting to campaigners' engagement with international institutions on the one hand and changing ideas about gender and sexuality on the other. In tackling the politics of gender and sexuality, this chapter does not claim that the two are identical. Sex, gender and sexual orientation nourished forms of activism that sometimes operated separately or – as was the case with the subjects of other chapters – even collided. That said, this chapter acknowledges points of convergence, from the protagonists in the sexual reform movements of the 1920s to acknowledgements of intersectionality in the twenty-first century.

Transnational bonds and organizational efforts

According to the historian Bonnie Anderson, 'the first international women's movement' emerged in the 1830s. She has drawn attention to a correspondence network comprising a core group of twenty women and another twenty-one on the periphery.[13] Tracing their links across three decades, Anderson has shown how they helped one another across considerable distances – from Massachusetts to Leipzig and from Sheffield to Paris. Experience of repression and exile reinforced such transnational bonds. The French activist Jeanne Deroin was a case in point. Inspired by the utopian socialism of the Saint-Simonians and as a protagonist in the French 1848 revolution, she promoted women's rights through periodicals – first *La Voix des Femmes*, then *Opinion des Femmes* – and by initiating the creation of a women's rights association. In 1850, she was charged and imprisoned for plotting against the government.[14] In this period, women's periodicals in Britain and the United States printed the letters she sent to her fellow campaigners from prison.[15] After her release, Deroin settled in London, where she remained until her death, maintaining ongoing French and English publishing activities for several decades – although, by the 1880s, her espousal of a spiritual form of feminism contrasted with the concerns of a new generation of activists.[16]

The international movement of the mid-nineteenth century was certainly a transnational phenomenon, yet it did not establish firm associational structures. It was in the 1870s and 1880s that the international women's movement attained a sounder organizational footing. Within just over three decades, several major organizations emerged: the Women's Christian Temperance Union (1874), the International Abolitionist Federation (1875), the International Council of Women (1888), the International Woman Suffrage Alliance (1904) and the International Bureau of Socialist Women (1907). According to the historian Leila Rupp, such efforts had a significant impact: 'What started as delicate shoots breaking through the thawing ground blossomed into a bounteous garden that we call the international women's movement.'[17]

When considering the causes that are associated with the emergence of an international women's movement, three elements require particular attention: social reform, suffrage and socialism. The first aspect was important because the promotion of women's rights was not only cast in terms of social betterment, but also because it had intrinsic connections to other reform movements. This aspect was exemplified by the Women's Christian Temperance Union (WCTU) which, according to Ian Tyrell, was 'the first mass organization among women dedicated to social reform'.[18] Nineteenth-century temperance could be linked to liberal, radical and socialist causes, driven by underlying views on progress and perfectibility.[19] As indicated by the WCTU's reference to Christianity, religious beliefs – including a commitment to modesty and sobriety – were important. Indeed, the organization's missionary impulses meant that, from its inception in the United States in 1874, it spread internationally. Why, however, can this be viewed as a woman's movement? One reason was the activists' argument regarding the impact of alcohol on the sphere of domesticity, that is, the potential havoc that alcoholism could cause within working-class families. Moreover, there were overlaps with other aspects of the women's movement. For instance, the New Zealand and Australian branches of the WCTU actively promoted women's suffrage, partly because some members deemed it necessary to get a wider hearing for their reform demands.[20] Their activism did have some success: New Zealand introduced women's suffrage in 1893, and Australia followed in 1902. This, in turn, had implications for European activists – not least because of Australia and New Zealand's role as settler colonies within the British Empire or, subsequently, as Dominions of the British Commonwealth.

Other social reform causes directly addressed discriminatory practices that targeted women. Within the Anglophone world, Josephine Butler was arguably the most famous woman activist. In Britain, she succeeded in effecting the repeal of the Contagious Diseases Act, which had targeted female prostitutes, in 1886. However, by that point, her efforts had extended to other countries for over decade: in 1875, she had founded the International Abolitionist Federation, which campaigned against the state regulation of prostitution and the trafficking of women. In terms of its terminology – which referred to women as victims of 'white slavery' and cast the campaigners as 'new abolitionists' – such activism consciously evoked the earlier endeavours of the anti-slavery movement.[21] Butler insisted on the need to look beyond Britain. As she put it, 'in defeating "White Slavery" in England alone, we should be merely lopping off a solitary branch, so to speak, of the poisonous tree' whereas 'the old parent tree, with its deep roots, and strong trunk' would still be 'standing in neighbouring countries'.[22] To some extent, she succeeded in building an international movement. The historian Anne Summers has argued that 'Butler's campaigns awakened women all over Europe, from the 1870s onwards, to the horrors and hypocrisies of the sexual double standard' and suggested that this cause 'rather than that of access to the professions and to the suffrage, was crucial in propelling many of them for the first time to a form of feminist action'.[23]

The reach of Butler's efforts was uneven across Europe and thus revealed deeper differences.[24] As Barbara Metzger has pointed out, the movement was 'by no means homogenous', with an 'abolitionist' strand arguing that the 'abolition of state regulation would curb the trafficking in women', whereas another faction focused on 'social purity'.[25] Moreover, in several countries, the adoption of abolitionist principles encountered divisions from the start. In Italy, activists formed a national branch of Butler's federation in 1875 but some campaigners rejected the moral line of Butler's arguments. An additional problem was 'the impossibility of finding an agreement with the Catholic majority of Italy in the struggle against regulated prostitution'.[26] In the Netherlands, Butler's abolitionism seemed to enjoy greater success: according to the researcher Petra de Vries, it provided 'the new generation of feminists' with 'a clear and public case of male sexual domination and a strategy for change'.[27] Yet de Vries has pointed out that this is a matter of perspective as 'a different story might be told, one in which the campaign against "the state regulation of vice" drifted away from a feminist perspective and was characterised by tensions between male and female abolitionists'.[28]

Notwithstanding such limitations, these efforts created legacies of transnational cooperation, especially on the issue of women's trafficking which, as an inherently transnational phenomenon, could only be addressed through international action. This impetus informed the International Congresses on the White Slave Traffic of 1899, 1902 and 1910, which also placed the issue on the diplomatic agenda, as reflected in the International Agreement for the Suppression of the White Slave Traffic (1904).[29] Such initiatives had long-term implications: as discussed further on in this chapter, they formed the backdrop to later strategies of working with and through international institutions. The focus on victims of sexual exploitation also had the potential to forge global connections. For instance, in the 1880s, Indian women's social reformer Pandita Ramabai travelled to England and the United States, attracting interest in her efforts for the victims of child marriage and receiving support from the WCTU.[30] However, both the notions of 'white slavery' and the encounter between Indian and British women's activists also reflected the ways in which empire and visions of 'civilization' shaped perspectives on women's rights.[31]

As the cases of the WCTU and the International Abolitionist Federation demonstrate, there was an emerging landscape of international women's organizations by the 1870s. Despite these early contacts, it took until 1888 before a broader international women's organization was established. That year, a congress in Washington, DC, created the International Council of Women (ICW). The ICW was initially made up of individual members and no national branches, with the exception of an American one. Soon thereafter, however, the organizational principle changed: instead, the ICW became a confederation of national women's councils which, in their turn, would bring together a number of different associations. While reflecting the national bases of internationalism in this period, it proved a relatively successful model: by 1914, twenty-three national councils had become affiliated.[32] In several cases, the ICW inspired the formation of national federations.[33] The ICW engaged with reform causes in different ways. For instance, in 1914, it reported that its president had contacted 'ladies of influence' in several countries, with a 'plea that the personal influence of these ladies might be exerted to secure the suppression of the White Slave Traffic in their respective countries', while in the same period, the Council shared its findings from an enquiry into different education systems.[34]

While ICW congresses considered a broad array of issues, the organization's position on women's suffrage remained equivocal, in line with the heterogeneity of its membership: not all ICW activists were feminists, and not all feminists were suffragists. At the same time, the ICW's early years coincided with the growth of organizations that promoted the enfranchisement of women. In the late nineteenth and early twentieth centuries, a range of societies pursued this aim at the national level, yet before the First World War, such activism yielded limited results: Finland, Norway and Denmark were the sole European countries with female suffrage before 1914. The ICW maintained a Standing Committee on Suffrage and Rights of Citizenship from 1906 onwards, collecting material on suffrage from national suffrage societies. However, given the contrasting views on the subject, it primarily studied women's suffrage, rather than actively campaigning for it. For instance, in 1911, the ICW sent out questionnaires to members in countries with full or partial women's suffrage, seeking to find out how far the introduction of women's suffrage had affected the social, economic and legal position of women more generally.[35]

Figure 5.1 Poster advertising the Budapest congress of the International Woman Suffrage Alliance in 1913. *Source:* Lithograph by Anna Sóos Korányi, reproduced by Sepia Times / Universal Images Group, via Getty Images.

Such activism suggested that information gathering could be a form of activism: without necessarily adopting an official campaigning stance, the material could be placed at the disposal of suffragists within the organization. Moreover, the 1911 ICW report cited transnational links as potential evidence for the benefits of women's suffrage: it pointed out that women's suffrage had been introduced in 'Sweden, Finland, Norway, Denmark, Iceland – nations which are familiar with the results of progressive movements in neighbouring countries and which would never follow a precedent that did not add to the general welfare'.[36]

The foundation of the International Woman Suffrage Alliance (IWSA) resulted from the ICW's reticence to engage in active campaigning on women's suffrage. In contrast to the older organization, the IWSA explicitly stated its intention 'to secure the enfranchisement of the women of all nations, and to unite the friends of women suffrage throughout the world in organized co-operation and fraternal helpfulness'.[37] Carrie Chapman Catt, president of the National American Woman Suffrage Association, was a driving force behind the creation of this new venture: in 1902, she invited representatives of various suffrage societies to the national convention organized by her organization in 1902, attracting delegates from ten countries, with the formal foundation taking place in 1904, at a conference that coincided with the ICW's congress in Berlin.[38] At a personal level, however, there were many links between the two organizations. Several campaigners – including Chapman Catt herself as well as the Dutch feminist Aletta Jacobs – participated in the ICW's Standing Committee on Suffrage and Rights of Citizenship alongside their role in the IWSA. Their transnational activism was not confined to conference settings: for instance, in 1913, Chapman Catt and Jacobs embarked on a 'world tour' that took them to China, Indonesia, South Africa and Egypt, where they addressed meetings and studied the state of the women's movement. While noting that they had visited 'countless extraordinary sights and met many people' and stressing that they 'greatly valued all we had learned', Jacobs concluded that their 'most powerful feeling was gratitude that we had been able to perform such useful work among the women of Africa and Asia'.[39] Such comments may have emphasized the campaigners' ambitions, yet they also underscored a limitation: as Leila Rupp has pointed out, 'the process of constructing an international collective identity reproduced global power relations' and featured 'unacknowledged assumptions about the superiority and natural leadership of Euro-American societies'.[40]

The suffrage cause sometimes overshadows other concerns that figured prominently within the women's movement. For example, the French and Belgian women's movements of this period have sometimes been portrayed as 'backward' because of their relatively limited activism on women's suffrage. The historian Julie Carlier, however, has challenged this view, stressing that these movements were often strongly commitment to promoting women's social and economic rights.[41] Transnational contacts mattered in this regard, as Belgian feminism was invigorated by its contacts with the Dutch activist Wilhelmina Drucker, whose activism extended to the labour movement.[42]

These links remind us that, alongside social reform and suffrage, there was a third aspect that inspired female activists to mobilize transnationally: class. The rise of international women's organizations occurred in an era when socialists also organized themselves across national borders. Indeed, socialism and feminism had some features in common. One aspect was the potential transnational dimension: for socialists, class solidarity overrode national boundaries, and for some feminists, sisterhood was a transnational concept. Furthermore, at least in theory, both socialists and feminists were targeting injustices in the existing electoral system. For instance, although some socialists believed in revolution, others focused on the ballot box, arguing against regulations that disenfranchised workers or that gave additional weight to property-owning classes. Moreover, socialist women began to organize themselves, arguing for the entwined nature of class-based and gendered oppression. As noted in Chapter 4, in 1907, leading campaigners – including Alexandra Kollontai from Russia, Clara Zetkin from Germany and Luise Zietz from Austria – established the International Bureau of Socialist Women to organize their joint efforts.

Diversity and congruence within the international women's movement

The activism of socialist women raises the wider question of ideological diversity within the women's movement. Many socialists were reluctant to join forces with the established non-socialist women's organizations, which they associated with 'bourgeois feminism'. As the historian Marylin Boxer has pointed out, 'bourgeois feminism' was something of a construct – used polemically by female socialists against their opponents.[43] To them, any activism that focused exclusively on feminist concerns needed denouncing because it ignored the overriding importance of class struggle. Clara Zetkin, for instance, argued that 'the middle class women advocates of suffrage' were merely 'engaged in a struggle from their own middle-class point of view'. To Zektin, they did 'not fight for the political emancipation of the female sex, but for the advancement of the interests of the middle class'.[44]

While there was some socialist hostility towards feminists who were deemed to ignore class-based injustice, such conflicts also entered internal socialist debates. This aspect was exemplified by the experiences of the Dutch socialist and feminist Wilhelmina Drucker, who in 1891 attended the Second International's Brussels congress on behalf of the *Vrije Vrouwenvereeniging* (Free Women's Association). Despite the socialist background of her association, several male socialists argued against her inclusion as a delegate, with a member of her own party, the *Sociaal-Democratische Bond* (Social Democratic Alliance), claiming that 'She does not desire that man and woman fight against capitalism, but that woman and man fight each other'.[45] The fact that Drucker's opponents included the leading Dutch socialist Ferdinand Domela Nieuwenhuis was particularly striking. In the 1880s, Domela Nieuwenhuis had met Josephine Butler and been involved in campaigns against the state regulation of prostitution, cooperating with feminists and evangelicals.[46] Moreover, as noted in Chapter 4, in the 1890s, he argued against the exclusion of anarchists – thus making the case for inclusivity in some areas but not when it came to the presence of feminists. His unwillingness to give a forum to socialist feminists seemed to indicate a wider issue: the historian Piet de Roy has argued that the *Sociaal-Democratische Bond* 'had nothing against women in theory, but it had problems with them in practice', noting that 'the competition between the sexes and the classes became more visible than it had initially been'.[47]

Tactical considerations created further tensions. For instance, while many socialists supported women's suffrage at least in principle, some were more reluctant. In countries such as Spain and France – where culture wars involving the Catholic Church played a prominent role in the political system – some activists argued that women's enfranchisement would strengthen the conservative vote as women would heed the advice of their priest.[48] Such arguments remind us that gender prejudices extended to the political left. Material concerns could be a factor, too. For instance, some protagonists of organized labour viewed women workers as potential economic competitors who would undercut the wages of male trade-union members.[49]

While these examples stress potential antipathy towards the feminist cause, these tensions cut both ways. Activists within the ICW largely adopted a course that provided the organization with 'a reputation for moderation and respectability'.[50] Seen from this angle, the socialist movement's association with revolution was a potential problem. Indeed, many leading figures within the ICW were of a moderate or downright conservative disposition. The fact that in the early years, the ICW was led by an aristocrat, Lady Aberdeen, seems to illustrate this. An example of this contrast with the members of socialist women's organizations is the Finnish activist Alexandra Gripenberg.[51] Gripenberg was a significant figure within the ICW and maintained an extensive correspondence with leading women activists from other countries. She combined this role with a prominent role in national politics. Following the enfranchisement of women in the Grand Duchy of Finland in 1906, Gripenberg entered the Finnish parliament. However, her overall political stance was conservative: she had previously questioned Finnish women's political maturity to exercise their right to vote, and her views on social relations were characterized by an aversion to class-based politics.

While it may therefore be tempting to see the period before 1914 in terms of a clash between socialist women and 'bourgeois feminism', we must not assume a clear-cut dichotomy and instead need to appreciate the overlaps between different currents. Marylin Boxer has argued that the differences were often rhetorical, whereas in practice, there were manifold links.[52] In Finland, women workers had played a key role in the successful quest for women's suffrage, which had been introduced after a strike wave had shaken Finland – along with other parts of the Russian Empire – in 1905.[53] Moreover, some activists straddled the boundaries between feminism, labour and socialism – for instance the British feminist Dora Montefiore, who combined membership in the Second International, the ICW and the IWSA. Having visited Finland in 1906, Montefiore also stressed the role and experiences of working women in the successful Finnish suffrage campaign.[54]

Contacts that connected feminism and socialism could also come from protagonists of the 'bourgeois' women's movement. The Dutch feminist Aletta Jacobs – a social reformer, rather than a socialist – worked with different groups on the left. During her first visit to London in 1879, she visited the Fabian Society (describing it as 'completely socialist in outlook') and attended 'meetings of various working-class groups'.[55] Her time in England predated Jacobs's leading role in Dutch suffragism – though it occurred at a point by which she had already gained some prominence in feminist circles, both by being the first Dutch woman to qualify as a medical doctor and as an advocate of birth control. Over subsequent years, she cooperated with segments of the labour movement, and her translation of *Woman and Labour*, a text by the South African activist Olive Schreiner, was influential in the Dutch reception of Scheiner's arguments.[56] In other words, labelling Jacobs a 'bourgeois feminist' would be reductive. Moreover, WILPF – the organization that Jacobs had co-founded – became a space in which faminists from different ideological backgrounds collaborated.[57]

While the debates on the relationship between 'bourgeois' feminism and socialist women's activism are well known, the existence of a separate international movement of Catholic women further complicates the picture. Its existence formed part of a wider process in which the Catholic Church embraced and sponsored lay activity. Given the transnational nature of the church itself, it is hardly surprising that Catholic women's activism extended to the international level, forming part of the wider phenomenon of Catholic internationalism.[58] In 1910, an International Federation of Catholic Women's Organizations was established in Brussels. Such efforts covered different political shades and concerns. On the one hand, the International Federation was linked to the nationalist and anti-feminist *Ligue patriotique des Françaises* and the conservative *Ligue des femmes chrétiennes*, while also involving associations from other countries that stressed 'women's duties' and adopted an anti-suffragist stance. On the other hand, the same era saw the emergence of Catholic advocacy for women's suffrage, as exemplified by the Catholic Women's Suffrage Society in Britain (1911) and the *Ligue Catholique du suffrage feminine* (1912) in Belgium. By the interwar years, two new Catholic women's organizations in France, *Action Sociale de la Femme* (Woman's Social Action) and the *Union Nationale pour le Vote des Femmes* (National Union for Women's Vote), promoted woman's suffrage, and it has been argued that their move towards this position reflected 'the interconnectedness of women's national and international work'.[59] Such a stance was linked both to the international contacts that these activists had built but also interpreted the cause in terms of French national prestige on the international stage.

The framing of women's suffrage in both national and international terms reflected a wider feature of women's internationalism: even women activists who were engaged in transnational contacts and who participated in international congresses often stressed their national allegiances. Leila Rupp's research has highlighted the presence of various kinds of national rhetoric and representation at the events associated with the international women's movement.[60] She has also pointed out that for some activists, 'internationalism coexisted with a strong national loyalty, unless the two came into conflict, in which case nationalism took precedence'.[61]

Indeed, for many activists, recognition within the national sphere and the ability to speak the language of nationhood were vitally important. These concerns bore consequences during the First World War. As had been the case for socialists and pacifists, the outbreak of the military conflict in 1914 triggered internal divisions in the women's movement.⁶² While most activists swung behind the national war effort – leading to a rupture in the work of the ICW and IWSA, for example – some activists insisted on the continuing relevance of sisterhood. For example, as editor of the IWSA journal *Jus Suffragii*, the British activist Mary Sheepshanks secured the magazine's publication during the war years and used the periodical to publish news from opposing sides as well as covering pacifist initiatives, despite criticism by some suffragists.⁶³ *Jus Suffragii*'s coverage extended to featuring news of the women's congress at The Hague in 1915 which, as noted in Chapter 3, attracted over 1,100 women in a joint anti-war stance. Transnational links – involving Aletta Jacobs and other Dutch organizers as well as American social reformers such as Jane Addams – were important in making this event happen.

Many prominent suffrage activists rejected the invitation to the Hague congress, underlining the ruptures caused by the war.⁶⁴ Nonetheless, the congress had important consequences. Chapter 3 has already mentioned the campaign of 'citizens' diplomacy' that arose from the congress, with feminists travelling to the capitals of the warring nations to push for peace negotiations.⁶⁵ The activists also launched a bulletin that helped maintain transnational dialogue in wartime.⁶⁶ Moreover, the congress had a durable impact as it spawned the Women's Committee for a Permanent Peace, which in 1919 became the Women's International League for Peace and Freedom (WILPF). Chapter 3 has noted WILPF's features as a pacifist association, yet at the same time, the organization also construed itself as part of the women's movement. As Sarah

Figure 5.2 Members of the Women's Peace Party (USA), including Jane Addams, travel to the Women's Peace Congress at The Hague, 28 April 1915. *Source:* Corbis Historical / Library of Congress, via Getty Images.

Hellawell has shown with regard to its British branch, gender-based rhetoric featured prominently within WILPF.[67] In this respect, the activists picked up older tropes, for instance arguments about a maternal commitment to peace.

Notwithstanding their differences during the First World War, those international organizations that – unlike WILPF – had suspended their actions during the conflict slowly rebuilt their ties after 1918. For individual campaigners, this was often a difficult process, with only a gradual acceptance of the value of transnational cooperation.[68] With regard to woman's suffrage, the ventures of feminist organizations had to confront an ever-more diverse landscape. Whereas women gained the vote in large parts of the continent, there were notable exceptions: France, Belgium, Switzerland, Bulgaria and Yugoslavia did not grant nationwide voting rights to women. The IWSA adapted to these complex circumstances by broadening its remit, renaming itself to become the International Alliance of Women for Suffrage and Equal Citizenship.

At a time of contrasting developments in terms of women's suffrage and other political rights, activists shared perspectives from their respective countries. For instance, in 1920, the Czech activist Františka Plamínková – a prominent figure in both the ICW and the International Alliance of Women – presented recent accomplishments in her own country in an English publication. She argued that her country's position in Central Europe had invested it with a particular experience and purpose:

> We are like an island in the midst of surging waves, we feel the shock as it were of the breakers. How many foreigners penetrate across the frontiers to us! But we do not force them to abandon their original sentiments of race and nationality. We have always erred on the side of an excess of hospitality. But this centre of Europe, perhaps by virtue of its geographical situation and the collision of most varied influences is like a gigantic workshop in which these influences are re-moulded and give rise to progressive ideals.[69]

Such discourse articulated a sense of national mission which, at the same time, could be projected within an international setting, reflecting Plamínková's own combination of national and transnational concerns.[70]

While the interwar years were a period of reconstruction for international feminism, they also indicated a broadening in several respects. The historian Marie Sandell has highlighted the extent to which international women's organizations sought to expand beyond Europe and North America during the 1920s and 1930s.[71] Having attended the 1930 congress of the International Alliance for Suffrage and Equal Citizenship, which was held in Istanbul, the British MP Lady Astor framed the event in terms of her organization's growing focus on 'the East'. To her, 'The choice of Istanbul, the junction of East and West' had a 'striking effect' particularly on the 'Eastern women' who had 'seen for themselves how the advantages of freedom are benefiting their Turkish sisters'.[72] There were evident problems with such discourse: portrayals of delegates from Asia and Africa, for instance, involved exoticizing the 'other' and revealed a thinking in terms of civilizational differences.

Moreover, when it came to 'race', the internal culture and external actions of international women's organizations covered a broad spectrum, from racist behaviours to active involvement in anti-racist campaigning.[73] Likewise, responses to the rise of fascism varied. During the 1930s, WILPF members increasingly shifted towards anti-fascist activism, in some instances cooperating with the leftist ventures of the Women's World Committee against War and Fascism.[74] Yet these anti-fascist commitments did not extend to all women's organizations, some of whom maintained contacts with Germany and Italy. When Gertrud Scholtz-Klink, leader of the centralized women's organization of Nazi Germany, visited London in March 1939, it generated protests but also involved some meetings with a smaller group of British women's activists. These ambivalent responses have been interpreted as indicative of a broader issue, namely the existence of 'two kinds of gendered international activism prevalent' in the interwar years: on the one hand a 'feminist/anti-fascist discourse' and, on the other hand, a 'more conservative motherly/pacifist discourse'.[75]

Engaging with international organizations – from the League of Nations to the UN

Both the scope and limitations of international women's organizations reflected broader features of interwar internationalism. Organizations such as WILPF actively engaged with the international system, starting with attempts to inform debates at the Paris Peace Conference and later manifesting itself in WILPF's campaigning on such issues as disarmament.[76] While activists had limited success in shaping the creation of the League of Nations – the organization that embodied the new international order – the League did become an important partner in several respects: efforts against the trafficking of women, the quest for social protection and the potential for active involvement in the new institutions.

As far as the first of these cases is concerned, we have already seen that prostitution and the trafficking of women had featured in transnational women's activism well before the First World War. Even before the League's foundation, representatives of different women's organizations had sought to make this issue part of the future League's remit.[77] In 1921, their efforts resulted in an International Convention on the Traffic of Women and Children – 'the first League Convention dealing with a human rights issue', according to the historian Barbara Metzger.[78] Moreover, activists gained a forum to inform debates on the convention and its future through the Advisory Committee on the Traffic in Women and Children, which – while only meeting once a year – provided a framework for interactions between officials and activists.[79] The ongoing prominence of this issue was reflected in another convention, passed in 1933 and dealing with the 'Traffic in Women of Full Age'.[80]

The second aspect concerned economic and employment rights. In this respect, the newly established International Labour Organization (ILO) – which formed part of the wider League of Nations system – emerged as a target and tool. The ILO's tripartite structure meant that it offered opportunities for political representation: alongside government delegates and representatives of business, trade unions had a role within the organization. Campaigners for women's rights could thus engage with the ILO by working with and through trade unions.[81] Moreover, even without formally serving as delegates to ILO meetings, they could make their voices heard. For instance, in 1919, the Women's Trade Union League of North America hosted an International Congress of Working Women that was timed to coincide with the International Labour Conference.[82] Yet some ILO measures on labour protection proved divisive: among women's activists, a controversy ensued between those who advocated legal equality and those who sought special protection for women.[83]

The third aspect was the opportunity for women activists to gain external recognition by participating in the work of the League. Much of the recent literature on the League has stressed its significance as a space in which officials, experts and activists interacted with one another.[84] One way was through specialist committees that featured representatives of women's organizations. This included the debates on the trafficking of women and children, but it lasted until the end of the League, as campaigners' demands resulted in the creation of a special Committee for the Study of the Legal Status of Women in 1937.[85] There were also activists who managed to participate as delegates of their respective countries in the Assembly of the League of Nations. These included WILPF members such as the British campaigner Helena Swanwick and the Danish feminist Henni Forchhammer, who had also served as vice-president of the ICW.

Some women took on official roles within the League system. While the Covenant of the League of Nations made League positions available to men and women on an apparently equal basis, the actual practice looked rather different, as the League's higher echelons were dominated by men. Exceptions to this rule included Rachel Crowdy, who headed the League of Nations' Social Section, and Marguerite Thibert at the ILO.[86] Moreover, the Mandates section of the League involved two women's activists from Nordic countries, Anna Bugge-Wicksell from Sweden and Valentine Dannevig from Norway.[87] There were evident links to earlier forms of activism: before the war, Bugge Wicksell had been a member of the IWSA, while Dannevig had been involved in the Norwegian branch of WILPF. Their respective involvement in the League showed how activists and international institutions intersected very directly.

After the Second World War, activists sought to engage with the new institutional organizations in ways that echoed the attempts of the pre-war years. For example, during the 1950s, the Swedish activist and politician Alva Myrdal played an influential role in promoting women's rights, development and disarmament within the UN system, notably UNESCO, before continuing her promotion of disarmament as a Swedish government minister.[88] The UN also perpetuated the system of working through expert committees, offering new opportunities for women's groups that had gained recognition as international NGOs. Such NGOs played a particular role in the context of the large-scale World Conferences on Women, with the first such meeting in Mexico in 1975 constituting a landmark event.[89] The growth of NGO representation – with 6,000 women in attendance at the conference in Mexico City, followed by 8,000 in Copenhagen (1980), 15,000 in Nairobi (1985) and 30,000 in Beijing (1995) – testified to this development.[90]

Significantly, international women's organizations influenced the UN's staging of special conferences dedicated to women. While the UN was certainly a site of Cold War struggles, it also enabled international women's organizations to work across the power blocs. The WIDF's role in collaborating with the UN was a case in point. The federation was undoubtedly dominated by communist activists and largely supportive of the Soviet Union and its allies, yet it was also effective in using the UN in a way that transcended Cold War binaries.[91] For instance, WIDF pressure gave rise to the Convention on the Elimination for All Forms of Discrimination against Women (1979). Significantly, the body that monitored its work include women leaders from different power blocs and non-aligned countries. Invaka Coti – whose comments on equality featured at the start of this chapter and who was a democratic socialist rather than a communist – joined the committee in 1987.[92] Between 1993 and 1996, Corti served as its chairperson and, in looking back on its activities, highlighted the 'great contribution to the universal recognition' provided by the UN's international women's conferences that had taken place between 1975 and 1995.[93]

Another major development was the growing interaction of traditionally European-dominated international women's organizations and actors from the Global South. This included the WIDF, which engaged actively with Third World currents as part of a wider attempt by protagonists from the Second World to go global.[94] From a different political vantage point, the non-communist protagonists of Socialist International Women also launched attempts to involve protagonists from the Global South. For instance, in 1986, the organization's conference in Lima, Peru, featured the Senegalese politician Catherine Diop with a speech on 'The Third World Viewpoint', emphasizing the need of 'health for all', access to education and highlighting 'the economic and racial crisis [that] endangers the political and social stability of many African countries'.[95] While some of this involvement can be seen in terms of Cold War competition for Third World support, such events also exemplified the extent to which, increasingly, women's rights were construed in terms of their connection to development. Debates on these issues evidently continued after the Cold War, sometimes in ways that reflected different strategies and priorities. For example, in 1994, women's NGOs that had gathered for the UN's Conference on Population and Development in Cairo were divided between those who focused on particular areas – such as reproductive rights – and those that argued for a holistic approach to combating inequality.[96]

New attitudes and the shift from rights to liberation

Campaigns that were waged at the international level also related to shifting attitudes on gender and sexuality. When considering this aspect, it makes sense to first return to the interwar years which, in Susan Grayzel's words, were 'a time of tense renegotiating of the meanings of masculinity and femininity in states preparing for and/or experiencing violence and conflict'.[97] In this era, the prevalence of traditionalist attitudes contrasted with fresh challenges to gendered expectations and moral assumptions, from the figure of the 'New Woman' to the emergence of a gay subculture in some European cities.[98] These developments were by no means uniform and they encountered manifold obstacles. For example, French anxieties about the national body manifested themselves in natalist policies that revolved around traditional notions of the family and, for instance, imposed penalties on advocacy for birth control.[99]

That said, measures against proponents of birth control also highlighted the fact that, in several countries, reproductive rights as well as broader questions of sexuality seized the attention of activists. In the Soviet Union – where abortion was legal until its recriminalization under Stalin in 1936 – the most prominent proponent of a new morality was Alexandra Kollontai.[100] Her stance, which included the promotion of 'free love', contrasted with traditionalist attitudes within the Bolshevik leadership, and broader Soviet debates on sexual reform already ended during the era of the New Economic Policy in the early 1920s.[101] Recent research, however, has highlighted the transnational impact of Kollontai's ideas on sexual reform, for instance her feminist campaigners for sexual reform in interwar Germany.[102]

Weimar Germany was itself the site of important developments for the promotion of sexual reform. In 1919, the physician Magnus Hirschfeld established his Institute for Sexology in Berlin and hosted an international congress two years later.[103] While the Institute and congress were cast as scientific endeavours, their concerns extended into the political sphere, promoting acceptance of different sexualities and support for birth control. In 1928, Hirschfeld's efforts gave rise to an organization that brought activists from different countries into contact with one another: the World League for Sexual Reform. Looking back at the World League's London congress of 1929, the British activist Dora Russell concluded that 'If anyone wishes to know who were the standard-bearers of progressive opinion in the chief European countries at that date, the index of the participants is a reliable guide'.[104]

Along with the Australian medic Norman Haire, Russell was one of the event's organizers.[105] As she noted, there was an underlying tension between those who emphasized scientific concerns and those who considered sexual reform as a political project.[106] Notwithstanding such differences, delegates agreed on a range of topics, passing 'resolutions on marriage and divorce, sex and censorship, sex education, birth control, abortion, prostitution and venereal disease, which might serve as a basis for a tolerance and humane society'. To Russell, it was clear that the event had 'expressed an internationalism that went beyond mere politics, and kept open the channel between us and the Soviet Union and the politicians'.[107] Soviet involvement in the event was indeed evident in several respects: Kollontai sent a message to the congress, Soviet speakers attended the gathering, and activists even staged a private screening of a banned Soviet film about abortion.[108] Such ventures should not obscure the relative marginality of such activism at a time when authoritarian or totalitarian currents – often built around a traditionalist view of gender roles – were on the rise. In May 1933, Hirschfeld's Institute fell victim to Nazi attacks, and Hirschfeld himself died in French exile two years later.

After the end of the Second World War, the initial social and political contexts provided some challenges for debates on sexuality. However, it did not stifle debate altogether, as demonstrated by Simone de Beauvoir's book *Le deuxième sex* in 1949, published in an abridged English translation as *The Second Sex* four years later.[109] The influence of Beauvoir's work has been described as 'remarkable, even paradigmatic', with the philosopher Barbara Andrew arguing that her book 'influenced all subsequent feminist philosophy'.[110] In tackling the social construction of gender roles, Beauvoir was as an inspirational figure for the women's liberation movement that emerged in the late 1960s and that has sometimes been referred to as a 'second wave'. As the historian Sylvie Chaperone has shown, the protagonists of French women's liberation, the *Mouvement de libération des femmes*, valued and cooperated with Beauvoir, notwithstanding generational differences that manifested themselves in their interactions.[111]

The women's liberation movement was an international phenomenon, and its emergence was linked to the developments of the 1960s, including more tolerant attitudes to sexuality in the counterculture. At the same time, male domination within ostensibly egalitarian groups pushed feminists to organize separately.[112] For instance, Mariarosa Dalla Costa – a key figure in the Italian women's liberation movement of the 1970s – had initially been interested in the 'workerist version of Marxism', supporting the emphasis on workplace agitation by parts of the Italian New Left. However, in looking back, 'I experienced, as did many other women in extra-parliamentary groups in the early 1970s, the contradiction of not feeling that my condition as a woman was represented or understood – neither by activism nor by this Marxist thought.'[113]

During the 1970s, protagonists of women's liberation shared strategies with one another. For instance, in 1971, the French campaign for the legalization of abortion received a major stimulus when 343 French women – including Beauvoir – jointly proclaimed in the news magazine *Le Nouvel Observateur* that they had had an illegal abortion. The initiative inspired similar public declarations in both West Germany and the United States, where these actions significantly affected the debate on abortion rights.[114] The activities of French campaigners also influenced abortion rights campaigning in Italy, but, as the historian Maud Bracke has shown, feminist protests on the issue remained more limited. Another transnational transmission process had a greater impact: the notion of 'self-help' – as advocated and practiced by American feminists – was implemented in reproductive health clinics that Italian feminists set up across the country.[115]

Transnational links were important in another venture that involved Italian feminists, namely the 'Wages for Housework' campaign. In 1972, the book that helped to launch the campaign included essays by the UK-based American activist Selma James and Mariarosa Dalla Costa. In her introduction, James pointed out that ideas that she had articulated in her piece on 'A Woman's Place' (1953) were now being 'taken by a woman in Italy [Dalla Costa] and used as a starting point for a restatement of Marxist theory and a reorientation of struggle'.[116] The conceptualization of housework as unwaged labour made it a potential focus for class struggle. In 1975, this point was reiterated by the feminist Silvia Federici, who had moved from Italy to the United States in 1967. Her *Wages*

Against Housework treatise argued that the 'unwaged condition of housework' had been 'the most powerful weapon in reinforcing the common assumption that housework is not work, thus preventing women from struggling against it'.[117]

Louise Toupin – a former activist as well as a historian of the campaign – has stressed the international reach of 'Wages for Housework', with 'groups active in Italy, England, the United States, England, Canada, Switzerland, and Germany'.[118] The emphasis on transnational cooperation resulted in the creation of the International Feminist Collective in 1972 – according to Toupin, a 'feminist "Internationale" ahead of its time'.[119] As Maud Bracke has shown, the campaign's adoption depended on local contexts: the specific circumstances of Italian women, whose employment rate was lower, as well as the nature of the Italian women's liberation movement meant that the demand was taken up widely, at least for some years, whereas in Britain, the campaign attracted counter-arguments within the women's liberation movement early on.[120] In many ways, Wages for Housework proved successful in alliance building, for instance by considering different forms of oppression through the inclusion of lesbian and African American women's groups in these campaigns. By 1977, however, the campaign slowly evaporated. To Silvia Federici, the experience of the International Feminist Collective 'showed the importance of having an international network', but also 'the limits of any organization that exists in the absence of a mass movement'.[121]

Notwithstanding these differences, the women's liberation movement was keen to stress transnational bonds, with a range of new feminist periodicals trying to reinforce this sense of connection. Such notions of global sisterhood also meant that Western activists displayed an interest in the activities of women's groups in the socialist world. For instance, when feminists from the French group *Psychoanalyse et Politique* (Psychoanalysis and Politics) visited the Soviet Union in 1979, they were excited to discover a local group in Leningrad whose independent feminist activism could be construed as a Soviet manifestation of women's liberation, with activities that focused on the publication of the women's almanac *Zheshchina i Rossia* (Women and Russia).[122] In 1983, an American observer described it as 'the first feminist journal to emerge on the Soviet scene since Stalin's rise to power' and noted that its first issue had been 'published in full or in part in France, Norway, Sweden, Brazil, Japan, England, and West Germany'.[123] Operating outside the structures of the Soviet state, the feminists met with recriminations, with four members being forced abroad. In that context, international women's solidarity became all important, with Tatiana Mamonova – the Leningrad group's co-founder – promoting the vison of 'an international feminist union of solidarity with the women of Soviet Russia'.[124]

Towards gay liberation

Women's organizations experienced tensions when it came to matters of sexual orientation – which famously was the case when the American feminist Betty Friedan denounced lesbianism as a 'Lavender Menace' in 1969, sparking protests by lesbian feminists. Recent research, however, has emphasized the importance of lesbianism for the evolution of radical feminism in both North America and Western Europe during the 1970s.[125] Such observations point to another development in this period: the rise of gay liberation. This section considers the latter's transnational dimensions, with a focus on the activism of homosexual men.

International activism on the subject of sexual orientation pre-dated gay liberation: during the 1950s and 1960s, 'homophile' activists in various countries had argued for the decriminalization and acceptance of same-sex relations. In 1951, an International Congress for Sexual Equality – initiated by Dutch activists and held in Amsterdam – led to the creation of the International Committee for Sexual Equality. According to historian Leila Rupp, the body 'occupied a middle position, linking activism around same-sex sexuality in the [interwar] World League for Sexual Reform ... to the emergence of a contemporary transnational gay and lesbian movement in the 1970s'.[126]

In the late 1960s and early 1970s, most European countries which had not yet legalized same-sex relations did so, but decriminalization did not amount to full equality. In this context, the emerging gay liberation movement adopted a more explicit stand, with important transnational features. Developments in the United States were crucial in inspiring activists in Western Europe. In 1969, a police raid on the Stonewall Inn on Christopher Street, New York, not only resulted in violent clashes but also sparked the staging of 'gay pride' marches and the formation of the Gay Liberation Front. The terminology reflected a shift from the previous generation of homophile activists: as Laura Belmonte has pointed out, '"Gay" signaled the activists' rejection of the homophiles' accommodationist views and of medical discourses defining homosexuality as pathology'.[127] Meanwhile, the term 'liberation' pointed to the activists' 'broad aims for personal freedom, political equality, and social justice'.[128]

These undertakings provided a model for activists in Western Europe, who began to stage their own marches – for instance by celebrating the anniversary of the Stonewall riots as 'Christopher Street Day' – and who adopted the term 'Gay Liberation Front' for new groups, for instance in Britain (1970) and Denmark (*Bøssernes Befrielsesfront*, 1971). Having examined activism in both Denmark and the Netherlands, the historian Andrew Shield has argued that both Stonewall and news about the Gay Liberation Front in the United States 'contributed to the radicalization of Danish and Dutch activism in the 1970s'.[129] A similar turn towards more radical forms of activism manifested itself in the name of new French and Italian groups that described themselves as 'revolutionary homosexual action fronts'. Seen from this angle, gay liberation reflected transnational processes, and this was further demonstrated by the shared use of symbols. For instance, in the 1970s, activists in different countries adopted the 'pink triangle', which had previously been used to stigmatize homosexual inmates of Nazi concentration camps. According to the historian Craig Griffiths, 'before the rainbow flag emerged on the scene later in the 1980s, the pink triangle became arguably the most influential gay symbol'.[130] In recalling past periods of repression, the use of the pink triangle pointed to 'a wider transnational "memory boom" in homosexual politics'.[131]

Beyond transnational inspirations, the 1970s saw various efforts to internationalize the campaign for equality and liberation. As had been the case for feminists, international organizations were an important target for such efforts. During the 1970s, gay rights campaigners unsuccessfully urged the United Nations to address discrimination on the grounds of sexual orientation and also began to coordinate their efforts, for instance through an International Gay Rights Congress of 1974.[132] Lesbian activists participated in the NGO debates of the UN's International Conference of Women in 1975, which included disputes on the role of sexual liberation.[133] The creation of the International Gay Association (IGA) in 1978 was the outcome of manifold internationalization efforts that had preceded it. Exercising pressure on different UN bodies was part of IGA's work from the outset, for instance the campaign against the World Health Organization's 'continued categorization of homosexuality as a disease'.[134] During the 1980s, IGA's relationship with such bodies was further shaped by the HIV/AIDS crisis. In such contexts, the documentation of homophobic policies went hand in hand with the staging of protests, for instance in September 1984, when 1,000 activists marched from the site of the Stonewall Inn to the UN headquarters.[135]

That said, several tensions affected the attempts to organize internationally. The inclusion of women within the IGA was one such issue. While IGA's 1980 conference in Barcelona was meant to mark the transformation into 'a fully integrated male-and-female organization', delegates dismissed suggestions to include lesbians in the association's name.[136] One year later, lesbian activists withdrew from IGA and established the International Lesbian Information Service in Helsinki – although by 1982, both organizations reiterated their desire to cooperate.[137] Subsequent efforts led to IGA becoming the International Lesbian and Gay Association (ILGA) in 1986. As such, it contributed to events such as the UN Women's Conference in Beijing (1995) and reiterated its 'strongest commitment ... to ensuring that lesbian rights and visibility are a priority issue in forums and movements around the world'.[138] During the 1990s, the growing inclusion of transgender rights was reflected in events such as the Transgender Pride Conference of 1995, which coincided with ILGA's Helsinki congress that year.[139] As a result of this broadening, the organization is now known as the International Lesbian, Gay, Bisexual, Trans and Intersex Association.

The emphasis on promoting LGBT rights worldwide sometimes clashed with the activists' largely Western European and North American backgrounds. IGA's first annual conference debated the organization's stance vis-à-vis the 'sexual exploitation and colonization of local gays' in developing countries: some speakers argued that advice on the purchasing of sex in gay travel guides was supporting sex tourism and thus reinforced exploitative power relations.[140] The ambivalent attitude towards such issues was underpinned by the exoticization of 'racial others' within some European gay magazines.[141] Given the wider question of attitudes and perceptions, IGA resembled other international associations in facing issues with extending its base beyond the West. By the mid-1980s, Ian Gunn – a veteran of the international gay rights movement – argued that it was 'too White and too dominated by North Europeans, however well-meaning and hard-working'.[142] Some of these features reflected the obstacles for open discussions of sexuality in parts of the Global South. Moreover, in Central and Eastern Europe in the 1980s, LGBT activists often operated under hostile circumstances. In this context, transnational ties could be important, as highlighted by the British campaigner Peter Tatchell staging a gay rights protest at the World Festival of Youth in East Berlin (1973) and by the influences that led to the creation of the first gay rights group in 1980s Poland.[143] Conscious of the challenging circumstances for activists in Eastern Europe, IGA members were heartened when a group from Leningrad approached them in 1984.[144]

Until the mid-1990s, one issue that caused significant problems for IL(G)A was the existence of paedophile groups that, in evoking the language of 'sexual liberation', sought to use the association as a platform. Their presence at its meetings proved controversial from the outset. In 1979, a report from IGA's first annual conference noted that a proposal on greater cooperation with paedophile groups had triggered substantial debate, with some delegates seeing paedophilia as the 'ultimate form of sexism' and arguing that a distance from such groups was important 'to avoid the constant charge of "child molester" levelled at homosexuals'.[145] While the resolution for closer cooperation was indeed rejected, some of the organization's positioning remained ambivalent: at the 1981 congress, for instance, participants unsuccessfully sought to evict one group of paedophile activists for the aggressive behaviour of its members; at the same event, delegates agreed to call an 'international day of action' to protest the fact that the leader of the Paedophile Information Exchange in Britain had been imprisoned 'for conspiracy to corrupt public morals'.[146] Such associations ultimately jeopardized some of the organization's international work: having attained NGO status at the UN in 1993, ILGA was hit by revelations that its 400 member organizations also included four groups of paedophile activists.[147] In 1994, an ILGA conference took steps to expel these groups, successfully reaching the 80 per cent voting threshold that was required for such expulsions.[148] These actions did not prevent it from losing its UN recognition in 1994, and subsequent applications for consultative status met with opposition: governments that were more generally hostile to LGBT rights cited these past ties in support of their resistance, until the organization regained its consultative status in 2011.

Division and unity since the 1990s

The collapse of communism across Central and Eastern Europe generated opportunities for overt activism on both women's and LGBT rights. Moreover, the 1990s and 2000s saw the introduction of anti-discrimination legislation as well as the legal recognition of same-sex partnerships in a range of European countries. However, such developments should not tempt us to adopt narratives of consistent progress, given the significant variations in the development of legal rights and public attitudes. Among some groups and individuals, these differences have informed the desire to create transnational 'spaces of resistance'.[149]

Moreover, political achievements do necessarily testify to the strength of activist groups. As Conor O'Dwyer has pointed out, Czech LGBT activists managed to attain 'greater progress since the fall of communism than most of their counterparts in the region' – yet, strikingly, this development did not coincide with broader success at mobilization.[150] For instance, Gay Pride parades started in Prague only in 2011 – a decade later than in Poland, where LGBT activists staged such marches in a difficult public environment.[151] According to O'Dwyer, the Czech successes in legal terms can be attributed to an 'effective NGO-oriented activism, which achieved both legislative breakthroughs and built an almost corporatist relationship with the state', whereas activists spent less time 'articulating a shared identity uniting the group and mobilizing it to achieve greater acceptance in mainstream society'.[152] When the Czech Republic adopted provisions for same-sex partnerships in 2006, it was hence based on 'an elite-based strategy of persuasion'.[153]

The question of an 'elite-based strategy of persuasion' is also relevant when it comes to a particularly significant level of activist engagement: during the 1990s and 2000s, when the European Union deepened its integration process and expanded geographically, various activist groups worked with EU institutions to attain their aims. With regard to women's rights, Christine Delphy – the sociologist who had been a leading figure in

Figure 5.3 Gay Pride Parade in Warsaw, 15 June 2013. *Source*: Nek Skarynski / AFP, via Getty Images.

the French women's liberation movement of the 1970s – noted in 1996 that national or regional differences as well as the evolving nature of the European project had created some obstacles, but stated that 'so far the European record has been amazingly good', with 'Europe, as an entity that is more than the sum of its parts' having managed to launch 'more progressive legislation than any of the Member States, or than all of them together'.[154] EU gender equality policies continued to evolve in the 2000s, with directives from the European Commission as a key factor.[155]

Similarly, EU institutions became a vehicle for LGBT campaigners, for instance with regard to anti-discrimination measures. The development of ILGA reflected this process. As noted, the organization had waged international lobbying since the late 1970s. In the course of the 1990s, ILGA developed closer links with the European Commission and, to this end, established a separate network, ILGA-Europe. By 2001, it entered formal relations with the EU, which also provided it with funding.[156] Such examples sparked further initiatives, for instance the creation of the Transgender Europe network in 2005, with representation vis-à-vis the EU and the Council of Europe as a major aim for activists.[157] In such contexts, the European institutions could appear as an ally, especially vis-à-vis governments that were less receptive or even hostile to gender equality or LGBT rights.

At the same time, this development also gave rise to a dilemma: the fact that campaigners partly operated via international institutions allowed some of their opponents to cast such activism as alien. This, for instance, was the case in Poland, where conservative politicians presented their efforts in terms of the defence of 'traditional' family values against an external threat.[158] Along similar lines, in 2021 the Hungarian government of Viktor Orbán passed a law banning the 'promotion' of 'LGBT ideology' in schools and the media, attracting international protest.[159] These debates reflected a wider issue: especially from the 2010s, gender equality and LGBT rights could be integrated into a right-wing or 'populist' discourse in which it was conflated with other issues, including hostility to the EU. While such actors framed their convictions in national terms, there were transnational dimensions to this discourse, as illustrated by Orbán addressing the Conservative Political Action Committee in Dallas, Texas, in 2022. At this meeting of American conservative activists, Orbán argued that 'the nation, Christian roots and family can be successful on the political battlefield' and cast himself as a defender of 'Western Civilizations' whose 'Christian roots' were being threatened by 'today's progressives'.[160]

The example points to a wider aspect, namely the role of a 'culture wars' rhetoric in which particular issues – for instance transgender rights – assumed symbolic importance.[161] Yet in recent years, transgender rights have also generated debate between groups and individuals who see themselves as progressive. This point has been reflected in conflicts between feminists who embrace, on one side, 'gender critical' and, on the other side, 'trans inclusive' views. The former group has emphasized sex-based rights; in some instances, its protagonists have sought to stress continuities with the earlier movement for women's liberation, especially in regard to the defence of biological rights and a questioning of gender roles.[162] By contrast, the latter group has seen such arguments as deceptive, claiming that they run the risk of further marginalizing a minority group.[163] In this context, advocates of trans rights have placed their own efforts within a broader history of ongoing activist struggles. For example, the British activist Shon Faye has argued for the connection between 'true trans liberation' and 'the demands of workers, socialists, feminists, anti-racists and queer people'.[164]

In the UK, conflicts on trans rights have tied in with wider, contested understandings of free speech.[165] Moreover, these debates have highlighted the ambivalent role of social media, which can amplify misunderstandings and misrepresentations. Yet platforms such as Twitter have also been used as tools of empowerment. With regard to trans rights, this aspect was exemplified by the #GirlsLikeUs campaign – launched by the American activist Janet Mock in 2012 – which sought to amplify the visibility of trans people.[166]

#GirlsLikeUs exemplifies the wider phenomenon of 'hashtag activism', which gained prominence during the 2010s. As such, it coincided with the rise of 'fourth wave' feminism, whose use of social media was epitomized by #MeToo, the campaign targeting everyday sexual harassment. Although popularized when some celebrity users began to embrace the phrase in 2018, the slogan originated with the African American feminist Tarana Burke who had used it since 2006 to allow women to share their experiences of sexual violence.[167] Recent research has highlighted the global reach of #MeToo, which was taken up by feminists well beyond Europe. Crucially, its meaning in different non-Western contexts has been used to critique traditional notions of 'global sisterhood'.[168] Such concerns are important as intersectionality – in which, for instance, gender-based oppression is seen in conjunction with inequalities relating to class, race or sexual orientation – is an important aspect of 'fourth wave' feminism.[169] Such aspects highlight the need to consider other forms of discrimination, which the next chapter will examine from other perspectives.

Notes

1. Ivanka Corti, 'Equality', in *United Nations Decade for Women 1976–1985: Equality, Development and Peace*, ed. Socialist International Women (London: SIW, 1985), 2.
2. 'A Short History of Socialist International Women', in Socialist International Women, *United Nations Decade for Women*, 15.
3. Francisca de Haan, 'The Women's International Democratic Federation (WIDF): History, Main Agenda, and Contributions, 1945–1991', as featured in the digital resource *Women and Social Movements, International* (Alexandria, VT: Alexander Street, 2012).
4. Judith Zinsser, 'From Mexico to Copenhagen to Nairobi: The United Nations Decade for Women, 1975–1985', *Journal of World History* 13, no. 1 (2002): 139–68.
5. Francisca de Haan, 'Left Feminism: Rediscovering the Women's International Democratic Federation', *Yearbook of Women's History* 40 (2021): 108. See also Gradskova, *The Women's International Democratic Federation*, 158–69.
6. On the origins of this term, see Geneviève Fraisse, *Reason's Muse: Sexual Difference and the Birth of Democracy*, trans. Jane Marie Tod (Chicago, IL: University of Chicago Press, 1994), 194–5.

7. Ann Taylor Allen, Anne Cova and June Puvis, 'International Feminisms', *Women's History Review* 19, no. 4 (2010): 493–501; June Hannam, *Feminism* (2nd edn; Abingdon: Routledge, 2012). On the connotations and terms in different languages, see also Kristina Schulz, 'The Women's Movement', in Klimke and Scharloth, *1968 in Europe*, 281–93.

8. For an acknowledgement of such critiques, see e.g. Barbara Molony and Jennifer Nelson, 'Introduction', in *Women's Activism and 'Second Wave' Feminism*, ed. Barbara Molony and Jennifer Nelson (London: Bloomsbury, 2017); Jo Reger, 'Finding a Place in History: The Discursive Legacy of the Wave Metaphor and Contemporary Feminism', *Feminist Studies* 43, no. 1 (2017): 193–221; Kathleen Laughlin et al., 'Is It Time to Jump Ship? Historians Rethink the Waves Metaphor', *Feminist Formations* 22, no. 1 (2010): 75–135.

9. Stacy Gillis, Gillian Howie and Rebecca Munford, eds, *Third Wave Feminism: A Critical Exploration* (2nd edn; Basingstoke: Palgrave, 2007); Astrid Henry, *Not My Mother's Sister: Generational Conflict and Third-Wave Feminism* (Bloomington, IN: Indiana University Press, 2004); Kristin Aune and Rose Holyoak, 'Navigating the Third Wave: Contemporary UK Feminist Activists and "Third Wave Feminism"', *Feminist Theory* 19, no. 2 (2018): 183–203. Most scholarship acknowledges that the meaning of a 'third wave' is by no means clear cut: see Jonathan Dean, 'Who's Afraid of Third Wave Feminism? On the Uses of the "Third Wave" in British Feminist Politics', *International Feminist Journal of Politics* 11, no. 3 (2009): 334–52.

10. See e.g. Prudence Chamberlain, *The Feminist Fourth Wave: Affective Temporality* (Cham: Palgrave, 2017).

11. For the importance of such clarifications, see Karen Offen, 'Understanding International Feminisms as "Transnational" – an Anachronism? May Wright Sewall and the Creation of the International Council of Women, 1889–1904', in Janz and Schönpflug, *Gender History in a Transnational Perspective*, 25–45.

12. See for instance, the notion of uncovering groups that were 'hidden from history' in both women's and LGBT histories: Sheila Rowbotham, *Hidden from History: 300 Years of Women's Oppression and the Fight against It* (London: Pluto Press, 1973); Martin Duberman, Martha Vicinus and George Chauncey, Jr, eds, *Hidden from History: Reclaiming the Gay and Lesbian Past* (New York: Meridian, 1989).

13. Bonnie S. Anderson, *Joyous Greetings: The First International Women's Movement, 1830–1860* (New York: Oxford University Press, 2000), 4–5.

14. Pamela Pilbeam, 'Jeanne Deroin: French Feminist and Socialist in Exile', in Freitag and Muhs, *Exiles from European Revolutions*, 286.

15. Anderson, *Joyous Greetings*, 151.

16. Pilbeam, 'Jeanne Deroin', 290.

17. Leila Rupp, 'The Making of International Women's Organizations', in Geyer and Paulmann, *The Mechanics of Internationalism*, 207. See also Leila Rupp, *Worlds of Women: The Making of an International Women's Movement* (Princeton, NJ: Princeton University Press, 1997); and Leila Rupp, 'Constructing Internationalism: The Case of Transnational Women's Organizations, 1888–1945', *American Historical Review* 99, no. 5 (1994): 571–600.

18. Ian Tyrrell, *Woman's World – Woman's Empire: The Woman's Christian Temperance Union in International Perspective, 1880–1930* (Chapel Hill, NC: University of North Carolina Press, 1991), 2.

19. Mark Lawrence Schrad, *Smashing the Liquor Machine: A Global History of Prohibition* (New York: Oxford University Press, 2021).

20. Tyrell, *Woman's World – Woman's Empire*, 221–41.

21. British, Continental and General Federation for the Abolition of Government Regulation of Prostitution, *The New Abolitionists: A Narrative of a Year's Work* (London: Dyer Brothers, 1876).
22. Josephine Butler in a letter to Henry J. Wilson, summer 1876, as cited in British, Continental and General Federation, *The New Abolitionists*, 226.
23. Anne Summers, 'Introduction: The International Abolitionist Federation', *Women's History Review* 17, no. 2 (2008): 149–52, at 150.
24. Anne Summers, 'Which Women? What Europe? Josephine Butler and the International Abolitionist Federation', *History Workshop Journal* 62, no. 1 (2006): 214–31.
25. Barbara Metzger, 'Towards an International Human Rights Regime during the Inter-War Years: The League of Nations' Combat of Traffic in Women and Children', in *Beyond Sovereignty: Britain, Empire and Transnationalism, c. 1880–1950*, ed. Kevin Grant, Philippa Levine and Frank Trentmann (Basingstoke: Palgrave, 2007), 56.
26. Bruno Wanrooij, 'Josephine Butler and Regulated Prostitution in Italy', *Women's History Review* 17, no. 2 (2008): 162. See also Stephanie Limoncelli, *The Politics of Trafficking: The First International Movement to Combat the Sexual Exploitation of Women* (Stanford, CA: Stanford University Press, 2010), 133–42.
27. Petra de Vries, 'Josephine Butler and the Making of Feminism: International Abolitionism in the Netherlands (1870–1914)', *Women's History Review* 17, no. 2 (2008): 266.
28. de Vries, 'Josephine Butler and the Making of Feminism', 272.
29. Metzger, 'Towards an International Human Rights Regime', 57.
30. Clare Midgley, 'Indian Feminist Pandita Ramabai and Transnational Liberal Religious Networks in the Nineteenth-Century World', in *Women in Transnational History: Connecting the Local and the Global*, ed. Clare Midgley, Alison Twells and Julie Carlier (Abingdon: Routledge, 2013), 13–32; Antoinette Burton, 'Colonial Encounters in Late-Victorian England: Pandita Ramabai at Cheltenham and Wantage 1883–6', *Feminist Review* 49, no. 1 (1995): 29–49.
31. For these broader issues, see Antoinette Burton, *Burdens of History: British Feminists, Indian Women, and Imperial Culture, 1865–1915* (Chapel Hill, NC: University of North Carolina Press, 1994).
32. ICW, 'Quinquennial Report of the Corresponding Secretary Presented at the Quinquennial Sessions, 1914', 1, as featured in Alexander Street's *Women and Social Movements, International* digital collection.
33. Anne Cova, 'International Feminisms in Historical Comparative Perspective: France, Italy and Portugal, 1880s–1930s', *Women's History Review* 19, no. 4 (2010): 595–612.
34. ICW, 'Quinquennial Report', 12 and 17.
35. For the responses to this questionnaire, see International Council of Women, *Third Annual Report 1911–1912* (Washington, DC: ICW, 1912), 136–40.
36. International Council of Women, *Third Annual Report*, 136.
37. 'Constitution of the International Woman Suffrage Alliance', in *IWSA, Report: Second and Third Conferences of the International Woman Suffrage Alliance, Berlin, Germany, June 3, 4, 1904, Copenhagen, Denmark, Aug. 7, 8, 9, 10, 11, 1906* (Copenhagen: Bianco Luno, 1906), 116.
38. Rupp, *Worlds of Women*, 22.
39. Jacobs, *Memories*, 162.
40. Rupp, 'Constructing Internationalism', 1576–7.

41. Julie Carlier, 'Forgotten Transnational Connections and National Contexts: An "Entangled History" of the Political Transfers That Shaped Belgian Feminism, 1890–1914', *Women's History Review* 19, no. 4 (2010): 503–22; Julie Carlier, 'Entangled Feminisms: Rethinking the History of the Belgian Movement for Women's Rights through Transnational Intersections', *Revue belge de philologie et d'histoire* 90, no. 4 (2012): 1139–52.
42. Mieke Aerts, 'Feminism from Amsterdam to Brussels in 1891: Political Transfer as Transformation, *European Review of History* 12, no. 2 (2005): 367–82; Myriam Everard and Mieke Aerts, 'Forgotten Intersections: Wilhelmina Drucker, Early Feminism, and the Dutch-Belgian Connection', *Revue belge de philologie et d'histoire* 77, no. 2 (1999): 440–72.
43. Marilyn Boxer, 'Rethinking the Socialist Construction and International Career of the Concept "Bourgeois Feminism"', *American Historical Review* 112, no. 1 (2007): 131–58.
44. Clara Zetkin, *Social-Democracy and Woman Suffrage: A Paper Read by Clara Zetkin to the Conference of Women Belonging to the Social-Democratic Party Held at Mannheim before the Opening of the 1906 Annual Congress of the German Social-Democracy*, trans. Jacques Bonhomme (London: Twentieth Century Press, 1907), 10. On Zetkin's views, with references to the Mannheim speech, see Hunt, *Equivocal Feminists*, 63–70.
45. Piet de Roy, *A Tiny Spot on the Earth: The Political Culture of the Netherlands in the Nineteenth and Twentieth Century* (Amsterdam: Amsterdam University Press, 2015), 148. See also Aerts, 'Feminism from Amsterdam to Brussels in 1891'; Everard and Aerts, 'Forgotten Intersections'.
46. de Vries, 'Josephine Butler and the Making of Feminism', 262.
47. de Roy, *A Tiny Spot on the Earth*, 149.
48. See e.g. Mary Nash, '"Ideals of Redemption": Socialism and Women on the Left in Spain', in *Women and Socialism, Socialism and Women; Europe between the Two World Wars*, ed. Helmut Gruber and Pamela Graves (New York: Berghahn, 1998), 365.
49. See e.g. the efforts of the French printer's union to exclude women from their trade in 1912: Offen, *European Feminisms*, 234.
50. Hannam, *Feminism*, 24.
51. Tiina Kinnunen, 'The National and International in Making a Feminist: The Case of Alexandra Gripenberg', *Women's History Review* 25, no. 4 (2016): 652–70.
52. Boxer, 'Rethinking the Socialist Construction and International Career', esp. 151–2.
53. Irma Sulkunen, 'Suffrage, Nation and Citizenship – The Finnish Case in an International Context', in *Suffrage, Gender and Citizenship: International Perspectives on Parliamentary Reforms*, ed. Irma Sulkunen, Seija-Leena Nevala-Nurmi and Pirjo Markkola (Newcastle upon Tyne: Cambridge Scholars Publishing, 2008), 83–105.
54. Karen Hunt, 'Suffrage Internationalism in Practice: Dora Montefiore and the Lessons of Finnish Women's Enfranchisement', in *The Politics of Women's Suffrage: Local, National and International Dimensions*, ed. Alexandra Hughes-Johnson and Lyndsey Jenkins (London: University of London Press / Institute of Historical Research, 2021), 285–308. On Montefiore within the context of socialist women's activism more broadly, see June Hannam and Karen Hunt, *Socialist Women: Britain, 1880s to 1920s* (London: Routledge, 2002).
55. Jacobs, *Memories*, 34.
56. Małgorzata Drwal, 'The Feminism of Olive Schreiner and the Feminism of Aletta Jacobs: The Reception of Schreiner's Woman and Labour in the Netherlands', *Dutch Crossing* 45, no. 1 (2021): 77–92. Schreiner's original text appeared as Olive Schreiner, *Woman and Labour* (London: Unwin, 1911).

57. Laura Beers, 'Bridging the Ideological Divide: Liberal and Socialist Collaboration in the Women's International League for Peace and Freedom, 1919–1945', *Journal of Women's History* 33, no. 2 (2021): 111–35.

58. The phenomenon of Catholic internationalism dated back to the nineteenth century: Vincent Viaene, 'Nineteenth-Century Internationalism and Its Predecessors', in *Religious Internationals in the Modern World: Globalization and Faith Communities since 1750*, ed. Abigail Green and Vincent Viaene (Basingstoke: Palgrave, 2011), 82–110.

59. Emily Machen, 'Catholic Women, International Engagement and the Battle for Suffrage in Interwar France: The Case of the Action Sociale de la Femme and the Union Nationale pour le Vote des Femmes', *Women's History Review* 26, no. 2 (2017): 229–44, at 230.

60. Rupp, *Worlds of Women*, e.g. 121; Rupp, 'Constructing Internationalism', 1593–5.

61. Rupp, 'Constructing Internationalism', 1587.

62. Alison Fell and Ingrid Sharp, eds, *The Women's Movement in Wartime: International Perspectives, 1914–19* (Basingstoke: Palgrave, 2007).

63. Sibyl Oldfield, 'Mary Sheepkshanks Edits an Internationalist Suffrage Monthly in Wartime: Jus Suffragii 1914–19', *Women's History Review* 12, no. 1 (2003): 119–39. For the broader example of women's pacifist journals during wartime, see Bruna Bianchi, 'Towards a New Internationalism: Pacifist Journals Edited by Women, 1914–1919', in *Gender and the First World War*, ed. Christa Hämmerle, Oswald Überegger and Birgit Bader-Zaar (Basingstoke: Palgrave, 2014), 176–94.

64. Wilmers, *Pazifismus in der internationalen Frauenbewegung*, 105–20.

65. Patterson, *The Search for Negotiated Peace*, 82–103.

66. Grace Brockington, Sarah Hellawell and Daniel Laqua, 'Pacifist Journals', in *The Edinburgh Companion to First World War Periodicals*, ed. Marysa Demoor, Cedric van Dijck and Birgit Van Puymbroeck (Edinburgh: Edinburgh University Press, 2023), esp. 357–9.

67. Sarah Hellawell, 'Antimilitarism, Citizenship and Motherhood: The Formation and Early Years of the Women's International League (WIL), 1915–1919', *Women's History Review* 27, no. 4 (2018): 551–64. For another gendered dimension of WILPF activism, see Ingrid Sharp, 'Love as Moral Imperative and Gendered Anti-War Strategy in the International Women's Movement 1914–1919', *Diplomacy & Statecraft* 31, no. 4 (2020): 630–47.

68. Ingrid Sharp, '"An Unbroken Family"? Gertrud Bäumer and the German Women's Movement's Return to International Work in the 1920s', *Women's History Review* 26, no. 2 (2017): 245–61; Ingrid Sharp and Matthew Stibbe, eds, *Women Activists between War and Peace: Europe, 1918–1923* (London: Bloomsbury, 2017).

69. Františka Plamínková, *The Political Rights of Women in the Czechoslovak Republic* (Prague: Gazette de Prague, 1920), 14–15.

70. Barbara Reinfeld, 'Františka Plamínková (1875–1942), Czech Feminist and Patriot', *Nationalities Papers* 25, no. 1 (1997): 13–33.

71. Marie Sandell, '"A Real Meeting of the Women of the East and West": Women and Internationalism in the Interwar Period', in Laqua, *Internationalism Reconfigured*, 161–86; Marie Sandell, 'Regional versus International: Women's Activism and Organisational Spaces in the Inter-War Period', *International History Review* 33, no. 4 (2011): 607–25; Sandell, *The Rise of Women's International Activism*, 46–77.

72. 'Lady Astor in Turkey: Women's Progress from Slaves to Deputies in Fifteen Years', *Manchester Guardian*, 23 April 1935, 13.

73. Christine Bolt, *Sisterhood Questioned? Race, Class and Internationalism in the British and American Women's Movements, c. 1880s–1970s* (Abingdon: Routledge, 2004), esp. chapters 4 and 5; Joyce Blackwell, *No Peace without Freedom: Race and the Women's International League for Peace and Freedom, 1915–1976* (Carbondale, IL: Southern Illinois University Press, 2004).

74. Laura Beers, 'Frauen für Demokratie: Möglichkeiten und Grenzen des zivilgesellschaftlichen Engagements', in *Normalität und Fragilität: Demokratie nach dem Ersten Weltkrieg*, ed. Tim Müller and Adam Tooze (Hamburg: Hamburger Edition, 2015), 119; Calver, *Anti-Fascism, Gender, and International Communism*.

75. Julie Gottlieb and Matthew Stibbe, 'Peace at Any Price: The Visit of Nazi Women's Leader Gertrud Scholtz-Klink to London in March 1939 and the Response of British Women Activists', *Women's History Review* 26, no. 2 (2017): 175. See also Julie Gottlieb, *'Guilty Women', Fascist Policy, and Appeasement in Inter-War Britain* (Basingstoke: Palgrave, 2015).

76. Jo Vellacott, 'A Place for Pacifism and Transnationalism in Feminist Theory: The Early Work of the Women's International League for Peace and Freedom', *Women's History Review* 2, no. 1 (1993): 23–56; Jo Vellacott, 'Feminism as if All People Mattered: Working to Remove the Causes of War, 1919–1929', *Contemporary European History* 10, no. 3 (2001): 375–94.

77. Thomas Fischer, 'Frauenhandel und Prostitution: Zur Institutionalisierung eines transnationalen Diskurses im Völkerbund', *Zeitschrift für Geschichtswissenschaft* 54, no. 10 (2006): 876–87, at 877.

78. Metzger, 'Towards an International Human Rights Regime', 73.

79. Fischer, 'Frauenhandel und Prostitution', 880; Metzger, 'Towards an International Human Rights Regime', 60; Magaly Rodríguez Garcia, 'The League of Nations and the Moral Recruitment of Women', *International Review of Social History* 57, S. 20 (2012): 97–128.

80. Metzger, 'Towards an International Human Rights Regime', 69.

81. Eileen Boris, Dorethea Hoehtke and Susan Zimmerman, eds, *Women's ILO: Transnational Networks, Global Labour Standards and Gender Equity, 1919 to Present* (Leiden: Brill, 2018).

82. Ulla Wikander, 'Demands on the ILO by Internationally Organized Women in 1919', in *ILO Histories: Essays on the International Labour Organization and Its Impact on the World during the Twentieth Century*, ed. Jasmien Van Daele et al. (Bern: Peter Lang, 2010), 67–90.

83. Carol Miller, '"Geneva – the Key to Equality": Inter-War Feminists and the League of Nations', *Women's History Review* 3, no. 2 (1994): esp. 223–6; Offen, *European Feminisms*, 352–4.

84. Kott, 'Les organisations internationales'; Laqua, ed., *Internationalism Reconfigured*.

85. Regula Ludi, 'Setting New Standards: International Feminism and the League of Nations' Inquiry into the Status of Women', *Journal of Women's History* 31, no. 1 (2019): 12–36.

86. On Crowdy, see e.g. Daniel Gorman, *The Emergence of International Society in the 1920s* (Cambridge: Cambridge University Press, 2012), 52–81. On Thibert, see Françoise Thébaud, *Une traversée du siècle: Marguerite Thibert, femme engagée et fonctionnaire internationale* (Paris: Editions Belin, 2017).

87. Susan Pedersen, 'Metaphors of the Schoolroom: Women Working the Mandates System of the League of Nations', *History Workshop Journal* 66, no. 1 (2008): 188–207.

88. Glenda Sluga, 'The Human Story of Development: Alva Myrdal at the UN, 1949–1955', in *International Organizations and Development, 1945–1990*, ed. Marc Frey, Sönke Kunkel and Corinna Unger (Basingstoke: Palgrave, 2014), 46–74.

89. Aoife O'Donoghue and Adam Rowe, 'Feminism, Global Inequality and the 1975 Mexico City Conference', in *Women and the UN: A New History of Women's International Human Rights*, ed. Rebecca Adami and Dan Plesch (Abingdon: Routledge, 2022), 88–103.
90. Jutta Joachim, 'Taming of the Shrew? International Women's NGOs, Institutional Power and the United Nations', in Olesen, *Power and Transnational Activism*, 220–1.
91. Francisca de Haan, 'Continuing Cold War Paradigms in Western Historiography of Transnational Women's Organisations: The Case of the Women's International Democratic Federation (WIDF)', *Women's History Review* 19, no. 4 (2010): 547–73; Gradskova, *The Women's International Democratic Federation*, 158–92.
92. *Report of the Committee on the Elimination of Discrimination against Women* (Sixth Session) (New York: United Nations, 1987), 90.
93. Ivanka Corti, 'Statement on the Occasion of the 25th Anniversary of the Adoption of the Convention on the Elimination of All Forms of Discrimination against Women by the General Assembly of the United Nations', 13 October 2004, United Nations, New York, available via https://www.un.org/womenwatch/daw/cedaw/cedaw25anniversary/cedaw25-IC.pdf (last accessed 9 January 2023).
94. Yulia Gradskova, 'Women's International Democratic Federation, the "Third World" and the Global Cold War from the late-1950s to the mid-1960s', *Women's History Review* 29, no. 2 (2020): 270–88; Celia Donert, 'Women's Rights and Global Socialism: Gendering Socialist Internationalism during the Cold War', *International Review of Social History* 67, S30 (2022): 1–22; Kristen Ghodsee, *Second World, Second Sex: Socialist Women's Activism and Global Solidarity during the Cold War* (Durham, NC: Duke University Press, 2019).
95. Caroline Diop, 'The Third World Viewpoint', in *XIII Conference of Socialist International Women, Lima, 16/17 June 1986: Equality – a Socialist Decade for Women* (London: Socialist International Women, 1986), 73–8 at 77.
96. Joachim, 'Taming of the Shrew?', 225.
97. Susan Grayzel, 'Total Warfare, Gender, and the "Home Front" in Europe during the First and Second World Wars', in *The Oxford Handbook of Gender, War, and the Western World since 1600*, ed. Karen Hagemann, Stefan Dudink and Sonya Rose (Oxford: Oxford University Press, 2020), 441.
98. See, for example, research that has explored these dimensions with regard to Germany: Katharina von Ankum, *Women in the Metropolis: Gender and Modernity in Weimar Culture* (Berkeley, CA: University of California Press, 1997); Katie Sutton, *The Masculine Woman in Weimar Germany* (New York: Berghahn, 2011); Robert Beachy, *Gay Berlin: Birthplace of a Modern Identity* (New York: Vintage, 2014).
99. Mary Louise Roberts, *Civilization without Sexes: Reconstructing Gender in Postwar France, 1917–1927* (Chicago, IL: Chicago University Press, 1994); Siân Reynolds, *France between the Wars: Gender and Politics* (London: Routledge, 1997).
100. On Kollontai's career, see Cathy Porter, *Alexandra Kollontai: A Biography* (Pontypool: Merlin Press, 2013).
101. Studer, *The Transnational World of the Cominternians*, 46.
102. Elisabeth Cheauré, 'Longue durée eines Transfers: Aleksandra Kollontaj und die deutsche(n) Frauenbewegung(en)', in *Russische Revolutionen 1917: Kulturtransfer im europäischen Raum*, ed. Elena Korowin and Jurij Lileev (Leiden: Brill, 2020), 195–217.
103. Elena Mancini, *Magnus Hirschfeld and the Quest for Sexual Freedom: A History of the First International Sexual Freedom Movement* (New York: Palgrave, 2010); Ralf Dose,

'The World League for Sexual Reform: Some Possible Approaches', *Journal of the History of Sexuality* 12, no. 1 (2003): 1–15.

104. Dora Russell, *The Tamarisk Tree: My Quest for Liberty and Love* (New York: Putnam, 1975), 217.
105. Ivan Crozier, '"All the World's a Stage": Dora Russell, Norman Haire, and the 1929 London World League for Sexual Reform Congress', *Journal of the History of Sexuality* 12, no. 1 (2003): 16–37. See also Stephen Brooke, 'The Body and Socialism: Dora Russell in the 1920s', *Past & Present*, no. 189 (2005): 147–77.
106. Russell, *The Tamarisk Tree*, 218.
107. Ibid., 220.
108. Ibid., 217–18 and 220.
109. Simone de Beauvoir, *Le deuxième sexe* (Paris: Gallimard, 1949); Simone de Beauvoir, *The Second Sex*, trans. Howard Parshley (New York: Alfred Knopf, 1953). On the American reception, see Rosie Germain, 'Reading "The Second Sex" in 1950s America', *The Historical Journal* 56, no. 4 (2013): 1041–62.
110. Barbara Andrew, 'Beauvoir's Place in Philosophical Thought', in *The Cambridge Companion to Simone de Beauvoir*, ed. Claudia Card (Cambridge: Cambridge University Press, 2003), 37.
111. Sylvie Chaperone, '*Momone* and the *Bonnes Femmes*; or Beauvoir and the MLF', in *The Women's Liberation Movement: Impacts and Outcomes*, ed. Kristina Schulz (New York: Berghahn, 2017), 73–91.
112. Kristina Schulz, 'Feminist Echoes of 1968: Women's Movements in Europe and the United States', in *A Revolution of Perception? Consequences and Echoes of 1968*, ed. Ingrid Gilcher-Holtey (New York: Berghahn, 2014), 124–47. Chaperone has spoken of the 'rejection of revolutionary machismo' in this context: Chaperone, '*Momone* and the *Bonnes Femmes*', 75.
113. Interview with Mariarosa Dalla Costa, as featured in Louise Toupin, *Wages for Housework: A History of an International Feminist Movement, 1972–77*, trans. Käthe Roth (London: Pluto Press, 2018), 224.
114. 'La liste des 343 françaises qui ont le courage de signer le manifeste "Je me suis fait avorter"', *Le Nouvel Observateur*, 5 April 1971; 'Wir haben abgetrieben!', *Stern*, 6 June 1971; 'We've Had Abortions', *Ms. Magazine*, spring 1972. See also Schulz, 'Feminist Echoes of 1968', 140 on the Franco-German links. On the American initiative, see a recent reappraisal: Jodie Tillman, '"We Have Had Abortions": 1972 Petition Changed Abortion Rights Movement', *Washington Post* website ('Retropolis' blog), 16 May 2022, https://www.washingtonpost.com/history/2022/05/16/ms-magazine-abortion-petition/ (last accessed 9 January 2023).
115. Maud Bracke, 'Our Bodies, Ourselves: The Transnational Connections of 1970s Italian and Roman Feminism', *Journal of Contemporary History*, 50, no. 3 (2015): 560–80.
116. Selma James, 'Introduction', in *The Power of Women and the Subversion of Community*, ed. Mariarosa Dalla Costa and Selma James (Bristol: Falling Wall Press, 1972), 13.
117. Silvia Federici, *Wages against Housework* (Bristol: Falling Wall Press, 1975), 2.
118. Toupin, *Wages for Housework*, 2.
119. Ibid., 83.
120. Maud Anne Bracke, 'Between the Transnational and the Local: Mapping the Trajectories and Contexts of the Wages for Housework Campaign in 1970s Italian Feminism', *Women's History Review* 22, no. 4 (2013): 625–42.

121. Interview with Silvia Federici, as featured in Toupin, *Wages for Housework*, 242.
122. Kirsten Harting, 'Echoes of Ourselves? Feminisms between East and West in the Leningrad Almanac Woman and Russia', in Schulz, *The Women's Liberation Movement*, 243–60.
123. Jeffra Flaitz, review of *Zhenshchina I Rossia: Almanakh Zhenshchinam O Zhenshchinakh* (Woman and Russia: An Almanac by Women about Women), *Journal of Thought* 18, no. 1 (1983): 116.
124. Harting, 'Echoes of Ourselves', 252.
125. Claire Bond Potter, 'Not in Conflict but in Coalition: Imagining Lesbians at the Centre of the Second Wave', in *The Legacy of Second-Wave Feminism in American Politics*, ed. Angie Maxwell and Todd Shields (Cham: Palgrave, 2018), 205–30; Christine Bard, 'Lesbianism as Political Construction in the French Feminist Context', in Schulz, *The Women's Liberation Movement*, 157–77.
126. Leila Rupp, 'The Persistence of Transnational Organizing: The Case of the Homophile Movement', *The American Historical* Review 116, no. 4 (2011): 1014–15. Leila Rupp, 'The European Origins of Transnational Organizing: The International Committee for Sexual Equality', in *LGBT Activism and the Making of Europe: A Rainbow Europe?*, ed. Philip Ayoub and David Paternotte (Basingstoke: Palgrave, 2014), 20–49.
127. Laura Belmonte, *The International LGBT Rights Movement: A History* (London: Bloomsbury, 2021), 121.
128. Belmonte, *The International LGBT Rights Movement*, 121.
129. Andrew Shield, 'The Legacies of the Stonewall Riots in Denmark and the Netherlands', *History Workshop Journal* 89 (2020): 196.
130. Craig Griffiths, *The Ambivalence of Gay Liberation: Male Homosexual Politics in 1970s West Germany* (Oxford: Oxford University Press, 2021), 153.
131. Griffiths, *The Ambivalence of Gay Liberation*, 127.
132. Belmonte, *The International LGBT Rights Movement*, 126.
133. Ibid., 128. See also Jocelyn Olcock, *International Women's Year: The Greatest Consciousness-Raising Event in History* (Oxford: Oxford University Press, 2017), 175–81.
134. 'IGA Enters World Arena', *Gay News*, 17 May 1979, 7.
135. Belmonte, *The International LGBT Rights Movement*, 146–7.
136. 'Women to Give Support to IGA', *Gay News*, 6 September 1979, 2. On the decision to retain the old name, see Jim Shearer, 'Spain: An Exhilarating IGA Conference', *Gay Scotland* (June 1980): 5–6.
137. 'IGA Loses Women's Branch', *Gay News*, 30 April 1981, 11; 'Women in the IGA', *Gay Scotland*, no. 5 (November 1982): 8.
138. '17 Years of Pursuing Lesbian and Gay Rights', *Gay Scotland*, no.104 (May 1996): 9.
139. '150 at ILGA's Helsinki Meeting', *Gay Scotland*, no. 91 (April 1995): 8.
140. 'IGA Enters World Stage', 7. On this issue, see Christopher Ewing, '"Toward a Better World for Gays": Race, Tourism and the Internationalization of the West German Gay Rights Movement, 1969-1983', *Bulletin of the German Historical Institute* 61 (2017): 109–34.
141. Christopher Ewing, '"Color Him Black": Erotic Representations and the Politics of Race in West German Homosexual Magazines, 1949-1974', *Sexuality and Culture* 21, no. 2 (2017): 382–403; Christopher Ewing, 'Highly Affected Groups: Gay Men and Racial Others in West Germany's AIDS Epidemic, 1981–1992', *Sexualities* 23, nos. 1–2 (2020): 201–23.

142. Ian Dunn, 'IGA Diminished?', *Gay Scotland* (September 1984), 16.
143. Josie McLellan, 'Glad to Be Gay behind the Wall: Gay and Lesbian Activism in 1970s East Germany', *History Workshop Journal* 74 (2012): 105–30; Lukasz Szulc, *Transnational Homosexuals in Communist Poland: Cross-Border Flows in Gay and Lesbian Magazines* (Cham: Palgrave, 2018), 100–6. For the contrasting cases of Poland and Czechoslovakia in the 1980s, see Conor O'Dwyer, *Coming Out of Communism: The Emergence of LGBT Activism in Eastern Europe* (New York: New York University Press, 2018), 84–94.
144. 'Gay Stirrings in the Communist Countries', *Gay Scotland* (March 1984): 5.
145. 'IGA Enters World Arena', 7.
146. 'IGA Loses Women's Branch', 11.
147. Belmonte, *The International LGBT Movement*, 159–60.
148. 'Outright to Support Boy-Love Group Expulsion from ILGA', *Gay Scotland*, no. 81 (June 1994): 3; 'ILGA Kicks Out Paedophiles', *The Pink Paper*, 8 July 1994, 2.
149. Selin Çağatay, Mia Liinason and Olga Sasunkevich, *Feminist and LGBTI+ Activism across Russia, Scandinavia and Turkey: Transnationalizing Spaces of Resistance* (Cham: Palgrave, 2022).
150. Conor O'Dwyer, 'From NGOs to Naught: The Rise and Fall of the Czech Gay Rights Movement', in *Beyond NGO-ization: The Development of Social Movements in Central and Eastern Europe*, ed. Kerstin Jacobsson and Steven Saxonberg (Farnham: Ashgate, 2013), 118.
151. O'Dwyer, *Coming Out of Communism*, 16.
152. O'Dwyer, 'From NGOs to Naught', 119.
153. Ibid., 131.
154. Christine Delphy, 'The European Union and the Future of Feminism', in *Sexual Politics and the European Union: The New Feminist Challenge*, ed. R. Amy Elman (New York: Berghahn, 1996), 148.
155. Alessandra Viviani, 'Women and the EU', in *Gender and the European Union*, ed. Sonia Lucarelli (Florence: Firenze University Press, 2014), 13–34; Anna van der Vleuten, *The Price of Gender Equality: Member States and Governance in the European Union* (Abingdon: Routledge, 2007); Gabriele Abels, Andrea Krizsán, Hether MacRae and Anna van der Vleuten, eds, *The Routledge Handbook of Gender and EU Politics* (Abingdon: Routledge, 2021).
156. O'Dwyer, *Coming Out of Communism*, 36–7.
157. Carsten Balzer and Jan Simon Hutta, 'Trans Networking in the European Vortex: Between Advocacy and Grassroots Politics', in Ayoub and Paternotte, *LGBT Activism and the Making of Europe*, 119–44.
158. Conor O'Dwyer, 'Does the EU Help or Hinder Gay-Rights Movements in Postcommunist Europe? The Case of Poland', *East European Politics* 28, no. 4 (2012): 332–52; Jon Binni and Christian Klesse, 'Transnational Solidarities and LGBTQ Politics in Poland', in Ayoub and Paternotte, *LGBT Activism and the Making of Europe*, 193–211.
159. 'Hungary: Orbán's Government Passes Anti-LGBTI Law Marking a "Dark Day" in the Country', *Amnesty International* press release, 15 June 2021, available at https://www.amnesty.org.uk/press-releases/hungary-orbans-government-passes-anti-lgbti-law-marking-dark-day-country (last accessed 9 January 2023).
160. 'Speech by Prime Minister Viktor Orbán at the Opening of CPAC Texas', 4 August 2022, as featured on the Hungarian prime minister's website, https://miniszterelnok.hu/speech-by-prime-minister-viktor-orban-at-the-opening-of-cpac-texas/ (last accessed 9 January 2023).

161. See, for instance, for the introduction covering such issues with regard to former Soviet republics, for instance Latvia, Belarus and Georgia: Rico Isaacs, Jonathan Wheatley and Sarah Whitmore, 'Culture Wars in the Post-Soviet Space', *Europe-Asia Studies* 73, no. 8 (2021): 1407–17.
162. For an example of references to past activism in such contexts, see Holly Lawford-Smith, *Gender-Critical Feminism* (Oxford: Oxford University Press, 2022), 28–46.
163. For a recent example, see Deborah Shaw, 'A Tale of Two Feminisms: Gender Critical Feminism, Trans Inclusive Feminism and the Case of Kathleen Stock', *Women's History Review* (advance access online, 2022), 10.1080/09612025.2022.2147915 (last accessed 9 January 2023). For a recent piece that criticizes the term 'gender critical' and the views associated with it, see Claire Thurlow, 'From TERF to Gender Critical: A Telling Genealogy?', *Sexualities*, advance access online (2022), https://doi.org/10.1177/13634607221107827 (last accessed 9 January 2023).
164. Shon Faye, *The Transgender Issue: Trans Justice Is Justice for All* (New York: Verso, 2022), xiv.
165. For contrasting views on this subject, see, on the one hand, Judith Suissa and Alice Sullivan, 'The Gender Wars, Academic Freedom and Education', *Journal of Philosophy of Education* 55, no. 1 (2021): 55–82; and, on the other hand, Shaw, 'A Tale of Two Feminisms'.
166. Jackson, Bailey and Foucault Welles, *#Hashtag Activism*, 65–96.
167. Shireen Roshanravan, 'On the Limits of Globalizing Black Feminist Commitments: "Me Too" and Its White Detours', *Feminist Formations* 33 no. 3 (2021): 239–55.
168. Chaitanya Lakkimsetti and Vanita Reddy, '#MeToo and Transnational Gender Justice: An Introduction', *Feminist Formations* 33 no. 3 (2021): 224–38.
169. The term 'intersectionality' predates the so-called 'fourth wave', having been introduced by the African American theorist Kimberlé Crenshaw in her article 'Demarginalizing the Intersection of Race and Sex: A Black Feminist Critique of Antidiscrimination Doctrine, Feminist Theory and Antiracist Politics', *Chicago Legal Forum* (1989): 139–67.

CHAPTER 6
ENCOUNTERING RACISM AND DISCRIMINATION

Throughout his long life, the African American scholar and civil rights activist W. E. B. Du Bois repeatedly travelled to Europe – starting with the period from 1892 to 1894, when he combined his academic research in Berlin with trips in and beyond Germany.[1] In 1952, he reflected on these experiences in a tribute to the Jewish participants of the Warsaw Ghetto Uprising (1943).[2] Looking back on his earlier time in Germany, he claimed that several encounters had left him 'not a little puzzled as to my own race problem and its place in the world'.[3] Du Bois argued that subsequent Central European travels – both to Germany in 1936 and to Poland in 1949 – further demonstrated the nature of anti-Semitism and its implications for his conception of the struggle he was involved in. As he put it, 'the problem of slavery, emancipation, and caste in the United States was no longer in my mind a separate and unique thing as I had so long conceived it.'[4] This change in perspective had led Du Bois to conclude that 'the race problem in which I was interested cut across lines of color and physique and belief and status and was a matter of cultural patterns, perverted teaching and human hate and prejudice, which reached all sorts of people'.[5]

One might argue that these comments were partly shaped by the forum for Du Bois's remarks, the left-wing periodical *Jewish Life*. Around the time of his 1936 trip to Germany, Du Bois's equivocal pronouncements on the Nazi regime had caused consternation among American Jewish organizations and antifascists.[6] Notwithstanding such inconsistencies, recent scholarship has acknowledged his forthright criticisms of Nazi policies in the 1930s and 1940s.[7] In the latter respect, Du Bois was not a solitary case. A range of African American activists expressed their 'concern about the plight of European Jewry' which, according to the historian Clive Webb, reflected the 'broadening and deepening of a longstanding internationalist outlook'.[8]

Representations of shared suffering could sometimes overshadow the distinctness of anti-Semitic violence. Writing in 1944, du Bois associated anti-Semitism in Nazi-occupied Europe with other forms of racism, including Western European assumptions 'that most of the rest of the world is biologically different' as well as beliefs 'that black and brown and yellow people are ... naturally inferior and inefficient; that they are a danger to civilization, to civilization as understood in Europe'.[9] Yet such remarks also indicate how anti-racism could, in turn, be connected to other causes, including the struggle against both imperial domination and class-based oppression: according to Du Bois, 'race fiction' was a tool 'to prolong economic inequality and injustice in the world'.[10] These comments reflect his growing embrace of socialist ideas. Political affinities first took him to the Soviet Union in 1926, followed by further visits in 1936, 1949 and 1959.[11] In Cold War America, his communist ties resulted in him being deemed an 'unregistered foreign agent', with the US authorities withholding of his passport from 1951 to 1958.[12]

Even beyond his travels and his connections to socialist and communist worlds, internationalism was a prominent feature of Du Bois's activism. His central role in the Pan-African movement was a case in point. Moreover, especially in the latter stages of his life, he increasingly framed and conceived his activism in global terms.[13] In 1961, Du Bois moved to Ghana, which its founding leader Kwame Nkrumah promoted as a centre for both anticolonial and Pan-African ventures.[14] Having been invited to pursue his project of an *Encyclopedia Africana* from Accra, Du Bois was one of several African Americans who travelled to the newly independent country.[15] For Du Bois, then, encounters with racism shaped a transnational trajectory that spanned several continents. For other activists, however, transnationalism was a matter of survival, as repression and persecution forced them into exile. Moreover, while transnational activism could drive anti-racist agendas, transnational ties and tools remained malleable. At times, fascists and neo-fascists cooperated across borders while promoting visions that sought to exclude or extinguish particular 'others'.

This chapter investigates such dynamics from several angles. It first highlights the efforts by Jewish activists to counter the discrimination that they experienced across different countries and empires. In this context, the chapter discusses humanitarianism and Zionism as strands of Jewish internationalism, while noting that anti-Semites deployed transnational contacts of their own. Secondly, the chapter considers different forms of Black activism, with a focus on two causes that resonated widely in Europe: the situation of African Americans on the one hand and of Black South Africans on the other. The final section shifts to the more recent past, with a focus on activisms that engaged with the multicultural nature of European societies.

The making of Jewish internationalisms

In 1840, the anti-Semitic 'blood libel' myth gave rise to the 'Damascus Affair', in which Jewish residents of the Ottoman city faced charges for the alleged murder of a Christian monk. Their imprisonment and torture as well as local anti-Jewish riots generated international protests. In the end, sustained pressure from abroad led to the release of the accused and precipitated reforms in the Ottoman Empire.[16] The Damascus Affair was an early example of transnational mobilization against anti-Semitism and, as such, underscores the need to look beyond Europe when considering the development of Jewish internationalism.[17] Moreover, the historian Abigail Green has stressed the 'long-term impact' of events that highlighted 'the interconnectedness of the Jewish world in an age of incipient globalization'.[18] Along similar lines, Tobias Brinkmann has suggested that the affair 'sparked the transnational consciousness of Jews throughout the Western diaspora and marked the symbolic birth of a public Jewish sphere that transcended national and imperial borders'.[19] The development of the Jewish press was one manifestation of this development.

Moses Montefiore and Adolphe Crémieux – two figures who had mobilized public opinion during the Damascus Affair – continued to play important roles in the growth of Jewish internationalism. Montefiore was a British banker, philanthropist and leader of the Board of Deputies of British Jews. His subsequent campaigning was exemplified by his intervention in another scandal, the Mortara Affair of 1858. In December 1858, the authorities in Bologna – then part of the Papal States – had removed a Jewish boy from his family, after learning of his secret baptism by a Catholic servant. The cruelty of these measures triggered widespread protests, and Montefiore travelled to Rome to lobby the papal authorities and arranged a large-scale petition in Britain.[20] Montefiore's French ally during the Damascus Affair, Adolphe Crémieux, became a protagonist of the Alliance Israélite Universelle (AIU), which had been founded in Paris in 1860 and initially focused on educational and philanthropic activities. While the AIU has often been portrayed as a largely French venture, it was genuinely transnational, with a large share of its supporters coming from outside France and a particular focus on activities in the Middle East.[21]

The AIU provided practical support during several waves of Jewish emigration from Eastern Europe – first in 1868–9 and 1881–2, and then on a larger scale in the 1890s, after anti-Semitic pogroms in the Russian Empire. In many instances, such efforts sought to facilitate onward travel to the Americas. The AIU was but one actor in this field, with newly founded bodies such as the Anglo-Jewish Association (1871), the *Hilfsverein der Deutschen Juden* (Aid Association of German Jews, 1901) and the American Jewish Committee (1906) forming a transnational network of aid associations.[22] As Abigail Green has argued, this development exemplified the 'proliferation of international Jewish groups and agencies', which amounted to 'the institutionalization of the Jewish international' in the late nineteenth and early twentieth centuries.[23] Jewish activists in Western Europe treaded a careful line, fearing that the arrival of migrants might affect the perception of Jewish communities. Their ambivalent stance became evident during the creation of the Central Bureau for Jewish Migration in 1904. The body originated in a conference held in Frankfurt/Main, organized by the *Hilfsverein* with the support of the AIU and B'nai B'rith, a Jewish fraternal association that had been founded in New York in 1843. In creating the Bureau, the organizers insisted that it 'must in no way take any measures that would be suited to lead to an increase in emigration'.[24] Instead, the body aimed to 'educate the emigrants about the preconditions under which alone a departure from their Eastern European home is advisable'. The meeting noted the difficult conditions of Jewish immigrants in British and American cities, concluding that it might be better to work towards 'an improvement of the conditions of East European Jews in their home countries'.[25]

By the turn of the nineteenth century, humanitarian ventures were joined by another strand of Jewish internationalism: Zionism. In 1896, the Austrian journalist Theodore Herzl published his book *Der Judenstaat*, the formative text of the Zionist movement.[26] Chaim Weizmann, later the first president of Israel, likened the impact of Herzl's book to 'a bolt from the blue'.[27] At the time of its publication, Weizmann – who had been born in the Russian Empire – studied in Berlin, where he was involved in diasporic circles that embraced the vision of a Jewish home in Palestine. In that respect, Herzl's book 'contained not a single new idea for us' – and yet, the author's 'daring, clarity and energy' solicited a positive response among Weizmann and his friends: 'The very fact that this Westerner came to us encumbered by our preconceptions had its appeal'. In retrospect, Weizmann appreciated Herzl 'as a man of action, as the founder of the Zionist Congress, and as an example of daring and devotion'.[28]

One year after publishing *Der Judenstaat*, Herzl staged the first Zionist Congress in the Swiss city of Basel, giving rise to the Zionist Organization – which, in this period, raised funds to purchase land in the Ottoman province of Palestine and negotiated with the Ottoman authorities. Subsequent Zionist conferences revealed significant differences about strategies, ideology and the role of religion. This, for instance, was the case in 1906, as Herzl unveiled a controversial plan for a settlement scheme in Uganda, rather than Palestine, during the Sixth World Zionist Congress.[29] Beyond congresses, newspapers provided another forum for Zionist debate, starting with Herzl's *Die Welt* (1897–1914). Moreover, between 1908 and 1914, Vladimir Jabotinsky – a Zionist activist from the

Figure 6.1 Zionist Congress, held in Basel, Switzerland, from 29 to 31 August 1897.
Source: Universal Images Group, via Getty Images.

Russian Empire – published *Le Jeune Turc* from Istanbul, seeking to create an alliance between the Zionist cause and the efforts of the Young Turks.[30]

Zionism was by no means universally accepted among Jewish activists, some of whom rejected the premise of Jewish nationhood. Yet, as a movement, it gained momentum at a time when political anti-Semitism grew across different parts of Europe. This included Herzl's hometown of Vienna, where the Christian Social politician Karl Lueger deployed it as an electoral tool, winning a majority for his Christian Social Party on the city council in 1895 and serving as the city's mayor from 1897 until his death in 1910.[31] Meanwhile, in France, the Jewish army captain Alfred Dreyfus had been wrongfully convicted for the sale of military secrets in December 1894. The Dreyfus Affair had transnational dimensions even beyond its extensive coverage in the international press.[32] One of the first detailed dissections of the injustice suffered by Dreyfus appeared abroad: the French author Bernard Lazare issued his attack on the authorities initially through a Belgian publisher.[33] Lazare also attended the first World Zionist Congress in 1897. Despite his support for Zionist principles and Herzl's efforts, Lazare broke with the Zionist Organization in 1899, criticizing its strategy and presumptions. Three years later, he attacked the fact that the Zionist Congress had praised Sultan Abdülhamid II while remaining silent about the massacres of Armenians in the Ottoman Empire.[34]

Alarm about the rise of anti-Semitism extended to activists whose efforts largely focused on other causes. The peace activist Bertha von Suttner was one such example: in 1891, her husband Arthur had co-founded the *Verein zur Abwehr des Antisemitismus* (Association for the Defence against Anti-Semitism) in Vienna. Suttner and Herzl maintained a regular dialogue, despite underlying differences: with its focus on a national homeland, Zionism contrasted with Suttner's supranational concerns; meanwhile Herzl considered the Viennese *Verein* to be too tacit in its endeavours and viewed pacifism as a secondary aim. Nonetheless, both sides were broadly sympathetic to one another; in 1903, Suttner even contacted Nicholas II to request an audience for Herzl after the latest anti-Semitic massacres in Russia.[35] Suttner's biographer has argued that the Austrian pacifist saw 'strong parallels between Herzl and herself' in terms of the dedicated pursuit of their respective cause.[36]

Suttner was not the only pacifist who attacked anti-Semitism. For example, the *Ligue internationale de la Paix et la Liberté* intervened in the Dreyfus Affair which, in its view, highlighted the dangers of militarism.[37] That said, the *Ligue* largely refrained from a systematic analysis of anti-Semitism. Similar limitations were evident within the international socialist movement: while some of its protagonists spoke out against anti-Semitism, others embraced stereotypes about 'Jewish capitalism'.[38] In this context, Brendan McGeever and Satnam Virdee have referred to a 'complex and sometimes troubling record' among European socialists and noted that 'such unevenness … was also reflected at the level of the supranational, at the congresses of the Second International'.[39] Like pacifists and socialists, humanitarians had their blind spots. In 1906, Max Nordau – a Zionist activist and intellectual from Hungary – criticized such inconsistencies in a discussion of the 'European conscience'. As Nordau pointed out, this notion was often used for incidents outside Europe, whereas political leaders and diplomats seemed unwilling to evoke the 'European conscience' when it came to the anti-Semitic pogroms in the Russian Empire.[40]

There was a particular challenge for transnational alliances against anti-Semitism: as Abigail Green has noted, 'the idea of international Jewish solidarity served as an argument against Jewish emancipation'.[41] Anti-Semitic tropes portrayed Jewish people as 'cosmopolitans' and cast suspicion on their national loyalties. Before intervening in the Dreyfus Affair, Lazare had acknowledged this issue in a study on anti-Semitism, which he published in 1894.[42] In 1898, a discussion in the *Jüdische Allgemeine Zeitung*, the principal Jewish periodical in Imperial Germany, further discussed this issue. The paper noted that it should not have been forced to comment on matters of patriotism because Jewish people's 'sentiment towards the fatherland' did not differ from that of 'any other citizens' – and yet 'the distinction, which factually does not exist, is being made by our enemies'.[43]

Anti-Semitic claims regarding Jewish people's alleged lack of attachment to the nation went hand in hand with notions of an international Jewish conspiracy. Such assertions were themselves disseminated across national borders, as exemplified by two infamous anti-Semitic texts – *La Conquête du monde par les Juifs* (The Conquest of the World by the Jews, 1873) and *The Protocols of the Elders of Zion* (1903). The former was written in French by an Anglo-Turkish author, Osman Bey (originally: Frederick Millengen) and first published in Switzerland.[44] The latter originally circulated in the Russian Empire and subsequently spread internationally, with an impact that continues to this day.[45] Significantly, both texts evoked existing transnational ties for anti-Semitic purposes: *The Conquest* falsely claimed to reveal the truth about the AIU's agenda, while the forged *Protocols* purported to feature secret discussions from the Zionist congress of 1897. In such representations, transnational activism was cast as a negative.

Combating anti-Semitism in the age of extremes

The First World War caused great suffering for many Jewish people. While the location of fighting on the Eastern Front – in areas that were home to the largest Jewish population in Europe – was one aspect, outpourings of anti-Semitism were another, linked to the proliferation of rumours and conspiracy theories that cast Jewish people as war profiteers.[46] In Eastern Europe, this development produced numerous pogroms, yet wartime anti-Semitism also manifested itself elsewhere on the continent, including among activists of the left.[47]

Yet the war years were also a time when Jewish activism impacted on government policy. Chaim Weizmann is usually credited as a key influence in shaping the Balfour Declaration (1917), in which the British Foreign Secretary promised support for the creation of a Jewish state in Palestine. Having been involved in the Zionist Organization since attending the Second Zionist Congress in 1899, Weizmann's academic career took him to Britain, where he became a naturalized citizen. The historian Thomas Fraser has argued that the Balfour Declaration was not merely a trade-off for Weizmann's willingness to make his recently invented process for acetone production available to the British war industry: 'The rather more prosaic truth was that by 1916 Weizmann had rendered a significant service to the British state and was now a respected figure in the eyes of those at the heart of the government.'[48] Weizmann's example thus illustrates how the standing of individual activists could help build credibility for a cause.

Notwithstanding the hopes raised by the Balfour Declaration, the aftermath of the Great War was an ambivalent era for Jewish internationalism. The League of Nations became a focus for some Jewish activists – both because of its role in minority protection and because Palestine, while administered by Britain, was a League mandate. The historian Jaclyn Granick has highlighted the spectrum covered by Jewish activists in their interactions with the League, from a 'policy of discrete intercession' and cooperation around expertise to the generation of publicity.[49] Yet such interactions were subject to limitations, in particular when considering activists' efforts to ensure that the League's minority protection arrangements would safeguard Jewish communities in Central and Eastern Europe.[50]

The League of Nations was but one forum in which Jewish activism intersected with different forms of interwar internationalism. Especially for Jewish activists from Eastern Europe, this included links to the worlds of socialist as well as liberal internationalism.[51] Key figures within the Labour and Socialist International (LSI) saw Zionism as an emancipatory movement, although others argued that the focus on Jewish statehood would distract from the transnational pursuit of class politics.[52] This tension manifested itself in the LSI's relationship with two Jewish member organizations, namely the General Jewish Labour Bund and Poale Zion. Both associations were organized internationally but with conflicting stances vis-à-vis Zionism. The Bund had been founded as a socialist Jewish organization in 1897. Facing repression within the Russian Empire, many of its founders operated from abroad: the Bund's Foreign Committee was based in Geneva, and one of its branches, the *Fraynd fun bund* (Friends of the Bund), undertook fundraising in the United States.[53] As the Bund rejected Zionism in 1901, dissenting factions established Poale Zion by 1906. Their party sought affiliation to both the Zionist Organization and the Second International. The latter's membership principles – which were based on national representation – provided obstacles for Poale Zion and, from a different angle, also affected the Bund.[54] In the 1920s, however, both Poale Zion and the Bund acceded to the LSI, although the former initially shared its seat on the International's executive with the Armenian *Dashnaktsutyun*.[55] Meanwhile, the relationship with communism varied across the two Jewish organizations. One Bundist faction affiliated to the Comintern, whereas the Bund itself adopted an increasingly critical stance vis-à-vis communists.[56] Meanwhile, relations between Poale Zion and communist parties were tense from the outset, exemplified by the Polish Communist Party's view of Zionism as a tool of British imperialism.[57]

The interwar years generated new patterns of transnational cooperation among Jewish activists, yet the era was also characterized by closer transnational ties among racists. As Arnd Bauerkämper and Grzegorz Rossoliński-Liebe have stressed, fascism was 'both a national and transnational phenomenon, as it transcended national borders but was rooted in national communities'.[58] One recent study on exchanges between fascists and neo-fascists in Italy and Spain has even interpreted internationalism as 'a crucial part of the nature of fascism and neo-fascism'.[59] Contacts between fascist groups and organizations were partly driven from the top, backed by the governments of Fascist Italy and later Nazi Germany.[60] Yet the beneficiaries of such state-led ventures included members of far-right movements who considered themselves 'activists' or intellectuals. The role of anti-Semitism in such exchanges tended to vary according to period and context, with anti-communism and corporatism forming alternative rallying points. That said, ideas about 'racial' purity as well as the rejection of 'cosmopolitanism' were common features of transnational fascism.

The contacts of Ion Moța – a key figure in the Legion of the Archangel Michael, Romania's principal fascist grouping – offer a case in point. Anti-Semitism had already been a feature of the Romanian far right before Moța's lifetime, as exemplified by attempts of Romanian activists to form an international counterpart to the AIU in the 1880s.[61] In the 1930s, Moța promoted the idea of an anti-Semitic 'brotherhood' that would even transcend the political conflict between Romania and Hungary.[62] He contributed to the *Welt-Dienst*, an anti-Semitic news agency, and in 1934 attended the International Fascist Conference in Montreux, where his participation highlighted 'the primacy of anti-Semitism as the main impetus for transnational cooperation of the [Romanian] legionary movement'.[63] Moța's transnational commitments further manifested themselves in his volunteering for the Francoist side during the Spanish Civil War, where he fell in 1937.

The role of 'race' became increasingly prominent during the Second World War when, according to the historian Benjamin Martin, 'the vision of culture that undergirded the Axis's inter-nationalist claim to European leadership was wholly penetrated by racism, in Italy as well as Germany'.[64] Yet Italian–German interactions were not without tensions. For example, the National Socialists had been notably absent at the Montreux conference of 1934 – an event at which the question of anti-Semitism proved divisive.[65] Moreover, the formation of the Axis did not necessarily result in closer transnational exchanges, with German protagonists seeking 'to block the penetration of Italian fascist ideological influence' at home.[66] This observation draws attention to a broader issue: while transnational fascism involved 'friendly encounters and all kinds of cultural, political and military cooperation' between allied movements, parties and governments, it also produced 'inter-fascist conflicts'.[67]

The rise of fascism invested transnational Jewish activism with particular urgency, especially after the National Socialist accession to power in 1933. Faced with the Nazi persecution of Jews, refugee aid was a major transnational undertaking. In this context, activists sought to prevent the impression that the arrival of refugees might pose a burden for their host societies and, for example, raised separate funds to settle Jewish refugees.[68] Attempts by Jewish organizations to work with the League of Nations and the High Commissioner of Refugees Coming from Germany had clear limitations, linked to the limited scope for the High Commissioner's role, as noted in Chapter 2.[69] Since aid efforts targeted symptoms rather than root causes, another strand of transnational Jewish activism aimed at raising public awareness and undertaking political lobbying. From 1936 onwards, the newly created World Jewish Congress drove such efforts. The historian Zohar Segev has argued that it 'operated as an American Jewish organization' but has also highlighted its transnational features.[70] It maintained an office in Geneva, organized rescue efforts, lobbied governments and maintained clandestine contacts in Germany and, later, Nazi-occupied Europe. By 1942, information gathering enabled the World Jewish Congress to highlight Nazi Germany's 'policy of constant and deliberate annihilation of all European Jewish communities' and to convey such information to Allied governments.[71] Yet the direct impact on governments during wartime remained limited. Likewise, the association's efforts to convince the International Committee of the Red Cross to address Nazi crimes bore little fruit.[72]

After 1945, the legacies of the Holocaust created a new context for transnational Jewish activism. With Europe's Jewish population vastly depleted, the centres for Jewish activism moved elsewhere. For example, the International Jewish Labour Bund reconstituted itself by hosting its first world conference in Brussels in 1947, but at the time, it was 'a small, weakened movement', notwithstanding its 'central role in the lives of its members' and the presence of Bundists communities in different countries, especially the United States.[73] Moreover, the foundation of Israel in 1948 marked the accomplishment of the Zionist movement's principal objective. Jewish organizations in other countries did not have an unambiguous relationship with the new state. One example of potential tensions emerged during the campaign on behalf of the Soviet Union's Jewish population. The Israeli government and some Jewish leaders in the United States focused on facilitating migration to Israel, whereas other activists promoted a broader agenda that sought to highlight day-to-day anti-Semitism in the Soviet Union.[74]

The so-called 'Soviet Jewry Movement' evidently had a wider historical context, with Soviet anti-Semitism manifesting itself in the so-called 'anti-cosmopolitan' campaign of the late Stalin era.[75] Yet it was in the late 1960s that the situation of Jewish people within the Soviet Union attracted wider international attention, with a particular focus on the *refuseniks*, that is, Jewish people whose demand for emigration had been denied by the Soviet authorities. While it is sometimes viewed within the context of rising human rights activism, Nathan Kurz has highlighted the campaign's distinct focus on one specific right, namely the freedom to emigrate from the Soviet Union.[76]

The campaign had several transnational features. Its connection to broader histories of Jewish activism is illustrated by its founding figure, Jacob Birnbaum, whose grandfather Nathan had coined the term 'Zionism' as a Viennese student activist during the 1880s. Born in Hamburg, Jacob Birnbaum escaped Nazi Germany in the *Kindertransport* of 1938, through which Jewish activists from Britain rescued Jewish children. He later settled in the United States, where he launched the Student Struggle for Soviet Jewry in 1964. By the 1970s, Birnbaum was one of several US-based activists in a movement that was notable in several respects, for instance by providing a forum for the activism of Orthodox Jews.[77] While the Soviet Jewry Movement was particularly prominent in the United States, it was a wider phenomenon that also encompassed Australia, Canada, Israel, Latin America and Western Europe.[78] In this context, Jewish activists from the Soviet Union developed ties to supporters in other countries. The diversity of its views and styles also generated conflict, which became evident when representatives of the movement met at an international conference in Brussels in 1971. As the activist Yuli Kosharovsky later recorded, the 'anodyne proposals for the conference organizers for quiet diplomacy and designing a symbol for the movement' contrasted with the stance of activists who favoured a more confrontational course.[79]

The Soviet case illustrates that a country's self-proclaimed anti-fascism did not preclude anti-Semitic policies. Likewise, in Poland, a government-instigated 'anti-Zionist campaign' drew on and mobilized anti-Jewish prejudice in the late 1960s.[80] This was but one example of the different meanings of 'anti-Zionism'. During the Cold War, communist governments attacked Israel for its alliance with Western countries and its alleged 'imperialism'. The stance of governments in both the Eastern bloc and the Arab world meant that for Jewish activists, the United Nations provided a more ambivalent interlocutor than its forerunner, the League of Nations. While Jewish activists had initially viewed the UN as forum to combat anti-Semitism, subsequent developments created growing disappointments – by 1975, a majority in the UN General Assembly denounced Zionism as a form of racism.[81] These developments were not only affected by Cold War dynamics and postcolonial politics: solidarity with the Palestinian cause animated various forms of transnational activism, especially after the Six-Day War of 1967. With Israeli occupation and settlement policies attracting scrutiny, pro-Palestinian mobilization received further stimuli through the First and Second Intifadas, the Palestinian uprisings of 1987–93 and 2000–5. As with other solidarity campaigns, the meanings and connotations of pro-Palestine solidarity varied: it could focus on areas of humanitarian concern, on active political lobbying for Palestinian statehood or contribution to peacebuilding efforts. However, some currents of 'anti-Zionist' activism deployed images of a 'Jewish lobby' that echoed well-established anti-Semitic tropes.[82] Such examples highlight the persistence of some stereotypes across different political currents, including in activist circles.

From a different angle, the vilification of George Soros – a Hungarian-born financier and philanthropist – shows how voluntary action could be portrayed in anti-Semitic terms. Having survived the Holocaust as a Jewish child, Soros grew up in the United States. After making his fortune on the financial markets, Soros funded various civil society efforts from the 1980s, including support for dissidents in Central and Eastern Europe. After the collapse of state socialism in the Eastern bloc, Soros's Open Society Foundation – launched as the Open Society Institute in 1993 – was one major vehicle for efforts to promote democracy in the region and elsewhere. Indeed, Soros's support for groups critical of Israeli policies also put him into conflict with Israel's government.[83] Yet right-wing circles in his native Hungary, the United States and elsewhere cast Soros's backing for humanitarian and human rights initiatives as the pursuit of a hidden agenda, revealing the durability of claims about a 'Jewish conspiracy'.[84]

Questioning 'race' and articulating Black identity

In 1911, the United Races Congress in London brought together activists, academics and political leaders, in an attempt to examine 'race' and racist prejudices from different perspectives. Jewish identity figured in these discussions, as reflected in a congress paper by Israel Zangwill, a British author whose parents had been immigrants from the Russian Empire. Three years before the London event, Zangwill's play *The Melting Pot* had premiered in the United States. Set among Jewish immigrants in America, its success gave rise to a well-known phrase that continues to feature in discourse on the role of immigrants in American society.[85] Zangwill himself was also an activist in the Zionist Organization, and his stance was illustrated by his comments at the London congress, as he described 'the absence of a territory in which the race can live' as the 'tragedy of Jewish existence today'.[86] Zangwill's paper highlighted the contrasting representations of Jewish identity. On the one hand, he referred to a 'cosmopolitan habit of mind'; on the other hand, he also stressed Jewish attachment to the nation, for instance proclaiming that there were 'no Ottomans so Young-Turkish as the Turkish Jews, no Americans so spread-eagle on the American soil, no section so Jingo as Anglo-Jewry'.[87]

In its wide-ranging consideration of 'race', the Universal Races Congress involved a significant American presence. W. E. B. Du Bois served as one of its 'honorary secretaries', and he was far from the only transatlantic visitor.[88] Other prominent American participants included the social reformer Jane Addams and the suffragist Mary White Ovington, who had cooperated with Du Bois in co-founding the National Association for the Advancement of Colored People (1909). The event provided American campaigners with opportunities to draw international comparisons. To Du Bois, the conference papers demonstrated 'that America is fifty years behind the scientific world in its racial philosophy'.[89] Du Bois's journal *The Crisis* noted that the active participation of non-white people at the event undermined racist claims about their inadequacy.[90] The coverage thus underscored a wider point raised at the conference, namely an acknowledgement that 'difference in civilization does not … necessarily connote either inferiority or superiority'.[91] The 1911 congress was not the first time that Du Bois travelled to London for an international gathering. Eleven years earlier, he had participated in the Pan-African Conference, an event staged by the Trinidadian activist and lawyer Henry Sylvester Williams.[92]

Both the Pan-African Conference of 1900 and the Universal Races Congress of 1911 illustrate how transnational cooperation enabled activists to challenge the premises of racist thinking in the early twentieth century. Such efforts contrasted with the contemporaneous spread of racist doctrines, including concepts of 'scientific racism'. While the implications for Jewish activists have already been noted, constructions of race also necessitated a response from other groups. Commenting on Africans and African American activism, Daniel Gorman has even argued that 'race' was more central for the construction of 'international alliances of opposition' in the early twentieth century than colonialism, although he has described one as being the 'cognate' of the other.[93] While Chapter 1 has highlighted the role of empire and colonialism in stimulating activism, including among people of African descent, intellectual currents that challenged racism became a major feature of transnational campaigning.

The growth of the Pan-African movement under Du Bois's leadership constituted one key development in this context. In 1919, the Pan-African Congress in Paris argued for the inclusion of Black voices in the making of a new post-war order. Further events of this kind followed in the 1920s, although in somewhat improvised ways, with meetings 'organized on shoestring budgets' and delegations whose composition involved activists who were visiting Europe for other reasons.[94] Pan-African Congresses were divided on the future of empire (as noted in Chapter 1), yet delegates concurred in denouncing racism. For example, upon conclusion of the 1921 congress, a letter to the League of Nations urged the organization 'to take a firm stand on the absolute equality of races'.[95] In this context, delegates criticized racism in terms of attempts to cast 'civilized men as uncivilized'.[96] Such language indicates that notions of civilizational hierarchies also affected Pan-Africanists. In a careful analysis of the Pan-African congresses, Jake Hodder has noted that organizers made 'a sharp distinction between "primitive" indigenous Africans on the one hand, and more enlightened Congress delegates on the other'.[97]

Even beyond gathering activists from different countries, Pan-Africanism had important transnational features, notably through the participation of diasporic communities. West African activists – including students from British colonies – analysed and challenged the racism that they encountered in the metropole.[98] Corresponding developments could be observed in France. In the 1930s, students from West Africa and the Caribbean articulated criticisms of racist thinking through the *Négritude* movement. As the historian Andreas Eckert has pointed out with regard to Léopold Sedhar Senghor – poet, politician in the French parliament and the first president of independent Senegal – Senghor's 'image of Africa' remained 'ambivalent and speculative', on the one hand promoting syncretism but on the other hand 'constitute *Négritude* as what divides the African spirit from the European one'.[99]

Pan-Africanism and *Négritude* contrasted with the transnational dissemination of racist ideas and policies in the interwar period. While racism in 1930s Europe prominently targeted Jews, it also affected Black people, especially as it combined discrimination of non-white minorities in European societies with a justification of imperial domination. For example, British fascists – whose stance had been shaped by transnational influences – promoted visions of white superiority that were underpinned by colonial racism.[100] Black activism in the 1930s was sensitive to such interconnections. The views by Pan-Africanist campaigner George Padmore are a case in point. As the historian Leslie James has argued, by the late 1930s, Padmore believed that 'imperial structures of power explained the numerous iterations of contemporary European racism in Nazi Germany, colonial Africa, and the West Indies'.[101]

As noted in Chapter 1, Padmore cooperated with another Trinidad-born activist, C. L. R. James, for instance by co-founding the International African Service Bureau in London in 1937. This body built upon the earlier alliances that had been created in the campaign against Italian imperialism in Abyssinia. Yet the bureau linked transnational activism with domestic challenges to racism. For example, it cooperated with the League of Coloured Peoples, a British anti-racist organization, in challenging the 'colour bar' that limited the access of non-white people to particular employment.[102] More broadly, the late 1930s were a period of alliance-building for anti-racist campaigners, with events from various internationalist groups, from the left to liberal internationalism.[103] In 1945, Padmore was among the organizers of the Pan-African Congress in Manchester. Held at a time of growing momentum for decolonization, the event highlighted the extent to which notions of 'race' were being questioned and contested. Alongside many resolutions that focused on colonialism, the event also raised the issue of the 'colour bar', demanding 'equal opportunities for all Colonial and Coloured people in Great Britain' and therefore requesting 'that discrimination on account of race, creed or colour be made a criminal offence by law'.[104]

The links between Pan-African ideas and wider anticolonial struggles remained relevant in the post-war years. This was evident in the work of Frantz Fanon, whose critique of imperialism and racism was influenced by his own experiences of colonialism but also engaged with ideas of African unity. As noted in Chapter 1, Fanon's writings had a transnational impact. In 1968, an American edition of *Les Damnés de la terre* cast Fanon's text as *The Handbook for the Black Revolution That Is*

Figure 6.2 Participants of the Pan-African Congress held at Chorlton-on-Medlock Town Hall, Manchester, 1 October 1945. *Source:* John Deakin / Stringer, via Getty Images.

Changing the Shape of the Earth.[105] In the late 1960s and early 1970s, radical groups such as the Black Panther Party (BPP) in the United States studied Fanon and cited him as an inspiration for their own struggle.[106] BPP member Kathleen Neal Cleaver later stated that 'Fanon's penetrating dissection of the intertwining of racism and violence in the colonial scheme of domination was compelling to Blacks fighting in America; it provided a clearly reasoned antidote to the constant admonition to seek changes peacefully'. According to Cleaver, the BPP's engagement with Fanon's book was based on the argument 'that the same racist imperialism that people in Africa, Asia, and Latin America were fighting against was victimizing Blacks in the United States'.[107]

Whereas some activists cast their struggle as one against imperial domination, Black Feminism drew attention to the intersections of discrimination based on race and gender.[108] One significant protagonist was Claudia Jones who, having been born in Trinidad, moved to the United States, where she joined the Communist Party, which she regarded as a vehicle for anti-racist struggles. Threatened with expulsion from the United States, she moved to Britain in 1955, where she became a central figure in anti-racist activism. Both Marxism and anti-racism shaped Jones's feminism, which highlighted the 'superexploitation' of Black women.[109] As her biographer Carole Boyce Davies has argued, Jones's diasporic experience not only 'meant pain and separation from family but ... also ... a host of other things', as she was able to forge manifold connections in the struggles she waged abroad.[110]

Black Feminism gained momentum in the late 1960s and 1970s.[111] This is not to say that interactions with Western European women's liberation were unambiguous. For example, a study of French feminist magazines has noted the 'problematic construction of African women as passive victims of uncivilised and backward cultures' well into the 1980s.[112] One alternative was the development of intersectional approaches to inequality, as articulated by the American academic and poet Audre Lorde. According to Lorde, racism and sexism had to be considered alongside heterosexism, ageism and classism.[113] In 1984, Lorde temporarily moved to West Berlin, having received a visiting fellowship at the Free University. As she later recalled, 'One of my goals for this trip was to meet Black German women.'[114] These encounters enabled Lorde to contribute to the emerging Afro-German women movement: Dagmar Schultz, the West German feminist academic who had arranged Lorde's stay, later praised her 'lasting contributions to the German political and cultural scene' in this period.[115] As the historian Heide Fehrenbach has argued, the development of Afro-German identity showed how 'reformulations of race, identity and nation in Germany were part of a larger transnational dialogue with African American and the American experience of race and gender'.[116]

The transatlantic dimensions of African American struggles

From Du Bois to Lorde, African American activists construed their struggle in global terms and therefore developed manifold transnational ties. European interest in the United States helped to sustain these interactions. Whereas in the nineteenth century,

European activism on the situation of African Americans had mostly revolved around the humanitarian efforts of abolitionists, by the interwar years, it targeted racist discrimination, in campaigns that were increasingly framed in terms of solidarity. Both Pan-Africanism and the transnational politics of the left were important factors in this period. European responses to the Scottsboro Affair illustrate this point. Campaigners in both the United States and Europe mobilized on behalf of nine young African Americans who became victims of a miscarriage of justice in 1931, having been sentenced to death for the alleged rape and murder of a white girl. The mobilization against their wrongful conviction included Pan-Africanists such as Padmore.[117] The fate of the 'Scottsboro boys' generated expressions of support within different groups and movements, as exemplified by the 1937 congress of the Women's International League for Peace and Freedom (WILPF).[118] The same WILPF event also passed motions on the right to asylum, political prisoners and on the aftermath of the Italian invasion of Abyssinia, illustrating the interconnectedness of different concerns in the radical politics of the 1930s.[119]

From the 1950s onwards, the growth of the African American civil rights movement reverberated across Cold War Europe in different ways. Political leaders in the Soviet bloc cited racist discrimination in the United States to highlight the deficiencies of the Western system, while hosting and celebrating activists such as W. E. B. Du Bois and Paul Robeson. Yet beyond state-sanctioned proclamations of solidarity, the civil rights movement and its methods also inspired oppositional groups in the Eastern bloc.[120] Moreover, government-sanctioned rhetoric sat at odds with the presence of racism in states that proclaimed their anti-fascism. At times, these contradictions generated activism among diasporic groups. For example, in 1963, the death of a Ghanaian student in the Soviet Union sparked protests amongst African students, including the unusual event of a demonstration on Red Square.[121] The protestors' comparisons between their experience in the USSR and the American South were widely noted in the British and American press – a delicate echo of the prominence that Soviet publications accorded to Western racism.[122]

In Western Europe, the African American freedom struggle spoke to different groups of activists and created direct interactions, albeit in somewhat ambiguous ways. Malcolm X's visit to Oxford in 1964 was a case in point. While some students at the University of Oxford saw his presence as an opportunity to generate publicity, anti-racist campaigners had concerns that the visitor's radical reputation might undermine local efforts.[123] Three years later, another transatlantic visitor from the United States, Stokely Carmichael, provided 'a tremendous catalyst for the Black Power movement in Britain'.[124] Carmichael's trip was occasioned by the 'Dialectics of Liberation' congress in London, a diverse countercultural event, which he addressed with a speech on Black Power.[125]

Transatlantic trips clearly had local impacts, yet they also had meanings for the visitors themselves, as they could 'enhance ... [their] status at home' and offer a platform to reach 'a wider audience'.[126] Such travels provided encouragement and a sense of validation during moments of isolation in the political struggles at home.[127] Moreover, they potentially broadened activists' perspectives: for instance, Stephen Tuck has noted that Malcolm X's travels to Britain and France led him to include Europe in his understanding of 'racial distinction and black resistance'.[128]

Within activist circles in Europe, a shared analysis of oppression sustained engagement with the African American freedom struggle. Such a sense of likeness involved an echoing of language and methods. For example, in 1963, American expatriates cooperated with the Asian Caribbean Organization – an anti-racist group co-founded by Claudia Jones – in staging a protest in London, three days after the civil rights movement's March on Washington.[129] In the same year, another British protest saw South Asian and Caribbean activists organize a bus boycott in Bristol. While targeting the 'colour bar', the use of this means of protest evoked the campaign that Rosa Parks had helped to launch in Montgomery, Alabama.[130]

Transatlantic inspirations in both language and methods also manifested themselves in the campaigns of Catholic civil rights activists in Northern Ireland during the late 1960s.[131] The historian Marc Mulholland has likened the American case to 'a mirror held up to [the] Northern Ireland experience, rather than a rigid template distorting Ulster's civil rights movement'.[132] Expressions of solidarity could provoke controversy, which became evident when the Northern Irish civil rights leader and freshly elected member of parliament Bernadette Devlin visited the United States in 1969. Whereas Devlin saw African American activists as natural allies in a shared struggle against oppression, local leaders of the Irish community were wary of radical associations and, in some cases, held prejudices that clashed with Devlin's sense of solidarity.[133]

Notions of likeness underpinned the different transnational entanglements of the Black Panther Party (BPP). In 1969, a group of Black Panthers moved to Algeria.[134] Bearing in mind Fanon's influence on the BPP and his association with the Algerian liberation struggle, a move to this country seemed to consolidate existing intellectual ties. Moreover, in the eyes of former activist Elaine Mokhtefi, 'Algeria's treatment of the Panthers flowed naturally from its position as a Third World Leader.'[135] The visit thus highlighted transnational inspirations for the BPP, yet in its turn, the Black Panthers' brand of Black militantism influenced movements elsewhere. In both Britain and Israel, Black Panther groups embraced a broader conception of 'Blackness' – in Britain, it comprised South Asians as well as people of African descent; in Israel, it focused on the position of Mizrahi Jews from North Africa and the Middle East.[136]

This is not to say that all expressions of likeness were viewed through the prism of racial discrimination, as the solidarity campaign for the Black feminist Angela Davis indicates. Davis had been arrested for supplying guns that had been used in a courtroom kidnapping and shooting. Davis's case attracted significant attention in Europe, including West Germany, to which she had pre-existing links. In 1965–7, she had studied philosophy in Frankfurt/Main which, while amounting to a 'very intensive learning experience' in academic terms, also put her in touch with German student activists. Looking back on this time, she acknowledged their attempts to reach 'some form of practical resistance capable of ultimately overturing the economic system' as well as their commitment to an internationalist awareness.[137] In 1972, Davis herself became subject to expressions of this awareness, as West German activists staged a large-scale demonstration and congress in support of her. Held in Frankfurt, the congress did not confine itself to discussing the politics of race and treated Davis's case as an 'example' of broader issues.[138] This also involved a discussion of political violence – an issue of particular concern given the actions of the Red Army Faction in this period.[139] According to the historian Martin Klimke, the event thus used an external case to enable West German New Left 'to come to a deeper understanding of its own situation'.[140] Moreover, after her release, Cold War dynamics shaped another transnational connection: in 1973, Davis became a guest at the World Festival of Youth in East Berlin. Her presence reflected her own Marxist views but also the GDR authorities' attempt to associate themselves with a figure who was widely celebrated among the left in this period. As the historian Katrina Hagen has pointed, representations of her sought 'to counter the subversive potential of Davis's politics'; instead, they 'familiarized Davis, both personally and politically, and exoticized her'.[141]

In the twenty-first century, the Black Lives Matter movement reignited European engagement with African American campaigns. Having emerged in 2013 in response to police brutality in the United States, Black Lives Matter gained even greater prominence during widespread protests in American cities in the summer of 2020. The campaign drew on social media and connections to popular culture. The movement's engagement with structural racism made it possible to translate its applicability beyond the immediate American context. Accordingly, European manifestations of Black Lives Matter did not only include a questioning of racist present-day practices, but also applied to a reconsideration of colonial-era racism and the challenge to the monuments that represented it.[142]

Challenging apartheid

One of the most durable transnational campaigns against racism targeted apartheid, South Africa's system of white minority rule and forced segregation. Apartheid was connected to the legacies of European colonialism in several ways. The policy itself dated back to 1948 – an era when South Africa was still a self-governing Dominion within the British Commonwealth of Nations. It was instituted by South Africa's National Party, which received the bulk of its support from the descendants of Dutch settlers. These historical ties explain why anti-apartheid resonated particularly in Britain and the Netherlands.[143] Yet as a political cause, anti-apartheid was international in scale, leading the sociologist Håkan Thörn to view it as 'part of the construction of a global civil society during the post-war era'.[144] At first sight, this assessment seems to contrast with the perceptions of some campaigners. For example, in 1976, French anti-apartheid activists recorded attempts at international collaboration but acknowledged that 'for the lack of time, money and power, the majority of our European movements are forced to neglect their international relations to dedicate themselves entirely to the priorities of their national situation'.[145] Taken together, however, both Thörn's interpretation and the French acknowledgement of limitations help us understand key features of anti-apartheid campaigning. Anti-apartheid did not give rise to international organizational structures in the way that some other movements did – yet, at the same time, activists from countries were nonetheless conscious of the need for transnational cooperation and saw their cause as having global significance.

One major axis of transnational efforts was built by South African opponents of apartheid. The African National Congress (ANC) began a strategy of internationalization even before the brutality of the South African authorities attracted greater international attention after the Sharpeville Massacre of 1960.[146] Having been banned in the wake of these events, the ANC moved major parts of its operations abroad, as did the Pan Africanist Congress of Azania (PAC), whose focus on Black nationalism contrasted with the ANC's stance. Over the subsequent decade, African nations such as Tanzania hosted ANC and PAC activists in a wider policy of supporting liberation struggles on the continent.[147] As the ANC adopted a policy of armed resistance from 1961 onwards, it also cooperated with militant organizations elsewhere on the continent, notably in Rhodesia and Angola.

Moreover, the transnational alliances of South African activists reached into Europe. Both the ANC and the PAC established a presence in London. Margaret Ling – a British woman who joined the movement during her student days in the early 1970s and played a prominent role in the UK's Anti-Apartheid Movement (AAM) during the 1980s – noted the importance of personal interactions in such contexts:

If you look at any activist, somewhere along the line they would have met somebody from Southern Africa, or they had a letter, or they had been there or something would have happened to make them feel personally and emotionally involved in the situation. And then having so many South Africans and other people from the region here in Britain was extremely important, to keep people continuously motivated and engaged and involved.[148]

One of Ling's predecessors as editor of the British *Anti-Apartheid News*, Christabel Gurney, noted that 'there were a lot of South African exiles in London and they were very committed to the cause'. Gurney believed that 'their commitment ... kind of rubbed off on some of us British people' as 'they were very good at involving people and making you think that you were part of the struggle'.[149] Such contacts with Black South Africans did not necessarily mean that the AAM was without its limitations. Ethel de Keyser, a white South African who became well-known in British anti-apartheid circles after moving to London, argued, 'We were certainly very white ... I don't think the black community in this country ever really saw the Anti-Apartheid Movement as leading the struggle against apartheid.'[150]

While the British example highlights links among activists, Swedish support for the ANC went beyond campaigners: it extended to the government.[151] Such backing was part of a foreign policy vision that espoused notions of moral leadership for a country that remained neutral in Cold War terms. In other instances, it was precisely the rivalry between the era's two power blocs that generated links: the Soviet Union and its allies attacked apartheid and denounced Western complicity with the South African regime.[152] At one level, these proclamations could help the communist governments shift attention from their own human rights records; at another, it resonated with their public endorsement of anti-imperialist struggles. In some cases, political affinities included the hosting of exiled activists. Yet while this applied to former members of the Community Party of South Africa – some of whom had joined the ANC – it did not extend to the PAC, which embraced an 'anti-Soviet Communism'.[153]

There were also ambiguities in the response among *activist* circles in the Eastern bloc. For example, notwithstanding their criticisms of state socialism, some dissidents concurred with government policy in opposing apartheid.[154] Yet by the 1980s, other groups – for instance in Hungary – thought that the Western left's interest in South Africa overshadowed their own struggle against injustice.[155] In Poland, some members of the banned trade union *Solidarność* spoke of a shared experience of oppression, yet such views were not universal; matters were complicated by the fact that the South African government had welcomed anti-communist Polish refugees.[156]

Meanwhile, Western European activists were often confronted with the existing diplomatic and business relations that linked their own countries to the apartheid state.[157] As an expression of such concerns, activists demanded that oil companies such as Shell, BP, Total and Elf cut their ties with South Africa.[158] One prominent way of addressing the question of complicity was the participation in consumer boycotts against South African products and against Western companies that had substantial business interests in South Africa.[159] Looking back at such actions, Margaret Ling argued that they were 'very good for mobilising people' as they were 'an action that everybody can take. Everybody goes shopping, everybody had the opportunity in Britain to buy or not to buy a South African product.'[160]

One prominent consumer boycott originated in the Netherlands: from 1972 onwards, the *Boycot Outspan Aktie* ('Boycott Outspan Action') targeted the sale of South African oranges and sparked similar efforts elsewhere. In 1975, the launch of a French anti-Outspan campaign provided a rallying point for local and national anti-apartheid groups. It received support from activists in the Netherlands and Switzerland, where campaigners had nearly 'lost hope to ever see the creation of a veritable anti-apartheid current'.[161] Indeed, the French anti-Outspan campaigners acknowledged early on that South Africa was 'far from the concerns of the French'; in this respect, the focus on Outspan oranges was partly 'a pedagogical tool to attract their attention'.[162] In doing so, activists did not confine themselves to moral arguments: they 'tried to get the rural population to join the movement by adding to its campaign the claim that the boycott of South African oranges would strengthen French agriculture'.[163] The campaign itself proved durable: a decade after its launch, the French *Mouvement Anti-Apartheid* affirmed its continuation of this strand of action, 'given its public impact', even if the Outspan boycott was no longer 'at the centre of the anti-apartheid struggle'.[164]

In the British case, consumer action developed a further thread in 1986 through the development of AA Enterprises, which embraced the concept of a 'buycott'. According to

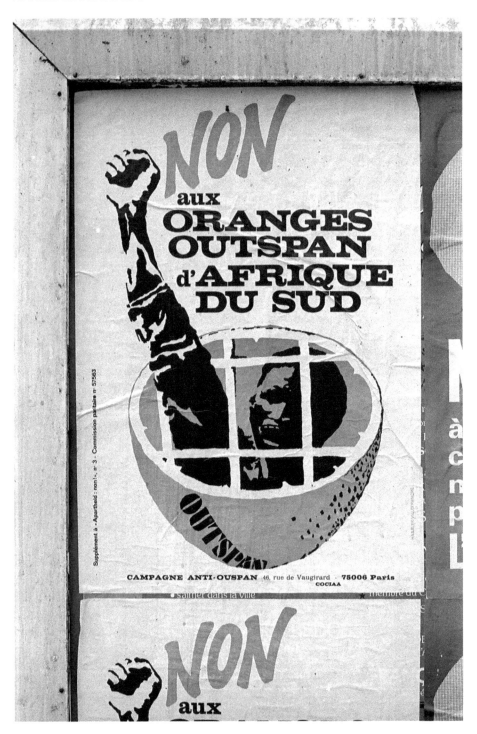

Figure 6.3 Poster against the purchase of South African Outspan oranges (Paris, c. 1976). *Source:* Roger Viollet, via Getty Images.

Margaret Ling, it was built around the 'concept of positive purchase, of using your power as a consumer, in a positive sense, as well as in a negative sense', through the purchase of anti-apartheid merchandise and goods from the African Frontline States that actively supported the struggle against apartheid.[165]

Consumer boycotts tied in with the ANC's endeavour to ensure the international isolation of the South African regime, with sporting and cultural boycotts as further elements of this strategy.[166] As far as the former was concerned, such action ranged from British protests against visits by South African cricketeers and rugby players to efforts to ban South African participation in international sporting tournaments. By 1980, activists from different countries resolved to create better structures for sharing information on teams or organizations that violated the sporting boycott.[167] In the cultural realm, the question of boycotts raised complex issues: matters became contested when it came to collaboration with South African artists who themselves were opponents or victims of apartheid. This dilemma gained particular attention in 1986, as the American singer-songwriter Paul Simon had travelled to South Africa to record his best-selling *Graceland* album with South African musicians, thus breaking the cultural boycott. Subsequent debates on the boycott also ensued among European anti-apartheid activists, for example when it came to planning events with South African performers.[168]

The large-scale publicity surrounding consumer boycotts, sports and culture highlighted a wider issue: as the historian Daniel Hucker has argued, 'the movement against apartheid was also a movement of public opinion, or at least an effort to galvanize public opinion in support of a cause'.[169] By the 1980s, music and celebrity activism were prominent ways of spreading the anti-apartheid message.[170] The most widely publicized example was the Seventh Birthday Concert for Nelson Mandela. Staged at London's Wembley Stadium in 1988 and broadcast across sixty-seven countries, the event was an all-star affair. In the eyes of former activist Margaret Ling, it was 'the peak of the movement'.[171] The AAM's prominent involvement in this event raised wider issues about the relationship between music and politics. A critic from the conservative British tabloid *Daily Mail* praised the music of Western stars but criticized the 'lectures of usually quite breathtaking banality from a wide variety of pop stars and specially imported American film actors' and noted that the audience 'must have suffered through the numerous ethnic sessions'.[172] Dismissive comments of this kind suggested that not only the political message but also attempts at the inclusion of South African musicians could solicit ambivalent responses. Nonetheless, both the 1988 event and another Wembley concert in 1990 held on the occasion of Mandela's release – illustrated how the captive ANC leader had come to embody the anti-apartheid cause. While a focus on the figure of Mandela helped to make the wider cause tangible, some campaigners viewed the 'Mandelafication' of their struggle as a potential narrowing.[173]

Appeals to public opinion also used another vehicle: international institutions, especially the United Nations. Anti-apartheid protesters were not the first to address this forum in the struggle against racism: in 1947, W. E. B. Du Bois and other African American civil rights activists issued an *Appeal to the World* and submitted it to the

UN's Commission on Human Rights.[174] Moreover, in 1946, Jawaharlal Nehru used the UN General Assembly to denounce discriminatory measures against the South Asian community in South Africa.[175] Anti-apartheid campaigners had some success in generating publicity through the UN General Assembly, facilitated by the support of the growing number of postcolonial states. As early as 1962, the General Assembly passed a resolution against apartheid and established a Special Committee against Apartheid. Further initiatives followed, from the International Conference for Economic Sanctions Against South Africa (1964) to the International Convention against Apartheid in Sports (1985) – although Cold War divisions and national sovereignty to some extent limited UN action.[176] Meanwhile, given the concern about business entanglements, the European Economic Community became an increasingly prominent target for campaigners, especially after the adoption of the Single European Act in 1986 had created greater momentum for Western European integration. In 1987, the European Council's Copenhagen summit sparked efforts by a coalition of Danish associations to undertake joint actions with partners from other countries. Such efforts were not free from disappointment: organizers concluded that it had been difficult to gain publicity as a budget crisis at the European Summit had absorbed much media attention.[177] Nonetheless, by November 1988, different national anti-apartheid groups set up a Liaison Group in Athens, aiming to pressurize the European Community and its member states more effectively.[178] Such issues indicated how engagement with international institutions enabled activists to formalize some of their ties.

The UN's role as a forum for debates in racism extended beyond the formal end of apartheid in the 1990s. In 2001, the South African city of Durban hosted the third UN Conference against Racism. References to the wider historical context featured in the meeting's final declaration, which noted 'the heroic struggle of the people against the institutionalized system of apartheid' and acknowledged 'the important role that different actors of civil society' had played in ending it.[179] Yet the Durban conference mostly attracted attention for conflicts that led to the departure of the US and Israeli delegates, with some observers concluding that the conference might 'have done more harm than good to the United Nations' credibility'.[180] The controversy was primarily associated with the efforts of some Arab governments to label Zionism a form of racism. The fact that these debates occurred at an event in South Africa also points to another sub-text: some forms of solidarity campaigning likened the situation of Palestinians to the past experiences of Black South Africans. In Durban, this became evident in an NGO forum that ran parallel to the diplomatic meeting and that described Israel a 'racist, apartheid state'.[181] In subsequent years, this analogy further manifested itself in the adoption of consumer boycotts as a contentious tool among some activists.[182] Apart from the intense debates on Israel and Palestine, the Durban conference raised controversy in its linking of racism and the legacies of empire, with compensation demands on slavery as one source of contention. In all of these respects, past struggles were an important and highly contested sub-text to the debates among activists, diplomats and political leaders.

A multicultural Europe

In 2001, the Durban Declaration described 'xenophobia against non-nationals, particularly migrants, refugees and asylum-seekers' as 'one of the main sources of contemporary racism'.[183] Migration and multiculturalism had been longstanding features of European history, well before the twentieth century.[184] However, from the 1950s onwards, substantial migration both within Europe and from other continents generated growing debates on national and cultural identity. With regard to Britain, the historian Elizabeth Buettner has spoken of 'imaginative racial geographies' that located national concerns within a 'transnational arena that encompassed the metropole, its declining empire and the Commonwealth'. Comparisons with external developments informed such discussions, with references to the Nazi persecution of Jews, the African American freedom struggle and South African apartheid all informing British discourses on 'race' during the 1960s.[185]

Immigration in post-1945 Europe produced different forms of transnational activism. For example, some immigrants – as well as their descendants, when they identified as members of a diasporic community – targeted the situation in the nation they viewed as their homeland. This kind of diasporic activism was nothing new, but post-war migration in this context raised awareness of causes such as the condition of Kurdish people living in Turkey, Iraq and Syria.[186] That said, diasporic activism did not necessarily *target* the actions of governments – it could also be deployed by them. Indeed, it has been argued that in the globalized politics since the 1990s, 'homeland governments, political parties, and social movements' have all been in a growing position 'to co-opt, pressure, or mobilize support from … constituencies abroad'.[187] Crucially, political activism of diasporic communities was not the only form of transnational activism shaped by immigration. Another example was the development of self-help structures within immigrant communities. Such forms of voluntary action were particularly important in cases where state support remained limited, and they could thus counter discriminatory aspects of welfare policies.[188]

Migrant welfare could combine with more overt forms of anti-racist campaigning. This, for instance, was the case in terms of emerging alliances between New Left activists and immigrant groups in 1960s France.[189] As the historian Daniel Gordon has shown, there were also some transnational exchanges between French and British anti-racist campaigners, albeit halting and uneven ones.[190] In some domains, anti-racist mobilization and other campaigns against the far right drew on popular culture that, in many ways, was transnational, as exemplified by the role of reggae in the British 'Rock against Racism' campaign of the 1970s or Anglo-American musical influences on West German campaigns against the far right towards the end of that decade.[191] Yet, in its turn, the far right also availed itself to aspects of youth culture, as reflected in the transnational spread of skinhead subculture among neo-Nazi groups during the 1980s.[192]

The latter observation relates to a wider aspect: while immigration spawned new anti-racist alliances, it also became an issue on which far right activists mobilized, in some cases across national borders. With intellectual roots in 1960s France, the 'European

New Right' viewed 'European civilization' as being under threat, and anti-immigration discourse both nourished and expressed such anxieties.[193] The New Right overlapped with neofascist circles, which maintained various transnational contacts. For example, in the 1960s and 1970s, neo-fascist parties in France and Italy drew on each other's experiences.[194] In the same period, Italian neo-fascists who had embarked on a campaign of political violence – 'black terrorism' – avoided arrest by migrating to Portugal, Spain or Latin America.[195] As Fabian Virchow has argued, in organizational terms, far-right links 'remained low for a long time', yet by the 2000s, they manifested themselves in neo-Nazi rallies with international participation.[196]

Moreover, in the 2010s, the so-called 'Identitarian' movement drew on these existing far right currents, while reflecting the broader geopolitical situation in the early twenty-first century: the Identitarians' main concerns were an aversion to 'globalization' and to a perceived 'Islamization' of European societies.[197] Islamophobia also manifested itself in the transnational dissemination of conspiracy theories, such as the notion of a 'Great Replacement'.[198] In some instances, Islamophobia and traditional anti-Semitic tropes intersected, as reflected in claims that George Soros was seeking to destroy European civilization by funding charities that would support an influx of Muslim immigrants.[199] Evidently, the internet facilitated the dissemination of rumours and false allegations. As early as 2000 – at a time when European consumer access to the World Wide Web was still growing – Holocaust denial had developed a significant online presence.[200] Moreover, in the 2010s, the Identitarian movement's growth beyond France and Austria initially occurred online.[201]

That said, it is important not to overemphasize the depth of transnational links of far-right groups. A recent study of far-right propaganda on social media has described 'transnationalism on Twitter' as being 'moderate at best'.[202] While far-right groups shared a hostility to particular 'others' and while some of its protagonists repeatedly sought to forge joint action, language and the prioritization of national concerns imposed limits on the growth of transnational links. Of course, as this chapter has shown, anti-racist campaigners had their own disputes and divisions – which also meant that in the 1970s and 1980s, joint transnational action among groups that confronted neo-fascists was somewhat slow to develop. At the same time, what set different forms of anti-racist transnationalism apart from its far-right opponents was the ability to link different causes and concerns in a global vision. Importantly, this also included the ability to frame resistance to racism in terms of universal rights – which is an evident connection to the next chapter's theme.

Notes

1. On Du Bois's first stay in Germany, see David Levering Lewis, *W. E. B. Du Bois: A Biography* (New York: Henry Holt, 2009), 67–110. See also Kenneth Barkin, 'W. E. B. Du Bois and the Kaiserreich', *Central European History* 31, no. 3 (1998): 155–70; Kenneth Barkin, 'W. E. B. Du Bois' Love Affair with Imperial Germany', *German Studies Review* 28, no. 2 (2005): 285–302.

2. W. E. B. Du Bois, 'The Negro and the Warsaw Ghetto', *Jewish Life* 6, no. 7 (1952): 14–15, reprinted in *W. E. B. Du Bois Speaks: Speeches and Addresses 1920–1963*, ed. Philip Foner (New York: Pathfinder, 1970), 296–7. For an interpretation of Du Bois's piece from the perspective of Holocaust Studies, see Michael Rothberg, 'W. E. B. Du Bois in Warsaw: Holocaust Memory and the Color Line', *The Yale Journal of Criticism* 14, no. 1 (2001): 169–89.
3. Du Bois, 'The Negro and the Warsaw Ghetto', 294 and 295.
4. Ibid., 297.
5. Ibid.
6. Harold Brackman, '"A Calamity Almost beyond Comprehension": Nazi Anti-Semitism and the Holocaust in the Thought of W. E. B. Du Bois', *American Jewish History* 88, no. 1 (2000): esp. 64–7; Clive Webb, 'The Nazi Persecution of Jews and the African American Freedom Struggle', *Patterns of Prejudice* 53, no. 4 (2019): esp. 341–2.
7. Apart from Brackman, 'A Calamity', 53–93, see Benjamin Sevitch, 'W. E. B. Du Bois and Jews: A Lifetime of Opposing Anti-Semitism', *The Journal of African American History* 87, no. 3 (2002): 332–7.
8. Webb, 'The Nazi Persecution of Jews', 343.
9. Du Bois, 'Prospect of a World without Racial Conflict', *American Journal of Sociology* 49, no. 5 (1944): 450–6, as reprinted in Foner, ed., *W. E. B. Du Bois Speaks,* 154–5.
10. Du Bois, 'Prospect', 163.
11. For discussions of Du Bois and Russia see, Joy Gleason Carew, *Blacks, Reds, and Russians: Sojourners in Search of the Soviet Promise* (New Brunswick, NJ: Rutgers University Press, 2010), 49–63; Kate A. Baldwin, *Beyond the Color Line and the Iron Curtain: Reading Encounters between Black and Red, 1922–1963* (Durham, NC: Duke University Press, 2002).
12. Bill Mullen, *Un-American: W. E. B. Du Bois and the Century of World Revolution* (Philadelphia, PA: Temple University Press, 2015).
13. Eve Darian-Smith, 'Re-reading W. E. B. Du Bois: The Global Dimensions of the U.S. Civil Rights Struggle', *Journal of Global History* 7, no. 3 (2012): 483–503. On Du Bois's Pan-Africanism, see Wilson Jeremiah Moses, 'Africa and Pan-Africanism in the Thought of Du Bois', in *The Cambridge Companion to W. E. B. Du Bois*, ed. Sahmoon Zamir (Cambridge: Cambridge University Press, 2008), 117–30.
14. These efforts are discussed in Matteo Grilli, *Nkrumaism and African Nationalism: Ghana's Pan-African Foreign Policy in the Age of Decolonization* (Cham: Palgrave, 2018).
15. For a discussion in this wider context, see Kevin Gaines, *American Africans in Ghana: Black Expatriates and the Civil Rights Era* (Chapel Hill, NC: University of North Carolina Press, 2006), 147–52.
16. The most detailed analysis of the affair is Jonathan Frankel, *The Damascus Affair: 'Ritual Murder', Politics, and the Jews in 1840* (New York: Cambridge University Press, 1997). For a recent reinterpretation, see Yaron Tsur, 'Who Introduced Liberalism into the Damascus Affair (1840)? Center, Periphery and Networks in the Jewish Response to the Blood Libel', in *Jews, Liberalism, Antisemitism: A Global History*, ed. Abigail Green and Simon Levis Sullam (Cham: Palgrave, 2020), 263–87.
17. Abigail Green, 'Nationalism and the "Jewish International": Religious Internationalism in Europe and the Middle East *c.* 1840–*c.* 1880', *Comparative Studies in Society and History* 50, no. 2 (2008): 535–58; Abigail Green, 'Old Networks, New Connections: The Emergence of the Jewish International', in Green and Viaene, *Religious Internationals in the Modern World*, 53–81.

18. Abigail Green, *Moses Montefiore: Jewish Liberator, Imperial Hero* (Cambridge, MA: Harvard University Press, 2010), 134–5.
19. Brinkmann, 'The Road from Damascus', 157.
20. Green, *Moses Montefiore*, 258–81.
21. Brinkmann, 'The Road from Damascus', 159; Green, 'Nationalism and the "Jewish International"', 543–4.
22. Brinkmann, 'The Road from Damascus', 164.
23. Green, 'Nationalism and the "Jewish International"', 555.
24. 'Die Woche', *Allgemeine Zeitung des Judentums*, 16 December 1904, 602.
25. Ibid.
26. Theodor Herzl, *Der Judenstaat: Versuch einer modernen Lösung der Judenfrage* (Leipzig and Vienna: M. Breitenstein's Verlags-Buchhandlung, 1896).
27. Chaim Weizmann, *Trial and Error: The Autobiography of Chaim Weizmann*, vol. 1: *1874–1917* (Lexington, MA: Plunkett Lake Press, 2013), 44.
28. Weizmann, *Trial and Error*, 44.
29. For the wider context, also in the run-up to the 1906 conference, see the document gathered in Michael Heyman, ed., *The Minutes of the Zionist General Council: The Uganda Controversy*, 2 vols (Jerusalem: Israel University Press, 1970).
30. Ozan Ozavci, 'A Jewish "Liberal" in Istanbul: Vladimir Jabotinsky, the Young Turks and the Zionist Press Network, 1908–1911', in Green and Levis Sullam, *Jews, Liberalism, Antisemitism*, 289–314.
31. Lueger's role in turning existing anti-Semitic sentiment among Viennese artisans into a wider political phenomenon is a key theme in John Boyer, *Political Radicalism in Late Imperial Vienna: Origins of the Christian Social Movement 1884–1897* (Chicago, IL: University of Chicago Press, 1981). See also Steven Beller, *Vienna and the Jews 1867–1938: A Cultural History* (Cambridge: Cambridge University Press, 1989).
32. Michel Denis, Michel Lagrée and Jean-Yves Veillard, eds, *L'Affaire Dreyfus et l'opinion publique en France et à l'étranger* (Rennes: Presses universitaires de Rennes, 1995).
33. Bernard Lazare, *Une Erreur judiciaire: La vérité sur l'affaire Dreyfus* (Brussels: Veuve Monnom, 1896).
34. Shlomo Sand, 'Bernard Lazare: Le premier sioniste français', *Revue française de l'histoire des idées politiques*, no. 4 (1996): 294–5.
35. Hamann, *Bertha von Suttner*, 226.
36. Ibid., 227.
37. Marcella Simoni, 'The Inner Frontier: Jews in *Les Etats-Unis d'Europe*', in Petricioli et al., *Les Etats-Unis d'Europe*, 153–4.
38. Brendan McGeever and Satnam Virdee, 'Antisemitism and Socialist Strategy in Europe, 1880–1917', *Patterns of Prejudice* 51, nos. 3–4 (2017): 225.
39. McGeeve and Virdee, 'Antisemitism and Socialist Strategy', 225.
40. Max Nordau, 'Das europäische Gewissen', *Ethische Kultur* 14, no. 13 (1 July 1906): 97–9. Hamann notes that Bertha von Suttner commented on this essay in a private letter to her fellow campaigner Alfred Fried, arguing that the 'European conscience' was to be found among pacifists and that activists such as Nordau should therefore join their cause. Hamann, *Bertha von Suttner*, 227.

41. Abigail Green, 'Nationalism and the "Jewish International"', 535.
42. Bernard Lazare, *L'Antisémitisme: son histoire et ses causes* (Paris: Léon Chailley, 1894), 301. For a survey of the wider issues, see Cathy S. Gelbin and Sander L. Gilman, *Cosmopolitanism and the Jews* (Ann Arbor, MI: University of Michigan Press, 2017).
43. 'Vaterlandsliebe (Zum Kaisergeburtstag)', *Allgemeine Zeitung des Judenthums*, 21 January 1898, 26.
44. Simon Levis Sullam, 'Osman Bey's *The Conquest of the World by Jews* (1873): A Liberal Antisemitism?', in Green and Levis Sullam, *Jews, Liberalism, Antisemitism*, 47–68.
45. Esther Webman, *The Global Impact of the Protocols of the Elders of Zion: A Century-Old Myth* (London: Routledge, 2011); Randall Bytwerk, 'Believing in "Inner Truth": The Protocols of the Elders of Zion in Nazi Propaganda, 1933–1945', *Holocaust and Genocide Studies* 29, no. 2 (2015): 212–29; Robert Singerman, 'The American Career of the *Protocols of the Elders of Zion*', *American Jewish History* 71, no. 1 (1981): 48–78.
46. Granick, *International Jewish Humanitarianism*, 3–4.
47. See, for example, the insightful analysis of wartime anti-Semitism among British Marxists, in Daniel Edmonds, 'Unpacking "Chauvinism": The Interrelationship of Race, Internationalism, and Anti-Imperialism among Marxists in Britain, 1899–1933' (PhD thesis, University of Manchester, 2018), 76–125. For the broader context in Britain, see Colin Holmes, *Anti-Semitism in British Society, 1876–1939* (London: Edward Arnold, 1979), chapter 8.
48. Thomas G. Fraser, *Chaim Weizmann: The Zionist Dream* (London: Haus, 2009), 49.
49. Jaclyn Granick, 'Les associations juives à la Société des Nations, 1919–1929: l'accès sans l'influence', *Relations internationales* 151, no. 3 (2012): 106.
50. Carole Fink, *Defending the Rights of Others: The Great Powers, the Jews, and International Minority Protection, 1878–1938* (Cambridge: Cambridge University Press, 2004), esp. 283–94.
51. Abigail Green, 'Liberals, Socialists, Internationalists, Jews', *Journal of World History* 31, no. 1 (2020): 38.
52. Paul Kelemen, 'In the Name of Socialism: Zionism and European Social Democracy in the Inter-War Years', *International Review of Social History* 41, no. 3 (1996): 331–50; Paul Simpson, 'Socialism, Internationalism and Zionism: The Independent Labour Party and Palestine, *c.* 1917–1939' (PhD thesis, Northumbria University, 2020), esp. 123–31.
53. Claudie Weill, 'Russian Bundists Abroad and in Exile, 1898–1925', in *Jewish Politics in Eastern Europe: The Bund at 100*, ed. Jack Jacobs (Basingstoke: Palgrave, 2001), 46–55; Frank Wolff, 'Relief Funds as Weapons: From Revolutionary Fundraising to Transnational Cultural Work', in *Yiddish Revolutionaries in Migration: The Transnational History of the Jewish Labour Bund*, ed. Loren Balhorn and Jan-Peter Herrmann (Leiden: Brill, 2020), 359–407.
54. Mario Keßler, *Zionismus und internationale Arbeiterbewegung 1897–1933* (Berlin: Akademie Verlag, 1994), 85–92. See also Simpson, 'Socialism, Internationalism and Zionism', 124.
55. Keßler, *Zionismus und internationale Arbeiterbewegung*, 142.
56. Abraham Brumberg, 'The Bund: History of a Schism' and Mario Keßler, 'The Bund and the Labour and Socialist International', both in Jacobs, *Jewish Politics in Eastern Europe*, 81–9 and 183–94 respectively.
57. Keßler, *Zionismus und internationale Arbeiterbewegung*, 125.
58. Arnd Bauerkämper and Grezegorz Rossoliński-Liebe, 'Fascism without Borders: Transnational Cooperation between Movements and Regimes in Europe, 1918–1945',

in Bauerkämper and Rossoliński-Liebe, *Fascism without Borders*, 2. See also Arnd Bauerkämper, 'Transnational Fascism: Cross-Border Relations between Regimes and Movements in Europe, 1922–1939', *East Central Europe* 37, nos. 2–3 (2010): 214–46; and Arnd Bauerkämper, 'Interwar Fascism in Europe and Beyond: Toward a Transnational Radical Right', in *New Perspectives on the Transnational Right*, ed. Martin Durham and Margaret Power (Basingstoke: Palgrave, 2010), 39–66.

59. Matteo Albanese and Pablo del Hierro, *Transnational Fascism in the Twentieth Century: Spain, Italy and the Global Neo-Fascist Network* (London: Bloomsbury, 2016), 2.
60. On the Italian case, see for example Aristotle Kallis, 'From CAUR to EUR: Italian Fascism, the "Myth of Rome" and the Pursuit of International Primacy', *Patterns of Prejudice* 50, nos. 4–5 (2016): 359–77.
61. Raul Cârstocea, 'Native Fascists, Transnational Anti-Semites: The International Activity of Legionary Leader Ion I. Moța', in Bauerkämper and Rossoliński-Liebe, *Fascism without Borders*, 222.
62. Cârstocea, 'Native Fascists, Transnational Anti-Semites', 223.
63. Ibid., 229. On the *Welt-Dienst*, see Hanno Plass and Bill Templer, '*Der Welt-Dienst*: International Anti-Semitic Propaganda', *The Jewish Quarterly Review* 103, no. 4 (2013): 503–22.
64. Martin, *The Nazi-Fascist New Order*, 152.
65. Philip Morgan, *Fascism in Europe, 1919–1945* (London: Routledge, 2003), 169. See also Hedinger, *Die Achse*, 114–15; and Martin, *The Nazi-Fascist New Order*, 17.
66. Martin, *The Nazi-Fascist New Order*, 250.
67. Grzegorz Rossoliński-Liebe, 'Inter-Fascist Conflicts in East-Central Europe: The Nazis, the "Austrofascists", the Iron Guard, and the Organization of Ukrainian Nationalists', in Bauerkämper and Rossoliński-Liebe, *Fascism without Borders*, 185.
68. Skran, *Refugees in Inter-War Europe*, 202–8; Kushner and Knox, *Refugees in an Age of Genocide*, 126–71; Michael Marrus, *The Unwanted: European Refugees from the First World War through the Cold War* (Philadelphia, PA: Temple University Press, 2002), 151 and 155–6; Selwyn Troen and Benjamin Pinkus, eds, *Organizing Rescue: Jewish National Solidarity in the Modern Period* (London: Frank Cass,1992); Isabella Löhr, 'Solidarity and the Academic Community: The Support Networks for Refugee Scholars in the 1930s', *Journal of Modern European History* 12, no. 2 (2014): 231–46; Anne Schenderlein, 'German Jewish "Enemy Aliens" in the United States during the Second World War', *Bulletin of the German Historical Institute* 60 (2017): 101–16.
69. Burgess, *The League of Nations and the Refugees from Nazi Germany*, 162.
70. Zohar Segev, *The World Jewish Congress during the Holocaust: Between Activism and Restraint* (Berlin: De Gruyter, 2014), 5. See also Jürgen Matthäus, *Predicting the Holocaust: Jewish Organizations Report from Geneva on the Emergence of the 'Final Solution', 1939–1942* (Lanham, MD: Rowman & Littlefield, 2019).
71. World Jewish Congress, 'Note Regarding the German Policy of Deliberate Annihilation of European Jewry (Geneva, 22 October 1942)', original in The Central Zionist Archives, Jerusalem, RG no. 68.045 and digitized by the United States Holocaust Memorial and Museum, at *Holocaust Sources in Context*, https://perspectives.ushmm.org/ (last accessed 9 January 2023).
72. Monty Noam, 'The World Jewish Congress Confronts the International Red Cross during the Holocaust', *Jewish Social Studies* 4, nos. 3–4 (1979): 229–56.

73. David Slucki, *The International Jewish Labor Bund since 1945: Toward a Global History* (New Brunswick, NJ: Rutgers University Press, 2012), 11.
74. Pauline Peretz, *Let My People Go: The Transnational Politics of Soviet Jewish Emigration during the Cold War*, trans. Ethan Rundell (New Brunswick, NJ: Transaction Publishers, 2015). See also Stuart Altshuler, *From Exodus to Freedom: A History of the Soviet Jewry Movement* (Lanham, MD: Rowman and Littlefield, 2005), whose account contrasts 'grassroots activism' and the 'establishment' among American Jewish protagonists.
75. Benjamin Pinkus, *The Soviet Government and the Jews 1948–1967: A Documented Study* (Cambridge: Cambridge University Press, 1984), 147–92.
76. Nathan A. Kurz, *Jewish Internationalism and Human Rights after the Holocaust* (Cambridge: Cambridge University Press, 2021), 138–63.
77. Adam Ferziger, '"Outside the Shul": The American Soviet Jewry Movement and the Rise of Solidarity Orthodoxy, 1964–1986', *Religion and American Culture* 22, no. 1 (2012): 83–130.
78. On the British part of this movement, see Mark Hurst, *British Human Rights Organizations and Soviet Dissent, 1965–1985* (London: Bloomsbury, 2016), 79–114.
79. Yuli Kosharovsky, *'We Are Jews Again'! Jewish Activism in the Soviet Union*, trans. Stefani Hoffman and ed. Ann Komaromi (Syracuse, NY: Syracuse University Press, 2017), 90–1.
80. Dariusz Stola, 'Anti-Zionism as a Multipurpose Policy Instrument: The Anti-Zionist Campaign in Poland, 1967–1968', *Journal of Israeli History* 25, no. 1 (2006): 175–201.
81. Kurz, *Jewish Internationalism and Human Rights*, 112–37.
82. David Cesarani, 'Anti-Zionism in Britain, 1922–2002: Continuities and Discontinuities', *Journal of Israeli History* 25, no. 1 (2006): 131–60; Shindler, *Israel and the European Left*, chs 16–18.
83. Mairav Zonszein, 'Israel's War against George Soros', *New York Times*, 17 July 2017, available at https://www.nytimes.com/2017/07/17/opinion/george-soros-israel-hungary.html (last accessed 9 January 2023).
84. Armin Langer, 'The Eternal George Soros: The Rise of an Antisemitic and Islamophobic Conspiracy Theory', in *Europe: Continent of Conspiracies: Conspiracy Theories in and About Europe*, ed. Andreas Önnerfors and André Krouwel (Abingdon: Routledge, 2021), 163–84; Ivan Kalmar, 'Islamophobia and Anti-Antisemitism: The Case of Hungary and the "Soros Plot"', *Patterns of Prejudice* 54, nos. 1–2 (2020): 182–98.
85. Israel Zangwill, 'The Jewish Race', in *Papers on Inter-Racial Problems: Communicated to the First Universal Races Congress Held at the University of London July 26–29, 1911*, ed. Gustav Spiller (London: P. S. King & Son, 1911), 261–7. On Zangwill in this period, see Meri-Jane Rochelson, *A Jew in the Public Arena: The Career of Israel Zangwill* (Detroit, MI: Wayne State University Press, 2006).
86. Zangwill, 'The Jewish Race', 271.
87. Ibid., 273.
88. 'Officers, Council, and Supporters', in Spiller, *Papers on Inter-Racial Problems*, xviii.
89. W. E. B. Du Bois, 'Editorial', *The Crisis* 2, no. 4 (1911): 157.
90. 'The Races Congress', *The Crisis* 2, no. 5 (1911): 208.
91. Ibid., 209.
92. Extracts from his speech at the 1900 congress are included in Sherwood, *Origins of Pan-Africanism*, 87.
93. Ibid.

94. Hodder, 'The Elusive History of the Pan-African Congress', 114. On the composition of delegations, see ibid., 118–21.
95. W. E. B. Du Bois Papers, MS 312, Special Collections and University Archives, University of Massachusetts Amherst Libraries: letter from the Pan-African Congress to the League of Nations, c. September 1921. Digitized at https://credo.library.umass.edu/view/full/mums312-b017-i345 (last accessed 9 January 2023).
96. Letter from the Pan-African Congress to the League of Nations, c. September 1921.
97. Hodder, 'The Elusive History of the Pan-African Congress', 124.
98. Adi, *West Africans in Britain, 1900–1960*; Marc Matera, *Black London: The Imperial Metropolis and Decolonization in the Twentieth Century* (Oakland, CA: University of California Press, 2015).
99. Andreas Eckert, 'Panafrikanismus, afrikanische Intellektuelle und Europa im 19. und 20. Jahrhundert', *Journal of Modern European History* 4, no. 2 (2006): 224–40, at 237–8.
100. Liam Liburd, 'Beyond the Pale: Whiteness, Masculinity and Empire in the British Union of Fascists, 1932–1940', *Fascism* 7, no 2 (2018): 275–96.
101. James, *George Padmore and Decolonization from Below*, 46.
102. David Killingray, '"To Do Something for the Race": Harold Moody and the League of Coloured Peoples', in *West Indian Intellectuals in Britain*, ed. Bill Schwarz (Manchester: Manchester University Press, 2004), 51–70. See also Barbara Bush, *Imperialism, Race and Resistance: Africa and Britain, 1919–1945* (London: Routledge, 1999).
103. Matera, *Black London*, 74; Gorman, *International Cooperation in the Early Twentieth Century*, 33.
104. George Padmore, *Colonial and Coloured Unity: A Programme of Action. History of the Pan-African Congress* (Manchester: Pan-African Federation, 1947), congress resolution entitled 'Colour Bar Problem in Britain'.
105. Frantz Fanon, *The Wretched of the Earth: The Handbook for the Black Revolution That Is Changing the Shape of the Earth*, trans. Constance Farrington (paperback edn; New York: Gove Press, 1968 [orig. 1961]).
106. Meghelli, 'From Harlem to Algiers', 104–5.
107. Kathleen Neal Cleaver, 'Back to Africa: The Evolution of the International Section of the Black Panther Party (1969–1972)', in *The Black Panther Party Reconsidered*, ed. Charles E. Jones (Baltimore, MD: Black Classic Press, 1998), 214 and 216.
108. Akwugo Emejulu and Francesca Sobande, 'Introduction: On the Problems and Possibilities of European Black Feminism and Afrofeminism', in *To Exist Is to Resist: Black Feminism in Europe*, ed. Akwugo Emejulu and Francesca Sobande (London: Pluto Press, 2019), 3–10.
109. Carole Boyce Davies, *Left of Karl Marx: The Political Life of Black Communist Claudia Jones* (Durham, NC: Duke University Press, 2008), 2. See also Marika Sherwood, *Claudia Jones: A Life in Exile* (2nd edn; London: Lawrence & Wishart, 2021).
110. Davies, *Left of Karl Marx*, 165. A selection of Jones's writings is available in Carole Boyce Davies, ed., *Claudia Jones: Beyond Containment* (Banbury: Ayebia Clarke, 2010).
111. For the British case, see Tracy Fisher, *What's Left of Blackness: Feminism, Transracial Solidarities, and the Politics of Belonging in Britain* (Basingstoke: Palgrave, 2012), 65–91.
112. Jennifer S. Duncan, 'Confronting "Race": French Feminism's Struggle to Become Global', in de Haan et al., *Women's Activism*, 184.

113. See e.g. Audre Lorde, 'Age, Race, Class and Sex: Women Redefining Difference', in Audre Lorde, *Sister Outsider: Essays and Speeches* (Freedom, CA: Crossing Press, 1984), 114–23.

114. Audrey Lorde, 'Foreword to the English Language Edition', in *Showing Our Colors: Afro-German Women Speak Out*, trans. Anne V. Adams and ed. May Optiz, Katharina Oguntoye and Dagmar Schultz (Amherst, MA: University of Massachusetts Press, 1992), xiv. This book originally appeared in West Germany as *Farbe bekennen: Afro-deutsche Frauen auf den Spuren ihrer Geschichte* (Berlin: Orlanda, 1986).

115. Dagmar Schultz, '*Audre Lorde: The Berlin Years 1984 to 1992*: The Making of the Film and Its Reception', *Feminist Studies* 40, no. 1 (2014): 199–206. See also Jennifer Michaels, 'The Impact of Audre Lorde's Politics and Poetics on Afro-German Women Writers', *German Studies Review* 29, no. 1 (2006): 21–40; Katherina Gerund, 'Sisterly (Inter)Actions: Audre Lorde and the Development of Afro-German Women's Communities', *Gender Forum* 22 (2008): 56–72; Tiffany N. Florvil, *Mobilizing Black Germany: Afro-German Women and the Making of a Transnational Movement* (Champaign, IL: University of Illinois Press, 2020), 25–52.

116. Heide Fehrenbach, 'Black Occupation Children and the Devolution of the Nazi Racial State', in *After the Nazi Racial State: Difference and Democracy in Germany and Europe*, ed. Rita Chin et al. (Ann Arbor, MI: University of Michigan Press, 2009), 52.

117. Pennybacker, *From Scottsboro to Munich*, e. g. 24 and 48–50.

118. *Report of the Ninth Congress of the Women's International League for Peace and Freedom: Luhacovice, Czechoslovakia, July 27th to 31st, 1937* (Geneva: WILPF, 1937), 109–10.

119. *Report of the Ninth Congress*, 107–9.

120. Maria Schubert, 'Allies across Cold War Boundaries: The American Civil Rights Movement and the GDR', *Kirchliche Zeitgeschichte* 33, no. 1 (2021): 59–71.

121. Julie Hessler, 'Death of an African Student in Moscow: Race, Politics, and the Cold War', *Cahiers du Monde Russe* 47, nos. 1–2 (2006): 33–63. See also Daniel Laqua, 'The Politics of Transnational Student Mobility, Youth, Activism and Education in Ghana, 1957–1966', *Social History* 48, no. 1 (2023): 87–113.

122. See e.g. '500 Africans Fight Police in Moscow in Race Protest', *New York Times*, 19 December 1963, 1.

123. Stephen Tuck, *The Night Malcolm X Spoke at the Oxford Union: A Transatlantic Story of Antiracist Protest* (Oakland, CA: University of California Press, 2014), 197–9. For another example of Malcolm X's direct interactions with British issues and causes, see Joe Street, 'Malcolm X, Smethwick, and the Influence of the African American Freedom Struggle on British Race Relations in the 1960s', *Journal of Black Studies* 38, no. 6 (2008): 932–50.

124. Rosie Wild, '"Black Was the Colour of Our Fight": The Transnational Roots of British Black Power', in *The Other Special Relationship: Race, Rights, and Riots in Britain and the United States*, ed. Robin Kelley and Stephen Tuck (New York: Palgrave, 2015), 39.

125. Stokely Carmichael, 'Black Power', in *The Dialectics of Liberation*, ed. David Cooper (London: Institute of Phenomenological Studies, 1968), 150–74.

126. Tuck, *The Night Malcolm X Spoke at the Oxford Union*, 186.

127. See, for example, Martin Luther King's visit to Newcastle upon Tyne in this context: Brian Ward, *Martin Luther King in Newcastle upon Tyne: The African American Freedom Struggle and Race Relations in the North East of England* (Newcastle upon Tyne: Tyne Bridge Publishing, 2017).

128. Tuck, *The Night Malcolm X Spoke at the Oxford Union*, 181.
129. Kenetta Hammond Perry, '"U.S. Negroes, Your Fight Is Our Fight": Black Britons and the 1963 March on Washington', in Kelley and Tuck, *The Other Special Relationship*, 7–24.
130. Madge Dresser, *Black and White on the Busses: The 1963 Colour Bar Dispute in Bristol* (Bristol: Bristol Broadsides, 1986).
131. Brian Dooley, *Black and Green: The Fight for Civil Rights in Northern Ireland and Black America* (Cambridge: Pluto, 1998).
132. Marc Mulholland, 'A Heavy Load: The American Civil Rights Movement and the Northern Ireland Civil Rights Movement', in Kelley and Tuck, *The Other Special Relationship*, 114.
133. Matthew O'Brien, 'Irish Americans, Race, and Bernadette Devlin's 1969 American Tour', *New Hibernia Review* 14, no. 2 (2010): 84–101.
134. Donna Murch, 'When the Panther Travels: Race and the Southern Diaspora in the History of the BPP, 1964–1972', in *Black Power beyond Borders: The Global Dimensions of the Black Power Movement*, ed. Nico Slate (New York: Palgrave, 2012), 57–78; Michael Clemons and Charles Jones, 'Global Solidarity: The Black Panther Party in the International Arena', *New Political Science* 21, no. 2 (1999): 177–203.
135. Elaine Mokhetefi, *Algiers, Third World Capital: Black Panthers, Freedom Fighters, Revolutionaries* (London: Verso, 2018), 95.
136. Anne-Marie Angelo, *Black Power on the Move: Migration, Internationalism, and the British and Israeli Black Panthers* (Chapel Hill, NC: University of North Carolina Press, 2021); Oz Frankel, 'The Black Panthers of Israel and the Politics of Radical Analogy', in Slate, *Black Power beyond Borders*, 81–106.
137. Angela Davis, *An Autobiography* (New York: Random House, 1974), 142.
138. Sozialistisches Büro, *Am Beispiel Angela Davis: Der Kongreß in Frankfurt. Reden, Referate, Diskussionsprotokolle* (Frankfurt/Main: Fischer, 1972).
139. Klimke, *The Other Alliance*, 126.
140. Ibid.
141. Katrina Hagen, 'Ambivalence and Desire in the East German "Free Angela Davis" Campaign', in *Comrades of Color: East Germany in the Cold War World*, ed. Quinn Slobodian (New York: Berghahn, 2015), 157–87.
142. Saima Nasar, 'Remembering Edward Colston: Histories of Slavery, Memory, and Black Globality', *Women's History Review* 29, no. 7 (2020): 1218–25. On processes of local adoption and adaptation, see also Nicole Scheiber, 'Black Lives Matter: The (Trans) local Movement for Black Lives in Germany', *Kirchliche Zeitgeschichte* 33, no. 1 (2021): 72–88.
143. On British anti-apartheid, see Roger Fieldhouse, *Anti-Apartheid: A History of the Movement in Britain, 1959–1994* (London: Merlin, 2004); Rob Skinner, *The Foundations of Anti-Apartheid: Liberal Humanitarians and Transnational Activists in Britain and the United States, c. 1919–64* (Basingstoke: Palgrave, 2010); Elizabeth Williams, *The Politics of Race in Britain and South Africa: Black British Solidarity and the Anti-Apartheid Struggle* (London: I.B. Tauris, 2015). On Dutch anti-apartheid, see Wouter Goedertier, 'Divided by a Common Language: Flemish and Dutch Engagement with Apartheid in South Africa', in *International Solidarity in the Low Countries during the Twentieth Century*, ed. Kim Christiaens, John Nieuwenhuys and Charel Roemer (Berlin: De Gruyter, 2020), 343–70.
144. Håkan Thörn, *Anti-Apartheid and the Emergence of a Global Civil Society* (Basingstoke: Palgrave, 2006), 48.

145. ANMT, folder 2000-057-MAA-008: Le campagne anti-outspan c.a.o. / Le collective de recherche et d'information sur l'Afrique Austral C.R.I.A.A., *Dans la Lutte anti-apartheid en France: Rapport d'activités (1975–77)*, 2.
146. Thörn, *Anti-Apartheid*, 128.
147. Stephen Ellis, *External Mission: The ANC in Exile, 1960–1990* (Oxford: Oxford University Press, 2013); Thörn, *Anti-Apartheid*, chapter 2.
148. Margaret Ling, interviewed by Håkan Thörn on 29 February 2000, made available at the Anti-Apartheid Movement Archives, https://www.aamarchives.org/archive/interviews/margaret-ling/int06t-margaret-ling-transcript.html (last accessed 9 January 2023).
149. Christabel Gurney, interviewed by Hana Sandhu, 16 October 2013, https://www.aamarchives.org/archive/interviews/christabel-gurney/int01t-christabel-gurney.html (last accessed 9 January 2023).
150. Ethel de Keyer, interviewed by Håkan Thörn on 3 March 2000, https://www.aamarchives.org/archive/interviews/ethel-de-keyser/int03t-ethel-de-keyser.html (last accessed 9 January 2023).
151. Thörn, *Anti-Apartheid*, e.g. 76–80.
152. Paul Betts, James Mark, Idesbald Goddeeris and Kim Christiaens, 'Race, Socialism and Solidarity: Anti-Apartheid in Eastern Europe', in *A Global History of Anti-Apartheid: 'Forward to Freedom' in South Africa*, ed. Anna Konieczna and Rob Skinner (Cham: Palgrave, 2019), 158. See also Sebastian Gehrig et al., 'The Eastern Bloc, Human Rights, and the Global Fight against Apartheid', *East Central Europe* 46, nos. 2–3 (2019): 290–317.
153. Thörn, *Anti-Apartheid*, 53.
154. See e.g. the stance of East German Protestants: Betts, et al., 'Race, Socialism and Solidarity', 168.
155. Betts et al., 'Race, Socialism and Solidarity', 178.
156. Kim Christiaens and Idesbald Goddeeris, 'Solidarity or Anti-Apartheid? The Polish Opposition and South Africa, 1976–1989', in Konieczna and Skinner, *A Global History of Anti-Apartheid*, 291–316.
157. Knud Andresen, Sebastian Junke and Detlef Siegfrid, 'Introduction', in *Apartheid and Anti-Apartheid in Western Europe*, ed. Knud Andresen, Sebastian Justke and Detlef Siegfried (Cham: Palgrave, 2021), 1–21.
158. Jakob Skovgaard, 'Perceptions of Petroleum: The British Anti-Apartheid Campaign against Shell', in Andresen et al., *Apartheid and Anti-Apartheid in Western Europe*, 49–70.
159. Jodi Burkett, '"Don't Bank on Apartheid!": The National Union of Students and the Boycot Barclays Campaign', in *Students in Twentieth-Century Britain and Ireland*, ed. Jodi Burkett (Cham: Palgrave, 2018), 225–45.
160. Ling, interviewed by Thörn on 29 February 2000.
161. Archives nationales du monde du travail, Roubaix (hereafter: ANMT), folder 2000-057-MAA-008: Le campagne anti-outspan c.a.o. / Le collective de recherche et d'information sur l'Afrique Austral C.R.I.A.A., *Dans la Lutte anti-apartheid en France: Rapport d'activités (1975–77)*, 2.
162. c.a.o. / C.R.I.A.A., *Dans la Lutte anti-apartheid en France*, 2.
163. Namara Burki, 'Conflicting Solidarities: The French Anti-Apartheid Movement and the Liberation Struggle in South Africa, circa 1960–1991', in Andresen et al., *Apartheid and Anti-Apartheid in Western Europe*, 193.

164. ANMT, folder 2000-057-MAA-008: Mouvement Anti-Apartheid, *Rapport d'activités 1984–1985*, 24.
165. Ling, interviewed by Thörn on 29 February 2000. See also Benjamin Möckel, 'Shopping against Apartheid: Consumer Activism and the History of AA Enterprises (1986–1991)', in Andresen et al., *Apartheid and Anti-Apartheid in Western Europe*, 71–90.
166. Ellis, *External Mission*, 142.
167. ANMT, folder 2000-057-MAA-008: 'Création d'un Centre de Coordination International', in Mouvement Anti-Apartheid (C.A.O.), *Rapport d'activités: 11.1978–10.1981*, 36–7.
168. Detlef Siegfried, 'Anti-Apartheid and the Politicisation of Pop Music: Controversies around the Mandela Concert in 1988', in Andresen et al., *Apartheid and Anti-Apartheid in Western Europe*, 139–62.
169. Daniel Hucker, *Public Opinion and Twentieth-Century Diplomacy: A Global Perspective* (London: Bloomsbury, 2020), 103.
170. Christian Lahusen, *The Rhetoric of Moral Protest: Public Campaigns, Celebrity Endorsement, and Political Mobilization* (Berlin: De Gruyter, 1996), 90–113. For music, see Peter Gabriel, 'Biko' (Charisma / Geffen, 1980); The Special AKA, 'Nelson Mandela' (2 Tone, 1984); Eddy Grant, 'Gimme Hope Jo'anna' (Parlophone / EMI, 1988). On Gabriel's song, see Michael Drewett, 'The Eyes of the World Are Watching Now: The Political Effectiveness of "Biko" by Peter Gabriel', *Popular Music and Society* 30, no. 1 (2007): 39–51.
171. Ling, interviewed by Thörn on 29 February 2000.
172. Marcus Berkmann, 'A Great Days Music … Shame About the Politics', *Daily Mail*, 13 June 1988, 4.
173. Burki, 'From the Theory to the Practice of Liberation', 123.
174. W. E. B. Du Bois, ed., *An Appeal to the World! A Statement on the Denial of Human Rights to Minorities in the Case of Citizens of Negro Descent in the United States of America and an Appeal to the United Nations for Redress* (New York: NAACP, 1947). For the broader context, see Carol Anderson, *Eyes Off the Prize: The United Nations and the African American Struggle for Human Rights, 1944–1955* (Cambridge: Cambridge University Press, 2003) and also Darian-Smith, 'Re-reading W. E. B. Du Bois', 493–9.
175. Lorna Lloyd, '"A Most Auspicious Beginning": The 1946 United Nations General Assembly and the Question of the Treatment of Indians in South Africa', *Review of International Studies* 16, no. 2 (1990): 131–51; Mark Mazower, *No Enchanted Palace: The End of Empire and the Ideological Origins of the United Nations* (Princeton, NJ: Princeton University Press, 2009), 149–89.
176. Anna Konieczna, '"We the People of the United Nations": The UN and the Global Campaigns against Apartheid', in Konieczna and Skinner, *A Global History of Anti-Apartheid*, 67–104. On the role of UNESCO in anti-apartheid, see Betts et al., 'Race, Socialism and Solidarity', 164–6.
177. ANMT, 2000 57 MAA41: NGO Initiative on EC and Apartheid, 'Letter to European Contacts', 9 January 1988.
178. Lorenzo Ferrari, 'Anti-Apartheid Goes to Brussels: Forms of Transnational Cooperation between the Anti-Apartheid Movements of the European Community Countries, 1977–1992', in Konieczna and Skinner, *A Global History of Anti-Apartheid*, 239–64. See also ANMT, 2000 57 MAA41: *Report of the Liaison Group of the National Anti-Apartheid Movements of the European Communities Athens: 17–18 September 1988*.

179. UN Conference against Racism, Racial Discrimination and Related Intolerance, 'Declaration' (September 2001), https://www.un.org/WCAR/durban.pdf (last accessed 9 January 2023).

180. Maggie Farley, 'Durban Meeting Gets a Bitter Review', *Los Angeles Times*, 9 September 2001, 4. See also Rachel Swarns, 'After the Race Conference: Relief, and Doubt Over Whether It Will Matter', *New York Times*, 10 September 2001, 10; Pamela Constable, 'U.S., Israel Quit Forum on Racism: Language Attacking Jewish State Cited', *Washington Post*, 4 September 2001, 1 and 16.

181. Point 162 of the World Conference against Racism NGO Forum Declaration, 3 September 2001, available at the website of the Asia-Pacific Movement for WCRA, https://www.hurights.or.jp/wcar/E/ngofinaldc.htm (last accessed 9 January 2023).

182. Amro Sadeldeen, 'The Emergence of the BDS Movement through an Israeli Mirror', *Radical History Review*, no. 134 (2019): 203–19.

183. World Conference against Racism, Racial Discrimination, Xenophobia and Related Intolerance, 'Declaration' (September 2001), available online https://www.un.org/WCAR/durban.pdf.

184. For a broader overview, see e.g. Klaus Bade, *Migration in European History*, trans. Allison Brown (Malden, MA: Blackwell, 2003).

185. Elizabeth Buettner, '"This Is Staffordshire not Alabama": Racial Geographies of Commonwealth Immigration in Early 1960s Britain', *The Journal of Imperial and Commonwealth History* 42, no. 4 (2014): 712.

186. See, for example, the case of Kurdish diasporic activism, which at various points sought to highlight the treatment of Kurdish populations in Iraq, Turkey and Syria: Vera Eccarius-Kelly, 'The Kurdish Conundrum in Europe: Political Opportunities and Transnational Activism', in *Migration and Activism in Europe since 1945*, ed. Wendy Pojmann (New York: Palgrave, 2008); 57–80; Bahar Bašer, Idris Ahmedi and Mari Toivanen, 'The Transnational Activism of the Kurdish Diaspora and the Swedish Approach to the Kurdish Question', in *Migration from Turkey to Sweden: Integration, Belonging and Transnational Community*, ed. Bahar Bašer and Paul Levin (London: I.B. Tauris, 2017), 228–60.

187. Terence Lyons and Peter Mandaville, 'Introduction', in *Politics from Afar: Transnational Diasporas and Networks*, ed. Terence Lyons and Peter Mandaville (London: Hurst, 2012), 4.

188. Eva Ostergaard-Nielsen, 'The Politics of Migrants' Transnational Political Practices', *The International Migration Review* 37, no. 3 (2003): 760–86; Yasemin Akiš Kalaylıoğlu and Mahir Kalaylıoğlu, 'Organising Turkish Migrants in Metropolitan Stockholm: From National Federation to Women, Youth and Other Associations', in Bašer and Levin, *Migration from Turkey to Sweden*, 181–227; Camille Hamidi, 'Voluntary Associations of Migrants and Politics: The Case of North African Immigrants in France', *Immigrants & Minorities* 22, nos. 2–3 (2003): 317–32.

189. See e.g. the French case. Daniel Gordon, *Immigrants and Intellectuals. May 68 and the Rise of Anti-Racism in France* (London: Merlin Press, 2012).

190. Daniel Gordon, 'French and British Anti Racists since the 1960s: A Rendez Vous Manqué?', *Journal of Contemporary History* 50, no. 3 (2015): 606–31.

191. Ian Goodyer, *Crisis Music: The Cultural Politics of Rock against Racism* (Manchester: Manchester University Press, 2009); Daniel Laqua, 'Rocking against the Right: Political Activism and Popular Music in West Germany, 1979–1980', *History Workshop Journal* 86 (2018): 160–83.

192. On the transnational dimensions of skinhead culture, see John Pollard, 'Skinhead Culture: The Ideologies, Mythologies and Conspiracy Theories of Racist Skinheads', *Patterns of Prejudice* 50, nos. 4–5 (2016): 398–419; Riccardo Marchi and José Pedro Zúquete, 'The Other Side of Protest Music: The Extreme Right and Skinhead Culture in Democratic Portugal (1974–2015)', *JOMEC Journal*, no. 9 (2016): 48–69; Timothy Scott Brown, 'Subcultures, Pop Music and Politics: Skinheads and "Nazi Rock" in England and Germany', *Journal of Social History* 38, no. 1 (2004): 157–78; Ryan Shaffer, *Music, Youth and International Links in Post-War British Fascism: The Transformation of Extremism* (Cham: Palgrave, 2017), 107–56.

193. Joan Antón-Mellón 'The Idées-Force of the European New Right: A New Paradigm?', in *Varieties of Right-Wing Extremism in Europe*, ed. Andrea Mammone, Emmanuel Godin and Brian Jenkins (London: Routledge, 2013), 53–68; Tamir Bar-On, 'Transnationalism and the French Nouvelle Droite', *Patterns of Prejudice* 45, no. 3 (2011): 199–223.

194. Andrea Mammone, *Transnational Neofascism in France and Italy* (Cambridge: Cambridge University Press, 2015).

195. Pablo del Hierro, '"From Brest to Buchares"': Neofascist Transnational Networks during the long 1970s', *European Review of History* 29, no. 3 (2022): 520–47.

196. Fabian Virchow, 'Creating a European (Neo-Nazi) Movement by Joint Political Action?' in Mammone et al., *Varieties of Right-Wing Extremism in Europe*, 200.

197. Fabian Virchow, 'Past-Fascist Right-Wing Social Movements', in Berger and Nehring, *The History of Social Movements*, 631.

198. Anita Nissen, 'The Trans-European Mobilization of "Generation Identity"', in *Nostalgia and Hope: Intersections between Politics of Culture, Welfare, and Migration in Europe*, ed. Anders Hellström, Martin Bak Jørgensen and Ov Cristian Norocel (Cham: Palgrave, 2020), 85–100.

199. Ivan Kalmar, 'Islamophobia and Anti-Antisemitism: The Case of Hungary and the "Soros Plot"', *Patterns of Prejudice* 54, nos. 1–2 (2020): 182–98.

200. Val Burris, Emery Smith and Ann Strahm, 'White Supremacist Networks on the Internet', *Sociological Focus* 33, no. 2 (2000): 215–35; Manuela Caiani and Patricia Kröll, 'The Transnationalization of the Extreme Right and the Use of the Internet', *International Journal of Comparative and Applied Criminal Justice* 39, no. 4 (2015): 331–51. Within North America and Europe, in 2000, Norway and Canada were the sole countries where over 50 per cent of the population were internet users: see *Our World in Data*, https://ourworldindata.org/internet (last accessed 9 January 2023).

201. Fabian Virchow, 'Past-Fascist Right-Wing Social Movements', in Berger and Nehring, *The History of Social Movements*, 630.

202. Caterina Froio and Bharath Ganesh, 'The Transnationalisation of Far Right Discourse on Twitter', *European Societies* 21, no. 4 (2019): 531.

CHAPTER 7
THE RIGHTS OF OTHERS

In 1977, the Russian human rights activist Lyudmila Alexeyeva addressed a special committee of the US Senate. One year earlier, she had collaborated with the physicist Yuri Orlov and other dissidents in founding a 'Helsinki Watch' group in Moscow, which recorded human rights abuses in the Soviet Union. In her statement to the American senators, she elaborated on the features of this group:

> All Helsinki Group members are participants in the human rights movement which is essentially a moral, not a political movement. Human rights activists are persons with differing political views, ranging from socialists to monarchists, but they all share the belief that society can only develop through the effective exercise of elementary human and civil rights.[1]

The episode is indicative of the development of human rights activism in several respects. Firstly, it occurred at a point in time that many scholars associate with the 'breakthrough' of human rights on the international agenda – a decade when they assumed an increasingly prominent place on the agenda of activists, politicians and diplomats.[2] According to historian Samuel Moyn, it was 'in the middle of the 1970s that human rights came to define people's hopes for the future as the foundation of an international movement and a utopia of international law'.[3] To Moyn, human rights became 'the last utopia after predecessors and rivals collapsed', thus gaining prominence at a point when hopes into the promises of communism or anticolonialism had faded.[4] The way in which Alexeyeva framed the work of her committee illustrates these points, as she insisted that the activism of her group would make a broader contribution to social progress.

Secondly, the Moscow group's activism points to the methods of human rights activists. As Alexeyeva stated, her group sought the 'genuine fulfilment by the Soviet authorities of the [Helsinki] Final Act's provisions affecting human rights' and, to this end, its members 'intended to collect information on violations of these provisions and to communicate such information to the people and governments of those countries which had signed the Helsinki Final Act, including the Soviet Government and public'.[5] Her comments indicated that information gathering and documentation were central features of human rights activism. In the Soviet Union, such efforts could be traced back to the *Chronicle of Current Events*, in which Alexeyeva and other activists had recorded Soviet human rights abuses from 1968 onwards and which, by the 1970s, reached Western activists through the efforts of the human rights organization Amnesty International.[6] A concern for documentation also informed Alexeyeva's subsequent activism – which involved documenting the efforts of other campaigners.[7] More specifically, however, her comments indicated the importance that activists accorded to the Helsinki Final Act (1975) – the international diplomatic agreement in which governments in East and West had pledged themselves to respect certain rights. Across Central and Eastern Europe, 'Helsinki Watch' committees evoked these stipulations and, in doing so, formed a transnational network of activists.[8]

Thirdly, the fact that Alexeyeva made her comments in front of US senators highlights particular transnational dimensions. In 1977, she had fled persecution in the Soviet Union and settled in the United States. In an era of burgeoning human rights campaigns, she was one of many human rights activists whom the threat of imprisonment forced into exile. Moreover, while victims of Soviet communism had long figured in Cold War rhetoric, the American reception of Soviet émigrés in the 1970s reflected the growing prominence of human rights in US foreign policy – a development that was particularly associated with the administration of Jimmy Carter.[9] Unsurprisingly, Alexeyeva's testimony in 1977 did not remain a solitary occurrence. In the following year, she addressed another Senate sub-committee alongside Natalia Solzhenitsyn, wife of the famous novelist and dissident Alexander Solzhenitsyn, with a report recording the 'strong public and media interest in these hearings'.[10]

As the historian Jan Eckel has noted, the 1970s saw a 'new boom in human rights in which governments and non-governmental players alike were discovering morality as a vital political resource'.[11] Activists such as Alexeyeva found a receptive audience precisely because they framed their concerns in a way that could transcend political polarities. Yet while the opening episode allows us to pinpoint a particular moment, it is also possible to consider such activism from a broader historical perspective. In contrast to Moyn's emphasis on the centrality of the 1970s, Lynn Hunt has emphasized a longer and deeper history: she stresses the transformative impact of principles that were connected to the Enlightenment and French Revolution as well as broader changes in attitudes and sensibilities.[12] From the opposite angle, Stefan-Ludwig Hoffmann has argued that a focus on the 1970s and 1980s downplays the extent to which '"human rights" [in those decades] coexisted and overlapped with other moral and political idioms like "solidarity" and included competing notions of rights, which were in many ways still indebted to the legacies of socialism and anti-colonialism'. In Hoffmann's view, 'It was only after the end of the Cold War that "human rights" emerged as an explanatory framework for understanding what had just happened.'[13]

Such arguments are not just about chronology and periodization – they reflect different interpretations as to the meaning, nature and prominence of human rights in the political realm. Yet, whether it is Hunt's reference to revolutionary France, Moyn's focus on the departure from past 'utopias' or Hoffmann's arguments for a more recent perspective, it is clear that human rights were entwined with causes and convictions that have featured in the preceding parts of this book. The present chapter is sensitive to such nuances. While it largely concurs with accounts that place the developments of the 1970s and 1980s centre stage, it acknowledges prior campaigns that were waged for the rights of others. In these earlier periods, 'human rights' were not the only or most prominent frames used by activists, as they often featured alongside expressions of humanitarian concern or political solidarity. In other words, while actors in earlier periods did not necessarily cast themselves as human rights activists, a rights-based discourse formed part of their wider rhetorical toolkit.

To acknowledge these complexities and explore different facets of activism, the chapter proceeds in several steps. It first considers how, before the Second World War, human rights were entwined with other causes that were being pursued transnationally. It then comments on the institutional frameworks related to different 'rights regimes', from the League of Nations and the United Nations to NGOs. The second half of the chapter focuses on activism since the 1970s, with an emphasis on developments in East and West, as well as the broadening of human rights conceptions in more recent times.

Activism and connected conceptions of human rights

In 1789, both the French *Déclaration des Droits de l'Homme et du Citoyen* and the American Bill of Rights articulated particular rights and guaranteed specific freedoms. Notwithstanding the universalizing rhetoric of their authors, such rights were tied to categories of citizenship and supposedly guaranteed by states – with implications as to who was being addressed, and with what kinds of arguments. There were attempts to challenge the limitations of these provisions. For example, in 1790, the activist Olympe de Gouges drafted a document on the rights of women because the *Déclaration* had confined itself to men; two years later, the British writer Mary Wollstonecraft made a case for women's rights in her response to the French events.[14] De Gouges's conflict with the Jacobins ended with her death by guillotine in 1793, yet her public stance on women's rights, according to Lynn Hunt, showed that '[t]he logic of rights had pushed even women's rights out from the obscuring fog of habit, at least in France and England'.[15] Meanwhile, in the United States, some activists challenged the exclusion of slaves from the republic's conception of rights.[16] However, while these examples suggest that the definitions and extent of rights were being contested, such campaigns were rarely cast in terms of universal human rights. Moreover, throughout the nineteenth century and well into the twentieth century, humanitarians and other activists tended to accept notions of state sovereignty, which implied boundaries to the implementation of their concerns.[17]

Given these challenges for a universal politics, many activists staked their rights-based claims within national contexts. Nonetheless, especially from the late nineteenth century onwards, questions of rights entered the international arena on some occasions. In instances where activists emphasized the rights of people abroad, notions of 'foreign despotism' figured prominently. Transnational articulations by campaigners particularly targeted powers at the margins of Europe, notably the Russian and Ottoman empires. For example, when a diverse cast of British, Irish and Russian activists staged a demonstration in London's Hyde Park in 1890, it was initiated by the newly founded Friends of Russian Freedom, an organization that denounced 'Tsarist despotism' and documented Russia's repression of the opposition in its periodical *Free Russia*.[18] Furthermore, with regard to the Ottoman Empire, Chapter 2 has already noted how various activists highlighted the situation of Christian minorities under Ottoman rule, be they Greek, Bulgarian or Armenian.[19] Their discourse featured an element of 'othering' that tended to obscure histories of coexistence within the empire while also revealing misunderstandings of the nature of the nineteenth-century Ottoman reform measures.[20] It also made for ambivalent alliances: the Young Turk movement initially cooperated with activists from minority groups and met with sympathy abroad in its challenge to the Sultan's autocratic rule. By the twentieth century, however, Young Turk nationalism shifted towards a course that in itself became the source of suffering for ethnic and religious minorities.[21]

Along the Russian and Ottoman cases, Spain was another country that frequently attracted external criticisms. Yet, whereas attacks on Ottoman actions expressed a particular concern for fellow Christians, religion figured very differently in the Spanish case: visions of Spanish 'despotism' were shaped by concerns about the role of the Catholic Church. In 1913–14, the conservative Spanish author Julián Juderías was so incensed at such portrayals that he described them as a 'black legend' (*leyenda negra*) that, for many centuries, had cast Spain as a site of reactionary forces, especially the Roman Catholic Church. Juderías argued that in such representations, Spain appeared as 'inquisitorial, fanatical, incapable of belonging among the civilized peoples today as in the past, and always inclined towards violent repression; an enemy of progress and innovation'.[22]

Political activism played a role in fostering such perceptions. According to the historian Friedrich Edelmayer, 'the international protests in 1909 against the execution of the Europe-wide renowned pedagogue Francisco Ferrer y Guardia … were the impetus for Juderías to write his work'.[23] As noted in Chapter 4, the anarchist educator Ferrer had been sentenced to death for his alleged role during the popular unrest of Barcelona's 'Tragic Week' in 1909. Those who attacked the Spanish authorities' persecution of Ferrer did so in terms that integrated them into a wider historical narrative. To Emma Goldman, Ferrer was a 'victim of popery and militarism in Spain'.[24] Rudolf Rocker pointed out that many observers saw 'the shape of [the fifteenth-century Grand Inquisitor] Torquemada looming again over Spain'.[25] Both Goldman and Rocker were anarchists and thus shared Ferrer's political persuasions. But in this instance, they did not cast their defence of Ferrer in terms of ideological affinities, but by focusing on rights that they saw threatened by a combination of clerical influence and state actions. In such representations, political ideas, the anticlericalism of the European left and a rights-based discourse intersected. Crucially, it meant that the solidarity campaign for Ferrer ranged far beyond the left, with liberals also expressing their sympathy. For example, shortly after Ferrer's arrest in 1909, the British secularist journal *The Freethinker* cast his case in broader terms, arguing that the 'clerical – that is, the Catholic – party … allows as little religious liberty as it can throughout the country' and that in Barcelona, 'heretics in general, and Atheists in particular, are being arrested, imprisoned, and even murdered, under the pretence of "public safety"'.[26]

These comments indicate that to liberals and socialists, perceptions of rights were shaped by the 'culture wars' that in many European countries pitted secularist republicans against conservatives who were often associated with the Catholic Church.[27] Such cleavages manifested themselves in the Dreyfus Affair which, as Chapter 6 has noted, was not only a formative event in the French Third Republic but also had transnational dimensions. Moreover, in 1898, *l'affaire* inspired the creation of the *Ligue des Droits de l'Homme* (Human Rights League, LDH), which became the leading republican defence organization in France.[28] Three years later, Belgian activists established a counterpart, and the two leagues collaborated transnationally.[29] As discussed in Chapter 3, the LDH gained a German partner organization in 1922, when an existing campaign group – the *Bund Neues Vaterland* (New Fatherland Alliance) – renamed itself *Deutsche Liga für Menschenrechte* (German League for Human Rights). Domestically, the German association sought to defend the Weimar Republic against its enemies on the right, highlighting issues such as far-right terror and politicized justice. Meanwhile, internationally, the French and German associations cooperated on questions of international relations, for instance during the Ruhr Crisis of 1923.[30] In other words, a concern for civil liberties at home combined with pacifist endeavours. The confluence of these causes was evident in 1922, as ten national human rights leagues formed an international federation – a body whose international campaigning reached into the post-1945 era.[31]

In 1928, the Italian socialist Luigi Campolonghi articulated the vision of the *Fédération internationale des Ligues des Droits de l'Homme* (International Federation of Human Rights Leagues) when he addressed the annual LDH congress on its behalf. Campolonghi had a longstanding connection to France, having first moved there in 1898 to escape political persecution in Italy. In 1909, he had also been active in the international campaign for Francisco Ferrer. From 1922, shortly after Mussolini's ascent to power, he became a leading figure in the newly founded *Lega italiana dei diritti dell'uomo* (Italian Human Rights League), which participated in the antifascist resistance.[32] At the 1928 LDH congress, Campolonghi emphasized that transnational cooperation was crucial to defending democracy, which he deemed intrinsically connected to the causes of human rights and peace. As he put it, liberty was always 'the first ransom of a rising dictatorship', while peace was 'the final victim' when dictatorships collapsed. He argued that in the past, 'the fault of all democracies' had been 'to limit the scope of their specific activities strictly to the national radius'. The *Fédération internationale* had addressed this issue by creating 'a united democratic front against the united reactionary front'.[33]

At the time of Campolonghi's speech, the Italian league had been operating from exile for six years. Campolenghi noted that transnational contacts helped to support political refugees, with human rights leagues 'abroad and especially in France' providing 'refuge for free spirits in revolt against triumphant dictatorships'.[34] Indeed, following the Nazis' ascent to power in 1933, members of the *Deutsche Liga für Menschenrechte* played an active role in the community of German antifascists in Paris, supported by leading LDH activists.[35] By the end of the decade, the *Fédération internationale* included Paris-based political exiles from Armenia, Germany, Italy, Poland, Romania, Russia and Spain.[36] The fate of Czechoslovakia was a major concern, with the federation's president denouncing the Munich Agreement of September 1938.[37] The Czechoslovakian branch sought to organize support for refugees from the German-annexed Sudetenland, before the activists were themselves driven abroad by the Nazi occupation in March 1939.

Such examples indicate how the promotion of human rights became entwined with the struggle against fascism. It thus intersected with efforts waged by other campaigners. For instance, as noted in Chapter 4, socialists and communists built their own international efforts based on the defence of victims of political persecution. Moreover, the historian Laura Beers has shown how some WILPF members moved from anti-fascist campaigning in the 1930s to support for the nascent UN in the 1940s, driven by the commitment to 'promote consciousness for human rights and world citizenship'.[38]

These brief examples illustrate that causes and campaigns that have featured in the preceding six chapters could also be cast in terms of a defence of human rights. Such activism fused different elements. The mobilization of humanitarian sentiment and notions of solidarity were prominent features, but rights-based language featured within the wider activist vocabulary, which meant that it could be deployed when humanitarian or ideological arguments had reached their limitations.

International organizations and human rights

The aftermath of the First World War raised the question of rights in more than one way. The post-war refugee waves and border redrawings put the question of national minorities on the agenda.[39] Conceptually, the 1920s and 1930s saw efforts to alter this state of affairs. The minority protection arrangements of the League of Nations placed the rights of particular groups under the scrutiny of an international institution, based on a system of bilateral agreements that were subject to League monitoring. The existence of a separate authority in Geneva created opportunities for activists to highlight violations of minority rights by submitting petitions – although League officials had discretion as to whether or not to formally receive them.[40] However, the system did not amount to a scheme for universal human rights, as it was limited to particularly defined groups. Moreover, recent work has highlighted the ambivalent impacts of the system – from attempts to circumvent the arrangements to ways in which the national implementation of such provisions set minority groups apart from the majority population.[41]

The developments of the 1930s and 1940s added further urgency to debates on minority protection. Chapter 5 has discussed efforts to address the situation of Jewish people who were victims of Nazi persecution, yet such endeavours were mostly conceived as humanitarian undertakings rather than making a human rights case. One protagonist in broader rights-based debates was the Polish lawyer Raphael Lemkin, whose study on *Axis Rule in Occupied Europe* introduced the term 'genocide' in 1944.[42] As the historian Dietmar Müller has noted, Lemkin was one of several figures whose 'legal activism was informed by sensibilities about ethno-religious minorities and by their personal experience of politically motivated emigration and suppression'.[43] Without a formal position in diplomacy or international administration, these legal activists 'tried to develop alternative repertoires of legal activism by stressing their unique diplomatic skills and intellectual insights in institutions in the orbit of the LoN [League of Nations]'.[44] After the war, Lemkin became a driving force behind the Genocide Convention, which the UN General Assembly adopted in 1948 and which entered into force in 1951.

The historian Mark Mazower has interpreted the Genocide Convention in connection with the minority protection system and its legacies. In this context, he has contrasted it with the Universal Declaration of Human Rights, which was also adopted in 1948 and which 'gestured toward a much weaker regime, whose ardent rhetoric of moral aspiration was supposed in some measure to act as substitute for the force of law'.[45] Such observations are important in highlighting that the growth of human rights rhetoric after the Second World War did not necessarily increase activists' opportunities to secure such rights.

In some respects, the Universal Declaration built upon interwar connections. During the 1920s and 1930s, René Cassin – the document's principal author – had been an LDH member, a key figure in building links among veterans across different countries as well as a French delegate to the Assembly of the League of Nations.[46] Likewise, another key figure behind the Convention, Eleanor Roosevelt, also had links to interwar internationalism.[47] Even before her time as First Lady of the United States (1933–45), she had cooperated with the American civil rights, peace and women's movements.[48]

Twenty years after the drafting of the Universal Declaration, the United Nations designated 1968 as the 'Year of Human Rights', which also inspired campaigns at national and international levels.[49] It was somehow fitting that in the very same year, Cassin received the Nobel Peace Prize. Looking back upon the Declaration of 1948, he described its 'universality' as a 'salient characteristic', noting that its provisions applied 'to all human beings, without any discrimination whatever' and also 'to all territories, whatever their economic or political regime'.[50] These comments indicated that at least in theory, human rights were supposed to transcend Cold War binaries. In practice, both human rights activism and human rights politics reflected and sometimes shaped ideological tensions. The history of Freedom House – an American association founded in 1941, with Eleanor Roosevelt as its honorary chair – is a good example. While seen as a human rights organization, its emphasis on 'freedom' bore Cold War connotations, with the association's focus in the 1950s being on 'the Soviet Union and it satellites in East Europe' and its role being 'perceived as … a kind of moral compass for the government, a vote of conscience that continued to support or urge U.S. intervention to promote democracy and freedom'.[51] Freedom House's attacks on human rights violations in communist countries also played a role in later eras, including Republican foreign policy during the 1980s, even though 'it did not move in lockstep with the Reagan administration'.[52]

Such observations indicate that representations of human rights were closely linked to the Cold War situation in Europe. Unlike the UN – which featured countries from both power blocs and from a plethora of non-aligned countries, including growing representation from postcolonial nations – Europe had its own human rights provisions that mirrored the continent's political division. The system involving the Council of Europe (1949), the European Convention on Human Rights (1950) and the European Court of Human Rights (1959) was a manifestation of this development. Early on, the Council – to which governments from non-communist countries affiliated – became a target authority for activists who sought to raise the violation of human rights in the emerging Eastern Europe. For example, Eastern European exiles from the Assembly of

Captive European Nations established formal cooperation with the Council in 1958. While acknowledging that freedom would 'not be restored to the countries behind the Iron Curtain by means of statements and resolutions', the Assembly's chairman Stefan Korboński argued that 'condemnations and protests' could constitute 'a moral and political foundation under any kind of future action having liberation as its aim'.[53]

While Korboński's association remained a marginal actor, its campaigning indicated that human rights – or the broader principle of 'freedom' – provided a terrain on which Cold War politics could play out, with activists, politicians, diplomats and jurists as protagonists. In the diplomatic sphere, competing visions of what constituted 'human rights' delayed the passing of an international convention. As early as 1952, the *Fédération internationale des Droits de l'Homme* – the continuation of the interwar federation – deplored the lack of such provisions.[54] It took until 1966 before two international covenants were signed under the UN's auspices: one dedicated to 'civil and political rights', the other on 'economic, social and cultural rights' – a division that reflected the insistence of socialist countries to place socio-economic freedoms on an equal footing.[55] These legal instruments did not change the limited opportunities for activists to trigger UN action, given the persistence of state sovereignty. Indeed, at the framing the Universal Declaration, 'the United States and the Soviet Union [had] joined forces to foreclose the possibility that they would have to subject their domestic policies to international standards, preferring that human rights remain subordinate to the prerogatives of great-power hegemony'.[56] This is not to say that state interests went unchallenged: notwithstanding the opposition of some governments, NGOs were able to address grievances to the UN's Human Rights Commission in Geneva from 1970 onwards.[57]

Amnesty International and the 'prisoners of conscience'

Developments in the UN coincided with a growing role for human rights NGOs, with the rise of Amnesty International (AI) as the most prominent case. At its foundation in 1961, the organization focused on a specific category of activists: 'prisoners of conscience'. In the newspaper article that inspired AI's creation, the British lawyer Peter Benenson suggested that 'a sickening sense of impotence' about the fate of political prisoners could have a positive impact if such 'feelings of disgust all over the world could be united into common action'.[58] To promote this cause, AI developed a particular tool, namely letter-writing campaigns through which activists targeted individual governments. In such cases, transnationalism was a key feature of Amnesty's modus operandi: groups in the country that violated political rights provided information but did not themselves campaign domestic matters. Instead, it fell onto activists elsewhere to exert the pressure – which was also a way of preventing recriminations by authoritarian governments.

While a concern for political prisoners remained central, AI broadened its activities over time. Moreover, at an organizational level, it underwent substantial change. As Jan Eckel has noted, 'The streamlined and institutionally nuanced Amnesty International of the 1980s had little in common with the sedate, peripheral sect of the mid-sixties.'[59] Indeed, its growth was gradual and uneven. In some instances, the formation of national chapters built upon existing groups: for instance, the Belgian AI branch had initially started out in association with the existing Belgian Human Rights League.[60] By 1971, AI counted 'nearly 1,000 groups and national sections in 28 countries', yet its report noted a concentration in Western and Northern Europe, acknowledging that on other continents, 'development is slow, partly because of distance from headquarters and partly for other reasons relating to political climate or lack of funds'.[61]

While the growth of AI chapters was by no means equally distributed, it also encountered obstacles. Having been founded in London, the organization's association with the British state was a particular issue. Early on, the Foreign Office viewed AI as providing 'humanitarians with an organisation free from Communist exploitation; its activities were in fact unwelcome in Communist countries'. Given its wider principles, the officials considered AI 'as a body which deserved discreet support' while acknowledging that its 'activities … might from time to time embarrass us'.[62] Accordingly, the British government channelled some funds to AI, for instance to provide support to political prisoners under the Rhodesian regime that had split from the Commonwealth with its Unilateral Declaration of Independence (1965).[63] AI founder Peter Benenson later acknowledged a degree of faith in the government's intentions: 'at the advent of the Labour Administration I believed on the evidence of my friends' record and their public declarations that they would set an example to the world in the matter of human rights.'[64]

As the historian Tom Buchanan has shown, this episode triggered the first major crisis in AI's history, as revelations about the acceptance of government funds coincided with two other factors: a rupture with the British governments over AI criticisms of British policies in the colony of Aden as well as concerns within the organization about Benenson's leadership. In the end, the divisions led to the latter's departure from the organization that he had created. According to Buchanan, 'This kind of rupture between a charismatic leader and the organization that he has founded is hardly unique' and noted that one might regard 'the crisis of 1966–67 … as a necessary, if disagreeable, moment of change in the life of Amnesty'.[65]

By the early 1970s, AI was in a stronger position – and gained greater prominence in the international realm. One major event on this path was the organization's response to the dictatorship in Chile, which had come into being when General Augusto Pinochet overthrew the democratically elected leftist government of Salvador Allende in September 1973. At a meeting of its international executive in Vienna – a mere five days after the Pinochet coup – the organization decided its course of action: it arranged an investigative mission to the Latin American country, appealed to the UN and encouraged national AI sections to pressurize their governments, especially with regard to the granting of asylum.[66] In this respect, the organization mixed different elements, targeting national and international authorities while also undertaking information gathering. Moreover, the AI report revealed how circumstances force activists to venture beyond their focus on political prisoners. Its *Annual Report* noted that AI had 'never been a "refugee organization"' yet that 'AI sections had to devote much time to provide financial and legal assistance for Chilean and other Latin American refugees' in countries where no other groups supported these refugees. It also noted that such help had extended to covering 'the fare of many refugees from Latin American countries to Europe'.[67]

The international protests against the Pinochet dictatorship have been interpreted as a major moment in the rise of human rights during the 1970s.[68] AI criticisms reflected broader features of human rights activism in the 1970s. First, the regime's use of torture enabled AI to tie the case to its anti-torture campaign, which it had launched two years before the Pinochet coup and which, according to Jan Eckel, 'played a key role in catapulting the organization into a new era'.[69] Secondly, activism on Chile exemplified

Figure 7.1 Amnesty International poster protesting against Argentina's use of torture on the occasion of the Football World Cup of 1978. *Source*: West German AI section, 1978, reprinted for an exhibition in 2011, via Sozialarchiv Zürich.

the growing focus on human rights conditions in Latin America, with the military dictatorships in Brazil (1964–85) and Argentina (1974–83) also featuring prominently on activists' agendas.[70] The 'disappearances' of political opponents in both Chile and Argentina sparked significant documentation efforts within AI.[71] In 1978, Argentina's hosting of the FIFA World Cup provided opportunities to shine a spotlight on the actions of the junta.

The focus on Latin America also pointed to a third issue: the dictatorships in Chile, Argentina and Brazil retained friendly relations with the US government and other countries in the West. The ability of AI – an organization founded in Britain – to address human rights abuses in the West thus underscored the universalism of its concerns, beyond ideological boundaries. It thus seemed to signify 'the search for a European identity outside Cold War terms' which, according to Samuel Moyn, was one of the 'catalysts for the [human rights] explosion' of the 1970s.[72]

Between human rights and left-wing solidarity

A commitment to addressing human rights in the West did not only consider Latin American allies of the United States but also extended to European countries. Indeed, Benenson's founding appeal had highlighted the situation of political prisoners in Portugal, whose right-wing dictatorship under António Oliveira de Salazar (and later Marcelo Caetano) did not preclude it from being a NATO member. Likewise, AI attacked the repression in Francoist Spain: even before launching AI, Benenson had been involved in a support committee for the Spanish opposition; and in 1970, an AI poster campaign subverted the 'Spain is different' slogan of the Spanish tourist industry by highlighting political repression in the country.[73]

As early as 1961, the secretary-general of the *Fédération internationale des Droits de l'Homme* proclaimed his hope that 'international [public] opinion' would extend as much scrutiny to the Portuguese and Greek regimes, which were 'no less cruel than the one … in Spain'.[74] Compared to the Salazar dictatorship in Portugal, the inclusion of Greece was somewhat striking. Addressing the federation in 1960, its vice president Ilias Tsirimokos – who would briefly serve as Greek prime minister in 1965 – acknowledged that his country was 'nominally a democracy', yet he pointed to the use of 'arbitrary police power' against the opposition, as illustrated by the imprisonment of leftist politician Manolis Glezos.[75] Such concerns became more pronounced after the military coup that established a dictatorship in 1967.[76] Indeed, torture allegations in Greece triggered one of the earliest AI fact-finding missions and thus were a forerunner to the organization's anti-torture campaign of the 1970s.[77]

While such examples highlight the significance of human rights discourse, campaigns against dictatorships in Southern Europe and Latin America did not depend on human rights as a frame. For many activists who protested these regimes, leftist solidarity was a more prominent factor. For instance, actions on behalf of the Chilean opposition were largely driven by 'traditionally left-wing politicians and organizations

Figure 7.2 Dutch demonstration against Pinochet's coup in Chile (Amsterdam, 15 September 1975). *Source:* Sepia Times/Universal Images Group, via Getty Images.

as well as new-leftist groups'.[78] In Europe, such activism revealed the importance of prior campaigns and experiences – from the memory of right-wing coups in interwar Europe to scandals surrounding torture, for example French actions during the Algerian War of Independence.

The past was particularly important when it came to Spain, as the centrality of the Spanish Civil War in the history of the left shaped attitudes to, and activism against, the Franco regime. Looking at Belgian activists, the historian Victor Fernández Soriano has argued that any incidents – from Francoist actions against trade unions to political executions – triggered responses: 'whenever news of repression in Spain … arrived in Belgium, Spanish solidarity reacted'.[79] Other forms of left-wing solidarity involved cooperation with the large communities of immigrant workers who had moved from Spain, Portugal and Greece to various Western European countries during the 1950s and 1960s.[80] Political sympathies underpinned assistance to the Portuguese, Spanish and Greek communist parties operating underground. Moreover, reflecting the rise of post-1968 militancy, protagonists of the Italian New Left provided arms to the Greek opposition.[81]

While activists of different backgrounds and persuasions welcomed the demise of the Portuguese (1974), Greek (1974) and Spanish (1975) dictatorships, the most prominent transnational interactions promoted particular political and social visions, rather than the implementation of human rights. In Portugal, protagonists from both East and West participated in the struggle to forge the new political system.[82] Such actions could take different shapes – with, for example, activists from the Dutch *Partij van de Arbeid* (Labour Party) raising funds 'in aid of democratic socialism in Portugal', using radio broadcasts as well as a 'nationwide house-to-house collection'.[83] Meanwhile, after Franco's death in 1975, European socialists and the Socialist International actively supported the democratic transition in Spain.[84] While the violation of basic freedoms under the Portuguese, Greek and Spanish dictatorships had certainly mattered to human rights activists, traditional patterns of left-wing solidarity informed more extensive mobilizations.

Left-wing solidarity also deployed anti-imperialist tropes when facing Western-backed dictatorships, and it thus connected such activism to phenomena discussed in Chapter 1. This, for example, was the case with Greek student activists in the early 1970s, who saw themselves as 'part of a wider anti-imperialist front that was taking place worldwide'. By likening their own country's situation to the situation in Chile, they 'placed Greece firmly within a third-worldist paradigm'.[85] The Argentinian case further illustrates the resonance of anti-imperialist discourse. Whereas AI focused on torture and political prisoners in the country, other activists analysed the dictatorship in terms of imperial domination. This perspective was exemplified by the unsuccessful attempt of French leftist activists – along with partners in other countries – to launch a boycott of the 1978 FIFA World Cup. After the end of the football tournament, an international meeting in Paris inspired some campaigners to establish a 'collective' on 'sports, imperialism and repression'.[86] Their initiative was rooted in perceptions of 'American imperialism' as the 'principal oppressor and exploiter of the Argentinian people', with 'French imperialism – even if it occupies a more modest place – not letting up'.[87]

These examples explain why, rather than speaking of a 'human rights boom', one can also look at the 1970s and 1980s as the era of a 'solidarity boom'. Crucially, however, the two intersected, and in this respect, left-wing solidarity drew upon the growing resonance of human rights language. By the 1980s, 'human rights' were a prominent entry in the left-wing lexicon when it came to solidarity campaigns on behalf of Latin American revolutionaries. For example, Kevin O'Sullivan has interpreted the civil war in El Salvador (1979–92) – in which US-backed government forces fought against an alliance of revolutionary troops – as a crucial case in which political solidarity, humanitarian aid and concepts of human rights all intersected.[88] This interplay was also characteristic of another solidarity campaign that focused on Central America, in this case Guatemala. Similar to El Salvador, the country's government received US support while engaging in widespread human rights violations as well as conducting a prolonged civil war with left-wing guerrillas. In Western Europe, solidarity campaigns highlighted political affinities. As the leaflet from a Belgian solidarity group put it: 'In Guatemala, to be active in a trade union is to risk your life'. Activists therefore argued that 'international solidarity can save lives!'.[89]

At the same time, a rights-based discourse became increasingly important for bringing the Guatemalan case to a wider audience. Roberta Menchú, an exiled indigenous rights activist from Guatemala, embodied this development. In 1983, her memoir *I, Rogberta Menchú* became an international bestseller.[90] Crucially, the text had a transnational story.

In 1982, Menchú had visited Europe upon the invitation of various Guatemala solidarity committees, and her book was based on interviews that she conducted with Elisabeth Burgos-Debray, the Paris-based Venezuelan academic and activist.[91] On the one hand, Menchú's renown attested to the growing interest in indigenous rights as a distinct feature in human rights discourse.[92] On the other hand, it also demonstrated how the language of human rights continued to intermesh with other discourses, including those of national liberation.

Human rights and Eastern Europe

The situation in countries such as Spain and Chile meant that Eastern European governments were able to evoke human rights discourse in their attacks on the West.[93] At the same time, the situation in countries under communist rule gave rise to manifold forms of human rights activism. This could take various shapes: for instance, during the early 1950s, a new incarnation of the *Deutsche Liga für Menschenrechte* maintained a section on 'victims of Soviet concentration camps' as well as programmes on 'persecuted Jewish people' and 'political refugees' that largely focused on Eastern Europe, with the creation of refugee hostels in West Berlin as one field of action.[94] As the historian Lorna Wildenthal has shown, these activities were part of a struggle among different activists who sought to claim the legacy of the pre-war *Liga*, and they constituted a short-lived attempt to rebuild the association along anti-communist lines.[95]

Whereas in such instances, a focus on human rights reflected the political polarization of the Cold War era, the overall picture changed during the 1970s. Reviewing the prospects for oppositional activity in 1980, the imprisoned Polish activist Adam Michnik argued that hopes to overthrow the government through revolutionary action were ill-founded, suggesting that 'an increasing struggle for reform and evolution that seeks an expansion of civil liberties and human rights' were 'the only course East European dissidents can take'.[96] Michnik's assessment is instructive in two respects. First, it shows how human rights had become a tool through which activists – both at home and abroad – sought change while bypassing questions about the political system as such. Secondly, with regard to Central and Eastern Europe, human rights discourse was increasingly entangled with the figure of 'the dissident' – individuals such as Michnik and Alexeyeva, who themselves were protagonists and subjects of human rights campaigns.[97]

At a practical level, both during the Prague Spring of 1968 and in subsequent years, there was 'a striking awareness of transnational values',[98] with dissident groups proclaiming their solidarity with one another. This was not just a rhetorical matter, as dissidents and supporters from different countries helped with the production and distribution of underground texts – known as *Samizdat* – through which they circumvented censorship and documented political repression.[99] In some instances, such contacts connected with ideas of a shared European or Central European identity. In the 1970s, dissidents such as the Hungarian author György Konrad had integrated ideas about Europe into their visions of an alternative future.[100]

Transnational inspirations played an important role in this development. In 1973, the Soviet dissident Valentin Turchin initiated the creation of a Soviet Amnesty International group. As Yuri Orlov recounted, the initiative comprised 'twenty-five or thirty of us, mostly scientists and writers from Moscow, Leningrad, Kiev, and Tbilisi', forming 'part of our general plan to help create more and more unofficial human rights groups in order to involve people in peaceful activity independent of the government'.[101] In line with AI's working principles, the group did not address the situation in the Soviet Union itself; instead, it took up the case of 'a South Vietnamese trade-union leader, a Yugoslav rightist, an Indonesian Communist, and worker-strikers from Poland'. Such efforts were meant to give 'the Russian public an example of commitment to pluralism and tolerance of any ideas that were promoted without violence'.[102] In 1975, AI reported that its international executive had recognized the group yet noted the obstacles for the Russian activists, including the arrest of some of its members.[103] Despite AI campaigns on behalf of political prisoners in the Soviet Union, relations between the Soviet Amnesty Group and the international organization were 'often strained'.[104] Yuri Orlov later complained about a lack of backing. In his view, the AI executive 'found us troublesome'; he speculated that 'bewitched by the Soviet political game the Amnesty leadership had decided not to complicate its relations with the Soviets by establishing close ties with dissidents'.[105]

A subsequent venture initiated by Orlov created more durable transnational ties: namely the creation of the Moscow Helsinki Group in 1976. Its members were to build on the fact that 'The Helsinki Final Act invited the public to monitor their countries' performance' – although, as Lyudmila Alexeyeva commented, 'the Soviet authorities asked for not assistance' but rather 'stood poised to punish it'.[106] As she pointed out, the substance of the activists' concerns was not new as such: many of them had been promoting civil liberties for many years. However, Helsinki provided a framework through which they could articulate their demands and attract foreign support: 'By giving our movement a new focus, Orlov made it possible for Western politicians to understand what we wanted.'[107] Moreover, the Moscow Helsinki Group forged links with dissidents in other parts of the Soviet Union, with activists from Ukraine, Lithuania, Georgia and Armenia compiling their own documentations of human rights abuses, which the Moscow group then sought to forward to the countries that had signed the Helsinki Final Act.[108]

There were parallel developments in other countries of the Eastern bloc: in Czechoslovakia, the Charter 77 group formed in 1977 and framed its criticisms in terms of violations of the Helsinki accords.[109] Like other dissidents, it distributed some of its information abroad, both through sympathizers in the West and exiles such as Jiři Pelikán – a Czech socialist whom the historian Kacper Szulecki has described as the example of a 'dissident interpreter'.[110] From Rome, Pelikán edited the magazine *Listy* as a vehicle for the Czechoslovak opposition, yet in 1977 he also co-edited a German 'yearbook' that featured writings from Eastern European dissidents, both as 'a platform' to showcase their internal discussions and as 'an East–West' dialogue.[111] Such foreign contacts could put activists at risk: when leading Charter 77 figures were subjected to a trial in 1979, the indictment stressed their links to 'subversive centers abroad' and cited their publications in *Listy* as evidence.[112]

In 1978, the emphasis on Helsinki became the subject of new organizational ventures in the West, as American activists formed Helsinki Watch, which was dedicated to monitoring compliance with the Helsinki provisions at the international level. The organization's approach differed from the way in which AI operated. As Mark Mazower has argued, whereas Amnesty 'relied on moral suasion and the power of shameful publicity', Helsinki Watch pressurized American politicians and, in doing so, 'pioneered … a new model of rights activism that brought diplomats, politicians, and NGOs together in a single concerted effort'.[113] Helsinki Watch also worked with exiled dissidents, including Alexeyeva, and maintained links to human rights activists in Central and Eastern Europe.[114] By the early 1980s, the organization sought to refute accusations of Cold War biases by initiating Americas Watch, which investigated human rights violations closer to home and also raised concerns about US foreign policy in this regard.[115]

While American ties to European human rights movements were important, they formed part of much wider transnational networking – even beyond the ties of dissident groups from different countries. For instance, the historian Mark Hurst has drawn attention to British efforts to support the Russian opposition, some of it driven by religious motivations.[116] Moreover, in Central and Eastern Europe, many of the new human rights groups of the 1970s maintained links to one another. As a result of these manifold ties, the different Helsinki Watch groups developed a formal structure by creating the International Helsinki Federation for Human Rights in 1982.[117]

One key benefit of such connections was their ability to meet a broader aim: the attempt by dissidents to reach Western media and attract external support for their course – an example of the 'boomerang effect' discussed in the work of Margaret Keck and Kathryn Sikkink.[118] As Alexeyeva noted in her account of activist efforts in the mid-1970s, the work of the Helsinki Group 'was receiving constant coverage in the Western press', even if it initially remained removed from the frontpages; moreover, coverage increased at the end of 1976 when 'news stories that originated with the group began to move from page 19 to page 1 of US newspapers'.[119] The arrest and sentencing of Yuri Orlov in 1978 further provided activists with a broader international echo.[120] The Orlov trial was a good example of how the persecution of one individual could be used to draw attention to the human rights situation in specific countries, with the fate of Andrei Sakharov – like Orlov a dissident and scientist – as another case in point.[121] Moreover, alongside the dissemination of information through like-minded groups, Western-funded stations such as Radio Free Europe and Voice of America enabled exiled dissidents to reach audiences in their home countries.[122]

In the 1980s, the potential use of such media was exemplified by the Romanian academic Doina Cornea, who had been working as a lecturer at Cluj University and lost her job in 1982, after Radio Free Europe had inadvertently disclosed her name when it featured her letter about the Ceaușescu regime in one of its broadcasts.[123] Notwithstanding the personal recriminations, Cornea followed up on this with subsequent letters, including one to Belgian television in 1988, after her case had featured in a Belgian TV documentary on Romanian human rights violations. In the same year, Cornea gained several signatories for an open letter that was published in various Western newspapers, and she complemented such activism with appeals to Pope John Paul II and to the International Confederation of Free Trade Unions.[124]

Dissidents did not necessarily have to frame their critiques in terms of human rights – and support for the subjects of communist oppression did not necessarily have to foreground human rights as its principal frame. The case of East German singer-songwriter Wolf Biermann illustrates this point. In 1976, Biermann – who had been a vociferous critic of the East German authorities – became a German *cause celèbre* when, during a concert tour of West Germany, he was expatriated and forced to remain in the West, despite his insistence on changing the GDR from within. In an interview shortly after his expatriation, Biermann indicated that particular hope for internal change had come from Eurocommunism which, as noted in Chapter 4, was a reformist course adopted by some communist parties in the West. From Biermann's perspective, 'Helsinki has provided the form, supported the formal insistence on tolerance, freedom of speech, etc., while the Euro-Communists have provided the revolutionary content'.[125] Indeed, Eurocommunist parties initially provided some support to Biermann – including the Spanish one, which accepted him as a member.

This example illustrates the coexistence of human rights discourse and left-wing solidarity among dissidents who critiqued their regimes from a socialist standpoint.[126] These multiple, and sometimes overlapping notions of activist concern were also important in the 1980s, as illustrated by the response to the Polish state's repression of the independent trade union *Solidarność*.[127] In some instances, campaigns for the Polish opposition were driven by labour solidarity rather than human rights. This dimension was exemplified by debates within the Trade Union Congress in Britain, which ultimately sided with *Solidarność* over the state-sanctioned, communist trade unions of Poland and other countries in the communist bloc.[128]

A broadening or a narrowing?

In 1989, the state-socialist regimes across Central and Eastern Europe collapsed, with the Soviet Union itself dissolving in 1991. The demise of these dictatorships derived from a variety of factors – including domestic opposition, economic malaise and the changing policies of the Soviet Union which, under Mikhail Gorbachev's leadership, was unwilling to prop up unpopular governments in its orbit. Among human rights activists, these developments gave rise to some optimism. In 1990, the International Helsinki Federation met in Moscow, amounting to 'the first officially permitted nongovernmental international human rights conference ever held in the Soviet Union'.[129]

At the time, Orlov was optimistic about the future: at the Moscow meeting, he observed 'that many former human rights activists were now politicians and influential deputies of parliament' and commented that he wanted 'any future Russian politician to have some practical experience with human rights work'.[130] Around the same time,

Alexeyeva stated that she 'would not attempt to predict Russia's future' but noted 'many encouraging signs'.[131] In other countries, dissidents did indeed become leaders – as illustrated when the playwright Václav Havel, co-founder of Charter 77, acceded to Czechoslovakia's presidency in December 1989. One year later, the former *Solidarność* leader Lech Wałęsa was elected president of Poland.

Yet such developments were by no means universal or durable. While the subsequent marginalization of former dissidents in Central and Eastern Europe is well known, it happened particularly quickly in some countries. In January 1990, less than a month after Ceaușescu's fall and execution, Doina Cornea sent a letter to the Western media, expressing her concern that the emerging leader of post-communist Romania, Ion Iliescu, was stalling the momentum towards democratization. She therefore urged Western countries to withhold financial assistance to Romania until there had been a change in policy.[132] This appeal, however, backfired: as one account has noted, by March 1990, she 'had become not only the most unpopular public figure in Romania, but an object of hatred'.[133]

Further problems became evident elsewhere in Eastern Europe, most clearly in Russia. While the era of Boris Yeltsin's presidency (1991–9) was politically and economically unstable, it was also relatively liberal. By contrast, the system that subsequently emerged under Vladimir Putin's rule saw a reduction in the opportunities for oppositional activity, and a worsening of the human rights situation more generally. The historian Mark Hurst has noted the similarities of some campaigns in the present day, with human rights groups such as AI continuing to mobilize on behalf of Russian dissidents.[134] In 2013, Lyudmila Alexeyeva warned that Putin was intending to 'destroy all independent civic activity' and specifically evoked the past efforts of Helsinki Watch in this context.[135] She was far from the only former dissident who protested against political developments, or to cite the campaigns of the past. In the late 2010 and early 2020s, several former dissidents from Hungary and Poland drew attention to human rights issues in their countries, including threats to the independent judiciary and the free press. For example, in February 2021, Adam Michnik criticized a Polish tax law that targeted the independent media. As he argued, 'Thirty years after the fall of the Berlin Wall, the abolition of censorship, and the collapse of the Soviet Union, Poland's civil society is again defending its hard-won democracy from a state determined to do away with it.' At the same time, he noted a competing form of transnationalism by arguing that the Polish Law and Justice party was taking its cues from the policies that had been adopted by Vladimir Putin in Russia and Viktor Orbán in Hungary.[136]

While such examples highlight the risk of democratic backsliding, there are also other examples of how the potential for human rights activism to effect lasting change seems to have narrowed in some respects. The historian Celia Donert has pointed out this aspect with regard to the changing fate of Roma rights. In the 1970s, activists who sought recognition for the situation of the Roma had evoked the human rights stipulations of the Helsinki Final Act, as part of a wider effort to secure citizenship rights.[137] By contrast, in the post-communist landscape, representations of Roma people as internal 'other' have meant that progress in the area has stalled, if not been reversed.

Figure 7.3 Lyudmila Alexeyeva (*centre*) at a human rights protest in Moscow, 31 October 2009. *Source:* Konstantin Zavrazhin, via Getty Images.

Seen from this angle, potential optimisms around 1990 seem to have been ill-founded. In other respects, however, one can also see a broadening. Within the framework of different international organizations – both intergovernmental and nongovernmental – understandings of human rights became more inclusive after 1990. This, for instance, could be seen in the extension of AI's scope. For a long time, LGBT organizations such as IGA/ILGA had called on AI to include the repression of sexual minorities in its remit. In 1978, the Dutch AI section had placed the question on the agenda of the organization's international council which, however, assigned the subject to a working party.[138] It was only in the 1990s that AI gradually broadened its vision and agreed to campaign on behalf of individuals who were imprisoned for their sexual orientation. In the same period, women's rights were increasingly incorporated into the work of human rights bodies, partly in line with the campaigning efforts of women NGOs.[139] On the occasion of the World Conference on Human Rights – held in Vienna in 1993 under the auspices of the UN – feminist campaigners hosted a Global Tribunal on Violations of Women's Human Rights, featuring testimony on a various issues, for instance female genital mutilation.[140] In this respect, intersections between different kinds of human rights are more easily recognized which, in itself, reflects past campaigning efforts.

Furthermore, as noted in Chapter 3, the experience of genocide in Bosnia and Rwanda brought the question of human rights onto the diplomatic agenda in a forceful way. The notion of a 'responsibility to protect' meant that, for the first time, a discourse on enforcing human rights across state sovereignty gained political acceptance, at least in theory.[141] This discourse featured in diplomatic fora and intergovernmental organizations, but with activists as contributors to these debates. As the historian Stefan-Ludwig Hoffmann has pointed out, 'a class of experts in "global governance" – Western foreign policy-makers, international lawyers, social scientists, new NGOs, the "transnational civil society"' was involved in this process and treated human rights as 'the new moral idiom for the post–Cold War world of "globalization."'[142]

Yet Hoffmann has also argued that following some momentum in the 1990s, this cause lost some of its appeal in subsequent decades – meaning that 'the human rights idealism of the late 20th century has itself become historical'.[143] In some respects, this development can be ascribed to events since 2010. Starting in Tunisia in 2010, the 'Arab Spring' saw the toppling of several governments that had long been criticized for their violations of human rights. The subsequent instability meant that the hopes of many campaigners were soon disappointed, with the new regimes having human rights records that, in many cases, scarcely improved on their predecessors. Moreover, from 2011 onwards, the Syrian Civil War highlighted the inability (or unwillingness) of governments to put the 'responsibility to protect' into practice. Such observations might make the 1990s a somewhat distinct era. Yet, rather than viewing this development purely in terms of a waning, it arguably returns human rights to a position where it is one of several concepts that activists can deploy, sometimes in conjunction with others.

Notes

1. *Hearings before the Commission on Security and Cooperation in Europe: Ninety-Fifth Congress. First Session on Implementation of the Helsinki Accords*, vol. IV (Washington, DC: US Government Printing Office, 1977), 30. Alexeyeva's statement was presented by Edward Kline, a businessman who served as Alexeyeva's translator.
2. For the notion of a 'breakthrough', see Jan Eckel and Samuel Moyn, eds, *The Breakthrough: Human Rights in the 1970s* (Philadelphia, PA: University of Pennsylvania Press, 2015). For a critical analysis of debates on periodization, with a special focus on the 1970s, see Robert Brier, 'Beyond the Quest for a "Breakthrough": Reflections on the Recent Historiography of Human Rights', *Jahrbuch für europäische Geschichte / Yearbook of European History* 16 (2015): 155–73.
3. Samuel Moyn, *The Last Utopia: Human Rights in History* (Cambridge, MA: Harvard University Press, 2010), 7.
4. Moyn, *The Last Utopia*, 8.
5. *Hearings before the Commission on Security and Cooperation in Europe*, 30.
6. Hurst, *British Human Rights Organizations and Soviet Dissent*, 158–60.
7. Ludmilla Alekseeva [Lyudmila Alexeyeva], *Soviet Dissent: Contemporary Movements for National, Religious, and Human Rights* (Middletown, CT: Wesleyan University Press, 1985).
8. Sarah Snyder, *Human Rights Activism and the End of the Cold War: A Transnational History of the Helsinki Network* (Cambridge: Cambridge University Press, 2011).

9. Barbara Keys, *Reclaiming American Virtue: The Human Rights Revolution of the 1970s* (Cambridge, MA: Harvard University Press, 2014). See also Jan Eckel, 'Schwierige Erneuerung: Die Menschenrechtspolitik Jimmy Carters und der Wandel der Außenpolitik in den 1970er Jahren', *Geschichte in Wissenschaft und Unterricht* 66, nos. 1–2 (2015): 5–24.
10. *Hearings before a Sub-Committee of the Committee on Appropriations, United States Senate, Ninety-Sixth Congress, First Session* (Washington, DC: US Government Printing Office, 1979), 1870.
11. Jan Eckel, *The Ambivalence of Good: Human Rights in International Politics since the 1940s*, trans. Rachel Ward (Oxford: Oxford University Press, 2019), 155.
12. Lynn Hunt, *Inventing Human Rights: A History* (New York: W. W. Norton, 2007).
13. Stefan-Ludwig Hoffmann, 'Human Rights and History', *Past & Present*, 232, no. 1 (2016): 282.
14. Olympe de Gouges, Déclaration des droits de la femme et de la citoyenne (1791); Mary Wollstonecraft, *A Vindication of the Rights of Women* (1792). See also Sophie Mousset, *Women's Rights and the French Revolution: A Biography of Olympe de Gouges*, trans. Joy Poirel (New Brunswick, NJ: Transaction, 2007).
15. Hunt, *Inventing Human Rights*, 172.
16. For an example of the inclusion of abolitionism in a broader narrative of human rights, see e.g. Paul Gordon Lauren, *The Evolution of International Human Rights: Visions Seen* (Philadelphia, PA: University of Pennsylvania Press, 2003), 38–46. Moreover, Hunt's account also comments on abolitionism, with a particular focus on France: Hunt, *Inventing Human Rights*, 160–7.
17. Kevin Grant, 'Human Rights and Sovereign Abolitions of Slavery, c. 1885–1956', in Grant et al., *Beyond Sovereignty*, 80–102; Michael Geyer, 'Humanitarianism and Human Rights: A Troubled Rapport', in Klose, *The Emergence of Humanitarian Intervention*, 31–55.
18. Robert Henderson, 'The Hyde Park Rally of 9 March 1890: A British Response to Russian Atrocities', *European Review of History* 21, no. 4 (2014): 451–66.
19. Rodogno, *Against Massacre*.
20. For a recent survey, see Baskın Oran, *Minorities and Minority Rights in Turkey: From the Ottoman Empire to the Present State*, trans. John William Day (Boulder, CO: Lynne Rienner, 2021).
21. Dikran M. Kaligian, 'A Prelude to Genocide: CUP Population Policies and Provincial Insecurity, 1908–14', *Journal of Genocide Research* 10, no. 1 (2008): 77–9.
22. Julían Juderías, 'The Black Legend' (1914), in *Modern Spain: A Documentary History*, ed. Jon Cowans (Philadelphia: University of Pennsylvania Press, 2003), 111.
23. Friedrich Edelmayer, 'The "Leyenda Negra" and the Circulation of Anti-Catholic and Anti-Spanish Prejudices', in *EGO – European History Online* (2011), http://www.ieg-ego.eu/edelmayerf-2010-en (last accessed 9 January 2023).
24. Goldman, *Living My Life*, 458.
25. Rocker, *The London Years*, 115.
26. G. W. Foote, 'Catholic Toleration', *The Freethinker* 29, no. 38 (1909): 593.
27. Christopher Clark and Wolfam Kaiser, eds, *Culture Wars: Secular-Catholic Conflict in Nineteenth-Century Europe* (Cambridge: Cambridge University Press, 2009); Lisa Dittrich, *Antiklerikalismus in Europa: Öffentlichkeit und Säkularisierung in Frankreich, Spanien und Deutschland (1848–1914)* (Göttingen: Vandenhoeck & Ruprecht, 2014).

28. Emanuel Naquet, *Pour l'humanité: la Ligue des droits de l'homme de l'Affaire Dreyfus à la défaite de 1940* (Rennes: Presses Universitaires de Rennes, 2014); William Irvine, *Between Justice and Politics: The Ligue de Droits de l'Homme 1898–1945* (Stanford, CA: Stanford University Press, 2007).

29. Jost Depotter, 'De Ligue Belge des Droits de l'Homme, 1901–1939: Identiteit en activisme' (MA dissertation, Ghent University, 2014).

30. Laqua, 'Reconciliation and the Post-War Order', 212–18. See also Ingram, *The War Guilt Problem and the Ligue des Droits de l'Homme*, esp. ch. 5.

31. Davies, *NGOs*, 96; Miia Halme-Tuomisaari, 'Lobbying for Relevance: American Internationalists, French Civil Libertarians and the UDHR', in *Revisiting the Origins of Human Rights*, ed. Pamela Slotte and Miia Halme-Tuomisaari (Cambridge: Cambridge University Press, 2015), 330–61.

32. Michele Marzulli, 'Introduzione: La LIDU di Luigi Campolonghi', in *Luigi Campolonghi: Il massone fondatore della Lega Italiana dei Diritti dell'Uomo*, ed. Claudio Palandrani (Rome: Tipheret, 2019), 11–27; Eric Vial, 'La Ligue française des Droits de l'Homme et la L.I.D.U., son homologue italien, organisation d'exile antifasciste dans l'entre-deux-guerres', *Le Mouvement Social*, no. 183 (1998): 119–34.

33. Ligue des Droits de l'Homme, *Le Congrès national de 1928: compte rendu sténographique (15–17 juillet 1928)* (Paris: LDH, 1928), 22.

34. Ligue des Droits de l'Homme, *Le Congrès national*, 19–20.

35. Hans Manfred Bock, *Topographie deutscher Kulturvertretung im Paris des 20. Jahrhunderts* (Tübingen: Narr, 2010), 199–203.

36. La Contemporaine, Paris, LDH/135/73: document 'Fédération internationale', dated 30 June 1939.

37. LDH/135/73: Ligue internationale, 'Séance du Conseil, jeudi 6 octobre 1938'.

38. Beers, 'Frauen für Demokratie', 132. One example for this trajectory is the British Labour politician and activist Ellen Wilkinson: Laura Beers, *Red Ellen: The Life of Ellen Wilkinson, Socialist, Feminist, Internationalist* (Cambridge, MA: Harvard University Press, 2016); Matt Perry, *'Red Ellen' Wilkinson: Her Ideas, Movements and World* (Manchester: Manchester University Press, 2015).

39. Volker Prott, *The Politics of Self-Determination: Remaking Territories and National Identities in Europe, 1917–1923* (Oxford: Oxford University Press, 2016).

40. Carole Fink, *Defending the Rights of Others: The Great Powers, the Jews, and International Minority Protection, 1878–1938* (Cambridge: Cambridge University Press, 2004); Jane Cowan, 'The Success of Failure? Minority Supervision at the League of Nations', in *Paths to International Justice: Social and Legal Perspectives*, ed. Marie-Bénédicte Dembour and Tobias Kelly (Cambridge: Cambridge University Press, 2007), 29–56.

41. Carolin Liebisch-Gümüş, 'Embedded Turkification: Nation Building and Violence within the Framework of the League of Nations 1919–1937', *International Journal of Middle East Studies* 52, no. 2 (2020): 229–44; Lerna Ekmekcioglu, 'Republic of Paradox: The League of Nations Minority Protection Regime and the New Turkey's Step-Citizens', *International Journal of Middle East Studies* 46, no. 4 (2014): 657–79.

42. Raphael Lemkin, *Axis Rule in Occupied Europe: Laws of Occupation, Analysis of Government, Proposals for Redress* (Washington, DC: Carnegie Endowment for International Peace, 1944).

43. Dietmar Müller, 'In the Orbit of the League of Nations: International Law Debates and Networks in the Interwar Period', in *Transregional Connections in the History of East-Central Europe*, ed. Katja Castryck-Naumann (Berlin: De Gruyter, 2021), 190.
44. Müller, 'In the Orbit', 190.
45. Mazower, *No Enchanted Palace*, 130. See also Mark Mazower, 'The Strange Triumph of Human Rights', *The Historical Journal* 47, no. 2 (2004): 379–98.
46. Jay Winter and Antoine Proust, *René Cassin and Human Rights: From the Great War to the Universal Declaration* (Cambridge: Cambridge University Press, 2013). On the broader phenomenon of veterans' internationalism, see Julia Eichenberg and John Paul Newman, eds, *The Great War and Veterans' Internationalism* (London: Palgrave, 2013); Alcade, 'War Veterans as Transnational Actors'.
47. For a detailed account of her involvement, see Mary Ann Glendon, *A World Made New: Eleanor Roosevelt and the Universal Declaration of Human Rights* (New York: Random House, 2001).
48. Melissa Cooper, 'Reframing Eleanor Roosevelt's Influence in the 1930s Anti-Lynching Movement around a "New Philosophy of Government"', *European Journal of American Studies* 12, no. 1 (2017), https://doi.org/10.4000/ejas.11914 (last accessed 9 January 2023); Dario Fazzi, 'Eleanor Roosevelt's Peculiar Pacifism: Activism, Pragmatism, and Political Efficacy in Interwar America', *European Journal of American Studies* 12, no. 1 (2017), https://doi.org/10.4000/ejas.11893 (last accessed 9 January 2023).
49. Tom Buchanan, *Amnesty International and Human Rights Activism in Postwar Britain, 1945–1977* (Cambridge: Cambridge University Press, 2020), 153–81.
50. René Cassin, 'The Charter of Human Rights: Nobel Lecture, December 11, 1968', in *Nobel Lectures in Peace (1951–1970)*, ed. Frederick Haberman (Singapore: World Scientific Publishing, 1999), 400.
51. William Korey, *NGOs and the Universal Declaration of Human Rights: 'A Curious Grapevine'* (New York: St Martin's Press, 1998), 446.
52. Carl Bon Tempo, 'From the Centre-Right: Freedom House and Human Rights in the 1970s and 1980s', in *The Human Rights Revolution: An International History*, ed. Akira Iriye, Petra Goedde and William Hitchcock (New York: Oxford University Press, 2012), 236.
53. Korboński, *Warsaw in Exile*, 195.
54. La Contemporaine, Paris, ARCH/0103/900: Fédération internationale des Droits de l'Homme, 'Résolution proposée par le Bureau Fédéral et adoptee par l'Assemblée réunie à Paris le 17 juillet 1952'.
55. Weitz, *A World Divided*, 415.
56. Roger Normand and Sarah Zaidi, *Human Rights at the UN: The Political History of Universal Justice* (Boomington, IN: Indiana University Press, 2008), 197.
57. Fiona McGaughey, *Non-Governmental Organisations and the United Nations Human Rights System* (Abingdon: Routledge, 2021). For the ambiguous relationship between NGOs and the UN structures for human rights from a 1990s perspective, before criticisms triggered some changes in the UN's human rights architecture, see Felice Gaer, 'Reality Check: Human Rights Nongovernmental Organisations Confront Governments at the United Nations', *Third World Quarterly* 16, no. 3 (1995): 389–404.
58. Peter Benenson, 'The Forgotten Prisoners', *The Observer*, 28 May 1961, 23. On the foundation of AI, see Tom Buchanan, '"The Truth Will Set You Free": The Making of Amnesty International', *Journal of Contemporary History* 37, no. 4 (2002): 575–95.

59. Eckel, *The Ambivalence of Good*, 160.
60. Amnesty International, *Annual Report: 1 June 1970–31 May 1971* (London: AI, 1971), 13.
61. Amnesty International, *Annual Report: 1 June 1970–31 May 1971*, 4 and 14. More broadly on AI's growth in the 1960s, see Buchanan, *Amnesty International and Human Rights Activism*, 104–52.
62. The National Archives, London, 3632/157/27: Confidential note from 9 May 1967, citing an earlier note from 1963.
63. Tom Buchanan, 'Amnesty International in Crisis, 1966–7', *Twentieth Century British History* 15, no. 3 (2004): 267–89. See also Buchanan, *Amnesty International and Human Rights Activism*, 128–34.
64. The National Archives, London, 3632/157/27: letter from Peter Benenson, 6 January 1967.
65. Buchanan, 'Amnesty International in Crisis, 1966–7', 286–7.
66. Amnesty International, *Annual Report 1973–74* (London: AI, 1974), 39.
67. Amnesty International, *Annual Report for 1973–74*, 40–1.
68. Patrick William Kelly, 'The 1973 Chilean Coup and the Origins of Transnational Human Rights Activism', *Journal of Global History* 8, no. 1 (2013): 165–86.
69. Eckel, *The Ambivalence of Good*, 163. See also Buchanan, *Amnesty International and Human Rights Activism*, 182–96. The first major document resulting from the AI campaign was Amnesty International, *Report on Torture* (London: Gerald Duckworth & Co., 1973).
70. Patrick William Kelly, *Sovereign Emergencies: Latin America and the Making of Global Human Rights Politics* (Cambridge: Cambridge University Press, 2018). See also the range of AI reports from those countries, e.g. Amnesty International, *Report on Allegations of Torture in Brazil* (London: AI, 1972); Amnesty International, *Report of an Amnesty International Mission to Argentina, 6–15 November 1976* (London: AI, 1977).
71. AI, *Disappeared Prisoners in Chile* (London: AI, 1977); AI, *The 'Disappeared' of Argentina: List of Cases Reported to Amnesty International, December 1974–November 1979* (London: AI, 1980).
72. Moyn, *The Last Utopia*, 8.
73. Tom Buchanan, 'How "Different" Was Spain? The Late Franco Regime in International Context', in *Spain Transformed: The Late Franco Dictatorship, 1959–75*, ed. Nigel Townson (Basingstoke: Palgrave, 2007), 85.
74. La Contemporaine, Paris, ARCH/0103/900: Fédération internationale des Ligues des Droits de l'Homme, 'Compte Rendu du Congrès du 26 Décembre 1961'.
75. ARCH/0103/900: 'Deuxième Séance', taken from congress report, 3 June 1960.
76. ARCH/0103/900: Fédération internationale des Droits de l'Homme, 'Rapport sur la situation en Grèce', 20 March 1968.
77. Barbara Keys, 'Anti-Torture Politics: Amnesty International, the Greek Junta, and the Origins of the Human Rights "Boom" in the United States', in Iriye et al., *The Human Rights Revolution*, 201–23; Ann Marie Clark, *Diplomacy of Conscience: Amnesty International and Changing International Human Rights Norms* (Princeton, NJ: Princeton University Press, 2001), 39–42.
78. As Jan Eckel has noted, 'The overwhelming preponderance of solidarity with Chile was a product of the political left, involving both traditionally left-wing politicians and organizations as well as new-leftist groups': Eckel, *The Ambivalence of Good*, 250.

79. Victor Fernández Soriano, 'Human Rights for Spain: Anti-Francoism in Belgium, between Old and New Forms of Protest (1960s–1970s)', in Christiaens et al., *International Solidarity in the Low Countries*, 146.
80. See, for instance, the case of Portuguese workers in France: Victor Pereira, *La dictature de Salazar face à l'émigration: l'État portugais et ses migrants en France (1957–1974)* (Paris: Presses de Sciences Po, 2012). For the limits of official support for the Portuguese opposition prior to the Carnation Revolution of 1974, see Pedro Aires Oliveira, 'A Sense of Hopelessness? Portuguese Oppositionists Abroad in the Final Years of the Estado Novo, 1968–1974', *Contemporary European History* 26, no. 3 (2017): 465–87.
81. Kornetis, *Children of the Dictatorship*, 67.
82. Pavel Szobi, 'From Enemies to Allies? Portugal's Carnation Revolution and Czechoslovakia, 1968–1989', *Contemporary European History* 26, no. 4 (2017): 669–90.
83. 'Socialist Diary', *Socialist Affairs* 25, no. 1 (January 1975): 16.
84. Pilar Ortuño Anaya, *European Socialists and Spain: The Transition to Democracy, 1959–77* (Basingstoke: Palgrave, 2002); Stine Bonaksen, 'Logics of Influence: European Social Democrats and the Iberian Transitions to Democracy', in *Rethinking European Social Democracy and Socialism: The History of the Centre-Left in Northern and Southern Europe in the Late 20th Century*, ed. Alan Grandino, Stefan Nygård and Peter Stadius (Abingdon: Routledge, 2022), 84–104.
85. Kornetis, *Children of the Dictatorship*, 248.
86. La Contemporaine, Paris, LDH Archives, ARCH/0103/758: Collectif pour le boycott de l'organisation par l'Argentine de la Coupe Mondiale de Football (CORA), 'Bilan et perspectives', 7.
87. CORA, 'Bilan et perspectives', 6.
88. Kevin O'Sullivan, 'Civil War in El Salvador and the Origins of Rights-Based Humanitarianism', *Journal of Global History* 16, no. 2 (2021): 247. See also O'Sullivan, *The NGO Moment*, 137–56.
89. AMSAB, Ghent, Doss. 268 ('Archief van Vlaams Guatemalacomité'): leaflet 'TUSGUA: Trade Union Support for Guatemala', 1987.
90. The English translation appeared the year after the original: Rigoberta Menchú, *I, Rigobertá Menchú*, trans. Ann Wright (London: Verso, 1984).
91. Elisabeth Burgos-Debray, 'Introduction', in Menchú, *I, Rigoberta Menchú*, xiv.
92. Jochen Kemner, 'Fourth World Activism in the First World: The Rise and Consolidation of European Solidarity with Indigenous Peoples', *Journal of Modern European History* 12, no. 2 (2014): 262–79.
93. Paul Betts, 'Rights', in *Socialism Goes Global: The Soviet Union and Eastern Europe in the Age of Decolonization*, ed. Paul Betts et al. (Oxford: Oxford University Press, 2022), 180–220. See also the specific the case of East Germany: Ned Richardson-Little, *The Human Rights Dictatorship: Socialism, Global Solidarity and Revolution in East Germany* (Cambridge: Cambridge University Press, 2020).
94. 'Arbeitsbericht 1953', in Deutsche Liga für Menschenrechte, *40 Jahre um Menschenrechte 1913–1953* (Berlin: Deutsche Liga für Menschenrechte, 1953), 33–16.
95. Lora Wildenthal, *The Language of Human Rights in West Germany* (Philadelphia, PA: University of Pennsylvania Press, 2013), 17–44.
96. Adam Michnik, 'A New Evolutionism' (1976), as featured in Michnik, *Letters from Prison*, 142.

97. For a detailed study on this subject, with a focus on Central Europe, see Kacper Szulecki, *Dissidents in Communist Central Europe: Human Rights and the Emergence of New Transnational Actors* (Cham: Palgrave, 2019). See also Brier's comments on dissidents as 'icons': Brier, *Poland's Solidarity Movement*, 8.
98. Wardhaugh et al., 'Intellectual Dissidents and the Construction of European Spaces', esp. 36.
99. Friederike Kind-Kovács and Jessie Labov, eds, *Samizdat, Tamizdat, and Beyond: Transnational Media during and after Socialism* (New York: Berghahn, 2013).
100. Barbara Falk, *The Dilemmas of Dissidence in East-Central Europe: Citizen Intellectuals and Philosopher Kings* (Budapest: Central European University Press, 2003), 298–310.
101. Yuri Orlov, *Dangerous Thoughts: Memoirs of a Russian Life*, trans. Thomas Whitney (New York: William Morrow and Company, 1991), 168.
102. Orlov, *Dangerous Thoughts*, 168.
103. Amnesty International, *Annual Report 1974/75* (London: Amnesty International Publications, 1975), 119.
104. Robert Horvarth, *The Legacy of Soviet Dissent: Dissidents, Democratisation and Radical Nationalism in Russia* (Abingdon: Routledge, 2003), 93.
105. Orlov, *Dangerous Thoughts*, 176.
106. Ludmilla [Lyudmila] Alexeyeva and Paul Goldberg, *The Thaw Generation: Coming of Age in the Post-Stalin Era* (Pittsburgh, PA: University of Pittsburgh Press, 1993), 281.
107. Alexeyeva and Goldberg, *The Thaw Generation*, 283.
108. Orlov, *Dangerous Thoughts*, 203.
109. By the time of the collapse of the Czechoslovakian regime, it had collected over 500 cases of human rights violations: Eckel, *The Ambivalence of Good*, 302.
110. Szulecki, *Dissidents in Communist Central Europe*, 90.
111. Jiří Pelikán and Manfred Wilke, 'Vorbemerkung der Herausgeber', in Pelikán and Wilke, *Menschenrechte*, 10–11.
112. '6 Czech Dissidents on Trial in Prague', *New York Times*, 23 October 1979, 10.
113. Mazower, *Governing the World*, 328.
114. Snyder, *Human Rights Activism and the End of the Cold War*, 116.
115. Cynthia Brown, ed., *With Friends Like These: The Americas Watch Report on Human Rights and U.S. Policy in Latin America* (New York: Pantheon, 1985).
116. For example of the religious dimensions, see Hurst, *British Human Rights Organizations and Soviet Dissent*, 115–46.
117. Snyder, *Human Rights Activism and the End of the Cold War*, 129.
118. Keck and Sikkink, *Activists beyond Borders*, 12–13.
119. Alexeyeva and Goldberg, *The Thaw Generation*, 284 and 288 respectively.
120. Orlov, *Dangerous Thoughts*, 226.
121. Paul Rubinson, '"For Our Soviet Colleagues": Scientific Internationalism, Human Rights, and the Cold War', in Iriye, *The Human Rights Revolution*, 245–65.
122. Arch Puddington, *Broadcasting Freedom: The Cold War Triumph of Radio Free Europe and Radio Liberty* (Lexington, KY: University Press of Kentucky, 2000).
123. Dennis Deletant, *In Search of Romania: A Memoir* (London: Hurst, 2022), 68–72.

124. Deletant, *In Search of Romania*, 75–6.
125. Wolf Biermann interviewed by Thomas Hoernigk, 2 Febuary 1977, in 'Two Interviews with Wolf Biermann', trans. Jack Zipes, *New German Critique*, no. 10 (1977): 25.
126. Daniel Laqua, 'Transnational Dimensions of a "German Case": The Expatriation of Wolf Biermann and the Politics of Solidarity in the 1970s', *Labour History Review* 86, no. 3 (2021): 369–96.
127. Brier, *Poland's Solidarity Movement*.
128. Stefan Berger and Norman LaPorte, 'Great Britain: Between Avoiding Cold War and Supporting Free Trade Unionism', in Goddeeries, *Solidarity with Solidarity*, 129–58.
129. Orlov, *Dangerous Thoughts*, 324.
130. Ibid., 322.
131. Alexeyeva and Goldman, *The Thaw Generation*, 313–14.
132. Alina Mungu-Pippidi, 'Romanian Political Intellectuals before and after the Revolution', in *Intellectuals and Politics in Central Europe*, ed. András Bozóki (Budapest: Central European Press, 1999), 87.
133. Mungu-Pippidi, 'Romanian Political Intellectuals', 88.
134. Mark Hurst, 'Crossing the Curtain: British Activists and the Echoes of Soviet Dissent in Contemporary Russian Human Rights Activism', *Cambridge Review of International Affairs*, https://doi.org/10.1080/09557571.2022.2106820, advance access online 9 August 2022 (last accessed 9 January 2023).
135. Lyudmila Alexeeva [Alexeyeva], 'Vladimir Putin's Goal Is to Destroy Russian Civil Society', *The Guardian online*, 24 May 2013, available at https://www.theguardian.com/commentisfree/2013/may/24/vladimir-putin-goal-russian-civil-society (last accessed 9 January 2023).
136. Adam Michnik, 'Polish Democracy in the Crosshairs', *Project Syndicate*, 16 February 2021, https://www.project-syndicate.org/commentary/polish-independent-media-protest-by-adam-michnik-2021-02, at 8 October 2022.
137. Celia Donert, *The Rights of the Roma: The Struggle for Citizenship in Postwar Czechoslovakia* (Cambridge: Cambridge University Press, 2017). See also Celia Donert, 'Charter 77 and the Roma: Human Rights and Dissent in Socialist Czechoslovakia', in *Human Rights in the Twentieth Century*, ed. Stefan-Ludwig Hoffmann (Cambridge: Cambridge University Press, 2011), 191–211.
138. 'Amnesty Backs Off', *Gay Times*, 20 September–3 October 1979, 1 and 3.
139. See, for example, the transnational efforts of *Terre des Femmes*, an organization formed in West Germany in 1981 with the specific aim to promote the human rights of girls and women, with activities that involved 'the crossing of either international borders or the crossing of cultural lines inside Germany': Wildenthal, *The Language of Human Rights in West Germany*, 132.
140. Kelly J. Shannon, 'The Right to Body Integrity: Women's Rights as Human Rights and the International Movement to End Female Genital Mutilation, 1970–1990s', in Iriye et al., *The Human Right Revolution*, 296.
141. Daniel Stahl and Annette Weinke, 'Intervening in the Name of Human Rights: On the History of an Argument', in *Human Rights and Humanitarian Intervention: Legitimizing the Use of Force since the 1970s*, ed. Norbert Frei, Daniel Stahl and Annette Weinke (Göttingen: Wallstein, 2017), 9–26.

142. Stefan-Ludwig Hoffmann, 'Are Human Rights History?', *Los Angeles Review of Books*, 2 June 2019, https://lareviewofbooks.org/article/are-human-rights-history/ (last accessed 9 January 2023).
143. Hoffmann, 'Are Human Rights History?'.

CHAPTER 8
GOING GREEN

'It's all interrelated', the West German activist Petra Kelly pointed out in response to a question about the relationship between her peace activism, her concern for ecology and various other issues that she had discussed in a TV interview. Kelly elaborated:

> Ecology means it's a reconciliation with the planet earth that has no emergency exit, because the planet earth is limited. It also means …. reconciliation with the people and with one another, also with men and women, reconciliation with children, with the handicapped, with all the exploited people on this earth. And ecology in the wider sense means also that we've only got this one spaceship called the 'planet earth', and we better live on it peacefully, or else we blow each other to pieces. And ecology in the German sense means also to try to question hierarchy, centralization, living always on the backs of other people …[1]

Kelly's interview was part of a broadcast that sought to introduce West Germany's growing 'green' movement to a British audience in November 1982. During the wide-ranging conversation, Kelly commented on a range of subjects, from gender relations to the exploitation of the developing world. Her engagement with such questions was informed by her personal history of activism. Having been involved in the pro-European ventures of the Young European Federalists in the early 1970s, Kelly became increasingly concerned with environmental matters and in 1980 co-founded the West German party *Die Grünen* (The Greens). By the early 1980s, she was also a prominent figure in the international peace movement which, as noted in Chapter 3, had gained fresh urgency in an era of worsening Cold War tensions.[2] Moreover, Kelly's activism connected not only causes but also countries. Born in Germany, she completed school and her undergraduate studies in the United States, conducted postgraduate work in Amsterdam and worked for the European Commission in Brussels. As the historian Stephen Milder has noted, 'Throughout her political career, Kelly's willingness to think outside national boundaries and her ability to imagine foreign ideas in the local landscape would define her politics.'[3]

To Kelly, it was evident that one's own actions and lifestyles were entwined with political concerns. As she put it in 1982, politics 'comes from the personal experience' – with the consequence that 'we must become experts over our own lives, over our own security, become experts over our own work, and not have it done for us, from the top, from soulless technocrats and bureaucrats, who don't know what life is all about'.[4] In such visions, green politics amounted to an emancipatory project. Picking up on the notions articulated by Kelly, this chapter traces how environmental activism became entwined with broader political visions, from democratic politics to sustainable development. It is this connectedness of different causes that makes it appropriate to conclude the present book with a chapter on 'green' activism.

While the term 'environmentalism' only gained currency in the 1970s, activism on behalf of the environment and ideas about its interconnection with other causes have a longer history.[5] For instance, the historian Joachim Radkau has spoken of an 'environmentalism before the environmental movement' whose history can be traced back to the late eighteenth century.[6] This is not to say that the preoccupations, self-perceptions or methods of activists were identical. As Jan-Henrik Meyer has pointed out, 'preservation', 'conservation' and 'protection' of nature denoted different motivations and aims. Moreover, 'the environment' rather than 'nature' only became an activist frame from the 1960s.[7] This chapter acknowledges that, notwithstanding some continuities, broader mobilization for environmental causes has intensified in more recent times. Transnational cooperation was central to such efforts, because many activists realized that particular problems – from the dangers of nuclear radiation to the threat of climate change – exceeded national boundaries. This awareness of global interdependence explains why a focus on environmental protection can also shift our perspective on how 'Europe' relates to the wider world.[8]

A concern for nature

In itself, a concern for nature was hardly a new phenomenon: after all, many different cultures have sought to live in balance with their natural habitat.[9] However, in the nineteenth century, the defence of nature inspired different forms of action. Three factors contributed to this development. The first was the impact of industrialization and urbanization on the environment, from the resource intensity of economic production to increasing pollution.[10] The second was European colonialism, which raised questions about nature and wildlife in ways that connected Europe to the wider world.[11] Thirdly, scientific research led to growing awareness of the possibility that some animal species might become extinct – and this realization coincided with changes in attitudes, including 'a new ethical perspective about animal life'.[12] When it came to transnational efforts, these factors intersected. For instance, the IR scholar Charlotte Epstein has argued that European 'preoccupation with the species inhabiting the immediate environment ... was effectively carried beyond the national territory through the consolidation of colonial empires'. Such issues were not necessarily cast in moral terms, as illustrated by concerns about 'declining game for colonial hunts'.[13]

By the end of the nineteenth century, efforts on behalf of endangered species involved different audiences. For instance, at the International Congress of Women in 1899, women's activists heard speeches on 'Dress in Relation to Animal Life' and 'Our Duties to Wild Animals'.[14] At the event, the British activist Etta Lemon – a key figure in the Society for the Protection of Birds – criticized the use of bird feathers as a fashion accessory. As she argued, it was 'through women and their weak submission to the dictates of what is known as Fashion that much of the wholesale and disastrous slaughter of bird life has taken place'.[15] The representation of this issue in gendered terms was not confined to congress settings, with bird preservation efforts constituting a vehicle for women's activism in this period.[16] By 1904, German activists set up an association to address this subject internationally, the *Internationaler Frauenbund für Vogelschutz* (International Women's Alliance or the Protection of Birds). The organization subsequently acquired a Belgian branch and contributed to the development of international structures for the bird preservation movement.[17] In terms of its composition and orientation, the *Frauenbund* was hardly radical: it received patronage from various German dignitaries, featured well-connected men among its leadership (despite calling itself a 'women's organization') and praised Wilhelm II as an 'emperor of peace'.[18] Moreover, such activism continued to have colonial dimensions, as 'the most self-consciously international wildlife cause of the day' targeted the trade in birds-of-paradise feathers from German New Guinea and the Dutch East Indies.[19]

In 1900, the International Conference on the Preservation of Wild Animals, Birds and Fish in Africa illustrated the colonial roots of conservation efforts. As the historian Bernhard Gissibl has put it, the meeting in London 'was a product of internationalized and moral imperialism extended to wild animals' and thus amounted to 'the animal-related complement of the antislavery internationalism related to East Africa'.[20] In this respect, diplomatic action on animal protection intersected with causes that have been discussed in Chapter 1 of this book: steps against the East African slave trade on the one side and the ivory trade on the other shared a discourse and protagonists, including their potential to serve imperial agendas. In 1913, influences from the colonial sphere manifested themselves at the World Conference on the Protection of Nature in Bern, even beyond the presence of delegates from colonial powers. The fact that the event took place in Switzerland, a country without colonies, should not obscure this aspect: recent research has highlighted manifold Swiss entanglements with colonialism and imperialism.[21] These links were embodied by the driving force behind the conference, the Swiss conservationist Paul Sarasin, whose activism drew both on 'his experiences as a traveller in times of European colonialism' and on his role within 'the international community of natural scientists'.[22] Such interconnections were illustrated by Sarasin's unsuccessful attempt to include indigenous people among the targets of nature protection efforts.[23]

According to the historian Jan-Henrik Meyer, the London and Bern conferences revealed 'key characteristics of international nature protection during the years before the First World War', including the way in which such attempts were meant 'to solve novel problems that resulted from technological advances and colonialism, and that were beyond the reach of national authorities'.[24] While being diplomatic events, both conferences were sustained by scientists and preservation groups that had emerged in different countries. This is not to say that the concern for nature was necessarily framed as a transnational endeavour: after all, nature could also be imagined in national terms. Representations of the environment as both natural and national also became evident through the intersections between National Socialist ideology and conservationist efforts.[25] For instance, Lina Hähnle – who had founded Germany's largest bird preservation society in 1899 and played an active role in international efforts on this issue – headed a newly created Reich League for the Preservation of Birds and was celebrated as the 'German mother bird' (*Deutsche Vogelmutter*).[26]

Notwithstanding its appropriation for national causes, the interwar years also saw ongoing transnational efforts dedicated to ecological concerns. One example was the campaign for the protection of seabirds from the risks of oil spillages. Activists established transnational links and targeted the League of Nations to generate international action.[27] To this end, they maintained an International Council for Bird Protection from 1922 onwards, renamed the International Committee for Bird Preservation six years later.[28] This organization was but one attempt to create international structures: in 1923, the formation of the International Society for the Preservation of the European Bison was another case. Moreover, aiming for a broader remit, Belgian, Dutch and French activists helped to create the International Office of Documentation and Correlation for the Protection of Nature (1928), which seven years later became the International Office for the Protection of Nature.[29] In discussing efforts that predated the 1960s, the historian Raf de Bont has acknowledged that 'international conservation was a small-scale enterprise', being sustained 'by modest transnational networks' in this period. Yet while 'its realizations on the ground might seem relatively limited', these earlier undertakings were important 'as [a] generator of ideas, ideals, and practices'.[30]

Such endeavours did not involve large-scale popular mobilization and instead revolved around 'expert-activists' who sought to shape policy on nature. One example was the designation of national parks as an approach to nature conservation which, following pioneering efforts in the United States, was adopted within different colonial and European settings. In Switzerland, conservationists followed the American example by creating a national park in the Alps in 1914, which Italy followed with the Gran Paradiso (1922) and Stelvio (1933) national parks during the interwar years.[31] Moreover in 1932, a cross-border national park in the Tatra Mountains became an explicitly transnational venture, operating across the borders between Poland and Czechoslovakia.[32]

The interaction between scientists, officials and campaigners was characteristic of such exchanges. In 1948, this interplay underpinned the creation of the International Union for the Protection of Nature, which in 1956 became the International Union for Conservation of Nature (IUCN). As the historian Simone Schleper has argued, the IUCN 'continued and consolidated the loosely organized international conservation endeavors dating back to the early 1900s': it 'built on colonial networks of naturalists around the globe' and subsequently benefited from 'a far-reaching network with scientific members in many parts of the world'.[33] As with the pre-war efforts, species at risk of extinction featured prominently on the IUCN's agenda. From 1961 onwards, a new international NGO with head offices in Switzerland complemented its work in this field: the World Wildlife Fund (WWF; later World Wide Fund for Nature). Anna-Katharina Wöbse and Hans-Peter Ziemek have described WWF 'as a financially powerful extended arm of the

IUCN' which 'was able to fund concrete research projects and media campaigns, and as a non-government organization ... was relatively unhindered by the barrier of the Iron Curtain'.[34] Significantly, WWF operated at different levels, from educational work to fundraising efforts that extended to the field of popular culture.[35] At the same time, it was hardly an anti-establishment venture, as illustrated by the fact that Prince Bernhard of the Netherlands served as the organization's initial president.

While organizational ventures – which often straddled the boundaries of activism, science and diplomacy – were one transnational manifestation of environmental concern, publications could both inform and inspire activism. Two texts – published within a decade from one another – are particularly associated with the growth of environmentalism in the 1960s and early 1970s. The first of these was *Silent Spring*, which the American biologist Rachel Carson published in 1962. Her book focused on the impact of pesticides, raising wider questions about environmental pollution. To Carson, 'the contamination of man's total environment with ... substances of incredible potential for harm' was 'the central problem of our age', along with 'the possibility of the extinction of mankind by nuclear war'.[36] Carson's work was not novel in all aspects, as it built on existing ideas among American conservationists.[37] However, it was remarkable in conveying scientific research on ecology, including the impact of human actions, to broader audiences. Foreign translations appeared in quick succession and had a significant influence in several cases, with the extensive resonance of her work in Sweden being a case in point.[38]

Ten years after Carson's book, the Club of Rome's study on *The Limits to Growth* exerted an even greater influence on the activist imagination. The Club of Rome had been founded in 1968, bringing together academics and diplomats with the aim of studying global problems. Its composition reflected an ongoing emphasis on expertise, yet, in comparison to earlier efforts, the picture that it painted was particularly drastic: the report concluded that without any change to the existing 'growth trends in world population, industrialization, pollution, food production, and resource depletion', the earth would reach 'the limits to growth ... within the next one hundred years'.[39] While the report attracted some criticism for its perceived alarmism, it attained a significant international echo.[40] The text had evidently tapped into a wider concern about the human footprint on the planet – and highlighted the need to take action.

New associations, new forms of campaigning

Messages about the 'limits to growth' resonated with existing unease about the nature and development of modern industrial society. But whereas the Club of Rome had clouted such terms in the language of science, an increasingly prominent strand of activism drew on the countercultural currents that had emerged during the 1960s.[41] In the late 1960s and early 1970s, environmentalism came to be a 'new social movement' in which post-material attitudes combined with the adoption of radical forms of protest.[42] Universities were crucial spaces in this respect. In the United States, the celebration of Earth Day particularly targeted university campuses, having initially started as a national day of 'teach-ins' in 1970.[43] In Denmark, student activists in 1969 demonstrated at a meeting of the Natural History Society and went on to set up NOAH, an environmentalist group that adopted countercultural forms of protest.[44]

Both Earth Day and NOAH developed links to Friends of the Earth (FoE), the environmentalist organization that came into being in 1969. As for the former, a semi-official account of FoE's history has argued that on the occasion of Earth Day in 1970, the American 'media went wild', with FoE being 'the biggest beneficiary' of the realization that the United States 'had a mass environmental movement'.[45] Meanwhile, NOAH, while operating independently for the first two decades of its existence, ultimately became the Danish FoE chapter in 1988. Its accession reflected FoE's growth into an international organization. In 1969, David Brower had created FoE in the United States, based on his dissatisfaction with the cautious approach of the Sierra Club, the American conservationist association for which Brower himself had served as executive director. FoE's creation reflected wider developments at the end of the 1960s, characterized by 'growing interest in global activism and increasing debates over the proper tactics for environmental groups'.[46] By 1971, the organization had expanded to Britain, Sweden and France as well as establishing an international secretariat. Its links to the protest movements of the late 1960s were underscored by the fact that the French branch, *Les Amis de la Terre*, was headed by Brice Lalonde, formerly a student leader during the 1968 protests.[47]

According to the historian Frank Zelko, FoE served as 'a model for the establishment of more activist-oriented and internationally focused environmental organizations'.[48] In this respect, it set a potential example for the development of Greenpeace – which, like FoE, came into being at the end of the 1960s, merging countercultural politics and ecology.[49] The earliest incarnation of Greenpeace, the 'Don't Make a Wave Committee', sought to disrupt US nuclear testing in Alaska. Because of the test site's proximity to Canada, it was from British Columbia that activists launched their first efforts. In 1971, activists set sail to Amchitka (Alaska), where they aimed to bear witness to the nuclear tests and potentially disrupt them. These early ventures contained key elements of what came to define Greenpeace activism. One feature was the adoption of protest forms that would attract widespread attention – not without risk to those involved. In this respect, Greenpeace exemplified a form of activism in which the use of the mass media assumed a prominent place.

In 1972, Greenpeace launched further actions, notably targeting French nuclear testing in the Pacific and, in doing so, becoming 'an increasing source of irritation to the French [authorities]'.[50] The clashes between Greenpeace activists and the French military generated substantial media coverage and were followed by a halting of French tests in 1974. These conflicts continued during new rounds of French testing in 1985 and 1995. The fallout of these clashes was spectacular. In July 1985, French agents detonated two bombs on the Greenpeace vessel Rainbow Warrior, which had been harboured in Auckland, New Zealand, in anticipation of a protest journey to French Polynesia.

The subsequent revelations about French actions generated widespread sympathy for Greenpeace as well as major diplomatic tensions between the French and New Zealand governments.[51] A decade later, the French military stormed another Greenpeace boat, Rainbow Warrior II, which had planned to disrupt French testing in the South Pacific.[52] In discussing the publicity generated by the latter case, the British *Observer* noted that 'Greenpeace's ability to use the moment to get across its message has become near legendary'.[53] Indeed, in 1995, the protests against French testing were but one of two campaigns that resonated widely: having generated publicity through direct action and a consumer boycott, the organization prevented Shell from sinking the Brent Spar, a decommissioned oil rig, into the North Sea.[54] At the end of 1995, the organization's *Annual Report* therefore concluded that its work had gained 'a higher profile than ever before'.[55]

One shared feature of the conflicts on nuclear testing and the Brent Spar was the fact that they occurred in maritime settings. Meanwhile, another campaign on the oceans – namely against whaling – suggested that, while the forms of activism had changed, some concerns linked Greenpeace to earlier conservation efforts. Attempts to protect the species dated back to the interwar years, with the League of Nations developing the project of an international convention on whales – a pioneering step in making the 'the common and solidaric use of a global resource' part of a legal agreement.[56] Over subsequent decades, whales became 'an emotional resource and

Figure 8.1 The Greenpeace boat 'Rainbow Warrior', after French agents had sunk the boat by detonating two bombs in the night of 9 July 1985 (Auckland harbour, image taken on 10 July 1985).
Source: AFP, via Getty Images.

icons' for the environmental movement.[57] While there was hence a broader history, Greenpeace sought not only to ensure compliance with existing agreements but to extend such protection. By 1974, its activism on the seas answered the need to provide 'compelling images' for the cause, as reflected in clashes with Soviet and Japanese whalers.[58] While generally seen as a successful area of Greenpeace activism, internal disputes about campaigning methods produced ruptures: in 1978, a faction that favoured a more confrontational course vis-à-vis whalers departed to found the Sea Shepherd Conservation Society.[59]

Tensions were not, however, confined to tactics, but also derived from the challenges of transnational cooperation. The case of Norway, where a Greenpeace chapter had been established in 1988, highlights such issues. Ongoing Norwegian involvement in whaling resulted in direct Greenpeace actions that came to be known as the 'whale war'.[60] The cache that Greenpeace had accrued in the international realm meant that it was not necessarily the underdog in this context. According to Juliane Riese, who has closely studied this conflict, the Norwegian situation amounted to 'a reversal of Greenpeace's self-perception as environmental Davids fighting the Norwegian whale-butchering Goliaths' as 'Greenpeace and the anti-whaling protest community were perceived by Norwegians as foreign oppressive Goliaths and sentimental hippies attempting to impose cultural imperialism on Norway, the environmental David'.[61] In this context, Norwegian Greenpeace activists disagreed with the methods and concerns of the wider international organization.

Such divisions point to a wider issue, namely the workings of Greenpeace as an organization. During the 1970s, Greenpeace had grown into an international movement, yet, rather than forming a coherent organization, it initially amounted to 'a loose confederation of tribes, each with its own elders, its own internal culture, and its own idea of what Greenpeace was or should become'.[62] Co-founder Robert Hunter recalled that following its initial successes, 'new Greenpeace groups were suddenly forming in our name'.[63] As Frank Zelko has noted, until the creation of more formal structures in the late 1970s, 'the term "Greenpeace" could be used by anyone who supported the cause, without needing to ask the original Vancouver Greenpeace for permission'.[64]

In 1978, Greenpeace established an international secretariat in Amsterdam, and its subsequent growth into a global organization with formal structures generated fresh tensions. This, for instance, was the case when Greenpeace expanded into West Germany in 1980. Despite their enthusiasm about joining forces with the organization, many German activists resented its 'stringent adherence to political neutrality – at least in terms of party politics – and the centralised, hierarchical, corporate-like structure in which a few people made all the important decisions'.[65] Zelko has noted the 'disappointment' by some campaigners that 'Greenpeace Deutschland, like the rest of Greenpeace, never became the idealised version of a democratic, grassroots, and participatory movement that German environmentalists hoped it would'.[66] While such responses might have reflected false expectations, they also pointed at contrasting understandings of what it means to be an activist.

Challenging nuclear power

The professionalization of international organizations such as Greenpeace contrasted with environmentalist practices in which grassroots democracy continued to play a central role. Significantly, in Western Europe, such notions had gained prominence during the 1970s, partly through campaigns against the construction of nuclear power plants. As noted elsewhere in this book, the issue of nuclear radiation had already generated concern in other realms – from campaigns against the spectre of nuclear warfare to Greenpeace action against nuclear testing. Yet in the 1970s and 1980s, protest against nuclear power amounted to 'a global movement'.[67] This issue gained particular urgency when, after the oil crisis of 1973, several countries sought to reduce their dependency on foreign oil by expanding the civilian use of nuclear energy. In resisting such plans, many campaigners deployed repertoires of action that built upon the protest cultures of the late 1960s. According to Christopher Rootes, the rise of anti-nuclear activism was 'crucial in in transmitting the legacy of 1968 to the broad environmental movement'.[68]

The anti-nuclear protests had several transnational dimensions. One aspect was the activism in the border region of Switzerland, France and West Germany, where several new plants were being planned. Significantly, the mobilizations in these contexts involved not only environmentalists and students from nearby universities but also farmers who considered their livelihoods at risk.[69] Such alliances nourished forms of activism that were framed in global terms but rooted in local contexts. The historian Andrew Tompkins has emphasized this aspect by speaking of 'a movement that was both very local and transnational'.[70] The vibrancy of these protests left an impression on activists whose initial political home had been in other political movements. For instance, until the mid-1970s, Petra Kelly's activism had focused on European politics. In 1975, she visited Wyhl, a site of local anti-nuclear protests, together with Jo Leinen who, like Kelly, campaigned for European integration 'from below'. By that point, Wyhl had become the site of major confrontations, with local resistance against the plans for the construction of a new power plant. Kelly and Leinen were inspired by what they observed. As Stephen Milder has put it, the campaigners in these border regions 'physically embodied the internationalist concept of Europe that Kelly and her colleagues in Brussels could only write about in the abstract'.[71]

Transnational links among anti-nuclear campaigners resulted in the transfer of activist strategies. In 1974, German activists had witnessed and supported the occupation of a site designated for a French power plant in Marckolsheim, not far from the German border; in 1975, they drew on this experience when they occupied the site in Wyhl.[72] Yet not all contacts were advantageous, as illustrated by the 1977 protests against the *Superphénix*, a planned reactor in Ceys-Malville, France. A large contingent of Western German protesters came along to these events, alongside activists from Italy, Spain and Switzerland.[73] However, the influx of activists from abroad allowed the French media to portray the protests as alien – at worst, as another German invasion. Moreover, West German activists brought their experience of confrontations with the police to the

French setting, contributing to a situation in which violent clashes adversely affected the image of the protests. Such issues highlighted a wider issue, namely that interpretations of 'civil disobedience' and its meanings could vary across the anti-nuclear movements of different countries.[74]

Unsurprisingly, then, the balance sheet for the anti-nuclear campaigns of the 1970s was uneven. While anti-nuclear campaigners successfully countered some construction plans in West Germany and Switzerland, they were less successful in gaining political support in France. Yet, even in places where the nuclear issue had been less prominent, subsequent developments could change this. In March 1979, a nuclear accident in Harrisburg, Pennsylvania – the Three Mile Island accident – underscored the risks of nuclear technology. In the United States, this case inspired protests among younger activists who evoked the anti-war protests of the preceding generation in their demonstrations against nuclear power.[75] Moreover, the incident also 'created substantial public doubts' regarding the safety of nuclear power in Europe.[76] These events coincided with ongoing efforts to cooperate across national borders. For instance, in June 1979, activists in Western Europe organized 'international days of action' that were dedicated to 'international cooperation against nuclear energy'. To the Swiss participants of this venture, the undertaking stood 'under the banner of a lust for life, of determination and of international solidarity'.[77] To emphasize these values, their own contribution over three days included large-scale demonstrations, evening celebrations as well as an 'international anti-atom forum' with speakers from Austria, France, West Germany and Spain.[78] Transnational ties also became evident in 1980, when French nuclear campaigners invited international participants to join a demonstration against the nuclear fuel reprocessing plant at La Hague – whose designated operation had transnational dimensions as Western European countries and Japan were to send some of their spent nuclear fuel to the site.[79]

In April 1986, the disaster at the Soviet nuclear power plant in Chernobyl highlighted the destructive capacity of nuclear power. As the political scientist Hein-Anton van der Heijden put it, Chernobyl 'had a far-reaching impact on nuclear energy politics, on public opinion with respect to nuclear power, on the anti-nuclear movement and even on the stability of the Soviet and Eastern European political systems'.[80] Greenpeace activists stressed that Chernobyl was but one of many examples that demonstrated the threat posed by nuclear technology and, at the end of the 1980s, expressed the hope that 'the Nuclear Age may be drawing to a close'.[81] That said, the success of subsequent campaigns varied widely. In Italy, large-scale anti-nuclear protests were followed by a successful referendum against the future use of nuclear power in 1988.[82] With regard to French and British responses, the historian Karena Kalmbach has shown how prior histories of activism shaped public perceptions of the disaster.[83] In the Soviet Union and other countries under state-socialist rule, the disaster reinforced domestic discontent, providing further momentum to calls for *perestroika* and reform of the political system. In some parts of the Soviet Union, for instance Lithuania and Ukraine, the response to Chernobyl was entwined with activism for national independence.[84]

Chernobyl's legacy extended well beyond the Cold War, as it continued to shape debates on the risks of nuclear energy. Greenpeace maintained an ongoing effort to document the disaster's long-term impact.[85] Moreover, in 2011, memories of past anti-nuclear activism on the one hand and Chernobyl on the other informed the response to the nuclear disaster in Fukushima, Japan.[86] The combination of these two factors generated particularly widespread protests in Germany, with Chancellor Angela Merkel subsequently announcing a phasing out of nuclear power in her country.[87]

The significant differences in the resonance of anti-nuclear campaigns suggest that national frameworks did matter. This realization is also important in terms of recent scholarship that has highlighted variations in terms of the nature and strength of transnational contacts in the anti-nuclear movements of different countries.[88] At the same time, even beyond NGOs such as Greenpeace and FoE, there were ongoing attempts to launch transnational ventures, in ways that fused anti-nuclear activism with other concerns. The Belgian association *Voor Moeder Aarde* ('For Mother Earth') provides a striking case in this regard. Founded in Ghent in 1991, the group initially focused on indigenous people, with a particular interest in Native Americans. In 1992, it cooperated with American partners in a 'Walk Across America for Mother Earth', which – on the quincentenary of Columbus's transatlantic journey – was cast as a human rights march to protest against 'the violation of Indigenous Peoples' landrights'.[89] Nuclear matters, however, did feature at the march, albeit with a focus on military rather than civilian uses: the final destination of the walk was Nevada – a state that had been the site of nuclear tests since the 1950s. As *Voor Moeder Aarde* activists noted, nuclear testing particularly affected the lands of indigenous people, whether in North America or in the Pacific.[90]

By 1995, the group's extension integrated nuclear energy into another campaigning effort, namely the 'Walk Across Europe for a Nuclear-Free World'. This venture took an international group of activists from Brussels to Moscow, with local stops to stage 'demonstrations, street theatre … and an exhibition'.[91] The targeting of civilian uses of atomic technology in this march was reinforced by the collaboration with the Support Network on Renewable Energy (SNoRE), which aimed at 'spreading information and knowledge about renewable energy and energy efficiency' and contributed a travelling exhibition to the march.[92] Activists symbolically associated different forms of anti-nuclear protest with one another, as the march was timed to reach the vicinity of Chernobyl on 6 August 1995, thus coinciding with the fiftieth anniversary of the Hiroshima bombing.[93] Moreover, the terminus added another symbolic layer, with activists due to reach Red Square on 12 October 1995 – a date that denoted Indigenous Peoples' Day in the United States. Arrests by the Russian police delayed the arrival but one day later, walkers were 'overjoyed to take off their worn-out shoes and dance across the square, until the police compelled them to leave'.[94]

Disappointment about limited media coverage did not deter *Voor Moeder Aarde* from marking the tenth anniversary of Chernobyl with yet another march, this time solely in Ukraine, with the 30 km zone as the final destination of the two-week march, which included fifty protesters from ten countries.[95] This action coincided with *Voor*

Figure 8.2 Russian security forces arrest a participant of the 'Walk Across Europe for a Nuclear-Free World', Moscow, 12 October 1995. *Source:* Alexander Nemenov/AFP, via Getty Images.

Moeder Aarde actions in Belgium, notably 'an overnight vigil' outside a nuclear power plant, and 'Bicycle Tours for a Nuclear-Free World' around different nuclear sites in the Netherlands.[96] Significantly, such actions were far from disconnected from the wider world of pacifist and environmentalist activism: in the 1990s, *Voor Moeder Aarde* maintained connections to Greenpeace and CND; by the early mid-2000s, it became the Belgian section of FoE.[97]

Green politics

The way in which protests against nuclear power could combine with the promotion of other causes pointed to broader vision of 'green politics'.[98] At its most basic level, being 'green' meant to show a dedication to environmental concerns. This included both the older issues of conservation and the protection of nature against pollution but also, in many countries, resistance to nuclear power, with climate change as a particularly prominent issue from the 1990s onwards. Such concerns went together with scepticism about the power of state authorities and private corporations. The anti-nuclear protests of the 1970s deployed and fostered narratives along such lines as they combined local resistance with an attack on political authorities that sought to implement energy policies against the will of local residents.

Within the wider discourse of green politics, the environment was understood as being connected to a range of other causes – as articulated in Petra Kelly's comments cited at the outset of this chapter. Three dimensions were particularly noteworthy. The first was an implicit critique of capitalism and excessive consumption. Seen from this angle, green politics was attractive for activists who had been involved in socialist, communist or anarchist groups during the 1970s. However, such stances were not confined to the left, as they could also revolve around more responsible forms of consumption and stress the need for protecting consumers against profit-making businesses. Pacifism was a second strand: the fact that military conflict and nuclear testing caused damage to nature explains why it could be cast as a 'green issue'. When peace protests experienced a revival in the early 1980s – as discussed in Chapter 3 – green politics was well placed to incorporate it.[99] Thirdly, green politics was construed as part of wider emancipatory movements: in this respect, it could forge alliances with second-wave feminism and LGBT activism.[100]

By the 1980s, green politics had resulted in the creation of new political parties – which often cast themselves as different from established ones and in many cases blurred the boundaries between activism and parliamentary politics. West Germany's *Die Grünen* entered the federal parliament in 1983, with Kelly as one of its most prominent figures. Having been launched at the regional level in 1979, followed by the creation of a national party in 1980, *Die Grünen* brought together disparate elements: it included protagonists from citizens' initiatives, environmental groups and various left-wing factions, as well as a handful of conservatives whose involvement, however, remained more temporary. As a whole, the party reflected broader political shifts that had occurred in the preceding decade. As Stephen Milder has put it, its development was 'the first fruit of a long-developing alternative politics shaped outside the established traditions of electoral politics and leftist resistance'.[101]

Green parties became a home for activists with roots in the protest culture of the 1960s and the 'new social movements' of the 1970s. As noted earlier, Brice Lalonde moved from being a French student leader in 1968 to co-founding *Les Amis de la Terre*. He subsequently participated in campaigns against French nuclear testing, ran as a green candidate for the French presidency (1981), launched the *Génération Écologie* party (1990) and served as French minister of the environment (1991–2).[102] Another prominent face of 1968 who transitioned to green politics was Daniel Cohn-Bendit: having gained prominence during the Parisian student protests and then continued his activism in West German leftist circles, he joined the newly formed *Grünen*. His later career saw him represent both the French and German green parties in the European Parliament. Yet the emergence of green politics was not confined to one particular generation. For example, Freda Weissner-Blau – the co-founder of the Austrian 'greens' – was nearly two decades older than the likes of Lalonde and Cohn-Bendit. Her case further illustrates how environmentalist concerns fed into a worldview that encompassed various issues. For instance, during the 1950s, a stint in the Belgian Congo alerted her to 'the unbearable injustices, the exploitation and oppression that Africans had to suffer' and familiarized her with alternatives to European worldviews.[103] Moreover, while emerging as a prominent figure in the Austrian anti-nuclear movement of the 1970s, she also participated in the Pugwash movement and undertook feminist work in adult education – the latter an activity that she described as 'nearly the most enriching of my entire political and other work'.[104]

It would go beyond the remit of this book to cover the subsequent development of green parties – some of which ended up forming part of government coalitions – but it is worth stressing their heterogeneous nature in the 1970s and 1980s.[105] For instance, countercultural currents were initially less prominent in Ecology – a British party founded in 1973 and the forerunner of what became the Green Party in 1985. Meanwhile, in France, one of the leading figures in green politics, Antoine Waechter, cast his political efforts as being 'neither left nor right'.[106] One shared feature of green parties, however, was the intention to do things differently, by eschewing formal party hierarchies, promoting gender parity within their ranks and rejecting some of the formalities associated with established politics. This approach formed part of a wider vision in which parliamentary politics not seen as the main raison d'être for green parties. As Petra Kelly put it in 1982,

> We will not do societal change just through the parliament. Our hope it to change Europe and to change society, and to change the system, structurally and non-violently, on the street. Parliament is just part of the strategy; it's a place where you can make your goals known, but sharing power or becoming a green minister ... has nothing to do with societal change.[107]

Over time, most green parties shed many of their activist characteristics and began to resemble more traditional parties, reflecting a 'difficult path from amateur-activist to professional-electoral logics'.[108] One aspect that they maintained, however, was the embrace of a transnational frames and patterns of cooperation. According to Heikki Patomäki and Teivo Teivainen, ties between green parties from different countries could 'be considered distant offspring of the earlier internationalisms' – thus resembling the socialist and communist cooperation in previous periods – yet they also seem to 'have a more global and post-national identity than traditional Internationals'.[109]

After the end of the communist dictatorships, green parties also emerged in different parts of Central and European Europe. In some instances, they built on existing movements, as environmental pollution seemed to signify a wider malaise of the political system. In Czechoslovakia, some issues with environmental pollution under state socialism had been acknowledged publicly but attempts to disguise other problems from the wider public meant that the state of the environment fed in with wider dissident critiques.[110] For instance, in the 1980s, members of the Charter 77 human rights group shared a censored report on environmental pollution via the foreign media.[111] In such cases, environmental concerns could be integrated into the human rights discourses that have been discussed in the preceding chapter. In other instances, green perspectives could appeal to dissidents who had been looking for a different kind of politics. This aspect was exemplified in 1980, when the exiled East German dissident and philosopher Rudolf Bahro joined *Die Grünen* and published a book that cast political ecology as an alternative to state socialism.[112] After 1990, however, the fate of green parties in Central and Eastern European parties was mixed.[113] Indeed, a study of environmentalism in Slovakia has suggested that the transnational ties and outlook of many 'green' protagonists – whether in parties or groups – could become an obstacle in a context where national framings proved politically powerful.[114]

International organizations, NGOs and sustainable development

Nature and the environment were not only activist concerns: the management of the natural habitat emerged as a subject for state planning and intervention, giving rise to a phenomenon that some scholars have described as 'the nature state'.[115] Yet, with environmental issues transcending national boundaries, such action was not confined to the sphere of governmental action but also entered the intergovernmental realm. During the interwar period, the League of Nations became a potential target for promoting the protection of nature.[116] Moreover, with rural regions featuring prominently in emerging discourse on international development, 'the countryside' became the focus for different transnational exchanges and initiatives in this era.[117]

After the Second World War, the United Nations system built upon these efforts and moved beyond them. Anna-Katharina Wöbse has argued that Julian Huxley, first Secretary General of UNESCO, and some like-minded people 'set off on the small path towards global nature protection' that had been mapped out by the League of Nations but – in reflection of the post-war era's ambitions – extended that path 'into a multi-track road'.[118] These post-war efforts operated at the nexus of policy, expertise and activism. For instance, while UNESCO expressed its concern for nature under Huxley's leadership, he was also influential in the foundation of the (non-governmental) International Union for the Protection of Nature. Moreover, over the subsequent decades, the United Nations system provided formal channels for its interactions with NGOs, with the creation of the UN Environmental Programme (UNEP) in 1972 adding to existing arrangements that, by that point, already involved a range of agencies and commissions.[119]

UNEP was one of the outcomes of the UN Conference on the Human Environment, held in Stockholm in 1972. Simone Schleper has argued that the event 'has entered the history books as the moment when the world community turned the global environment into a topic for international politics and diplomacy'.[120] This was not just a shift in discourse, but also provided new openings for activists. According to the historian Stephen Macekura, 'The Stockholm Conference … signaled the rapid broadening of what quickly became called the "environmental movement"', moving beyond the approaches of well-established associations such as IUCN and WWF.[121] While IUCN and WWF played a prominent role in planning the conference, other groups 'focused on grassroots mobilization outside the conference walls'. As a result, an official NGO event, the so-called 'Environment Forum', was complemented by a 'People's Forum' that linked the environment and economic development with questions of peace and social equality.

According to Macekura, such interactions, as well as the growing room for voices from the Global South, gave shape to the concept of sustainable development, in which Western environmentalists began to acknowledge the significance of issues such as 'poverty eradication, the pursuit of socio-economic equality between countries, and economic development as a political right for developing nations'.[122] In the 1980s, the UN itself nourished an integrated treatment of these issues through its World Commission on Environment and Development, headed by the Norwegian politician Gro Brundtland.[123] The Brundtland Commission's 1987 report laid the ground for another landmark UN conference: the Earth Summit in Rio. As with the Stockholm Conference, the gathering in Rio provided room for representatives from within civil society. At the same time, it also involved fresh conflicts, because to some, 'the notion of environmental scrutiny of development projects in the Third World smacked of cultural imperialism', as the historian Jay Winter put it.[124] Such tensions also became evident among activists: for instance, in 2007, a controversy erupted within the Climate Action Network, which had been formed after the Rio Summit and brought together different environmental NGOs. At its meeting in Bali, some members argued that the network was neglecting critical perspectives, especially from the Global South.[125]

The approach of activists in the post-Rio era had several elements. Firstly, it included an ongoing role for 'expert-activists': individuals who could provide scientific credibility to particular causes and urge action, for instance on the defining environmental issue of the twenty-first century, namely climate change. Secondly, it included holding governments and international institutions to account – with environmental NGOs urging action or drawing attention to the inadequate implementation of international agreements. This development also involved groups that had not originated in the environmental realm.[126] Thirdly, the interaction between environmental NGOs and international institutions could build on notions of partnership. Groups such as Greenpeace increasingly geared some their efforts towards working with the European Union.[127] In that respect, groups that had been associated with protest could be integrated into an existing system, with both limitations and opportunities. For instance, a study of environmental NGOs in Bosnia has noted that such groups have only had limited success at mobilizing activists but, at the same time, have been successful in attracting funding from European sources.[128] These observations further illustrate how transnational ties could address relative marginality at the national level.

Yet alongside these three approaches, a fourth approach that gained prominence in the 2000s focused less on working *with* international organizations, but rather used the meetings of particular bodies to stage global protests. This included a more confrontational stance, as reflected in support for direct action, as well as links to the growing global justice movement whose activities have been discussed in Chapter 4. In 2008, this trend was exemplified by the creation of Climate Justice Action whose position, according to social scientist Ruth Reitan, 'bordered on antagonism towards the United Nations and the interstate system and instead championed solutions to the climate crisis emanating from grassroots, workers and popular social movements linked into a global movement of movements'.[129]

Tackling climate change

As ventures such as the Climate Action Network and Climate Justice Action indicate, the issue of global warming became a major focus for the environmental movement. At the same time, the cause itself highlighted the malleability of transnational activism: while environmentalists mobilized across national borders and deployed expertise to this end, so did various groups that denied the existence of global warming, or that downplayed its risks. In many instances, such campaigns were steered by groups that, while presenting themselves as independent, were bankrolled by businesses with a vested interest.[130] Importantly, climate change denial intersected with other forms of activism. The way in which the Sweden Democrats – a party with roots in neofascist groups – integrated hostility to climate action into a far-right agenda was but one example.[131] Such connections extended to the online sphere, as illustrated by the links between climate-change-denying and far-right blogs in Germany and the United States.[132]

These observations underscore the ambivalent nature of transnational activism. Moreover, even within groups that agreed on the need for action in the face of the climate emergency, there were evident tensions. Two ventures that both emerged at the end of the 2010s indicated this diversity of potential approaches – on the one hand Extinction Rebellion, which was created in 2018 by British activists Roger Hallam and Gail Bradbrook, and on the other hand the 'School Strike for Climate' (also known as 'Fridays for Future') that were launched by the Swedish school student Greta Thunberg as a protest against the older generation's inaction on climate change.

Extinction Rebellion has mostly attracted attention through the use of blockades and other forms of disruption.[133] While the movement has grown internationally, responses to its approach have been mixed, as some 'actions have resulted in backlashes, from both members and wider society'.[134] In this respect, the movement's approach echoed other campaigns in which activists saw the urgency of their cause as a justification for particular transgressions. Alongside its embrace of direct action, Extinction Rebellion picked up the discourse of grassroots democracy which, as noted above, also featured in other varieties of green discourse. As a reflection of such ideas, the movement proposed the creation of a Citizens' Assembly on Climate and Ecological Justice. It claimed that elected representatives were 'not representative' and that instead solutions for the climate crisis should be developed based on the discussion of 'people from different walks of life (gender, age, ethnicity etc)' who would be 'randomly selected like a jury'.[135] Such statements – along with self-representations of forming a decentralized movement – have created the 'fantasy of a leaderless organization'.[136] Yet on closer inspection, the movement has also been a site in which power is exercised in different, albeit perhaps less overt ways.[137]

From a very different perspective, the School Strikes for Climate have also raised the question of leadership, because the campaign has been widely associated with the figure of Greta Thunberg. A comparative perspective, however, reveals a more nuanced picture. A survey among 'Fridays for Future' participants from seven European countries suggested that only in Sweden, Thunberg's home country, did respondents attribute their participation in the school strikes to Thunberg's example. Moreover, on the question of whether Thunberg had stimulated their interest in climate change, only 37 per cent of the respondents from different countries answered in affirmative terms.[138] Such aspects point to a wider issue: while media representations have often focused on the figure of Thunberg, the campaign itself has operated in a highly decentralized fashion. Social media has played a strong role in this regard. An analysis of Twitter references on 5 May 2019 – a day that saw an estimated 1.4 million participants in over 100 countries – has shown that 53.1 per cent of tweets focused on local settings, with global references coming second (18.4 per cent).[139] Obviously, such statistics need to be approached with caution, as the global issue at stake is self-evident; nonetheless, such examples indicate the movement's ability to root itself in local settings.

The local reference points of 'Fridays for Future' protests also suggest that the background and origins of the participants matter. Scholars have acknowledged that 'young people's access to strikes is highly uneven', with a prevalence in cities and in the Global North.[140] Data from the summer of 2019 listed Germany, Italy and Sweden as the countries with the highest number of school strikes. As one recent study on 'uneven solidarity' has noted, 'For many young people around the world, accessing education is a priority and a luxury, often threatened by weather events and family poverty.'[141] In this

Figure 8.3 Greta Thunberg and other participants of the 'School Strike for Climate' outside the Swedish parliament, Stockholm, 28 August 2018. *Source:* Michael Campanella, via Getty Images.

respect, the ability to participate in a school strike could reflect particular privileges, which accounted for the prevalence of such activism in the Global North.[142]

More generally, campaigns on climate change raise questions about underlying continuities in the history of activism. Strikes have been a longstanding feature of social movements, and even before 'Fridays of Future', 'school strikes' had been used for particular causes, albeit on a smaller scale.[143] Moreover, these ventures can be seen as part of a wider story of young people acting as activists; as highlighted by other parts of this book, this phenomenon also included anticolonial student activists, youth participation in humanitarian relief, pacifist ventures aimed at youth as well as the generational dimensions of the 1968 protests.[144] Furthermore, like other forms of activism – both on the environment and more generally – international institutions were the focus of hopes for meaningful change. This was the case when, in 2019, Greta Thunberg addressed the UN's Climate Action Summit. Thunberg framed her concerns in drastic terms, proclaiming to the delegates that 'you are failing us' and arguing that 'the young people are starting to understand your betrayal'.[145] Her speech was far from the first time that activist rhetoric had been carried into an international assembly, yet the fact that UN press releases explicitly publicized the statement was notable, in a way amplifying such criticisms. At the same time, the focus on global warming as a matter of survival points at two different strands in transnational activism: on the one hand, one in which a particular issue – whether it is the struggle against climate change or the overcoming of class-based oppression – takes priority of other concerns, and, on the other, one that treats different ideas and interests as intrinsically connected phenomena.

Notes

1. Petra Kelly, interviewed by Trevor Hyett on 'Afternoon Plus', Thames Television, 25 November 1982, available online https://www.youtube.com/watch?v=D_HTSQbeZhI (last accessed 9 January 2023).
2. Saskia Richter, 'Petra Kelly als Mittlerin in der transnationalen Friedensbewegung gegen den NATO-Doppelbeschluss', *Moving the Social* 44 (2010): 21–42.
3. Stephen Milder, 'Thinking Globally, Acting (Trans-)Locally: Petra Kelly and the Transnational Roots of West German Green Politics', *Central European History* 43, no. 2 (2010): 301–26, at 308.
4. Petra Kelly interviewed by Trevor Hyett on Thames Television, 25 November 1982.
5. For overviews, see Ramachandra Guha, *Environmentalism: A Global History* (London: Longman, 2016); Marco Armiero and Lise Sedrez, 'Introduction', in *A History of Environmentalism: Local Struggles, Global Histories*, ed. Marco Armiero and Lise Sedrez (London: Bloomsbury, 2014), 1–20.
6. Joachim Radkau, *The Age of Ecology*, trans. Patrick Camiller (Cambridge: Polity Press, 2014), 11.

7. Jan-Henrik Meyer, 'From Nature to Environment: International Organizations and Environmental Protection before Stockholm', in *International Organizations and Environmental Protection: Conservation and Globalization in the Twentieth Century*, ed. Wolfram Kaiser and Jan-Henrik Meter (New York: Berghahn, 2017), esp. 33–6.
8. Anna-Katharina Wöbse and Patrick Kupper, 'Epilogue: The Nature of Europe', in *Greening Europe: Environmental Protection in the Long Twentieth Century – A Handbook*, ed. Anna-Katharina Wöbse and Patrick Kupper (Berlin: De Gruyter, 2022), 447–51.
9. Abigail Dowling and Richard Keyser, eds, *Conservation's Roots: Managing for Sustainability in Preindustrial Europe, 1100–1800* (New York: Berghahn, 2020).
10. Robert Falkner, *Environmentalism and Global International Society* (Cambridge: Cambridge University Press, 2021), 48–50.
11. Corey Ross, *Ecology and Power in the Age of Empire: Europe and the Transformation of the Tropical World* (Oxford: Oxford University Press, 2017); Bernhard Gissibl, *The Nature of German Imperialism: Conservation and the Politics of Wildlife in Colonial East Africa* (New York: Berghahn, 2016).
12. Bill Kovarik, 'Endangered Species, News, and Public Policy: A History', in *Communicating Endangered Species: Extinction, News and Public Policy*, ed. Eric Freedman, Sara Shipley Hiles and David Sachsman (Abingdon: Routledge, 2021), 23–43.
13. Charlotte Epstein, 'The Making of Global Environmental Norms: Endangered Species Protection', *Global Environmental Politics* 6, no. 2 (2006): 37.
14. Countess of Aberdeen, ed., *Women in Social Life: The Transactions of the Social Section of the International Congress of Women, London, July 1899* (London: T. Fisher Unwin, 1899), 236–62.
15. Speech by Etta Lemon (listed as 'Mrs F. E. Lemon') in Aberdeen, *Women in Social Life*, 237.
16. Mieke Rascher, 'Engagement und Emanzipation: Frauen in der englischen Tierbewegung', in *Tierische Geschichte: Die Beziehung von Mensch und Tier in der Kultur der Moderne*, ed. Dorothee Brantz and Christof Mauch (Leiden: Brill, 2010), 286–303.
17. 'Der Vogelschutz im Auslande', 'Der Vogelschutz auf internationalen Kongressen' and Carl Heuß, 'Die Notwendigkeit und Form einer permanenten internationalen Verbindung zwischen den Vogelschutzvereinigungen der Kulturstaaten', all in *Jahrbuch für die Jahre 1909/11*, ed. Internationaler Frauenbund für Vogelschutz (Deutsche Abteilung) (Berlin: Internationaler Frauenbund für Vogelschutz, 1912), 134, 156–8 and 165–72 respectively.
18. 'Zusammenfassung des Vorstandes' and 'Allgemeiner Geschäftsbericht', both in Internationaler Frauenbund, *Jahrbuch*, 1–3.
19. Corey Ross, 'Tropical Nature as Global Patrimoine: Imperialism and International Nature Protection in the Early Twentieth Century', *Past & Present* 226, supp. no. 10 (2015): 222. See also Bernhard Gißibl, 'Paradiesvögel: Kolonialer Naturschutz und die Mode der deutschen Frau am Anfang des 20. Jahrhunderts', in *Ritual – Macht – Natur. Europä- isch-ozeanische Beziehungswelten in der Neuzeit*, ed. Johannes Paulmann et al. (Bremen: Übersemuseum, 2005), 131–54.
20. Gissibl, *The Nature of German Imperialism*, 246.
21. Patricia Putschert and Harald Fischer-Tiné, eds, *Colonial Switzerland: Rethinking Colonialism from the Margins* (Basingstoke: Palgrave, 2015); Bernhard Schär, 'Switzerland, Borneo and the Dutch Indies: Towards a New Imperial History of Europe, c. 1770–1850', *Past & Present*, advance access via https://doi.org/10.1093/pastj/gtab045 (last accessed 9 January 2023). International protection efforts formed part of wider Swiss foreign policy

that revolved around international ventures in this specific field as well as other forms of internationalism: Madeleine Herren, *Hintertüren zur Macht: Internationalismus und modernisierungsorientierte Außenpolitik in Belgien, der Schweiz und den USA 1865–1914* (Munich: Oldenbourg, 2000), 344–62.

22. Anna-Katharina Wöbse, *Weltnaturschutz: Umweltdiplomatie im Völkerbund und den Vereinten Nationen 1920–1950* (Frankfurt: Campus, 2012), 43.
23. *Recueil des procès-verbaux de la Conférence internationale pour la protection de la nature, Berne, 17–19 novembre 1913* (Bern: K. J. Wyss, 1913). See also Anna-Katharina Wöbse, 'Separating Spheres: Paul Sarasin and His Global Nature Protection Scheme', *Australian Journal of Politics and History* 61, no. 3 (2015): 339–51; Fenneke Sysling, '"Protecting the Primitive Natives": Indigenous People as Endangered Species in the Early Nature Protection Movement, 1900–1940', *Environment and History* 21, no. 3 (2015): 381–99; Ross, 'Tropical Nature as Global *Patrimoine*', 225–8.
24. Meyer, 'From Nature to Environment', 39.
25. Frank Uekötter, *The Green and the Brown: A History of Conservation in Nazi Germany* (Cambridge: Cambridge University Press, 2006).
26. Anna-Katharina Wöbse, 'Lina Hähnle und der Reichsbund für Vogelschutz: Naturbewegung im Gleichschritt', in *Naturschutz im Nationalsozialismus*, ed. Joachim Radkau and Frank Uekötter (Frankfurt/Main: Campus, 2003), 309–28.
27. Wöbse, *Weltnaturschutz*, 77–90.
28. Meyer, 'From Nature to Environment', 41.
29. Falkner, *Environmentalism and Global International Society*, 100; Meyer, 'From Nature to Environment', 44.
30. Raf de Bont, *Nature's Diplomats: Science, Internationalism, and Preservation, 1920–1960* (Pittsburgh, PA: University of Pittsburgh Press, 2021), 7.
31. Patrick Kupper, 'Translating Yellowstone: Early European National Parks, *Weltnaturschutz* and the Swiss Model' and Anna-Katharina Wöbse, 'Framing the Heritage of Mankind: National Parks on the International Agenda', both in *Civilizing Nature: National Parks in Global Historical Perspective*, ed. Bernhard Gissibl, Sabine Höhler and Patrick Kupper (New York: Berghahn, 2012), 123–56.
32. Meyer, 'From Nation to Environment', 43.
33. Simone Schleper, *Planning for the Planet: Environmental Expertise and the International Union for Conservation of Nature and Natural Resources, 1960–1980* (New York: Berghahn, 2019), 5.
34. Anna-Katharina Wöbse and Hans-Peter Ziemek, 'Restoring, Reintroducing, Rewilding: Creating European Wildnerness', in Kupper and Wöbse, *Greening Europe*, 89.
35. See, for example, its release of a charity album featuring The Beatles: 'No One's Gonna Change Our World' (Starline/Regal LP, 1969).
36. Rachel Carson, *Silent Spring* (New York: Houghton Mifflin, 1962), 8.
37. Chad Montrie, *The Myth of Silent Spring: Rethinking the Origins of American Environmentalism* (Oakland, CA: University of California Press, 2018).
38. On this, see the '*Silent Spring*, an International Bestseller', part of the virtual exhibition by Mark Stoll, 'Rachel Carson's Silent Spring, a Book That Changed the World' (Rachel Carson Centre), online via https://www.environmentandsociety.org/exhibitions/rachel-carsons-silent-spring/silent-spring-international-best-seller (last accessed 9 January 2023). See also

Mark Hamilton Lytle, *The Gentle Subversive: Rachel Carson, Silent Spring and the Rise of the Environmental Movement* (New York: Oxford University Press, 2007).

39. Donella H. Meadows et al., *The Limits to Growth: A Report for the Club of Rome Project on the Predicament of Mankind* (Washington, DC: Pontomac Associates, 1972), 23.
40. Elodie Vieille Blanchard, 'Modelling the Future: An Overview of the "Limits to Growth" Debate', *Centaurus* 52, no. 2 (2010): 91–116; Patrick Kupper and Elke Seefried, '"A Computer's Vision of Doomsday": On the History of the 1972 Study *The Limits to Growth*', in *Exploring Apocalyptica: Coming to Terms with Environmental Alarmism*, ed. Frank Uekötter (Pittsburgh, PA: University of Pittsburgh Press, 2018), 49–74. Some critiques focused on potential neo-Malthusian readings of the report. One recent study has referred to the report as 'a computer-aided version of Malthusian environmental arguments': Thomas Robertson, *The Malthusian Moment: Global Population Growth and the Birth of American Environmentalism* (New Brunswick, NJ: Rutgers University Press, 2012), 180.
41. Christopher Rootes, 'The Transformation of Environmental Activism: An Introduction', in *Environmental Protest in Western Europe*, ed. Christopher Rootes (Oxford: Oxford University Press, 2007), 1–19.
42. Clare Saunders, *Environmental Networks and Social Movement Theory* (London: Bloomsbury, 2013).
43. Akira Iriye and Petra Goedde, *International History: A Cultural Approach* (London: Bloomsbury, 2022), 215–16 and 226. With a focus on Earth Day activities in the United States, including their limitations, see Amy Fried, 'US Environmental Interest Groups and the Promotion of Environmental Values: The Resounding Success and Failure of Earth Day', *Environmental Politics* 7, no. 4 (1998): 1–22.
44. Asger Hougaard, 'The Founding of the Danish Environmental Movement NOAH', *Arcadia*, no. 18 (2019), via *Environment & Society Portal*, http://doi.org/10.5282/rcc/8563 (last accessed 9 January 2023).
45. Robert Lamb, in association with Friends of the Earth, *Promising the Earth* (Abingdon: Routledge, 1996), 34.
46. Stephen Macekura, *Of Limits and Growth: The Rise of Global Sustainable Development in the Twentieth Century* (Cambridge: Cambridge University Press, 2015), 101.
47. Lamb, *Promising the Earth*, 35.
48. Frank Zelko, 'Scaling Greenpeace: From Local Activism to Global Governance', *Historical Social Research* 42, no. 2 (2017): 325.
49. Frank Zelko, *Make It a Green Peace! The Rise of Countercultural Environmentalism* (New York: Oxford University Press, 2013).
50. Zelko, 'Scaling Greenpeace', 327.
51. G. P. Taylor, 'Victim or Aggressor? New Zealand and the Rainbow Warrior Affair', *Journal of Imperial and Commonwealth History* 22, no. 3 (1994): 512–30.
52. See e.g. 'Greenpeace Ship Stormed by French Commandos', *The Guardian*, 10 July 1995, 1; 'France Seizes 2 Ships Owned by Greenpeace', *New York Times*, 2 September 1995, 1.
53. Polly Ghazi, 'Greenpeace Wins War of Words', *The Observer*, 3 September 1995, 16. For a similar assessment, see Wolfgang Sachs, 'All the World's a Stage: Why Is Greenpeace So Successful?', *The Guardian*, 20 September 1995, 4.
54. Grant Jordan, *Shell, Greenpeace and the Brent Spar* (Basingstoke: Palgrave, 2001); Anna-Katharina Wöbse, 'Greenpeace and the Brent Spar Campaign: A Platform for Several Truths', in Uekötter, *Exploring Apocalyptica*, 129–49.

55. Greenpeace, *Annual Report 95* (Amsterdam: Greenpeace, 1995), 2.
56. Wöbse, *Weltnaturschutz*, 234.
57. Ibid., 241. See also Keith D. Suter, 'The International Politics of Saving the Whale', *Australian Journal of International Affairs* 35, no. 3 (1981): 283–94.
58. Zelko, *Make It a Green Peace*, 225.
59. Rik Scarce, *Understanding the Radical Environmental Movement* (updated edn; Walnut Creek, CA: Left Coast Press, 2006), ch. 6.
60. Juliane Riese, *Hairy Hippies and Bloody Butchers: The Greenpeace Anti-Whaling Campaign in Norway* (New York: Berghahn, 2017), 51.
61. Riese, *Hairy Hippies and Bloody Butchers*, 30.
62. Zelko, 'Scaling Greenpeace', 333.
63. Robert Hunter, *The Greenpeace Chronicle* (London: Picador, 1980), 239.
64. Zelko, 'Scaling Greenpeace', 328.
65. Frank Zelko, 'The Umweltmulti Arrives: Greenpeace and Grass Roots Environmentalism in West Germany', *Australian Journal of Politics & History* 61, no. 3 (2015): 401.
66. Zelko, 'The *Umweltmulti* Arrives', 413.
67. Astrid Mignon Kirchhof and Jan-Henrik Meyer, 'Global Protest against Nuclear Power: Transfer and Transnational Exchange in the 1970s and 1980s', *Historical Social Research* 39, no. 1 (2014): 179.
68. Christopher Rootes, 'The Environmental Movement', in Klimke and Scharloth, *1968 in Europe*, 300.
69. Stephen Milder, *Greening Democracy: The Anti-Nuclear Movement and Political Environmentalism in West Germany and Beyond, 1968–1983* (Cambridge: Cambridge University Press, 2017).
70. Andrew Tompkins, *Better Active Than Radioactive! Anti-Nuclear Protest in 1970s France and West Germany* (Oxford: Oxford University Press, 2016), 7. See also Andrew Tompkins, 'Grassroots Transnationalism(s): Franco-German Opposition to Nuclear Energy in the 1970s', *Contemporary European History* 25, no. 1 (2016): 117–42.
71. Milder, 'Thinking Globally, Acting (Trans-)Locally', 318.
72. Tompkins, *Better Active Than Radioactive*, 88–9 and 159.
73. Andrew Tompkins, 'Transnationality as a Liability? The Anti-Nuclear Movement at Malville', *Revue belge de philologie et d'histoire* 89, nos. 3–4 (2011): 1365–79. See also Tompkins, *Better Active Than Radioactive!*, 90 and 168–71.
74. Michael L. Hughes, 'Civil Disobedience in Transnational Perspective: American and West German Anti-Nuclear-Power Protesters', *Historical Social Research* 39, no. 1 (2014): 236–53.
75. Dario Fazzi, 'The Nuclear Freeze Generation: The Early 1970s Anti-Nuclear Movement between "Carter's Vietnam" and "Euroshima", in *A European Youth Revolt: European Perspectives on Youth Protest and Social Movements in the 1980s*, ed. Knud Andresen and Bart van der Steen (Basingstoke: Palgrave, 2016), 149.
76. Russell Dalton, 'The Environmental Movement in Western Europe', in *Environmental Politics in the International Arena: Movements, Parties, Organizations, and Policy*, ed. Sheldon Kamieniecki (Albany, NY: State University of New York Press, 1993), 58.
77. Sozialarchiv, Zürich, AR201.130 ('Dokumentation Anti-AKW-Bewegung'): Nationale Koordination der Schweizer AKW-Gegner Bern, 'Pfingsten 79 gegen Atomenergie'.

78. AR201.130: 'Internationale Demonstrationstage gegen die Atomenergie: Pfingstmarsch 79'.
79. AR201.130:'Kommt mit nach La Hague' (1980).
80. Hein-Anton van der Heijden, 'The Great Fear: European Environmentalism in the Atomic Age', in Armiero and Sedrez, *A History of Environmentalism*, 198.
81. Andy Stirling, 'The End of the Nuclear Dream', in *The Greenpeace Book of the Nuclear Age: The Hidden History, the Human Cost*, ed. John May (London: Victor Gollancz, 1989), 337.
82. van der Heijden, 'The Great Fear', 200.
83. Karena Kalmbach, *The Meanings of a Disaster: Chernobyl and Its Afterlives in Britain and France* (New York: Berghahn, 2021).
84. van der Heijden, 'The Great Fear', 199; Tetiana Perga, 'The Fallout of Chernobyl: The Emergence of an Environmental Movement in the Ukrainian Soviet Socialist Republic', in *Environmental Policy and Social Movements in Communist and Capitalist Countries 1945–1990*, ed. Astrid Mignon Kirchhof and J. R. McNeill (Pittsburgh, PA: University of Pittsburgh Press, 2019), 55–72.
85. David Santillo et al., eds, *The Chernobyl Catastrophe: Consequences on Human Health* (Amsterdam: Greenpeace, 2006).
86. Kalmbach, *The Meanings of a Disaster*, 6.
87. van der Heijden, 'The Great Fear', 204.
88. Eva Oberloskamp, 'Ambiguities of Transnationalism: Social Opposition to the Civil Use of Nuclear Power in the United Kingdom and in West Germany during the 1970s', *European Review of History* 29, no. 3 (2022): 417–51.
89. AMSAB, 294.3.5/294.0087: Fax 'Our Story – For Mother Earth'.
90. AMSAB, Ghent, 294.3.5/294.0087: 'Nuclear Testing and Indigenous People', doc. *c*. October 1995.
91. AMSAB, Ghent, 294/125: Leaflet 'Walk across Europe … For a Nuclear-Free World (Nederland)'.
92. Fax, 'Our Story – For Mother Earth'; and 'Support Network on Reneweable Energy', https://snore.org/snore/ (last accessed 9 January 2023).
93. See the announcement in AMSAB, Ghent 294/125: 'Persbericht: Geert, Katrien, Kristof, Marjan en Annelies stapen volgend jar 5.500 km van Brussel naar Moskou' (1994).
94. 'Walk across Europe '95 – Slot: Negen maan internationaal stappen … Een terugblik', *Voor Moeder Aarde* 5, no. 2 (1996): 4.
95. 'Tsjernobyl 10+: Stappen naaar de 30 km zone van Tsjernobyl', *Bulletin Voor Moeder Aarde* 5, no. 2 (1996): 4.
96. AMSAB, Ghent, 294.3.7/294.00101: Press release dated 24 April 1995.
97. Friends of the Earth International, *Annual Report 2004* (Amsterdam: FoE, 2004), 6; 'Voor Moeder Aarde met nieuwe naam en logo', *De Standaard*, 1 January 2007, available at https://www.standaard.be/cnt/b361640070101 (last accessed 9 January 2023).
98. Peter Newell, *Global Green Politics* (Cambridge: Cambridge University Press, 2020); Andrew Dobson, *Green Political Thought* (4th edn; Abingdon: Routledge, 2007); Douglas Togerson, *The Promise of Green Politics: Environmentalism and the Public Sphere* (Durham, NC: Duke University Press, 1999).
99. Silke Mende and Birgit Metzger, 'Eco-Pacifism: The Environmental Movement as a Source for the Peace Movement', in *The Nuclear Crisis: The Arms Race, Cold War Anxiety, and the German Peace Movement of the 1980s*, ed. Christoph Becker-Schaum et al. (New York: Berghahn, 2016), 119–37.

100. K. J. Warren, *Ecofeminist Philosophy: A Western Perspective on What It Is and Why It Matters* (Lanham, MD: Rowman & Littlefield, 2000).
101. Milder, 'Thinking Globally, Acting (Trans-)Locally', 326.
102. Joseph Zarka, *The Shaping of Environmental Policy in France* (New York: Berghahn, 2002), 48–69.
103. Freda Meissner-Blau, *Die Frage bleibt: 88 Lern- und Wanderjahre. Im Gespräch mit Gert Dressel* (Vienna: Amalthea Signum Verlag, 2014), 146.
104. Meissner-Blau, *Die Frage bleibt*, 162 (on Pugwash) and 166 (on adult education).
105. For an overview, see Emilie van Haute, ed., *Green Parties in Europe* (Abingdon: Routledge, 2016).
106. Szarka, *The Shaping of Environmental Policy in France*, 63–5.
107. Petra Kelly interviewed by Trevor Hyett on Thames Television, 25 November 1982.
108. Benoit Rihoux, 'Green Party Organisations: The Difficult Path from Amateur-Activist to Professional-Electoral Logics', in van Haute, *Green Parties in Europe*, 298–314.
109. Heikki Patomäki and Teivo Teivainen, 'Researching Global Political Parties', in *Global Political Parties*, ed. Katarina Sehm-Patomäki and Marko Ulvila (London: Zed Books, 2007), 95.
110. Alexandra Wedl, 'Green Volunteers in Czechoslovakia: The Youth Magazine Mladý svět and Its Environmental Campaign, 1970s–1980s', *Labour History Review* 86, no. 3 (2021): 397–423.
111. Doubravka Olšáková, 'Environmental Journalism? Radio Free Europe, Charter 77 and the Making of an Environmental Agenda', *Environment and History* 28, no. 2 (2022): 203–27.
112. Rudolf Bahro, *Elemente einer neuen Politik: Zum Verhältnis von Ökologie und Sozialismus* (Berlin: Olle & Wolter, 1980).
113. E. Gene Frankland, 'Central and Eastern European Green Parties: Rise, Fall and Revival', in van Haute, *Green Parties in Europe*, 59–91.
114. Edward K. Snadjr, *Nature Protests: The End of Ecology in Slovakia* (Seattle, WA: University of Washington Press, 2008).
115. Wilko Graf von Hardenberg, Matthew Kelly, Claudia Leal and Emily Wakild, eds, *The Nature State: Rethinking the History of Conservation* (Abingdon: Routledge, 2017).
116. Wöbse, *Weltnaturschutz*.
117. Some of these developments can be traced back to the interwar years: Liesbeth van de Grift and Amalia Ribi Forclaz, eds, *Governing the Rural in Interwar Europe* (Abingdon: Routledge, 2017).
118. Wöbse, *Weltnaturschutz*, 287–8.
119. Maria Ivanova, *The Untold Story of the World's Leading Environmental Institution: UNEP at Fifty* (Boston, MA: MIT Press, 2021).
120. Schleper, *Planning for the Planet*, 96.
121. Macekura, *Of Limits and Growth*, 92. On the tensions that manifested themselves in this context, see e.g. Keck and Sikkink, *Activists beyond Borders*, ch. 4.
122. Macekura, *Of Limits and Growth*, 8.
123. Iris Borowy, *Defining Sustainable Development for Our Common Future: A History of the World Commission on Environment and Development (Brundtland Commission)*

(Abingdon: Routledge, 2014). The World Commission's report was entitled *Our Common Future* (Oxford: Oxford University Press, 1987).
124. Jay Winter, *Dreams of Peace and Freedom: Utopian Moments in the Twentieth Century* (New Haven, CT: Yale University Press, 2004), 180.
125. Ruth Reitan, 'Coordinated Power in Contemporary Leftist Activism', in Olesen, *Power and Transnational Activism*, 60.
126. Victor Silverman, 'Sustainable Alliances: The Origins of International Labor Environmentalism', *International Labor & Working-Class History* 66 (2004): 118–35.
127. Liesbeth van de Grift, Hans Rodenburg and Guus Wieman, 'Entering the European Political Arena, Adapting to Europe: Greenpeace International, 1987–93', in *The Environment and the European Public Sphere: Perceptions, Actors, Policies*, ed. Christian Wenkel et al. (Winwick: White Horse Press, 2020), 147–64.
128. Adam Fagan and Indraneel Sircar, 'Environmental Movement Activism in the Western Balkans: Evidence from Bosnia-Herzegovina', in Jacobsson and Saxonberg, *Beyond NGO-ization*, 213–36.
129. Reitan, 'Coordinated Power', 67.
130. Naomi Oreskes and Erik Conway, *Merchants of Doubt: How a Handful of Scientists Obscured the Truth on Issues from Tobacco Smoke to Global Warming* (London: Bloomsbury, 2010); David Michaels, *The Triumph of Doubt: Dark Money and the Science of Deception* (New York: Oxford University Press, 2020), 181–99.
131. Martin Hultman, Anna Björk and Tamya Viinikka, 'The Far Right and Climate Change Denial: Denouncing Environmental Challenges via Anti-Establishment Rhetoric, Marketing of Doubts, Industrial/Breadwinner Masculinities Enactments and Ethno-Nationalism', in *The Far Right and the Environment: Politics, Discourse and Communication*, ed. Bernhard Forchtner (Abingdon: Routledge, 2019), 121–35.
132. Jonas Kaiser, 'In the Heartland of Climate Scepticism: A Hyperlink Network Analysis of German Climate Sceptics and the US Right Wing', in Forchtner, *The Far Right and the Environment*, 257–74.
133. Oscar Berglund and Daniel Schmidt, *Extinction Rebellion and Climate Change Activism: Breaking the Law to Change the World* (Cham: Palgrave, 2020).
134. Marianna Fotaki and Hamid Foroughi, 'Extinction Rebellion: Green Activism and the Fantasy of Leaderlessness in a Decentralized Movement', *Leadership* 18, no. 2 (2022): 231.
135. 'Citizens' Assembly', *Extinction Rebellion* website, https://extinctionrebellion.uk/be-the-change/citizens-assembly/ (last accessed 9 January 2023).
136. Fotaki and Foroughi, 'Extinction Rebellion', 229.
137. Ibid., 241.
138. Michael Neuber, Piotr Kocyba and Beth Gharrity Gardner, 'The Same, Only Different: Die Fridays for Future-Demonstrierenden im europäischen Vergleich', in Haunss and Sommer, *Fridays for Future*, 85–7. The surveys were conducted in Austria, Belgium, Germany, Italy, Poland, Sweden and Switzerland.
139. Shelley Boulianne, Mireille Lalancette and David Ilkiw, '"School Strike 4 Climate": Social Media and the International Youth Protest on Climate Change', *Media and Communication* 8, no. 2 (2020), https://doi.org/10.17645/mac.v8i2.2768 (last accessed 9 January 2023).
140. Catherine Walker, 'Uneven Solidarity: The School Strikes for Climate in Global and Intergenerational Perspective', *Sustain Earth* 3, no. 5 (2020), https://doi.org/10.1186/s42055-020-00024-3 (last accessed 9 January 2023).

141. Walker, 'Uneven Solidarity'.
142. The question of the social background of participants is more difficult to answer. In the aforementioned European survey, the majority of participants in six out of the seven countries defined themselves as 'upper middle class': Neuber et al., 'The Same, Only Different', 75.
143. Simon Teune, 'Schulstreik: Geschichte einer Aktionsform und die Debatte über zivilen Ungehorsam', in Haunss and Sommer, eds, *Fridays for Future*, 131–46.
144. On this aspect, see also Daniel Laqua and Nikolaos Papadogiannis, 'Youth and Internationalism in the Twentieth Century: An Introduction', *Social History* 48, no. 1 (2023): 1–16.
145. 'Greta Thunberg Tells World Leaders "You Are Failing Us", As Nations Announce Fresh Climate Action', *UN* News, 23 September 2019, available at https://news.un.org/en/story/2019/09/1047052 (last accessed 9 January 2023).

CONCLUSION

The photo on the cover of this book depicts an episode from a larger protest against nuclear weapons, staged in London on 16 July 1983.[1] Capturing a scene of people passing along an inflatable globe that is labelled 'fragile', the image illustrates how activists used visual displays to reinforce their message.[2] At the same time, the choice of prop indicates that the participants in this protest deployed a 'global imaginary', to use a term associated with the political scientist Manfred Steger. According to Steger, 'global imaginaries' emerged after the Second World War and challenged thinking in national categories.[3] This book, however, has reached back further into the past, showing how at different points in time and in different ways, activists stressed the global nature of their concerns. In many cases, like the activists on the cover, they developed a symbolic language to put their point across.

Unsurprisingly, then, the imagery associated with the 1983 protest was far from unique. In 1890 – nearly a century before the anti-nuclear protest in London – the radical British artist Walter Crane produced his lithograph 'Labour's May Day', in which workers form a circle that spans the earth. Crane stressed the global ambitions of the labour movement, and he emphasized this aspect by casting the figures in his image as representatives of different countries, cultures and continents. Moreover, while a banner on the original version of Crane's piece proclaimed the 'Solidarity of Labour', another version bore the slogan 'Proletarier aller Länder, vereinigt euch!' (commonly translated as 'Workers of the world, unite!'), the famous appeal of the *Communist Manifesto*. As Chapter 4 has pointed out, May Day was in itself a transnational phenomenon: following on from its initial association with American labour, the founding congress of the Second International in 1889 resolved to make it 'an international demonstration day' for the labour movement.[4]

In the decades between the publication of Crane's image and the 1983 protest, a wide array of international movements, associations and institutions featured representations of the globe in their emblems and literature. Moreover, environmentalists and other activists were inspired by, and reproduced, the iconic 'Blue Marble' image of 1972 – a picture that depicted planet earth from space and evoked notions of global connectedness.[5] In other words, when British activists passed along a globe balloon during their protest in London, they had good reason to expect that their message would be understood: they affirmed the internationalism of their movement and expressed their fear of nuclear annihilation.

Beyond the use of the globe, the cover image and Walter Crane's picture have another aspect in common: both emphasize connection and cooperation between activists. In the 'Solidarity of Labour' print, workers are joining hands in a gesture that evokes

Activism across Borders

Figure 9.1 Walter Crane, 'Solidarität der Arbeit' (Solidarity of Labour), lithograph to mark May Day 1890. *Source*: Hulton Archive/ Stringer, via Getty Images.

proletarian fraternity. In the 1983 image, activists are forming a line – and while, at this particular moment, their focus is on moving a balloon, the wider protest on that day saw participants joining hands in a human chain between the Soviet and American embassies in London. Such human chains had obvious symbolic dimensions as they allowed activists to display strength in numbers and unity.[6]

Conclusion

As a form of nonviolent resistance, human chains had entered the repertoire of the African American civil rights movement two decades earlier, for instance as a way of blocking access to segregated spaces.[7] Thus, the demonstration in 1983 drew on a tool that had already been used by activists in other contexts. Moreover, later campaigns illustrated the appeal of human chains to further groups of activists. In August 1989, the 'Baltic Way' constituted a landmark demonstration for the national independence of Estonia, Latvia and Lithuania, with participants linking the capitals of the three Baltic republics.[8] In May 1998, another human chain – staged by the Jubilee 2000 campaign during the G8 summit in Birmingham – emphasized demands for the cancellation of Third World debt.[9] Moreover, in recent Indian history, human chains have been used to highlight a number of issues, from women's rights to solidarity with the country's Muslim minority.[10] Taken together, these examples illustrate how a picture from one particular protest can reveal a much deeper history of activist tropes, themes and tools.[11]

An awareness of such similarities and connections does not obliterate the need to acknowledge the historical constellations that generated specific campaigns. The cover image draws attention to a distinct historical moment in the early 1980s – a time when the so-called 'Second Cold War' generated growing fears of nuclear destruction.[12] The demonstration in London formed part of a resurgent international movement against nuclear weapons in this period: indeed, the scholar and activist David Cortright has spoken of 'the largest mobilization of peace sentiment in human history up to that

Figure 9.2 Latvian participants in the 'Baltic Way' human chain on 23 August 1989.
Source: Ints Kalins / Reuters, via Alamy.

time'.[13] As Chapter 3 has noted, campaigners acknowledged the transnational nature of this issue. In response, some promoted 'détente from below' through cooperation between independent peace groups in the Eastern bloc and activists in the West. Moreover, Western European peace movements coordinated their actions in the early 1980s, seeking to highlight the international reach of their movement.

The use of a human chain at the London event was but one of many such instances in 1982–3. For example, in December 1982, thousands of women encircled the Royal Air Force base at Greenham Common.[14] Five months later, a human chain connected Greenham Common with nuclear establishments in Burghfield and Aldermaston – the latter a major destination for British peace marches from 1958 onwards.[15] Even in linking the diplomatic missions of the two superpowers, the London chain of 1983 was not unique: Irish activists launched a similar effort in Dublin on the same day, while another embassy chain was at the heart of a Parisian protest in October that year.[16] The French action occurred on a weekend of peace demonstrations across Western Europe, including a human chain in which 250,000 participants covered the 120 km distance between two American military sites in southern Germany.[17]

Of course, 1983 is but one year in which external factors fed activism on an international scale. A volume edited by the historians Gerd-Rainer Horn and Padraic Kenney has examined 1945, 1968 and 1989 as three 'transnational moments of change'. The editors chose this approach partly because it allowed them to combine the interdependent nature of two potential approaches to transnational history: on the one hand 'structural change', associated with 'great economic ... or political ... events or structures that are by their very nature supranational and that may be expected to have similar effects in a number of countries'; on the other hand 'active efforts to spread change from country to country'.[18] Two of the years they selected for their study are often treated as synonymous with major activist waves – radical student protest in 1968, and popular challenges to state socialism in 1989. Moreover, even the treatment of 1945 in Horn and Kenney's volume considers the latter in terms of activism, with contributions that shed light on communists and organized labour in the aftermath of the Second World War.[19] Another study that explores transnational connections through particular moments is Jay Winter's consideration of 'minor utopias'. Winter focuses on six years in the twentieth century (1900, 1919, 1937, 1948, 1968 and 1992), each of them with a particular overarching theme.[20]

One could easily make the case for the consideration of other years as 'transnational moments' or 'utopian moments'. For instance, books dedicated to, respectively, 1956 and 1979 have highlighted the significance of historical transformations and their relationship with activism in those years.[21] Looking beyond the twentieth century, both 1889 and 2003 would also be plausible choices: the former for reasons noted in the introduction; the latter because of the international mobilization against the Iraq War as well as a growing global justice movement. That said, while particular years loom large in both popular memory and historiography, any moment can be a valid starting point for exploring transnational connections. Such observations also raise questions about activists themselves. Many of them were keen to craft narratives of historical continuity.

Conclusion

Figure 9.3 Participants in a human chain that linked the Women's Peace Camp outside the airbase at Greenham Common with the Nuclear Weapons Establishment at Aldermaston (both in Berkshire, UK), 1 April 1983. *Source:* Mirrorpix, via Getty Images.

Yet when protests culminated in a broader rupture, they could experience their own moment as exceptional and thus standing 'outside' of time.[22]

Rather than proposing an alternative set of key moments, this book has adopted a thematic approach. In doing so, it has acknowledged that notions of a shared past were central to many movements, organizations and campaigns.[23] By placing specific efforts and campaigns in a wider chronological framework, we can probe such narratives and thus adopt a nuanced understanding of activism. On the one hand, the transience of many alliances throws into question activist accounts that emphasize continuity. On the other hand, the persistence of various themes, tropes and tactics also invites scepticism regarding claims about the 'novelty' of a particular movement or campaign. Moreover, the broader thematic gaze means that my focus has not only been on protest or social movements: while the cover image is taken from a large-scale demonstration, the book as a whole has gone beyond the more spectacular manifestations of activism. In doing so, it has explored different ideas and forms of mutual support.

These observations relate to a wider question, namely the way in which we write about transnational activism. The initial idea for this book dates back to 2013 – a time when 'globalization' was a prominent frame through which politicians, commentators, activists and academics analysed their present.[24] Our present-day world is still characterized by many forms of economic and cultural integration, yet there has been some debate as to whether globalization is nearing its end.[25] In April 2022, the British political magazine *New Statesman* referred to 'the age of deglobalisation', arguing that various events – including 'the 2008 financial crisis, the election of Donald Trump, the Covid-19 pandemic and the war in Ukraine' – had contradicted assumptions about the onward march of global integration.[26] Political developments in recent years have certainly sensitized us to the limitations of global interactions and to the boundaries for transnational mobility and movements. Within a European context, the Brexit referendum of 2016, the conflicts of the Hungarian and Polish governments with the EU as well as the growth of various nationalist or 'populist' parties all testify to the ongoing appeal of national frameworks and ideas.[27] Moreover, limitations on the physical movement of people are strikingly obvious. In 2015, the dramatic rise in refugee migration to Europe led several EU governments to resurrect border controls. It also precipitated the enhanced policing of the EU's external borders. Such developments created alarming scenes in the Mediterranean and, in the winter 2021–2, at the Polish-Belarussian border. The obstacles of going 'across borders' became further evident during the Covid-19 pandemic, with European countries introducing restrictions on international travel in the spring of 2020.

While contemporary circumstances demonstrate the persistence and power of state borders, they have not caused a reduction in transnational activism. After all, as the introduction to this book has noted, our present is characterized by manifold campaigns that range beyond individual nations. Throughout, this book has featured activists who disseminated their ideas in the face of external constraints. The existence and ongoing power of national convictions does not in itself mean that there is *less* transnational activism. With its acknowledgement of ambivalence, the present study has shown how imperialists, nationalists and racists all waged transnational efforts of their own.

Conclusion

As early as 1966, an influential article by the sociologists Mayer Zald and Robera Ash pointed to the 'ebb and flow of sentiments' within social movements.[28] Such a metaphor is useful when looking at individuals or groups, making it possible to trace activist commitments and the point when the appeal of particular issue begins to fade.[29] Nonetheless, the book has consciously avoided speaking of 'ebbs and flows'. Transnational activism was a multifarious phenomenon and, as this study has shown, it was often launched from the margins, by individuals who were quite distant from the levers of power. Clearly, many movements remained ephemeral – and throughout the book, we have seen cases of alliances that were characterized by their transience. Rather than focusing on the high tide of a campaign, or raising the question of their success, the approach has been to look at different forms of activism as parts of a wider phenomenon. In doing so, we can understand transnational activism as a thread running through European social, cultural and political history. While its shape and nature depended on contexts and causes, it formed part of the fabric of European societies and connected them to many other parts of the world.

Notes

1. 'CND Chain', *The Observer*, 17 July 1983.
2. Nicole Doerr, Alice Mattoni and Simon Teune, 'Visuals in Social Movements', in *The Oxford Handbook of Social Movements*, ed. Donatella della Porta and Simon Teune (Oxford: Oxford University Press, 2015).
3. Manfred Steger, *The Rise of the Global Imaginary: Political Ideologies from the French Revolution to the War on Terror* (Oxford: Oxford University Press, 2008), 10–11.
4. *Protokoll des Internationalen Arbeiter-Congresses zu Paris*, 123. See also Herbert Reiter, 'The Origins of May Day', in *The Ritual of May Day in Western Europe: Past, Present and Future*, ed. Abby Peterson and Herbert Reiter (Farnham: Ashgate, 2016), 139–59. For another Crane image that celebrates May Day, see Laura Forster, 'Radical Object: Walter Crane's The Worker's Maypole (1894)', *History Workshop*, 1 May 2020, https://www.historyworkshop.org.uk/radical-object-walter-cranes-the-workers-maypole-1894/ (last accessed 9 January 2023).
5. Manfred Steger and Amentahru Wahlrab, *What Is Global Studies? Theory and Practice* (Abingdon: Routledge, 2016), 138–9.
6. As noted in the introduction, 'numbers' and 'unity' are two elements of the 'WUNC displays' in Charles Tilly's typology of social movements.
7. As early as 1964, *Life* magazine described the 'linking of arms' as the 'traditional stance of civil rights demonstrators': 'Mission in Mississippi', *Life* 57, no. 1 (3 July 1964): 32. For an example of the subsequent spread beyond the American South, see for instance the use of a human 'chain-in' in Milwaukee, Wisconsin in 1965, as part of a protest against school segregation: Patrick D. Jones, *Selma of the North: Civil Rights Insurgency in Milwaukee* (Cambridge, MA: Harvard University Press, 2009), 59–79.
8. On the 'Baltic Way', see Paula Christie, 'The Baltic Chain: A Study of the Organisation Facets of Large-Scale Protest from a Micro-Historical Perspective', *Lithuanian Historical Studies* 20 (2015): 183–211.

9. Reitam, *Global Activism*, 82.
10. See e.g. 'Sabarimala Temple: Indian Women Form "620km Human Chain" for Equality', *BBC News*, 1 September 2019, available at 'https://www.bbc.co.uk/news/world-asia-india-46728521; 'India: Human Chain Protects Hindu Temple amid Riots over Facebook Post', *France 24*, 13 August 2020, available at https://observers.france24.com/en/20200813-india-human-chain-temple-mob-violence (last accessed 9 January 2023).
11. Dieter Rucht has noted the use of a human chain of 120 km in a protest against nuclear power in Northern German: Dieter Rucht, 'Protest Movements and Their Media Images', in *Mediation and Protest Movements* ed. Bart Cammaerts, Alice Mattoni and Patrick McCurdy (Bristol: Intellect, 2013), 252.
12. Eckart Conze, Martin Klimke and Jeremy Varon, eds, *Nuclear Threats, Nuclear Fear and the Cold War of the 1980s* (Cambridge: Cambridge University Press, 2017).
13. Cortright, *Peace*, 148.
14. As April Carter has noted, along British activists, this protest also involved participants from Sweden, West Germany and the Netherlands: Carter, *Peace Movements*, 121.
15. Lawrence Wittner has stressed the diversity of the case in the human chain of April 1983, with protestors 'ranging from well-dressed grandmothers to babies in strollers': Wittner, *Towards Nuclear Abolition*, 131.
16. See e.g. 'Hand in Hand for Peace', *RTÉ News* report, originally broadcast on 16 July 1983 and available via https://www.rte.ie/archives/2018/0709/977442-cnd-human-chain-demonstration/ (last accessed 9 January 2023).
17. On this particular German protest, see Susanne Schregel, *Der Atomkrieg vor der Haustür: Eine Politikgeschichte der neuen Friedensbewegung in der Bundesrepublik 1970–1985* (Frankfurt/Main: Campus, 2011), 229.
18. Padraic Kenney and Gerd-Rainer Horn, 'Introduction: Approaches to the Transnational', in Horn and Kenney, *Transnational Moments of Change*, xi.
19. Aldo Agosti, 'Recasting Democracy? Communist Parties Facing Change and Reconstruction in Postwar Europe', and Patrick Pasture, 'Window of Opportunities or Trompe l'Oeil? The Myth of Labor Unity in Western Europe after 1945', both in Horn and Kenney, *Transnational Moments of Change*, respectively 3–26 and 27–50.
20. Jay Winter, *Dreams of Peace and Freedom: Utopian Moments in the Twentieth Century* (New Haven, CT: Yale University Press, 2006).
21. Simon Hall, *1956: The World in Revolt* (London: Faber, 2016); Frank Bösch, *Zeitenwende 1979: Als die Welt von heute begann* (Munich: C.H. Beck, 2019).
22. For considerations of this aspect, see Alexandra Paulin-Booth and Matthew Kerry, 'Introduction – Activist Times: Temporality and Political Action in Twentieth-Century Europe', *European Review of History* 28, no. 4 (2021): 475–83; Joachim Häberlen, 'Heterochronias: Reflections on the Temporal Exceptionality of Revolts', *European Review of History* 28, no. 4 (2021): 531–48.
23. See e.g. Nicole Doerr's comment that 'social movements have tried to commemorate their shared past in order to imagine future collective action and relationships with other groups': Nicole Doerr, 'Memory and Culture in Social Movements', in *Conceptualizing Culture in Social Movement Research*, ed. Britta Baumgarten, Priska Daphi and Peter Ulrich (Basingstoke: Palgrave, 2014), 206–26, at 207.
24. See e.g. World Economic Forum, *Global Agenda Outlook 2013* (Geneva: World Economic Forum, 2013).

25. For contrasting positions regarding the potential 'end' of globalization, see e.g. Michael O' Sullivan, *The Levelling: What's Next after Globalization* (New York: PublicAffairs, 2019); Jeremy Green, *Is Globalization Over?* (Cambridge: Polity, 2019).
26. 'The Age of Deglobalisation', *The New Statesman*, 1–7 April 2022, 3.
27. To cite but some examples of perspectives on nationalist and populist politics in a global age, see John B. Judis, *The Nationalist Revival: Trade, Immigration, and the Revolt against Globalization* (New York: Columbia Global Reports, 2018); Terry Flew, 'Globalization, Neo-Globalization and Post-Globalization: The Challenge of Populism and the Return of the National', *Global Media and Communication* 16, no. 1 (2020): 19–39.
28. Mayer Zald and Roberta Ash, 'Social Movement Organizations: Growth, Decay and Change', *Social Forces* 44, no. 3 (1966): 327–41.
29. See e.g. the example of Danish participation in solidarity campaigns for refugees: Hjalmar Bang Carlsen, Snorre Ralund and Jonas Toubøl, 'The Solidary Relationship's Consequences for the Ebb and Flow of Activism: Collaborative Evidence from Life-History Interviews and Social Media Event Analysis', *Sociological Forum* 35, no. 3 (2020): 696–720; James Downton and Paul Wehr, *The Persistent Activist: How Peace Commitment Develops and Survives* (Boulder, CO: Westview Press, 1998).

SELECT BIBLIOGRAPHY

Primary sources

Archival collections

AMSAB – Institute of Social History, Ghent: Émilienne Brunfaut papers (343); Vlaams Guatemalacomité papers (268); Voor Moeder Aarde papers (294).

Archives du Ministère des Affaires Étrangère 'Allemagne 1928' (R1507, P733); 'Conférence Anti-Esclavagiste de Bruxelles' (doss. 373, P304–P305).

Archives nationales du Monde du Travail, Roubaix: Mouvement Anti-Apartheid papers (2000-057-MAA008 and 2000-057-MAA41).

Bodleian Libraries, University of Oxford: Anti-Slavery Society papers (MS Brit Emp. S18, S20, S22).

La Contemporaine, Paris: Ligue des Droits de l'Homme papers (doss. ARCH/0103/758); Fédération internationale des Droits de l'Homme papers (doss. ARCH/0103/900).

Institut Emile Vandervelde, Brussels: Emile Vandervelde papers.

International Institute of Social History (IISG), Amsterdam: Labour and Socialist International papers (ARCH01368); Rassemblement Universel pour la Paix papers (ARCH01165); Sozialistische Jugend-Internationale papers (ARCH01370).

LSE Archives and Special Collections, London: E. D. Morel papers.

National Archives, Kew Gardens, London: files 3632/157/27 ('Correspondence with Peter Benneson of Amnesty International') and FCO7/3611('Chile Solidarity Campaign').

Peace Collection, Swarthmore College, Pennsylvania: Ruth Fry papers (DG046).

Sozialarchiv, Zürich: 'Dokumentation Anti-AKW-Bewegung' (AR201.130); 'Schweizer Solidaritätsbrigade in Nicaragua, 1982' (AR 201.259).

United Nations Archives, Geneva: International Peace Bureau papers (IPM/IPB); dossier 6B ('Slavery') in the League of Nations Archives.

Digital repositories

'Forward to Freedom: The History of the British Anti-Apartheid Movement, 1959–1994', Anti-Apartheid Movement Archives, https://www.aamarchives.org.

Warwick Digital Collections (with material from the Modern Records Centre, Warwick University), https://wdc.contentdm.oclc.org.

W. E. B. Du Bois Papers, Special Collections and University Archives, University of Massachusetts Amherst Libraries, https://credo.library.umass.edu/view/collection/mums312.

Wilson Anti-Slavery Collection, Nineteenth-Century British Pamphlets, JSTOR Primary Sources, https://www.jstor.org/collection/pamphas.

'Women and Social Movements, International – 1840 to Present' digital collection (ed. Kathryn Kish Sklar and Thomas Dublin), Alexander Street, https://search.alexanderstreet.com/wasi.

Select Bibliography

Periodicals

Articles from daily newspapers, including *The Guardian, L'Indépendance Belge, Los Angeles Times, Le Monde, New Statesman, New York Times, The Observer, Reichspost, The Times, Washington Post*.

Articles from specialist periodicals associated with different movements, including *Allgemeine Zeitung des Judentums* (Jewish activists), *Die Autonomie* (anarchists), *Bulletin Trimestriel* (Congo reformers), *The Freethinker* (secularists), *Freiheit* (anarchists), Die Friedens-Warte (pacifists), *Gay News* (LGBT), *Gay Scotland* (LGBT), *Die Gleichheit* (socialist women's movement), *Gott will es!* (Catholic humanitarians), *The Herald of Peace* (pacifists), *Intercontinental Press* (Trotskyists), *International Press Correspondence* (communists), *Journal de la Morale Chrétienne* (humanitarians), *Labour Leader* (labour movement), *Londoner Freie Presse* (socialists), *Die Menschenrechte* (pacifists/human rights activists), *Le Mouvement Antiesclavagiste* (humanitarians), *Socialist Afffairs* (socialists), *Der Sozialdemokrat* (socialists), *Spain and the World* (anarchists), *Die Versöhnung* (pacifists), *Die Waffen Nieder* (pacifists), *Young India* (anticolonialists).

Printed sources

Aberdeen, Countess of, ed. *Women in Social Life: The Transactions of the Social Section of the International Congress of Women, London, July 1899.* London: T. Fisher Unwin, 1899.

Addams, Jane, Emily Balch, and Alice Hamilton, eds. *Women at the Hague: The International Congress of Women and Its Results.* New York: Macmillan, 1915.

African-Asian Conference. *Selected Documents of the Bandung Conference: Texts of Selected Speeches and Final Communique of the Asian-African Conference, Bandung, Indonesia, April 18–24, 1955.* New York: Institute of Pacific Relations, 1955.

Alekseeva, Ludmilla [Alexeyeva, Lyudmila]. *Soviet Dissent: Contemporary Movements for National, Religious, and Human Rights.* Middletown, CT: Wesleyan University Press, 1985.

Alexeyeva, Ludmilla [Lyudmila] and Paul Goldberg. *The Thaw Generation: Coming of Age in the Post-Stalin Era.* Pittsburgh, PA: University of Pittsburgh Press, 1993.

Ali, Tariq. *Street Fighting Years: An Autobiography of the Sixties.* New edition. London: Verso, 2005.

Amnesty International. *Annual Report 1973–74.* London: AI, 1974.

Amnesty International. *Annual Report 1974/75.* London: AI, 1975.

Amnesty International. *Annual Report: 1 June 1970–31 May 1971.* London: AI, 1971.

Amnesty International. *Report of an Amnesty International Mission to Argentina, 6–15 November 1976.* London: AI, 1977.

Amnesty International. *Report on Allegations of Torture in Brazil.* London: AI, 1972.

Amnesty International. *Report on Torture.* London: Gerald Duckworth & Co., 1973.

Angell, Norman and Dorothy Buxton. *You and the Refugee: The Morals and Economics of the Problem.* Harmondsworth: Penguin, 1939.

Angell, Norman. *Europe's Optical Illusion.* London: Simpkin, Marshall, Hamilton, Kent & Co., 1909.

Bahro, Rudolf. *Elemente einer neuen Politik: Zum Verhältnis von Ökologie und Sozialismus.* Berlin: Olle & Wolter, 1980.

Bakunin, Mikhail. *Bakunin on Anarchy: Selected Texts by the Activist-Founder of World Anarchism*, edited by Sam Dolgoff. London: George Allen & Unwin, 1973.

Bakunin, Michael [Mikhail]. *Statism and Anarchy*, translated and edited by Marshall Shatz. Cambridge: Cambridge University Press, 1990.

Balabanoff, Angelica. *My Life as a Rebel.* New York: Harper and Brothers, 1938.

Select Bibliography

Barbusse, Henri. *Paroles d'un combattant: articles et discours (1917–1920)*. Paris: Flammarion, 1920.
Bartels, Wim, ed. *Tussen Oost- en West-Europa*. Amersfoort: De Horstink, 1983.
Bartolf, Christian, ed. *The Breath of My Life: The Correspondence of Mahatma Gandhi (India) and Bart de Ligt (Holland) on War and Peace*. Berlin: Gandhi-Informations-Zentrum, 2000.
Barton, Clara. *The Red Cross: A History of This Remarkable International Movement in the Interest of Humanity*. Washington, DC: American National Red Cross, 1898.
Bernstein, Eduard. *My Years of Exile: Reminiscences of a Socialist*, translated by Bernard Miall. New York: Harcourt, Brace and Howe, 1921.
Biermann, Wolf. 'Two Interviews with Wolf Biermann', trans. Jack Zipes. *New German Critique*, no. 10 (1977): 13–27.
Binet, Laurence, ed. *MSF and the War in the Former Yugoslavia, 1991–2003*. Paris: MSF, 2015.
Bloch, Jan. *Is War Now Impossible? Being an Abridgment of 'The War of the Future in Its Technical, Economic and Political Relations'*. London: Grant Richards, 1899.
Boulanger, Claire, Bernard Jacquemart, and Philippe Granjon. *L'Enfer yougoslave: les victimes de la guerre témoignent*. Paris: Belfond, 1994.
Bray, Mark and Robert H. Haworth, eds. *Anarchist Education and the Modern School: A Francisco Ferrer Reader*. Oakland, CA: PM Press, 2019.
Brinson, Charmian and Marian Malet, eds. *Rettet Ossietzky! Dokumente aus dem Nachlaß von Rudolf Olden*. Bibliotheks- und Informationssystem der Universität Oldenburg: Oldenburg, 1990.
British and Foreign Ant-Slavery Society. *Proceedings of the General Anti-Slavery Convention, Called by the Committee of the British and Foreign Anti-Slavery Society, and Held in London, from Friday, June 12th to Tuesday, June 23rd, 1840*. London: BFASS, 1841.
British, Continental and General Federation for the Abolition of Government Regulation of Prostitution. *The New Abolitionists: A Narrative of a Year's Work*. London: Dyer Brothers, 1876.
Bureau internationale de la Paix. *Bulletin Officiel du IVme Congrès Universel de la Paix, tenu à Berne (Suisse) du 22 au 27 août 1892*. Bern: Haller, 1892.
Carmichael, Stokely. 'Black Power'. In *The Dialectics of Liberation*, edited by David Cooper, 150–74. London: Institute of Phenomenological Studies, 1968.
Carson, Rachel. *Silent Spring*. New York: Houghton Miffin, 1962.
Cassin, René. 'The Charter of Human Rights: Nobel Lecture, December 11, 1968'. In *Nobel Lectures in Peace (1951–1970)*, edited by Frederick Haberman, 394–407. Singapore: World Scientific Publishing, 1999.
Clarke, Richard. *Cardinal Lavigerie and the African Slave Trade*. London: Longmans, Green & Co., 1889.
Cleaver, Kathleen Neal. 'Back to Africa: The Evolution of the International Section of the Black Panther Party (1969–1972)'. In *The Black Panther Party Reconsidered*, edited by Charles E. Jones, 211–54. Baltimore, MD: Black Classic Press, 1998.
Cockburn, Alexander and Robin Blackburn, eds. *Student Power: Problems, Diagnosis, Action*. London: Penguin, 1969.
Cohn-Bendit, Daniel and Gabriel Cohn-Bendit. *Obsolete Communism: The Left-Wing Alternative*, translated by Arnold Pomerans. London: André Deutsch, 1968.
Collins, Carole. '"Break the Chains of Debt!": International Jubilee 2000 Campaign Demands Deeper Debt Relief'. *Review of African Political Economy* 26, no. 81 (1999): 419–22.
Coudenhove-Kalergi, Richard. *Crusade for Pan-Europe: Autobiography of a Man and a Movement*. New York: George Putnam's Sons, 1943.
Coudenhove-Kalergi, Richard. *Kampf um Paneuropa: Aus dem 1. Jahrgang*. Vienna: Paneuropa-Verlag, 1925.

Select Bibliography

Dalla Costa, Mariarosa and Selma James. *The Power of Women and the Subversion of Community*. Bristol: Falling Wall Press, 1972.

Davis, Angela. *An Autobiography*. New York: Random House, 1974.

de Beauvoir, Simone. *Le deuxième sexe*. Paris: Gallimard, 1949.

Deletant, Dennis. *In Search of Romania: A Memoir*. London: Hurst, 2022.

Delphy, Christine. 'The European Union and the Future of Feminism'. In *Sexual Politics and the European Union: The New Feminist Challenge*, edited by R. Amy Elman, 147–58. New York: Berghahn, 1996.

Deutsche Liga für Menschenrechte. *40 Jahre Kampf um Menschenrechte 1913–1953*. Berlin: Deutsche Liga für Menschenrechte, 1953.

Direction générale de l'œuvre anti-esclavagiste. *Documents relatifs au Congrès libre anti-esclavagiste, tenu à Paris, en septembre 1890*. Paris: Direction générale de l'oeuvre anti-esclavagiste, 1890.

Doyle, Arthur Conan. *The Crime of the Congo*. London: Hutchinson & Co., 1909.

Doyle, Arthur Conan. *The South African War: Its Cause and Conduct*. London: Georg Newnes, 1902.

Du Bois, W. E. B. *W. E. B. Du Bois Speaks: Speeches and Addresses 1920–1963*, edited by Philip Foner. New York: Pathfinder, 1970.

Duffett, John, ed. *Against the Crime of Silence: Proceedings of the Russell International War Crimes Tribunal*. Flanders, NJ: O'Hare Books, 1968.

Dunant, Henri [Henry]. *The Origins of the Red Cross: 'Un Souvenir de Solferino'*, translated by Anna Heylin Wright. 1862. Philadelphia: John Winston, 1911.

Faber, Mient Jan. 'Human Security from Below: Freedom from Fear and Lifeline Operations'. In *The Viability of Human Security*, edited by Monica den Boer and Jaap de Wilde, 149–78. Amsterdam: Amsterdam University Press, 2008.

Fanon, Frantz. *The Wretched of the Earth: The Handbook for the Black Revolution That Is Changing the Shape of the Earth*, translated by Constance Farrington. 1961. Paperback edition. New York: Gove Press, 1968.

Faye, Shon. *The Transgender Issue: Trans Justice Is Justice for All*. New York: Verso, 2022.

Federici, Silvia. *Wages against Housework*. Bristol: Falling Wall Press, 1975.

Fricke, Dieter and Rudolf Knaack, eds. *Dokumente aus geheimen Archiven: Übersicht der Berliner politischen Polizei über die allgemeine Lage der sozialdemokratischen und anarchistischen Bewegung 1878–1913*, vol. 1: *1878–1889*. Weimar: Herman Böhlaus Nachfolger, 1983.

Fricke, Dieter and Rudolf Knaack, eds. *Dokumente aus geheimen Archiven: Übersichten der Berliner politischen Polizei über die allgemeine Lage der sozialdemokratischen und anarchistischen Bewegung 1878–1913*, vol. 2: *1890–1906*. Weimar: Hermann Böhlaus Nachfolger, 1989.

Fricke, Dieter and Rudolf Knaack, eds. *Dokumente aus geheimen Archiven: Übersichten der Berliner Polizei über die allgemeine Lage der sozialdemokratischen und anarchistischen Bewegung 1878–1913*, vol. 3: *1906–1913*. Berlin: Berliner Wissenschaftsverlag, 2004.

Fried, Alfred Hermann. *Das internationale Leben der Gegenwart*. Leipzig: Teubner, 1908.

Fried, Alfred Hermann. *Europäische Wiederherstellung*. Zürich: Füssli, 1915.

Fried, Alfred Hermann. *Handbuch der Friedensbewegung*. Vienna: Verlag der Oesterreichischen Friedensgesellschaft, 1905.

Fryth, Jim and Sally Alexander, eds. *Women's Voices from the Spanish Civil War*. London: Lawrence & Wishart, 1991.

Furtado, Jean, ed. *Turkey: Peace on Trial*. London: Merlin Press and END, 1984.

Goldman, Emma. *Living My Life*. New York: Alfred Knopf, 1930.

Goldman, Emma. *My Disillusionment in Russia*. Garden City: Doubleday, Page & Co., 1923.

Select Bibliography

Gordon, May Ogilvie. *The International Council of Women and the Meetings of the International Council of Women in Berlin, 1904.* Aberdeen: Free Press, 1904.

Gravelli, Asvero. *Verso l'internazionale fascista.* Rome: Nuova Europa, 1932.

Hecker, Marita. 'Im Geist der internationalen Brigaden: Erinnerungen an die Nicaragua-Solidaritätsarbeit im Gesundheitsbereich'. In *Aufbuch nach Nicaragua: Deutsch-deutsche Solidarität im Systemwettstreit*, edited by Eika Harzer and Willi Volks, 73–5. Berlin: Christoph Links Verlag, 2008.

Herzen, Alexander. *Letters from France and Italy, 1847–70*, translated and edited by Judith Zimmerman. Pittsburgh, PA: University of Pittsburgh Press, 1995.

Herzl, Theodor. *Der Judenstaat: Versuch einer modernen Lösung der Judenfrage.* Leipzig and Vienna: M. Breitenstein's Verlags-Buchhandlung, 1896.

Heyman, Michael, ed. *The Minutes of the Zionist General Council: The Uganda Controversy*, 2 vols. Jerusalem: Israel University Press, 1970.

Heyrick, Elizabeth. *Immediate, Not Gradual, Abolition; or, an Enquiry into the Shortest, Safest and Most Effective Means of Getting Rid of West Indian Slavery.* Leicester: T. Combe, 1824.

Hobhouse, Emily. *The Brunt of the War, and Where It Fell.* London: Methuen, 1902.

Huysmans, Camille. *The Policy of the International: A Speech of and Interview with the Secretary of the International*, translated by Fred Gorle. London: Allen & Unwin, 1916.

International Council of Women. *Third Annual Report 1911–1912.* Washington, DC: ICW, 1912.

Internationaler Frauenbund für Vogelschutz (Deutsche Abteilung). *Jahrbuch für die Jahre 1909/11.* Berlin: Internationaler Frauenbund für Vogelschutz, 1912.

Internationales Frauenkomitee für dauernden Frieden. *Bericht – Rapport – Report: Internationaler Frauenkongress. Haag vom 21. April – 1. Mai 1915.* Amsterdam: IWCPP, 1915.

Jacobs, Aletta. *Memories: My Life as an International Leader in Health, Suffrage, and Peace*, edited by Annie Wright and translated by Harriet Feinberg. 1924. New York: Feminist Press, 1996.

James, C. L. R. *The Black Jacobins: Toussaint L'Ouverture and the San Domingo Revolution.* 1938. Reprinted with a new preface. London: Penguin, 1980.

James, C. L. R. *Toussaint Louverture: The Story of the Only Successful Slave Revolt in History*, edited Christian Høgsbjerg. 1934. Reprinted with introduction. Durham, NC: Duke University Press, 2013.

James, C. L. R. *World Revolution, 1917–1936: The Rise and Fall of the Communist International*, ed. Christian Høgsbjerg. 1937. Durham, NC: Duke University Press, 2017.

Jones, Claudia. *Beyond Containment*, edited by Carole Boyce Davies. Banbury: Ayebia Clarke, 2010.

Jouhaux, Léon. 'Fifty Years of Trade-Union Activity in [sic] Behalf of Peace: Nobel Lecture, December 11, 1951'. In *Nobel Lectures in Peace (1951–1970)*, edited by Frederick Haberman, 10–23. Singapore: World Scientific Publishing, 1999.

Junod, Marcel. *Warrior without Weapons*, translated by Edward Fitzgerald. 1947. London: Jonathan Cape, 1951.

Kaldor, Mary, ed. *Europe from Below: An East–West Dialogue.* London: Verso, 1991.

Kaldor, Mary. *Global Civil Society: An Answer to War.* Cambridge: Polity, 2003.

Kaldor, Mary. *Human Security: Reflections on Globalization and Intervention.* Cambridge: Polity, 2007.

Kavan, Jan. 'Czechoslovakia 1968: Revolt or Reform? 1968—A Year of Hope and Non-Understanding'. *Critique* 36, no. 2 (2008): 289–301.

Kinkel, Johanna. *Hans Ibeles in London: Ein Familienbild aus dem Flüchtlingsleben.* Stuttgart: J.G. Cotta'scher Verlag, 1860.

Koenen, Gerd. *Das rote Jahrzehnt: Unsere kleine deutsche Kulturrevolution 1967–1977.* Cologne: Kiepenheuer & Witsch, 2001.

Kollontai, Alexandra. *Selected Articles and Speeches*, translated by Cynthia Carlile. New York: Progress Publishers, 1984.
Korboński, Stefan. *Warsaw in Exile*, translated by David Welsh. London: Gorge Allen & Unwin, 1966.
Kuron, Jacek and Karol Modzelewski. 'A Socialist Manifesto for Poland'. *International Socialism*, no. 28 (1967): 25–7.
Lavigerie, Charles. *L'Esclavage Africain: Conférence sur l'esclavage dans le Haut Congo*. Brussels: Société antiesclavagiste, 1888.
Lavigerie, Charles. *Slavery in Africa: A Speech. Made at the Meeting Held in London July 31, 1888*. Boston: Cashman, Keating and Company, 1888.
Lazare, Bernard. *L'Antisémitisme: son histoire et ses causes*. Paris: Léon Chailley, 1894.
Lazare, Bernard. *Une Erreur judiciaire: La vérité sur l'affaire Dreyfus*. Brussels: Veuve Monnom, 1896.
Lefèvre-Pontalis, Antonine. *Conférences antiesclavagistes*. Saint Cloud: Imprimerie Berlin Frères, 1891.
Lemkin, Raphael. *Axis Rule in Occupied Europe: Laws of Occupation, Analysis of Government, Proposals for Redress*. Washington, DC: Carnegie Endowment for International Peace, 1944.
Lenin, Vladimir Ilyich. 'Lessons of the Commune' (March 1908). In *Collected Works*, vol. 13: *June 1907–April 1908*, translated by Bernard Isaacs and edited by Clemens Dutt, 475–8. Moscow: Foreign Languages Publishing House, 1962.
Lenin, Vladimir Ilyich. 'Opportunism and the Collapse of the Second International' (January 1916). In *Lenin Collected Works*, vol. xix: *1916–1927*, translated by Moissaye Olgin and edited by Alexander Trachenberg, 15–27. London: International Publishers, 1942.
Lévy, Bernard-Henri. *Le lys et la cendre: journal d'un écrivain au temps de la guerre de Bosnie*. Paris: Grasset, 1996.
Liebknecht, Wilhelm et al. *Protokoll des Internationalen Arbeiter-Congresses zu Paris. Abgehalten vom 4. bis 20. Juli 1889*. Nuremberg: Wörlein, 1890.
Ligue des Droits de l'Homme. *Le Congrès national de 1928: compte rendu sténographique 15–17 juillet 1928*. Paris: LDH, 1928.
Lloyd, Lola Maverick and Rosika Schwimmer. *Chaos, War, or a New World Order: What We Must Do to Establish the All-Inclusive, Non-Military, Democratic Federation of Nations*. 4th edition. Chicago, IL: Campaign for World Government, 1942.
Lorde, Audre. *Sister Outsider: Essays and Speeches*. Freedom, CA: Crossing Press, 1984.
Lown, Bernard. *Prescription for Survival: A Doctor's Journey to End Nuclear Madness*. San Francisco: Berrett-Koehler Publishers, 2008.
Luxemburg, Rosa. *The National Question: Selected Writings by Rosa Luxemburg*, edited by Horace Davis. New York: Monthly Review Press, 1976.
Mandel, Ernest. *From Stalinism to Eurocommunism: The Bitter Fruits of 'Socialism in One Country'*, translated by Jon Rothschild. London: New Left Books, 1978.
Marcuse, Herbert. *One-Dimensional Man: Studies in the Ideology of Advanced Industrial Society*. London: Routledge & Kegan Paul, 1964.
Marx, Karl. *The Civil War in France: Address of the General Council of the International Working-Men's Association*. London: Edward Truelove, 1871.
May, John. *The Greenpeace Handbook of the Nuclear Age: The History of the Human Cost*. London: Victor Gollancz, 1989.
Meadows, Donella, Dennis Meadows, Jørgen Randers and William W. Behrens III. *The Limits to Growth: A Report for the Club of Rome Project on the Predicament of Mankind*. Washington, DC: Pontomac Associates, 1972.
Meissner-Blau, Freda. *Die Frage bleibt: 88 Lern- und Wanderjahre. Im Gespräch mit Gert Dressel*. Vienna: Amalthea Signum Verlag, 2014.

Select Bibliography

Menchú, Rigoberta. *I, Rigoberta Menchú*, translated by Ann Wright. London: Verso, 1984.
Michnik, Adam. *Letters from Prison and Other Essays*. Berkeley, CA: University of California, 1985.
Mladjenović, Lepa. 'Women in Black against War (Belgrade)'. In *Feminists under Fire: Exchanges across War Zones*, edited by Wenona Giles et al., 41–4. Toronto: Between the Lines, 2003.
Mokhetefi, Elaine. *Algiers, Third World Capital: Black Panthers, Freedom Fighters, Revolutionaries*. London: Verso, 2018.
Montandon, George. *Deux ans chez Koltchak et chez les bolchéviques pour la Croix-Rouge de Genève, 1919–1921*. 3rd edition. Paris, 1923.
Morel, E. D. *The Congo Slave State: A Protest against the New African Slavery; and an Appeal to the Public of Great Britain, of the United States, and of the Continent of Europe*. Liverpool: J. Richardson and Sons, 1903.
Morel, E. D. *The Horror on the Rhine*. London: Union of Democratic Control, 1920.
Münzenberg, Willi. *Livre Brun sur l'incendie du Reichstag et le terreur hitlérienne*. Paris: Éditions Carrefour, 1933.
Nordau, Max. 'Das europäische Gewissen'. *Ethische Kultur* 14, no. 13 (1 July 1906): 97–9.
Novicow, Jacques. *Der ewige Krieg: Antwort auf eine Schrift 'Der ewige Friede' des Herrn Prof. Karl Frh. v. Stengel*, translated by Alfred Hermann Fried. Berlin: Vita, 1899.
Novicow, Jacques. *War and Its Alleged Benefits*, translated by Thomas Seltzer. New York: Henry Holt & Co., 1911.
Optiz, May, Katharina Oguntoye, and Dagmar Schultz, eds. *Showing Our Colors: Afro-German Women Speak Out*, translated by Anne V. Adams. Amherst, MA: University of Massachusetts Press, 1992.
Orlov, Yuri. *Dangerous Thoughts: Memoirs of a Russian Life*, translated by Thomas Whitney. New York: William Morrow and Company, 1991.
Orwell, George. *The Lion and the Unicorn: Socialism and the English Genius*. 1941. Reprinted with introduction. London: Penguin, 1982.
OSCE Special Monitoring Mission to Ukraine. *Gender Dimensions of SMM Monitoring: Women's Perceptions of Security and Their Contributions to Peace and Security, 1 November 2018–15 June 2021*. Kiev: OSCE, 2021.
Padmore, George. *Colonial and Coloured Unity: A Programme of Action. History of the Pan-African Congress*. Manchester: Pan-African Federation, 1947.
Peace and Disarmament Committee of the Women's International Organisations. *Official Record of the Declarations and Petitions Presented by the Disarmament Committee of the Women's International Organisations to the Disarmament Conference, Geneva, February 6th, 1932*. Geneva: Imp. de la Tribune de Genève, 1932.
Pelikan, Jiří and Manfred Wilke. *Menschenrechte: Ein Jahrbuch zu Osteuropa*. Reinbek: Rowohlt, 1977.
Pettitt, Ann. *Walking to Greenham: How the Peace-Camp Began and the Cold War Ended*. Aberystwyth: Honno, 2006.
Peukert, Josef. *Erinnerungen eines Proletariers aus der revolutionären Arbeiterbewegung*. 1913. Reprinted. Frankfurt/Main: Verlag AV, 2002.
Plamínková, Františka. *The Political Rights of Women in the Czechoslovak Republic*. Prague: Gazette de Prague, 1920.
Recueil des procès-verbaux de la Conférence internationale pour la protection de la nature, Berne, 17–19 novembre 1913. Bern: K. J. Wyss, 1913.
Richter, Wolfgang, Elmar Schmähling, and Eckart Spoo, eds. *Die Wahrheit über den NATO-Krieg gegen Jugoslawien: Schrift des Internationalen Vorbereitungskomitees für ein Europäisches Tribunal über den NATO-Krieg gegen Jugoslawien*. Schkeuditz: Schkeuditzer Buchverlag, 2000.

Rocker, Rudolf. *The London Years*, translated by Joseph Leftwich. 1956. Reprinted with introduction and epilogue. Nottingham: Five Leaves, 2005.
Roden Buxton, Charles and Dorothy Buxton. *The World after the War*. London: George Allen & Unwin, 1920.
Rolland, Romain. *Gandhi*. Paris: Stock, 1924.
Rosdolsky, Roman. 'A Memoir of Auschwitz and Birkenau'. *Monthly Review* 39, no. 8 (1988): 33–8.
Rosdolsky, Roman. 'The Workers and the Fatherland: A Note on a Passage in the "Communist Manifesto"'. *Science and Society* 29, no. 3 (1965): 330–7.
Rouse, Ruth. *Rebuilding Europe: The Student Chapter in Post-War Reconstruction*. London: Student Christian Movement, 1925.
Roy, M. N. *Revolution and Counterrevolution in China*, translated by Paul Frölich. Berlin: Soziologische Verlagsanstalt, 1930.
Russell, Dora. *The Tamarisk Tree: My Quest for Liberty and Love*. New York: Putnam, 1975.
Santillo, David, Paul Johnston, Ruth Stringer, and Tony Sadownichik, eds. *The Chernobyl Catastrophe: Consequences on Human Health*. Amsterdam: Greenpeace, 2006.
Schmidt, Nelly, ed. *Abolitionnistes de l'esclavage et réformateurs des colonies, 1820–1851*. Paris: Katharla, 2000.
Schmidt, Nelly. *La Correspondance de Victor Schœlcher*. Paris: Maisonneuve et Larose, 1995.
Schücking, Walther. *Der Staatenverband der Haager Konferenzen*. Berlin: Duncker & Humblot, 1912.
Senghor, Lamine. *La Violation d'un pays, et autres écrits anticolonialistes*, edited by David Murphy. 1927. Reprinted with introduction and other texts. Paris: L'Harmattan, 2012.
Socialist International Women. *United Nations Decade for Women 1976–1985: Equality, Development and Peace*. London: SIW, 1985.
Socialist International Women. *XIII Conference of Socialist International Women, Lima, 16/17 June 1986: Equality – a Socialist Decade for Women*. London: Socialist International Women, 1986.
Société antiesclavagiste de France. *Congrès international antiesclavagiste tenu à Paris les 6, 7, 8 août 1900: Compte rendu des séances*. Paris: Société antiesclavagiste de France, 1900.
Sozialistisches Büro. *Am Beispiel Angela Davis: Der Kongreß in Frankfurt. Reden, Referate, Diskussionsprotokolle*. Frankfurt/Main: Fischer, 1972.
Spiller, Gustav, ed. *Papers on Inter-Racial Problems: Communicated to the First Universal Races Congress Held at the University of London July 26–29, 1911*. London: P. S. King & Son, 1911.
Stepniak. *Underground Russia: Revolutionary Profiles and Sketches from Life*. New York: Charles Scribner's Sons, 1883.
Swanwick, H. M. *Collective Insecurity*. London: Jonathan Cape, 1937.
Thompson, E. P. *Beyond the Cold War*. London: Merlin Press and END, 1982.
Trotsky, Leon. *The Revolution Betrayed: What Is the Soviet Union and Where Is It Going?*, translated by Max Eastman. London: Faber & Faber, 1937.
United States Congress, Senate. *Hearings before a Sub-Committee of the Committee on Appropriations, United States Senate, Ninety-Sixth Congress, First Session*. Washington, DC: US Government Printing Office, 1979.
United States Congress, Senate. *Hearings before the Commission on Security and Cooperation in Europe: Ninety-Fifth Congress. First Session on Implementation of the Helsinki Accords*, vol. IV. Washington, DC: US Government Printing Office, 1977.
von Ossietzky, Carl. *The Stolen Republic: Selected Writings of Carl von Ossietzky*, translated by John Preet and edited by Bruno Frei. Berlin: Seven Seas, 1971.
von Suttner, Bertha. *Der Menschheit Hochgedanken: Roman aus der nächsten Zukunft*. Berlin: Verlag der Friedens-Warte, 1911.

Select Bibliography

von Suttner, Bertha. *Die Barbarisierung der Luft*. Berlin: Verlag der Friedenswarte, 1912.

von Suttner, Bertha. *Die Waffen nieder! Eine Lebensgeschichte*. Dresden: Edgar Pierson, 1889.

von Suttner, Bertha. *Memoirs of Bertha von Suttner: The Records of an Eventful Life*, translated by Nathan Haskell Dole. Boston, MA: Ginn and Company, 1910.

Weizmann, Chaim. *Trial and Error: The Autobiography of Chaim Weizmann*, vol. 1: *1874–1917*. Lexington, MA: Plunkett Lake Press, 2013.

Women's International League for Peace and Freedom. *Report of the International Congress of Women, Report, May 12 to May 17, 1919*. Geneva: WILPF, 1919.

Women's International League for Peace and Freedom. *Report of the Ninth Congress of the Women's International League for Peace and Freedom: Luhacovice, Czechoslovakia, July 27th to 31st, 1937*. Geneva: WILPF, 1937.

Zetkin, Clara. *Social-Democracy and Woman Suffrage: A Paper Read by Clara Zetkin to the Conference of Women Belonging to the Social-Democratic Party Held at Mannheim before the Opening of the 1906 Annual Congress of the German Social-Democracy*, translated by Jacques Bonhomme. London: Twentieth Century Press, 1907.

Individual online items (all links last verified on 9 January 2023)

Caritas Europa. 'A People Sacrificed: Sanctions against Iraq' (report, 28 February 2021), available on *ReliefWeb*, https://reliefweb.int/report/iraq/people-sacrificed-sanctions-against-iraq-report-caritas-europa.

Corti, Ivanka. 'Statement on the Occasion of the 25th Anniversary of the Adoption of the Convention on the Elimination of All Forms of Discrimination against Women by the General Assembly of the United Nations', 13 October 2004, United Nations, New York, available via https://www.un.org/womenwatch/daw/cedaw/cedaw25anniversary/cedaw25-IC.pdf.

Extinction Rebellion. 'Citizens' Assembly', https://extinctionrebellion.uk/be-the-change/citizens-assembly/.

Global Call to Acton against Poverty. *The World We Want: GCAP Annual Report 2011*, 6, available at https://gcap.global/wp-content/uploads/2018/07/The-World-We-Want.pdf.

James, C. L. R. In Conversation with Stuart Hall, Channel 4, 1984, https://www.youtube.com/watch?v=_Gf0KUxgZfI&t.

Kelly, Petra. Interviewed by Trevor Hyett on 'Afternoon Plus', Thames Television, 25 November 1982, https://www.youtube.com/watch?v=D_HTSQbeZhI.

Kollontai, Alexandra. 'A Militant Celebration' (1920), trans. Alix Holt, *Marxist Internet Archive*, https://www.marxists.org/archive/kollonta/1920/womens-day.htm.

Licht, Sonja and Slobodan Drakulić. 'When the Word for Peacemaker Was a Woman: War and Gender in the Former Yugoslavia', originally published in 1996 and republished in the 'Selected Papers Anniversary Issue' of the *Belgrade Women's Studies Journal* (2002), https://web.archive.org/web/20210926055506/https://www.zenskestudie.edu.rs/en/publishing/online-material/women-s-studies-journal/296-when-the-word-for-peacemaker-was-a-woman-war-and-gender-in-the-former-yugoslavia.

Luxemburg, Rosa. 'Rebuilding the International'. *Die Internationale*, no. 1 (1915), https://www.marxists.org/archive/luxemburg/1915/xx/rebuild-int.htm.

Walsh, Joan. 'Jubilee 2012? A Leader of the Global Debt-Relief Movement Says OWS Can Point to Restructuring America's Consumer Debt Crisis'. *Salon.Com*, 12 October 2012, https://www.salon.com/2011/10/12/jubilee_2012/.

World Conference against Racism NGO Forum Declaration. 3 September 2001, available at the website of the Asia-Pacific Movement for WCRA, https://www.hurights.or.jp/wcar/E/ngofinaldc.htm.

World Conference against Racism, Racial Discrimination, Xenophobia and Related Intolerance. 'Declaration' (September 2001), available online https://www.un.org/WCAR/durban.pdf.

World Jewish Congress. 'Note Regarding the German Policy of Deliberate Annihilation of European Jewry (Geneva, 22 October 1942)', original in The Central Zionist Archives, Jerusalem, RG no. 68.045 and digitized by the United States Holocaust Memorial and Museum, https://perspectives.ushmm.org/.

Zetkin, Clara. 'From the International of the Word to the International of the Deed'. *The Communist International*, new series, no. 1 (1924), https://www.marxists.org/archive/zetkin/1924/xx/international.htm.

Secondary sources

Adi, Hakim. *Pan-Africanism and Communism: The Communist International, Africa and the Diaspora, 1919–1939*. Trenton: Africa World Press, 2013.

Adi, Hakim. *Pan-Africanism: A History*. London: Bloomsbury, 2018.

Adi, Hakim. *West Africans in Britain, 1900–1960: Nationalism, Pan-Africanism, and Communism*. London: Lawrence & Wishart, 1998.

Adi, Hakim and Marika Sherwood. *The 1945 Manchester Pan-African Congress Revisited*. London: New Beacon Books, 1995.

Aerts, Mieke. 'Feminism from Amsterdam to Brussels in 1891: Political Transfer as Transformation'. *European Review of History* 12, no. 2 (2005): 367–82.

Aires Oliveira, Pedro. 'A Sense of Hopelessness? Portuguese Oppositionists Abroad in the Final Years of the Estado Novo, 1968–1974'. *Contemporary European History* 26, no. 3 (2017): 465–87.

Aissaoui, Rabah. 'Exile and the Politics of Return and Liberation: Algerian Colonial Workers and Anti-Colonialism in France during the Interwar Period'. *French History* 25, no. 2 (2011): 214–23.

Albanese, Matteo and Pablo del Hierro. *Transnational Fascism in the Twentieth Century: Spain, Italy and the Global Neo-Fascist Network*. London: Bloomsbury, 2016.

Albert, Gleb. *Das Charisma der Weltrevolution: Revolutionärer Internationalismus in der frühen Sowjetgesellschaft 1917–1927*. Cologne: Böhlau, 2017.

Alcalde, Ángel. 'War Veterans as Transnational Actors: Politics, Alliances and Networks in the Interwar Period'. *European Review of History* 25, nos. 3–4 (2018): 492–511.

Alexander, Robert Jackson. *International Trotskyism, 1929–1985: A Documented Analysis of the Movement*. Durham, NC: Duke University Press, 1991.

Allen, Ann Taylor. Anne Cova and June Puvis. 'International Feminisms'. *Women's History Review* 19, no. 4 (2010): 493–501.

Alloul, Houssine, Edhem Eldem, and Henk de Smaele, eds. *To Kill a Sultan: A Transnational History of the Attempt on Abdülhamid II (1905)*. London: Palgrave, 2018.

Alston, Charlotte. '"A Great Host of Sympathisers": The Doukhobor Emigration and Its International Supporters'. *Journal of Modern European History* 12, no. 2 (2014): 200–15.

Alston, Charlotte. 'The Work of the Russian Liberation Committee in London, 1919–1924'. *Slavonica* 14, no. 1 (2008): 6–17.

Alston, Charlotte. *Tolstoy and His Disciples: The History of a Radical International Movement*. London: I.B. Tauris, 2014.

Anderson, Benedict. *Under Three Flags: Anarchism and the Anti-Colonial Imagination*. London: Verso, 2005.

Select Bibliography

Anderson, Bonnie. *Joyous Greetings: The First International Women's Movement, 1830–1860*. New York: Oxford University Press, 2000.

Andresen, Knud and Bart van der Steen, eds. *A European Youth Revolt: European Perspectives on Youth Protest and Social Movements in the 1980s*. Basingstoke: Palgrave, 2016.

Andresen, Knud, Sebastian Justke, and Detlef Siegfried, eds. *Apartheid and Anti-Apartheid in Western Europe*. Cham: Palgrave, 2021.

Andreyev, Catherine and Ivan Savický. *Russia Abroad: Prague and the Russian Diaspora, 1918–1938*. New Haven, CT: Yale University Press, 2004.

Angelo, Anne-Marie. *Black Power on the Move: Migration, Internationalism, and the British and Israeli Black Panthers*. Chapel Hill, NC: University of North Carolina Press, 2021.

Armiero, Marco and Lise Sedrez, eds. *A History of Environmentalism: Local Struggles, Global Histories*. London: Bloomsbury, 2014.

Ashton, Rosemary. *Little Germany: German Refugees in Victorian Britain*. Oxford: Oxford University Press, 1989.

Ayoub, Philip and David Paternotte, eds. *LGBT Activism and the Making of Europe: A Rainbow Europe?* Basingstoke: Palgrave, 2014.

Baldwin, Kate. *Beyond the Color Line and the Iron Curtain: Reading Encounters between Black and Red, 1922–1963*. Durham, NC: Duke University Press, 2002.

Balhorn, Loren and Jan-Peter Herrmann. *Yiddish Revolutionaries in Migration: The Transnational History of the Jewish Labour Bund*. Leiden: Brill, 2020.

Bandeira Jerónimo, Miguel and Damiano Matasci. 'Imperialism, Internationalism and Globalisation in Twentieth Century Africa'. *Journal of Imperial and Commonwealth History* 48, no. 5 (2020): 793–804.

Bandeira Jerónimo, Miguel and José Pedro Monteiro, eds. *Internationalism, Imperialism and the Formation of the Contemporary World: The Pasts of the Present*. Cham: Palgrave, 2018.

Bantman, Constance. *The French Anarchists in London, 1880–1914: Exile and Transnationalism in the First Globalisation*. Liverpool: Liverpool University Press, 2013.

Bantman, Constance. *Jean Grave and the Networks of French Anarchism, 1854–1939*. Cham: Palgrave, 2021.

Bantman, Constance. 'Louise Michel's London Years: A Political Reassessment (1890–1905)'. *Women's History Review* 26, no. 6 (2017): 994–1012.

Bantman, Constance and Bert Altena, eds. *Reassessing the Transnational Turn: Scales of Analysis in Anarchist and Syndicalist Studies*. New York: Routledge, 2015.

Bar-On, Tamir. 'Transnationalism and the French Nouvelle Droite'. *Patterns of Prejudice* 45, no. 3 (2011): 199–223.

Barnett, Michael. *Empire of Humanity: A History of Humanitarianism*. Ithaca, NY: Cornell University Press, 2011.

Barry, Gearóid. *The Disarmament of Hatred: Marc Sangnier, French Catholicism and the Legacy of the First World War, 1914–45*. Basingstoke: Palgrave, 2012.

Bauerkämper, Arnd. 'Transnational Fascism: Cross-Border Relations between Regimes and Movements in Europe, 1922–1939'. *East Central Europe* 37, nos. 2–3 (2010): 214–46.

Bauerkämper, Arnd and Grzegorz Rossolinski-Liebe, eds. *Fascism without Borders: Transnational Connections and Cooperation between Movements and Regimes in Europe from 1918 to 1945*. New York: Berghahn, 2017.

Baughan, Emily. *Saving the Children: Humanitarianism, Internationalism, and Empire*. Oakland, CA: University of California Press, 2022.

Beers, Laura. 'Bridging the Ideological Divide: Liberal and Socialist Collaboration in the Women's International League for Peace and Freedom, 1919–1945'. *Journal of Women's History* 33, no. 2 (2021): 111–35.

Beers, Laura. 'Frauen für Demokratie: Möglichkeiten und Grenzen des zivilgesellschaftlichen Engagements'. In *Normalität und Fragilität: Demokratie nach dem Ersten Weltkrieg*, edited by Tim Müller and Adam Tooze, 111–32. Hamburg: Hamburger Edition, 2015.

Belmonte, Laura. *The International LGBT Rights Movement: A History*. London: Bloomsbury, 2021.

Bensimon, Fabrice, Quentin Deluermoz, and Jeanne Moisand, eds. *'Arise Ye Wretched of the Earth': The First International in a Global Perspective*. Leiden: Brill, 2018.

Berger, Stefan and Holger Nehring, eds. *The History of Social Movements in a Global Perspective*. London: Palgrave, 2017.

Berger, Stefan and Sean Scalmer, eds. *The Transnational Activist: Transformations and Comparisons from the Anglo-World since the Nineteenth Century*. Cham: Palgrave, 2018.

Berglund, Oscar and Daniel Schmidt. *Extinction Rebellion and Climate Change Activism: Breaking the Law to Change the World*. Cham: Palgrave, 2020.

Berry, David and Constance Bantman, eds. *New Perspectives on Anarchism, Labour and Syndicalism: The Individual, the National and the Transnational*. Newcastle upon Tyne: Cambridge Scholars Publishing, 2010.

Bianchi, Bruna and Geraldine Ludbrook, eds. *Living War, Thinking Peace (1914–1924): Women's Experiences, Feminist Thought, and International Relations*. Newcastle upon Tyne: Cambridge Scholars Publishing, 2016.

Bieber, Florian and Dario Brentin, eds. *Social Movements in the Balkans: Rebellion and Protest from Maribor to Taksim*. Abingdon: Routledge, 2019.

Bilić, Bojan. *We Were Gasping for Air: (Post-)Yugoslav Anti-War Activism and Its Legacy*. Baden Baden: Nomos, 2012.

Bilić, Bojan and Vesna Jankovic, eds. *Resisting the Evil: [Post-]Yugoslav Anti-War Contention*. Baden Baden: Nomos, 2012.

Black, Maggie. *A Cause for Our Times: Oxfam – The First 50 Years*. Oxford: Oxfam and Oxford University Press, 1992.

Blackwell, Joyce. *No Peace Without Freedom: Race and the Women's International League for Peace and Freedom, 1915–1976*. Carbondale, IL: Southern Illinois University Press, 2004.

Boli, John and George M. Thomas, eds. *Constructing World Culture: International Non-Governmental Organizations since 1875*. Stanford, CA: Stanford University Press, 1999.

Bolt, Christine. *Sisterhood Questioned? Race, Class and Internationalism in the British and American Women's Movements, c. 1880s–1970s*. Abingdon: Routledge, 2004.

Bolt, Christine and Seymour Drescher, eds. *Anti-Slavery, Religion, and Reform: Essays in Memory of Roger Anstey*. Folkestone: Wm. Dawson & Sons, 1980.

Boris, Eileen, Dorethea Hoehtke, and Susan Zimmermann, eds. *Women's ILO: Transnational Networks, Global Labour Standards and Gender Equity, 1919 to Present*. Leiden: Brill, 2018.

Boxer, Marilyn. 'Rethinking the Socialist Construction and International Career of the Concept "Bourgeois Feminism"'. *American Historical Review* 112, no. 1 (2007): 131–58.

Boyce Davies, Carole. *Left of Karl Marx: The Political Life of Black Communist Claudia Jones*. Durham, NC: Duke University Press, 2008.

Bracke, Maud. 'Between the Transnational and the Local: Mapping the Trajectories and Contexts of the Wages for Housework Campaign in 1970s Italian Feminism'. *Women's History Review* 22, no. 4 (2013): 625–42.

Bracke, Maud. 'Our Bodies, Ourselves: The Transnational Connections of 1970s Italian and Roman Feminism'. *Journal of Contemporary History* 50, no. 3 (2015): 560–80.

Bracke, Maud. *Which Socialism, Whose Détente? West European Communism and the Czechoslovak Crisis of 1968*. Budapest: Central European University Press, 2007.

Braskén, Kasper. *The International Workers' Relief, Communism, and Transnational Solidarity: Willi Münzenberg in Weimar Germany*. Basingstoke: Palgrave, 2015.

Select Bibliography

Braskén, Kasper. 'Making Anti-Fascism Transnational: The Origins of Communist and Socialist Articulations of Resistance in Europe, 1923–1924'. *Contemporary European History* 25, no. 4 (2016): 573–96.

Brewis, Georgina. *A Social History of Student Volunteering: Britain and Beyond, 1880–1980*. Basingstoke: Palgrave, 2014.

Brier, Robert. 'Broadening the Cultural History of the Cold War: The Emergence of the Workers' Defence Committee and the Rise of Human Rights'. *Journal of Cold War Studies* 15, no. 4 (2013): 104–27.

Brier, Robert. *Poland's Solidarity Movement and the Global Politics of Human Rights*. Cambridge: Cambridge University Press, 2021.

Brock, Peter and Nigel Young. *Pacifism in the Twentieth Century*. Syracuse, NY: Syracuse University Press, 1999.

Brock, Peter and Thomas P. Socknat, eds. *Challenge to Mars: Pacifism from 1918 to 1945*. Toronto: University of Toronto Press, 1999.

Brockington, Grace, Sarah Hellawell, and Daniel Laqua. 'Pacifist Journals'. In *The Edinburgh Companion to First World War Periodicals*, edited by Marysa Demoor, Cedric van Dijck and Birgit Van Puymbroeck, 352–67. Edinburgh: Edinburgh University Press, 2023.

Brown, Timothy Scott. *Sixties Europe*. Cambridge: Cambridge University Press, 2020.

Brückenhaus, Daniel. *Policing Transnational Protest: Liberal Imperialism and the Surveillance of Anticolonialists in Europe, 1905–1945*. Oxford: Oxford University Press, 2017.

Brydan, David and Jessica Reinisch, eds. *Internationalists in European History: Rethinking the Twentieth Century*. London: Bloomsbury, 2021.

Buchanan, Tom. *Amnesty International and Human Rights Activism in Postwar Britain, 1945–1977*. Cambridge: Cambridge University Press, 2020.

Burkett, Jodi. 'Re-defining British Morality: "Britishness" and the Campaign for Nuclear Disarmament 1958–68'. *Twentieth Century British History* 21, no. 2 (2010): 84–205.

Burroughs, Robert. *African Testimony in the Movement for Congo Reform: The Burden of Proof*. London: Routledge, 2019.

Burton, Antoinette. *Burdens of History: British Feminists, Indian Women, and Imperial Culture, 1865–1915*. Chapel Hill, NC: University of North Carolina Press, 1994.

Byrne, Jeffrey James. *Mecca of Revolution: Algeria, Decolonization and Third World Order*. New York: Oxford University Press, 2016.

Cabanes, Bruno. *The Great War and the Origins of Humanitarianism, 1918–1924*. Cambridge: Cambridge University Press, 2014.

Çağatay, Selin, Mia Liinason, and Olga Sasunkevich. *Feminist and LGBTI+ Activism across Russia: Scandinavia and Turkey: Transnationalizing Spaces of Resistance*. Cham: Palgrave, 2022.

Callahan, Kevin. *Demonstration Culture: European Socialism and the Second International, 1889–1914*. Leicester: Troubador, 2010.

Calver, Jasmine. *Anti-Fascism, Gender, and International Communism: The Comité Mondial des Femmes Contre le Guerre et le Fascisme, 1934–1941*. Abingdon: Routledge, 2023.

Capotescu, Cristian. 'Migrants into Humanitarians: Ethnic Solidarity and Private Aid-Giving during Romania's Historic Flood of 1970'. *East European Politics and Societies* 35, no. 2 (2021): 293–312.

Carle, Emmanuelle. 'Women, Anti-Fascism and Peace in Interwar France: Gabrielle Duchêne's Itinerary'. *French History* 18, no. 3 (2004): 291–314.

Carlier, Julie. 'Entangled Feminisms: Rethinking the History of the Belgian Movement for Women's Rights through Transnational Intersections'. *Revue belge de philologie et d'histoire* 90, no. 4 (2012): 1139–52.

Carlier, Julie. 'Forgotten Transnational Connections and National Contexts: An "Entangled History" of the Political Transfers that Shaped Belgian Feminism, 1890–1914'. *Women's History Review* 19, no. 4 (2010): 503–22.

Carter, April. *Peace Movements: International Protest and World Politics since 1945*. London: Longman, 1992.

Castelli, Alberto. *The Peace Discourse in Europe, 1900–1945*. Abingdon: Routledge, 2019.

Ceadel, Martin. *Semi-Detached Idealists: The British Peace Movement and International Relations, 1854–1945*. Oxford: Oxford University Press, 2000.

Célestine, Audrey, Nicolas Martin-Breteau, and Charlotte Recoquillon. 'Black Lives Matter: un mouvement transnational?'. *Esclavages et post-esclavages*, no. 6 (2022): 1–18.

Christiaens, Kim. 'Between Diplomacy and Solidarity: Western European Support Networks for Sandinista Nicaragua'. *European Review of History* 21, no. 4 (2014): 617–34.

Christiaens, Kim. 'Europe at the Crossroads of Three Worlds: Alternative Histories and Connections of European Solidarity with the Third World, 1950s–1980s'. *European Review of History* 24, no. 6 (2017): 932–54.

Christiaens, Kim. 'States Going Transnational: Transnational State Civilian Networks and Socialist Cuba and Sandinista Nicaragua Solidarity Movements in Belgium (1960s–1980s)'. *Revue belge de philologie et d'histoire* 89, nos. 3–4 (2011): 1277–305.

Christiaens, Kim, Idesbald Goddeeris, and Magaly Rodríguez García, eds. *European Solidarity with Chile, 1970s–1980s*. Frankfurt/Main: Peter Lang, 2014.

Christiaens, Kim, John Nieuwenhuys, and Charel Roemer, eds. *International Solidarity in the Low Countries during the Twentieth Century: New Perspectives and Themes*. Berlin: De Gruyter, 2020.

Christie, Ryerson. *Peacebuilding and NGOs: State–Civil Society Interactions*. Abingdon: Routledge, 2013.

Clark, Ann Marie. *Diplomacy of Conscience: Amnesty International and Changing International Human Rights Norms*. Princeton, NJ: Princeton University Press, 2001.

Clavin, Patricia. 'Defining Transnationalism'. *Contemporary European History* 14, no. 4 (2005): 421–39.

Clavin, Patricia. 'Time, Manner, Place: Writing Modern European History in Global, Transnational and International Contexts'. *European History Quarterly* 40, no. 4 (2010): 624–40.

Clay, Dean. 'The Congo Free State Propaganda War, 1890–1909'. *The International History Review* 43, no. 1 (2021): 457–74.

Cœuré, Sophie and Rachel Mazuy. *Cousu de fil rouge: Voyages des intellectuels français en Union soviétique. 150 documents inédits des Archives russes*. Paris: CNRS Éditions, 2012.

Cohen, Laurie. 'Across a Feminist-Pacifist Divide: Baroness Bertha von Suttner's Tour of the United States in 1912'. *L'Homme* 20, no. 2 (2009): 85–104.

Cole, Peter, David Struthers, and Kenyon Zimmer, eds. *Wobblies of the World: A Global History of the IWW*. London: Pluto, 2017.

Confortini, Catia Celia. *Intelligent Compassion: The Women's International League for Peace and Freedom and Feminist Peace*. Oxford: Oxford University Press, 2012.

Conway, Martin. *Western Europe's Democratic Age: 1945–1968*. Princeton, NJ: Princeton University Press, 2020.

Conway, Martin and Kiran Klaus Patel, eds. *Europeanization in the Twentieth Century: Historical Approaches*. Basingstoke: Palgrave, 2010.

Conze, Eckart, Martin Klimke, and Jeremy Varon, eds. *Nuclear Threats, Nuclear Fear and the Cold War of the 1980s*. Cambridge: Cambridge University Press, 2017.

Coons, Lorraine. 'Gabrielle Duchêne: Feminist, Pacifist, Reluctant Bourgeoise'. *Peace & Change* 24, no. 2 (1999): 121–47.

Select Bibliography

Cooper, Sandi. *Patriotic Pacifism: Waging War on War in Europe, 1815–1914*. New York: Oxford University Press, 1991.

Cortright, David. *Peace: A History of Movements and Ideas*. Cambridge: Cambridge University Press, 2008.

Cova, Anna. 'International Feminisms in Historical Comparative Perspective: France, Italy and Portugal, 1880s–1930s'. *Women's History Review* 19, no. 4 (2010): 595–612.

Crossland, James, Melanie Oppenheimer, Neville Wylie, eds. *The Red Cross Movement: Myths, Practices and Turning Points*. Manchester: Manchester University Press, 2020.

Crozier, Ivan. '"All the World's a Stage": Dora Russell, Norma Haire, and the 1929 London World League for Sexual Reform Congress'. *Journal of the History of Sexuality* 12, no. 1 (2003): 16–37.

Cullinane, Michael. 'Transatlantic Dimensions of the American Anti-Imperialist Movement, 1899–1909'. *Journal of Transatlantic Studies* 8, no. 4 (2010): 301–14.

Dallywater, Lena, Chris Saunders, and Helder Adegar Fonseca, eds. *Southern African Liberation Movements and the Global Cold War 'East': Transnational Activism 1960–1990*. Berlin: De Gruyter, 2019.

Darian-Smith, Eve. 'Re-reading W. E. B. Du Bois: The Global Dimensions of the U.S. Civil Rights Struggle'. *Journal of Global History* 7, no. 3 (2012): 483–503.

Davey, Eleanor. *Idealism beyond Borders: The French Revolutionary Left and the Rise of Humanitarianism, 1954–1988*. Cambridge: Cambridge University Press, 2015.

David-Fox, Michael. *Showcasing the Great Experiment: Cultural Diplomacy and Western Visitors to Soviet Russia, 1921–1941*. Oxford: Oxford University Press, 2012.

David, Huw. 'Transnational Advocacy in the Eighteenth Century: Transatlantic Activism and the Anti-Slavery Movement'. *Global Networks* 7, no. 3 (2007): 367–82.

David, Thomas and Janick Schaufelbuehl. 'Swiss Conservatives and the Struggle for the Abolition of Slavery at the End of the Nineteenth Century'. *Itinerario* 34, no. 2 (2010): 87–103.

Davies, Thomas. *NGOs: A New History of Transnational Civil Society*. London: Hurst, 2014.

Davies, Thomas. *The Possibilities of Transnational Activism: The Campaign for Disarmament between the Two World Wars*. Leiden: Brill, 2007.

de Bont, Raf. *Nature's Diplomats: Science, Internationalism, and Preservation, 1920–1960*. Pittsburgh, PA: University of Pittsburgh Press, 2021.

De Giuseppe, Massimo and Girogio Vecchio. 'Die Friedensbewegungen in Italien'. *Mitteilungsblatt des Instituts für soziale Bewegungen* 32 (2004): 131–57.

de Haan, Francisca. 'Continuing Cold War Paradigms in Western Historiography of Transnational Women's Organisations: The Case of the Women's International Democratic Federation (WIDF)'. *Women's History Review* 19, no. 4 (2010): 547–73.

de Haan, Francisca. 'Left Feminism: Rediscovering the Women's International Democratic Federation'. *Yearbook of Women's History* 40 (2021): 107–12.

de Vries, Petra. 'Josephine Butler and the Making of Feminism: International Abolitionism in the Netherlands (1870–1914)'. *Women's History Review* 17, no. 2 (2008): 257–77.

Delius, Anna. 'Translating Human Rights between Local Workers and Transnational Activism in Late 1970s Poland'. *East Central Europe* 46, nos. 2–3 (2019): 188–211.

Della Porta, Donatella, ed. *Global Diffusion of Protest: Riding the Protest Wave in the Neoliberal Crisis*. Amsterdam: Amsterdam University Press, 2017.

Della Porta, Donatella, ed. *The Global Justice Movement: Cross-National and Transnational Perspectives*. Abingdon: Routledge, 2007.

Della Porta, Donatella and Alice Mattoni, eds. *Spreading Protest: Social Movements in Times of Crisis*. Colchester: ECPR Press, 2014.

Della Porta, Donatella and Manuela Caiani. *Social Movements and Europeanization*. Oxford: Oxford University Press, 2009.

Della Porta, Donatella and Mario Diani. *Social Movements: An Introduction*. Malden, MA: Blackwell, 2006.

Della Porta, Donatella, Massimiliano Andretta, Lorenzo Mosca, and Herbert Reiter. *Globalization from Below: Transnational Activists and Protest Networks*. Minneapolis, MN: University of Minnesota Press, 2006.

Derrick, Jonathan. *Africa's 'Agitators': Militant Anti-Colonialism in Africa and the West, 1918–1939*. New York: Columbia University Press, 2008.

Di Paola, Pietro. *The Knights Errant of Anarchy: London and the Italian Diaspora (1880–1917)*. Liverpool: Liverpool University Press, 2013.

Dittrich, Lisa. *Antiklerikalismus in Europa: Öffentlichkeit und Säkularisierung in Frankreich, Spanien und Deutschland (1848–1914)*. Göttingen: Vandenhoeck & Ruprecht, 2014.

Dols, Chris and Benjamin Ziemann. 'Progressive Participation and Transnational Activism in the Catholic Church after Vatican II: The Dutch and West German Examples'. *Journal of Contemporary History* 50, no. 3 (2015): 465–85.

Donert, Celia. 'Women's Rights and Global Socialism: Gendering Socialist Internationalism during the Cold War'. *International Review of Social History* 67, S30 (2022): 1–22.

Dose, Ralf. 'The World League for Sexual Reform: Some Possible Approaches'. *Journal of the History of Sexuality* 12, no. 1 (2003): 1–15.

Dromi, Shai. *Above the Fray: The Red Cross and the Making of the Humanitarian NGO Sector*. Chicago: University of Chicago Press, 2020.

Drwal, Małgorzata. 'The Feminism of Olive Schreiner and the Feminism of Aletta Jacobs: The Reception of Schreiner's Woman and Labour in the Netherlands'. *Dutch Crossing* 45, no. 1 (2021): 77–92.

Eckel, Jan. *The Ambivalence of Good: Human Rights in International Politics since the 1940s*, translated by Rachel Ward. Oxford: Oxford University Press, 2019.

Eckel, Jan and Samuel Moyn, eds. *The Breakthrough: Human Rights in the 1970s*. Philadelphia, PA: University of Pennsylvania Press, 2015.

Eley, Geoff. *Forging Democracy: The History of the Left in Europe, 1850–2000*. Oxford: Oxford University Press, 2002.

Ellis, Stephen. *External Mission: The ANC in Exile, 1960–1990*. Oxford: Oxford University Press, 2013.

Ellis, Sylvia. 'Promoting Solidarity at Home and Abroad: The Goals and Tactics of the Anti-Vietnam War Movement in Britain'. *European Review of History* 21, no. 4 (2014): 557–76.

Epstein, Charlotte. 'The Making of Global Environmental Norms: Endangered Species Protection'. *Global Environmental Politics* 6, no. 2 (2006): 32–54.

Evangelista, Matthew. *Unarmed Forces: The Transnational Movement to End the Cold War*. Ithaca, NY: Cornell University Press, 1999.

Everard, Myriam and Francisca De Haan, eds. *Rosa Manus: The International Life and Legacy of a Jewish Dutch Feminist*. Leiden: Brill, 2016.

Everard, Myriam and Mieke Aerts. 'Forgotten Intersections: Wilhelmina Drucker, Early Feminism, and the Dutch-Belgian Connection'. *Revue belge de philologie et d'histoire* 77, no. 2 (1999): 440–72.

Falk, Barbara. *The Dilemmas of Dissidence in East-Central Europe: Citizen Intellectuals and Philosopher Kings*. Budapest: Central European University Press, 2003.

Favez, Jean-Claude. *The Red Cross and the Holocaust*, translated by John and Beryl Fletcher. Cambridge: Cambridge University Press, 1999.

Fehrenbach, Heide and Davide Rodogno, eds. *Humanitarian Photography: A History*. Cambridge: Cambridge University Press, 2015.

Fell, Alison and Ingrid Sharp, eds. *The Women's Movement in Wartime: International Perspectives, 1914–19*. Basingstoke: Palgrave, 2007.

Fieldhouse, Roger. *Anti-Apartheid: A History of the Movement in Britain, 1959–1994*. London: Merlin, 2004.

Select Bibliography

Filatova, Irina. 'Indoctrination or Scholarship? Education of Africans at the Communist University of the Toilers of the East in the Soviet Union, 1923–1937'. *Paedagogica Historica* 35, no. 1 (1999): 41–66.

Finchelstein, Federico. *Transatlantic Fascism: Ideology, Violence, and the Sacred in Argentina and Italy, 1919–1945*. Durham, NC: Duke University Press, 2010.

Fink, Carole. *Defending the Rights of Others: The Great Powers, the Jews, and International Minority Protection, 1878–1938*. Cambridge: Cambridge University Press, 2004.

Fischer-Tiné, Harald. 'Indian Nationalism and the "World Forces": Transnational and Diasporic Dimensions of the Indian Freedom Movement on the Eve of the First World War'. *Journal of Global History* 2, no. 3 (2007): 325–44.

Fischer, Thomas. 'Frauenhandel und Prostitution: Zur Institutionalisierung eines transnationalen Diskurses im Völkerbund'. *Zeitschrift für Geschichtswissenschaft* 54, no. 10 (2006): 876–87.

Fletcher, Roger. 'Cobden as Educator: The Free-Trade Internationalism of Eduard Bernstein, 1899–1914'. *The American Historical Review* 88, no. 3 (1983): 561–78.

Fontaine, Marion. 'L'Internationale des syndicalistes: quel sens donner à l'internationalisme? Le cas des mineurs'. *Cahiers Jaurès*, nos. 212–13 (2014): 91–103.

Forster, Laura. 'The Paris Commune in the British Socialist Imagination, 1871–1914'. *History of European Ideas* 46, no. 5 (2020): 614–32.

Forsythe, David. *The Humanitarians: The International Committee of the Red Cross*. Cambridge: Cambridge University Press, 2005.

Fotaki, Marianna and Hamid Foroughi. 'Extinction Rebellion: Green Activism and the Fantasy of Leaderlessness in a Decentralized Movement'. *Leadership* 18, no. 2 (2022): 224–46.

Framke, Maria. *Delhi – Rom – Berlin: Die indische Wahrnehmung von Faschismus und Nationalsozialismus 1922–1939*. Darmstadt: WBG, 2013.

Framke, Maria. 'Political Humanitarianism in the 1930s: Indian Aid for Republican Spain'. *European Review of History* 23, nos. 1–2 (2016): 63–81.

Framke, Maria. '"We Must Send a Gift Worthy of India and the Congress!": War and Political Humanitarianism in Late Colonial South Asia'. *Modern Asian Studies* 51, no. 6 (2017): 1969–98.

Frazier, Jessica. *Women's Antiwar Diplomacy during the Vietnam Era*. Chapel Hill, NC: The University of North Carolina Press, 2017.

Freitag, Sabine and Rudolf Muhs, eds. *Exiles from European Revolutions: Refugees in Mid-Victorian Politics*. New York: Berghahn, 2003.

Fürst, Juliane. *Flowers through Concrete: Explorations in Soviet Hippieland*. Oxford: Oxford University Press, 2021.

Gatejel, Luminita. 'Bargaining for Humanitarian Aid across the Iron Curtain: Western Relief Workers in Romania in the late 1970s'. *Cold War History* 22, no. 1 (2022): 41–57.

Gatrell, Peter. *Free World? The Campaign to Save the World's Refugees*. Cambridge: Cambridge University Press, 2011.

Gatrell, Peter. *The Making of the Modern Refugee*. Oxford: Oxford University Press, 2015.

Gehrig, Sebastian, James Mark, Paul Betts, Kim Christiaens, and Idesbald Goddeeris. 'The Eastern Bloc, Human Rights, and the Global Fight against Apartheid'. *East Central Europe*, 46, nos. 2–3 (2019): 290–317.

Gerund, Katherina. 'Sisterly (Inter)Actions: Audre Lorde and the Development of Afro-German Women's Communities'. *Gender Forum* 22 (2008): 56–72.

Getty, J. Arch. 'Trotsky in Exile: The Founding of the Fourth International'. *Soviet Studies* 38, no. 1 (1986): 24–35.

Geyer, Martin and Johannes Paulmann, eds. *The Mechanics of Internationalism: Culture, Society, and Politics from the 1840s to the First World War*. Oxford: Oxford University Press, 2001.

Ghodsee, Kristen. *Second World, Second Sex: Socialist Women's Activism and Global Solidarity during the Cold War*. Durham, NC: Duke University Press, 2019.

Gilburd, Elonory. 'The Revival of Soviet Internationalism in the Mid to Late 1950s'. In *The Thaw: Soviet Society and Culture during the 1950s and 1960s*, edited by Denis Kozlov and Elonory Gilburd, 362–401. Toronto: University of Toronto Press, 2013.

Gildea, Robert, James Mark and Anette Warring, eds. *Europe's 1968: Voices of Revolt*. Oxford: Oxford University Press, 2013.

Gildea, Robert, James Mark and Niek Pas. 'European Radicals and the "Third World"'. *Cultural and Social History* 8, no. 4 (2011): 449–71.

Gill, Rebecca. *Calculating Compassion: Humanity and Relief in War, Britain 1870–1914*. Manchester: Manchester University Press, 2013.

Gill, Rebecca. 'Networks of Concern, Boundaries of Compassion: British Relief in the South African War'. *Journal of Imperial and Commonwealth History* 40, no. 5 (2012): 827–44.

Gill, Rebecca and Cornelis Muller. 'The Limits of Agency: Emily Hobhouse's International Activism and the Politics of Suffering'. *Safundi* 19, no. 1 (2018): 16–35.

Gkotzaridis, Evi. '"Who Will Help Me to Get Rid of This Man?": Grigoris Lambrakis and the Non-Aligned Peace Movement in Post-Civil War Greece: 1951–1964'. *Journal of Modern Greek Studies* 30, no. 2 (2012): 299–338.

Gleason Carew, Joy. *Blacks, Reds, and Russians: Sojourners in Search of the Soviet Promise*. New Brunswick, NJ: Rutgers University Press, 2010.

Goddeeries, Idesbald, ed. *Solidarity with Solidarity: Western European Trade Unions and the Polish Crisis, 1980–1982*. Lanham, MD: Lexington Books, 2010.

Goebel, Michael. *Anti-Imperial Metropolis: Interwar Paris and the Seeds of Third World Nationalism*. Cambridge: Cambridge University Press, 2015.

Goebel, Michael. 'Geopolitics, Transnational Solidarity or Diaspora Nationalism? The Global Career of M.N. Roy, 1915–1930'. *European Review of History* 21, no. 4 (2014): 485–99.

Gopal, Priyamvada. *Insurgent Empire: Anticolonial Resistance and British Dissent*. London: Verso, 2019.

Gordeeva, Irina. 'Solidarity in Search of Human Agency: "Détente from Below", and Independent Peace Activists in the Soviet Union'. *Labour History Review* 86, no. 3 (2021): 339–68.

Gordon, Daniel. 'French and British Anti-Racists since the 1960s: A Rendez-Vous Manqué?'. *Journal of Contemporary History* 50, no. 3 (2015): 606–31.

Gorman, Daniel. *The Emergence of International Society in the 1920s*. Cambridge: Cambridge University Press, 2012.

Gorman, Daniel. *International Cooperation in the Early Twentieth Century*. London: Bloomsbury, 2018.

Gorsuch, Anne and Diane Koenker, eds. *The Socialist Sixties: Crossing Borders in the Second World*. Bloomington, IN: Indiana University Press, 2013.

Götz, Norbert, Georgina Brewis, and Steffen Werther. *Humanitarianism in the Modern World: The Moral Economy of Famine Relief*. Cambridge: Cambridge University Press, 2020.

Gottlieb, Julie and Matthew Stibbe. 'Peace at any Price: The Visit of Nazi Women's Leader Gertrud Scholtz-Klink to London in March 1939 and the Response of British Women Activists'. *Women's History Review* 26, no. 2 (2017): 173–94.

Goyens, Tom. *Beer and Revolution: The German Anarchist Movement in New York City, 1880–1914*. Urbana, IL: University of Illinois Press, 2007.

Gradskova, Yulia. 'The WIDF's Work for Women's Rights in the (Post)Colonial Countries and the "Soviet Agenda"'. *International Review of Social History* 67, S30 (2022): 155–78.

Gradskova, Yulia. *The Women's International Democratic Federation, the Global South, and the Cold War: Defending the Rights of Women of the 'Whole World'?*. Abingdon: Routledge, 2021.

Granick, Jaclyn. *International Jewish Humanitarianism in the Age of the Great War*. Cambridge: Cambridge University Press, 2021.

Select Bibliography

Grant, Kevin. *A Civilised Savagery: Britain and the New Slaveries in Africa, 1884–1926*. New York: Routledge, 2005.

Grant, Kevin, Philippa Levine, and Frank Trentmann, eds. *Beyond Sovereignty: Britain, Empire and Transnationalism, c. 1880–1950*. Basingstoke: Palgrave, 2007.

Green, Abigail. 'Liberals, Socialists, Internationalists, Jews'. *Journal of World History* 31, no. 1 (2020): 11–41.

Green, Abigail. 'Nationalism and the "Jewish International": Religious Internationalism in Europe and the Middle East c. 1840 – c. 1880'. *Comparative Studies in Society and History* 50, no. 2 (2008): 535–58.

Green, Abigail. *Moses Montefiore: Jewish Liberator, Imperial Hero*. Cambridge, MA: Harvard University Press, 2010.

Green, Abigail and Simon Levis Sullam, eds. *Jews, Liberalism, Antisemitism: A Global History*. Cham: Palgrave Macmillan, 2020.

Green, Abigail and Vincent Viaene, eds. *Religious Internationals in the Modern World*. London: Palgrave, 2012.

Green, Lara. 'Russian Revolutionary Terrorism, British Liberals, and the Problem of Empire (1884–1914)'. *History of European Ideas* 46, no. 5 (2020): 633–48.

Gruber, Helmut and Pamela Graves, eds. *Women and Socialism, Socialism and Women; Europe between the Two World Wars*. New York: Berghahn, 1998.

Guha, Ramachandra. *Environmentalism: A Global History*. London: Longman, 2016.

Guieu, Jean-Michel and Christophe Le Dréau, eds. *Le 'Congrès de l'Europe' à La Haye (1948–2008)*. Brussels: P.I.E. Peter Lang, 2008.

Haas, Peter M. *Epistemic Communities, Constructivism, and International Environmental Politics*. Abingdon: Routledge, 2016.

Häberlen, Joachim. 'Between Global Aspirations and Local Realities: The Global Dimensions of Interwar Communism'. *Journal of Global History* 7, no. 3 (2012): 415–37.

Hagemann, Karen, Stefan Dudink, and Sonya Rose, eds. *The Oxford Handbook of Gender, War, and the Western World since 1600*. Oxford: Oxford University Press, 2020.

Hagen, Katrina. 'Ambivalence and Desire the East German "Free Angela Davis" Campaign'. In *Comrades of Color: East Germany in the Cold War World*, edited by Quinn Slobodian, 157–87. New York: Berghahn, 2015.

Hamann, Brigitte. *Bertha von Suttner: Ein Leben für den Frieden*. Munich: Piper, 1986.

Hämmerle, Christa, Oswald Überegger, and Birgit Bader-Zaar, eds. *Gender and the First World War*. Basingstoke: Palgrave, 2014.

Hannam, June. *Feminism*. 2nd edition. Abingdon: Routledge, 2012.

Harms, Victoria. 'Living Mitteleuropa in the 1980s: A Network of Hungarian and West German Intellectuals'. *European Review of History* 19, no. 5 (2012): 669–92.

Haslam, Jonathan. 'The British Communist Party, the Comintern, and the Outbreak of War, 1939: "A Nasty Taste in the Mouth"'. *Diplomacy & Statecraft* 3, no. 1 (1992): 147–54.

Haunss, Sebastian and Moritz Sommer, eds. *Fridays for Future – Die Jugend gegen den Klimawandel; Konturen der weltweiten Protestbewegung*. Bielefeld: transcript, 2020.

Heerten, Lasse. *The Biafran War and Postcolonial Humanitarianism: Spectacles of Suffering*. Cambridge: Cambridge University Press, 2017.

Hellawell, Sarah. 'Antimilitarism, Citizenship and Motherhood: The Formation and Early Years of the Women's International League (WIL), 1915–1919'. *Women's History Review* 27, no. 4 (2018): 551–64.

Helm, Christian. 'Booming Solidarity: Sandinista Nicaragua and the West German Solidarity Movement in the 1980s'. *European Review of History* 21, no. 4 (2014): 597–615.

Henderson, Robert. 'The Hyde Park Rally of 9 March 1890: A British Response to Russian Atrocities'. *European Review of History* 21, no. 4 (2014): 451–66.

Henderson, Robert. *The Spark That Lit the Revolution: Lenin in London and the Politics That Changed the World*. London: Bloomsbury, 2020.
Herren, Madeleine. *Internationale Organisationen seit 1865: Eine Globalgeschichte der internationalen Ordnung*. Darmstadt: Wissenschaftliche Buchgesellschaft, 2009.
Hessler, Julie. 'Death of an African Student in Moscow: Race, Politics, and the Cold War'. *Cahiers du Monde Russe* 47, nos. 1–2 (2006): 33–63.
Hilson, Mary. *The International Co-operative Alliance and the Consumer Co-operative Movement in Northern Europe, c. 1860–1939*. Manchester: Manchester University Press, 2018.
Hilson, Mary, Silke Neunsinger, and Greg Patmore, eds. *A Global History of Consumer Co-operation since 1850: Movements and Businesses*. Leiden: Brill, 2017.
Hilton, Matthew. 'International Aid and Development NGOs in Britain and Human Rights since 1945'. *Humanity* 3, no. 3 (2012): 449–72.
Hockenos, Paul. *Homeland Calling: Exile Patriotism and the Balkan Wars*. Ithaca, NY: Cornell University Press, 2003.
Hodder, Jake. 'The Elusive History of the Pan-African Congress, 1919–27'. *History Workshop Journal* 91, no. 1 (2021): 113–31.
Hoffmann, Stefan-Ludwig, ed. *Human Rights in History*. New York: Cambridge University Press, 2010.
Høgsbjerg, Christian. *C. L. R. James in Imperial Britain*. Durham, NC: Duke University Press, 2014.
Horn, Gerd-Rainer. *The Spirit of '68: Rebellion in Western Europe and North America, 1956–1976*. Oxford: Oxford University Press, 2007.
Horn, Gerd-Rainer. *The Spirit of Vatican II: Western European Progressive Catholicism in the Long Sixties*. Oxford: Oxford University Press, 2015.
Horn, Gerd-Rainer and Padraic Kenney, eds. *Transnational Moments of Change: Europe 1945, 1968, 1989*. Lanham, MD: Rowman & Littlefield, 2004.
Howe, Stephen. *Ireland and Empire: Colonial Legacies in Irish History and Culture*. Oxford: Oxford University Press, 2000.
Huber, Anja. *Fremdsein im Krieg: Die Schweiz als Ausgangs- und Zielland von Migranten, 1914–1918*. Zurich: Chromos, 2017.
Hucker, Daniel. *Public Opinion and Twentieth-Century Diplomacy: A Global Perspective*. London: Bloomsbury, 2020.
Hughes, Michael. 'British Opinion and Russian Terrorism in the 1880s'. *European History Quarterly* 41, no. 2 (2011): 255–77.
Hughes, Michael L. 'Civil Disobedience in Transnational Perspective: American and West German Anti-Nuclear-Power Protesters'. *Historical Social Research* 39, no. 1 (2014): 236–53.
Hunt, Karen. 'Suffrage Internationalism in Practice: Dora Montefiore and the Lessons of Finnish Women's Enfranchisement'. In *The Politics of Women's Suffrage: Local, National and International Dimensions*, edited by Alexandra Hughes-Johnson and Lyndsey Jenkins, 285–308. London: University of London Press/Institute of Historical Research, 2021.
Hunt, Lynn. *Inventing Human Rights: A History*. New York: W. W. Norton, 2007.
Hurst, Mark. *British Human Rights Organizations and Soviet Dissent, 1965–1985*. London: Bloomsbury, 2016.
Huzzey, Richard. *Freedom Burning: Anti-Slavery and Empire in Victorian Britain*. Ithaca, NY: Cornell University Press, 2012.
Imlay, Talbot. *The Practice of Internationalism: European Socialists and International Politics, 1914–60*. Oxford: Oxford University Press, 2018.
Ingram, Norman. *The Politics of Dissent: Pacifism in France, 1919–1939*. Oxford: Oxford University Press, 1991.
Ingram, Norman. *The War Guilt Problem and the Ligue des Droits de l'Homme, 1914–1944*. Oxford: Oxford University Press, 2019.

Select Bibliography

Iriye, Akira. *Global Community: The Role of International Organizations in the Making of the Contemporary World*. Berkeley, CA: University of California Press, 2004.

Iriye, Akira and Pierre-Yves Saunier, eds. *The Palgrave Dictionary of Transnational History: From the Mid-19th Century to the Present Day*. Basingstoke: Palgrave, 2010.

Iriye, Akira, Petra Goedde, and William Hitchcock, eds. *The Human Rights Revolution: An International History*. New York: Oxford University Press, 2012.

Irwin, Julia. *Making the World Safe: The American Red Cross and a Nation's Humanitarian Awakening*. Oxford: Oxford University Press, 2013.

Jackson, Sarah, Moya Bailey, and Brooke Foucault Welles. *#Hashtag Activism: Networks of Race and Gender Justice*. Cambridge, MA: The MIT Press, 2020.

Jacob, Frank and Mario Keßler, eds. *Transatlantic Radicalism: Socialist and Anarchist Exchanges in the 19th and 20th Centuries*. Liverpool: Liverpool University Press, 2021.

Jacobs, Jack, ed. *Jewish Politics in Eastern Europe: The Bund at 100*. Basingstoke: Palgrave, 2001.

Jacobsson, Kerstin and Steven Saxonberg, eds. *Beyond NGO-ization: The Development of Social Movements in Central and Eastern Europe*. Farnham: Ashgate, 2013.

James, Leslie. *George Padmore and Decolonization from Below: Pan-Africanism, the Cold War, and the End of Empire*. Basingstoke: Palgrave, 2015.

Janse, Maartje. '"Holland as a Little England? British Anti-Slavery Missionaries and Continental Abolitionist Movements in the Mid-Nineteenth-Century". *Past & Present*, no. 229 (2015): 123–60.

Janz, Oliver and Daniel Schönpflug, eds. *Gender History in a Transnational Perspective: Networks, Biographies, Gender Orders*. New York: Berghahn, 2014.

Jenkins, Jennifer, Heike Liebau, and Larissa Schmid. 'Transnationalism and Insurrection: Independence Committees, Anti-Colonial Networks, and Germany's Global War'. *Journal of Global History* 15, no. 1 (2020): 61–79.

Jenkinson, Jacqueline. 'Soon Gone, Long Forgotten: Uncovering British Responses to Belgian Refugees during the First World War'. *Immigrants & Minorities* 34, no. 2 (2016): 101–12.

Jennings, Lawrence. *French Anti-Slavery: The Movement for the Abolition of Slavery in France, 1802–1848*. Cambridge: Cambridge University Press, 2000.

Jensen, Richard Bach. *The Battle against Anarchist Terrorism: An International History, 1878–1934*. Cambridge: Cambridge University Press, 2014.

Jones, Heather. 'International or Transnational? Humanitarian Actors during the First World War'. *European Review of History* 16, no. 5 (2009): 697–713.

Kadelbach, Thomas. *Les brigadistes suisses au Nicaragua (1982–1990)*. Fribourg: Academic Press Fribourg, 2006.

Kaiser, Wolfram and Jan-Henrik Meyer, eds. *International Organizations and Environmental Protection: Conservation and Globalization in the Twentieth Century*. New York: Berghahn, 2017.

Kaldor, Mary. *New and Old Wars: Organized Violence in a Global Era*. 3rd edition. Cambridge: Polity, 2012.

Kallis, Aristotle. 'From CAUR to EUR: Italian Fascism, the "Myth of Rome" and the Pursuit of International Primacy'. *Patterns of Prejudice* 50, nos. 4–5 (2016): 359–77.

Kallis, Aristotle. 'The Transnational Co-production of Interwar "Fascism": On the Dynamics of Ideational Mobility and Localization'. *European History Quarterly* 51, no. 2 (2021): 189–213.

Kalmbach, Karena. *The Meanings of a Disaster: Chernobyl and Its Afterlives in Britain and France*. New York: Berghahn, 2021.

Karamouzi, Eirini. '"Out With the Bases of Death": Civil Society and Peace Mobilization in Greece during the 1980s'. *Journal of Contemporary History* 56, no. 3 (2021): 617–38.

Keck, Margaret and Kathryn Sikkink. *Activists beyond Borders: Advocacy Networks in International Politics*. Ithaca, NY: Cornell University Press, 1998.

Keene, Judith. *Fighting for Franco: International Volunteers in Nationalist Spain during the Spanish Civil War, 1936–1939*. London: Hambledon Continuum, 2001.

Kelemen, Paul. 'In the Name of Socialism: Zionism and European Social Democracy in the Inter-War Years'. *International Review of Social History* 41, no. 3 (1996): 331–50.

Kelly, Luke. 'Christianity and Humanitarianism in the Doukhobor Campaign, 1895–1902'. *Cultural and Social History* 13, no. 3 (2016): 339–55.

Kelly, Patrick William. *Sovereign Emergencies: Latin America and the Making of Global Human Rights Politics*. Cambridge: Cambridge University Press, 2018.

Kenney, Padraic. 'Borders Breached: The Transnational in Eastern Europe since Solidarity'. *Journal of Modern European History* 8, no. 2 (2010): 179–95.

Kenney, Padraic. *A Carnival of Revolution: Central Europe 1989*. Princeton, NJ: Princeton University Press, 2002.

Keßler, Mario. *Zionismus und internationale Arbeiterbewegung 1897–1933*. Berlin: Akademie Verlag, 1994.

Keys, Barbara. *Reclaiming American Virtue: The Human Rights Revolution of the 1970s*. Cambridge, MA: Harvard University Press, 2014.

Kind-Kovács, Friederike. *Budapest's Children: Humanitarian Relief in the Aftermath of the Great War*. Bloomington, IN: Indiana University Press, 2022.

Kind-Kovács, Friederike and Jessie Labov, eds. *Samizdat, Tamizdat, and Beyond: Transnational Media during and after Socialism*. New York: Berghahn, 2013.

Kinealy, Christine. *Daniel O'Connell and the Anti-Slavery Movement: 'The Saddest People the Sun Sees'*. London: Pickering & Chatto, 2011.

Kinna, Ruth and Matthew S. Adams, eds. *Anarchism, 1914–18: Internationalism, Anti-Militarism and War*. Manchester: Manchester University Press, 2017.

Kinna, Ruth. *The Government of No One: The Theory and Practice of Anarchism*. London: Pelican, 2019.

Kinnunen, Tiina. 'The National and International in Making a Feminist: The Case of Alexandra Gripenberg'. *Women's History Review* 25, no. 4 (2016): 652–70.

Király, Edit. 'An der Grenze des Erlaubten: Ungarische Kontakte der Aktion Sühnezeichen in den 1980er Jahren'. *Journal of Modern European History* 8, no. 2 (2010): 221–42.

Kirby, David. 'International Socialism and the Question of Peace: The Stockholm Conference of 1917'. *The Historical Journal* 25, no. 3 (1982): 709–16.

Klimke, Martin. *The Other Alliance: Student Protest in West Germany and the United States in the Global Sixties*. Princeton, NJ: Princeton University Press, 2010.

Klimke, Martin and Joachim Scharloth, eds. *1968 in Europe: A History of Protest and Activism, 1956–1977*. Basingstoke: Palgrave, 2008.

Klimke, Martin, Jacco Pekelder, and Joachim Scharloth, eds. *Between Prague Spring and French May: Opposition and Revolt in Europe, 1960–1980*. New York: Berghahn, 2011.

Klose, Fabian, ed. *The Emergence of Humanitarian Intervention: Ideas and Practice from the Nineteenth Century to the Present*. Cambridge: Cambridge University Press, 2016.

Klose, Fabian. *In the Cause of Humanity: A History of Humanitarian Intervention in the Long Nineteenth Century*, translated by Joe Kroll. Cambridge: Cambridge University Press, 2022.

Kodi, Muzong. 'The 1921 Pan-African Congress at Brussels: A Background to Belgian Pressures'. *Transafrican Journal of History* 13 (1984): 48–73.

Konieczna, Anna and Rob Skinner, eds. *A Global History of Anti-Apartheid: 'Forward to Freedom' in South Africa*. Cham: Palgrave, 2019.

Konishi, Sho. 'The Emergence of an International Humanitarian Organization in Japan: The Tokugawa Origins of the Japanese Red Cross'. *The American Historical Review* 119, no. 4 (2014): 1129–53.

Kornetis, Kostis. *Children of the Dictatorship: Student Resistance, Cultural Politics and the 'Long 1960s' in Greece*. New York: Berghahn, 2013.

Select Bibliography

Korowin, Elena and Jurij Lileev, eds. *Russische Revolutionen 1917: Kulturtransfer im europäischen Raum*. Leiden: Brill, 2020.

Kosharovsky, Yuli. *'We Are Jews Again'! Jewish Activism in the Soviet Union*, translated by Stefani Hoffman and edited by Ann Komaromi. Syracuse, NY: Syracuse University Press, 2017.

Kotek, Joël. *Students and the Cold War*, translated by Ralph Blumenau. Basingstoke: Palgrave, 1996.

Kott, Sandrine. *Organiser le monde: une autre histoire de la guerre froide*. Paris: Seuil, 2021.

Kraft, Alison and Carola Sachse, eds. *Science, (Anti-)Communism and Diplomacy: The Pugwash Conferences on Science and World Affairs in the Early Cold War*. Leiden: Brill, 2020.

Kruitenbrouwer, Vincent. *War of Words: Dutch Pro-Boer Propaganda and the South African War (1899–1902)*. Amsterdam: Amsterdam University Press, 2012.

Kunkel, Sönke and Christoph Meyer, eds. *Aufbruch ins postkoloniale Zeitalter: Globalisierung und die außereuropäische Welt der 1920er und 1930er Jahre*. Frankfurt/Main: Campus, 2012.

Kurz, Nathan. *Jewish Internationalism and Human Rights after the Holocaust*. Cambridge: Cambridge University Press, 2021.

Kushner, Tony and Katherine Knox. *Refugees in an Age of Genocide: Global, National and Local Perspectives during the Twentieth Century*. London: Frank Cass, 1999.

Lakkimsetti, Chaitanya and Vanita Reddy. '#MeToo and Transnational Gender Justice: An Introduction'. *Feminist Formations* 33, no. 3 (2021): 224–38.

LaPorte, Norman, Kevin Morgan, and Matthew Worley, eds. *Bolshevism, Stalinism and the Comintern: Perspectives on Stalinization, 1917–53*. Basingstoke: Palgrave, 2008.

Laqua, Daniel. *The Age of Internationalism and Belgium, 1880–1930: Peace, Progress and Prestige*. Manchester: Manchester University Press, 2013.

Laqua, Daniel. 'Democratic Politics and the League of Nations: The Labour and Socialist International as a Protagonist of Interwar Internationalism'. *Contemporary European History* 24, no. 2 (2015): 175–92.

Laqua, Daniel. 'Freethinkers, Anarchists and Francisco Ferrer: The Making of a Transnational Solidarity Campaign'. *European Review of History* 21, no. 4 (2014): 467–84.

Laqua, Daniel, ed. *Internationalism Reconfigured: Transnational Ideas and Movements between the World Wars*. London: I.B. Tauris, 2011.

Laqua, Daniel. 'Pacifism in Fin-de-Siècle Austria: The Politics and Limits of Peace Activism'. *The Historical Journal* 57, no. 1 (2014): 199–224.

Laqua, Daniel. 'The Politics of Transnational Student Mobility, Youth, Activism and Education in Ghana, 1957–1966'. *Social History* 48, no. 1 (2022).

Laqua, Daniel. 'Rocking against the Right: Political Activism and Popular Music in West Germany, 1979–1980'. *History Workshop Journal* 86 (2018): 160–83.

Laqua, Daniel. 'The Tensions of Internationalism: Transnational Anti-Slavery in the 1880s and 1890s'. *The International History Review* 33, no. 4 (2011): 705–26.

Laqua, Daniel. 'Transnational Dimensions of a "German Case": The Expatriation of Wolf Biermann and the Politics of Solidarity in the 1970s'. *Labour History Review* 86, no. 3 (2021): 369–96.

Laqua, Daniel and Charlotte Alston. 'Activism and Dissent under State Socialism: Coalitions and Campaigns in the 1970s and 1980s'. *Labour History Review* 86, no. 3 (2021): 295–311.

Laruelle, ed. Marlene, *Eurasianism and the European Far Right: Reshaping the Europe – Russia Relationship*. Lanham, MD: Lexington, 2015.

Lattek, Christine. *Revolutionary Refugees: German Socialism in Britain, 1840–1860*. Abingdon: Routledge, 2006.

Laucht, Christoph. 'Transnational Professional Activism and the Prevention of Nuclear War in Britain'. *Journal of Social History* 52, no. 2 (2018): 439–67.

Laursen, Ole Birk, ed. *Lay Down Your Arms: Anti-Militarism, Anti-Imperialism and the Global Radical Left in the 1930s*. Atlanta, GA: On Our Own Account, 2019.

Laycock, Jo. 'Saving the Remnant or Building Socialism? Transnational Humanitarian Relief in Early Soviet Armenia'. *Moving the Social* 57 (2017): 77–96.

Laycock, Jo and Francesca Piana, eds. *Aid to Armenia: Humanitarianism and Intervention from the 1890s to the Present*. Manchester: Manchester University Press, 2020.

Legg, Stephen, Mike Heffernan, Jake Hodder, and Benjamin Thorpe, eds. *Placing Internationalism: International Conferences and the Making of the Modern World*. London: Bloomsbury, 2022.

Levsen, Sonja and Kiran Klaus Patel. *Beyond Transnationalism: Mapping the Spatial Contours of Political Activism in Europe's Long 1970s*, themed issue of *European Review of History* 29, no. 3 (2022).

Levy, Carl and Matthew Adams, eds. *The Palgrave Handbook of Anarchism*. Cham: Palgrave, 2019.

Lewis, Su Lin and Carolien Stolte. 'Other Bandungs: Afro-Asian Internationalisms in the Early Cold War'. *Journal of World History* 30, no. 1 (2019): 1–19.

Liburd, Liam. 'Thinking Imperially: The British Fascisti and the Politics of Empire, 1923–35'. *Twentieth Century British History* 32, no. 1 (2021): 46–67.

Liddington, Jill. *The Road to Greenham Common: Feminism and Anti-Militarism in Britain since 1820*. Syracuse, NY: Syracuse University Press, 1989.

Limoncelli, Stephanie. *The Politics of Trafficking: The First International Movement to Combat the Sexual Exploitation of Women*. Stanford, CA: Stanford University Press, 2010.

Löhr, Isabella. 'Solidarity and the Academic Community: The Support Networks for Refugee Scholars in the 1930s'. *Journal of Modern European History* 12, no. 2 (2004): 231–46.

Lössing, Felix. *A 'Crisis of Whiteness' in the 'Heart of Darkness': Racism and the Congo Reform Movement*. Bielefeld: transcript, 2020.

Louro, Michele. *Comrades against Imperialism: Nehru, India, and Interwar Internationalism*. Cambridge: Cambridge University Press, 2018.

Louro, Michele, Carolien Stolte, Heather Streets-Salter, and Sana Tannoury-Karam, eds. *The League against Imperialism: Lives and Afterlives*. Leiden: Leiden University Press, 2021.

Lovell, Julia. *Maoism: A Global History*. New York: Alfred A. Knopf, 2019.

Ludi, Regula. 'Setting New Standards: International Feminism and the League of Nations' Inquiry into the Status of Women'. *Journal of Women's History* 31, no. 1 (2019): 12–36.

Lynch, Cecilia. *Beyond Appeasement: Interpreting Interwar Peace Movements in World Politics*. Ithaca, NY: Cornell University Press, 1999.

Macekura, Stephen. *Of Limits and Growth: The Rise of Global Sustainable Development in the Twentieth Century*. Cambridge: Cambridge University Press, 2015.

Makris, Alexandros. 'The Greek Peace Movement and the Vietnam War, 1964–1967'. *Journal of Modern Greek Studies* 38, no. 1 (2020): 159–83.

Mammone, Andrea. *Transnational Neofascism in France and Italy*. Cambridge: Cambridge University Press, 2015.

Mammone, Andrea, Emmanuel Godin, and Brian Jenkins, eds. *Varieties of Right-Wing Extremism in Europe*. Abingdon: Routledge, 2013.

Mancini, Elena. *Magnus Hirschfeld and the Quest for Sexual Freedom: A History of the First International Sexual Freedom Movement*. New York: Palgrave, 2010.

Manela, Erez. *The Wilsonian Moment: Self Determination and the International Origins of Anticolonial Nationalism*. New York: Oxford University Press, 2007.

Manjapra, Kris. *M. N. Roy: Marxism and Colonial Cosmopolitanism*. Abingdon: Routledge, 2010.

Select Bibliography

Marchal, Jules. *E. D. Morel contre Léopold II: L'histoire du Congo 1900–1910*. Paris: L'Harmattan, 1996.

Mark, James and Péter Apor. 'Socialism Goes Global: Decolonization and the Making of a New Culture of Internationalism in Socialist Hungary, 1956–1989'. *Journal of Modern History* 87, no. 4 (2015): 852–91.

Mark, James, Paul Betts et al. *Socialism Goes Global: The Soviet Union and Eastern Europe in the Age of Decolonisation*. Oxford: Oxford University Press, 2022.

Mark, James, Péter Apor, Radina Vučetić, and Piotr Osęka. '"We Are with You, Vietnam": Transnational Solidarities in Socialist Hungary, Poland and Yugoslavia'. *Journal of Contemporary History* 50, no. 3 (2015): 439–64.

Marks, Shula, Paul Weindling, and Laura Wintour, eds. *In Defence of Learning: The Plight, Persecution, and Placement of Academic Refugees, 1933–1980s*. Oxford: Oxford University Press, 2011.

Marrus, Michael. *The Unwanted: European Refugees from the First World War through the Cold War*. Philadelphia, PA: Temple University Press, 2002.

Matera, Marc. *Black London: The Imperial Metropolis and Decolonization in the Twentieth Century*. Oakland, CA: University of California Press, 2015.

Matthäus, Jürgen. *Predicting the Holocaust: Jewish Organizations Report from Geneva on the Emergence of the 'Final Solution', 1939–1942*. Lanham, MD: Rowman & Littlefield, 2019.

Maul, Daniel. *The Politics of Service: US-amerikanische Quäker und internationale humanitäre Hilfe 1917–1945*. Berlin: De Gruyter, 2022.

May, Rob. 'Saving Our Empire from the Bolsheviks: The British Fascisti from a Transnational Perspective'. *The Journal of Imperial and Commonwealth History* 49, no. 1 (2021): 70–92.

Mazower, Mark. *Governing the World: The History of an Idea*. London: Penguin, 2012.

Mazower, Mark. 'The Strange Triumph of Human Rights'. *The Historical Journal* 47, no. 2 (2004): 379–98.

McCarthy, Helen. *The British People and the League of Nations: Democracy, Citizenship and Internationalism, c. 1918–1945*. Manchester: Manchester University Press, 2011.

McDermott, Kevin and Jeremy Agnew. *The Comintern: A History of International Communism from Lenin to Stalin*. New York: St Martin's, 1997.

McGaughey, Fiona. *Non-Governmental Organisations and the United Nations Human Rights System*. Abingdon: Routledge, 2021.

McGeever, Brendan and Satnam Virdee. 'Antisemitism and Socialist Strategy in Europe, 1880–1917'. *Patterns of Prejudice* 51, nos. 3–4 (2017): 221–34.

McMahon, Patrice. *The NGO Game: Post-Conflict Peacebuilding in the Balkans and Beyond*. Ithaca, NY: Cornell University Press, 2017.

Michaels, Jennifer. 'The Impact of Audre Lorde's Politics and Poetics on Afro-German Women Writers'. *German Studies Review* 29, no. 1 (2006): 21–40.

Midgley, Clare, Alison Twells, and Julie Carlier, eds. *Women in Transnational History: Connecting the Local and the Global*. Abingdon: Routledge, 2013.

Miers, Suzanne. *Britain and the Ending of the Slave Trade*. London: Longman, 1975.

Miers, Suzanne. *Slavery in the Twentieth Century: The Evolution of a Global Problem*. Walnut Creek, CA: AltaMira, 2003.

Mignon Kirchhof, Astrid and J. R. McNeill, eds. *Environmental Policy and Social Movements in Communist and Capitalist Countries 1945–1990*. Pittsburgh, PA: University of Pittsburgh Press, 2019.

Mignon Kirchhof, Astrid and Jan-Henrik Meyer. 'Global Protest against Nuclear Power: Transfer and Transnational Exchange in the 1970s and 1980s'. *Historical Social Research* 39, no. 1 (2014): 165–90.

Milder, Stephen. *Greening Democracy: The Anti-Nuclear Movement and Political Environmentalism in West Germany and Beyond, 1968–1983*. Cambridge: Cambridge University Press, 2017.

Milder, Stephen. 'Thinking Globally, Acting (Trans-)Locally: Petra Kelly and the Transnational Roots of West German Green Politics'. *Central European History* 43, no. 2 (2010): 301–26.

Miller, Carol. '"Geneva – the Key to Equality": Inter-War Feminists and the League of Nations'. *Women's History Review* 3, no. 2 (1994): 219–45.

Milner, Susan. *The Dilemmas of Internationalism: French Syndicalism and the International Labour Movement, 1900–1914*. New York: Berg, 1990.

Mitchell, Katharyne and Key MacFarlane. 'The Sanctuary Network: Transnational Church Activism and Refugee Protection in Europe'. In *Handbook on Critical Geographies of Migration*, edited by Katharyne Mitchell, Reece Jones and Jennifer Fluri, 410–24. Cheltenham: Edward Elgar, 2019.

Möller, Esther. 'Humanitarismus ohne Grenzen? Die Rotkreuz- und Rothalbmondbewegung und der Israel-Palästina-Konflikt 1948–1949'. *Geschichte in Wissenschaft und Unterricht* 66, nos. 1–2 (2015): 61–77.

Möller, Esther, Johannes Paulmann, and Katharina Stornig, eds. *Humanitarianism in the Twentieth Century: Practice, Politics and the Power of Representation*. Cham: Palgrave, 2020.

Monforte, Pierre, *Europeanizing Contention: The Protest against 'Fortress Europe' in France and Germany*. New York: Berghahn, 2014.

Morina, Christina. *Die Erfindung des Marxismus: Wie eine Idee die Welt eroberte*. Munich: Siedler, 2017.

Moss, Nicolas. *Solidarity Is More than a Slogan: International Workers Aid during and after the 1992-1995 War in Bosnia and Herzegovina*. Brussels: Rosa Luxemburg Stiftung, 2021.

Moura Mota, Isadora. 'On the Verge of War: Black Insurgency, the "Christie Affair", and British Antislavery in Brazil'. *Slavery & Abolition* 43, no. 1 (2022): 120–39.

Moyn, Samuel. *The Last Utopia: Human Rights in History*. Cambridge, MA: Harvard University Press, 2010.

Mullen, Bill. *Un-American: W. E. B. Du Bois and the Century of World Revolution*. Philadelphia, PA: Temple University Press, 2015.

Mulligan, William and Maurice Brigg, eds. *A Global History of Anti-Slavery in the Nineteenth Century*. Basingstoke: Palgrave, 2013.

Murphy, David. 'Defending the "Negro Race": Lamine Senghor and Black Internationalism in Interwar France'. *French Cultural Studies* 24, no. 2 (2013): 161–73.

Murray, Hannah-Rose. *Advocates of Freedom: African American Transatlantic Abolitionism in the British Isles*. Cambridge: Cambridge University Press, 2020.

Murray, Hannah-Rose and John McKivigan, eds. *Frederick Douglass in Britain and Ireland, 1845–1895*. Edinburgh: Edinburgh University Press, 2021.

Naquet, Emanuel. *Pour l'humanité: La Ligue des droits de l'homme de l'Affaire Dreyfus à la défaite de 1940*. Rennes: Presses Universitaires de Rennes, 2014.

Natalia Shapovalova and Olga Burlyuk, eds. *Civil Society in Post-Euromaidan Ukraine*. Stuttgart: ibidem, 2018.

Nation, R. Craig. *War on War: Lenin, the Zimmerwald Left, and the Origins of Communist Internationalism*. Durham, NC: Duke University Press, 1989.

Nehring, Holger. *Politics of Security: British and West German Protest Movements and the Early Cold War, 1945–1970*. Oxford: Oxford University Press, 2013.

Nehring, Holger and Benjamin Ziemann. 'Do All Paths Lead to Moscow? The NATO Dual-Track Decision and the Peace Movement – A Critique'. *Cold War History* 12, no. 1 (2012): 1–24.

Neumann, Matthias. 'Youthful Internationalism in the Age of "Socialism in One Country": Komsomol'tsy, Pioneers and "World Revolution" in the Interwar Period'. *Revolutionary Russia* 31, no. 2 (2018): 279–303.

Newell, Peter. *Global Green Politics*. Cambridge: Cambridge University Press, 2020.

Nicolas Delalande. *La Lutte et l'entraide: l'âge des solidarités ouvrières*. Paris: Seuil, 2019.

Select Bibliography

Nietsch, Julie. 'The Mother Teresa Society: Volunteer Work for the Kosovo-Albanian "Parallel Structures" in the 1990s'. *Comparative Southeast European Studies* 68, no. 2 (2020): 200–24.

Nye, Joseph and Robert Keohane. 'Transnational Relations and World Politics: An Introduction'. *International Organization* 25, no. 3 (1971): 329–49.

O'Brien, Matthew. 'Irish Americans, Race, and Bernadette Devlin's 1969 American Tour'. *New Hibernia Review* 14, no. 2 (2010): 84–101.

O'Dwyer, Conor. *Coming Out of Communism: The Emergence of LGBT Activism in Eastern Europe*. New York: New York University Press, 2018.

O'Reilly, Maria. *Gendered Agency in War and Peace: Gender Justice and Women's Activism in Post-Conflict Bosnia-Herzegovina*. London: Palgrave, 2013.

O'Sullivan, Kevin. *The NGO Moment: The Globalisation of Compassion from Biafra to Live Aid*. Cambridge: Cambridge University Press, 2021.

Offen, Karen. *European Feminisms, 1750–1950: A Political History*. Stanford, CA: Stanford University Press, 2000.

Olcock, Jocelyn. *International Women's Year: The Greatest Consciousness-Raising Event in History*. Oxford: Oxford University Press, 2017.

Oldfield, John. *The Ties That Bind: Transatlantic Abolitionism in the Age of Reform, c. 1820–1865*. Liverpool: Liverpool University Press, 2020.

Oldfield, Sibyl. 'Mary Sheepkshanks Edits an Internationalist Suffrage Monthly in Wartime: Jus Suffragii 1914–19'. *Women's History Review* 12, no. 1 (2003): 119–39.

Oleinikova, Olga and Jumana Bayeh, eds. *Democracy, Diaspora, Territory: Europe and Cross-Border Politics*. Abingdon: Routledge, 2019.

Olesen, Thomas. 'Globalising the Zapatistas: From Third World Solidarity to Global Solidarity?'. *Third World Quarterly* 25, no. 1 (2004): 255–67.

Olesen, Thomas, ed. *Power and Transnational Activism*. Abingdon: Routledge, 2011.

Ortuño Anaya, Pilar. *European Socialists and Spain: The Transition to Democracy, 1959–77*. Basingstoke: Palgrave, 2002.

Ostergaard-Nielsen, Eva. 'The Politics of Migrants' Transnational Political Practices'. *The International Migration Review* 37, no. 3 (2003): 760–86.

Osterhammel, Jürgen. *The Transformation of the World: A Global History of the Nineteenth Century*, translated by Patrick Camiller. Princeton, NJ: Princeton University Press, 2014.

Othen, Christopher. *Franco's International Brigades: Adventurers, Fascists, and Christian Crusaders in the Spanish Civil War*. London: Hurst, 2013.

Paisley, Fiona and Pamela Scully. *Writing Transnational History*. London: Bloomsbury, 2019.

Palmier, Jean-Michel. *Weimar in Exile: The Antifascist Emigration in Europe and America*, translated by David Fernbach. London: Verso, 2006.

Pasture, Patrick. *Histoire du syndicalisme chrétien international: La difficile recherche d'une troisième voie*. Paris: L'Harmattan, 1999.

Patterson, David. *The Search for Negotiated Peace: Women's Activism and Citizen Diplomacy in World War I*. New York: Routledge, 2008.

Paulmann, Johannes, ed. *Dilemmas of Humanitarian Aid in the Twentieth Century*. Oxford: Oxford University Press, 2016.

Paulmann, Johannes, ed. *Humanitarianism and Media: 1900 to the Present*. New York: Berghahn, 2018.

Pavard, Bibia, Florence Rochefort, and Michelle Zancarini-Fournel. *Ne nous libérez pas, on s'en charge: Une histoire des féminismes à nos jours*. Paris: La Découverte, 2020.

Pavlakis, Dean. *British Humanitarianism and the Congo Reform Movement, 1896–1913*. Farnham: Ashgate, 2013.

Pedersen, Susan. *The Guardians: The League of Nations and the Crisis of Empire*. Oxford: Oxford University Press, 2015.

Pennybacker, Susan. *From Scottsboro to Munich: Race and Political Culture in 1930s Britain.* Princeton, NJ: Princeton University Press, 2009.

Pereira, Victor. *La dictature de Salazar face à l'émigration: l'État portugais et ses migrants en France (1957–1974).* Paris: Presses de Sciences Po, 2012.

Peretz, Pauline. *Let My People Go: The Transnational Politics of Soviet Jewish Emigration During the Cold War*, translated by Ethan Rundell. New Brunswick, NJ: Transaction Publishers, 2015.

Perrier, Hubert, Catherine Collomp, Michel Cordillot, and Marianne Debouzy. 'The "Social Revolution" in America? European Reactions to the "Great Upheaval" and to the Haymarket Affair'. *International Labor and Working-Class History* 29 (1986): 38–52.

Petersson, Frederick. 'Hub of the Anti-Imperialist Movement: The League against Imperialism and Berlin, 1927–1933'. *Interventions* 16, no. 1 (2014): 49–71.

Petricioli, Marta, Donatella Cherubini, and Alessandra Anteghini, eds. *Les Etats-Unis d'Europe: Un Project Pacifiste/The United States of Europe: A Pacifist Project.* Bern: Peter Lang, 2004.

Piana, Francesca. 'The Dangers of "Going Native": George Montandon in Siberia and the International Committee of the Red Cross, 1919–1922'. *Contemporary European History* 25, no. 2 (2016): 253–74.

Pons, Silvio. *The Global Revolution: A History of International Communism 1917–1991*, translated by Allan Cameron. Oxford: Oxford University Press, 2014.

Prashad, Vijay. *Red Star over the Third World.* London: Pluto, 2019.

Prettenthaler-Ziegerhofer, Anita. *Botschafter Europas: Richard Nikolaus Coudenhove-Kalergi und die Paneuropa-Bewegung in den zwanziger und dreißiger Jahren.* Cologne: Böhlau, 2004.

Priestland, David. *The Red Flag: Communism and the Making of the Modern World.* London: Allen Lane, 2009.

Proctor, Tammy. *Civilians in a World at War, 1914–1918.* New York: New York University Press, 2010.

Quinn-Judge, Sophie. *Ho Chi Minh: The Missing Years.* London: Hurst, 2003.

Radkau, Joachim. *The Age of Ecology*, translated by Patrick Camiller. Cambridge: Polity Press, 2014.

Raeff, Marc. *Russia Abroad: A Cultural History of the Russian Emigration, 1919–1939.* Oxford: Oxford University Press, 1990.

Rappaport, Helen. *Conspirator: Lenin in Exile.* New York: Basic Books, 2010.

Rees, Tim and Andrew Thorpe, eds. *International Communism and the Communist International, 1919–1943.* Manchester: Manchester University Press, 1998.

Reitan, Ruth. *Global Activism.* Abingdon: Routledge, 2007.

Rhéaume, Charles. 'Western Scientists' Reactions to Andrei Sakharov's Human Rights Struggle in the Soviet Union, 1968–1989'. *Human Rights Quarterly* 30, no. 1 (2008): 1–21.

Ribi Forclaz, Amalia. *Humanitarian Imperialism: The Politics of Anti-Slavery Activism, 1880–1940.* Oxford: Oxford University Press, 2015.

Richard, Anne-Isabelle. 'The Limits of Solidarity: Europeanism, Anti-Colonialism and Socialism at the Congress of the Peoples of Europe, Asia and Africa in Puteaux, 1948'. *European Review of History* 21, no. 4 (2014): 519–37.

Richardson-Little, Ned. *The Human Rights Dictatorship: Socialism, Global Solidarity and Revolution in East Germany.* Cambridge: Cambridge University Press, 2020.

Richter, Saskia. 'Petra Kelly als Mittlerin in der transnationalen Friedensbewegung gegen den NATO-Doppelbeschluss'. *Moving the Social* 44 (2010): 21–42.

Riese, Juliane. *Hairy Hippies and Bloody Butchers: The Greenpeace Anti-Whaling Campaign in Norway.* New York: Berghahn, 2017.

Risse-Kappen, Thomas, ed. *Bringing Transnational Relations Back In: Non-State Actors, Domestic Structures and International Institutions.* Cambridge: Cambridge University Press, 1995.

Select Bibliography

Rodogno, Davide. *Against Massacre: Humanitarian Interventions in the Ottoman Empire, 1815–1914*. Princeton, NJ: Princeton University Press, 2012.

Rodogno, Davide. *Night on Earth: A History of International Humanitarianism in the Near East, 1918–1930*. Cambridge: Cambridge University Press, 2022.

Rodogno, Davide, Bernhard Struck, and Jakob Vogel, eds. *Shaping the Transnational Sphere: Experts, Networks and Issues from the 1840s to the 1930s*. New York: Berghahn, 2015.

Rodríguez Garcia, Magaly. 'The League of Nations and the Moral Recruitment of Women'. *International Review of Social History* 57, S. 20 (2012): 97–128.

Rootes, Christopher, ed. *Environmental Protest in Western Europe*. Oxford: Oxford University Press, 2007.

Rosenberg, Emily, ed. *A World Connecting: 1870–1945*. Cambridge, MA: Belknap Press, 2012.

Roshanravan, Shireen. 'On the Limits of Globalizing Black Feminist Commitments: "Me Too" and Its White Detours'. *Feminist Formations* 33, no. 3 (2021): 239–55.

Roy, Baijayanti. 'At the Crossroads of Anti-Colonialism, Axis Propaganda and International Communism: The Periodical Azad Hind in Nazi Germany'. *Media History* (advance access online 2022), https://doi.org/10.1080/13688804.2022.2158793 (last accessed 9 January 2023).

Rucht, Dieter. 'The Transnationalization of Social Movements: Trends, Causes, Problems'. In *Transnational Movements in a Globalizing World*, edited by Donatella Della Porta, Hanspeter Kriesi and Dieter Rucht, 206–22. Basingstoke: Palgrave, 1999.

Rupp, Leila. 'Constructing Internationalism: The Case of Transnational Women's Organizations, 1888–1945'. *American Historical Review* 99, no. 5 (1994): 571–600.

Rupp, Leila. 'The Persistence of Transnational Organizing: The Case of the Homophile Movement'. *The American Historical* Review 116, no. 4 (2011): 1014–39.

Rupp, Leila. *Worlds of Women: The Making of an International Women's Movement*. Princeton, NJ: Princeton University Press, 1997.

Sampson, Steven. 'Weak States, Uncivil Societies and Thousands of NGOs: Benevolent Colonialism in the Balkans'. In *The Balkans in Focus: Cultural Boundaries in Europe*, edited by Sanimir Resic and Barbara Törnquist-Plewa, 27–44. Lund: Nordic Academic Press, 2002.

Sand, Shlomo. 'Bernard Lazare: Le premier sioniste français'. *Revue française de l'histoire des idées politiques*, no. 4 (1996): 281–96.

Sandell, Marie. *The Rise of Women's Transnational Activism: Identity and Sisterhood between the World Wars*. London: I.B. Tauris, 2015.

Sasson, Tehila. 'Milking the Third World? Humanitarianism, Capitalism, and the Moral Economy of the Nestlé Boycott'. *The American Historical Review* 121, no. 4 (2016): 1196–224.

Sasson, Tehila. 'From Empire to Humanity: The Russian Famine and the Imperial Origins of International Humanitarianism'. *Journal of British Studies* 55, no. 3 (2016): 519–37.

Saunders, Clare. *Environmental Networks and Social Movement Theory*. London: Bloomsbury, 2013.

Saunier, Pierre-Yves. *Transnational History*. Basingstoke: Palgrave, 2013.

Scalmer, Sean. *Gandhi in the West: The Mahatma and the Rise of Radical Protest*. Cambridge: Cambridge University Press, 2011.

Schleper, Simone. *Planning for the Planet: Environmental Expertise and the International Union for Conservation of Nature and Natural Resources, 1960–1980*. New York: Berghahn, 2019.

Schmidt, Nelly. *L'abolition de l'esclavage: Cinq siècles de combats, XVIe – XXe siècles*. Paris: Fayard, 2005.

Schmidt, Nelly. *Victor Schœlcher et l'abolition de l'esclavage*. Paris: Fayard, 1994.

Schönemann-Behrens, Petra. *Alfred H. Fried: Friedensaktivist – Nobelpreisträger*. Zürich: Römerhof, 2011.

Schrad, Mark Lawrence. *Smashing the Liquor Machine: A Global History of Prohibition*. New York: Oxford University Press, 2021.

Schubert, Maria. 'Allies across Cold War Boundaries: The American Civil Rights Movement and the GDR'. *Kirchliche Zeitgeschichte* 33, no. 1 (2021): 59–71.

Schulz, Kristina. 'Feminist Echoes of 1968: Women's Movements in Europe and the United States'. In *A Revolution of Perception? Consequences and Echoes of 1968*, edited by Ingrid Gilcher-Holtey, 124–47. New York: Berghahn, 2014.

Schulz, Kristina, ed. *The Women's Liberation Movement: Issues and Outcomes*. New York: Berghahn, 2017.

Sedlmaier, Alexander, ed. *Protest in the Vietnam Era*. Basingstoke: Palgrave, 2022.

Segev, Zohar. *The World Jewish Congress during the Holocaust: Between Activism and Restraint*. Berlin: De Gruyter, 2014.

Service, Robert. *Comrades! A History of World Communism*. Cambridge, MA: Harvard University Press, 2007.

Sharp, Ingrid and Matthew Stibbe, eds. *Women Activists between War and Peace: Europe, 1918–1923*. London: Bloomsbury, 2017.

Sharp, Ingrid. '"An Unbroken Family"? Gertrud Bäumer and the German Women's Movement's Return to International Work in the 1920s'. *Women's History Review* 26, no. 2 (2017): 245–61.

Sharp, Ingrid. 'Love as Moral Imperative and Gendered Anti-War Strategy in the International Women's Movement 1914–1919'. *Diplomacy & Statecraft* 31, no. 4 (2020): 630–47.

Shaw, Caroline. *Britannia's Embrace: Modern Humanitarianism and the Imperial Origins of Refugee Relief*. Oxford: Oxford University Press, 2015.

Shekhovtsov, Anton. *Russia and the Western Far Right: Tango Noir*. Abingdon: Routledge, 2018.

Sherwood, Marika. *Claudia Jones: A Life in Exile*. 2nd edition. London: Lawrence & Wishart, 2021.

Sherwood, Marika. *Origins of Pan-Africanism: Henry Sylvester Williams, Africa and the African Diaspora*. New York: Routledge, 2011.

Shield, Andrew. 'The Legacies of the Stonewall Riots in Denmark and the Netherlands'. *History Workshop Journal* 89 (2020): 193–20.

Shindler, Colin. *Israel and the European Left: Between Solidarity and Delegitimization*. London: Continuum, 2012.

Sibeud, Emmanuelle. 'Entre geste impériale et cause internationale: défendre les indigènes à Genève dans les années 1920'. *Monde(s)*, no. 6 (2014): 23–43.

Siegfried, Detlef. 'Understanding 1968: Youth Rebellion, Generational Change and Postindustrial Society'. In *Between Marx and Coca-Cola: Youth Cultures in Changing European Societies, 1960–1980*, edited by Axel Schildt and Detlef Siegfried, 59–81. New York: Berghahn, 2006.

Salvatici, Silvia. *A History of Humanitarianism, 1755–1989: In the Name of Others*, translated by Philip Sanders. Manchester: Manchester University Press, 2019.

Simms, Brendan and D. J. B. Trim, eds. *Humanitarian Intervention: A History*. Cambridge: Cambridge University Press, 2011.

Skinner, Rob. *The Foundations of Anti-Apartheid: Liberal Humanitarians and Transnational Activists in Britain and the United States, c. 1919–64*. Basingstoke: Palgrave, 2010.

Skran, Claudena. *Refugees in Inter-War Europe: The Emergence of a Regime*. Oxford: Oxford University Press, 1995.

Slate, Nico, ed. *Black Power beyond Borders: The Global Dimensions of the Black Power Movement*. New York: Palgrave, 2012.

Slobodian, Quinn. *Foreign Front: Third World Politics in Sixties West Germany*. Durham, NC: Duke University Press, 2012.

Slotte, Pamela and Miia Halme-Tuomisaari, eds. *Revisiting the Origins of Human Rights*. Cambridge: Cambridge University Press, 2015.

Sluga, Glenda. *Internationalism in the Age of Nationalism*. Philadelphia, PA: University of Pennsylvania Press, 2013.

Sluga, Glenda and Patricia Clavin, eds. *Internationalisms: A Twentieth-Century History*. Cambridge: Cambridge University Press, 2017.

Select Bibliography

Snyder, Sarah. *Human Rights Activism and the End of the Cold War: A Transnational History of the Helsinki Network*. Cambridge: Cambridge University Press, 2011.

Social Movement Studies Editorial Collective, ed. *Occupy! A Global Movement*. Abingdon: Routledge, 2015.

Sorrels, Katherine. *Cosmopolitan Outsiders: Imperial Inclusion, National Exclusion, and the Pan-European Idea, 1900–1930*. New York: Palgrave, 2016.

Stamatov, Peter. *The Origins of Global Humanitarianism: Religion, Empires, and Advocacy*. Cambridge: Cambridge University Press, 2013.

Steger, Manfred. *The Rise of the Global Imaginary: Political Ideologies from the French Revolution to the War on Terror*. Oxford: Oxford University Press, 2008.

Steinacher, Gerald. *Humanitarians at War: The Red Cross in the Shadow of the Holocaust*. Oxford: Oxford University Press, 2017.

Stierl, Maurice. 'A Sea of Struggle – Activist Border Interventions in the Mediterranean Sea'. *Citizenship Studies* 20, no. 5 (2016): 561–78.

Stola, Dariusz. 'Anti-Zionism as a Multipurpose Policy Instrument: The Anti-Zionist Campaign in Poland, 1967–1968'. *Journal of Israeli History* 25, no. 1 (2006): 175–201.

Stolte, Carolien. '"The People's Bandung": Local Anti-Imperialists on an Afro-Asian Stage'. *Journal of World History* 30, no. 1 (2019): 12–56.

Stolte, Carolien. 'Trade Unions on Trial: The Meerut Conspiracy Case and Trade Union Internationalism, 1929–32'. *Comparative Studies of South Asia, Africa and the Middle East* 33, no. 3 (2013): 345–59.

Studer, Brigitte. *Reisende der Weltrevolution: Eine Globalgeschichte der Kommunistischen Internationale*. Frankfurt/Main: Suhrkamp, 2020.

Studer, Brigitte. *The Transnational World of the Cominternians*. Basingstoke: Palgrave, 2015.

Stutje, Jan Willem. *Ernest Mandel: A Rebel's Dream Deferred*, translated by Christopher Beck and Peter Drucker. London: Verso, 2009.

Stutje, Klaas. *Campaigning in Europe for a Free Indonesia: Indonesian Nationalists and the Worldwide Anticolonial Movement, 1917–1931*. Copenhagen: NIAS Press, 2019.

Sulkunen, Irma, Seija-Leena Nevala-Nurmi, and Pirjo Markkola, eds. *Suffrage, Gender and Citizenship: International Perspectives on Parliamentary Reforms*. Newcastle upon Tyne: Cambridge Scholars Publishing, 2009.

Summers, Anne. 'Which Women? What Europe? Josephine Butler and the International Abolitionist Federation'. *History Workshop Journal* 62, no. 1 (2006): 214–231.

Sysling, Fenneke. '"Protecting the Primitive Natives": Indigenous People as Endangered Species in the Early Nature Protection Movement, 1900–1940'. *Environment and History* 21, no. 3 (2015): 381–99.

Szulc, Lukasz. *Transnational Homosexuals in Communist Poland: Cross-Border Flows in Gay and Lesbian Magazines*. Cham: Palgrave, 2018.

Szulecki, Kacper. *Dissidents in Communist Central Europe: Human Rights and the Emergence of New Transnational Actors*. Cham: Palgrave, 2019.

Taithe, Bertrand. 'Reinventing (French) Universalism: Religion, Humanitarianism and the "French Doctors"'. *Modern & Contemporary France* 12, no. 2 (2004): 147–58.

Tarrow, Sidney. *The New Transnational Activism*. Cambridge: Cambridge University Press, 2005.

Tarrow, Sidney. *Power in Movement: Social Movements and Contentious Politics*. 3rd edition. Cambridge: Cambridge University Press, 2013.

Taylor, Becky. *Refugees in Twentieth-Century Britain*. Cambridge: Cambridge University Press, 2021.

Thébaud, Françoise. *Une traversée du siècle: Marguerite Thibert, femme engagée et fonctionnaire internationale*. Paris: Éditions Belin, 2017.

Thörn, Håkan. *Anti-Apartheid and the Emergence of a Global Civil Society*. Basingstoke: Palgrave, 2006.

Tilly, Charles. *The Politics of Collective Violence*. Cambridge: Cambridge University Press, 2003.

Tilly, Charles and Sidney Tarrow. *Contentious Politics*. 2nd edition. Oxford: Oxford University Press, 2015.

Tilly, Charles, Ernesto Castañeda, and Lesley J. Wood. *Social Movements, 1768–2018*. New York: Routledge, 2020.

Tismaneanu, Vladimir, ed. *In Search of Civil Society: Independent Peace Movements in the Soviet Bloc*. New York: Routledge, 1990.

Todorova, Maria. *The Lost World of Socialists at Europe's Margins: Imagining Utopia, 1870s–1920s*. London: Bloomsbury, 2020.

Tompkins, Andrew. *Better Active Than Radioactive! Anti-Nuclear Protest in 1970s France and West Germany*. Oxford: Oxford University Press, 2016.

Tompkins, Andrew. 'Grassroots Transnationalism(s): Franco-German Opposition to Nuclear Energy in the 1970s'. *Contemporary European History* 25, no. 1 (2016): 117–42.

Tompkins, Andrew. 'Transnationality as a Liability? The Anti-Nuclear Movement at Malville'. *Revue belge de philologie et d'histoire* 89, nos. 3–4 (2011): 1365–79.

Tóth, Heléna. *An Exiled Generation: German and Hungarian Refugees of Revolution, 1848–1871*. New York: Cambridge University Press, 2014.

Toupin, Louise. *Wages for Housework: A History of an International Feminist Movement, 1972–77*, translated by Käthe Roth. London: Pluto, 2018.

Tremlett, Giles. *The International Brigades: Fascism, Freedom and the Spanish Civil War*. London: Bloomsbury, 2021.

Troen, Selwyn and Benjamin Pinkus, eds. *Organizing Rescue: Jewish National Solidarity in the Modern Period*. London: Frank Cass, 1992.

Tuck, Stephen. *The Night Malcolm X Spoke at the Oxford Union: A Transatlantic Story of Antiracist Protest*. Oakland, CA: University of California Press, 2014.

Turcato, Davide. 'Italian Anarchism as a Transnational Movement, 1885–1915'. *International Review of Social History* 52, no. 3 (2007): 407–44.

Tyrrell, Ian. *Woman's World – Woman's Empire: The Woman's Christian Temperance Union in International Perspective, 1880–1930*. Chapel Hill, NC: University of North Carolina Press, 1991.

Unangst, Matthew. 'Manufacturing Crisis: Anti-Slavery "Humanitarianism" and Imperialism in East Africa, 1888–1890'. *Journal of Imperial and Commonwealth History* 48, no. 5 (2020): 805–25.

van Dam, Peter. 'Attracted and Repelled: Transnational Relations between Civil Society and the State in the History of the Fair Trade Movement since the 1960s'. In *Shaping the International Relations of the Netherlands, 1815–2000: A Small Country on the Global Stage*, edited by Ruud van Dijk, Samuël Kruizinga, Vincent van Kuitenbrouwer and Rimko van der Maar, 83–200. Abingdon: Routledge, 2018.

van Dam, Peter. 'No Justice Without Charity: Humanitarianism after Empire'. *The International History Review* 44, no. 3 (2022): 653–74.

van Dam, Peter. *Wereldverbeteraars: een geschiedenis van fair trade*. Amsterdam: Amsterdam University Press, 2018.

van de Grift, Liesbeth, Hans Rodenburg, and Guus Wieman. 'Entering the European Political Arena, Adapting to Europe: Greenpeace International, 1987–93'. In *The Environment and the European Public Sphere: Perceptions, Actors, Policies*, edited by Christian Wenkel, Eric Bussière, Anahita Grisoni and Hélène Miard-Delacroix, 147–64. Winwick: White Horse Press, 2020.

van der Linden, Marcel. *Transnational Labour History: Explorations*. Aldershot: Ashgate, 2003, 12.

Select Bibliography

van Dongen, Luc, Stéphanie Roulin and Giles Scott Smith, eds. *Transnational Anti-Communism and the Cold War: Agents, Activities, and Networks*. Basingstoke: Palgrave, 2014.

Van Goethem, Geert. *The Amsterdam International: The World of the International Federation of Trade Unions, 1913–1945*. Aldershot: Ashgate, 2006.

van Haute, Emilie, ed. *Green Parties in Europe*. Abingdon: Routledge, 2016.

van Holthoon Frits and Marcel van der Linden. *Internationalism in the Labour Movement, 1830–1940*. Leiden: Brill, 1988.

van Voss, Lex Heerma, Patrick Pasture, and Jan De Maeyer, eds. *Between Cross and Class: Comparative Histories of Christian Labour in Europe, 1840–2000*. Bern: Peter Lang, 2005.

Vangroenweghe, Daniël. *Rood rubber: Leopold II en zijn Kongo*. Brussels: Elsevier, 1985.

Varon, Jeremy. *Bringing the War Home: The Weather Underground, the Red Army Faction, and Revolutionary Violence in the Sixties and Seventies*. Berkeley, CA: University of California Press, 2004.

Vellacott, Jo. 'Feminism as if All People Mattered: Working to Remove the Causes of War, 1919–1929'. *Contemporary European History* 10, no. 3 (2001): 375–94.

Vellacott, Jo. 'A Place for Pacifism and Transnationalism in Feminist Theory: The Early Work of the Women's International League for Peace and Freedom'. *Women's History Review* 2, no. 1 (1993): 23–56.

Vial, Eric. 'La Ligue française des Droits de l'Homme et la L.I.D.U., son homologue italien, organisation d'exile antifasciste dans l'entre-deux-guerres'. *Le Mouvement Social*, no. 183 (1998): 119–34.

Vučetić, Radina. 'Violence against the Antiwar Demonstrations of 1965–1968 in Yugoslavia: Political Balancing between East and West'. *European History Quarterly* 45, no. 2 (2015): 255–74.

Wanrooij, Bruno. 'Josephine Butler and Regulated Prostitution in Italy'. *Women's History Review* 17, no. 2 (2008): 153–71.

Watenpaugh, Keith. *Bread from Stones: The Middle East and the Making of Modern Humanitarianism*. Oakland, CA: University of California Press, 2015.

Webb, Clive. 'The Nazi Persecution of Jews and the African American Freedom Struggle'. *Patterns of Prejudice* 53, no. 4 (2019): 337–62.

Weiss, Holger. *Framing a Radical African Atlantic: African American Agency, African Intellectuals and the International Trade Union Committee of Negro Workers*. Leiden: Brill, 2013.

Weiss, Holger, ed. *International Communism and Transnational Solidarity: Radical Networks, Mass Movements and Global Politics, 1919–1939*. Leiden: Brill, 2016.

Weitz, Eric. *A World Divided: The Global Struggle for Human Rights in the Age of Nation-States*. Princeton, NJ: Princeton University Press, 2019.

Wernicke, Günter and Lawrence Wittner. 'Lifting the Iron Curtain: The Peace March to Moscow of 1960–1961'. *The International History Review* 21, no. 4 (1999): 900–17.

Wernicke, Günter. 'The Communist-Led World Peace Council and the Western Peace Movements: The Fetters of Bipolarity and Some Attempts to Break Them in the Fifties and Early Sixties'. *Peace and Change* 23, no. 1 (1998): 265–311.

Wigger, Iris. *The 'Black Horror on the Rhine': Intersections of Race, Nation, Gender and Class in 1920s Germany*. London: Palgrave, 2017.

Wikander, Ulla. 'Demands on the ILO by Internationally Organized Women in 1919'. In *ILO Histories: Essays on the International Labour Organization and Its Impact on the World during the Twentieth Century*, edited by Jasmien Van Daele, Magaly Rodríguez García, Geert Van Goethem and Marcel van der Linden, 67–90. Bern: Peter Lang, 2010.

Wildenthal, Lora. *The Language of Human Rights in West Germany*. Philadelphia, PA: University of Pennsylvania Press, 2013.

Williams, Elizabeth. *The Politics of Race in Britain and South Africa: Black British Solidarity and the Anti-Apartheid Struggle*. London: I.B. Tauris, 2015.

Williams, Theo. *Making the Revolution Global: Black Radicalism and the British Socialist Movement before Decolonisation*. London: Verso, 2022.
Wilmers, Annika. *Pazifismus in der internationalen Frauenbewegung (1914–1920): Handlungsspielräume, politische Konzeptionen und gesellschaftliche Auseinandersetzungen*. Essen: Klartext, 2008.
Winter, Jay. *Dreams of Peace and Freedom: Utopian Moments in the Twentieth Century*. New Haven, CT: Yale University Press, 2004.
Winter, Jay and Antoine Proust. *René Cassin and Human Rights: From the Great War to the Universal Declaration*. Cambridge: Cambridge University Press, 2013.
Wittner, Lawrence. *Resisting the Bomb: A History of the World Nuclear Disarmament Movement, 1954–1970*. Stanford, CA: Stanford University Press, 1997.
Wittner, Lawrence. *Toward Nuclear Abolition: A History of the World Nuclear Disarmament Movement, 1971–Present*. Stanford, CA: Stanford University Press, 2003.
Wöbse, Anna-Katharina. 'Separating Spheres: Paul Sarasin and His Global Nature Protection Scheme'. *Australian Journal of Politics and History* 61, no. 3 (2015): 339–51.
Wöbse, Anna-Katharina. *Weltnaturschutz: Umweltdiplomatie im Völkerbund und den Vereinten Nationen 1920–1950*. Frankfurt: Campus, 2012.
Wöbse, Anna-Katharina and Patrick Kupper, eds. *Greening Europe: Environmental Protection in the Long Twentieth Century – A Handbook*. Berlin: De Gruyter, 2022.
Wolin, Richard. *The Wind from the East: French Intellectuals, the Cultural Revolution, and the Legacy of the 1960s*. 2nd edition. Princeton, NJ: Princeton University Press, 2018.
Worley, Matthew, ed. *In Search of Revolution: International Communist Parties in the 'Third Period'*. London: I.B. Tauris, 2004.
Zachariah, Benjamin. 'A Voluntary Gleichschaltung? Indian Perspectives towards a Non-Eurocentric Understanding of Fascism'. *Journal of Transcultural Studies* 5, no. 2 (2014): 63–100.
Zelko, Frank. *Make It a Green Peace! The Rise of Countercultural Environmentalism*. New York: Oxford University Press, 2013.
Zelko, Frank. 'Scaling Greenpeace: From Local Activism to Global Governance'. *Historical Social Research* 42, no. 2 (2017): 318–42.
Zelko, Frank. 'The Umweltmulti Arrives: Greenpeace and Grass Roots Environmentalism in West Germany'. *Australian Journal of Politics & History* 61, no. 3 (2015): 397–413.
Ziemann, Benjamin, ed. *Peace Movements in Western Europe, Japan and the USA during the Cold War*. Essen: Klartext, 2007.
Ziemann, Benjamin. 'A Quantum of Solace? European Peace Movements during the Cold War and Their Elective Affinities'. *Archiv für Sozialgeschichte* 49 (2009): 351–89.
Zimmermann, Susan. *GrenzÜberschreitungen: Internationale Netzwerke, Organisationen, Bewegungen und die Politik der globalen Ungleichheit vom 17. bis zum 21. Jahrhundert*. Vienna: Mandelbaum, 2010.

INDEX

1848 revolutions 10, 141–2, 191
1956 uprising (Hungary) 76, 163
1968 protests 2, 48, 115–16, 163, 166–8, 270, 272, 292, 295, 299, 305, 318

abolitionism *see* anti-slavery
Aborigines' Protection Society 33, 35, 38
abortion 204–5
Abyssinia *see* Ethiopia
activism (general definition) 2–6
Addams, Jane 108, 199, 233
Adler, Friedrich 159
Afghanistan 117
Africa (views / portrayals of) 25, 30–3, 35, 41, 43–5, 79, 195, 200, 233–4, 236, 299
African American activism 28–9, 40, 44, 46, 80, 115, 206, 212, 223–4, 233, 236–9, 243, 245, 333
African National Congress (ANC) 240–1, 243
Albania 164
alcohol 15, 32–3, 38, 191–2
Aldermaston 110–11, 318–19
Alexander II 144–5
Alexeyeva, Lyudmila 259–60, 272–4, 276–7
Algeria 30, 39, 41, 43, 45–6, 72, 238, 270
Ali, Tariq 115–16
Alliance Israélite Universelle (AIU) 225, 228, 230
American Congo Reform Association 34–5
American Relief Administration 70, 77
Amnesty International 259, 266–9, 273, 277
Amsterdam 49, 106, 109, 149–50, 207, 270, 287, 294
Amsterdam-Pleyel Movement 106, 109
anarchism 1, 6, 95, 100, 105–6, 140–54, 156, 160–1, 170, 196, 262, 299
Angell, Norman 75–6
Anti-Apartheid Movement (AAM) 240, 243
anti-fascism 43, 45, 76, 140, 148–62, 189, 201, 232, 237
anti-imperialism 40–9, 72–3, 99, 105, 116, 120, 153, 241, 271
anti-nuclear protest, *see* nuclear weapons, nuclear power
anti-Semitism 69, 74, 223–32
anti-slavery
  before the 1880s 26–30
  interwar period 38–9
  late nineteenth and early twentieth centuries 25–6, 30–3, 46
  references, allusions and analogies 33–4, 42–3, 80, 192–3, 223, 289
Anti-Slavery Society (Britain) 38–9, 44, *see also* British and Foreign Anti-Slavery Society
anticlericalism 6, 160, 262
anticolonialism 15, 37, 39–46, 49, 102, 224, 235, 305
antimilitarism 105–6, 115, 120, 154, 162
apartheid 3, 239–44
Arab Spring 172, 278
arbitration 96–8, 101, 107
Argentina 143, 268–9, 271
Armenia 70, 74, 79, 144, 153, 227, 229, 262–3
Arnaud, Émile 95–6
Assembly of Captive European Nations 162, 265–6
Attac 170
Australia 38, 72, 163, 192, 204, 232
Austria 11, 25, 68, 76, 78, 93–4, 98–9, 101, 140, 143–4, 148, 159, 196, 225, 227, 246, 296, 299–300
Austria-Hungary *see* Habsburg Monarchy
Axis Powers 101, 161, 230, 264

Bahro, Rudolf 300
Bakunin, Mikhail 105, 145–6, 152–3
Balabanoff, Angelica 146, 154
Balkan federation (concept of) 103, 153
Barbusse, Henri 106
Barcelona 117, 151, 160, 208, 262
Basch, Victor 104
Bates, Winifred 72
Beauvoir, Simone de 115, 205
Belgian Congo 42, 299, *see also* Congo Free State
Belgium 1, 5, 25, 30–2, 34–6, 38, 41–2, 44, 73–4, 77, 95–6, 104, 106, 108, 143–4, 146, 148–9, 154, 163–4, 195, 198, 200, 227, 263, 267, 270–1, 274, 289–90, 297–8
Belgrade 118–19, 122, 158
Benenson, Peter 266–7, 269
Berlin 34, 37, 42, 70, 71, 98, 102–3, 107, 115–16, 119, 151, 158, 167, 195, 204, 209, 223, 226, 236, 239, 272, 276
Bern 96, 145, 154, 289
Bernstein, Eduard 147, 150
Biermann, Wolf 275
bird preservation 289–90

Index

Black Lives Matter 1, 239
Black Panther Party (BPP) 236, 238
Bolsheviks 42, 68, 145–6, 155–6, 158, 168, 204
Bosnia 83, 103, 117–22, 143, 277, 302
boycotts 26, 36, 50, 238, 241, 243–4, 271, 293
Brazil 25–6, 30, 79, 171, 206, 269, 302
Brussels 32–4, 42–4, 46, 142, 145, 147–8, 196, 198, 231–2, 287, 295, 297
Bulgaria 74, 144, 153, 159, 200, 262
Bureau international pour la défense des indigènes 35, 38–9
Butler, Josephine 192, 196
Buxton, Dorothy 75–8

Cadbury, William 77
Campaign for Nuclear Disarmament (CND) 104, 110–11, 298
Campolonghi, Luigi 263
Carmichael, Stokely 115, 237
Carnegie Endowment for International Peace 97, 103
Carson, Rachel 291
Cassin, René 265
Catholic activism 6, 30–2, 46–7, 103, 116, 160, 165, 192, 197–8, 238, 262
Challaye, Félicien 35
Chapman Catt, Carrie 195
Charter 77 group 273–4, 276, 300
Chazov, Yevgeniy 112
Che Guevara 47
Chernobyl 296–7
Chicago 149, 151–2
children 37, 70–2, 74–5, 77–9, 98, 151, 189, 193, 201–2, 209, 231, 287, *see also* youth
Chile 76, 267–72
China 42–3, 45–6, 72, 158, 164, 195, 206
Christian labour movement 149, 165
civil rights 46, 114–15, 223, 237–8, 243, 265, 317, 321
climate change 288, 298, 302–5
Club of Rome 291
Cohn-Bendit, Daniel 168, 299
Cold War 5, 11–12, 46–7, 76, 78, 104, 107–8, 110–14, 116–18, 162–3, 169, 189, 203, 224, 232, 237, 239–40, 244, 260, 265–6, 269, 272, 274, 278, 287, 297, 317
Communist International (Comintern) 42–3, 70, 106–7, 140, 146, 155–62, 229
Communist Manifesto 139, 315
communist parties 43, 106–7, 113, 115, 139, 155–7, 164, 167–8, 229, 236, 270, 275
Communist University of the Toilers of the East 42, 157
Congo Free State 33–6
Congo Reform Association 34–5

conservation (nature) 288–90, 293–4, 298
consumption and consumers 26, 50, 150, 241, 243–4, 246, 293, 299
Cornea, Doina 274–6
Corti, Ivanki 189–90, 203
cosmopolitanism
    definitions 8–9
    expressions of 37, 98, 118, 139, 142, 153
    negative representations of 228, 230–1
Coudenhove-Kalergi, Richard 98–9
Council of Europe 211, 265
Crane, Walter 315–16
Crémieux, Adolphe 225
Croatia 117, 119
Cuba 26, 47, 143, 152
Czech Republic 120, 210
Czechoslovakia 48, 113–14, 120, 156, 263, 273, 276, 290, 300

Dalla Costa, Mariarosa 205
Damascus Affair 224–5
Dashnaktsutyun 153, 229
Davis, Angela 238–9
de Keyser, Ethel 240
de Ligt, Bart 100–2
deglobalization 11, 320
Delphy, Christine 210–11
Denmark 79, 110–11, 193, 195, 202, 207, 244, 292
Deroin, Jeanne 191
Deutsche Liga für Menschenrechte 103–4, 263, 272
Devlin, Bernadette 238
diaspora 38, 41, 43, 45, 70, 119–20, 141, 144, 153, 224, 226, 234, 236–7, 245
Dimitrov, Georgi 159
disasters 66, 77–9, 296–7
dissidents 12, 48, 112–14, 118, 163–5, 232, 241, 259–60, 272–6, 300
Dollfuss, Engelbert 99, 140, 159
Domela Nieuwenhuis, Ferdinand 147, 196
Douglass, Frederick 28–9
Doyle, Arthur Conan 36–7
Dreyfus Affair 227–8, 262–3
Drucker, Wilhelmina 195–6
Du Bois, W. E. B. 44–5, 223–4, 233–4, 236–7, 243
Dublin 149, 318
Duchêne, Gabrielle 109
Duff, Peggy 108, 115
Dugin, Alexander 120
Dunant, Henry 66–7

Earth Day 292
Earth Summit (Rio) 302
education 1, 3, 42, 73, 98, 150–1, 157, 160, 167–8, 193, 203–4, 211, 225, 291–2, 300, 303–5
Egypt 31, 67, 70, 143, 151, 195, 203

359

Index

Einstein, Albert 112
El Salvador 48, 271
Engels, Friedrich 139, 142, 147
environmentalism (terminology and concepts) 3, 288, 291, 294–5, 299, 302, 315
Estonia 111, 317
Ethiopia 30, 39, 68
   famine 79, 81
   Italian attack 39–40, 42, 65, 67, 234, 237
Eurocommunism 164, 275
Europe (boundaries of) 12
European integration and Europeanism 12, 97–8, 211, 244, 295
European Nuclear Disarmament (END) 113–14, 118, 120
European Union 83, 117, 120–1, 172, 210–1, 302, 320
Europeanization 10, 12
exile 47, 73–4, 76, 102–3, 105, 140–7, 150–1, 153–4, 157–8, 162–3, 165, 191, 204, 224, 240–1, 260, 263, 265, 271, 273–4, 300
Extinction Rebellion 303

Faber, Mient Jan 118
fair trade 50
famine 66, 70, 77–81
Fanon, Frantz 46, 49, 235–6, 238
fascists and neo-fascists (transnational cooperation) 8, 98–9, 160–2, 229–30, 245–6, 303
Fauset, Jessie 44
Fédération internationale des Ligues des Droits de l'Homme 263, 266, 269
Federici, Silvia 205
feminism 1, 3, 15
   Black feminism 236, 238–9
   development of organizations 27–8, 191–6
   geographical broadening 200
   links to green politics 299–300
   links to pacifism 14, 93, 95, 98, 107–10, 112, 120, 189, 199–202, 318–19
   relationship with intergovernmental organizations 189, 201–3, 208, 277
   relationship with socialism 148–9, 196–8
   sexuality 203–209, 211–12
   terminology and 'waves' metaphor 190, 205, 212, 299
   see also women's liberation movement, women's suffrage
Ferrer y Guardia, Francisco 151, 262–3
Finland 79, 111, 118, 120, 193, 195, 197, 208
First International *see* International Workingmen's Association
First World War 5, 37, 68, 73, 77, 93, 99–100, 103, 106, 108, 154–5, 198–9, 228–9
   aftermath 11, 36–8, 44, 70, 74, 77–8, 96, 103, 149, 229, 264
Fourth International 141, 158, 163
France
   anti-apartheid activists 239, 241–2
   Catholics 30–3, 103, 198
   colonialism and imperialism 26, 38, 41–6, 234, 238, 270–1
   environmentalism 290, 292–3, 295–6, 299–300
   exiles, refugees and immigrants 74, 143, 145, 151, 157–9, 245–6
   far right 161–2, 228, 245–6
   French Revolution 146, 151, 260–1
   human rights 227, 260–1, 263, 265
   humanitarianism 25, 27–33, 35–6, 68–9, 72–3, 75, 79, 81–2, 118, 225
   peace movement 95–6, 98, 100, 103, 109, 115, 263
   protests 1, 116, 166, 168, 170, 299, 318
   socialists, anarchists and communists 105–6, 140, 142–4, 146–7, 149, 151, 163–4, 197
   women's activism 93, 190–1, 195, 198, 200, 204–7, 211, 236, 261
   see also Dreyfus Affair
Franco-Prussian War 11, 68, 93
Franco, Francisco 72, 160, 230, 269–71
Freedom House 265
Freiheit (periodical) 144, 150
Fridays for Future *see* School Strikes for Climate
Fried, Alfred Hermann 11, 93, 95–7, 103
Friedens-Warte, Die (journal) 93, 103, 105
Friends of Russian Freedom 261
Friends of the Earth 292, 297–8

Gandhi, Mohandas 3, 46, 100–2
Garibaldi, Giuseppe 11, 101, 141–3
Garvey, Amy Ashwood 45
Garvey, Marcus 41–2
Gay Liberation Front 207
Gay Pride 207, 210
General Jewish Labour Bund 229, 231
Geneva 35, 66–7, 97–8, 101, 103, 106, 108, 145, 229, 231, 264, 266
genocide 37, 68–70, 74, 82, 104, 117, 119, 231–2, 246, 264–5, 277
Geremek, Bronisław 118
Germany
   1848 revolution 141–2
   conservation movement 289–90
   environmentalism 287, 294–7, 299, 304
   Federal Republic of Germany 78, 82, 104–5, 115–16, 168–9, 205–6, 238–9, 245, 268, 275, 318
   German Democratic Republic (GDR) 76, 78, 165, 239, 275, 300

humanitarian and human rights activists 30–1, 73, 78, 82, 225, 263, 268, 273
 Jewish associations 225, 228, 231
 Nazi Germany 45, 65, 68, 75, 98–9, 104, 107, 159, 161–2, 201, 223, 230–1, 234, 263
 peace activism 93, 96–8, 103–5, 109–10, 115–16, 120
 protests 110, 167–9, 172, 318
 socialists, anarchists and communists, 42, 71, 105, 142–4, 146–8, 150–7, 159, 196
 war, conflict and post-conflict 5, 11, 36–8, 68, 74, 77, 103, 108, 140, 154, 162–3, 263
 women's movement(s) 152, 154, 201, 204, 205–6, 263
Ghana 45, 224, 237
Gleichheit, Die (periodical) 151
Global Call to Action against Poverty 79–80
global justice movement 79–81, 117, 169–72, 318
globalization 1, 9–12, 49, 150, 169–71, 224, 246, 278, 320
Goldman, Emma 143–4, 146, 150–1, 156, 160–1, 262
Gorbachev, Mikhail 165, 275
Gouges, Olympe de 261
Grange, Dominique 166
Gravelli, Asvero 161
Great Britain
 anticolonial activists 40–5, 100, 235
 anti-apartheid 239–45
 Black activism 236–8
 environmentalism 287, 292, 296, 300, 303
 human rights activism 261–2, 267–9, 274–5
 humanitarian groups and organisations 25–39, 69, 71, 74, 77–80
 international conferences, congresses or speakers 27–9, 44, 68, 141, 204, 233, 235
 Jewish activism 75, 225, 228–9, 231, 233
 LGBT activism 207, 208–9, 212
 peace activism 95–6, 98, 100–2, 104–11, 113–14, 118, 315, 317
 protests 1, 36–7, 40–1, 110, 115–16, 238, 261, 315, 317–8
 representations of British Empire 26, 29–30, 35, 38, 42, 234
 site of exiles and refugees 74–6, 141–5, 147–8, 150
 socialists, anarchists and communists 105, 142–3, 146–8, 156, 160, 164, 315–16
 women's activism 191–3, 197–202, 206, 261, 288, 318
Greece 74, 78, 103–4, 110–11, 167, 172, 262, 269–71
green parties 287, 299–301
green politics 1, 298–301
Greenham Common 109–10, 113, 318–9
Greenpeace 292–8, 302

Gripenberg, Alexandra 197
Gulf War (1991) 116, 119

Habsburg Monarchy 11, 37, 96, 98, 102–3, 139
Hähnle, Lina 289–90
Haiti 25, 40, 79
Halifax Ladies' Anti-Slavery Society 28–9
Halliday, Fred 168
Harris, Alice 34
Harris, John 34, 55
Hauke-Bosak, Jozef 102
Havel, Václav 114, 276
Haymarket Affair 151–2
Helsinki Federation for Human Rights 274–5
Helsinki Final Act 259–60, 275
Helsinki Watch 259, 273–4, 276
Herzen, Alexander 145
Herzl, Theodore 225–7
Heyrick, Elizabeth 26
High Commissioner for Refugees Coming from Germany 75, 230
Hirschfeld, Magnus 204
Ho Chi Minh 41
Holocaust 69, 168, 231–2, 246
human chains 119, 316–9
human rights 7–8, 15, 241
 activist groups, movements and organizations 81, 103, 231–2, 259–60, 263–4, 266–9, 272–4
 connection to solidarity campaigns 165, 261–2, 269–72, 275
 documents 201, 259, 261, 266
 links to other causes 14, 80, 112–14, 119–20, 122, 169, 277–8, 297, 300
 relationship with intergovernmental organizations 201, 244, 264–6, 277
 since the 1990s 275–8
humanitarian intervention 30, 69, 118–20
humanitarianism (definitions and concepts) 12, 25, 65–6, 69, 77, 79
Hungary 11, 68, 71, 76, 93–4, 99, 113, 141, 156, 163, 165, 211, 227, 230, 232, 241, 272, 276, 320
Huysmans, Camille 154

Iceland 195
Identitarian movement 264
Immigration 6, 10, 41, 74–5, 83, 141–44, 149, 158, 169, 225, 231, 233, 245–6, 270, 320, *see also* exile, diaspora, refugees
imperialism
 accusation of cultural imperialism 294, 302
 age of high imperialism 10, 25, 30–7, 289
 challenges in the interwar period 37–45, 157, 234–5
 in postcolonial contexts 45–50

361

Index

perceptions / representations of the US 13, 47–8, 119–20, 142, 236, 271
representations of relationship with Zionism 229, 232
India 3, 26, 37, 42, 45, 317
Indignados 171–2
Inter-Parliamentary Conferences 96
Interkerkelijk Vredesberaad 114, 118
International Abolitionist Federation 191–3
International African Friends of Abyssinia 39–40
International African Service Bureau 42, 45, 234
International Alliance of Women for Suffrage and Equal Citizenship 200, *see also* International Women Suffrage Alliance
International Bureau of Socialist Women 148, 191, 196
International Committee of the Red Cross (ICRC) 65–9, 231
International Conference of Socialist Women 150–2, 189
International Council of Women (ICW) 107, 191, 193, 195, 197, 199–200, 202, 288
International Federation of Christian Trade Unions (CISC) 149
International Federation of Trade Unions (IFTU) 149, 159
International Gay and Lesbian Association / International Gay, Bisexual, Trans and Intersex Association (ILGA) 208–9, 211, 277
International Gay Association (IGA) 208–9, 277
International Labour Organization (ILO) 39, 201–2
International Office for the Protection of Nature 290–1, 301
International Peace Bureau 96–7, 103
International Physicians for the Prevention of Nuclear War (IPPNW) 112
International Relations (theory, research) 7, 168, 274, 288
International Union for the Conservation of Nature (IUCN) 290
International Woman Suffrage Alliance (IWSA) 191, 194–5, 197, 199–200, 202
International Women's Day 152
internationalism 1, 14, 95, 108–9, 116, 198, 201, 204, 235, 265, 289, 300, 315
communist internationalism 155–64, 224, see also *Comintern*
cultural dimensions 150–2
definitions 8–9, 14
fascist internationalism 160–1
'informal internationalism' 143, 172
Jewish internationalism 224–30
labour internationalism 149
relationship with empire 13–14, 38, 45

relationship with nationhood 153–4, 193, 198
socialist internationalism 109, 139–40, 142, 152–5, 159, 224, *see also* International Workingmen's Association, Labour and Socialist International, Second International, Socialist International, Socialist International Women
Iraq 116–17, 245, 318
Ireland 28, 49, 79, 144, 160, 169, 238, 261, 318
Israel 67, 119, 231–2, 225, 238, 244
Istanbul 74, 144, 200, 227
Italy 11, 25, 30–1, 39–41, 50, 65–6, 68, 93, 98, 101–2, 118–19, 140–6, 159–61, 164, 168–70, 189, 192, 201, 205–7, 230, 234, 237, 246, 263, 270, 290, 295–6, 304

James, C. L. R. 40, 43, 158, 234
James, Selma 205
Japan 38, 45, 65–6, 71, 98, 114, 145, 161, 206, 294, 296–7
John Paul II 165–6, 275
Jones, Claudia 236, 238
Jonhaux, Léon 149
Jubilee 2000 campaign 80–1, 317
Judérias, Julián 262
Junod, Marcel 65, 67

Kaldor, Mary 9, 113–14, 118–21
Kautsky, Karl 147
Kelly, Petra 287, 295, 299–300
Kinkel, Gottfried 142
Kinkel, Johanna 142
Kollontai, Alexandra 148–9, 152, 196, 204
Konrad, György 272
Korboński, Stefan 76, 162, 266
Kosovo 119–21
Kossuth, Lajos 141
Kouchner, Bernard 82
Kropotkin, Peter 144–5
Kun Béla 99, 156
Kurón, Jacek 114, 164

Labour and Socialist International (LSI) 106, 155–6, 159, 229
Lalonde, Brice 292, 299
Lambrakis, Grigoris 110
Latvia 111, 317
Lavigerie, Cardinal 30–3
Lazare, Bernard 227–8
League Against Imperialism (LAI) 42–3, 46, 157
League of Nations 8
civil, minority and human rights 234, 261, 264–5
humanitarian causes 38–9, 70, 201
Jewish activists 229–30, 232

Mandates 38, 202
nature and wildlife 290, 293, 301
support and criticisms 13, 78, 96–8, 106, 108
war 39, 98
women activists 108, 202
Lemkin, Raphael 70, 264
Lenin, Vladimir 42, 145–6, 152, 154
Leningrad 158, 206, 209, 273, *see also* Petrograd, St Petersburg
Leopold II of Belgium 31, 34
LGBT rights 3, 190, 206–12, 277, 299
Liebknecht, Karl 105, 155
Ligue des Droits de l'Homme 103–4, 263, 265
Ligue internationale de la Paix et de la Liberté 100–2, 105, 227
Ling, Margaret 240–1, 243
Lithuania 111, 273, 296, 317
Lloyd, Lola Maverick 99
London 27–8, 40–41, 44, 72, 74, 79, 95, 110, 116–17, 142–7, 150–2, 158, 168, 191, 197, 201, 204, 233–4, 237–8, 240, 267, 289, 315–8
Lorde, Audre 236
Lown, Bernard 112
Luxemburg, Rosa 153–5

Malatesta, Errico 142–4
Malcolm X 237–8
Manchester 45, 235
Mandel, Ernest 163–4, 167
Mandela, Nelson 3, 243
Maoism 46, 49, 163–4, 169
Marcuse, Herbert 167
maritime activism 81–3, 292–4
Marx, Karl 139, 142, 152
Marxism 12, 43, 139, 145–8, 153, 163–5, 205, 236, 239
May Day 152, 154, 315–16
Mazzini, Giuseppe 101, 141
McDonald, James 75
Médecins du Monde 82
Médecins Sans Frontières (MSF) 81–3
Menchú, Roberta 271–2
MeToo campaign 212
Mexico 42, 157, 166, 169–70, 202–3
Michel, Louise 144, 151
Michnik, Adam 118, 163–5, 272, 276
migration *see* diaspora, exile, immigration, refugees
Mille, Pierre 35
Mladjenović, Lepa 118–19
Modzelewski, Karol 164
Moneta, Ernesto Teodoro 101–4
Montandon, Georges 68–9
Montefiore, Dora 197
Montefiore, Moses 225
Morel, E. D. 34–6

Moscow 42–3, 107, 110–11, 113–14, 140, 156–8, 259, 273, 275, 277, 297–8
Most, Johann (John) 144–5, 150
Moța, Ion 230
Mouvement anti-apartheid 241–2
Münzenberg, Willi 42, 70, 157, 159
music 79, 151, 166–7, 243, 245, 275
Mussolini, Benito 39, 159, 161–2, 263
Myrdal, Alva 202

Nansen, Fridtjof 75
Nardal, Paulette 39
National Socialists 5, 42, 45, 65, 68–9, 75, 99, 104, 106–7, 140, 155, 159, 162, 167–8, 201, 204, 207, 223, 230–1, 234, 245–6, 263–4, 289–90
nationalism 10–12, 98, 100–5, 121–2, 139, 153–4, 198, 240, 262, 320
anticolonial nationalism 41–4, 102
Négritude 234
Nehru, Jawaharlal 43, 45–6, 244
Netherlands 27–9, 36, 41, 49–50, 74, 97, 100, 106, 108–9, 114, 147, 154–5, 192, 195–9, 207, 239, 241, 270–1, 277, 289, 291, 298
New Left 76, 115, 136
New Right 246
new social movements (concept) 3, 291, 299
New Zealand 38, 192, 292–3
NGOs 5, 13–14, 75, 78, 80–1, 120–1, 170, 202–3, 208–10, 244, 261, 266, 274–5, 277–8, 290, 297, 300–2
Nicaragua 47–8, 50, 73
Nkrumah, Kwame 45, 224
Nobel Peace Prize 93, 102, 104, 112, 265
Nordau, Max 227
North Atlantic Treaty Organization (NATO) 101, 111, 114–15, 119, 121, 269
Northern Ireland 49, 169, 238
Norway 79, 104, 110–11, 157, 193, 195, 202, 206, 294
nuclear power 295–300
nuclear weapons 35, 65, 75, 95, 101, 107, 110, 112–13, 297, 302, 315, 317, 319

O'Connell, Daniel 28
Occupy movement 1, 171–2
Orbán, Viktor 211, 276
Ossietzky, Carl von 103–4
Ottoman Empire 11, 32, 37–8, 67–70, 74, 102, 141, 144, 153, 224, 226–7, 233, 261–2
Oxfam 78

pacifism 2, 11, 15
absolute / non-violent approaches 46, 99–101
definition / terminology 93–6
focus on organizations and law 95–9

363

Index

links with feminism 14, 93, 95, 98, 107–10, 112, 120, 189, 199–202, 318–19
relationship with other campaigns 27, 39, 105–7, 115, 155, 227, 263, 298–9
responses to war 102–4, 198–9
Padmore, George 42–3, 45, 234–5, 237
Palestine 67, 119, 169, 226, 228–9, 232, 244
Pan Africanist Congress of Azania (PAC) 240
Pan-Africanism 43–6, 224, 233–5, 237
Pan-Europe 12, 98–9
Panda Farnana, Paul 41–2, 44
papacy and the Vatican 30, 149, 165, 225, 275
Paris 25, 32–3, 39, 41, 44, 70, 100, 106–7, 109–10, 146, 151–2, 158, 166–8, 191, 201
    Paris Peace Conference (1919) 37, 44, 201
Pelikán, Jiří 200
periodization 10–13, 318, 320
Petrograd 152, *see also* Leningrad, St Petersburg
Pettifor, Ann 80
Pettitt, Ann 110, 113
Peukert, Josef 143–4
Pinochet, Augusto 76, 267–8, 270
Plamínková, Františka 200
Poale Zion 229
Poland 77, 93, 102, 108, 114, 118, 139–42, 153–4, 162–5, 209–11, 223, 229, 232, 241, 263–4, 272–3, 275–6, 290, 320
political violence 6, 144–5, 164, 168–9, 239, 246, 263
Popular Front 106, 159, 161–2
populism 211, 320
Portugal 36, 47–8, 246, 269–71
postcolonial contexts 1, 26, 49–50, 81, 232, 244, 265
Prague 93, 107, 140, 158, 210
    Prague Spring 48, 163, 166, 272
Pratt, Hodgson 96
prisoners of war 67–8
Proudhon, Pierre-Joseph 142
Pugwash Conferences on Science and World Affairs 112, 300

Quakers 29, 74, 100, 110

race (concepts of) 29, 31, 36, 109, 200–1, 212, 223, 230, 233, 235–6, 245
Rainbow Warrior 292–3
Rassemblement Universel pour la Paix 106, 109
Red Cross movement (societies and movement) 65–70, 72, 77, 81–2, 100, 231
refugees 66, 70, 72–7, 81, 83, 141–3, 146, 158–9, 163, 230, 241, 245, 263–4, 267–8, 272, 320
Rhodesia 240, 267
Robeson, Paul 40, 237
Rocker, Rudolf 147, 150–1, 262
Rolland, Romain 100, 103, 106

Roma 276
Romania 78, 103, 143, 160, 230, 263, 274–6
Rome 11, 80, 102, 117, 225, 273
Roosevelt, Eleanor 265
Rosdolsky, Roman 139–41, 153, 163
Roy, M. N. 42–3
Russell, Bertrand 110, 112, 115, 119
Russell, Dora 204
Russia
    Cold War era 112–14, 162, 259–60, 273, *see also* Soviet Union
    exiles and refugees 74, 141, 145–6, 158, 225
    famine 70, 77
    peace activism 93, 100, 120
    post-communist 120, 275–6, 297–8
    Russian Civil War 68, 70, 77, 156, 158
    Russian Empire 37, 73–4, 145, 197, 225–9, 261
    Russian Jews 73, 225–9, 231–3
    Russian Revolution (1917) 38, 74, 152, 156, 158, 168
    socialists, anarchists and communists 42, 71, 105, 143–6, 148, 150, 156–8, 196
    solidarity with oppositional groups 100, 113, 261, 263, 274
    Soviet Russia *see* Soviet Union
    women's activism 148, 196, 204, 206
Russian Social Democratic Labour Party 145–6, 150
Rwanda 82, 117, 277

Sagnier, Marc 103
Sakharov, Andrei 112–13, 274
Sarajevo 118–19, 122
Sartre, Jean-Paul 81, 115
Save the Children 37, 71, 77–8
Schücking, Walther 96
Schurz, Carl 141–2
Schwimmer, Rosika 99–100
Scottsboro Affair 237
Sea Watch 83
Second International 105, 146–9, 151–5, 162, 196–7, 227, 229, 315
Second World War 2, 11–13, 46, 67, 69, 72, 76, 78, 95, 99, 101, 107, 140, 202, 205, 230, 261, 265, 301, 315, 318
Senghor, Lamine 42–3
Serbia 117–9
sexuality (attitudes to) 190, 203–5, 207, 211–12, 236
Six-Day War 48, 232
Slovenia 117, 119
social movements (definition and research) 2–5, 9, 15, 321, *see also* new social movements
socialist internationalism *see under* internationalism
Socialist International 271

Index

Socialist International Women 189, 203
Société Antiesclavagiste de Belgique 33–4
Société de la Morale Chrétienne, 27, 95
Société française pour l'abolition de l'esclavage 27–8
Solidarność 165–6, 241, 275, 276
Solzhenitsyn, Natalia 260
Soros, George 232, 246
South Africa 36–8, 195, 198, 224, 239–44
Soviet Jewry Movement 231–2
Soviet Union 5, 42–3, 46–8, 70, 76, 78, 107, 111–14, 139, 155–60, 162–4, 168, 203–4, 206, 224, 231–2, 237, 240, 294, 296, 316
  human rights activism 259–60, 265–6, 272–3, 275–6
Spain 25–6, 30, 144–5, 151–2, 159, 171, 197, 230, 245, 262–3, 269–72, 275, 295–6
  Spanish Civil War 45, 65, 67, 71–3, 75, 159–61, 230, 270
sports 157, 243–4, 268–9, 271
St Petersburg 145, *see also* Leningrad, Petrograd
Stalin, Joseph and Stalinism 106, 157–9, 163–5, 204, 206, 231
Stepniak 145
Stockholm 106–7, 115, 145, 154–5, 301–2, 304
students 41, 43, 46, 48, 78, 98, 104, 114–16, 148, 163, 167–8, 231, 234, 237–8, 240, 271, 292, 295, 299, 303, 305, 318
Sturge, Joseph 27
Support Network on Renewable Energy (SNoRE) 297
Suttner, Bertha von 93–7, 102, 105, 107, 122, 227
Swanwick, Helena 98, 202
Sweden 3, 27, 110, 112, 115, 120, 154–5, 195, 202, 206, 240, 291, 292, 303–4
Switzerland 31, 35, 47–8, 50, 65, 67–8, 73, 103, 106, 141, 143–7, 150, 154, 171, 200, 206, 226, 228, 241, 289–90, 295–6

The Hague 97, 99, 108, 119, 122, 146, 199
Third World 46–50, 78, 80–1, 165, 169, 203, 238, 271, 302, 317
Thompson, E. P. 113
Thunberg, Greta 3, 303–5
Tolstoy, Leo 100–1
Toupin, Louise 206
trade unions 39, 43, 45, 50, 106, 118, 140, 143, 146, 149–51, 156–7, 159, 165, 170, 202, 241, 270–1, 273, 275
trafficking of women 192–3, 201–2
transgender rights 208, 211–12
transnational history 6–7, 318
Trinidad 40, 42, 44, 233–4, 236
Trotskyism 140–1, 157–8, 160, 163–5
Turchin, Valentin 273

Turkey 74, 114, 143, 157, 158, 200, 228, 233, 245, *see also* Ottoman Empire, Young Turks

Ukraine 73, 120, 139, 273, 296, 297, 320
United Front (Comintern) 106, 157
United Nations (UN)
  conferences 170, 202–3, 208, 244, 277, 301–2
  cooperation with activists 76, 78–9, 189–90, 202–3, 208–9, 232, 243–4, 265–7, 301, 305
  hopes and criticisms 99, 116–18, 232, 264, 302
  post League of Nations 8, 13, 261
  United Nations Educational, Cultural and Scientific Organization (UNESCO) 202, 301
  United Nations Environmental Programme (UNEP) 301
  United Nations Relief and Rehabilitation Administration (UNRRA) 76, 78
United Races Congress 233
United States (general)
  American activists in Europe 40, 44, 68, 108, 143–4, 156, 160, 223–4, 233, 236–8
  destination for immigrants and travelling activists 34, 42, 99–100, 139, 141–3, 150, 163, 167, 193, 205–6, 232–3, 259–60, 287
  initiatives / impacts of US activists 1, 44, 109, 112, 195, 199, 205, 207, 212, 231, 236–9, 243, 274, 291–2, 316
  international relations / foreign policy 13, 47–9, 70, 72, 77–8, 95, 97, 107, 114–16, 265–6, 269, 271, 316, 318
  transatlantic cooperation 26–9, 34–7, 44, 99, 102, 115, 168, 191, 193, 205–6, 211, 225, 229, 231–2, 260, 274, 296–7, 303, 315
Universal Peace Congress 34, 96, 98, 102–4

Vandervelde, Emile 35
Vienna 94, 140, 227, 267–7
Vietnam 41, 81–2, 273
  Vietnam War 47–8, 72–3, 104, 109, 111, 114–16, 119
voluntary action (definition) 4–5
Voor Moeder Aarde 297–8

Wages for Housework 205–6
War Resisters' International (WRI) 100, 110
Weizmann, Chaim 225–6, 228–9
Wells, H. G. 93
West African Students' Union (WASU) 41, 234
whales 293–4
Wilson, Woodrow 37, 97
Women in Black 118–19, 122
Women Strike for Peace 109
Women's International Democratic Federation (WIDF) 48, 189, 203

365

Index

Women's International League for Peace and Freedom (WILPF) 108–9, 120, 198–202, 237, 264
women's liberation 108–10, 190, 205–6, 211, 236
Women's Peace Congress (The Hague, 1915) 108, 199
women's suffrage 107, 148–9, 194–200
Workers' International Relief (WIR) 70–1, 157
World Christian Temperance Union (WCTU) 191–3
World Conference on the Protection of Nature 289
world federalism 99
World Festival of Youth 168, 209, 239
World Jewish Congress 231
World Social Forum 170–1
World Trade Organisation (WTO) 170
World Wildlife Fund / World Wide Fund for Nature (WWF) 290–1, 301
World Zionist Congress 226–7
WUNC displays 4–5, 321 n.6

xenophobia 74, 83, 245–6, *see also* racism, anti-Semitism

Young Turks 227, 233, 262
youth 50, 78, 103, 121, 148–9, 156–7, 167–8, 209, 239, 245, 303–5, *see also* children, students
Yugoslavia 79, 114, 117–22, 158, 200

Zangwill, Israel 233
Zapatistas 169
Zasulich, Vera 154
Zetkin, Clara 152, 154–6, 196
Zietz, Luise 196
Zimmerwald Left 106, 154–5
Zionism 224–9, 231–3, 244
Zionist Organization 226–9, 233
Zürich 48, 103, 108, 145, 152